International A

DANCING THE
Second E

Nearly half a century ago, Rupert Raj was one among the ... t generation of transsexual men taking matters into their own hands. Without any role models, or even a concept of trans masculinity, he delved into the unknown, searching for his personal truth, trusting only on instinct. We owe a debt to pioneers like Rupert that nowadays trans men and women around the globe have ways of understanding and finding themselves. His life story is a crucial testimony that deserves to be read.

~**ALEX BAKKER, MA**
Historian and writer (The Netherlands)
Author of *My Untrue Past* and *Transgender in Nederland*

Rupert Raj is one of trans history's most important figures. His tireless activism in the 1970s and 1980s, in particular, paved the way for generations of activists not only in the U.S. and Canada, but globally as well. Dancing the Dialectic *is a beautifully written, first-person account of that activism, joining other classics in the genre—from* Emergence *to* Redefining Realness.

~**ELSPETH BROWN, PhD**
Professor of History, University of Toronto
Board Member, The ArQuives: Canada's LGBTQ2+Archives

Born around the time that Christine Jorgensen's story made world headlines and retiring at a time when trans people are reaching an emancipation watershed worldwide, Rupert Raj is one of a select few whose life neatly tracks the arc of modern trans history. Weaving those *two together, this updated memoir refers to a veritable 'Who's Who' of trans activism across borders and oceans.* Dancing the Dialectic *is the true 'warts and all' story of a man whose whole adult life has been devoted to advocacy and community support. Highly recommended.*

~**CHRISTINE BURNS, MBE**
Writer and equalities advocate (UK)
Author of *Pressing Matters*, Editor of *Trans Britain*

When it comes to advocating for people with gender identities and presentations outside the binary norm, Rupert Raj is indefatigable. When he gets knocked down, he gets right back up and goes back to work. He has been on the front lines for nearly 50 years, and his work has been transformational. Raj's story is fascinating and inspirational and educational, all at once.

~DALLAS DENNY, MA
Founder, American Educational Gender Information Service
(now Gender Education & Advocacy, Inc.)
Author of *Current Concepts in Transgender Identity*

A 'Who's Who' of Canadian and American trans* activisms and histories, Rupert Raj makes an original, exciting and extremely important contribution simply by telling us his story. Dancing the Dialectic *is a unique and compelling read; do not miss this trans* tour de force!*

~BOBBY NOBLE, PhD
Associate Professor and Coordinator, Sexuality Studies, York University
Author of *Masculinities Without Men?* and *Sons of the Movement*

In this text Rupert Raj brings us into an intimate personal space: his life experiences. And in that telling, he traces the development of his political involvement, over decades, in building transpositive healthcare. Raj's influence has been significant, and profoundly appreciated, across Canada and beyond. Thank you for your passion and commitment, Rupert. And for Dancing the Dialectic*: recommended reading!*

~JIM OULTON, MSW
Past President, Canadian Professional Association for Transgender Health

It is impossible to fully capture Rupert Raj's transformational impact on trans communities throughout Canada and globally. With his memoir, Dancing the Dialectic*, Raj offers readers candid and captivating insight into his extraordinary life.*

~K.J. RAWSON, PhD
Associate Professor of English, College of the Holy Cross
Director, Digital Transgender Archive

Praise for First Edition

Anyone interested in trans history in Canada should definitely read Dancing the Dialectic *by Rupert Raj. He demonstrates, in detail, the struggles, both personal and institutional, which he, and many others in Canada and worldwide, had to undertake to become the man or woman they are.*

~**MICHAEL A. GILBERT, PhD**
Professor Emerita of Philosophy, York University
Author of "Defeating Bigenderism," in
Hypatia: Journal of Feminist Philosophy
Past Director, Fantasia Fair

A veritable whirlwind of activism: victories and defeats, struggles and resiliency, frustration and hope. In Dancing the Dialectic, *Rupert Raj gives readers a blow-by-blow account of what it's like to build a trans community and a movement from nothing but a facile mind, drive and compassion. Trust me, it's a lot easier to read about than it is to do! Thank you, Rupert, for everything you have given us.*

~**JAMISON GREEN, PhD**,
Past President, World Professional Association for Transgender Health
Author of *Becoming a Visible Man*

Rupert Raj chronicles his life as an activist fiercely devoted to the struggle for trans equality and the liberation of all forms of life on this earth. A fight spanning five decades, the trails this pioneering trans activist has blazed are full of twists and turns. His relentless pursuit of the road ahead has not been without alienation, conflict and anger, loneliness and failure, which he relates with brutal honesty. Nonetheless, his is a story of resilience—and of love for himself, his (chosen) family, friends and community. A key piece of trans history, Raj's memoir blends recollection of the past with advice for future activists fighting for justice for all.

~**DAN IRVING, PhD**,
Associate Professor and Coordinator of Sexuality Studies Minor,
Carleton University
Co-editor of *Trans Activism in Canada*

Trans people today are deeply indebted to pioneers like Rupert Raj, who forged a path where none existed and dared to make the world a better place for all of us. His efforts were tireless, his vision just, his mark indelible—may Rupert's legacy be as profound as the life he led.
~**BRICE D. SMITH, PhD**
Author of *Lou Sullivan: Daring To Be A Man Among Men*

Back in the early 1990s, when I was a young trans thing just learning my community's history, I discovered an amazing magazine, Metamorphosis *(1982-1988) filled with resources for trans life. The pioneering community leader spearheading that project was Rupert Raj. Dancing the Dialectic tells the story of his remarkable life—and most remarkable of all is that something as vital as* Metamorphosis *was just a small part of his many accomplishments!*
~**SUSAN STRYKER, PhD**,
Founder, Transgender Studies Initiative,
University of Arizona,
Author of *Transgender History*

Rupert Raj is a quintessential trailblazer, deeply immersed in life's paradoxes and challenges, intensely engaged in movements for social change—he continuously asks questions and takes risks to find answers to the riddle of his life. A trans man who began his journey to manhood in a time that was risky and fraught with opposition from every corner, when medical transition was obscure, Raj's story is important. Filled with significant events and interactions with both famous and obscure trans people who have created our world—trans history is alive here.
~**MAX WOLF VALERIO**
Author of *The Testosterone Files*

DANCING THE DIALECTIC:

True Tales of a Transgender Trailblazer

Second Edition

DANCING THE DIALECTIC

True Tales of a Transgender Trailblazer

(Second Edition)

Rupert Raj

With a Preface by Margot Wilson, PhD

Published by
TransGender Publishing
www.transgenderpublishing.ca

TGP

an imprint of
Castle Carrington Publishing
Victoria, BC, Canada

2020

DANCING THE DIALECTIC
True Tales of a Transgender Trailblazer
(Second Edition)

Copyright © Rupert Raj, 2020
Preface copyright © Margot Wilson, 2020
Cover portrait of Rupert Raj copyright © Valerie Soo, 2017
All photographs (except where otherwise noted): Author's collection

Second Edition, 2020
Includes preface, author's epilogue, intersectional bibliography and appendices
TransGender Publishing, Victoria, BC, Canada
www.transgenderpublishing.ca

ISBN: 978-1-9992472-1-8 (paperback)
ISBN: 978-1-9992472-2-5 (e-book)

First Edition, 2017
CreateSpace Independent Publishing Platform
North Charleston, South Carolina
Library of Congress Control Number: 2017907019
ISBN-13: 978-1545435496
ISBN-10: 1545435499

All rights reserved. No part of this publication may be reprinted, reproduced, stored in a retrieval system or transmitted in any form, or by any means, electronic, mechanical, photocopying, and recording or otherwise, now known or hereafter invented without the express prior written permission of the author, except for brief passages quoted by a reviewer in a newspaper or magazine. To perform any of the above is an infringement of copyright law.

Raj, Rupert.
Dancing The Dialectic: True Tales of a Transgender Trailblazer
(Second edition)

1. Transsexualism – Autobiography. 2. Transgenderism – History/Activism. 3. Intersex – History/Activism. 4. Two-Spirit – Activism. 5. *Hijra* – Activism. 6. Gender/Sexuality. 7. Eco-activism/Animal Liberation.

Dedication

To my cherished life partner and soulmate, KJ, who came back into my life when I needed her most.

To my beloved sister and best friend, A.G., who has always been there for me since we were kids.

To my first social worker therapist, Miss Stephens, who validated me as a vulnerable transsexual teenager when the transphobic psychiatrists did not.

To my G.P. psychotherapist, Dr. Paul Wozniak, who continuously supported me over the past 19 years from my middle into my senior years.

To my family doctor, Dr. Abbas Ghavam-Rassoul, who holistically cared for me for the past 17 years as a patient who is also a person.

To all those transgender and cisgender activists (Gender Workers and Queer Activists) who gave/give their blood, sweat and tears (and sometimes their lives) to make this a safer world for members of the gender- and sexual-minority communities.

To all transsexual, transgender, crossdressing, genderqueer, gender non-binary, gender-transgressive, intersex, and Two-Spirit people—and our loved ones, friends, and allies.

To all those eco-activists and animal liberationists (Earth scientists, ecofeminists, environmentally-engaged Buddhists, Indigenous Rainbow Warriors and others) who fought/fight to free Mother Earth's enslaved animals and expand the circle of compassion.

And, to all Earthlings, human and animal—especially those trans-species sentient beings who strive to co-exist peacefully on our self-conscious planet (aka Gaia).

Contents

Preface to the Second Edition xiii
Author's Notes xv
Acknowledgements xix

Part I:

Dialectical Dancer 1

    1. Existential Angst…Gender Distress…High School Crush (1952-1968) 2

    2. Tragic Family Loss…Bittersweet First Love (1968-1971) 27

    3. Gender Transition…Higher Learning…Sexual Liaisons (1971-1975) 43

Part II:

Gender Worker 71

    4. Trans FACTivism…More Surgery…Two Romances and A Brief Affair (1975-1982) 72

    5. Metamorphosis…More Schooling…A Special Friendship (1982–1988) 106

    6. Gender Worker/Gender Consultants…First Marriage (1988–1990) 127

    7. Intense Burnout…Secular Humanism, Ethical Vegetarianism, Career Counselling…A Brief Affair and Divorce (1990–1998) 138

    8. Trans Re-Activism…Even More Schooling…Ricochet Romance (1998-2001) 154

Part III:

Therapeutic Healer, Teacher & Writer 177

    9. Psychotherapy…Gender Consulting…Second Marriage and Divorce (2001-2011) 178

    10. RR Consulting Redux…Even More Surgery…The Love of My Life (2011–2013) 210

    11. Archival Accolades…Trans Anthologies…Intersex and Two-Spirit Inclusivity…Mental Breakdown (2013-2017) 224

Part IV:
Rainbow Warrior 263
    12. Retirement…Eco-Activism & Animal Liberation (2017-) 264
Epilogue (2017-2019) 288
Appendix I 299
Appendix II 302
Intersectional Bibliography 304
About the Author 351

Preface to the Second Edition

Rupert Raj comes to the world in multiple and varied guises: a self-described activist and advocate for trans people and animals, a committed pescetarian, perennial angry man, voracious reader, writer, philosopher, gender worker; therapeutic healer, teacher, indefatigable networker (both nationally and internationally), dialectical dancer; and rainbow warrior. His biography provides a whirlwind journey, through the ups and downs, successes and challenges, disappointments and drama that characterize Rupert's struggle to make sense of his own gender journey towards personal and professional authenticity. Beyond this, Rupert has made his life's work the support and advocacy of others walking the same path. His work addresses the intersection of race, Indigeneity, gender identity, sexual orientation, and the rights of transsexual/transgender, genderqueer, intersex, *Hijra*, Indigenous, and Two-Spirit people, as well as environmental and animal justice.

Growing up in Ottawa (Canada's capital), during a time before the internet and global connectivity, in a time when gender and sexual preference were firmly situated within a male/female binary, where heterosexual attraction between man and woman provided the only form of socially sanctioned union, Rupert begins his story as an "unsuspecting" infant and "angry at the world" toddler. A "crying on the inside" child and gender distressed teenager, Rupert knew instinctively that he was really a boy in a girl's body and questioned whether there was any resolution to this persistent and intense gender distress. Ultimately, this led him to question whether he was a "freak of nature." Resolving that he was, in fact, a "female to male transsexual"—"a trans boy"—he began secretly crossdressing as a reflection of the male self imprisoned within. This early self-consciousness, soon followed by the loss of his parents, set Rupert on a path of exploration, experimentation, and self-discovery that gave rise to the man Rupert is today.

Dancing the Dialectic is an uninhibited, no holds barred journey through the intimate details of Rupert's coming of age as a trans man and the interwoven and varied paths along which that transition has led him throughout his life. It is a rare individual who is willing to be as open, honest, and transparent in telling their life story as Rupert. What he provides is a detailed, straight forward, unvarnished exposition of the man he is today and the journey he undertook in order to arrive at his current destination. Characterized by recurring periods of burnout and re-energized comeback, Rupert, as a self-described dialectical dancer, pirouettes in a spiral of alternating vulnerability and resilience. Multiple tributes in the form of awards, honourable mentions, and induction into The ArQuives further attest to community recognition of Rupert's persistence in the dance.

What follows is the story of a 41 year transition, including legal, social, medical, and surgical interventions that ultimately led to a 15 year professional clinical career as a psychotherapist and gender consultant, supporting the LGBTTI2SQQAA (lesbian, gay, bisexual, transsexual, transgender, intersex, Two-Spirit, queer, questioning, asexual, and allied) community.

As part of his commitment to supporting the trans community, Rupert has produced three books, including *Trans Activism in Canada: A Reader* (co-edited with Dan Irving, PhD, 2014), *Of Souls & Roles, Of Sex & Gender: A Treasury of Transsexual, Transgenderist & Transvestic Verse from 1967 to 1991* (2017, revised in 2018), and the first edition of *Dancing The Dialectic: True Tales of A Transgender Trailblazer* (2017). He has also authored numerous newsletters, articles, clinical research papers, and book chapters, appeared on radio, television, and film documentaries, and co-founded, a number of trans counselling services, service organizations, and peer-support groups.

This second edition of *Dancing the Dialectic* provides additional textual materials and chapter notes, new photographs, an expanded intersectional bibliography, excerpts from *Of Souls & Roles, Of Sex & Gender* (Appendix I), affirmations (Appendix II), and an epilogue that covers the years since the publication of the first edition. Editorial input has been largely around punctuation, word choice, and referencing. I made a concerted effort to retain the narrative, idiom, and language of Rupert's story as he originaly told it.

Overall, Rupert's story provides his views on trans cultural imperialism, marginalization and co-option, invisibility and erasure, visibility and re-emergence (especially of trans people of colour, Indigenous, Two-Spirit, *Hijra*, intersex, and trans people with disabilities), transmisandry, transmisogyny, and transfeminism, positive paradigm shifts, and other activists (Canadian, American, and international) who share similar intersectional perspectives as his own. Not my prerogative to divulge the details of Rupert's life story, my responsibility here lies in introducing you to Rupert as the author and inviting you to immerse yourself in this frankly uninhibited, courageously candid, recounting of the life story of a Canadian transgender pioneer. This is quintessential Rupert Raj at his primal best, his fearlessly straightforward self.

Margot Wilson, PhD
October 10, 2019
Victoria, BC

Editor's Caveat: After several rounds of editorial review, revision, and negotiation, I have acquiesced to authorial preferences for non-standard punctuation, italics, capitalization, and spelling. Accordingly, the text that follows reflects the final decisions/preferences of the author. Moreover, there has been an evolution in the terms used by members of the trans community to describe themselves. The choice of words used throughout this volume are those of the author.

Author's Notes

First Edition

This journal records not only my personal history as a Eurasian (Polish and East Indian) Canadian, existential Outsider, counsellor/consultant, researcher/educator, writer/editor, trans/intersex/Two-Spirit activist and eco-activist/animal liberationist, but also acknowledges the lives and works of many of my North American and (to a lesser extent) British, Australian, and New Zealander peers (citing additional information and resources in the chapter notes). As well as many Americans, I also mention a substantial number of Canadian activists (and allies) in tribute to their individual advocacy efforts within Canada and their collective contribution towards global trans/intersex/Two-Spirit equality and/or animal liberation.

To preserve their privacy, I have used pseudonyms or omitted surnames for many non-public persons—including living relatives, friends, my partner, and ex-partners—and have opted not to include photographs of my partner or ex-partners because they all prefer anonymity. I have also refrained from naming certain problematic trans/intersex/Two-Spirit activists because, despite their dishonourable words or actions, I do not wish to individually humiliate them. I have called out several cisgender mental health professionals though, for genderphobic or other wrongdoings, staying true to the facts without intent to libel. And, I have also critiqued certain organizations, not out of malice, but rather, to flag problematic practices and recommend positive alternatives or cite other organizations' higher standards, while duly crediting their exemplary practices.

To portray my ever-evolving multidimensional identities in some semblance of chronological order, I've divided the book into four parts: I: Dialectical Dancer (existential philosopher/psychologist/anthropologist/sociologist), II: Gender Worker (trans/intersex/Two-Spirit activist), III: Therapeutic Healer, Teacher & Writer (psychotherapist/gender consultant/educator/trainer/published clinical researcher/book editor), and IV: Rainbow Warrior (eco-activist/animal liberationist). Part IV continues the intersectionality of diverse types of activism, specifically, advocacy for the rights of both the transgender community and the animal world (as exemplified by Calvin Neufeld), and liberation for trans people, sex workers, and animals (as evidenced by Mirha-Soleil Ross and Xanthra Mackay). The comprehensive bibliography roughly accords to each part of the book (with some overlap) and is cross-referenced by subject category.

The main threads of this memoir trace my intersecting identities and roles—"dancing the dialectic" between existentially-dynamic polarities; the evolution of my identities and roles over the lifespan—my "transjectory" from trans youth to trans elder, and from peer gender worker to professional gender consultant to aspiring eco-activist/animal liberationist; my driving need for validation and visibility, and the disconcerting co-existence of appreciation for *and* erasure of my life and work; and recurring burnout and vicarious traumatization, and my attendant need for sustainable self-care.

Additional themes include: transphobia/transpositivity, transmisogyny/transfeminism, transmisandry, invisibility/visibility of intersex people, erasure/reclaiming of Indigenous transgender and Two-Spirit people, exclusion/inclusion of people of colour, sexual/gender policing, communal infighting, trans cultural imperialism—erasure/appropriation—and intersectionality of identities (trans and intersex, trans and *Hijra*, trans and Two-Spirit, trans and racialized, trans and queer, trans and feminist, trans and vegan, etc.) and activist efforts (trans/queer activism, trans/HIV activism, trans/sex-worker activism, trans activism/art, trans activism/gender studies, trans activism/sports, trans/animal liberation, etc.).

As a social scientist and social historian, I also mention a number of cisgender people (now departed), compelled as I am to compare and contrast myself with a few select philosophers, psychologists, psychiatrists, anthropologists, sociologists, physicists, writers, actors, artists, and activists with whom I share certain beliefs or values, traits or temperaments. My intention is not to equate myself with any of these particular existential Outsiders—as I value not only our commonality but our uniqueness as idiosyncratic individuals—but rather, to locate myself on the "lunatic fringe"—genius or madness?—of the normal distribution curve as one of a limited number of social change agents, while encouraging other aspirants to strive for changes for the better, personally and politically, locally and globally, for both human and animal sentient beings.

Rupert Raj
August 1, 2017
Toronto, Ontario

Second Edition

Of special note in Parts II and III of this revised and updated edition, are the enriched discussions in the text—with accompanying relevant resources in the chapter notes and intersectional bibliography—around intersex people, genderqueer folks, trans people of colour, South Asian *Hijras*, Indigenous trans people, and Two-Spirit people, as well as individuals with dual/multiple identities: trans-intersex, trans-*Hijra*, trans-Two-Spirit, trans mixed-race, trans people of colour, etc. Also included are important issues, such as: intergenerational LGBTTI2SQQAA community engagement; (anti-)sexism, (anti-) transmisogyny (trans-exclusionary radical feminism vs. transfeminism), (anti-)transmisandry; (anti-)racism and (anti-)Indigeneity, and intersectional collaboration among trans/intersex people of colour and Two-Spirit people; anti-oppressive co-operation among the gender communities (transgender/genderqueer/intersex/*Hijra*/Two-Spirit people) and our cisgender allies; trans cultural imperialism (appropriation/erasure); more visible presence of Canadian trans, intersex, and Two-Spirit activists, politicians, lawyers, judges, primary and mental healthcare professionals, social workers, educators, academics, researchers, social historians, writers, musicians, filmmakers, and professional athletes; a greater inclusion of trans people worldwide in community activism, politics, law, healthcare, social work, education, academia, journalism, multimedia arts, sports, science, and religion; and continuous movement towards a more gender positive media. These significant issues are briefly summarized as a series of 20 positive sociopoliticohistorical paradigm shifts over the past 50 years to effectively close chapter 11.

The original bibliography—which roughly corresponded to each of the book's four parts with some cross-referencing by subject category—has been reconfigured as an intersectional bibliography, in which Part II (Gender Worker) and Part III (Therapeutic Healer, Teacher & Writer), now combined, have been newly-categorized by specific topics and subtopics and, also, in some sections, by subpopulations within the overall gender community, in terms of race, nationality, gender, age, or other specific identities. Not all works cited in the main text are referenced in the chapter notes, so please consult the relevant section(s) or subsection(s) in the intersectional bibliography for a full citation.

The appendices consist of three poems excerpted from my 2017/2018 international trans poetry anthology, and three affirmations written for my former counselling clients.

To portray my ever-evolving multidimensional identities in some semblance of chronological order, I've divided the book into four parts: I: Dialectical Dancer (existential philosopher/psychologist/anthropologist/sociologist), II: Gender Worker (trans activist/intersex & Two-Spirit ally), III: Therapeutic Healer, Teacher & Writer (psychotherapist/gender consultant/educator/trainer/published clinical researcher/book editor), and IV: Rainbow Warrior (eco-activist/animal liberationist). (Recently influenced by intersex activist/trans ally, Emi Koyama, mentioned elsewhere in this book, I'm reworking my former self-descriptor as a trans/intersex/Two-Spirit activist to one of a trans activist/intersex & Two-Spirit *ally*—referencing my trans identity, as well as my past advocacy specifically for transsexual, transgender, intersex, and Two-Spirit people—including former counselling clients. Of course, I also support genderqueer, *Hijra*, and other gender non-binary adults, as well as gender-creative kids/teens. I made this change so people don't mistakenly assume that I'm claiming to be trans, intersex *and* Two-Spirit—as some multiple-identity individuals are.) Part IV continues the intersectionality of diverse types of activism, specifically, advocacy for the rights of both the transgender community and the animal world (as exemplified by Calvin Neufeld), and liberation for trans people, sex workers, and animals (as evidenced by Mirha-Soleil Ross and Xanthra Mackay).

I would like to specially note here my variable usage of certain terminology, specifically, in terms of historical and cultural context, and of political correctness. Occasionally, I have used the words, "fags" and "dykes," in an affirmatory way to show the reader the cultural context of self-descriptors of some of these gay men and lesbians, respectively, at a particular time in history. Similarly, to trace the historical evolution of popular gender labels, for the most part, I've employed, chronologically, the terms: "transsexual," "transvestite," "androgyne," and "hermaphrodite." Subsequently, I've used their present labels: "transgender," "crossdresser," genderqueer/ gender-creative/gender non-binary, and "intersex," respectively. I have also rarely used the historically-popular jargon of "transgenderist" and "she-male," and "he-she"—now all anachronistic and/or politically incorrect—solely to locate specific gender identities on the diverse gender spectrum of the 1970s, 1980s, and 1990s, and their attendant self-descriptors. Additionally, at times I've used the terms, "transsexuals," "transvestites," "androgynes," "genderqueers," "transqueers," and "transbis," etc., as nouns for the sake of variety, but have usually employed their adjectival forms to reflect current politically-correct usage. In general, I use the catch-all label, "transgender," to signify that collective group of people who individually identify as transsexual, transgender, genderqueer, intersex, Two-Spirit, or *Hijra* (or a combined identity), as well as crossdressers and other gender non-binary individuals. Similarly, I often use short forms, such as "trans women," "trans men," "trans people," "T-girls," "T-boys," and "T-community" as popular alternatives.

Hopefully, this new, enriched second edition will be used in high school, college, and university curricula as a teaching tool to promote a deeper understanding of the people, events, and culture, the history, politics, and human rights activism around gender identity and sexual orientation—and of deep ecology and animal liberation—in Canada, the USA, and beyond.

Rupert Raj
October 1, 2019
Vancouver, BC

Acknowledgements

First Edition

A labour of love, writing one's life story is also an arduous task—dancing between facts and feelings, artistry and technicality. I am obliged to the following people, who helped transform my creative vision into a living legacy.

I am particularly grateful to Scott Kettles, Helen Lensky, Dr. Nick Matte, Alan Miller, Jade Pichette, Dr. Rebecka Sheffield and Raegan Swanson all of The ArQuives: Canada's LGBTQ2+ Archives (formerly, Canadian Lesbian & Gay Archives) for their assistance in retrieving requested items from my collection of papers as research aids to inform this memoir. I am also grateful to Alan and Dr. Cait McKinney for scanning the photographs for inclusion in this book. And an extra-special thank-you to Elspeth Brown, who processed my archival collection (The Rupert Raj fonds) and created the Finding Aid, and for listing me and this memoir on Wikipedia.

I also appreciate the extensive biographical data compiled on Zagria's "A Gender Variance Who's Who" website and have regularly referenced this in the chapter notes so readers can access further information on selected transgender and cisgender individuals.

My genuine gratitude goes out to my literary editors, Loren Bornstein and Lynne Stahl, for their invaluable input to my first edition—especially to Lynne for suggesting a number of effective editorial changes, while still preserving the overall content and my own literary style.

A word of thanks is due to my geek friend, Stephanie Mott, whose image manipulation expertise saved my ass by morphing the photographs in the book into Tiff files of 300 dpi resolution.

My warm appreciation goes out to my graphic illustrator, Valerie Soo, for her flattering portrait of me on the front cover—considering that I'm not that photogenic!

I am also grateful to my writer friends, David Bateman and Mary W. Walters, for encouraging me to self-publish the original edition in my desperation after my initial publisher and I parted ways due to differences in creative vision, editorial direction and production timelines. I'm ever so thankful for the excellent professional standards and personal customer relations of the publishing team at CreateSpace (an Amazon company), which supported me throughout all phases of the design, production and marketing process in a timely turn-around.

I'm deeply indebted to my trans activist-writer friends for their testimonials promoting my book. For your significant contributions to the trans, intersex and/or Two-Spirit communities over the years, I salute each one of you: Dr. Michael (Miqqi Alicia) Gilbert, Dr. Dan Irving, Dr. Jamison Green, Dr. Brice D. Smith, Dr. Susan Stryker and Max Wolf Valerio. I use the title,

"Dr.," throughout the book to signify those people with PhDs—as well as those with MDs and PsyDs—in deference to their hard-earned professional credentials. I apologize if I've unintentionally omitted anyone's proper designation.

Lastly, I thank you, dear reader, for vicariously travelling my life journey with me—and for possibly exceeding your comfort zone by being open to an existential and intellectual autobiography—and now invite you to "dance the dialectic" with me.

Rupert Raj
August 1, 2017
Toronto, Ontario

Second Edition

For this revised edition, I greatly appreciate the additional testimonials provided by my transgender colleagues: Alex Bakker (Dutch), Christine Burns (English), Dr. Bobby Noble (Canadian), Dallas Denny, and Dr. K.J. Rawson (both American); and my two Canadian cisgender allies: Dr. Elspeth Brown and Jim Oulton. Thank you for your activism and allyship over the years.

I'm especially beholden to University of Victoria anthropology associate professor emerita, Margot Wilson, founder of TransGender Publishing—the only trans press in Canada—for her caring, commitment, and creativity in bringing this revised edition to print. She painstakingly edited this complex manuscript in close collaboration with me, and worked magic with many of the photographs! Our mutual interest in anthropology was an added bonus. Moreover, I'm grateful to Margot for taking the initiative to publish the life stories of not only American (and Dutch) trans people—especially elders—but also of trans Canadians, given that we have been here right from the start—fighting hard for transgender, genderqueer, intersex, and Two-Spirit people's human rights—although typically eclipsed by our southern neighbours!

Finally, I wish to thank archivist Lucie Handley-Girard for researching several of my resources in The Rupert Raj fonds in The ArQuives in Toronto and virtually relaying the requested information to me in Vancouver.

Rupert Raj
October 1, 2019
Vancouver, BC

Part I:

Dialectical Dancer

* * *

<u>*DIALECTICAL DANCER*</u>

*Dancing the dialectic
between existential desperation
and philosophical resignation—
spinning at the centre
like a whirling dervish—
embracing the tension
of the polar opposites.*

* * *

1. Existential Angst...Gender Distress...High School Crush (1952-1968)

A multidimensional man, I knew, as soon as I was born, what my core identity was: logistics manager. It was February 10, 1952, and to survive the vagaries of life and all the bureaucratic bullshit, I had to learn how to navigate the system, how to negotiate the world in my own way. Fortunately, I grew resilient; becoming adept at walking the razor's edge, like German philosopher Friedrich Nietzsche's tightrope walker.[1] Yet, as an existential Outsider, balancing between absurdity and meaning, despair and hope, cynicism and compassion, I still struggle to survive on this plagued planet. "Dancing the dialectic" between madness and sanity, confusion and clarity, complacency and commitment, I continually strive towards being and becoming.

Existential Outsiders are those rare, countercultural revolutionaries of our world, socially-alienated, creative visionaries, who Swiss psychologist, Carl Jung, called "individuators." British existentialist philosopher, Colin Wilson, was the first writer to devote a popular book to the Outsider, as the blurb on the book's back cover attests:

> *The [Existential] Outsider is an individual engaged in an intense self-exploration—a person who lives at the edge, challenges cultural values, and stands for Truth. Born into a world without perspective, where others simply drift through life, the Outsider creates his own set of rules and lives them in an unsympathetic environment...*
>
> *Through the works and lives of various artists—including Kafka, Camus, Eliot, Hemingway, Hesse, Lawrence, van Gogh, Nijinsky, Shaw, Blake, Nietzsche, and Dostoyevski—Wilson... illuminates the struggle of those who seek not only the transformation of Self but also the transformation of society as a whole.*
>
> The Outsider, Wilson, 1956[2]

Outsiders exist across cultures and countries, time and space, comprising about 10% of the population.[3] Some (3-5%) are malevolent outsiders (psychopaths, sociopaths),[4] and some (5%) are benevolent existential Outsiders (empaths).[5] These latter number among the prophets, philosophers, and poets; the Earth scientists, physicists, and psychologists; the teachers, preachers, and healers; the cultural artists, social rebels, and spirit-warriors; the environmental, political, and sexual activists—and the sexual inverts and gender benders. And, as Wilson's existentialist classic shows, these dialectical dancers and dreamers struggled to survive in a world alien to them.

I, too, felt like a stranger in a strange land, So, I intuitively knew I had to figure out some way to make sense of this crazy world without inherent meaning to keep from falling into the abyss of absurdism. I stopped believing in the supernatural (a supreme being or afterlife) when I turned seven, relying instead on the Earth Mother as my guide. So, I turned away from religion, eventually gravitating towards philosophy and science to help explain and fill the meaningless void of this random universe. Notwithstanding my naturalistic worldview, I still cannot resist dancing the dialectic between empiricism and mysticism, between physics and metaphysics, much like Austrian-American physicist/deep ecologist Fritjof Capra.[6] I inherited my love for science (and physics[7]) from my East Indian father (Dr. Amal Chandra Ghosh), a nuclear physics professor at Carleton University in Ottawa. He met my mother in 1947 while he was conducting research at the Nobel Institute of Physics in Stockholm; they married two years later and immigrated to Canada in 1951. My father and I had a special bond, and at nighttime, he occasionally took me to the Dominion Observatory to gaze at the planets, moon, and stars through the giant telescope. My passion for psychology and sociology I inherited from my Polish mother (Maria Teresa Sulima-Gottowt), whose hopes to continue social science studies were dashed due to the onset of bipolar disorder and the duties of motherhood. So, I became the "psychologist" in the family, eventually graduating with a Bachelor's degree in psychology and a Master's degree in counseling psychology.

    I was equally drawn to psychology and philosophy. My philosophical predilections were: logic, ethics, phenomenology, existentialism, humanism, and socialist feminism (and later, ecofeminism and transfeminism), as well as the philosophies inherent in Taoism and Zen Buddhism (the religion of no religion). I also appreciated the philosophical system of dialectics, variously espoused by Eastern and Western dialecticians.[8] It's purely my philosophical nature that keeps me from total misanthropy! I dance the dialectic between idealism and cynicism, straddling the middle road of positive realism. As an existentialist-humanist, I'm so thankful for the writings and practical works of particular existentialist/humanist philosophers, psychologists/psychiatrists, activists, and writers.[9] Four of these Outsiders particularly stand out: Franz Kafka,[10] Dr. Viktor Frankl,[11] Edward Carpenter,[12] and Jiddu Krishnamurti.[13] An idiosyncratic eclectic, I'm also a practical philosopher: "As my work is, so am I" (Vincent van Gogh, August 17, 1883).[14] As a man of honour, I strive to personify my beliefs and values by living according to my conscience: "I would rather be a man of conviction than a man of conformity" (Martin Luther King, Jr., 1998).[15]

    From birth onwards, forced to manage the logistics of living, in addition to being a logistics manager, I also had to become a task manager. Austrian psychiatrist, Dr. Alfred Adler, conceived of our three life tasks as love (family, romance), work (including school), and community (friendship, volunteerism, activism). Neo-Adlerians have added two more: selfhood and spirituality. My task of selfhood is ongoing—beyond the physical task of metamorphosing into my identified gender—as my psyche continues to evolve and my inner core becomes increasingly visible, shining through like bright points in the starry night. My striving towards visibility and validation is a continual life challenge, relentlessly fueled by anger born out of gender distress and lack of cisgender (non-transgender) privilege,[16] childhood abuse, and existential angst; of not being seen and valued for the whole person I am in all of my dimensions: personal, professional, political, creative. Hence, I'm the perennial Angry Man—on a par with those two righteously-enraged, African American activists/writers, James Baldwin[17] and Ralph Ellison,[18] the intense, British thinking actor/writer, Dirk Bogarde,[19] and that desperate Dutch painter, Vincent van Gogh.[20] How do I transform this rage and despair into meaning and self-empowerment? Following the shamanistic archetypes of the Four-Fold Way®,[21] crosscultural anthropologist Angeles Arrien's Native American medicine-wheel helps me integrate the four major aspects of myself: Visionary (philosopher-psychologist-anthropologist), Healer (counsellor-consultant), Teacher (educator-trainer-mentor), and Warrior (activist). My Writer and Lover sub-selves are the underlying threads weaving me together into a living tapestry. I have adapted the wheel slightly to reflect the four parts of this memoir, applying personal metaphors to describe my various functional roles: Dialectical Dancer (visionary/existential Outsider), Gender Worker (trans activist/intersex & Two-Spirit ally), Therapeutic Healer/Teacher/Writer (as cited above), and Rainbow Warrior (eco-activist/animal liberationist).

My primary task, from age two onwards, was survival—specifically, surviving my mother's physical abuse (she was jealous of my father's love for me even though she favoured my older brother). I also had to learn to cope with her emotional neglect as she virtually never showed affection. She had been quite loving and physically demonstrative towards me until I turned two, then her bipolar disorder emerged violently. Swearing loudly in an uncontrollable rage, she would become aggressive: slapping, kicking, pulling my hair, twisting my arm, and she once even tried to choke me! The latter incident was especially traumatic because I was only nine, and never expected a mother to hurt her child that way. Witnessing my sister and me squabbling over a puppet, my mother lost it, and screaming up a storm, tore into me. Putting her hands around my throat, she started to squeeze, but thankfully, stopped before I suffocated. Regaining control, she applied iodine where her fingernails had dug into my throat and a bandage to cover my bruises. When my parents prevaricated about my injury—"Oh, she had an accident"—friends of the family never challenged this cover-up of child abuse. Bad as the physical abuse was though, I'm thankful that it wasn't either emotional or sexual abuse!

My mother's violent outbursts towards me and my four siblings were not maliciously motivated as I sensed that she really loved us but simply didn't know how to show it. She also could not control her angry impulses and should never have had children. Not the maternal type, she was further impaired by poor mental health, including (I suspect) narcissistic personality disorder, deeming she was too pure to confess her sins to the priest and too "normal" to consult a psychiatrist. Moreover, she never expressed empathy towards others, or ever apologized for abusing us kids. Her psychological problems were also largely due to her strict Roman Catholic upbringing. Her mother had sent her to be reared by nuns during her formative years, tainting her with rigid, puritanical attitudes bordering on negation of self, sexuality, and life itself. I observed that many Eastern Europeans (including my Polish relatives and my mother's friends) had been victimized by this oppressive patriarchal religion that historically devalued women, children, and animals—not to mention people who were other than Christian, White, heterosexual, or cisgender!

Always scientifically objective, I can now concede that my mother was not all bad. Not subscribing to divine or human absolutes, such as purely good or evil, insofar as everything is relative, I embrace, instead, a continuum consciousness reflecting the idiosyncrasy and variability of humans and animals, nature, and culture. Notwithstanding, I don't condone abuse or neglect, meanness or humiliation, or my mother's violent behaviour. One of her positive personality traits came to the fore when she stood up to her mother, a devout Catholic, unequivocally telling her that she was going to marry my father, an agnostic raised in the Hindu faith (read: heathen). Thankfully, my grandmother was so taken with my father that she gave her unconditional consent. My father, in his turn, resisted his parents' wish that he marry a Hindu woman of their choice—they never wholeheartedly embraced my mother as their daughter-in-law. I'm so grateful that my parents passed on their independent spirit to me—one that transcends both race and religion!

My vulnerability as a child of an abusive parent was commonplace during the 1950s and 1960s. The Ottawa Children's Aid Society didn't protect me simply because it wasn't aware of the abuse. People tended to sweep domestic violence under the carpet in those days. My father didn't report it because his love for his wife minimized the reality of her abusive behaviour, precluding appropriate intervention. The few times he did intervene on my behalf, my mother would lash out physically at him and, eventually, he gave up, retreating to a place of defeat and denial. I never told him so, but I always felt unsafe when I was by myself in my mother's presence and let down that he wasn't there to protect me. Too bad he hadn't read any of Polish-Swiss-Jewish, child psychiatrist Dr. Alice Miller's books on cruel parenting and childhood abuse![22] I eventually forgave my father for his fallibility, but it took a long time. Nonetheless, his paternal neglect forced me to learn to fend for myself, which is why I'm so resilient to this day. From quite an early age I had to be my own parent, psychotherapist, and priest.

Desperately trying to stay out of my mother's way, I sought refuge in the neighbouring fields, woods, ravines, and marshes, and on the railway tracks. A lone wolf, I communed with nature. Soothed by the solitude, I would sit in my tree fort, nestled deep in the forest, my nose buried in a comic or children's book, escaping to a fantasy world free from violence and fear. Mother Nature and books were my saving grace, rescuing me from despair. And, sometimes, on a weekday, I would seek sanctuary in the nearby church, enwrapped in the eerie stillness within. I felt safe there, far from the maddening crowd.

The dialectical dilemma of religion: the attraction of certain symbols and rituals, yet the repulsion of dogmatic rules and punitive sanctions! An ex-Christian friend of mine called herself an intellectual atheist, but still an emotional Catholic. For me, I was pulled in by the sensuality of it all: the stained-glass windows, the gold-inlaid statues, the burning incense and candles, the pipe-organ music, the Gregorian chants, even the wine-soaked Eucharistic wafer. But then, the hypocritical elitism, dogmatism, and misogyny of the misnamed "Mother Church" and "her" all-powerful, often-pedophilic priests and sexually-starved, strap-happy nuns would always push me away—into a safe zone of democratic freethinkers (secular humanists/atheists). A notable exception to the perverse perfidy of Christian denominations are the pacifistic Quakers. And, of course, the non-creedal, humanistic, pantheistic, liberal-leaning, LGBTTI2SQQAA-friendly, Unitarian Universalist Association, which incorporates Christianity, Hinduism, Buddhism, Taoism, Judaism, Islam, and Earth-centred spirituality.

The same thing goes for my visceral attraction to, and my cerebral repulsion from, Hinduism, Bahá'í, Islam, Judaism, and male-centred paganism. The enchantments of exploring certain mythological, androgynous deities like the Hindu god, Krishna (Vishnu), the friendship firesides of the Bahá'í, faith, the whirling dervishes of Islamic Sufism, the mystical tree of life of Judaic Kabbalism, and the sacred fire and Maypole dances of Celtic Druidism would all inevitably be tainted by the oppressive doctrinal practices waged against innocent animals, boys, girls, women, non-heterosexual and non-cisgender people, and other Outsiders. Not that all Taoists, Buddhists, Zenists, goddess worshippers, Indigenous spirit-believers, agnostics, and atheists are guiltless by any means! Still, the psychological anthropologist in me could not quite resist the allure of the quest for the Holy Grail (eternal truth), and like the alchemical psychologist, Dr. Carl Jung (both scientist and mystic), I would be plagued by a lifelong pursuit of the Philosopher's Stone.

My childhood memories, though, are not all bad. There were good times too, such as the camaraderie of siblings playing together in the house, or reading comic books, or watching TV. My brother, Jakub, was two years older than me, my sister, Arjuna, two-and-a-half years younger, my middle brother, Casimir, five years younger, and my youngest brother, Andrzej, 11 years younger. I recall one time when we kids had a creative impulse to put on a puppet show—a whodunit mystery-thriller—for our parents. They loved it! It was one of our happier times as a close family unit.

Beyond that, there were birthdays and religious holidays, replete with Polish and Swedish culinary delights—and occasionally East Indian cuisine—including delicious desserts, which we kids loved to help bake. My mother would dish out borscht, cabbage rolls, sauerkraut, and perogies, with pickled-herring rollmops, liverwurst pâté, Limburger cheese, and dark Pumpernickel rye bread on the side, topped up with tasty pastries: babka, baba rum, and poppy-seed or plum-jam rolls. My father periodically prepared such Indian delicacies as wafer-thin cream-of-wheat crêpes fried in butter and spiced with cardamom, and would put out delectable sweets: *rossogolla*, *suji halwa* and coconut *ladoo*.

Another positive childhood memory are the photographs my father took of our family, including home movies (I disliked the ones of me, however, because my external female presentation did not match my internal male persona). I also appreciated the paintings and reprints throughout our house, including van Gogh's *Reaper with Sickle*. My mother also painted (pastel landscapes), and I so wish I had inherited her talent to portray natural beauty through art. Oh well, at least I can see the world through Vincent's eyes, vibrantly transformed by his larger-than-life colours and textures. Vincent was a kindred spirit who resonated with me on so many levels: our dual attraction to women and men, our passion for plants and nature, and our compassion for everyday people and the downtrodden. Vincent was religious and spiritual, whereas I was secular and existential, but we both harboured a love for Mother Nature and a lust for life and art. There was music in our house too. The phonograph serenaded us at nighttime with my parents' records of European classical composers, as well as traditional folk music from Poland and Sweden—but, surprisingly, no East Indian music. These days, I still listen to traditional folk music (particularly Celtic), but prefer contemporary folk, jazz, blues, R&B, soul, rock 'n' roll, popular and world music (especially, Ghazal's Indian-Persian jamming). My life story is a blend of downbeat blues and soulful shouts, a dance of life and death, of love and loss.

Life was a challenge growing up because of who I was in the world. At age three, while riding my trike in the living room as I watched my father sitting nearby, I instinctively knew that I was *really* a boy, and I naïvely presumed that I was the only boy trapped in a girl's body on the planet. Such a lonely existence! When taking baths with my older brother, I was devastated that I did not have what he had between his legs. Was I a freak of nature? No!

I was a transsexual[23]—specifically, a female-to-male transsexual (a trans boy). However, it wasn't until some 15 years later that I would learn that I had been *born* this way. So, until then, I feared that I would never escape my gender dysphoria, this persistent, intense gender distress caused by the dissonance between my mind and body. I was desperate! A prisoner of gender, I was faced with an incredible challenge: to somehow find a way to overcome my (rare) birth limitation of being a transsexual male born into a female body. Would I succeed?

Growing up in Ottawa, I was the proverbial tomboy and played with both boys and girls. Although not sexually precocious, when I was eight, I concocted "the Naked Room Club" (using the same initials as my father's part-time government post at the National Research Council), where, in the privacy of the cold cellar, my playmates and I would reveal our privates as a primitive form of sex education. Of course, I was hugely embarrassed at having to bare my business, not to mention bitterly jealous of my male playmate's little "dick and balls." Nevertheless, vicarious pleasure compelled me, while penis envy plagued my heart! Like many tomboyish girls, I played with toys on both sides of the gender divide: my brother's Mechano set and Dinky Toy cars as well as my tea sets and dolls. Of my two dolls though, one was male (Ronnie) and the other sexually indeterminate (androgynous? intersex?). Intuitively identifying as male, I magically changed my gender-neutral doll into a boy, naming him Robin and reframing the original "dress" my mother had made for "her" as a Roman-styled male tunic made for "him." If only I could change myself that easily!

Sometime later, during my gender transition, I almost took the name Robin because, growing up, I had identified with Robin Hood and other legendary male figures like Ivanhoe, Lancelot and Zorro. As a child, I would also masquerade as the macho cartoon character, Mighty Mouse, swooping through the air in my flowing red cape to gallantly save Minnie Mouse and other damsels in distress. Besides comic book superheroes like Superman, Flash Gordon and the Green Lantern, I loved comics about Mickey Mouse, Donald Duck, and, especially, Uncle Scrooge McDuck (whose fantasy adventures to far-off and mythical lands—and discovery of the alchemical Philosopher's Stone—sparked the would-be anthropologist and metaphysicist in me). I was definitely a nerd, rather than a jock, and when I did occasionally engage in sports, they were typically medieval sports like fencing and archery. Two other male names I nearly chose were Richard and Dirk (after the handsome British screen idols, Richard Greene[24] and Dirk Bogarde.[25]

A TV and film aficionado as a teenager, I also identified with several other male cultural icons; namely, British actor, Laurence Harvey, and American, gay film star, Montgomery Clift. I was an avid reader too, identifying with many classic, male fictional heroes: Pip in *Great*

Expectations,[26] Prince Nikolaevich Myshkin in *The Idiot*,[27] Rudolf Rassendyll in *The Prisoner of Zenda*,[28] Rupert in *Rupert of Henzau*,[29] and Philip Carey in *Of Human Bondage*.[30] Not only did I identify with these dashing male heroes, I was also in love with them! My romantic feelings, however, remained long-repressed because back then, I could not figure out how a man could love another man, never having heard of homosexuality or bisexuality, let alone transsexualism or hermaphrodism (now intersex[31]).

When I was about two years old, we moved from Churchill Avenue into our brand new home on Niagara Drive in suburban Ottawa: a yellow-brick house bordering a field and woods, in which nestled Whitehill Glade Restaurant, complete with a wishing-well and goldfish pond, and weddings in the summertime. Later, I would seek sanctuary in the nearby greenhouse in the woods in those halcyon days before school!

At five-and-a-half, I was petrified when I first began Kindergarten at St. Thomas Aquinas, a bilingual, Roman Catholic school. My mother took me to class that first dreadful day, leaving me to face the cold cruel world all by myself. Innocently enough, I had worn a pair of blue-and-yellow plaid pants, only to be told by my teacher, Miss Manning, that I could not come back to class unless I wore a skirt or dress. Her words struck me like the cold blade of a knife: I had no choice but to comply with this early instance of gender policing. I also had to wear sandals and carry a purse-type satchel like the *other* girls, but I desperately craved the laced boots and backpack-style schoolbag with which the boys were privileged. Even worse, girls and boys were segregated in certain ways; namely, washrooms and physical exercises. I was a fish out of water, longing for the school day to end so I could resume the privacy of my own home, free to be me: the boy that I really was.

In the first grade, I admired a classmate named Bobby, but my feelings were mixed with envy. I wanted to look like him; even more so, I wanted to *be* like him; a boy. I also had feelings for the first of many teachers, Mrs. Papineau. In a recurring dream (the power of the subconscious!), in which she was Ginger Rogers and I, Fred Astaire, I would start off in my female form, beginning to pirouette as part of my repertoire. Then, halfway through, I would magically turn myself inside-out to present my true male self in the guise of the celebrated hoofer himself, wearing a top hat and tails, and flourishing my cane as I tap danced with the glamorous Ginger. The dream was a dynamic metaphor for future change: the Dialectical Dancer, currently caught between female sex and male gender, one day ultimately able to transmute into male.

My parents, being immigrants, wanted their children to learn English. So, when my school turned Francophone just before I finished the first grade, we kids were transferred to an English-speaking Catholic school. Alas, our new school teachers were super-strict nuns, lashing our hands with a leather strap for the slightest transgression. And, we had to wear regulation school uniforms (girls wore black jumpers and white blouses, white knee socks and black shoes), which, ironically, was better than wearing our own street clothes because at least I could blend in as an anonymous black-and-white blur. Lady Luck soon smiled on me though, as my siblings and I were reprieved after only a few months.

Our reprieve took the form of a temporary relocation to Montreal, in the suburb of Longueuil, for a year-and-a-half (1958-1960), while my father pursued his doctorate degree in physics at McGill University. While in Quebec, I attended a Catholic school and fell in love with my second-grade teacher, Miss Packard. To my ignominy, female students had to take First Communion and Confirmation. So, I had to suffer wearing a lace gown and veil as a Bride of Christ, forcing a fake smile for my father's camera. I only had one close friend: Jeannie. When we played house or hospital with her girlfriends, I assumed the role of father or doctor. There was a boy, Peter, who I liked, but it was also that I wanted to *be* him; like my feelings for Bobby, I coveted his male birthright.

Back home in Ottawa again, I was allowed to skip the third grade because of the different educational standards between Ontario and Quebec at the time and my higher than average grades. I began to like classes for the first time, especially literature, and my reading comprehension was excellent. My fourth-grade teacher, Miss Conrad (whom I also dreamt about), told me that my vocabulary was that of a 12-year-old, which made me feel pretty good. So good that I too wanted to be a teacher when I grew up. My only two friends were Sheryl (also a tomboy) and Doug. Sheryl and I spent time at her house, playing softball, watching TV, and walking her pet collie. She even tried to teach me to play her piano. Doug was sweet on me, walking me to school every day for a time and, once, he even gave me a Valentine, but our friendship soon fizzled out because I didn't want to be his *girl*friend.

Beyond schoolmates, I had several neighbourhood playmates: David and Jane (siblings), and Ian. In the wintertime, we built snow forts and had snowball fights, tobogganed and played ice-hockey. I would pretend to be Rocket or Pocket Richard of the Montréal Canadiens. In the summertime, we rode our bikes, played baseball and road-hockey, and swam in the school pool. I hated wearing a girls' bathing suit, often hiding beneath a towel. We used to collect empty Coke and beer bottles in order to buy bubble gum, licorice, sweet tarts, cherry bombs, and comic books at the Lebanese corner store with the refund deposit.

There were also Jim and Janet, a brother and sister, who lived a few houses down from me. Jim and I would play chess and mechanical hockey, run his model trains, blow up his toy tanks with firecrackers, and gaze at the tropical fish in his aquariums. Two buddies just hanging out, he never really saw me as a girl. Janet and I occasionally played dress up: she pressuring me to wear her mother's fur coat and walk in her pumps. I hated this ordeal, suffering through it simply to humour her. Trying to balance myself on heels, I felt like a female impersonator! I felt safe with Janet and Jim because they did not judge my dissonant gender identity. Their German mother used to call me *das mannchen* ("little man") because of my boyish demeanour—a welcome compliment to mitigate my intensifying gender distress!

Madame Fortune was looking out for me once again because I was never bullied in school. I don't know how I managed to escape this insidious form of violence because if there was ever a potential victim, it would have been me—the proverbial misfit, a "he-she." Ironically, it was I who, in one instance, picked a fight with a boy slightly younger than me and pushing him onto the ground, pummelled him until he surrendered. I don't know why I committed such a heinous crime, but I felt a sense of empowerment at proving my mettle as one of the guys. Happily, my bullying bent was short-lived, an aberrant departure from my true character as a gentle man. Bullies are always cowards. Their aggressive actions typically stem from emotional insecurity (often resulting in anxiety, depression, and anger), usually brought on by dysfunctionality, abuse, or neglect at home, at school, or at work. Sometimes, antisocial behaviour is due to confusion or conflict around emergent identity issues, such as possibly being gay or lesbian, trans or intersex, or otherwise sexually or gender transgressive. Sadly, anti-bullying legislation to protect students in Ontario schools would not be enacted until the early 2000s.[32]

In the sixth grade, I had to again deal with my own persistent feelings around gender identity and sexual orientation. I had a crush on my first male teacher (Mr. White), but suppressed my attraction because I simply could not reconcile how I, a boy at my core, could possibly fall for another male. Disorienting dissonance! Many gay/bi trans-males have struggled over the years, relentlessly searching for validation from their cisgender male peers. At that time, I shared a bedroom with my sister, and turning 11, in the privacy of our room, I began to crossdress. Wearing a white shirt, blue tie, navy blazer, beige Levi's, and black penny loafers, I would beam at my male visage in the mirror, hoping to someday vanquish my unbearable gender distress. I swore Arjuna to secrecy and she faithfully kept my confidence. A true ally, she offered to wear pants—as I did—instead of a dress, when we walked to church in wintertime (the only time my mother permitted a departure from our regular female summer attire), so I wouldn't be noticeable as the odd "man" out.

In the seventh grade, my classmate Shawn and I competed to see who could recite the most poetry and tied at 1000 lines. A romantic, I love poetry! We enjoyed a sense of camaraderie, clambering up into his tree fort with his male buddies just as if I were another boy. I also had a thing for my library teacher, Miss Guignard, who invited the library club (of which I was a member) to a party at her Gothic-styled house on Sunset Boulevard in Ottawa's upscale district. I seriously contemplated becoming a librarian myself because of my intense love for books—not to mention for a certain lovely librarian!

During my last year in grade school, I befriended a neighbourhood boy, Chris, who was two years younger than me (who, some years later, came out as gay). We were simply buddies, no hanky-panky. Sadly, his mother would not let me play with her son after a time because she disapprovingly noted that I was "developing." At 13, my chest was just starting to swell. A well-bred English lady, she viewed our friendship as improper, declaring me off limits even though she was unaware of my unexpressed transsexualism and her son's unarticulated homosexuality. Too bad neither Chris nor I knew how to verbalize our authentic identities at the time. Had we been able to, we could have allied ourselves against a heterosexist and cisgender world.

Graduating from childhood to adolescence, I was ambivalent about starting secondary school. Feeling both excitement and trepidation, I biked to class that first day of September in 1965. Ridgemont High's motto was "Knowledge is power" and I welcomed enlightenment because, at the tender age of 13, my future seemed unclear. What was in store for me? Would I finally be able to become the *real* me? I bumbled through most of my academic year, but as final exams approached, my crossgender feelings intensified and I had thoughts of wanting to die. Desperate, I felt trapped and alone. Believing I was the only person caught in this conundrum, I didn't know how to solve the problem. My distress increased to the point where I could not concentrate on my studies and on my final Geography exam, I simply scribbled my name, leaving the rest of the paper blank. An indirect cry for help, I felt unsafe to disclose my gender dysphoria to anyone other than my sister. Reluctantly, I went to summer school to make up my failed Geography grade.

Puberty inevitably reared its ugly head as "the curse" finally struck! Riding home on the school bus, I suddenly felt an icky sensation and upon standing up, I was aghast to see menstrual blood oozing through my jumper; a sickening sight of red on yellow. I felt so humiliated! The trials and tribulations of a transsexual teenager trying to make it in this world! Fortunately, mine was the next stop. I now wonder if perhaps this was the start of my internalized transphobia. It wasn't shame at being born a trans boy (or an ostensible girl) but, rather, angry embarrassment at this unwanted dilemma; female reproductive organs intruding in such a tacky way! Because my mother was away visiting her mother in Sweden that summer, my father had to explain the facts of life, providing me with sanitary napkins. Both father and mother to us kids, my dad's androgyny rubbed off on me, and even though my core gender identity was male, I complemented my *animus* (masculinity) with a measure of *anima* (femininity). Like my father, I was learning to be both protector and nurturer. As liberated "males," my father and I embraced *yin* and *yang* in balanced measure. Over time, my binary, male gender identity evolved into more of an androgynous one, while still identifying primarily as a (trans) man. Not a "femmy" man myself, I warmly embrace my trans and cis brothers who are.

My budding sex drive began to poke through at this time. From Kindergarten onwards, I had crushes on all my teachers, female *and* male. Although I occasionally harboured romantic feelings for boys in grade school, I preferred girls and was attracted to several female classmates. But women were even better! In ninth grade, I really fell hard for my English and Physical Education teacher, Miss Ritchie (affectionately dubbed J.J. by her students), who was also my guidance counsellor. Sweet and pretty, I was so besotted with her that one day after class, as she boarded the bus, I got on too and sat down opposite her. I presented her with a bunch of pink carnations I had bought earlier (unbeknownst to my family). She responded appropriately as my English teacher: "Thank you for the lovely flowers. By the way, how are your gerunds and verbals coming along?" Painfully shy and confounded by inconsequential questions about grammar, I mumbled something in response, blushing red as a beet. Miss Ritchie said goodbye as she got off at her stop, while I rode home, arriving late for supper. Thankfully, my parents didn't challenge my alibi that I had been studying in the school library, and my secret love was safe.

As someone not fitting the stereotype of a "normal" teenage girl, I felt like a stranger[33]—a gender-ambiguous Outsider desperately trying to survive in a cisgender world. French-Algerian existential philosopher, Albert Camus (one of my role models), would have appreciated the awkward absurdity of it all! I certainly looked atypical with my short hair, desert boots, knee socks, shirt-like blouses, and mandatory skirt or jumper. I tried to wear less traditionally feminine textures like leather and coarse fabrics, and more traditionally masculine colours like blue, green and brown. One time, before setting off for school, my mother nearly found me out: I sweated buckets as she straightened the collar of my green, floral print blouse that was hiding my plain green one underneath! I also tried to flatten my abhorrent budding breasts by binding my chest with a cloth belt, but this didn't work as well as I had hoped, so I gave up. At home, I practiced lowering my voice, talking and singing in a deeper octave. Again, my mother nearly caught me in the act as she walked into the room as I was pulling a Pavarotti! Hardest for me was having to change in the girls' school locker room before mandatory physical education classes, which I frequently tried to miss, calling in sick or conveniently forgetting my gym suit at home. It was sheer hell trying not to catch a glimpse of my female classmates undressing, and even more hellish trying not to let them see me while I changed! On these occasions, I wished I was invisible.

Ironically, in some ways, I *was* the Invisible Man. A shy loner, I had only one real friend in high school, Hilda. Like me, she was an Outsider too. Not a raving beauty by then current standards of femininity, she didn't have a boyfriend—preferring animals to boys—and wanted to be a veterinarian. Whereas she might not have been seen as a lesbian, I was very likely perceived as a butch dyke—transsexual boys being unheard of back then. For the remaining years of high school, my inner maleness would remain unseen until I was finally able to begin university as the man I knew myself to be.

My invisibility also extends to my ethnoracial identity given that, although biracial, my Brownness is diluted by my Whiteness, and to my chagrin, I virtually always pass for White. This erasure goes even further as I have been the victim of racism not only by White people but also by people of colour (in particular, other South Asians) and those of mixed race (especially, other Eurasians). Whoever accused marginalized groups of eating our own was right on the mark! My lack of visibility is comprehensive: even today, I'm usually seen as a White, straight, cisgender male. While this erasure certainly provides some measure of privilege, it also conceals the diverse dimensions of my overall being, dulling the brilliance of the multifaceted amethyst that I am!

The only instance of biracial validation I have ever received was at the 2015 and 2017 mixed-race, multimedia, M.I.X.E.D. Art conferences in Toronto, where I was invited to co-facilitate a roundtable discussion on activism and burnout. Gender identity and sexual orientation were also recognized by conference delegates as key components of a multidimensional identity—along with intersections of race, class, gender, and sex—especially for trans and queer people who are mixed race or partly Indigenous. Overall, though, I was fortunate enough to largely escape ethnoracial bigotry, only rarely being subjected to such slurs as "Polak" or "Paki." If I had had the gumption at the time, I would have fittingly rebutted: "I'm proud to have a mixture of Polish *and* Indian ancestry!" And even more so, given the legacy of outstanding social change agents (many of whom are also existential Outsiders) from both countries, namely, Polish-Swiss child psychiatrist/trauma therapist, Dr. Alice Miller, and various Indian prophets, religious leaders, philosophers, ecofeminists, state leaders, and politicians: Buddha, Mahatma Gandhi, Krishnamurti, Vandana Shiva, Indira Gandhi, and several *Hijra* politicians.

In 1968, when I was 16, I got a real eye-opener as I chanced upon two retrospective newspaper articles about hermaphroditic (intersex) people. The first news story reported that Polish sprinter, Ewa Klobukowska,[34] was the first Olympic athlete to fail a sex-chromatin gender test in 1967, registering an extra chromosome (a genetic mosaic of 47, XX/XXY), and was banned from professional sports. The second news report outed another intersex athlete, an Austrian downhill-skier named Erika Schinegger,[35] who was also disqualified in 1967 by the International Olympic Committee Medical Commission because "she" was, in fact, male. He had Complete Androgen Insensitivity Syndrome (CAIS) with an XY karyotype and was found to have internal male sex organs. Until quite recently, intersex and transgender athletes, like Canadian trans women, Michelle Dumaresq,[36] Kristen Worley[37] and Dr. Rachel McKinnon,[38] had to fight for their right to compete in professional sports as their self-identified gender. Following "her" disqualification, Erika surgically reassigned as male, legally changed his name to Erik, married and became a father. Incredibly, the same year as these news stories came out, another intersex person (an Australian)—misassigned as female at birth, and later reassigned as 47, XXY (Kleinfelter's type Syndrome)— was socially (but not medically) transitioning to male. He legally changed his name to Peter Stirling[39] and later married a woman. Regrettably, I didn't learn about him until many years later, when his 1989 autobiography was sexploited by the tabloids. Moreover, I was unaware of several even earlier intersex people who were also initially presumed to be female at birth until medical examinations at puberty or death revealed an intersex condition,[40] as well as other early gender transgressors: so-called female husbands[41] and passing women.[42]

Although I did not know whether I too, might be intersex, I resonated with Ewa and Erik and their stories provided me with a ray of hope. Perhaps a similar medical condition could explain my crossgender identity? If so, there might also be a cure for me! Suppressing my hopes, I still dared to mention the news articles to my family. Now, all these years later, I don't recollect the specific reactions of my mother and siblings. Privately, I disclosed to my father that I believed I was bisexual (meaning to me, with my limited understanding and language, that I was male on the inside, female on the outside). I hadn't yet come across the terms, "transsexual" or "androgynous," but I wonder why I didn't use the term, "hermaphroditic." Simply responding that Oscar Wilde was a homosexual—my father's only point of reference at the time—neither he nor I had heard of the widely-sensationalized, 1952 Christine Jorgensen "sex change" story (or if he had, it had slipped his memory). Dad added, "We'll try to find a psychiatrist to show you that the life of a girl can be just as rewarding as that of a boy." As feminist and humanist as this view seemed, his proposed solution did not resolve my problem: I was a female-to-male transsexual, not a masculine lesbian! Too bad that neither of us knew of Dr. Benjamin's groundbreaking, 1966 medical text, *The Transsexual Phenomenon,* published only two years earlier! My only reply was, "Please don't tell Mom." Nothing came of my father's offer, though—perhaps he thought I would soon get over my adolescent gender anxiety. I never had a chance to broach the subject again because just four months later, on top of grinding gender distress, my world suddenly fell out from under me!

Chapter 1 Notes

[1] Nietzsche, Friedrich, *Thus Spoke Zarathustra,* (translated by Walter Kaufmann), London, UK: Penguin Books, 1978.

[2] Quoted here: http://www.wilderdom.com/wilson/. Colin Wilson wrote six sequels to his seminal existential work, *The Outsider*, New York, NY: J. P. Tarcher, 1956. https://en.wikipedia.org/wiki/The_Outsider_(Colin_Wilson). These include: *Religion and the Rebel* (Bath, UK: Ashgrove Press, 1957); *Beyond the Outsider* (London, UK: Macmillan Publishing, 1965); and *Introduction to the New Existentialism* (London, UK: Hutchinson, 1966). https://en.wikipedia.org/wiki/Colin_Wilson. A controversial figure, he ran the gamut from Left to Right, and while I don't agree with everything he wrote, I'm intrigued by his positive existential stance as he moved from angry young man (*The Angry Years: The Rise and Fall of the Angry Young Men*, London, UK: Robson Books, 2007) to optimistic realist to "superman" (*Super Consciousness: The Quest for the Peak Experience*, London, UK: Watkins Publishing, 2007). The last book was inspired by the self-actualization theories of American humanistic, transpersonal psychologist, Abraham Maslow (noted in chapter 3). For additional existentialists, see https://en.wikipedia.org/wiki/Existentialism.

[3] The normal distribution curve (aka the bell curve) is a probability distribution schema used to model phenomena such as physical characteristics, test scores, and some psychological traits**.** See https://brilliant.org/wiki/normal-distribution/. Google "normal distribution example psychology" to see the statistical breakdown of the normal curve: 0.5% and 2% (respectively) at each end of the normal curve (totalling the anormative 5%), 13.5% to each side of the middle (totalling 27% of the normative majority), and 34% at each nearest side to the middle (totalling 68% of the normative majority).

Anormative outsiders probably lie within the 5% of outliers (beyond the normative average) and beyond—moving inwards towards the centre of the curve—totalling 11% or so. It's estimated that 3-6% of the overall population have antisocial personality disorder (with psychopaths comprising about 1% and sociopaths 2-5%). See also note 4 below. In contrast, empaths make up about 5% of the population. (Although 15-20% of people are empathic, not all are classified as empaths). To further complicate things, there are two subsets of the general category of empaths: psychic or spiritual empaths (estimated around 1-2% of the population), and supernatural empaths, as portrayed in science fiction. See also note 5 below.

[4] For psychopaths, see https://www.psychologytoday.com/ca/blog/mindmelding/201301/what-is-psychopath-0. For sociopaths, see https://www.psychologytoday.com/ca/basics/sociopathy. For differences between the two, see https://psychcentral.com/blog/differences-between-a-psychopath-vs-sociopath/.

[5] For empaths (a higher level of normatively empathic people), see https://drjudithorloff.com/top-10-traits-of-an-empath/. For empathic people, see https://www.psychologytoday.com/ca/blog/emotional-freedom/201602/10-traits-empathic-people-share. For differences between the two, see https://www.psychologytoday.com/us/blog/human-kind/201901/having-empathy-and-being-empath-what-s-the-difference. For psychic empaths, see https://www.learnreligions.com/what-is-a-psychic-empath-2561944. For spiritual empaths, see https://www.empathdestiny.com/difference-between-being-an-empath-and-being-a-spiritual-

healer/. For supernatural empaths in science fiction, see
https://www.empath.nyc/blog/2017/10/11/what-is-an-empath-really.
 While a very small number of existential Outsiders could possibly be malevolent (psychopathic or sociopathic), the majority are much more likely to be benevolent inasmuch as they are concerned with the personal meaning of life (and death), and individual freedom and responsibility. Many are conscientious citizens and some are social justice and deep ecological activists. Consequently, a number are empathic and some are even empaths.

[6] See: Capra, Fritjof, *The Tao of Physics: An Exploration of the Parallels Between Modern Physics and Eastern Mysticism*, Boulder, CO: Shambhala Publications, 1975.

[7] I was awe-struck by the physical wonders of the universe upon reading, several years later, the classical theories of cosmological physicists Dr. Albert Einstein (theory of relativity) and Dr. Stephen Hawking (quantum mechanics, time, black holes, and ongoing research towards formulating a grand unified theory of the universe). See: Einstein, Albert, and Leopold Infeld, *The Evolution of Physics: First Concepts to the Theories of Relativity and Quanta* (translated from the German by Maurice Solovine), Paris, FR: Flammarion Group (Éditions Gallimard), 1938. Reprint, Amazon (Kindle Edition), 1983; and Hawking, Stephen, *The Theory of Everything: The Origin and Fate of the Universe*, Beverly Hills, CA: New Millennium Press, 1997. (Ecophilosophers, ecopsychologists, Gaia Earth scientists and eco-activists, also dear to my heart, are mentioned in chapter 12.)

[8] Dialectics (also known as the "dialectical method") is a type of minor logical discourse practiced by both Western philosophers (e.g., Zeno of Elea, Socrates, Plato, Aristotle, Boethius, Abelard, William of Ockham, Thomas Aquinas, Georg Wilhelm Friedrich Hegel, Immanuel Kant, Karl Marx, Friedrich Engels, Edward Carpenter, Murray Bookchin, Karl Barth and Emil Brunner), and proponents of Eastern traditions (e.g., Buddha, Confucius, Lao Tzu, D.T. Suzuki, Indian Vedantists, and Krishnamurti). From classical to medieval to modern philosophy, Western dialectics takes many forms, including the Socratic method, the Hegelian dialectic, Marxist dialectical materialism, Bookchin's dialectical naturalism (social ecology), and Karl Barth and Emil Brunner's dialectical theology. As well, there's the recent clinical application of Dr. Marsha Linehan's Dialectical Behavioral Therapy (DBT) (noted in chapter 12). Hegel's dialectic comprises three developmental stages (configured as a triangle): a thesis—giving rise to its reaction, an antithesis—which contradicts or negates the thesis, and the tension between the two being (ideally) resolved by means of a synthesis, or simply formulated: problem –> reaction -> solution. Dancing the dialectic, at times I ambivalently embrace the tension of the polar opposites; at other times, I long for a hoped-for reconciliation of these polarities. My paradoxical perspective is inspired by earlier dialectical dancers: philosophers Edward Carpenter and Jiddu Krishnamurti, and physicists Fritjof Capra and Albert Einstein. See also https://en.wikipedia.org/wiki/Dialectic.

[9] The select list includes: existentialist and/or humanist philosophers, Hazel Barnes, Albert Camus (alternatively self-styled as "absurdist"), Edward Carpenter, Simone de Beauvoir, Jiddu Krishnamurti, Jean-Paul Sartre and Colin Wilson; existentialist and/or humanist psychologists/psychiatrists, Dr. Erik Erikson, Dr. Viktor Frankl, Dr. Erich Fromm, Dr. Abraham Maslow and Dr. Rollo May; existentialist writers, Fyodor Dostoyevsky, James Joyce, Franz Kafka and Leo Tolstoy; and Black existentialist writers, W. E. B. Du Bois, Ralph Ellison, Toni Morrison and Richard Wright.

[10] Franz Kafka (1883-1924) was a shy Bohemian-Jewish novelist, who variously lived in former Czechoslovakia (now the Czech Republic), Germany and Austria, but was never

completed accepted by Czechs, Germans or Austrians. One biographer suggests that Kafka inclined towards vegetarianism—as a protest against his brutal father, a butcher—as well as bisexuality, but that neither inclination was properly manifested due to his internally-conflicted nature. See: Friedländer, Saul, *Franz Kafka: The Poet of Shame and Guilt*, New Haven, CT: Yale University Press, 2012. https://glreview.org/article/how-straight-could-kafka-have-been/. Kafka's German-language short stories and novels explore themes of alienation, anxiety, guilt and absurdity: *The Metamorphosis (or The Transformation)*, New York, NY: W. W. Norton, 2014; and *The Complete Novels: The Trial; Amerika; The Castle; Falmouth*, UK: Minerva Press, 1992. My 1982-1988 gender counselling-educational service for trans men was called Metamorphosis (later renamed Metamorphosis Medical Research Foundation), alluding to gender transition from female to male due to certain birth-assigned females' sense of self-alienation and gender anxiety arising from being born in the "wrong body."

[11] Dr. Viktor Frankl (1905-1997) was a German-Jewish psychiatrist and writer who survived a Nazi concentration camp during the Holocaust, and later immigrated to the USA, where he established clinical and training centres offering Logotherapy, his innovative therapeutic model of striving for hope and meaning. Frankl's books include: *Man's Search for Meaning: An Introduction to Logotherapy* (3rd ed.) (translated from the German by Ilse Lasch), New York, NY: Touchstone Books (Simon & Schuster), 1984; *The Doctor and the Soul: From Psychotherapy to Logotherapy* (translated from the German by Richard Winston and Clara Winston), New York, NY: Vintage Books, 1986; *Psychotherapy and Existentialism: Selected Papers on Logotherapy*, New York, NY: Simon & Schuster, 1967; and *The Will to Meaning: Foundations and Applications of Logotherapy*, New York, NY: New American Library, 1988.

[12] Edward Carpenter (1844-1929) was a socially-androgynous, gay, British philosopher, poet, political activist, mathematician, mystic and writer. He was also a democratic socialist (but also, at times, an anarchist-communist), pacifist, pro-suffragette feminist, humanitarian, theoretical ecologist, vegetarian and anti-vivisectionist. Like me, he danced the dialectic between Western intellectual science (especially, physics, and in his case, also mathematics) and Eastern intuitive mysticism (particularly, Buddhism, Taoism, and in his case, also Hinduism), driven to try to reconcile these (and other) seemingly opposing polarities. He advocated for the rights of queer and androgynous ("intermediate" sexed) people, prisoners, working-class labourers, women (including suffragettes and prostitutes), and animals. A naturalist, he closely communed with animals and nature, and a humanist, he "consummately" communicated with people. We would have been cerebral and visceral soul mates! See: Carpenter, Edward, *My Days and Dreams: Being Autobiographical Notes*, London, UK: Allen and Unwin, 1916 (3rd ed.), 1918. https://archive.org/stream/mydaysanddreamsb00carpuoft/mydaysanddreamsb00carpuoft_djvu.txt.

[13] Jiddu Krishnamurti (1895-1986) was an irreligious Indian philosopher, spiritual leader, public speaker and writer, who transcended both religion and science. See: Krishnamurti, Jiddu, *The Core of the Teachings*, UK: Krishnamurti Foundation Trust, 1980. https://www.jkrishnamurti.org/about-core-teachings; and Williams, Christine V., *Jiddu Krishnamurti: World Philosopher (1895-1986): His Life and Thoughts*, Delhi, India: Motilal Barnarsidass, 2004.

[14] Quoted in van Gogh, Vincent, *Letter from Vincent van Gogh to Theo van Gogh*, The Hague, NL, August 17, 1883.

http://www.webexhibits.org/vangogh/letter/12/312.htm?qp=attitude.Father.

[15] King, Jr., Martin Luther, and Clayborne Carson, ed., *The Autobiography of Martin Luther King Jr.*, New York, NY: Warner Books, 1998. https://www.goodreads.com/quotes/7145128-it-is-simply-my-way-of-saying-that-i-would.

[16] Trans woman activist, Julia Serano, coined the terms, "cisgender" and "cissexual," to identify normative birth privilege accorded to non-transgender (cisgender) people. Related terms are "cissexist" and "ciscentric." Read Serano's books: *Whipping Girl: A Transsexual Woman on Sexism and the Scapegoating of Femininity*, New York, NY: Seal Press, 2007; and *Excluded: Making Feminist and Queer Movements More Inclusive*, New York, NY: Seal Press, 2013.

Latinx-American, intersex activist, Hida Viloria, author of *Born Both: An Intersex Life*, New York, NY: Hatchette Books, 2017, wonders if intersex people without medical intervention are actually cisgender (or cissex), while still promoting alliance with transgender people. By contrast, Canadian intersex activist, Prof. Morgan Holmes (noted in chapter 11), urges the inclusion of intersex individuals under the overall transgender (or transsex) umbrella, but critiques the gender/sex binary inherent in the trans-cis continuum, which doesn't seem to include intersex—a serious limitation of language when describing conceptual complexities of gender and sex!

[17] See: Baldwin, James, *Giovanni's Room*, New York, NY: Dial Press, 1956; and Leeming, David A., *James Baldwin: A Biography*, New York, NY: Alfred A. Knopf, 1994.

[18] See: Ellison, Ralph, *Invisible Man,* New York, NY: Random House, 1947; and Rampersad, Arnold, *Ralph Ellison: A Biography*, New York, NY: Alfred A. Knopf, 2007.

[19] Read Dirk's seven-volume autobiography, and also Coldstream, John, *Dirk Bogarde: The Authorised Biography*, London, UK: Weidenfeld & Nicolson, 2004. He was knighted in 1992.

[20] See: Naifeh, Steven, and Gregory White Smith, *Van Gogh: The Life*, London, UK: Random House, 2011.

[21] See: Arrien, Angeles, *The Four-Fold Way: Walking the Paths of the Warrior, Teacher, Healer and Visionary*, New York, NY: Harper, 1993.

[22] Dr. Alice Miller's books include: *The Untouched Key: Tracing Childhood Trauma in Creativity and Destructiveness*, New York, NY: Anchor Books, 1988; and *The Drama of the Gifted Child: The Search for the True Self* (rev. ed.), New York, NY: Basic Books, 1994.

[23] Transsexuals (trans people) experience a gender identity inconsistent with their birth-assigned sex, and desire to "transition" to their identified gender, usually seeking medical assistance (cross-sex hormone therapy and/or gender-confirming surgeries) to align their bodies with their identified gender. A medical diagnosis of gender dysphoria can be made if one experiences distress, discomfort, dissonance, or impaired functioning due to one's crossgender identity and a wish to live in society as one's self-identified gender. "Transsexualism" is a subset of an umbrella category of "transgenderism": gender dissonance expressed by crossdressers (formerly, "transvestites"), transsexuals and transgenderists, as well as people who identify as genderqueer (formerly, "androgynes," now gender non-binary), intersex (formerly, "hermaphroditic"), *Hijra* or Indigenous Two-Spirit. Additional terms include "gender-variant," "gender-diverse," and "gender-transgressive" (mainly for adults)

and "gender non-conforming," "gender-independent" and "gender-creative" (mainly for children and adolescents). However, some transsexuals—and a number of gender non-binary, intersex, *Hijra* and Two-Spirit people—reject "transgender" as a self-descriptor.

An unknown number of transsexuals are also intersex and I believe the medical link (genetic and/or hormonal) between transsexualism and intersex will someday be proven—or that a similar genetically-predisposed or congenital condition will be discovered.

See: Benjamin, Harry, *The Transsexual Phenomenon*, New York, NY: Julian Press, 1966 (reprint, Düsseldorf, DEU: Symposium Publications, 1999); and Green, Richard, and John Money, eds., *Transsexualism and Sex Reassignment*, Baltimore, MD: Johns Hopkins University Press, 1969. For more resources on transsexualism, see the Intersectional Bibliography.

[24] Richard Greene starred in the 1950s British TV series, *The Adventures of Robin Hood*, produced by Sapphire Films.

[25] As well as playing the cute "Dr. Simon Sparrow" in the 1950s-1960s British *"Doctor"* films (directed by Ralph Thomas, produced by Betty Box), Dirk Bogarde also portrayed several queer characters: the internalized biphobic barrister ("Melville Farr") in the landmark 1961 British film, *Victim* (directed by Basil Dearden, produced by Allied Film Makers); the bisexual manservant ("Hugo Barrett") in the 1963 British movie, *The Servant* (directed and produced by Joseph Losey); and the boy-loving, dying older man ("Gustav von Aschenbach") in the 1971 Italian-French film, *Death in Venice* (directed and produced by Luchino Visconti).

[26] Dickens, Charles, *Great Expectations,* London, UK: Chapman & Hall, 1861.

[27] Dostoyevsky, Fyodor, *The Idiot* (translated from the Russian by Constance Garnett and Alan Myers). New York, NY: Vintage Classics, 2002.

[28] Hope, Anthony, *The Prisoner of Zenda,* Bristol, UK: J. W. Arrowsmith, 1894.

[29] Hope, Anthony, *Rupert of Hentzau,* Bristol, UK: J. W. Arrowsmith, 1898 (sequel to above).

[30] Maugham, W. Somerset, *Of Human Bondage,* New York, NY: George H. Doran Company, 1915.

[31] Intersex or intersexuality (formerly "hermaphrodism," "true hermaphrodism," and "pseudohermaphrodism") in humans and animals describes variations of sex characteristics that don't fit typical binary notions of "male" or "female" bodies. Variations include genital and/or gonadal ambiguities, hormonal anomalies, and/or combinations of chromosomal "genotype" and sexual "phenotype" other than XY-male and XX-female, including genetic mosaicism. Contrary to popular belief, not all intersex people are sterile, although many are. The medical descriptor for intersex traits as "disorders of sex development" has been controversial since its emergence in 2006, so some intersex activists use the non-pathological descriptor, "differences of sex development." The earliest recorded mention of an intersex (formerly, hermaphroditic) person was Herculine Barbin's personal journal, *Herculine Barbin: Being the Recently Discovered Memoirs of a Nineteenth-Century French Hermaphrodite* (introduced by Michel Foucault; translated from the French by Richard McDougall), New York, NY: Pantheon Books, 1980.

Pioneering transsexual man, Dr. Michael Laurence Dillon, published *Self: A Study in Endocrinology and Ethics*, Amsterdam, NL: Elsevier Science, 1946, a semi-autobiographical treatise conflating intersex and transsexualism (the latter is a subset of the psychiatric syndrome, gender dysphoria), because neither condition had been clinically identified at that time. He believed "masculine inverts" (female-to-male transsexuals or trans men) were born with "the mental outlook and temperament of the other sex," and because this form of "inversion" was innate (a hidden physical condition similar to intersex), it could not be "cured" by psychiatry or psychology, but should be treated medically with cross-sex hormones and sex-reassignment surgery.

A number of trans people also identify (or have been diagnosed) as intersex, and I believe that transsexuals (as a small subcategory under the larger transgender umbrella, which also includes transgender, genderqueer (gender non-binary) and Two-Spirit people and crossdressers) are actually intersex, and that science will ultimately prove this, finally "exorcising" gender dysphoria from the *Diagnostic and Statistical Manual of Mental Disorders* (*DSM*), published by the American Psychiatric Association (APA), and the *International Classification of Diseases* (*ICD*), published by the World Health Organization (WHO). There are a few people who have socially (but not surgically) transitioned and were proven to be intersex at birth, puberty or after death (e.g., Herculine Barbin and Sir Ewan Forbes); some people who were very likely intersex (e.g., Robert Allen and Mark Woods), or possibly intersex (e.g., Bill Allen and Wynsley Michael Swan), whose potentially verifying medical documents as to diagnosis and treatment are unavailable; and others whose suspected intersexuality is controversially contested (e.g., Dr. James Miranda Barry). There are also those people who have been medically confirmed as intersex—but are sometimes also considered transsexual—who might or might not identify as both (e.g., Erik Schinegger and Peter Stirling). Moreover, there are those often presumed to be transsexuals, whose claims of intersexuality have never been conclusively medically substantiated (e.g., Lili Elvenes (Elbe) and Dawn Simmons (Hall) despite a medical certificate purportedly verifying an intersex diagnosis (e.g., Roberta Cowell) so the sex-reassigning surgeon would not be charged with violating the law prohibiting transsexual surgery! And, there are those whose intersexuality has been medically verified, who have been actively transphobic (e.g., Georgina Somerset)! Finally, there are those politically-incorrect, "self-constructed intersex," gender non-binary, polymorphous-perverse transqueers like Del LaGrace Volcano!

American intersex activist, Cheryl Chase (now Bo Laurent), founded the now-defunct Intersex Society of North America (ISNA). See https://zagria.blogspot.ca/2009/01/bo-laurent-1956-intersex-activist.html. Cheryl (Bo) edited ISNA's journal, *Hermaphrodites with Attitude*, from 1994 to 2005 (http://www.isna.org/library/hwa), featuring articles by such notable authors as Dr. Tiger Devore (formerly Howard), Dr. Alice Domurat Dreger, Dr. Anne Fausto-Sterling, and Dr. Morgan Holmes. Cheryl (Bo) and ISNA fought against "intersexphobia": negative attitudes towards people who possess intersex traits (biological sex traits not typically male or female), and especially against the involuntary "corrective" surgery of often-ambiguous genitalia on intersex infants, children and teenagers. In 2007, Hida Viloria (see note above on "cisgender"), founder of the Intersex Campaign for Equality, took issue with Bo over the pathologization implied by the new medical label for intersex, "disorders of sex development."

In 2017, Organisation Intersex International Australia and Intersex Awareness New Zealand jointly called for legal reform in Australia and New Zealand, including the criminalization of deferrable intersex medical interventions on children, an end to legal classification of sex, and improved access to peer support.

Closer to home, Emi Koyama is a Japanese-American intersex activist, who has written extensively on intersex, including the instructive manuals, *Introduction to Intersex Activism* (2nd ed.), and *Teaching Intersex Issues* (2nd ed.), both published in 2003 by Intersex Initiative Portland. http://www.intersexinitiative.org/publications/index.html. She is also an ardent trans ally (see note on "transfeminism" in chapter 4). In addition to the aforementioned, other noted international sex researchers have written on both intersexuality and transsexualism, under an over-arching category, including Dr. Milton Diamond and Dr. Hazel Beh; Dr. Peggy T. Cohen-Kettenis and Dr. Friedmann Pfäfflin; Dr. Roberto Farina; and Dr. Joan Roughgarden. And, American historian Dr. Gilbert H. Herdt has compared intersexuality (sex) and androgyny (gender).

Several American, Australian and New Zealander film documentaries on intersex people have recently come out, and there are a number of intersex organizations online. For more resources on intersex, see: Intersectional Bibliography.

[32] See: Bill 14, "Anti-Bullying Act, 2012, An Act to Designate Bullying Awareness and Prevention Week in Schools and to Provide for Bullying Prevention Curricula, Policies and Administrative Accountability in Schools." (This Act amends the Education Act). Legislative Assembly of Ontario. https://www.ola.org/en/legislative-business/bills/parliament-40/session-1/bill-14.

[33] I'm alluding to the English translation of the title of Albert Camus's 1942 French novel, *L'Étranger (The Stranger)* (Paris, FR: Éditions Gallimard), in which he creates the tragic, existential anti-hero, Mersault. Of course, I'm nothing like this criminal character, but we do share an existential displacement in the "ordinary" world of men and women. A self-styled "absurdist," Camus's book dramatized his existential notion of the absurdity of living in a meaningless world and a random universe. His book was subsequently published in English under alternate titles: *The Outsider* (London, UK: Hamish Hamilton Publishing, 1946); and *The Stranger* (New York, NY: Vintage Books, 1988; translated from the French by Matthew Ward).

[34] Ewa Klobukowska (1946-) and I were indirectly related by our Polish ethnicity. See https://zagria.blogspot.ca/2009/08/ewa-kobukowska-1946-athlete.html. (Note: Klobukowska's surname is misspelled in the URL).

[35] Erik Schinegger's autobiography, co-authored by Marco Schenz, was published in two non-English languages: *Mein Sieg über mich. Der Mann, der Weltmeisterin wurde* (German), München, DEU: Herbig, 1988; and *L'Homme Qui Fut Championne du Monde* (French), Paris, FR: *Éditions Michel Lafon*, 1989. (The English translation of the title is *My Victory Over Myself: The Man Who Became a Female World Champion*). Watch director/producer Kurt Mayer's 2005 film, *Erik(A)*, documenting Erika Schinegger's gender transition to Erik Schinegger (1948-). See also https://zagria.blogspot.ca/2010/02/erik-schinegger-1948-skier.html.

[36] Nearly four decades after Ewa's and Erik's battles with Olympic officials, Vancouver trans woman, professional downhill mountain bike champion, Michelle Dumaresq, sparked another "sex change" furor with her fellow female racers when she won the world championship, making history as the first transgender athlete on a national team. Watch: Dumaresq, Michelle, Karen Duthie, dir., Diana Wilson, prod., and Lesley Ewen, *100% Woman*, Vancouver, BC: Artemis Dreams Productions/Producers on Davie Pictures, and the Canadian Television Fund, 2004. Distributed by Moving Images. https://www.movingimages.ca/. For further developments—involving a fracas with a female second-place finisher in the 2006 Canadian National Championships—see https://en.wikipedia.org/wiki/Michelle_Dumaresq.

[37] In 2008, after Kristen Worley, a Toronto trans-female, professional cyclist (post-transitionally, an XY female), failed to make the Beijing Olympic team because of a higher-than-allowed testosterone level for female athletes, she filed an Ontario Human Rights suit

against the provincial arm of the International Olympic Committee (IOC) in 2016, arguing that professional sports should be based on ability, not sex. Kristen has had mediation talks with the IOC, Union Cycling Internationale and the Canadian government on May 24, 2017, in her continued battle. See: Worley, Kristen, and Joanna Schneller, *Woman Enough: How a Boy Became a Woman and Changed the World of Sport*, Toronto, ON: Random House (Canada), 2019. See also https://zagria.blogspot.ca/2012/08/sports-gender-and-trans-part-3-recent.html.

[38] British Columbian, trans-feminist activist, Dr. Rachel McKinnon, is the first trans-female, professional world champion athlete, winning the UCI Masters Track Cycling World Championship (women's sprint, 35-44) in 2018, followed by a backlash of vicious transphobia from her competing cis-female athlete, and numerous others. https://www.cyclingweekly.com/news/latest-news/transgender-athlete-rachel-mckinnon-faced-death-threats-abuse-historic-win-399888. She hopes to compete for Canada in the 2020 and 2024 Olympics, making her the first openly-trans Olympian if she wins! Rachel is also Assistant Professor of Philosophy at the College of Charleston in South Carolina, and a public speaker and academic writer on transgenderism and philosophicopolitical issues. https://rachelmckinnon.com/publications. See also: Intersectional Bibliography.

[39] Peter Stirling (1936-) was the first known transsexual or intersex person in Australia to medically transition, in this case, to male, in 1968, soon after he had given birth to his daughter (sensationalized in the *Weekly World News*, Sept. 26, 1989). Read Peter Stirling's memoir, *So Different: An Extraordinary Autobiography*, Melbourne, AU: Simon & Schuster (Australia), 1989. See also https://zagria.blogspot.ca/2015/11/peter-stirling-1936-shoe-retailer.html.

[40] Early intersex (formerly, hermaphroditic) people included French citizen, Herculine Adélaîde (aka Alexina) Barbin (1838-1868) (see note above), and English citizens, Mark Woods, Mark Weston, and Robert Allen, and Scottish citizen, Sir Ewan Forbes. During the early to mid-1900s, these four Britons had all reassigned as males, socially, legally and/or medically.

Mark Woods (1905-19??) was very likely intersex given that "he" told a newspaper reporter that at 18, "his" sex had spontaneously changed from female to male, and 10 years later, at 28, "he" was legally changing "his" gender to male and beginning to live as a man. The photostat of the news article, "Woman's Physical Transformation: Starting Life Afresh as a Man," *Dundee Evening Telegraph*, Sept. 11, 1933, is reprinted in Christine Burns, ed., *Trans Britain: Our Journey from the Shadows*, London, UK: Unbound, 2018, 14.

Mark Weston (1905-1978) was quite possibly intersex, born with a genital abnormality, assigned a female sex-designation and raised as a girl. In 1936, following two gender-confirmation surgeries at Charing Cross Hospital in London, he married and sired three children. A photostat of the news article, "Man, Once Girl, Weds Friend: He was Formerly Woman Athlete," *Portsmouth Evening News*, August 1936, is reprinted in Burns, *Trans Britain*, 15. See also https://zagria.blogspot.com/2008/08/mark-weston-1906-shot-putter-and.html.

Robert Allen (1914-19??) was apparently intersex given that he never took male hormones or underwent genital surgery but was certified as "male" by a physician. He legally changed his gender to male in 1944, started living as a man and married a woman. See: Allen, Robert, *But for the Grace: The True Story of a Dual Existence*, London, UK: W. H. Allen, 1954. See also https://zagria.blogspot.com/2015/06/robert-allen-1914-film-maker.html.

Sir Ewan Forbes, 11th Baronet of Craigievar (1912-1991) had to fight to inherit his elder brother's baronetcy—typically passed on to the oldest living male relative)—because his male cousin contested his legal right, citing Ewan's birth-assigned sex as female, which was later medically and legally reassigned as intersex in adulthood. Ewan finally won his lawsuit after a three-year battle—a blatant case of genderphobia and intersexphobia! See also https://zagria.blogspot.ca/2008/02/men-in-kilts.html.

For information on intersex and dual-identity, trans-intersex people, see the Intersectional Bibliography.

[41] "Female husbands" were birth-assigned females who had socially transitioned from female to male without medical intervention. Some of these included: English horse groom, James Allen, and alehouse manager, Harry Stokes, in the 18th and 19th centuries, and English novelist, "John" Radclyffe Hall, and World War I colonel, Sir Victor Barker, in the early 20th century.

James (née Abigail) Allen (1787-1829) was one of a series of so-called "female husbands" in the UK, who had married women in the 18th and 19th centuries. See: Duberman, Martin, "The Female Husband," in Martin Duberman, ed., *About Time: Exploring the Gay Past*, New York, NY: Meridian Books, 1986, 24-30. See also https://zagria.blogspot.com/2017/08/james-allen-1787-1829-labourer.html.

Harry (née Harriett) Stokes (circa 1799-1859) was a bricklayer/beerhouse manager/special constable, who was assigned female at birth but lived as a man and had two long-term relationships with women. In 1838 and 1859, newspapers described "him" as a "man-woman" and a "female husband." See https://en.wikipedia.org/wiki/Harry_Stokes.

Radclyffe (née Marguerite) Hall (1880–1943) wrote the iconic novel, *The Well of Loneliness*, London, UK: Jonathan Cape, 1928, featuring "Stephen Gordon" as a semi-autobiographical fictional hero. Although many lesbian feminists assert that Radclyffe was a masculine lesbian, many trans people (Dr. Aaron Devor, myself and others) claim "him" as an early, medically non-transitioned, female-to-male transsexual, who lived part-time as a man, and went by the nickname "John," given to him by his female partner, Lady Una Troubridge.

Sir Victor Barker (née Valerie Lilias Arkell-Smith) (1895–1960) was historically recorded as a "passing" woman, but might actually have been an early, medically non-transitioned, transsexual man given that "he" was a soldier in a British regiment during and after World War I, and had a wife and son. In 1929, "he" was outed as a woman, and arrested and sent to jail for nine months for falsifying a marriage certificate to marry "his" fiancée. See: Collis, Rose, *Colonel Barker's Monstrous Regiment: A Tale of Female Husbandry*, London, UK: Virago Press, 2002. See also: Parts I, II, III & IV on Sir Victor Barker on Zagria's website, "A Gender Variance Who's Who." https://zagria.blogspot.ca/. For more general information, see https://18centurybodies.wordpress.com/2013/06/05/cross-dressing-and-female-husbands/; https://www.huffingtonpost.com/2015/01/30/female-husbands_n_6581974.html; and the Intersectional Bibliography.

[42] "Passing women" (a misnomer because they actually passed as men) were birth-assigned females who had socially transitioned from female to male without medical intervention, some dating as far back as the 15th century, like French war-hero(ine) Jeanne d'Arc. Later examples included: Irish military surgeon, Dr. James Miranda Steuart Barry, in the 19th century, and in America, journalist, Jack Bee Garland, longshoreman, Harry Livingston (aka Harry Allen), and jazz bandleader, William Lee "Billy" Tipton, in the early 20th century.

Saint Jeanne d'Arc (aka Joan of Arc) (1412-1431) was a French war hero(ine) (or "military maid") who fought for France in the Hundred Years' War against England. She was canonized as a Roman Catholic saint after being burned at the stake by the Burgundian Faction (French nobles allied with the English) for the heretical crime of dressing in male (military) clothing. See: Feinberg, Leslie, *Transgender Warriors: Making History from Joan of Arc to Dennis Rodman*, Boston, MA: Beacon Press, 1996.

Dr. James Miranda Steuart Barry (née Margaret Ann Bulkley) (1795–1865) lived "his" entire adult life as a man, and "his" female birth-assigned sex only became known after death. See: Duncker, Patricia, *James Miranda Barry*, London, UK: Bloomington Publishing, 1999. Published in the USA as *The Doctor*, New York, NY: Harper, 1999. It's highly controversial whether James was a "passing woman," or actually intersex. See https://en.wikipedia.org/wiki/James_Barry_(surgeon); and https://zagria.blogspot.com/2008/01/james-miranda-stuart-barry-1795-1865.html.

Jack Bee Garland (née Elvira Virginia Mugarietta) (1869-1936) was very likely an early gay trans man given that he lived as a man and had sexual relations with "other" men. Read Louis Sullivan's groundbreaking biography, *From Female To Male: The Life of Jack Bee Garland*, New York, NY: Alyson Books, 1990. See also https://zagria.blogspot.com/2012/06/jack-bee-garland-1869-1936-journalist.html.

Harry Livingston (later known as Harry Allen) (née Nell Pickerell) (1882–1922) unapologetically rejected "his" female gender assignment and insisted that the media not misgender "him" when newspapers referred to "him" with his birth name and feminine pronouns. See https://en.wikipedia.org/wiki/Harry_Allen_(trans_man).

William Lee "Billy" (née Dorothy Lucille) Tipton (1914-1989) successfully passed as male without hormones or surgery for the last 49 years of his life, outed as transgender only upon his death. See: Middlebrook, Diane Wood, *Suits Me: The Double Life of Billy Tipton*, Boston, MA: Houghton Mifflin Harcourt, 1998. For more general information, see: Thompson, C. J. S., *The Mysteries of Sex: Women Who Posed as Men and Men Who Impersonated Women*, New York, NY: Causeway Books, 1974; and: Wheelright, Julie, *Amazons and Military Maids: Women Who Dressed as Men in Pursuit of Life, Liberty and Happiness*, London, UK: Pandora Press, 1989.

Although many cisgender feminist, lesbian and gay historians have dubbed these early gender transgressors "passing women" or "female husbands," might not some of these individuals have possibly been transsexual (early trans men) or intersex, and who were determined—often against overwhelming odds—to live in society according to their "true" (felt) gender without the benefit of modern-day sex-hormone therapy and sex-reassignment surgery? In fact, some trans people claim Dr. James Barry, Radclyffe Hall, Jack Garland, Harry Livingston (Allen) and Billy Tipton as one of our own: early "transgender warriors." And I assume that some intersex people have a similar claim as early intersex transgressors. Given that medical records are not always publicly accessible, and that some individuals might have misrepresented their sexual status due to perceived stigma, we might never know for sure. For more information on "passing women," see the Intersectional Bibliography.

2. Tragic Family Loss…Bittersweet First Love (1968-1971)

August 1968: I was 16. My father was driving us kids to a summer cottage we had rented in Perth, Ontario, not far from Ottawa. We were eager to explore this Lanark County town before having to return to school. My older brother, Jakub, stayed home to paint our kitchen and my mother was undergoing some important medical tests. My father would collect her tomorrow, rejoining us at the cottage. That evening, he had a creative impulse to sketch a dream house in which he envisioned himself as an old man, residing with my mother, along with us kids and our kids—an extended family in the Asian tradition. Sadly, his dream was not to be.

During their drive back to the cottage, it was raining hard in the township of Carleton Place when, suddenly, the car skidded, crashing into a bridge abutment and flipping over. My father was killed instantly. My mother was thrown from the car and died four days later, after lying in a coma. A farmer, witnessing the accident, called the police, who notified Jakub. He asked our neighbour to drive up and bring us home. On the anxiety-ridden ride back, we were told a half-truth: that our parents had been hospitalized following an automobile accident. The task to break the tragic news fell to my older brother. I believe that neither he nor my middle brother, Casimir, have ever fully healed from this untimely loss, ultimately resulting in each one permanently breaking off from all of the siblings except one. Still in shock, my youngest brother, Andrzej (then only six), did not shed a tear, but I cried a river, as did my other siblings. At the funeral, the emotional stress caused my arthritis to flare up as I painfully limped up the church aisle towards my parents' coffins aided by my father's cane. During the reception, we suffered through the typical small talk and forced civility that characterize funerals. Most people are so terrified by their own mortality that they rarely talk about death, opting for denial rather than realism. My father had been loved and respected by his colleagues and students: so, including my mother's few friends, there was a good turnout of mourners.

My maternal Polish grandmother (*Babcia,* in Polish) and paternal Indian uncle (*Jethu,* in Bengali) travelled overseas to pay respects to their departed loved ones and commiserate with us kids. Each of them invited us to go and live with them in Sweden or India, respectively, but none of us wanted to leave our siblings, friends or our familiar homeland. Similarly, neither our grandmother nor uncle were willing to leave behind their families to come and live in Canada. We all mournfully parted forevermore, separated once again by culture and geography. It's hard enough being part of a multicultural extended family but even more challenging when relatives live in disparate parts of the globe. Sad circumstances indeed for a long overdue family visit.

My sister's godfather was appointed our legal guardian and estate executor to manage our legal and financial affairs. Friends of the family looked in on us once in a while to make sure we were all right. But we weren't, being recently orphaned and feeling quite alone in the world.

It took me about two years to fully mourn my parents' passing and I displayed several photographs of them during that time to keep their memories alive. Although I sorely grieved that I would never again see my father—the person I had most cherished in the world—I was so relieved to be free at last of my mother—that mad monster I had both feared and hated, whom I've long since forgiven intellectually but never quite yet emotionally. It was one of the saddest, yet one of the happiest, days of my life; a bittersweet dialectical dilemma. Newly orphaned, my primary task was to find a way to finally be me: a teenage boy. My resolve was renewed: "in the depths of winter, I finally learned there was, within me, an invincible summer."[1] Camus expressed this dialectical tension of despair and hope, vulnerability and resilience after concluding that the only way to stay sane and not dismiss this absurd life is to purposefully embrace the maddening meaninglessness of it all, to transcend the violent suffering of this hell on earth, and to live life to the full regardless! Fervent hope spiced with sardonic humour is the medicine needed to cure our existential anxiety.

The first thing I did on my road to freedom was to start wearing my father's tweed jacket and tie as a signifier of my male core, the young man within. This didn't go down well with Jakub, who verbally attacked me: "Mom and Dad couldn't figure out if you were a girl or a boy because you don't really look like either, and you act like a tomboy." This resulted in a down-and-dirty wrestling match. I was fighting for my life—and my right to be me—and he was fighting to maintain his *status quo* as the alpha male. To clearly convince my brother that my true gender identity was *not* female, I conceded to his request to wear a jumper, jewelry and make-up (the first time ever!) for a party he was planning at our house as the acid test of my true feelings while publicly dressed as a woman. Feeling like a drag queen (minus the big wig, feather boa, and spiked heels), my flesh crawled under this uncomfortable get-up and I couldn't wait to don my "normal" boy duds again. The length I was prepared to go for sibling satisfaction!

Besides my brother, I got flack for my crossdressing from our foster parents, Chuck and Cathy, whom the Catholic Children's Aid Society sent to look after us for a year. Chuck thought that "it" (my transsexual identity) was all in my head and that I would get over this adolescent phase in time. Sadly, they could not see that I needed help badly. Desperate, I turned to my legal guardian, asking him to find me a psychiatrist.

I was referred to Dr. Roberts, chief psychiatrist at the Royal Ottawa Hospital (ROH), who administered the Draw-A-Person Self-Concept Test (of course, I drew a male stick-figure). He then sent me to a clinical psychologist, who gave me the Rorschach test: all the ink blots looked like butterflies or flowers or sex organs. Finally, he assigned me to a clinical social worker (Miss Stephens[2]) for time-limited psychotherapy. She was the first person, other than my father, Arjuna and Hilda, to really hear me—without judgement, with empathy. I felt that I could trust her unreservedly and that made me feel safe. I didn't feel quite so alone in the world, having to hide my deep, dark secret. Perhaps there was light at the end of the tunnel after all. Not knowing how to crawl out of this well of loneliness, I looked to her, my beacon of hope, to help me find a way. She did indeed get things started, the first domino in a series. When I told her that I was "a boy trapped in a girl's body," she showed me *Transsexualism and Sex Reassignment*, the 1969 medical book by Dr. Richard Green[3] and Dr. John Money.[4] This was the first time that I clearly knew what I was and had the language to express it: a transsexual! A glimmer of hope sparked that one day I would escape from my spectral half-life in the shadows and find my place in the sun. But not quite yet: I first had to suffer through two psychiatrists, one complacent, the other pathologizing.

The first was a Polish psychiatrist at the Ottawa General Hospital, who paid more attention to my Polish grandmother than to me. So, I fired his ass forthwith! The second was a psychoanalyst in private practice, a pompous, cigar-chomping neo-Freudian, who made me lie on the couch with his back turned to me. When I told him about Green and Money's book with the postsurgical photographs of trans-male patients at Johns Hopkins Hospital in Baltimore, this "medical healer" wielded his transphobia like a sledgehammer: "You want to get butchered? Okay, go ahead. I'll even drive you to the airport." His unexpected violent reaction made me feel more vulnerable and desperate than ever.

Before Chuck and Cathy completed their term as interim foster parents, I asked our legal guardian if I could move in with Hilda's family as arrangements were already being made for my siblings to live with other families. Although the Hendersons welcomed me warmly, I chose not to disclose my crossgender identity to Hilda's parents and siblings, wearing my boy clothes only in the privacy of my bedroom. In public, I tried to be invisible—quite a challenge as I presented as a weird-looking girl.

Serendipitously, I chanced upon a teletyped news release at CFRA's radio station during career day when I was exploring broadcast journalism as a potential vocation. The release read:

> *Hope for Transsexuals—Gender Identity Clinic soon to open in Portland, Oregon. Male-to-female and female-to-male transsexuals may finally find a way out of their intense, lifelong gender distress through medical science in the form of life-saving sex-change operations.*

I sensed that Mother Nature was looking out for me, encouraging me not to give up. Forcing myself to reach beyond despair, I grabbed onto hope, inspired by Austrian-Jewish psychiatrist Dr. Viktor Frankl's Logotherapy—an existential model for hope and meaning.

February 1970. Turning 18, I had only four months to go until my high school graduation. But once more, my gender dysphoria hit rock-bottom! I had to reach out to someone—anyone. Sinking into a quagmire, I struggled to keep my head above the murky depths. Now that Hilda had temporarily relocated to Kingston, there was nobody at school whom I felt I could trust. But I took a chance anyway and wrote to Miss Ritchie, telling her that I was, "really a boy inside a girl's body" and that I had romantic feelings for her. She could have made my life a living hell, stigmatizing me as a seemingly butch lesbian, but, to her credit, she remained sensitively professional, sharing my love letter with the senior guidance counsellor for direction and asking her to speak with me. The latter meant well but could have chosen her words more carefully: "I think you are all twisted up inside." She quickly clarified that she didn't mean that I was bad or sick, simply confused. I was blessed to have had such non-judgmental teachers because they could have tried to have me committed as a sexual deviant!

As it turned out, I committed myself to save me from suicide. I needed help badly and I needed it now! While living with the Hendersons, I threatened to take my life and asked my legal guardian to admit me as an in-patient to the Royal Ottawa Hospital to help me resolve my gender identity problem. A month later, my guardian drove me to the ROH and helped me get settled in. Remarkably, I was never subjected to either tranquilizers or electroshock therapy during my six weeks there! But my treatment plan obligated me to attend a female therapy group. When the facilitating psychiatrist probed participants about possible sexual abuse by their fathers or other male relatives and then interrogated me, I became distraught and bolted from the room. Unnerved, I climbed over the barbed-wire fence and scaled the ladder of the water-tower on the hospital grounds. I didn't go all the way up though, because I feared heights and didn't really want to jump to an early death. Eventually, I climbed down and returned to my room, trying to sooth myself to sleep. Incredulously, nobody noticed my desperate act of contemplated annihilation: an orphan's cry in the wilderness. Desolate, I felt abandoned and alone.

Men and women were segregated into separate hospital wings, but, occasionally, I forayed into the men's ward to have a smoke with the male patients. In their midst, I felt empowered, accepted as one of the fellows—a heart-warming feeling of finally coming home, like lounging in a comfy chair in front of a cozy fire without a care in the world. Sadly, I couldn't get to the male wing that often, so I had to find male companionship elsewhere. Happily,

I chanced across *another* teenage boy, Vic. We hung out, playing badminton, archery, and darts, and spilling our guts. Telling him my story, he accepted me without hesitation: it all seemed perfectly natural to him. What wasn't natural was my female form, which I so desperately wanted to change.

Unlike the female patients attired in blouses and skirts, I wore a shirt and jeans, violating a strict dress code. But I didn't care. I was just following my instincts. This rubbed a fellow patient the wrong way. Her name was "Dina." She gently accosted me, urging me not to rock the boat and to wear feminine garb like everyone else in the female wing. Ignoring her exhortation, I took up my rightful place in the universe, assuming my nascent male privilege. The police had brought Dina to the hospital drunk and disorderly, and screaming blue murder following a fight with her husband, whom she was divorcing. She was 28 and had three kids. Soon afterwards, Dina kissed me full on the mouth (my first kiss!), sending shivers through me. She thought I was a butch dyke because I wore mannish clothes and short hair. I boldly corrected her, saying that I was a female-to-male transsexual and wanted a "sex change" operation, mentioning the photographs of surgically-constructed penises in Green and Money's book. She expressed consternation: "But what if you get caught in the middle and end up half-man and half-woman?" I replied that I would just have to take my chances and hope for the best. Dina reiterated her sexual attraction to me but said she wasn't sure if I was truly transsexual, perceiving me more as a masculine lesbian. Conflicted though I was, I pretended to be the butch dyke she wanted me to be because I did not want to lose the only lover I had ever had. I felt so lonely and needed someone—a nurturing woman—to love me. Was this blatant falsehood internalized transphobia or simply survival? I told myself that I had to be strategic to satisfy my romantic needs. I later came to regret this misrepresentation (an inauthentic self-erasure) but, right at that moment, I was drowning and had to keep afloat by any means. Dina's pet name for me was "Nicki." We became secret lovers, going for walks on the grounds, surreptitiously holding hands in the lounge, and stealing a passionate kiss or two in the washroom when nobody was around. Our lovemaking was constrained by our circumstances but even minimum contact stoked my fire, making my spirits soar.

During my hospital stay, I was under the care of Dr. Arboleda-Flórez, a psychiatrist who would not prescribe me testosterone because I was not yet legal age (21 at that time). I was desolate at having to wait another three years to masculinize my body. As always, I felt imprisoned, not wanting to live in a world where I could not be myself, where I had to live a lie. Suppressed rage turned inwards as depression: despair smothered me in a gray smog and suicidal thoughts flooded my brain.

I finally got my walking papers; discharged, but not cured. Returning to the Hendersons, I pined for Dina. I felt that I couldn't go on without her. Just a teenager in love! With only two more weeks to go before her hospital release, Dina wrangled a day pass. We rendezvoused on Parliament Hill, then ambled along the Rideau Canal, holding hands and exchanging kisses among the fragrant lilacs. If only this feeling could last! Upon her discharge, Dina asked me to come and live with her. We rented a farmhouse in Russell, a village in the Ottawa Valley, and moved in early July. Except for my ever-persistent gender dysphoria, that summer was pure bliss; just Dina and me and the kids, with our German shepherd, Sheba, and our tabby, Jenny, on our own private acre. On the farm, I saw calves being born for the first time and witnessed Sheba giving birth to a litter of pups. A real hands-on education for a city boy like me!

At first, Dina supported me in my fervent wish for malehood. She fashioned me a breast-binder from a cotton dishtowel to flatten my 32C bumps. Everything seemed to be going well. Alas, it wasn't all a bed of roses because I felt conflicted about our sexual relationship, particularly when Dina tried to suck my nipples, rationalizing, "I don't love just your breasts, or a hand, or a foot; I love all of you, the whole person." I wanted to believe her but I had my doubts. My instincts proved right when she vigorously probed my front hole with her finger. I felt violated, betrayed, enraged, desperate, uncertain, unsafe. Dina later confessed, "When I touched you there, I deliberately wanted to hurt you so you'd feel that you are really a woman." Her convoluted explanation sickened me as I sadly realized that she did not understand what I was going through, having no idea whatsoever what it's like to be transsexual. I was a man and felt totally disconnected from my female parts, with no desire to make love until I could change them to male ones through surgery. Once again, I felt misunderstood and invalidated.

On top of alienation, I experienced a sense of consternation when, after several weeks had passed, Dina castigated me for wearing my beloved grey flannel or blue plaid pants and my desert boots or penny-loafers—mannish enough to let me pass for male in public. It took her some time to go from initial skepticism to partial acceptance, then back to ambivalent resistance and, finally, total rejection. Erased yet again, the true me did not exist for her. An optimistic realist, I tried to cheer up by listening to inspiring teen-rock tunes like Alice Cooper's "School's Out for Summer," and "I'm Eighteen"—with its jubilant lyrics of a boy becoming a man. This was supposed to be my time, my coming-of-age as a man, except that I had nobody to come out to, no place to go. I still had miles to go before I could self-actualize as Nick.

A blip in my isolation occurred when Arjuna came for a visit. My friend, Sheryl, also visited us shortly thereafter with her mother. These visits did little to improve my mood though, as I could not confide in them what was really going on with me, having to put on a false positive face so as not to burden them with my troubles. This was indeed a vulnerable time for me, having lost my parents only two years earlier and, one day, I felt particularly abandoned. Dina was visiting her parents in Ottawa and, by midnight, when she still hadn't returned, I called to see when she was coming home. She was livid when she returned early the next morning, chastising me for acting like a baby. She then told me that she believed homosexuality, bisexuality, and transsexualism were not normal and went against God, even though her brother was gay! It's very challenging to fight religious or secular bigotry given the widespread, crosscultural indoctrination, peer-pressure, and non-critical thinking based on fear, ignorance, and/or hate. Both societal oppression (such as homophobia, biphobia and transphobia, etc.)—which is directed towards others—and internalized oppression (such as internalized biphobia, for example)—which is directed towards oneself (as in Dina's case)—are equally soul destroying.

Our romance lasted only six months from our first meeting in April until early October when, one day, Dina told me that she was not in love with me anymore—but still loved me like a mother—and forthwith moved me out of her bedroom to one upstairs. Denying her bisexual inclination (she had confided earlier having had a secret crush on her closest female friend), she now claimed that she was heterosexual after all and did not want to be sexually involved with women—even though I had emphatically stated that I was male inside. I was devastated! I had to make the best of it though, because I had nowhere else to go. I asked my legal guardian to find somewhere else for me to live in the Winchester area so that I could stay in the same school to finish my graduation year, but nothing turned up. Panicking, I felt doubly-imprisoned; an unrequited love-struck teenager trapped in the wrong body, stuck in the country house of my rejecting ex-lover miles from the city. Was there no way out for this prisoner of love, this prisoner of gender?

I tried my damnedest to win Dina back to no avail. When I threatened to kill myself, she tossed a razor-blade at me: "Go ahead, do us all a favour and get it over with." Her callous challenge punched a hole in my personal power: I felt beaten. Shortly afterwards, I learned that she was secretly carrying on with a farmer (Frank) in the village. Confronting her, she retorted that she was going to ask him to go to bed with me to make me realize, once and for all, that I was a *straight girl*—not a lesbian or a female-to-male transsexual. Miserable, I tore up Dina's photo in an act of injured male pride and rebellious rage. The next day, I ran away for a few hours, hiding in the bushes nearby to teach her a lesson. I didn't need the bitch after all, to hell with her! I felt lost with nobody close by to talk to, so I reached out to my family, writing of my despair to Jakub, who was living in Syracuse, NY with his girlfriend, Lilly. While sympathetic, he lived too far away to offer me any practical assistance.

During my year-long stay with Dina, I made the best of a bad situation, not wanting to leave until I earned my high school diploma. Eventually, we got to know some of the neighbours (the Walton family), including a girl my age named Mona, who befriended me, easing my broken heart somewhat. Like me, she was a tomboy—but not a fellow transsexual as I had hoped—and I gave her my black, leather Beatle cap to mark our friendship. Mona, Frank, Dina, and I would play hands of Poker or Hearts while drinking Molson Canadian beers and smoking Export cigarettes. We listened to country 'n' western music on the radio and danced to live rock bands at the Russell Hotel.

Things went from bad to worse as Dina grew increasingly judgmental and controlling. She threatened to call my teacher to check that, upon reaching the warmth of the school building, I had taken off the winter pants that I wore underneath my skirt. Coming across my letter from the federal government, she was enraged to discover that I had applied to legally change my name to Nicholas Christopher Ghosh on my social insurance card. Mortified that she had found out my secret, I also felt endangered. Things were quickly coming to a head!

My unbearable gender distress forced me to show my true colours despite my efforts at self-restraint. In a class essay for English literature, I had identified with Heathcliff, Catherine's swarthy, doomed lover in Emily Bronte's 1847 Gothic romance, *Wuthering Heights*. Confused, my teacher questioned my identification with this male character, misgendered as it was in her eyes. Was I subconsciously crying out for help? Perhaps. In desperation, I then reached out to the guidance counsellor. Blushing like crazy, I nervously mumbled that I was a transsexual and wanted male hormones and surgery to physically become a man. But, never having heard of trans people, he perceived me to be a masculine lesbian, conflating gender identity with sexual orientation. And yet, I had never identified as a dyke in my life! If I had been lesbian, instead of transsexual, I would very likely have become a "stone butch"[5]: a masculine lesbian whose anatomical female parts are sexually off limits to her femme partner. I also briefly toyed with the notion of presenting as androgynous or third gender[6] (beyond feminine or masculine)—but did I really want to be an androgyne[7] (now, genderqueer[8])? Interestingly, I would not come across *Hijras* (third-gender South Asians)[9] or Indigenous Two-Spirit people[10] until many years later. Instinctively feeling not like a woman, but at the same time not liking men all that much (they were so sexist!), I felt more evolved than either sex. Intellectually, I was somewhat androgynous but, experientially, I was transsexual—specifically, a trans-*male*. There still existed that persisting sense of being a stranger in a strange land. Would I ever reach my goal of male self-actualization?

Too bad that when I really needed to know (knowledge is power!), I was unaware of my transsexual (and intersex) predecessors who had already been reassigned to their identified gender socially, legally, *and* medically. Some of these medical pioneers included trans women such as: Danish painter Lili Elvenes (Elbe),[11] in 1930; English World War II fighter pilot/race-car driver, Roberta (Betty) Cowell,[12] in 1951; American ex-GI/photojournalist, Christine Jorgensen,[13] from 1951 to 1952; English surgeon-lieutenant, Georgina Carol Somerset,[14] in 1957; French nightclub singer, "Coccinelle" (Jacqueline Charlotte Dufresnoy),[15] in 1958; English model, April Ashley,[16] in 1960; American showgirl, Hedy Jo Star,[17] in 1962; Welsh travel writer, Jan Morris,[18] from 1964 to 1972; and English antiques dealer, Dawn Langley Simmons (Hall),[19] in 1968. And, trans men such as: English mill worker, Bill Allen,[20] in 1935; American radiologist, Dr. Alan L. Hart,[21] in 1917; English Lieutenant-Colonel, Wynsley Michael Swan,[22] in 1923; English domestic servant, Harry Weston,[23] in 1939; English ship doctor, Michael Laurence Dillon,[24] from 1939 to 1949; American philanthropist, Reed Erickson,[25] from 1963 to 1965; and American ex-nun/nurse, Dr. Angelo (Tony) Tornabene (aka Mario Martino),[26] from 1967 to 1971.

Before our romance soured, when Dina was still open to my identity as a trans man, we had sent away for Green and Money's book, a real eye-opener. Highly informative, as well as male-to-female transsexuals, it featured photographs of female-to-male transsexuals like me! There were illustrations of various sex-reassignment surgeries: for trans women, mammoplasty (breast implants), orchiectomy (removal of the testes), and penile inversion/vaginoplasty (reconfiguration of the penis to create a neovagina,); and for trans men, bilateral mastectomy/male chest construction (removal of breast tissue and creation of male pecs), pan-hysterectomy (removal of the ovaries, uterus, cervix, and fallopian tubes), and phalloplasty (construction of a neopenis). Even though these early transsexual surgeries were fairly rudimentary—and the outcomes sometimes questionable—they seemed to me a life-saver, and I felt alive for the first time. I would be born again as a whole person, as a man.

The domino effect continued to open doors as Green and Money's book mentioned endocrinologist, Dr. Harry Benjamin. He had a practice in downtown Manhattan serving transsexual patients but, regrettably, he had just retired. Fortunately, his colleague, Dr. Charles Ihlenfeld, also an endocrinologist (who later became a psychiatrist), took over his clinical practice. Dr. Ihlenfeld was to be one of my medical saviours, facilitating my emergence from the labyrinth, my exit from hell. But I was not out of the fire yet.

That summer of 1971, following my high school graduation, I developed tonsillitis and had to have my tonsils removed. That same month, there was a gale in Winchester, which I wished would blow me away to another galaxy where I could physically become male. No such luck! I had to serve my time in the Valley for another month before starting university in Ottawa. I got a jump on things by taking a pre-university credit-course in archeological anthropology through Trent University. This six-week practical course involved an archeological dig on an old Jesuit site in Perkinsfield, outside of Peterborough. We camped out in tents while working on the site. I loved it and almost decided to pursue anthropology, but psychology won out as my intended major. Perhaps I should have chosen psychological anthropology, thereby combining both specialties. Our futures have many potential paths. Mine led me to eventually become a psychotherapist and a gender consultant and, before that, a trans community activist. Then, 30 years later, I was invited to speak at the TransIdentities Symposium at Trent U., my *alma mater*. When Dina visited me at our dig, I bitterly resented her intrusion, especially when she alluded to me as "she" and "her," calling attention to my birth-assigned sex in front of my professor and classmates while I was trying to keep my head down so as to be inconspicuous in the world.

In mid-August, a week before my scheduled lazy eye operation at the Ottawa Civic Hospital, Dina and I took her kids to the Capital Fair in downtown Ottawa. It was my last dance as Dina's ex-lover. Amidst the fairground tents, goofing around like some randy teenager, I grabbed a spare section of a tent pole, pretending it was my overlong penis: "This is my rod—are you ready for a poke?" Not amused, Dina made some castrating retort, wounding my male pride. "Oh well," I reflected, "I'll soon be departing this scene." I literally followed through, running from the fairgrounds to my sister's place in town, where I laid low until the day of my eye surgery. Unbeknownst to Dina, I had stashed some ties, shirts, pants, and a pair of black Chelsea boots in a trunk at Arjuna's apartment. Dressing in my normalizing guy gear gave me a brief reprieve from gender hell.

Following the operation, I awoke in the hospital to find my boy clothes gone, replaced by a blouse, skirt, pantyhose, and sandals. I was livid! I had never felt so invaded, so betrayed. My inherent resilience overcame my vulnerability that day as I summoned up courage to rebel—trans resistance! Telephoning Dina, I called her a "fucking bitch," angrily slamming down the phone. I then called my older brother, who was in town, asking him to bring me one of his shirts, some pants, and a pair of shoes. It seemed an eternity until Jakub arrived with the life-saving attire to cover my female nakedness, my gender discomfiture. As we were about to make our getaway, Dina charged into the hospital room in a rage, demanding that I put on the girls' clothes she had brought and return with her to the farm. Happily, my brother and I managed to escape this mad woman, hiding out at his place until the heat blew over.

Next morning, Jakub drove me to the farmhouse in Russell to retrieve my belongings because this boy was breaking out! It was a tense moment as Dina attempted to stop us from entering the house. Reluctantly, she eventually allowed us inside to gather my things, which we hastily threw into the back of my brother's pick-up truck. Dina was grimly silent. Then, as we drove away, I shouted a parting, "Fuck you, bitch! I'm out of here!" Free at last of my prison warden (and rejecting lover), I felt a sudden surge of hope and a thrill of adventures to come.

Chapter 2 Notes

[1] Camus, Albert, *L'Été* (*Summer*), Paris, FR: Éditions Gallimard, collection Blanche, 1954, n.p.n. French-language edition only. Here's the rest of the quote: "And that makes me happy. For it says that no matter how hard the world pushes against me, within me, there's something stronger—something better, pushing right back." https://www.goodreads.com/quotes/508603-in-the-midst-of-winter-i-found-there-was-within.

[2] Regrettably, I'm uncertain if "Miss Stephens" is her correct name; I previously cited it as "Dr. Hall" in my dedication to her in my earlier book, co-edited with Dan Irving, *Trans Activism in Canada: A Reader*, Toronto, ON: Canadian Scholars' Press, 2014. It's a pity my memory is so hazy around the name of someone who was so pivotal in my early life!

[3] For information on Dr. Richard Green, see https://zagria.blogspot.ca/2011/04/richard-green-1936-part-1-psychiatrist.html; and https://zagria.blogspot.ca/2011/04/richard-green-1936-part-2-academic.html.

[4] For information on Dr. John Money and the Johns Hopkins University psychohormonal research clinic, see https://zagria.blogspot.ca/2010/07/johns-hopkins-psychohormonal-research.html; and https://zagria.blogspot.ca/2010/07/johns-hopkins-part-2-1966-1979.html.

[5] Read stone butch Leslie Feinberg's semi-autobiographical novel, *Stone Butch Blues*, Ann Arbor, MI: Firebrand Books, 1993. Leslie also identifies as genderqueer (see note on genderqueer below).

[6] See: Singer, June, *Androgyny: Toward a New Theory of Sexuality*, New York, NY: Anchor Books, 1976 (republished as *Androgyny: The Opposites Within*, Jung on the Hudson Book Series, Lake Worth, FL: Nicolas Hays, 2000); and Herdt, Gilbert, ed., *Third Sex, Third Gender: Beyond Sexual Dimorphism in Culture and History*, Brooklyn, NY: Zone Books, 1994.

[7] For information on androgynes, see https://gender.wikia.org/wiki/Androgyne. Most of the androgynes in the 1970s through the 1990s, were birth-assigned males. See: Kane, Ariadne/J. Ari, and Margot Wilson, *Gender Odyssey: Journey of an Intrepid Androgyne*, Victoria, BC: TransGender Publishing, forthcoming. The only term I'm aware of for birth-assigned females at that time was "he-she" (as mentioned in Leslie Feinberg's novel: see note above).

[8]. "Genderqueer" (gender non-binary) is a catch-all category for gender identities not exclusively masculine or feminine (outside the gender binary and cisnormativity). Genderqueer people might express a combination of masculinity and femininity, or neither, in their gender expression. Genderqueers might identify as either having an overlap of, or indefinite lines between, gender identity; having two or more genders (bigender, trigender or pangender); having no gender (agender, non-gendered, genderless, genderfree, neutrois); moving between genders or having a fluctuating gender identity (gender fluid); or, being third-gender or other-gendered. Some genderqueers prefer gender-neutral pronouns (singular-usage "they," "their," "them"), and also: "ze," "sie," "hir," "co," "ey." Others prefer conventional gender-specific pronouns ("her," "him," "he," "she"), or prefer only their name and no pronouns. Many genderqueer people prefer additional neutral language, such as the title, "Mx." instead of "Mr." or "Ms." Some genderqueers are medically treated for gender

dysphoria with hormones and/or surgery, like transsexual/transgender people. See also https://www.psychologytoday.com/us/blog/sex-sexuality-and-romance/201807/guide-genderqueer-non-binary-and-genderfluid-identity; and: Intersectional Bibliography.

[9] *Hijras* (also known as "Aravanis," "Jagappas" or "Kinnars") are a partly religious subculture made up of birth-assigned males in India, Bangladesh, Pakistan, and Nepal, who are neither masculine nor feminine but live and dress as women, and are legally accepted as "third gender" by those governments. *"Hijra"* was once translated in English as "eunuch" or "hermaphrodite," although LGBT historians and human rights activists have sometimes included them under the "transgender" umbrella. In 2014, the Indian Ministry of Social Justice and Empowerment transgender experts committee, *Hijras* and other trans activists requested that the term, "eunuch," be discontinued from use in government documents because it is not one with which the communities identify. Traditionally, most *Hijras* become sexually neutered by having their genitals surgically removed to show their devotion for, and to ritually identify with, the Hindu goddess, Bahuchara Mata, whose procreative powers are thereby transferred to them. *Hijras* consider themselves ascetic, but some also (often with shame) engage in prostitution with men to supplement their meagre wages earned by singing, dancing and offering blessings at births and deaths.

Recently, a few *Hijras* have identified as feminine and as transgender, and have surgically transitioned to female. Several *Hijras* have entered politics, but some have been contested as "ineligible" for women's seats because of their male birth sex. Only a small number are known to be born intersex. Since 2013, when homosexuality was re-criminalized in India, *Hijras* have encountered physical, psychological and sexual violence by the police. In Bangladesh, they have suffered abuse in government hospitals, and in Pakistan, they have been victims of religious oppression by Christians and Muslims (Shia and Sunni), who pressured landlords to evict them. On April 15, 2014, the Supreme Court of India ruled that transgender people should be treated as a third category of gender, or as a socially and economically "backward" class entitled to proportional access and representation in education and employment. *Hijras* are unknown in Sri Lanka because the Buddhist sects there condemn them as "sexually abnormal."

There is no precise female-born counterpart to the male-born *Hijra*, but the "Sadhin," a gender-variant female, transforms herself, not into a man, but into a celibate woman, opting for the ascetic life as a "saint" as an alternative to marriage and motherhood. She can dress like a man, cut her hair short and take on a man's social roles and behavioural attributes.

For more resources on *Hijras* and dual-identity, trans-*Hijra* people, see the: Intersectional Bibliography. For a transgender perspective on the difference between Indian trans women and *Hijras*, see Monalisa Das's July 12, 2016 article. https://www.thenewsminute.com/article/awesome-it-can-get-indian-website-and-transgenders-46350.

[10] "Two-Spirit" (or "Two-Spirited") is a pan-Indian, umbrella term used by some Indigenous North Americans to describe certain people in their communities fulfilling a traditional third-gender, ceremonial cultural role, and only makes sense when contextualized within a First Nations framework. The term was adopted in 1990 to replace the anachronistic, inappropriate anthropological label, "berdache." "Two-Spirit" is not interchangeable with "LGBT Native American" or "gay Indian" because this title differs from most Western definitions of sexuality and gender identity insofar as it isn't so much about whom one is sexually interested in, or how one personally identifies; instead, it's a sacred, spiritual and ceremonial role confirmed by Two-Spirit community Elders. Third- and fourth-gender roles traditionally embodied by Two-Spirit people incorporate wearing clothing and performing work associated

with both men and women. Not all Indigenous tribes/nations have rigid gender roles, but amongst those that do, the spectrum commonly delineates four genders: feminine woman, masculine woman, feminine man, and masculine man. Indigenous identity is predominantly cultural, rather than a racial classification, based on membership in a particular community, cultural fluency or citizenship, and some Native American or First Nations people might not even consider themselves to be people of colour. Notwithstanding, they still experience discrimination, harassment and abuse (anti-Indigeneity). Some Two-Spirit people identify as gay, lesbian, bisexual, pansexual or asexual. A few might also identify as transgender (and/or intersex); however, contrary to popular misconception, not all Indigenous trans people identify as Two-Spirit.

For more information on Two-Spirit, dual-identity, trans-Two-Spirit, and multiple-identity, trans-intersex-Two-Spirit people, see the Intersectional Bibliography.

[11] Lili Ilse Elvenes (Elbe) (born Einar Wegener) (1882-1931) was the third known transsexual in the world (and the second Dane) to undergo gender-confirming surgeries (orchiectomy, penectomy, scrotectomy, vaginoplasty, and a transplanted uterus and ovary) in Germany from 1930 to 1931, but died shortly afterwards of postsurgical complications. Rumoured to be intersex, this has never been confirmed. Read Lili's posthumously-published autobiography, *Man into Woman: An Authentic Record of a Change of Sex,* London, UK: Jarrolds Publishers, 1933. David Ebershoff's fictionalized account of Lili and her wife, Gerda Gottlieb, *The Danish Girl*, London, UK: Allen & Unwin, 2000, was adapted into a 2015 American film of the same name by director, Tom Hooper, and producers, Gail Mutrux and Neil LaBute. See also: Part I (Einar Wegener), Part II (Lili Ilse Evenes) and Part III (Lili Elbe) on "A Gender Variance Who's Who." https://zagria.blogspot.ca/.

[12] Roberta Elizabeth (Betty) Cowell (1918-2011) was the first transsexual woman in the UK to have sex-reassignment surgery. She had an inguinal orchiectomy (removal of the testes) circa 1950 or 1951 and vaginoplasty (creation of a vagina) in May 1951. Roberta allegedly falsely stated she was intersex so that her surgeon wouldn't be penalized by the legal and medical authorities because transsexual surgery was not legally or medically sanctioned then. Read Roberta's memoir, *Roberta Cowell's Story,* London, UK: Heinemann, 1954. See also https://zagria.blogspot.ca/2012/07/betty-cowell-1918-2011-motor-racer-pilot.html.

[13] Christine Jorgensen (1926-1989) had an orchiectomy in September 1951 and a penectomy in November 1952, both in Copenhagen, Denmark, and eventually (once this surgical procedure became available) a vaginoplasty in the USA. In 1976, Christine sent me a signed copy of her autobiography, *Christine Jorgensen: A Personal Biography*, New York, NY: Bantam Books, 1967 (reprinted by Cleis in San Francisco, CA in 2002, with an introduction by Dr. Susan Stryker), and we exchanged several letters. Christine's life was fictionalized in director Irving Rapper's melodrama, *The Christine Jorgensen Story*, USA: Edward Small Productions, 1970. Compare this with Susan Stryker's experimental video documentary, *Christine in the Cutting Room*, USA, 2013.

[14] Georgina Carol Somerset (1923-2013) was also intersex and surgically transitioned to female in London, UK in 1958, marrying Christopher Somerset in 1962. Asserting that she was not transsexual, and therefore, a "normal" woman, she opposed the UK Gender Recognition Bill in 2003, claiming that transsexuals were sexually "abnormal" and should not be granted a legal change of sex-designation to match their identified gender. See: Somerset, Georgina, *A Girl Called Georgina: An Illustrated Autobiography, with Study Update,* Leicester, UK: The Book Guild, 1992. Watch her TV documentary profile: *A Girl Called Georgina*, directed by Gordon Mason, UK: ITV, 1995. http://www.bfi.org.uk/films-tv-

people/4ce2b7e73bd35. See also: Parts I, II & III on Georgina Somerset on "A Gender Variance Who's Who." https://zagria.blogspot.ca/.

[15] Jacqueline Charlotte Dufresnoy ("Coccinelle") (1931-2006) was the first French transsexual to become a major film star in the 1960s. Her 1960 marriage was the first transgender union to be legally sanctioned in France. Read Jacqueline's memoir, *Coccinelle par Coccinelle* (French) (*Ladybug by Ladybug*), Paris, FR: Editions Filipacchi, 1987. See also https://zagria.blogspot.ca/2009/03/jacqueline-charlotte-dufresnoy-1931.html.

[16] April Ashley (1935-) published her autobiography, *First Lady*, London, UK: Blake Publishing, 2006, two-and-a-half decades after Duncan Fallowell's biography, *April Ashley's Odyssey*, London, UK: Jonathan Cape, 1982, relating many more post-transitional adventures and love affairs in this later version. See also https://zagria.blogspot.ca/2012/06/april-ashley-more-has-been-awarded-mbe.html.

[17] Hedy Jo Star (1920-1999) wrote several versions of her autobiography: *I Changed My Sex!*, Chicago, IL: Allied Books, 1955 (reissued as *I Changed My Sex!: The Autobiography of Stripper Hedy Jo Star, Formerly Carl Hammonds,* Chicago, IL: Allied Books, 1980); and one using both her birth name and adopted name, Star, H. J./Carl Hammonds, *My Unique Change*, Chicago, IL: Novel Books, 1965. See also https://zagria.blogspot.com/search?q=hedy+jo+star.

[18] See: Morris, Jan, *Conundrum*, San Diego, CA: Harcourt Brace Jovanovich, 1974. Because British doctors wouldn't operate on her unless she had first divorced her wife, Elizabeth Tuckniss—which Jan refused to do—she decided to undergo sex-reassignment surgery with Dr. Georges Burou in Morocco, who did not impose this legal restriction. See also: Parts I, II & III on Jan Morris on "A Gender Variance Who's Who." https://zagria.blogspot.ca/.

[19] Dawn Langley Pepita Simmons (Hall) (1922-2000) was English film star Margaret Rutherford's nephew-cum-niece. She had sex-reassignment surgery in the USA in 1968, but to preclude potential transphobic stigma, falsely claimed that she was intersex. In 1969, she wed a young Black man, making theirs the first legal interracial marriage in South Carolina. Read Dawn's memoirs: *Man into Woman: A Transsexual Autobiography*, New York, NY: Macfadden-Bartell, 1971; and *Dawn: A Charleston Legend*, Charleston, SC: Wyrick, 1995. See also: Parts I & II on Dawn Langley Simmons on "A Gender Variance Who's Who." https://zagria.blogspot.ca/.

[20] It's uncertain whether Bill Allen (1906-1949) was transsexual or intersex insofar as there are no available personal or medical reports of his mysterious hospital stay or his post-hospital claim to be a man. See https://zagria.blogspot.com/2008/07/bill-allen-1906-1949-mill-worker.html.

[21] Dr. Alan L. Hart (1890-1962) was the first known transsexual to have gender-confirmation surgery: a pan-hysterectomy in the USA in 1917, but no male genital surgery. See https://zagria.blogspot.com/2008/10/alan-lucill-hart-1890-1962-doctor.html.

[22] Lieutenant-Colonel Wynsley Michael Swan (??-1949) was a transsexual man whom Roberta Cowell had met in England, briefly mentioning him in her autobiography. Pre-transitionally, Wynsley had served in the British Women's Army Corps in World War I, and in 1927, married a woman. Details of his gender transition are unavailable so it's possible that he might have been intersex. See https://zagria.blogspot.com/2009/02/wynsley-michael-swan-

1949-lieutenant.html.

[23] Harry Weston (1917-1943), following the example of his older (very likely) intersex sibling, Mark Weston (see note in chapter 1), changed his name and gender presentation from female to male in the 1930s and underwent sex-reassignment surgery at Charing Cross Hospital in London, UK in 1939. Sadly, he hung himself three years later, while suffering from depression. It's uncertain whether Harry was transsexual or intersex. See https://zagria.blogspot.com/2012/07/harry-weston-1917-1943-domestic-servant.html.

[24] Dr. Michael Laurence Dillon (1915-1962) began taking male hormones in 1939, had a mastectomy in 1942, and underwent several phalloplastic operations to surgically create a neopenis from 1946 to 1949. After being outed as transsexual in England, he moved to India and became the first Englishman to be ordained as a Tibetan Buddhist monk, taking the name Lobzang Jivaka. His health failed and he died at Dalhousie, India in 1962, aged 47. See Hodgkinson, Liz, *Michael née Laura: The World's First Female to Male Transsexual*, London, UK: Virgin Books, 1989. Michael Dillon and Roberta Cowell had a brief rocky romance, the first- known transsexual couple; see: Kennedy, Pagan. *The First Man-Made Man: The Story of Two Sex Changes, One Love Affair, and a Twentieth-Century Medical Revolution*. London, UK: Bloomsbury Publishing, 2007.

[25] For information on Reed Erickson (1917-1992), see: Devor, Aaron H., and Nicholas Matte, "ONE Inc. and Reed Erickson: The Uneasy Collaboration of Gay and Trans Activism, 1964-2003," *GLQ: A Journal of Lesbian and Gay Studies*, 2004, 10(2): 179-209; and also https://zagria.blogspot.com/2008/06/reed-erickson-1917-1992-engineer-scion.html. To learn about the Erickson Educational Foundation, see the text and accompanying note in chapter 3.

[26] Dr. Angelo (Tony) Tornabene (1937-2011), writing under the pseudonym, "Mario Martino," published his memoir, co-written by harriet, *Emergence: A Transsexual Autobiography,* New York, NY: Crown Publishers, 1977. Although the cover promoted the book as "the first complete female-to-male story," two earlier writers had beaten him to the punch: intersex Robert Allen in 1954 and transsexual Michael Dillon in 1946. See also https://zagria.blogspot.ca/2013/08/mario-martino-1938-usa.html.

3. Gender Transition…Higher Learning…Sexual Liaisons (1971-1975)

A new chapter was about to begin for this existential adventurer, one combining university and gender transition. At 19, I knew self-empowerment was within my grasp: I would be Superman for real, once I got pumped with kryptonite (testosterone).

I rented a basement apartment in a house owned by an Italian couple on Bank Street in Ottawa, fairly close to Carleton University. My sister nearly blew my cover when she corrected the landlady (who perceived me as male), referring to me as "she" and "her." Hiding beneath my cap and gender-neutral trench coat, I was beyond embarrassed! Oh well. There to offer me moral support out of the goodness of her heart, Arjuna didn't do it on purpose. Unfortunately, I had to use my female birth name because they wanted to see identification; once I settled in, I would tell them my chosen name (Nick). The rent was only $100 a month, including utilities, with a key to the wine cellar thrown in. I had it made in the shade!

Before starting classes, I informed the Dean of Student Services that I was a female-to-male transsexual wishing to go by my adopted male name, Nicholas Christopher Ghosh. He kindly changed my school records accordingly even though my name change was not yet legal. As Nick, I presented in a super-male persona, wearing three-piece suits and carrying a briefcase to class. I was mistaken for a professor more than once because the other male students dressed casually and carried backpacks. Not out as transsexual to my former high school classmates, only a few recognized me on campus, although several showed a flicker of recognition as our eyes met. This was even before I began male hormones! Many trans men successfully pass as male prior to testosterone therapy, unlike many of our trans sisters, who face formidable challenges passing as female prior to feminizing estrogen medication.

Initially, I registered for the Bachelor of Sciences program in the pre-med stream, wanting to become a doctor and eventually a psychiatrist in order to help other people like me. Regrettably, I failed miserably in mathematics, chemistry, and physics: so, I switched to the Bachelor of Arts program with a major in psychology, hoping instead to become a clinical psychologist. Sadly, this never came to be: but, at least, I eventually made it into the field of mental health as a practicing psychotherapist—a viable alternative.

While studying Psychology 101, I asked Professor Bill Walther if I could give a talk on transsexualism for my classmates. Initially, he agreed; but on further reflection, he discouraged me, believing that the students were not ready for such a *new* phenomenon. I gave up on the idea: but, in hindsight, I wish I had kicked the ass off those asinine assumptions of psychology/psychiatry, which cavalierly conflate gender identity and sexual orientation. Constrained, these behavioural sciences are often limited by polarized conceptions of black and white, straight and gay, male and female, masculine and feminine, thereby dismissing the rich colours of the evolutionary rainbow—reflecting sexual and gender diversity in nature and culture. This diversity is enriched by instances of homosexuality, transsexualism, and intersex across all species.[1]

In my first year of university, I was only selectively out as a transsexual man: so, only a few classmates knew my personal history. I was still woman-focussed, fancying several female students, to whom I shyly made brave overtures, but everyone turned me down flat. I couldn't fathom why because I appeared super-straight and wasn't all that bad-looking (a couple of my friends told me that I looked like Neil Sedaka or Richard Dreyfuss). Feeling dejected after a young woman's non-reciprocation, I was so distraught that I was almost broadsided by another car while driving through an intersection. Fortunately, I suffered only a bruised male ego. I eventually decided to try my luck with guys, making out with several gay men over the course of my university career, although this wouldn't happen until the following year after the first stage of my surgical transition.

In the meantime, I thought I would try the gay and lesbian community to meet friends and possibly a lover. I found a group at Pestalozzi College where gay dances were held. There, I met pioneering gay activist, Charlie Hill, who, alongside others, presented the historical "We Demand" manifesto[2] to the federal government on August 28, 1971, demanding long-overdue legal reforms for the Canadian homophile community. Sadly, I missed out on this milestone event as I was still recovering from my eye surgery and my post-Dina trauma! I also came across Gays of Ottawa (GO),[3] a political advocacy and social support group, where I met co-founder, Denis LeBlanc, and other homophile activists. My first-ever article, "On Transsexualism"[4] (written around October 1971), was published in the *GO Info* newsletter in April 1973. I wasn't happy that the editors sat on my article for over a year before publishing it! Back then, the gay media was often as bad as mainstream media (and at times even now) either declining to print, or delaying printing, feature articles on gay/bisexual trans people. In the 1970s, 1980s, and 1990s, when transsexual men like Lou Sullivan and I submitted articles and reviews to North American queer periodicals, such as *The Advocate, The Body Politic*, and *GO Info,* these were frequently rejected as having little or no interest value for their cisgender readership. In the early 2000s, when trans-males like Kyle Scanlon and I reached out to gay TV cable channels, like Canada's PrideVision (which morphed into OUTTV), asking producers to interview us, we were often summarily dismissed as not sexy enough—compared to hot cis gay men, or glamorous drag queens or über-femme trans women! My article in *GO Info* was the first of lots of writing and editing I would do on gender and sexual identity over the next 50 years.

In addition to psychology, I took various humanities courses: sociology, anthropology, political science, philosophy, and comparative religion. (I was intrigued by psychological anthropology: a crosscultural overview of diverse attitudes and behaviours, including mental illness). A Renaissance man, higher education was preparing me for the community activism that was soon to follow. I loved sociology and anthropology, and devoured American mythologist Joseph Campbell's works on comparative mythology and religion. Professor Nalini Devdas taught our comparative religion class, opening my eyes to a world I had never seen before. Impoverished, recovering Roman Catholic that I was, I learned about Christian mysticism, Judaic Kabbalism, Islamic Sufism, Hindu nihilism, Taoism, and Buddhism. Too bad the curriculum did not include the neopagan goddess religions and Native spirituality. A participant observer, I also explored, firsthand, other diverse faith communities, such as Hare Krishna, Bahá'í, Islam, Zen Buddhism, Quakerism, and Unitarian Universalism, in my soul searching. Ultimately, I repudiated the religionism of both my mother's Christianity[5] and my father's Hindu[6] upbringing (agnostic though he was), and forged my own beliefs and values, informally embracing an eclectic mix of secular humanism (atheism), Taoism, and Zen Buddhism.[7] In my view, the latter two are more non-theistic philosophy than religion, *per se*—and Zen is often referred to as the religion of no religion. Lao Tzu's *Tao Te Ching (The Way of Life)* (1955), Alan Watts's *The Way of Zen* (1957), and Nancy Wilson Ross's *The World of Zen: An East-West Anthology* (1960) were books that changed my life—especially the latter's intersection of Eastern and Western philosophy. Given my penchant for duality and plurality, ambiguity and ambivalence, Dialectical Dancer that I am, I was intrigued by their dialectical tension: the Taoist dichotomy of *yin/yang* and the Zen polarities of and/or and both/neither. American spiritual ecofeminist, Starhawk, likewise values this "on-off pulse of polar energy" that "dissolves dualities and sees opposites as complements...the rhythm of the dance."[8] And, given my transgender identity, I was also enamoured of the bigender, Indian Buddhist *bodhisattva*, Avalokiteshvara[9] (who had various names incarnations in other South Asian countries) and the androgynous/intersex nature of the mythic Hindu deities, such as Ardhanarishvara, Lakshmi-Narayana, and many others.[10]

My present trajectory was split between my academic/vocational path and my gender journey. I wanted to begin my gender transition right away as the gender dissonance was intensifying, splitting apart *psyche* (mind) and *soma* (body), like a severe stroke disconnecting the right and left brain hemispheres, impairing basic functions such as walking and talking. In rare instances, gender dysphoria can cause pre-transitional trans people to experience temporary emotional paralysis or selective mutism, rendering them motionless or speechless. I was often numb (unable to feel hope or joy) and mute (unable to voice my anguish and anger). A walking zombie, I was in suspended animation until my salvation finally came on October 5, 1971.

On that auspicious day, I took a plane to New York City to ask Dr. Ihlenfeld to prescribe male hormones for me. When I arrived at the doctor's office, Jakub was already there (loyal brother that he was), ready to sign off for me because I was underage (19) and needed permission from an older relative or legal guardian. That day was one of the happiest of my life: I felt like a million bucks after I got my first testosterone enanthate injection. Two hundred mg/ml biweekly was my prescription and I would likely be on male hormone therapy the rest of my life. "T"—as trans men call this wonder drug—gave me the desired male secondary sex-characteristics: beard, Adam's apple, low voice, body hair, muscles, increased sex drive. The invisible man was finally becoming visible after years of blood, sweat, and tears. Persistence pays off!

The next few months were pure bliss as I went through my second puberty: a transformational rite-of-passage from female to male adolescence. My sex drive zoomed from zero to 100 in a nanosecond; I couldn't stop jacking off—a novel experience as I had never masturbated before. The university washrooms were a lifesaver as I greedily grabbed a magic moment between classes during which to scratch my constant itch. No wonder so many men are constantly sex-crazed!

The Christmas season upon me, my landlords invited me upstairs for some holiday cheer. I told them all about myself: I was a man trapped in a female body, was now going by Nick, and would be having chest surgery next summer. When I showed them pictures of transsexuals in Benjamin's book, they were surprised, not fully understanding: but they accepted me regardless, even though they were practicing Catholics. That was the best Christmas present ever!

My 20th birthday was fast-approaching and that February I bought myself a car: a brand-new, shiny, red Toyota Corolla with a standard shift. After only a few driving lessons, I drove downtown during rush hour, turning left into a busy intersection on one of the iciest days. Mother Earth was surely watching out for me that day as I almost hit another car during that daredevil turn, grinding the gears, starting and stopping, as I nervously inched across the intersection, blocking oncoming traffic. I could feel the sweat pouring off me. Michael Andretti I was not! After this harrowing experience, I soon learned to shift manually like a pro.

Nonetheless, I did explore my physical side, trying out traditional medieval sports like fencing and archery: but, not excelling at either, I gave up in frustration. I also nearly signed up for boxing lessons, but changed my mind because I'm not the macho "Rocky" type. Looking back, I wish I had taken up soccer and field hockey, but back then field hockey was only for girls (and ice hockey only for boys). I didn't pursue ice hockey (even though I had played a bit as a youngster) because, lacking athletic prowess, I was apprehensive that I wouldn't be good enough to compete on an all-male team. The same went for soccer. Too bad I let fear and frustration get in the way of mastering a new skill and having some fun.

Overall, I was feeling good as my gender transition proceeded according to plan. The next step was the psychological evaluation to approve me for a bilateral mastectomy and male chest construction (now called "top" surgery). Following my birthday, I flew to NYC to see Dr. Wardell Pomeroy, the eminent clinical psychologist and fellow sex-researcher with Dr. Alfred Kinsey. He was cordial while assessing me for eligibility for sex-reassignment surgery. Elated when he gave me the green light, nothing could stop me now from realizing my goal of self-actualization, of becoming my authentic self through surgical masculinization. The drabness of that grey wintry day brightened with the promise of good things to come.

That summer, as my first year of university wound down, feeling lonely and desiring friendship, I moved into a student housing co-operative, the Bertrand Russell House, with five other Carleton U. students. The co-op next door was the Albert Einstein House. I was the only trans (and quasi-queer) resident, but my housemates welcomed me wholeheartedly. The names of both houses resonated with me, philosopher and (social) scientist that I was. Given my dual perspective of an empiricist and metaphysicist—akin to American psychologist/religious philosopher, Dr. William James, and Swiss psychologist/religious mystic, Dr. Carl Jung, both of whom investigated psychological *and* spiritual phenomena[11]—I wished to combine a major in psychology with a minor in philosophy. But the faculty advisor vehemently denied my request, disparaging philosophy for its non-empirical, esoteric approach to the pursuit of knowledge. A similar state of affairs is the final emergence, after many decades, of the now-validated, empirical science of parapsychology,[12] arising out of its pre-scientific predecessor: occult practices known as spiritualism or theosophy.[13]

To this day, I resent his discouragement and take myself to task for allowing him to deter me from my desired academic path. There's got to be a hell for pompous academics, overinvested in their narrow field of study! What about interdisciplinary studies? As stated earlier, I should have specialized in psychological anthropology and become a psychological alchemist like Jung, who paralleled the alchemical process of transmuting base metals into gold with the psychological processes of individuation of the self and transcendence of the psyche.[14] As it turned out, I became a *psychophysical* alchemist, transforming parts of my bodily self from female to male—like some of those images of surgically transformed, trans-male pecs and "junk in the trunks" depicted in Loren Cameron's *Body Alchemy: Transsexual Portraits* (1966). Overall, though, I was really enjoying university because I could select my courses and, for the most part, follow my personal learning path. Like Magister Ludi in *The Glass Bead Game,* Hermann Hesse's 1943 novel of the intelligentsia, I was an (aspiring) intellectual but had to augment my limited inheritance with part-time earnings if I was to continue my academic career on a full-time basis.

So, I took a summer job as a live-in farmhand in the Ottawa Valley. This was my fourth part-time job so far, having previously worked as a library clerk, banquet waiter, and security guard. This job, however, involved heavy farm work, which was alien to me, city boy that I was. I only lasted three days before heading for the hills, my dignity barely intact, but I had good reason for my sudden departure. During breakfast with my employers, two of the middle eyehooks of my breast-binder suddenly pulled apart, causing my two bumps to balloon out unexpectedly. Dismayed, I quickly leaned forward to conceal the unsightly bulges and, happily, my compromised circumstances went undetected. What a close call; my body all scrunched up, perspiration pouring over me! Moreover, my employers were hiring another farmhand and having to share the bedroom and bathroom with another bunkie petrified me! I still had a larger-than-life chest and if my binder was to slip off during the night, it would not be a welcome sight to an unsuspecting roommate unless he happened to be transensual (sexually turned on by trans folks).

Free until school resumed in September, I decided to drive to Toronto to meet the trans women who ran the Association of Canadian Transsexuals (ACT),[15] formed in 1970. I had learnt of ACT's existence from the newsletter put out by the Erickson Educational Foundation (EEF),[16] founded in 1964 by American trans-male philanthropist, Reed Erickson, to fund psychomedical research on transsexualism. EEF sponsored sexological symposia in Europe and North America, and listed gender identity clinics and trans peer-support groups throughout the world.

My first trip to Toronto, I was excited as I drove down in my little red car, speeding along the Trans-Canada Highway in high spirits. Young and free and in my prime, my future looked bright. Arriving late that evening, I drove down Yonge Street in search of a cheap hostel for the night. Next morning, I drove to the Community Homophile Association of Toronto (CHAT),[17] housed in a community centre on Cecil Street in Chinatown. Formed in 1970 and directed by George Hislop, CHAT was one of Toronto's earliest gay liberation organizations, which ran until 1977. The centre was also where ACT met. There, I met the founding organizers of Canada's first transsexual organization: Diana LaMonte (president), Lynne Pellerin[18] (vice-president) and Louise N. (secretary). We soon all became friends and I remained close to

Lynne until her death in 2012. For a very short time, Louise and I were romantically involved. ACT held regular meetings and the following year, we invited EEF secretary, Zelda Suplee, to put on a workshop for our transsexual members. She came all the way from Baton Rouge, LA, lugging a big box of informational pamphlets on the medical and legal aspects of transsexualism and gender transitioning.

During my time in Toronto, I also met some cisgender queer folks, including Philip Cairns, a young poet, artist, and actor. He presented as somewhat androgynous, and drew pictures of intersex flowers, sprouting both pistils and stamens, which he later exhibited in art shows. We quickly became close friends. Invited to a friend's cottage, we frolicked in the pool while the stereo blasted out '60s and '70s rock (Creedence Clearwater Revival, Van Morrison, etc.). For the first time, I felt that I belonged: I was part of an intentional community of gay men, lesbians, and transsexuals. (Most bisexual, intersex, and Two-Spirit people[19] were only selectively out in those days.) I invited Louise to Ottawa for a week-long visit and we hung out together, a boy-girl trans couple. Me, in my black leather jacket and white corduroy fisherman's cap, and her, in her fake leopard-skin jacket and heels, strolling down Bank Street, holding hands, and feeling good. Our romance was short-lived though, because the chemistry just wasn't there, but we remained friends for several years afterwards.

My surgery date with Dr. David Wesser at Yonkers Professional Hospital in NY was fast-approaching. I could hardly wait, sweltering in the humidity, constrained by my breast-binder. My inheritance would cover the surgical fee ($1,400 US) and the plane ticket. Arjuna kindly offered to accompany me for this milestone event. So, I was all set.

I had learned of Dr. Wesser from Angelo (Tony) Tornabene (aka Mario Martino), a post-operative transsexual man and nursing supervisor at the hospital (who later received a doctorate in Counseling Psychology in 1979). Tony led The Labyrinth Foundation Counseling Service for trans men with his first wife, Rebecca, providing aftercare in their home for trans men who had undergone chest surgery. Following his frustration at the surgical complications he had experienced with his two phalloplasties (the first one became infected and had to be removed and he lost the glans of the second), Tony decided to create a viable alternative. Towards this end, he attempted to design a non-surgical prosthetic penis or peeing packer[20] for the purposes of urination and sexual penetration. He sought a medical sculptor to enhance his newly-designed Penile Prosthetic Device (PPD),™ a silicone penis in beige or black. The PPD would be a boon for those trans men who did not opt for phalloplasty, which, being experimental surgery, was cosmetically and functionally extremely limited at the time (more about this later).

I was elated, as well as scared shitless, as they wheeled me into the operating theatre for my top surgery: elated finally to be rid of those loathsome lumps on my chest, replaced by regular male pecs like any other (cis) guy; scared because I had never undergone a major operation like this before and was a bit worried about the outcome. So, I was thankful to have my sister, Tony and his wife there for support. Upon waking from the anaesthetic, although in pain, I felt on top of the world because, after 20 unbearable years, my body was finally masculinizing to match my inner core. I was on cloud nine! Arjuna and I stayed at Tony's place, watching *I Love Lucy* re-runs while I healed. My recovery went smoothly and I finally began to feel more comfortable in my body. Now, all I needed was a penis! Following my recovery, with Arjuna's help, I wrote to a number of phalloplastic surgeons around the world. Everyone replied, including a surgeon in Israel, who used a rib as a stiffening rod for the surgically-fashioned neopenis.

Finally free of those unwanted mammaries, I went swimming at a public pool for the first time as a man. It felt gloriously liberating, although changing in the men's change room was daunting—trying to hide my privates beneath an oversized towel while putting on my underwear—so, thereafter, I drove home in my wet bathing trunks. A bad idea in wintertime, which quashed my attempts at public swimming for a while.

Now, less top heavy, I began feeling better about myself and settled into the co-op. One of my housemates had some hash, which I tried for the first time, but after a few tokes, I became paranoid, running out onto our snow-covered front lawn. Disoriented, I called the Distress Centre and spoke to a nice fellow, a gay Black man from the Bahamas studying at the University of Ottawa. When I disclosed my transsexual status, he didn't care one whit. Breaking boundaries, we exchanged phone numbers and after getting together for a few beers, we ended up in bed. George was sweet and charming, a tasty, hot chocolate treat! We went to his place and I told him that I had never been with a man before. He said he would be gentle and he was. He fucked me in the ass while I lay on my back with my chest scars in full view, but he didn't bat an eye. For the first time, someone accepted me completely as male in a sexual way! My spirits soared as I marked another milestone in my passage to malehood—and perhaps my first towards bisexuality.

We got together two more times but, sadly, I first had to muster some Dutch courage by drinking a couple of beers before sexing because I still harboured a poor body image from the waist down, lacking a cock and balls.

As well as George, a couple of other gay men topped me as I explored the joys of anal sex. One was Gordon, a well-bred, polite man, who gave me a bottle of Russian bear oil to bring out the sheen in my black hair. We only indulged once but remained friends for a while, as did George and I. George eventually returned to the Caribbean and we wrote a few times before finally losing touch. Beyond kissing and cuddling and anal penetration, I didn't do the whole-body thing because my genitals and the other hole were off limits, but I did give them good head for the asking! Was I turning queer after all?

Around this time, my activist gene was stirring, so I decided to educate the world about transsexuals. I called CFRA Radio to see if they wanted to feature me as a trans spokesperson and, definitely interested, we pre-taped an interview at the station. However, I subsequently told them to scrap it, disliking their focus on my bathroom behaviour, pruriently probing as to exactly how I pee in the men's room: "Do you use the urinal or the stall?" Little did they know that I was still penis-less!

This was my first introduction to the malevolent media—sensationalist talk shows, like *The Jerry Springer Show, Dr. Laura, The Howard Stern Show,* etc. and the gutter press, trashy tabloids, like the *Globe*, *National Enquirer*, *News of the World,* etc.—which sensationalize "sex changes" in a tacky way, trashing "trannies" as so-called freaks of nature. Even some mainstream reporters, writing for respectable newspapers, like David Keith Cohler of the *Chicago Tribune,* perpetrated a brand of trans pathology, this time in book format. I seriously considered writing to him, taking him to task for his transmisandrist book, *Freemartin,*[21] a trashy novel about a psychopathic, trans-male serial killer(!), but I was worried that outing myself as trans might jeopardize my potential career as a journalist if I decided to pursue this line of work. At these times, cowardice crushes courage for the sake of professional advancement and economic survival! Back then, I didn't know of any openly transgender journalists or media critics, like today's English trans activist, Helen Belcher,[22] founder of the UK Trans Media Watch in 2008, and Indian Tamil trans activist, Rose Venkatesan,[23] who hosted two TV talk shows from 2008 to 2010, and a radio program established in 2011. Rose plans to produce films featuring trans characters, and a reality TV series on gender-reassignment surgery. Similar to transphobic media monsters, like Cohler, there were screenwriters and film directors, like Brian De Palma, whose twisted erotic thriller, *Dressed to Kill,*[24] was so trans pathologizing that it was a travesty! Its ludicrous depiction of a split-personality transsexual—a female patient trapped in the body of a male psychiatrist, who slashes her male counterpart's girlfriend in a jealous rage—is almost laughable. Thankfully, there are now more transpositive representations of trans characters in film and television.[25]

In retrospect, perhaps I should have agreed to do the radio show after all, considering that so many people are ignorant of the intriguing idiosyncrasies of transgender bodies. I then decided to reach out to other trans people for mutual support and called the *Ottawa Journal* and the *Ottawa Citizen* to place my personal ad: "Female-to-male transsexual seeking other transsexuals and transvestites for friendship." Disconcertingly, neither newspaper would print my advertisement in the "seeking friends" section, stating that because the terms, "transsexuals," and "transvestites" (now "crossdressers"), were explicitly sexual (in their view), I must advertise in the "sexual contacts" section, which was not at all what I wanted. So much for accessing peer-support! Undaunted, I was determined to find others like me in the city.

So, I went back to Gays of Ottawa to try my luck there. My transsexual article in the *GO* newsletter had attracted the attention of two trans women, Sandi and Micheline Johnson. Micheline, and another trans woman, whom I would meet later, both worked for the federal government. The latter was stealth (not out as trans) and threatened to stop me from forming a trans group inasmuch as she didn't want to alert the public to people like us, fearing reprisals in the form of transphobia or genderphobia.[26] Such bigotry could be individual or systemic, implicit or explicit. Her attitude shocked me because I was out as a transsexual man to many people, unashamed that I was born this way; however, I was able to sympathize with her felt vulnerability as a trans woman in this cisgender, genderphobic world. Micheline and I became friends. Sandi and I grew even closer and, some years later, had a brief romantic fling.

As well as local media, I reached out further afield to western Canada, writing a letter about transsexualism to the newspaper editor of the Vancouver *Georgia Straight*, seeking correspondence with other transsexuals and trans-friendly gays and lesbians. A cisgender gay man, James Loewen, who (like many other gay males) was exploring his own gender identity, responded favourably, and flew out from Vancouver to meet me, staying over for a few days that summer. I reciprocated by flying west to his home for the Christmas holidays. Shortly afterwards, he became a professional portrait photographer and his several rare photos of me in my prime are immortalized in my collection at The ArQuives.[27] Years later, James became an intactivist,[28] fighting against the surgical oppression waged against infants and children: involuntary penile circumcision in boys, non-consensual genital mutilation in girls, and involuntary surgical "correction" of sexually-indeterminate genitalia in boys and girls, intersex babies, and children. A fellow secular humanist (atheist), feminist, and deep ecologist (vegan animal liberationist), this passionate advocate for vulnerable sentient beings is a benevolent Outsider, blowing the whistle on medical and religious oppression. This is the main reason we're still friends today, nearly 50 years later.

My Ottawa friends and I had some good times together over the next few years, drinking and dancing at queer clubs like the Coral Reef Club—where drag queens, female impersonators, and pre-transitional transsexual women (like Genevieve), would put on drag shows, histrionically lip-synching torch songs—then cruising down Bank Street in my red-hot Toyota and over the bridge to Hull (Quebec) to check out our favourite watering-holes: *Hotel Chez*

Henri, the Standish, and the Ottawa House. There, I met a number of French-Canadian lesbians, including several very macho diesel dykes.[29] In the 1970s, I personally didn't observe any political tensions between these masculine lesbians and transsexual men (both sometimes vying for the same desired femme), but growing frictions eventually manifested as the infamous border wars in the 1980s and 1990s—a bleak time in our queer-trans communal history.[30] At the time though, things seemed relatively peaceful and I was expanding my circle, embracing a diversity of folks and enjoying youthful adventures along the way. Life was good!

Inclined to embark on further sexual adventures, I ended up in bed with a bisexual man and, then, shortly afterwards with his straight wife. The couple was divorcing because John had just come out as gay and his wife, Mary, didn't want to stay in the marriage. This time, I didn't need to get drunk to sleep with a man insofar as my bisexual identity was steadily evolving. Sadly, though, I wasn't able to achieve physical or emotional intimacy with either John or Mary. This wasn't due to my lingering gender dysphoria and still partially-negative body image, but simply because neither of them was right for me. I even took part in a *ménage à trois* on two occasions: one with two lesbian friends who wanted to try it on with a trans guy, and the other with a bisexual male friend (a leather-daddy biker) and a pansexual[31] trans woman friend who lusted after everybody! Since alcohol was involved in both instances, disappointingly, we all passed out before things really got going.

After this series of sexual experiments, I realized that I felt more "humansexual"[32] (now pansexual) than gay, straight, or bisexual, inasmuch as I was attracted not only to non-transsexual (cisgender) women and men, but also to female and male transsexuals. Even so, I did not always broadcast my all-encompassing sexual preference to others—especially to other trans people—because I feared their likely disapprobation. This was my early internalization of pansexualphobia, and I didn't start using the self-descriptor, pansexual, until the early 2000s.

But I was really after love; not mere lust. Desperate for a meaningful relationship, I wasn't always that selective when it came to potential lovers or partners. In my youthful desperation, I asked out one of my housemates, a young woman who caught my fancy, but she turned me down. I was deflated: "What's wrong with me? Am I not man enough?" Resentful of her rejection, I locked myself in the bathroom and in a gesture of angry despair, cut my wrist—but not deeply, hating the sight of blood. Another housemate (Cal) talked me through this crisis, getting me to eventually open the door. But I still felt humiliated and demoralized. Unlucky in love so far, would I always be single?

Fortunately, my loneliness dispelled when I befriended two delightful gay roommates: Mike and Rex. Mike was a real character, always camping it up and occasionally dressing in drag, his long hair complimented by a string of pearls and a purse. He used to enhance the drawings in my *Tom of Finland*[33] magazines—gay male porn with larger-than-life pictures of lusty men with big dicks in leather jackets and jack boots, revving their motorbikes, whipping and fucking other men, both White and Black. Rex was a soft-spoken, gentle soul with long, tied-back, red hair. I was gathering a core group of friends, although I would remain single for some time to come.

Summertime was approaching and that meant the annual Gay Pride March. In solidarity with my trans and queer friends, we proudly marched on Parliament Hill alongside other activists, determined to win our legal rights—these being still early days in the Gay Liberation Movement. Interestingly, both the 1966 Compton's Cafeteria Riot in San Francisco[34] and the 1969 Stonewall Inn Riots in New York City were sparked by police violence against street queens and transsexual sex workers, who fought back for the first time as a united front. Ironically, drag queens, transvestites, and transsexuals (many of whom were Black, Hispanic, and Latinx) would not be officially welcomed into the fold until the 1980s or 1990s. Even then, many cisqueer folks still perpetuated genderphobic exclusion, a prime example being gay bars I saw in Montreal, Ottawa, Toronto, Calgary, and Vancouver sporting warning signs: "No drag queens, transvestites, or transsexuals permitted." Not until the new millennium would a trans-specific (sex) club open in Canada.[35] As well as queer legal reforms, my transsexual friends and I advocated for trans rights, speaking out at campaign meetings to the representatives of the three major political parties. We asked for anti-discrimination laws and equitable access to healthcare for trans people in Ontario and across Canada. The New Democratic Party (NDP) was the most sympathetic to our cause, the Liberals flagging behind, and the Tories (the Progressive Conservative Party) often opposing or, at best, non-committal. It took decades of lobbying, provincially and federally, before politicians conceded that trans rights are human rights, finally addressing our needs as a heretofore invisible and underserved community.

One reason it took so long was that being disenfranchised and fragmented, we lacked critical mass. Many transsexuals were not readable as such, opting to pass as cisgender men and women: however, this invisibility drastically changed some decades later as many more trans people chose to come out as proud T-boys and T-girls, alongside transqueer, genderqueer, intersex, Two-Spirit, and other gender liberators.[36]

Moreover, the cisgender, gay/lesbian community and the transvestite/transsexual community were quite separate; intersecting socially or sexually in various contexts, but rarely politically. (Moreover, bisexual, intersex, and Two-Spirit people were barely visible as such—an intriguing sociopolitical dynamic). Was this because these two marginalized sectors were too close for comfort, both competing for larger societal acceptance as so-called normal? Or, was it because one group focussed on sexual orientation, sex partners, queer politics, and gay reforms, while the other focussed on gender identity, medical and legal transition, peer-support, and trans rights? Or, perhaps it was because the trans body politic did not fully emerge until sometime later with its own formalized identity and identity politics? Over time, this split would heal as bridges were built to promote unity and solidarity within the still-evolving LGBTTI2SQQAA[37] community. Even so, this evolution towards a communal rainbow was fraught with challenges and setbacks. Sadly, even today, we are still witnessing genderphobia, transphobia, and intersexphobia displayed by some cisqueer folks, paralleled by homophobia, lesbophobia, and biphobia on the part of some trans people; not to mention anti-Indigeneity, racism, classism, sexism, ableism, and ageism perpetuated by both parties. Promisingly though, both communities have been working towards becoming more transpositive and more queerpositive, respectively, as the overall gender/queer community becomes increasingly integrated. Still another reason for this slow turning-of-the-wheel was the constant in-fighting and gender policing within the transsexual, transgenderist,[38] and transvestite populations, frequently derailing a united transgender movement. Solidarity is an ideal not easily realized, especially when political ideologies and party affiliations were as polarized as those were within the early trans community, dividing those on the Right from those on the Left, with a few middle-grounders holding their own in the Centre. Nonetheless, our diligent fight for trans people's human rights eventually paid off as we eventually won some legal battles—but not without sustaining substantial casualties: those often unsung gender heroes who burned out or passed on along the way. And, our fight for justice continues.

All activists have personal lives besides their political ones—although it's hard for many of us to keep these separate, as many feminists will attest—and I was no exception. As a student-of-life and knowledge-seeker, entering my third year of university, my psychology, sociology, political science, and philosophy courses were informing my developing activism, enabling me to put theory into practice.

In terms of philosophy, intrigued as I am by logic, ethics, epistemology, and phenomenology,[39] my passions are existentialism[40] and humanism[41] (often interrelated).[42] These latter two include the writings of existentialist philosophers, theologians, and novelists such as Martin Buber, Albert Camus, Fyodor Dostoyevsky, Martin Heidegger, James Joyce, Franz Kafka, Søren Kierkegaard, Friedrich Nietzsche, Jean-Paul Sartre, Simone de Beauvoir, and Paul Untilich, as well as a number of humanist psychologists and psychiatrists (cited further on). Humanist existentialism can be a bridge intersecting philosophy and psychology, and often embraces the political philosophy of socialism.[43] Fundamental themes of life and death, hope and despair, faith and cynicism, meaning and absurdity, empowerment and powerlessness, resigned humour and impotent rage, humility and pride, passion and compassion are the only real concerns of humankind—except for the instinct to survive and peacefully co-exist with Mother Earth's other inhabitants. Many of these pairs can function as complementary traits (rather than polarized opposites) but are also dialectical, requiring reconciliation. And, what single-mindedly drives the altruistic activist (and all caring creatures) is the over-arching moral imperative to never relinquish concern and lapse into complacency!

Yes, I am the Dialectical Dancer, dancing for my very life, trying to reconcile the seemingly irreconcilable. Like all human beings, I'm encumbered with the single most important task of making my own meaning in life. Like all of us, I'm charged with the responsibility of maintaining hope and faith in the face of overwhelming ontological odds. No wonder I am in chronic burnout mode, suffering constant lived and vicarious trauma, due to lifelong existential angst! Even so, as a community activist serving trans people, I must prevail, and the philosopher in me helps me to do just that.

As for the psychology program, I did not fancy psychometrics, statistics, research methodology or experimental psychology all that much. What really grabbed me were the analytical, behavioural, developmental, existential, humanistic, social, organizational, phenomenological, personal, and counselling psychologies. I abhorred abnormal psychology's inherent tendency towards psychopathology. Our psychology textbooks in those days were medieval in terms of human sexology; specifically, homosexuality, lesbianism, and transvestism. I do not recall either bisexuality or transsexualism even being mentioned and, if so, they were assuredly psychopathologized as deviant or abnormal! Most of the early pseudo-scientific theories about gay men, lesbians, bisexuals, androgynes, transvestites, and transsexuals would soon be disproved by sexologists, psychologists, sociologists, and anthropologists conducting more rigorous research—and still later, by participatory action research (PAR) methodology involving a collaborative mix of straight, queer, cisgender, and transgender participants.

With regards to counselling psychology, I was attracted to a variety of psychological theories and psychotherapeutic modalities: existential/humanistic therapy, Adlerian therapy, Jungian therapy, Gestalt therapy, rational-emotive behavior therapy/cognitive behavior therapy, and client-centred therapy. I was also interested in child developmental psychology, adult developmental psychology, and thanatological psychology/psychotherapy.[44]

An eclectic thinker, I have a particular proclivity for Jung's dream analysis and psychological alchemy[45]—combining Eastern religions with

Western psychology, replete with alchemical metaphors and mystical mandalas; Frankl's Logotherapy[46]—transforming vulnerability to resilience by embracing existential hope and creating meaning in life; Maslow's life-long self-actualizing psychology[47]—aspiring upwards through a hierarchy of human needs; Erikson's dynamic, dialectical approach towards continually reworking and resolving developmental life-stage themes and identity crises throughout the life cycle[48]—as well as his intriguing concept of pseudo-speciation[49]; and Adler's individual psychology[50]—fulfilling our life tasks and manifesting personal power and meaning through social interest (or political activism).

Not surprisingly, it is the practical philosopher, psychologist, and psychotherapist (visionary and healer), in me that infuse my personal and social agency as a gender transgressor cum social change agent. Dialectical Dancer is morphing into Gender Worker.

Even though my male gender identity (internal) and male gender role (external) were firmly established, I wasn't yet legally male. My Ontario Health Insurance Plan (OHIP) card still showed my female birth name and birth-assigned sex and I still got government mail addressed to "Miss Ghosh." Directly confronting the OHIP director in his office, I requested that he change my name on my health card to Mr. Nicholas Christopher Ghosh. To my surprised delight, he consented: "Of course! You certainly don't look like a 'Miss' to me; anyone can see that you are a man." The benefit of passing privilege! Now, all I had to do was legally change my name and sex designation. First, I applied for a legal change-of-name, which, at that time, required one to appear before a provincial court judge. Embarrassed at telling the world my private business, I steeled myself to the task, telling the judge that I was a female-to-male transsexual, had been going by the name of Nicholas Christopher Ghosh for three years and had had a sex reassignment operation two years ago. I took the legal change-of-name certificate to the Office of Vital Statistics and soon after received my amended birth certificate. I was now legally male! Four years later, following my hysterectomy in 1978, I finally attained legal status as male, preventing future humiliation at school registrar's offices, human resources departments, welfare offices, health centres, and hospitals, not to mention airports and border crossings when accosted by pompous clerks and power-hungry officials, who might enjoy making my life hell with their petty bureaucracy. Or, if stopped by the traffic police to check my driver's license. Nobody could cross me now!

On a roll as a legally *bona fide* male, I decided to have some fun for a change: "All school and work and no play makes Nick a dull boy!" I convinced my housemates to throw a 1950s/1960s dress-up party. It was a blast! Coiffed in ducktails or beehives, and dressed in leathers or feathers, and boots or spiked heels, we rocked and rolled, while the platters spun (Elvis, the Supremes, the Beatles, and Cliff Richards). Dressed all in leather, my pompadour Brylcreemed, I jived to the jukebox all night long with my good friends. I felt like the king of the prom!

My manly confidence growing, I thought I would try my hand at love again and reach out to Dina once more because I still carried a torch for my first love (oh, my foolish heart!). I compiled an audiotape of 1950s and 1960s love songs, crooning along in my most love-struck voice and sent it to Dina. She called me up and I invited her to another upcoming house party, but she turned me down. Male hormones raging, I wasn't to be deterred so one evening, I drove to her apartment and knocked on the door. She nearly had a heart attack when she saw me (now a young man) standing there in the flesh. To my surprise, she invited me in. Before I knew it, I was sitting on her lap as she cooed, "Oh, you and your hats!" (I was wearing my favourite white fisherman's cap). Offering me her living room couch she invited me to sleep over, but I politely declined because it was nearly three a.m. and I had classes early next morning. She then told me that a butch dyke acquaintance, Rick, had slept beside her in bed one night recently—but only after Dina had placed a divider between them. This was her way of protesting that she really wasn't lesbian or bisexual and that she still saw me as a potential threat: a perceived masculine lesbian even though I was post-op! Some people are in perpetual denial.

Next evening, I returned to Dina's house and she halfheartedly asked me in. Then, over coffee, she snarled at me that her psychiatrist at the Royal Ottawa Hospital (Dr. S.) had informed her that I was "not a real man" because I did not have a penis! Was my flesh-and-blood micropenis a fake organ? When I got really mad at her transmisandrist slur, she got angry in turn, demanding that I leave immediately. When I wouldn't go right away, her brother (who lived with her) overpowered me, pinning me to the floor, shouting, "Leave my sister alone, you fucking butch dyke!" And this from a queer man! His words cut me like a knife because I had never identified as lesbian, let alone as female. Born a transsexual male, I had instinctively known this fact since I was three years old. I yelled back at him, "Get off me, you goddamn bastard!" Dina called the police and two officers arrived, ordering me to face the wall. As Dina referred to me by female pronouns, they checked my identification—thankfully, now male—and were obviously perplexed: "This guy isn't a woman!" Asking Dina if she wanted to press charges, she replied in the negative—fortunately for me or I would have been tender meat for those stand-up guys behind bars and I did not fancy myself as some Daddy's bitch! My Earth Mother was surely looking out for me that day as I narrowly escaped arrest and possible imprisonment. Finally free of my masochistic obsession for the Dragon Lady, I snuffed out my torch for Dina for good.

Processing these events, I went to see Dr. S. to give him a piece of my mind. I was pissed off at his reportedly transphobic remarks, which were untrue anyway, given that a number of transgender men and cisgender men (such as genitally-injured war vets) do not have a functioning penis. Even so, they are still very much male. Repeating what Dina had told me he had said about me, Dr. S. flatly denied it, stating that he had no patient by the name of Dina. Had she lied to me or was his tongue tied by patient confidentiality? Psychiatry being what it was at the time (and sometimes still is today), he was assuredly not going to make any concessions to me: the patient, the younger person, the psychopathological transsexual. After all, he was the doctor, the older person, the normal (cisgender) one. As the all-powerful psychiatrist, he could have committed me simply because I had the "balls" to challenge him. Our confrontation ended in a stand-off and I left feeling empowered—but also defeated—because his mind and heart were closed to understanding and empathy. Sometimes direct action works, sometimes it doesn't. The main thing is not to become discouraged when advocating for ourselves. Always be ready to rise up again like the fallen spirit-warrior or the burning Phoenix.

Beginning my fourth year at Carleton U., I had to pin down my thesis topic if I was to graduate by next summer. I asked my thesis advisor, Professor Bob Wakefield, if I could do a research study comparing transsexual men with masculine lesbians, showing how they differed psychologically and sexually, even though many trans men had initially identified as butch dykes and some even as staunch feminists. Conceding my idea as an intriguing comparison, he backed me 100%. Disappointingly, I couldn't find any research participants because when I called the university's gay/lesbian line, the queer woman who answered declared that androgyny was now "the thing" in the lesbian world and that butches were out, so that quashed it.[51] Alas, I have a lifetime of regrets around missed opportunities, but ultimately I have to let them go. Perhaps writing this memoir is a way to do that: a cleansing of the soul.

Disheartened, I abandoned the research project and souring on the whole idea of a thesis, I cut my losses and ran. I transferred my four-year Honours program to a three-year Bachelor's program so I could graduate sooner and, finally, be done with it. Nonetheless, still wishing to pursue graduate studies in clinical psychology, I applied to four universities in Ontario, but was turned down by everyone because of my low grade-point average. My dream of becoming a clinical psychologist was dashed! I decided to take a break from school and visit my friend, Louise, in Vancouver. The west coast had always called to me: so, I headed out there looking for adventure.

Shortly before I left for British Columbia, my trans-male friend, Lee D., appealed to the Ontario Ministry of Health to include sex-reassignment surgery

(SRS) as an insured health service under OHIP for *all* transsexual Ontarians, including those trans people (like him) who had not been assessed through the Adult Gender Identity Clinic (AGIC) at Toronto's Clarke Institute of Psychiatry (now the Centre for Addiction and Mental Health [CAMH]).[52] Such unqualified universal coverage would mean that he and other impoverished Ontarians would not have to pay out of pocket for transsexual surgeries. (OHIP continued to cover the cost of SRS for trans people in Ontario until it was delisted in 1998 as a "non-essential" health service: (medically unnecessary; therefore, deemed cosmetic). Sadly, Lee was unsuccessful: health insurance coverage was still limited to only those transsexuals approved by the Clarke's AGIC (the sole provincial assessor until 2015). Many trans people (like me) opted not to access the Clarke Gender Clinic, disinclined to go through the arduous and time-consuming approval process, thereby delaying their gender transition. Some others were accepted into the clinic, but did not meet the stringent approval criteria, failing the Real-Life Test. This test required surgical candidates to provide documented proof of having publicly lived full-time in their identified gender role. This meant studying, working, or volunteering 40 hours a week for at least two years, often without the benefit of cross-sex hormone (and electrolysis treatments for trans women). Regrettably, not everyone could afford these necessary interventions—especially those who were unemployed, disabled, or newly-immigrated—forcing some people (mostly transsexual women) to illicitly obtain underground market hormones and/or turn to sex work to finance their gender transition. Other trans people who failed the Real-Life Test because they could not publicly pass as their identified gender were condemned to simply live a double life (as sometimes male, sometimes female), or otherwise languish in a genderless land—often turning to alcohol, drugs, and unsafe sex to suppress their gender dysphoria.

To add insult to injury, Lee was not permitted to legally change his sex designation to male following his first transsexual operation (top surgery) because he still had female reproductive organs. So, I had to loan him the money. A pioneering trans warrior, Lee went to the press in November 1974 and his story was featured in the *Ottawa Journal*. To assist Lee, I called Dr. Morton Shulman, a Member of Provincial Parliament (MPP) with the New Democratic Party (NDP), but, disappointingly, he was just leaving politics and could not help us. Temporarily stonewalled, I was nonetheless determined to push for Ontario health insurance for my trans sisters and brothers. An activist was born!

Chapter 3 Notes

[1] See: Nanda, Serena, *Gender Diversity: Crosscultural Variations* (2nd ed.), Long Grove, IL: Waveland Press, 2014; and Roughgarden, Joan, *Evolution's Rainbow: Diversity, Gender and Sexuality in Nature and People,* Berkeley, CA: University of California Press, 2004.

[2] See: "We Demand," *The Body Politic*, November-December 1971, (1): 4-7; and Brian Waite's "Remembrance and Reflection on We Demand and Strategy for Gay Liberation," *The Body Politic*, August 28, 2011, n.p. And the photo history http://onthebookshelves.com/wedemand.htm.

[3] For information on Gays of Ottawa (GO) and the *GO Info* newsletter, see https://arquives.andornot.com/en/list?q=gays+of+ottawa&p=1&ps=20; and https://biblio.uottawa.ca/atom/index.php/gays-of-ottawa.

[4] My transsexual news article is housed in the Rupert Raj fonds: The ArQuives in Toronto. https://arquives.andornot.com/en/list?q=on+transsexualism+article&p=1&ps=20.

[5] See: Russell, Bertrand, *Why I Am Not a Christian –and Other Essays on Religion and Related Subjects*, Abingdon, UK: Routledge, 1927. Reprint, New York, NY: Touchstone Books (Simon & Schuster), 1957. (Edited by Paul Edwards).

[6] See: Ilaiah, Kancha, *Why I Am Not a Hindu: A Sudra Critique of Hindutva Philosophy, Culture and Political Economy,* Kolkata, India: Samya, 1996; and Singh, Bhagat, Why I Am an Atheist, Lahore, India: *The People,* 1930. Reprint, General Press, 2019 (Kindle edition).

[7] Several other transgender/gender non-binary people interested in Buddhism are listed below.

English transsexual doctor, Michael Laurence Dillon, was the first European to become a Tibetan Buddhist. He was ordained as a novice monk of the Gelukpa order at the Rizong Gompa Monastery in Ladakh, India, taking the name, Lobzang Jivaka. See: Jivaka, Lobzang/Dillon, Michael, *Out of the Ordinary: A Life of Gender and Spiritual Transitions*, New York, NY: Fordham University Press, 2016. (Written in 1962 and published posthumously).

English male crossdresser, Upasaka Devamitra, is a member of the Triratna Buddhist Order. He lives in London, UK and teaches at the London Buddhist Centre. See his website https://devamitrablog.wordpress.com/. Read his memoir, *Confessions of a Transvestite Buddhist: A Quest for Manhood*, London, UK: Achilles Publishing, 2014. https://www.waterstones.com/book/confessions-of-a-transvestite-buddhist/upasaka-devamitra/9780993502200.

Dutch trans woman, Caitriona Reed, is a trailblazing, transgender Zen Buddhist teacher, who transitioned 20 years ago. She co-founded (with her partner Michele Benzamin-Miki) the Manzanita Village Retreat Center in southern California, which focusses on Vipassana meditation and Zen practice as a means to promote sustainable ecologies, non-violence, and social justice. Read her article, "Coming Out Whole," *Inquiring Mind*, Spring 1998, 14(2). https://www.inquiringmind.com/article/1402_15_reed_coming-out-whole/. See also Emily DeMaio Newton's interview with Caitriona in *The Buddhist Review Tricycle*, July 26, 2019. https://tricycle.org/trikedaily/caitriona-reed/.

Canadian gender non-binary social worker, Corey Keith, is interested in sex and spirituality, and has explored secular humanism, Buddhism, Tantric yoga, paganism, and Indigenous spirituality (especially of Two-Spirit people). Corey is also a wellness coach and a consultant on sexuality, gender, and beyond. See their website https://spectraconsulting0.wixsite.com/home. Read their story, "Glimmerings of Balance," in Margot Wilson and Aaron Devor, eds., *Glimmerings: Trans Elders Tell Their Stories*, Victoria, BC: TransGender Publishing, 2019, 75-88.

I have also known (or known of) trans, genderqueer, intersex, *Hijra*, and Two-Spirit people who followed other diverse religions, namely, the Bahá'í faith, Christianity, Hinduism, Judaism, Islam, the pagan goddess religions, Indigenous spirituality, and Unitarian Universalism. And also irreligious agnostics and atheists.

[8] Starhawk, *The Spiral Dance: A Rebirth of the Ancient Religion of the Great Goddess*, New York, NY: Harper & Rowe, 1979. Incidentally, a number of trans women worship diverse Earth goddesses and some even belong to witches' covens.

[9] For information on this Buddhist bodhisattva, see https://en.wikipedia.org/wiki/Avalokite%C5%9Bvara.

[10] For information on these Hindu deities, see https://en.wikipedia.org/wiki/LGBT_themes_in_Hindu_mythology.

[11] See: James, William, *The Varieties of Religious Experience: A Study in Human Nature*, Harlow, UK: Longmans, Green & Co., 1902; and *Psychology and Religion: West and East*, New York, NY: Pantheon Books, 1969.

[12] See: Broughton, Robert S., *Parapsychology: The Controversial Science*, New York, NY: Ballantine Books, 1991.

[13] See: Wilson, Colin, *The Occult: A History*, London, UK: Random House, 1971.

[14] Jung, Carl. G., *Psychology and Alchemy*, Collected Works of C. G. Jung, vol. 12, Princeton, NJ: Princeton University Press, 1968.

[15] Some few exceedingly rare materials on the Association of Canadian Transsexuals (ACT) are part of The Rupert Raj fonds (the second entry listed with 1972 as the date range) at The ArQuives. https://arquives.andornot.com/en/list?q=Association+of+Canadian+Transsexuals&p=1&ps=20 There is no known extant information on the founders, except for Lynne Pellerin, who died in 2012.

[16] See: Devor, Aaron H., and Nicholas Matte. "Building a Better World for Transpeople: Reed Erickson and the Erickson Educational Foundation," *International Journal of Transgenderism*, 2007, 10(1), 47-68. The Reed Erickson Collection is preserved in the Transgender Archives at the University of Victoria Library in Victoria, BC, which includes EEF newsletters and pamphlets. http://transgenderarchives.ca/. After the EEF folded in 1977, it was taken over by the Janus Information Facility (1977-1980), then by J2CP Services (1981-1991), and ultimately by the American Educational Gender Information Service (AEGIS) (renamed Gender Education & Advocacy) (1991-1998).

[17] For information on the Community Homophile Association of Toronto (CHAT), see https://arquives.andornot.com/en/list?q=Community+Homophile+Association+of+Toronto+%

28CHAT%29&p=1&ps=20.

[18] Lynne Pellerin used to put on performances for mostly straight audiences in Toronto and Hamilton as part of "the Great Imposters" (a troupe of female impersonators, drag queens, transvestites and transsexuals) in the 1970s and 1980s. She also appeared in a 2001 film documentary about mostly French-Canadian trans sex workers, *Madame Lauraine's Transsexual Touch*, directed by Mirha-Soleil Ross and co-produced by Viviane Namaste and Monica Forrester.

[19] See: Jacobs, Sue-Ellen, Sabine Lang, and Wesley Thomas, eds., *Two-Spirit People: Native American Gender Identity, Sexuality, and Spirituality*, Bloomington, IN: University of Illinois Press, 1997; Roscoe, Will, *The Zuni Man-Woman*, Albuquerque, NM: University of New Mexico Press, 1992; and Williams, Walter L., *The Spirit and the Flesh: Sexual Diversity in American Indian Culture*, Boston, MA: Beacon Press, 1992. Some Two-Spirit people also identify as transgender; see: 2-Spirited People of the 1st Nations, *Our Relatives Said: A Wise Practices Guide*, *Voices of Aboriginal Trans-People*, Toronto, ON, 2008.

[20] A non-surgical penile prosthetic device (PPD) is distinct from a surgical penile prosthesis. The former is a type of substantially revolutionized, malleable, strap-on dildo (now called a "packer"), cosmetically and functionally engineered to allow a trans man to sexually penetrate a partner, and often also to urinate through (a "stand-to-pee" or "STP" packer). The latter (a "penile implant" to facilitate erection and penetration) is either a non-inflatable implant, consisting of a silicone, semi-rigid bendable rod inserted into the surgically-constructed neopenis; or alternatively, an inflatable implant, consisting of two cylinders inserted into the neopenis, and a hydraulic pump and release valve inserted into the scrotum. In the two-piece model, a reservoir is inserted into the neopenis; in the three-piece model, the reservoir is inserted into the stomach. Urine passes through the re-routed urethra. See: "The Total Guide to Penile Implants For Transsexual Men." http://www.trans-health.com/2013/penile-implants-guide/. Phalloplastic surgeon/reconstructive urologist, Dr. Curtis Crane, performs penile implant surgery in San Francisco.

[21] David Cohler's novel, *Freemartin* (Boston, MA: Little, Brown and Co., 1981) takes its title from a real-life "freemartin": an intersex, sterile female calf with XX/XY chromosomes (the twin of a male calf whose hormones affected her development) and masculinized behaviour. Freemartin Syndrome can sometimes also occur in sheep, goats, pigs, deer and camels, and only rarely in humans. This transmisandrist crime novel depicts a fictional, post-phalloplasty, trans-male, sociopathic serial killer ("Carl Newman"), who is both homophobic and misogynist; he strangles three cisgender women and then cuts off their breasts and genitals because they have purportedly verbally emasculated him or tried to cut off his neopenis. I critiqued this transphobic trash in *Metamorphosis Magazine*, May-June 1987, vol. 6(3).

[22] For more information on English trans Liberal Democrat, Helen Belcher, see https://helenbelcher.uk/en/. For the UK Trans Media Watch, see http://www.transmediawatch.org/.

[23] For more information on Indian Tamil, trans, talk-show host, Rose Venkatesan, see https://zagria.blogspot.com/2013/09/rose-venkatesan-1980-engineer.html#.XS_Y-OipGyI.

[24] Genderphobic erotic thrillers, such as Brian De Palma's 1980 *Dressed to Kill* and Alfred Hitchcock's 1960 *Psycho*, are a clear indictment of the (mostly American and British) popular

film industry's persistent penchant for "sexploiting" gender *dissonance*, rather than celebrating gender *diversity*. In the early 2000s, I had considered approaching trans videomaker Boyd Kodak to curate a presentation at Toronto's Inside Out LGBT Film Festival comprising a series of clips of selected transphobic and transpositive films from the 1960s to the 2000s, similar to the treatment of queer and trans movies in the 1995 USA film documentary *The Celluloid Closet*, directed and written by Rob Epstein and Jeffrey Friedman (the film was based on Vito Russo's book, *The Celluloid Closet: Homosexuality in the Movies*, New York, NY: Harper & Row, 1981). Regrettably, my inspired notion never materialized.

[25] See Wikipedia: "Media Portrayals of Transgender People;" "A List of Transgender Characters in Film and Television;" and "Transsexual and Transgender Actors." Google: "transgender movies in India."

[26] "Transhobia" is discrimination, harassment and/or abuse against transsexuals based on fear, ignorance and hatred of the gender non-binary (gender fluidity). "Genderphobia" is a broader term, which includes negatively "othering" genderqueer and intersex people, as well as "gender transgressors," such as effeminate gay men and masculine lesbians.

[27] See https://arquives.andornot.com/en/list?q=rupert+raj&p=1&ps=20. Four of James Loewen's photographs of me immediately follow chapter 8 and there is a group photo of him and me and three friends following the Epilogue.

[28] Canadian photographer James Loewen is the unofficial video documentarian of Intact America's anti-circumcision group. http://www.intactamerica.org/loewen.

[29] Dykes" is another term for lesbians; "diesel dykes" refer to extremely masculine or "butch" lesbians (aka "butch dykes"), usually wearing leather jackets and often riding motorbikes (aka "leather-daddies."). I'm employing the descriptor, "diesel dykes," in a sexually-affirming way, as many lesbians and their allies did back then—and perhaps some still do.

[30] See: Bobby (formerly Jean Bobby) Noble's *Sons of the Movement: FtMs Risking Incoherence on a Post-Queer Cultural Landscape*, Toronto, ON: Women's Press (Canadian Scholars' Press), 2006; and *Masculinities Without Men?: Female Masculinity in Twentieth-Century Fictions*, Vancouver, BC: UBC Press, 2003.

[31] "Pansexual" means being potentially, sexually or romantically attracted to anyone or everyone, whether male, female or intersex, cisgender or transgender. https://en.wikipedia.org/wiki/Pansexuality.

[32] I first came across the term "humansexual" on a pamphlet from the University of Waterloo in the early 1970s. The term is now generally replaced by "pansexual." https://en.wiktionary.org/wiki/humansexual

[33] The *Tom of Finland* homeoerotic magazine, based on the gay leather biker culture, was founded in 1950 by Finnish gay man, Touko Laaksonen. I used this print pornography to fulfill my gay-male fantasies in the early 1970s while exploring my incipient homophilic inclinations. See https://www.tomoffinlandfoundation.org/foundation/N_Home.html.

[34] Watch: Silverman, Victor, and Susan Stryker, dirs., *Screaming Queens: The Riot at Compton's Cafeteria* (San Francisco, CA: Frameline, 2005), documenting the first major transgender protest in North America.

[35] In 2006, Toronto trans-female cabaret performer, Mandy Goodhandy (aka Amanda Taylor), opened the first-ever transgender (sex) club in Canada, Goodhandy's. A sex-worker activist, Mandy wished to provide a safe place for trans women to meet people for drinking, dancing, and possibly on-site sex play. The club also featured performances by drag queens and drag kings. In 2012, it was renamed Club 120 (and dubbed "Toronto's pansexual playground"), and hosted sex parties. In 2018, the club converted to a restaurant called Diner 120, featuring open-mic nights and songs sung by Mandy. https://nowtoronto.com/music/features/local-hero-mandy-goodhandy/. Read Mandy's memoir, *Just Call Me Lady: A Work of Completion*, Pennsauken, NJ: BookBaby, 2018.

[36] See: Feinberg, Leslie, *Trans Liberation: Beyond Pink or Blue,* Boston, MA: Beacon Press, 1998.

[37] The acronym stands for "lesbian, gay, bisexual, transsexual, transgender, intersex, Two-Spirit, queer, questioning, asexual, allied." An alternative umbrella term for this long acronym is "rainbow."

[38] Before the term "transgender," became the popular umbrella term for all crossgender people in the late 1980s, as early as the mid-1970s, "transgenderist" emerged as a label describing a group of birth-assigned males who either identified as bigender women, or as "she-males" (for many people, this term is now politically incorrect). Transgenderists were an intermediate category between transsexuals and transvestites (now known as crossdressers) on the crossgender spectrum—although some transvestites also used this label in the late 1980s to be more inclusive of transsexuals and transgenderists. For example, the Transvestite's [sic] Independence Club (TVIC) in Albany, NY —(which published the *TVIC Journal*— in the mid-1970s), changed its name circa the late 1980s to the Transgenderist's [sic] Independence Club (TGIC)— (and published the *TGIC Magazine*); see https://www.digitaltransgenderarchive.net/files/tx31qh75x. Transgenderists commonly underwent only partial female sex-reassignment, usually including estrogen therapy, facial and body hair removal, and breast enlargement, but kept their penises—either to sexually satisfy their wives or girlfriends, or, if they were sex workers, to please those male customers known as "tranny chasers" (for many people, this term is now politically incorrect) who preferred a "chick with a dick." The latter was the title of a popular sex magazine advertising the services of transgenderist sex workers. Some transgenderists also underwent orchiectomy (removal of the testes) to suppress erections, but stopped short of the creation of a neovagina; see https://en.wikipedia.org/wiki/Transgender.

[39] See: Zahavi, Dan, *Husserl's Phenomenology*, Stanford, CA: Stanford University Press, 2003.

[40] See: Wilson, Colin, *Introduction to the New Existentialism*, London, UK: Hutchinson (Penguin Random House), 1966.

[41] See: Lamont, Corliss, *Humanism as a Philosophy*, New York, NY: Philosophical Library, 1949. Reprinted as *The Philosophy of Humanism* (8th ed.), Washington, DC: Humanist Press, 1997 (edited by Beverley Earles and Beth K. Lamont, with gender neutral references). https://www.corliss-lamont.org/philos8.htm; and Allen, Jr., Norm R., ed., *African-American Humanism: An Anthology,* Buffalo, NY: Prometheus Books, 1991.

[42] See: Barnes, Hazel E., *Humanistic Existentialism: The Literature of Possibility,* Lincoln, NE: University of Nebraska Press, 1959; and Sartre, Jean-Paul, *Existentialism Is a Humanism* (translated from the French by Carol Macomber), New Haven, CT: Yale University Press, 2007; See also Sartre's existential novel, *Nausea* (translated from the French by Robert Baldick), London, UK: Penguin Books, 1965.

[43] See: Fromm, Erich, *Socialist Humanism*, London, UK: Allen Lane (Penguin Random House), 1965.

[44] For books on these and other psychological theories and psychotherapeutic modalities, see: Intersectional Bibliography.

[45] See: Jung, Carl G., *Psychology and Alchemy*, Collected Works of C. G. Jung, vol. 12, Princeton, NJ: Princeton University Press, 1968; and Jung, Carl G., *Dreams*, Bollingen Series, vol. 20, Princeton, NJ: Princeton University Press, 1974.

[46] See: Viktor Frankl's *The Will to Meaning: Foundations and Applications of Logotherapy,* New York, NY: New American Library, 1988; and *Psychotherapy and Existentialism: Selected Papers on Logotherapy,* New York, NY: Simon & Schuster, 1967.

[47] For information on Maslow's principle of self-actualization and his life tasks, see Maslow, Abraham, *Toward a Psychology of Being*, New York, NY: Van Nostrand-Reinhold, 1962; *Religions, Values, and Peak Experiences*, Columbus, OH: Ohio State University Press, 1964; and *The Farther Reaches of Human Nature*, New York, NY: Esalen (Viking Press), 1971.

[48] See: Erikson, Erik, *The Life Cycle Completed,* New York, NY: W. W. Norton, 1985, 32-33 (Figure 3: The Life Cycle 3). This figure schematizes his theoretical life cycle from youth to adulthood to old age over eight developmental stages: psychosexual stages/modes, psychosocial crises, radius of significant relations, and diametrically-opposed basic strengths and basic antipathies—and their potential dialectical resolution in related principles of social order, benign binding ritualizations, and their complementary regressive "ritualism." This scheme can alternatively lead to a celebration of life as conflict and defiance (as played out in the challenging defeats and victories of community activism, for example), rather than as having to inevitably lead to integration and acceptance, thereby comprising another kind of positive-realistic life strategy (ever dancing the dialectic). See also Erikson's *Identity: Youth and Crisis,* New York, NY: W. W. Norton, 1968; and *Vital Involvement in Old Age* (co-authored by Joan M. Erikson and Helen Kivnick), New York, NY: W. W. Norton, 1986.

[49] I reference Erikson's psychosocial notion of "pseudo-speciation" in my discussion of speciesism, anti-speciesism and "trans-speciesism" in chapter 7.

[50] For Adler's concept of "social interest" (community conscience), see *The Individual Psychology of Alfred Adler*, Ansbacher, H. L., and Ansbacher, R. R., eds., New York, NY: Harper & Row, 1956.

[51] These divergent populations were eventually compared by Dr. Aaron H. Devor in his paper, "Gender Blending Females: Women and Sometimes Men," *American Behavioral Scientist*, 1987, 31(1): 12-40; and "More Than Manly Women: How Female-to-Male Transsexuals Reject Lesbian Identities," in Bonnie Bullough, Vern Bullough, and James Elias, eds., *Gender Blending*, Buffalo, NY: Prometheus Books, 1997, 87-102.

[52] For various posts on the gender clinicians and transsexual patients of Toronto's former not-always-trans-friendly Clarke Institute of Psychiatry, see https://zagria.blogspot.com/search?q=clarke+institute+of+psychiatry#.XTD_x-ipGyI.

*Me, as an unsuspecting baby (L), with my older brother, Jakub.
Ottawa, Ontario, 1953*

*Me, as an angry at the world toddler, held fast by my scolding father,
with my mother and brother, Jakub.
Ottawa, Ontario, 1954*

My First Communion, smiling on the outside, crying on the inside!
Montreal, Quebec, 1958

(L to R): My sister, Arjuna, an unidentified friend, my younger brother,
Casimir, a gawky-looking me, and my older brother, Jakub.
Montreal, Quebec, 1959

*Posing for my yearbook as a pre-transitional, high school student.
Ottawa, Ontario, 1966 and 1967*

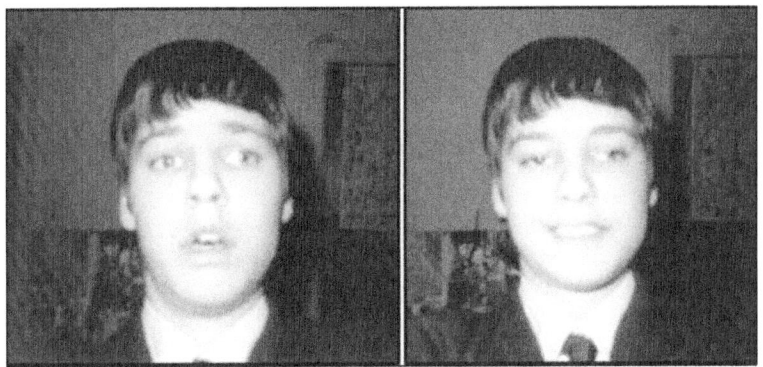

*Secretly crossdressed in blazer and tie—my mirror
reflecting an image of the male imprisoned within.
Ottawa, Ontario, 1969*

Part II:

Gender Worker

* * *

<u>*GENDER WORKER*</u>

*Professional Transsexual
Gender Consultant
Trans Activist:
different titles, same work–
working for the good
of the gender community.*

* * *

4. Trans FACTivism…More Surgery…Two Romances and A Brief Affair (1975-1982)

"Go west, young man!" my inner voice urged again. In October 1975, I rode the CP rail line from Ottawa to Vancouver, chain-smoking, guzzling beers, and playing poker with riders traversing the country from Newfoundland to British Columbia and back. Some Indigenous folks strumming guitars and wailing out country songs invited me to join in. After a couple of thousand miles crossing the prairies, we passed through the Rockies in Alberta and chugged onwards into British Columbia. The train's rhythmic click-clack lulled me to sleep, curled up with my copy of *War and Peace*. A few hundred miles more and we arrived in Vancouver at last. The smell of the Pacific Ocean and the sight of the mountain peaks soared my spirits like one of the swooping seagulls.

I lugged my steamer trunk into a cab and got a room downtown at the Granville Hotel, a sleazy dump for $4 a night. I had to share the bathroom on my floor and use the communal male shower—so much for privacy! I went to the restaurant where Louise worked and she graciously invited me to stay with her and her boyfriend, Mel, until I could find other accommodations. I soon rented a room in a rooming house at the intersection of Nelson and Bute Streets in the West End, not far from the gay village. Louise told me about Bob Whitelaw, a nice social worker who counselled transsexuals. He referred me to Dr. Bill Maurice, a trans-friendly psychiatrist at Vancouver General Hospital, who renewed my testosterone prescription before I ran out, seeing that I didn't have a family doctor. That would follow shortly but, at that moment, I needed a job because my savings were dwindling fast. I could not find work right away, so I applied for interim welfare benefits until I eventually found employment working at a series of low-paying jobs. I bussed tables at a downtown greasy spoon, cleaned houses for the rich bitches and bastards in North Vancouver, sold Collier's encyclopaedias door to door in Richmond, unloaded furniture shipments for an antique store, painted stage-sets at The Vancouver Theatre Arts Club, and processed herring at an oceanside fish processing plant in rubber coveralls and boots. A jack-of-all-trades.

My 24th birthday passed uneventfully. I desperately needed a doctor: so, I checked out the Pine Free Clinic in Kitsilano and was referred to Dr. Kenford Nedd, a transpositive doctor, who provided the healthcare I needed. Determination and the domino effect won out again. I asked a nurse if she knew of any other transsexuals I could meet. She asked one of her patients (a young, pre-transitional trans man) if she could pass on his phone number to me. He called himself Eugene and lived in my neighbourhood, close to the beach. When I knocked on his door, he wasn't home; so, I left a note with my name and number underneath his door. He called me the next day and invited me to his place. I went over, eager to meet another trans guy because I didn't know any trans people there other than Louise. When Eugene opened the door, I was immediately taken by his androgynous presentation: this was the start of my transensuality!

Eugene asked me to stay over and we soon got it on. This was the first time I had climaxed with another person and it felt great! Eugene and I spent all our time together over the next few days and, then, he asked me to move in. I eagerly agreed and we set up house together with his two children. He was receiving social assistance while taking a college retraining program towards potential employment upon graduation. I was the stay-at-home house husband, and we grooved to '50s, '60s and '70s classic rock, while dancing, drinking and toking. We also dug the social-protest folk songs of Bob Dylan, Joan Baez, and Phil Ochs, and John Lennon's songs of peace and love. And, as bisexual, transsexual guys, we devoured the written and dramatic works of queer male writers and actors Bill Burroughs, Allen Ginsberg, Jack Kerouac, Gore Vidal, Walt Whitman, Tennessee Williams, Christopher Isherwood, Dirk Bogarde, and Quentin Crisp. When I surprised Eugene with Ginsberg's and Whitman's sexually-controversial poetry collections[1]—with their flamboyant homoerotic verses—for his birthday, he was "sexstatic"! Sadly, Eugene didn't share my budding interest in feminism; however, as I eagerly delved into the books of cisgender-female activists around the world, including those who were transpositive or non-committal.[2] Trans-female (trans)feminists would not emerge until the 1990s, and trans-male (trans)feminists not until the 2000s—indeed, in those early days, some transsexual men were both anti-feminist and anti-lesbian: an ill-conceived, compensatory strategy to protect their often vulnerable, new malehood. In summertime, we would saunter down to Kitsilano Beach and lazily sun ourselves on the sand before going in for a dip. I was on top of the world! We eventually had to move from our cozy basement apartment but found even nicer digs on West Eighth Street.

We frequented gay bars and clubs in The Village on Davie Street with our cis gay friends, James and Jerry. James Loewen was an Adonis, and Jerry had such a sunny smile. They were the sweetest guys ever and (for cisgender men) very transpositive! Although Eugene and I identified as a gay-male couple, we were mostly read as straight because he was still pre-testosterone and looked gender fluid, whereas I presented as unquestionably male. We were denied entrance to one gay club because we were perceived as a hetero couple—turned away as interlopers despite our protests of being genuine fags.[3] Oh, the double-edged sword of passing privilege—for those who have it and for those who don't! Many trans men have a privileged advantage over many of our trans sisters in terms of passing as our identified male gender. It's a bitter irony, however, when some gay and bi trans men are perceived as non-queer by our queer brothers—a unique form of invisibility (erasure)!

Budding activist that I was, I had to balance my love, social, and work lives with my advocacy work. I needed to carry on the trans lobby efforts I had begun back east because, whether or not I returned to my home province, I had made a commitment to fight for health insurance coverage for sex-reassignment surgery for my trans sisters and brothers back in Ontario. Towards this end, I ventured out to make connections with the local community. Unaware of any trans groups in the city and not street-savvy—I didn't know any local trans sex workers who could direct me—I reached out to the queer community and found Gay Alliance Towards Equality (GATE).[4] Formed in 1971, it was the first Canadian homophile group to work for gay and lesbian rights (with sister groups in Edmonton and Toronto), eventually folding in 1980. The folks there welcomed me unconditionally and I felt truly blessed. When I told them that I wanted to petition the Ontario Ministry of Health to include transsexual operations for Ontarians under the Ontario Health Insurance Plan (OHIP) and needed photocopies, envelopes, and stamps to mail the petition to potential supporters in North America, they readily complied with my request.

Gung ho, I mailed out petitions to transpositive physicians, psychiatrists, psychologists, surgeons, politicians, and trans activists across Canada and the USA, many of whom returned signed copies in support. The next step was to mail the petitions to the OHIP director and Ontario Health Minister. Sadly, I dropped the ball: physical fatigue ground me down and I ran out of steam after my grinding work day. Such stymied follow-through is common in community activism, especially grassroots trans lobbying in the early days when neither infrastructure nor sustainability were forthcoming. We had no government or corporate support and—except for some limited support from the queer community—we were totally on our own; sisters and brothers doing it for ourselves. For many, such unpaid activism was simply beyond their meagre means, barely being able to afford to go to university, or make enough money to pay the bills. For me, the well-intentioned activist, it meant yet another aborted project due to inadequate resources. Nevertheless, the remains of this petition project survive intact in my archived collection, testifying to my thwarted efforts at early trans advocacy.

Periodic delisting of sex-reassignment surgery (SRS) for trans Canadians as an insured provincial health benefit has been a historical trend since SRS was first partially covered in Manitoba in 1969. Transsexual surgeries can be deemed as either medically non-essential or not an economic priority in the annual health budget. In the past, provincial governments have often expediently denigrated so-called "sex change" surgery as a lifestyle choice—often due to religious objections of right-wing senators—indicting trans people as a burden on the health system. As of 2019, all 10 provinces and two of the three territories wholly or partially fund various gender-confirming surgical procedures.[5]

Vancouver grew on me despite the rain. I loved the west coast vibe: the "supernaturalness" of BC (as the tourist board touts it), the countercultural ethos of Left-leaning entrepreneurs, artists, healers, environmental advocates, sexual activists, and queers. I fit so well into this alternative lifestyle of Lefties that I would have made this my permanent home if certain unexpected circumstances hadn't later intervened. Eugene and I made a point of enjoying city life and accessing both culture—Gastown, with its cobblestone streets, gaslit lamps, and live jazz—and nature—Stanley Park, with its lush rainforest, sky-high totem poles and languid Lost Lagoon.

Coming up to a year in Vancouver, I went back to school so I could get off poverty row and establish a professional career. Just because I couldn't get into psychology didn't mean that I couldn't pursue another meaningful vocation. In the fall of 1976, I applied to Teacher's College at the University of British Columbia and taught grade six students for my practicum. But teaching kids was not for me: so, I dropped out after first term. My vocational aspirations thwarted, I felt frustrated. What was I to do? It is rare that school, work, community activism, family, friends, love, and money all coincide! But life would soon show me a way….

One day in 1976, Eugene and I came across an article in the *Calgary Herald* that piqued our interest: sex-reassignment surgeons at Calgary's Foothills Hospital were performing phalloplasty for transsexual men. Unaware that medical technology had somewhat improved since the rudimentary operations at Johns Hopkins Hospital in Baltimore, we were ecstatically hopeful: "Yay! Alberta, here we come!" I would go on ahead and set up a home base for Eugene and the kids, who would follow once they had wound up things in Vancouver. It was hard to leave Eugene behind and I felt a bit blue as I hugged him goodbye, ready to set off on a new adventure. I was on the rails again as I rode the train through the Rocky Mountains to our new home in Calgary. At 25, the world was mine and I was feeling fine!

Upon my arrival in Calgary, I got a room in a downtown rooming house and began looking for work the next day. I landed a full-time job as a security-guard, working at condominium construction sites for the Capital Security Company. After six weeks of minimum-wage pay, I had enough for a deposit on a three-bedroom townhouse. I also had to come up with a $200 damage deposit (half of the $400 monthly rent—steep for that time). Utilities were extra and heating costs in the freezing winters were sky-high in this landlocked prairie town, so I needed another job to pay for all of this. Luckily, I got work as a weekend desk clerk at the Calgary Stampeder Hotel down the road from our new home. I was a working-class workaholic, although not by choice! I spent my leisure time reading and wrote long letters to my absent partner. I felt so alone, with no friends except for Jerry, who had also moved from Vancouver.

When Eugene and the kids arrived, I was overjoyed after being a bachelor for three long months! We made up for lost time in passionate love play. He immediately applied for welfare, which was necessary for our economic survival given that my $3 hourly wage was not enough to support a family of four.

Having established our home front, we turned our attention to gender transitioning. The Gender Identity Program at the University of Calgary's Faculty of Medicine was affiliated with Foothills Hospital, where the transsexual surgeries were performed. The four primary program staff members[6] consisted of two psychiatrists, an endocrinologist, and a genitoplastic surgeon. Eugene and I applied and were accepted once we paid the program fee of $1,000 each, which included the cost of the psychiatric assessments, therapy sessions, and surgeries. We told the staff that we identified as gay trans men and lived in the same house. Dr. Angus later probed me to determine if we were lovers, to which I falsely responded that we had once been sexual partners but were now just friends. I intuitively knew these gender clinicians would be homophobic (conflating gender identity and sexual orientation). So, playing their game, I told them what they needed to hear. Nowadays, most transqueer people do not feel the need to hide their gender identity or their sexual orientation, proud to be out as trans fags, trans dykes, and transbis.

Despite some minor challenges, I was optimistic about the prospect of future surgery and coasted along for a while seeing as no crises were looming on the horizon. Then, suddenly, I had a *grand mal* epileptic seizure and blacked out. Awakening in the emergency room after an undetermined interval, I experienced the worst headache of my life and felt disoriented, not knowing where I was. Eugene told me what had happened. The neurologist prescribed me the anticonvulsant, Dilantin. Fortunately, I only had the one convulsion and discontinued the medication after two years. So, for a brief time, I had this condition in common with Dostoyevsky and possibly also van Gogh (both heroes of mine).

Still hoping to earn more than subsistence wages, I applied to Canada Post for a letter carrier job. I was initially declined because I had naïvely listed my BA in psychology on my résumé. The old school postie interviewing me seared me with sarcasm: "So you have a psychology degree. Does this mean you're going to psychoanalyze the other workers?" Reeling from this incredible query, I replied in the negative. I applied again to the post office for another position as a mail handler, this time strategically omitting my university education. The interviewer made me lift a 75 lb. sack of mail off the floor onto his desk. A mere 100 lbs. myself, I staggered underneath its weight.

While my back was turned, I heard him snickering at my physical incapacity. I was mortified! When he told me that he didn't think I could do the job, I retreated, dispirited and defeated once more. This soldier-of-fortune was battle-weary, tired of all the bullshit of the system! What does a man have to do to earn a living? It's remarkable that I didn't resort to pushing drugs or selling my body as many of the disenfranchised feel compelled to do. Alternatively, I could have been a criminal mastermind if I had chosen that route, but I opted to operate within the law, contributing to society in a meaningful way as a responsible citizen.

Driven to try higher education once more, I applied to the University of Calgary's Bachelor of Social Work program. Sadly, I bombed out again because of my substandard grade point average. Even though I had been out of school for two years and had done some trans community activism, the faculty head was unwilling to give me a break as a mature student. I was infuriated! Whether higher education or viable employment, I was equally blocked. I was really feeling the vocational dysphoria blues! Yes, I was a citizen with certain privileges, but no aid was forthcoming from either academia or corporate Canada to help me improve my chances for a better life. Years later, as a Humanist Association of Canada member, my fellow humanists and I called upon the federal government to incorporate in the Canadian Charter of Rights and Freedoms the basic right for all Canadians to be guaranteed gainful employment. We're still waiting for a favourable response! I felt like someone not of this world, an alien. Where did I fit in? Would I ever find my niche?

New Year was almost upon us and I wanted to make my resolutions for 1978. Partly inspired by Gandhi's passive (yet transformative) resistance against the imperialist British Raj in the days of colonialist India—and that of my Indian grandparents, who had also fought Gandhi's war, as well as the resistance of my Polish grandfather, killed in the fight for freedom against the Nazis—I was determined to achieve my vocational goals even if I had to employ alternative strategies. Instead of entering the front door like the privileged elite, I would climb through the bathroom window. Come hell or high water, I would prevail! Through a lifetime of dogged persistence and creative resistance, I ultimately won the battle, bringing home the prize of a Master's degree—but that was still many years in the future. Right now, I had to do something practical, rather than tilting at windmills. Pumped up by my inner pep talk, I took action. In January, I established the Foundation for the Advancement of Canadian Transsexuals (FACT).

I got the idea from the Association of Canadian Transsexuals (ACT), which soon fizzled out after its brief lifespan due to the founders' collective burnout. I wanted to continue the trailblazing work that Diana, Lynne, and

Louise had begun in Toronto in 1970. The acronym FACT was partly engineered by Eugene (soon to be our secretary under the pseudonym, Chris E. Black), who was inspired by the phrase, "for the advancement of," in the organizational name of the National Association for the Advancement of Colored People. It was a time-honoured idea to use the momentum of another social cause (the American civil rights movement) even though the notion of intersectionality—interlinking population demographics, social determinants of health, societal oppression, and social justice—was not well-understood back then. Now, all we needed was a treasurer to complete our founding board. We soon found him: Kyle Spooner, a pre-transitional transsexual man, who was also enrolled in the University of Calgary's Gender Program. With me as president, we now had a full slate of officers. So, I registered FACT as a non-profit corporation with the Alberta government, opened a business bank account and rented a post-office box. We needed one more thing: a board of professional advisors. I invited the university gender program's medical professionals to officially support our organization and they unanimously agreed. We were on our way!

Inspired by the *Renaissance: Gender Identity Services* newsletter put out by California trans activists Joanna Clark[7] and Jude Patton,[8] I published my own trans periodical, *Gender Review: A FACTual Journal*, which I edited from June 1978 to June 1981.

The first issue (June 1978) featured a photo of me baring my hairy chest. The fourth issue (March 1979) depicted a statue of the intersex Greek god/goddess of love, Hermaphrodite, a full-breasted person holding up their toga to proudly display their penis. This *avant garde* issue contained an article entitled "Androgyny" by yours truly, including a somewhat androgynous photo of me sporting a Van Dyke beard, longish hair, an earring, an ankh pendant, and a saffron Indian shirt. I copped some bad vibes from Dr. Tony Tornabene for my non-binary gender focus in a note he furiously dashed off to me: "It's a 1,000% crock of shit! Transsexual men are male, period!" Oh well, old school as Tony was, I suppose we can't all transgress the gender binary. He was hell-bent on imposing traditional sex stereotypes onto trans men and trans women, whereas I was heralding a new wave of gender fluid folks: gender benders, gender blenders, gender fuckers. Following this instance of transgender policing, which denied the reality of other gender expressions, I was soon to experience another kind of denial (or rather, rationalization), this time from the cisgender community. Responding to my letter to American Jungian psychologist Dr. June Singer (author of *Androgyny: Towards a Theory of Sexuality*, 1976), she summarily dismissed my objection that transsexuals, transvestites, and transgenderists—the latter sometimes also identifying as androgynes[9]—were not mentioned in her book, rationalizing that her focus was on exploring Jung's *animus* (masculine aspect) in non-trans women and *anima* (feminine aspect) in non-trans men. Whatever the rationale, it still smacks of erasure—and a missed opportunity in psychosocial research to compare how androgyny might variably play out in cisgender versus transgender people (particularly, transgenderists/androgynes).

Gender Review was a labour of love, painstakingly produced on my Brother electric typewriter and lettered with Letraset transfers. Copies were mailed to our foundation members and subscribers in North America, Europe, and even as far off as the South Pacific. My modest little periodical truly had an international scope and readership! In addition to helping professionals—endocrinologists, surgeons, sexologists, psychiatrists, psychologists, psychotherapists, social workers, lawyers—my newsletter featured or mentioned many trans-female activists[10] from Canada and the USA, and a few from the UK, Australia, and New Zealand—as well as several American trans-male activists (cited later). Non-elitist, I covered the whole gamut of trans people: prisoners, pornographers, prostitutes, police officers, politicians, poets, physicians, pastors, principals, teachers, scientists, counsellors, computer programmers, graphic designers, musicians, ex-soldiers, athletes, artists, and activists.

I also exchanged newsletters with other transsexual and transvestite editors; thereby, increasing our mutual meaningful connections and creating a nascent transgender community, locally and globally. In those early days of community building, prior to the advent of the Internet in the 1990s (with its e-zines, blogs, live journals, list serves, chat rooms, and websites), trans newsletters and magazines were our lifeline!

With regards to my pending surgical transition, I met periodically with the two psychiatrists at the gender clinic as part of my ongoing clinical assessment and therapy. One of them asked me if I or a family member had ever suffered from mental illness. I responded in the negative regarding myself, and mentioned that my mother likely had manic depression (now bipolar disorder) but had never been diagnosed or prescribed medication. He then asked me whether I had ever been on anti-depressants or anxiolytics. When I replied, "No," he, nonetheless, suggested that I go on a mood stabilizer and prescribed Elavil (Amitriptyline). Against my better judgement, I tried it briefly because I figured that compliance would be the best strategy to win psychiatric approval for my desired surgeries. Reflecting on this later, I felt uneasy because it did not seem right for physicians to push drugs onto those patients who were not clinically depressed or anxious (which I wasn't). As a vulnerable transsexual patient, I did not feel safe enough to resist an oppressive medical system! Karmic law prevailed in the long run because some years later (in the 1990s) the Calgary gender clinic was reportedly shut down[11] following a complaint lodged by two transsexual patients (Eugene and his then girlfriend

Cassie). This was not the first gender clinic closure: nor would it be the last!

There has been a series of gender identity clinic (GIC) closures in Canada since the 1970s, mostly due to governmental expediency but sometimes because of community pressure from trans people and our cis allies, sparking an investigation. Such was the case when CAMH's controversial Child, Youth, and Family Gender Identity Clinic—headed by psychologist Dr. Kenneth Zucker and psychiatrist Dr. Susan Bradley since the mid-1970s—was discontinued by CAMH Medical Director Dr. Kwame McKenzie in 2015. The clinic's closure followed a CAMH-commissioned review by extra-agency psychiatrists Dr. Suzanne Zinck and Dr. Antonio Pignatiello, whose findings "did not disconfirm" the alleged use of reparative or conversion therapy with gender non-conforming youth.[12] Such behaviour-modification therapies strive to change the crossgender behaviour of children and teenagers to accord with that of their birth-assigned sex and are also used to deter young people from identifying as lesbian, gay, bisexual, or pansexual. The trans community, clinic survivors, parents, allies, and professional organizations, like Rainbow Health Ontario,[13] rejoiced at this long-overdue outlawing of the ongoing reported psychiatric abuses of a vulnerable population! In March 2007, Toronto trans activists Kyle Scanlon,[14] Christina (Tina) Strang,[15] and more than a dozen other trans people crashed a celebration at the Hospital for Sick Children honouring the clinic's founder (Dr. Bradley).[16] Following Dr. Zucker's lecture on gender identity disorders in children and adolescents (part of the celebration), Kyle and Tina passed out leaflets protesting Bradley and Zucker's outmoded gender-pathologizing theories and practices.[17] Even though I was unable to join the peaceful protest, this act of trans resistance paved the way for future change. In 2015, Ontario New Democratic Party (NDP) Member of the Provincial Parliament (MPP) Cheri DiNovo's Bill 77,[18] prohibiting conversion therapy for youth in Ontario, became law—with the advocacy support of the Canadian Professional Association for Transgender Health (CPATH).[19] Consequently, conversion therapy was delisted as an insured health service under OHIP. At present, this is a hot political issue across our country (and the rest of the world). As of 2019, besides Ontario, there are partial bans on conversion therapy in Manitoba, Nova Scotia, and the city of Vancouver; and other jurisdictions might soon follow. Regrettably, this past March, the Canadian federal government rejected a public petition to ban conversion therapy nationwide, deeming it a provincial/territorial issue.[20] In the USA, a number of cities and states already have some form of anti-conversion therapy laws, and there's a push for federal legislation.[21]

While I simultaneously pursued penile constructive surgery and my unpaid career as a "professional transsexual" (then a popular title for a dedicated trans activist), my private life was complicated by relationship dynamics. One day, Eugene and I got into a fight. Hurt and angry, I took an overdose of Dilantin and Elavil pills in a half-hearted suicide attempt, a passive-aggressive appeal to my partner for an apology and future considerateness. He rushed me to the hospital to have my stomach pumped. After several days of psychiatric observation, I was discharged. Then, Eugene followed suit a few weeks later with his own suicide attempt, after another altercation. Fortunately, we began to learn safer, more effective ways to resolve future conflicts. We decided to improve our relationship dynamics by developing mutual respect, trust, open dialogue, consensus decision-making and conflict-resolution strategies. Celebrating our recommitment to a healthier relationship, we dined at a downtown piano bar by the Husky Tower. While sipping Kahlúas, we listened to a moving rendition of Janis Joplin's "Turtle Blues," savouring the tinkling of the piano. Then, we slow-danced to a cool jazz tune.

We didn't have a large circle of friends, partly because we did not want to be judged by a super-straight trans community for being queer, gender policing was in full force back then! But we still occasionally invited trans people to our house for beers and reefers, including Candy and Dee Dee, two party girls, who were also patients of the university gender program. Then, there was Rusty, a trans man who had a neopenis surgically constructed at Foothills Hospital, involving multiple operations to make it functional for both urination and sexual intercourse. Although I fully understand why he went to the extent he did towards achieving male genitals to dispel his gender dissonance, I was put off by its Frankensteinian appearance. Consequently, I began having second thoughts: perhaps I should wait until medical technology improved.

Following my pan-hysterectomy in the spring of 1978, my question was answered. I couldn't have the phalloplasty after all! Weighing only 100 lbs., I lacked sufficient tissue on my thighs and buttocks for a skin graft to fashion the neophallus. I did not want to use my arm for a donor site because it would have required a deep wound, leaving an unsightly scar. My surgeon, Dr. Birdsell, contacted Dr. Donald Laub, a phalloplastic surgeon in Stanford, California, to see if anything could be done, such as cultivating skin tissue in a petri dish, but the medical technology was not yet that advanced. After raising my hopes and relocating to another province just to have this surgery, only to be let down, I felt devastated! Ever the warrior, I cut my immediate losses but did not abandon my long-term goal. I would eventually attain further masculinization, but I still had many long years to wait.

We invited Rusty to move in to help pay our exorbitant rent. An introvert, I found it somewhat crowded—not to mention hard to concentrate on producing the newsletter, and answering letters and calls from trans people all over the world when he and Eugene were making noise downstairs. So, I was relieved when Rusty eventually moved out. But we still needed a roommate. Enter Cassie, a truck-driver and gender program patient. She had long red hair and a sweet smile but a mean temper. One time, she and I got into a fight because she had made a racial slur against Sikhs. Knocking the wind out of me, she sent my eyeglasses flying. Another time, she kicked me in the shins for no reason at all other than a lot of displaced anger.

As for racist comments directed towards me, I was virtually exempt from such bigotry due to my passing privilege as a perceived White person (I take after my Polish mother in terms of skin colour). I did occasionally experience some racism though; once from a customer of the Stampeder Hotel, who called me an "elephant rider," and once from a transperson at the Foothills Hospital, who called me a "Paki." As for the trans person, I was shocked that the oppressed can also be the oppressor! I wrote about this displaced discrimination by the disenfranchised transgender community in my newsletter, calling upon transsexuals not to put down transvestites, female impersonators, and drag queens, who, in turn, often discriminate against transsexual women. On and on it goes, the dysfunctional drama of oppression: each contender clamouring for the moral high ground as the most oppressed victim! Although somewhat better today, racism, classism, sexism, genderism, and all the other "isms" still persist in trans and queer communities. Shouldn't we have evolved somewhat more than this by now?

After nearly two years of slogging it out at the security company for subsistence wages, often waiting for a bus in 40 degrees below zero (Fahrenheit), with icicles hanging on my beard, I was asked to do a double shift one morning because my replacement did not show up. Dead tired and bored out of my mind after my all-night shift, in an act of civil disobedience (I think Gandhi, Tolstoy, and Thoreau would have been proud of me), I flatly refused and walked off the site, heading home for a good night's sleep. Damned if I was going to kill myself for a lousy $3 an hour! I was so tired of this capitalist, consumerist patriarchy! A Social Democrat, I was a man with a conscience, a fighter for the underdog—not some pushover lackey.

The company owner, an ex-RCMP officer, withheld my paycheque for insubordination. So, I had to complain to the Alberta Ministry of Labour, which ordered him to pay me my rightful wages. In the office, awaiting my paycheque, his six feet six inches towered above my five feet three inches: "I've put better men than you in my pocket!" I didn't bother to retort to this adolescent, macho power play, other than to declare, "I quit!" sauntering out with my head held high. I was done with petty officials, self-serving profiteers, and men of no vision! Was this the world I signed up for? Me, the Renaissance man, the philosopher? At 27, I was still too much of an idealist to survive in the real world where dreams are seldom realized, and when they are, not without a vale of blood, sweat, and tears. John Lennon's inspired song,

"Imagine," was still playing on the radio, but the humanistic lyrics of this atheistic Outsider did not fully register in the hearts of most people—social conformists with no imagination.

Without a job—I had also recently quit my part-time desk clerk job due to sheer exhaustion—I decided to better my future odds by enriching my résumé with social work experience. I volunteered as a patient visitor at the Baker Sanatorium for people with permanent disabilities and terminal diseases. It took me 90 minutes each way to get there and back by bus during the frigid winter months, but I did it anyway for six long weeks, determined to become a social worker or mental health counsellor someday.

To compound my woes, one day, I ventured down to the basement where Cassie's room was and found Eugene in bed with her! My heart stopped! I was consumed with rage and despair. Betrayed, I shouted obscenities at them and stomped upstairs. So much for community activism if your relationship is the price you pay! I soothed myself by listening to some downbeat blues (Billie Holiday and Nina Simone); then I upped the beat by grooving to Joan Armatrading and Etta James. Cooling off, I thought that maybe we could all live together in an open marriage, with Cassie and I both sharing Eugene. But, I soon realized that I was the jealous type, not made for polyamory.

May 1979: the decade was winding down and me with no job, no relationship, no prospects. Why remain in this barren cowboy town, beaten down yet again? I felt somewhat like Jack Kerouac and his fellow Beats, who rebelled in the 1950s against the complacency and mediocrity of the Establishment—countering mainstream culture by taking hallucinatory drugs, beating bongo drums, writing sex-charged poetry, balling their brains out, and taking to the road to see America. Too bad I didn't just fuck off to San Francisco, one of the trans/queer friendliest cities in the world—and join trans-male queers, like Lou Sullivan (except that we wouldn't become acquainted until three years later—bad timing, as always!). Another deep regret I must let go. Instead, my path led me back to Ottawa, where I hoped to kindle a romance with my trans woman friend Sandi. Once more, I was headed for an uncertain future. I took the train back, riding those long miles of track through the Rockies and across the prairies, eager to return home to Ontario.

Before reaching Ottawa, I stopped off in Winnipeg to visit fellow trans activist, Linda O'Connell, her husband Rodger, and their German shepherd, who nearly knocked me over. Linda went by the title, Reverend, having recently completed a mail order divinity degree. Newly incorporating her North American Transsexual Society (NATS), she tried to liaise with the Gender Identity Program at the University of Manitoba's Health Sciences Centre but to no avail. In those days, grassroots community and establishment psychiatry rarely danced together and, when they did, they were often out of step. Not one to be excluded for long, Linda reached out to other trans activists like me (more on this later).

* * *

I opened up myself to new possibilities, new adventures. Always the existential adventurer, I was ready to join the dance again, to see what the universe had to offer. Upon arriving in Ottawa, I headed straight for Sandi's co-op and shacked up with her, hoping to spark a romance, considering that we had been close friends before I left three-and-a-half years earlier. We gave it a shot but we just didn't click that way—oh well, we were still pals. Ottawa had changed a lot in the years I had been away, becoming much more French-speaking and it was harder for me to get a good job. Too, I had no family there anymore that I was close to except for my sister. After two months, I got the wanderlust again and moved to Toronto—the New York of the north. My lesbian friend offered to put me up until I could find my own place.

I was excited at the prospect of becoming a Torontonian, arriving in July 1979. After a summer stay at a student co-op, I found a cheap house to rent in the west end and moved in with two trans women (Janice and Rita) and two queer folks (Peter and Barb). We had some fun times at our Concord Avenue house, including a few rollicking good parties. One stellar event took place that fall when Rita (a bit of a diva), her friend Cheli and Peter performed *The Rocky Horror Picture Show*[22]—the 1975 cult classic featuring the transvestite-transsexual hero/ine Dr. Frankenfurter. Rita, strikingly done up in Kiss makeup, lip-synched the entire score without missing a beat, followed by a full encore! A memorable moment, I wish someone had captured it on film!

We would bar hop amidst the straight-owned taverns, like the Gerard House—working-class guys and gals, a smoke in one hand, a beer in the other, boogieing to '50s and '60s rock; the Continental Inn—leather-daddy butch bikers fighting over lipstick lesbians; the St. Charles Tavern—drag queens dressed to the nines in feathers, sequins and stiletto heels, strutting their stuff; and the London Pub/Bay House—sexy trans pros servicing out-of-town businessmen in the back parking lot. Or, we would go clubbing at gay dance clubs and discos, such as the Quest—party queers toking up in the bathroom while pissing out their beers; Colby's—bears on the prowl, cruising nubile hot twinkies; the Manatee—virtually-naked go-go boys swinging in cages; and Katrina's—silver daddies looking for pubescent rough trade. Taking to the night life, we had a ball!

Sometime later, I gave in to my impulse to check out gay male cruising joints—bars with balls—like Traxx, the Tool Box, and the Black Eagle, but I was too nervous to cruise, so I simply watched the action around me, sipping my beer. Curious about the other half, I even ventured alone into dyke clubs like the Rose, Woman's Common, and Pope Joan—with its drag-king performers—but I never felt quite at ease there, as if I was intruding on sacred space. Over the course of my nighttime clubbing, I came across a few other trans-fag and trans-dyke acquaintances, who were not always out as trans while cruising or schmoozing with cisqueer folks. This was not usually due to shame, but rather, because there was still a lot of transphobia among cisgender gay men and lesbians back then. So, like me, many transqueer people led a double life. During the day, "we walk among you"[23] of the dominant, cis heteronormative culture—often imperceptible to your less-than-discerning gaze—but come the night, we "walk on the wild side"[24] in a world beyond the mundane mainstream—trans and queer subcultures colliding and colluding in wild and woolly ways! During these excursions, we would bump into trans divas, like Dianna Boileau[25]—a secretary who frequently visited Toronto—and one of the first Canadians to have had transsexual surgery in 1970; Didi Hunter—a sex worker in Cabbagetown, who passed away shortly after her gender-confirming surgery in the mid-1980s; and Michelle DuBarry[26]—one of the world's two oldest performing drag queens and co-founder of The Great Imposters.

Rita and I quickly became an item, but our romance was short-lived. One night, three days after vanishing to paint the town red in Montreal, I awoke at 3 a.m. to find she had become a bleached blonde! Shortly afterwards, she asked me for a "divorce" and moved out of our bedroom. I was a lone wolf again. I didn't mind because I was already over our relationship. What the hell! Two lonely trans folks who had reached out for some sexual intimacy.

Broke and in between jobs, I gave school another try, enrolling in a Printing program at George Brown College, but lacking the hands-on skills to effectively manage the Heidelberg press and AB Dick printer, I quit halfway through. I was disappointed at my thwarted effort to learn a technical trade. Cerebral as I was, I simply was not cut out for mechanical/technical stuff. More's the pity. I went back on welfare briefly to tide myself over.

Soon afterwards, I landed a job as a shipper-receiver for the Reliable Toy Company. I loaded and unloaded 45-foot tractor-trailers along with some pretty uncouth male characters, who would make obscene gestures at their female co-workers, swear like sailors, and tell sexual tales in a ritual display of adolescent machismo. Fortunately, they were unaware of my transsexual history as I was still stealth. Even so, a bizarre incident did take place at the workplace. One hot, humid day while I was bare-chested, groaning under the boxes we were piling onto the skids, a male co-worker spotted the faded scars on my chest, remarking curiously, "Hey buddy, did you have open-heart surgery?" to which I lied in in the affirmative. Then, another co-worker piped up, "No, I think Nick had a 'sex change'!" Shocked out of my wits and scrambling to regain my composure, I laughed it off, not deigning to counter this outrageous allegation. Lady Luck had my back that day as not one more word was said, the whole incident forgotten. This crummy job didn't pay much, but it got me off welfare and pumped up my muscles. What was really cool was that I was accepted as one of the guys. Still, I don't know how I stuck it out for almost five years.

Now able to pay the bills, I turned once more to activism because I wanted to resume FACT and the work I had begun out west. Continuing to develop my self-taught skills as a networker supreme, I began meeting key players who would hopefully be instrumental in furthering my aims to serve the transsexual community. The first person I met was Dr. Betty Wilson Steiner,[27] then head psychiatrist of the Clarke's Adult Gender Identity Clinic. I had been sending her complimentary copies of *Gender Review* because I wanted her to spread the word about FACT to her transsexual patients. Dr. Steiner said she would refer interested trans patients to me and wished me luck when I told her that I was considering going into social work. I felt gratified at this favourable response and apparent good intentions towards collaboration. Later, however, I learned that once my non-profit gender services had switched from annual membership dues to professional fees for similar resources and supports, she changed her stance, intentionally not referring my gender consulting services because they were not covered by OHIP. So much for free enterprise and consumer choice! A unique and valuable service was rendered inaccessible to the patient population who needed it most. Once again, I was excluded, erased!

Another instance of erasure of gender-transgressive people by Dr. Steiner was exemplified in her book *Gender Dysphoria: Development, Research, Management* (1985), wherein she mentions male transvestites[28] (birth-assigned males who dress in female clothing, now known as crossdressers)—but categorically denied the existence of their female counterparts. Upon reading this non-fact, I sent off a sardonic note to Lou Sullivan—who had initially identified as a female transvestite before re-identifying as a transsexual man sometime later—and two other American female transvestites: "You might as well publish your obituaries right now because in Betty's all-knowing mind you don't exist!" They all responded to my bleak humour with chagrin. This type of reverse misogyny[29] was prevalent. Such erasure of females by many behavioural scientists even extended to a misperceived male-female ratio of transsexualism as three trans women to one trans man. Just because we can't always see masculine-identified birth-assigned females doesn't mean they don't exist! There were even more trans erasures to come.

Being an activist often means that one is disenfranchised oneself and therefore even more driven to right the balance of power. As such, one must offset one's moral indignation and righteous rage with a dash of healthy cynicism and sardonic humour. Otherwise, we would all call it quits and dive into a dark pit of despair. Humour can be a healing agent, a soothing balm to take the sting out of a sense of embittered futility. For this reason, my cronies and I would joke about some of the trans-negative psychiatrists and psychologists who seemed hell-bent on driving us over the edge!

One was Dr. Steiner: another was Dr. Leslie Martin Lothstein. A clinical psychologist at Case Western Reserve University's Gender Identity Program in Cleveland, Dr. Lothstein wrote the transphobic textbook, *Female-to-Male Transsexualism: Historical, Clinical, and Theoretical Issues* (1984). Jude Patton told me that he had flung the book against the wall in disgust, and both Lou Sullivan and I wrote scathing reviews[30]. One joke we shared revolved around the hypothetical possibility of a concealed transsexual identity for either or both Steiner and Lothstein, given that "Wilson" (Steiner's middle name) was a male-sounding name (for a woman), while "Leslie" was an androgynous one. But, would someone who was actually transgender be transphobic? Well, not unless they were stealth, like closet crossdressers or trans persons who suffered from internalized transphobia. Of course, as far as I know, neither of these two gender clinicians were transgender. I qualify this statement because I do know several trans-identified psychologists and psychotherapists who either assess or counsel transgender clients, and who *are* stealth—which has a bearing on the issue of provider self-disclosure and the trust implicit in a professional relationship with mental health practitioners.

Joking aside, when it comes to helping professionals, we must not minimize the adverse impact on patients of powerful people like the late Dr. Kurt Freund,[31] an early sexologist at the former Clarke Institute of Psychiatry (now CAMH), who developed his controversial penile plethysmography (or phallometry) to measure the penile sexual arousal in males in order to identify homosexuals and pedophiles, respectively. In addition to effeminate gay men and male crossdressers, phallometry was sometimes used on self-identified trans women to determine if they were truly transsexual, or, rather, transvestic or homosexual. Freund conducted research into the so-called paraphilias—voyeurism, exhibitionism, frotteurism, sadism, masochism, fetishism, transvestism, pedophilia—reportedly lumping certain transsexuals into this catch-all bag of so-called perverts and child molesters. The Clarke was not a safe place from the late 1960s into the early 2000s for most people who identified as other than heterosexual or cisgender. Fortunately, I escaped this fate, unlike many of my trans peers, who still suffer severe post-traumatic stress following their early psychiatric internment there.

Soon after, I had a serendipitous meeting with Vicki Bellefeuille, owner of the Electrolysis Educational Institute. She taught students the paramedical art of electrolysis (a technique to remove unwanted facial or body hair) and many of her graduates intended to treat cisgender and transgender women and cisgender gay and bi men. A true trans ally, she hosted our inaugural Toronto-based FACT meeting that fall in her school. Vicki and I co-led the meeting, which was well-attended by trans women and trans men, partners and family members. Periodically, Vicki threw parties for members of the queer and trans communities at her Rosedale apartment. Several years later, she married a male transvestite and I celebrated their wedding at the trans-affirming First Unitarian Congregation of Toronto.

I met more people, including Stacie, a trans client of Vicki's, and Lyle, a trans man who roomed with Stacie in her Kensington Market apartment, along with his girlfriend, Cora. We held our second FACT meeting at their apartment, and holding hands in a friendship circle, we pledged solidarity to ourselves and the larger trans community. Someone suggested that we fashion a coded collar-pin to discreetly signal our transsexual identity to other trans people. An intriguing idea but nobody followed through at the time. Decades later, someone else designed a trans logo, which was emblazoned on pin-on buttons.

Around this time, I met Susan Huxford-Westall, an older trans woman from Hamilton, just retiring from a teaching career and newly embarking on her gender transition. Dr. Steiner had referred her to me. I invited Susan to join FACT as treasurer and she enthusiastically agreed. We joined forces and she suggested expanding FACT to become a truly national transsexual foundation. So, we set up chapters (havens) in Toronto, Hamilton, Kitchener, and Ottawa in Ontario, then spread into Quebec (Montreal) and Manitoba (Winnipeg), but never quite made it to the farther reaches of eastern, western, and northern Canada. A designated trans person led each chapter. Susan and I co-founded the FACT Toronto chapter. I chaired it for a short time before handing it over to Susan, who ran it until she retired in 1986, succeeded by Denise Hudson as chair until 1979. Robin S. led FACT Kitchener, Micheline Johnson and Marg G. successfully facilitated FACT Ottawa, and Janice Anderson ran FACT Hamilton for a while, before becoming our national secretary. Susan took over when Janice passed away in 1981. We still do not know if Janice's death was suicide—as Susan and I believed it to have been—or an accidental drug overdose. Her Mormon parents buried her in male clothing and reverted to her male birth name in the obituary and at the funeral service—a tragic example of transphobic violence against a deceased family member and a wake-up call to all trans people to make living wills, outlining explicit end-of-life directives to protect their privacy posthumously. Montrealer Patricia Fisher led FACT Quebec, and I can't recall who ran FACT Winnipeg.

Susan and I held biweekly FACT Toronto meetings at the Electrolysis Educational Institute and, later, at The 519 Community Centre. These meetings functioned as a therapeutic support group where transsexuals and transvestites could access information and resources, and share challenges and successes. We also did community outreach and public education across southern Ontario through newspaper articles, and radio and television programs. We even appeared on two TV talk shows with Dr. Ray Blanchard,[32] a clinical psychologist at the Clarke AGIC. This was before I knew how trans-negative he really was: still, he eventually got his comeuppance in 2009, following an internal investigation by CAMH's medical director and Diversity Office.[33] Even though I was leading a double life, in stealth mode at school and at work, but out in the community and in the media, I chose to show my face—unlike my trans man friend who hid behind dark sunglasses—when featured on a 1984 TV show with Dr. Robert Dickey, the new chief psychiatrist at the Clarke AGIC, succeeding Dr. Steiner. In 1982, opting for anonymity because of the double life I led, I had adopted the alias, Rupert Raj. After a while though, I got tired of having two names and, in 1988, my alias became my legal name.

Regrettably, those early television programs made no mention of the diverse sexual orientations of trans people—who could be straight, gay, lesbian, bisexual, pansexual, transensual, or asexual—because, incredibly, neither the media nor the specialized discipline of sexology really knew much about the true nature of trans people's lived experiences, especially when it came to their sexuality. And, with rare exceptions (noted below), those few sexologists who were so aware did not want to reveal that trans people might be other than heterosexual because this would have deconstructed their overly-invested theories of heteronormative psychosexuality within the trans population. At the time, there was considerable anti-gay bias in research! Lou Sullivan told me that he had written to Dr. Blanchard in 1988, declaring that gay trans men, like himself, do exist and have existed as far back as Jack Bee Garland in the late 19th century in San Francisco, but that, over the years, Dr. Blanchard consistently denied this fact. Compare this form of erasure to Dr. Steiner's assertion that female crossdressers did not exist. Thanks to Lou's living example and his proactive education of gender clinicians like Dr. Ira Pauly, Dr. Eli Coleman, and Dr. Walter Bockting, transhomosexuality was classified in sexological taxonomy as a valid sexual orientation in 1989,[34] although psychiatrist Dr. Robert Stoller had written about bisexual transsexuals 17 years earlier![35]

Besides media outreach, Susan and I presented Trans 101 educational workshops for university students in psychology, psychotherapy, social work, sexology, and sexuality studies; for doctors and nurses, and sometimes psychotherapists (but rarely, psychiatrists and psychologists) in hospitals, health centres, and mental health institutions; and for social workers in community agencies that supported female ex-prisoners, including pre-transitional trans men and post-transitional trans women—and male ex-prisoners—including pre-transitional trans women but not post-transitional trans men (see chapter 5 for our advocacy work on behalf of trans prisoners).

In those early days before intersectional analyses and anti-oppression frameworks, racism, anti-Indigeneity, classism, sexism, homophobia, transphobia, etc. were rarely mentioned, if at all. It's not surprising that such human psychosexual dimensions as basic as gender identity and sexual orientation were typically conflated, making our training efforts particularly challenging. For example, an educational workshop took place in 1981 at the Clarke AGIC, but Susan and I were not invited to present. This was a subtle form of exclusion, wherein only certain trans people were selected—usually those who were duly accepted as professional peers because of their higher degrees, and/or those who would not challenge the psychomedical status quo: transsexualism as a psychiatric disorder. So they chose Dr. Tony Tornabene (Mario Martino) as their sole presenter, who spoke about phalloplasty for transsexual men. His presentation was informative, but his grandstanding as the trans alpha male made my blood boil! In typical macho braggadocio, he likened himself to the notorious gangster, Al Capone, leaning on his Italian heritage. A male diva, T.T. was assuredly not a transfeminist, as evidenced by his transmisogynist[36] indictment of transsexual women in his autobiography.[37] Regretfully, I'm ashamed to say that, in those very early days, even I was guilty of some negative attitudes towards trans women.[38]

And, there were/are still other people unfriendly towards transsexual women, as evidenced by their vitriolic books. These included several transmisogynist, American and Australian cisgender radical feminists: Dr. Mary Daly,[39] Dr. Janice Raymond,[40] Dr. Germaine Greer[41] and Dr. Sheila Jeffreys.[42] Until the emergence of transfeminism[43] in the 1990s—and the recent outpouring of transfeminist anthologies in the 2000s by mostly queer, cisgender women—the only early cisgender female, feminist allies of trans women are/were American, trans-friendly, radical feminist Andrea Dworkin[44] and American, third-wave transfeminist Judith Butler,[45] With xenophobia running rampant in the 1980s, in addition to transphobia and transmisogyny, femmephobia[46] was another anti-feminine attitude present in both the straight and queer worlds. Such genderphobic bigotry—directed towards trans women, male crossdressers, and drag queens (but not always female impersonator entertainers)—is perpetuated by virtually all sectors of society: cisgender and transgender males, and cisgender females. Of course, trans women can also be genderphobic towards people other than themselves. As a result of these messages of hate against trans women, gender wars broke out around the world between cis rad fems and trans women, some of whom were feminists themselves, like American trans woman Dr. Allucquére Rosanne (Sandy) Stone, who penned the trans-empowering "The 'Empire' Strikes Back: A Posttranssexual Manifesto" in 1987 (revised in 1991 and 1994).[47]

Dialogue between cisgender and transgender women continued over the years into the new millennium, and 2006 was a watershed year for transfeminism in Canada. In Toronto, York University's Professor Krista Scott-Dixon published her milestone anthology, Trans/forming Feminisms: Trans-feminist Voices Speak Out (2006),[48] the first-ever, explicitly transfeminist collection, which included contributions by trans women, trans men, third-gender/genderqueer people, and female and male cisgender allies. Moreover, York University and the Centre for Feminist Research co-sponsored the transformative Trans/Equity: Past, Present and Possibilities conference in Toronto,[49] which included a focus on gender equality for trans women. Presenters included trans-female academics and activists (Dr. Heather Davies, Dr. Viviane Namaste, Dr. Trish Salah, and Monica Forrester), a male to female crossdresser/transgender activist (Dr. Michael A. Gilbert), trans-male academics and activists (Dr. Aaron Devor, Zack Marshall, Syrus Marcus Ware, and me), and a cisgender ally (Dr. Sheila Cavanaugh). Dr. Namaste presented a brief history of early Québécois trans women, in particular, Montreal cabaret artists (who were also often sex workers) in the 1950s and 1960s—a segment of Canadian trans history that is often unacknowledged (erased) by the rest of (English-speaking) Canada. Another presenter particularly relevant to my discussion here, was crossdressing York University professor, Dr. Michael A. Gilbert,[50] who, some years earlier, had dramatically revealed "hir" bigender identity (and double life) to hir philosophy students by coming to class one day dressed as Miqqi Alicia (her female identity). The real eye-opener was that a seemingly all-male man could have a feminine alternate persona, but more importantly, could be a male feminist.[51]

In fact, from the late 1960s into the 1980s, Dr. Virginia (Charles) Prince[52] and a number of other male transvestites and transgenderists in the USA were also identifying this way. Glenda René Jones published the *Journal of Male Feminism*.[53] But, the real question is: What was their critical understanding of *true* equality for women (transsexual and cisgender) who lived full-time in the female role, given the sociosexual male privilege still accorded to male transvestites/transgenderists living a double life? Sometime in the 1990s, as gender identities, social sex-roles, and societal gender relations evolved, American trans woman Davina Anne Gabriel published the first-ever transfeminist periodical, *TransSisters: The Journal of Transsexual Feminism*.[54] Canadian trans women Mirha-Soleil Ross and Xanthra Mackay produced probably the first-ever transfeminist porn video, *Gender Troublemakers*.[55] This progressive gender politics was still evolving into the 2000s, with American, trans-female transfeminists, such as Kate Bornstein,[56] Diana Courvant,[57] Julie Serano, and Dr. Sandy Stone (an intersex activist/trans ally[58]): and Canadian, trans-female feminists like Jade Pichette,[59] Dr. Rachel

McKinnon, Dr. Trish Salah, and Dr. Viviane Namaste. On December 5, 2017, a milestone in transgender equality occurred when French-Canadian, transfeminist Gabrielle Bouchard[60] became the new president of the *Fédération des femmes du Québec*—the first trans-female to lead the province's primary women's rights organization! Exactly a month before (November 5, 2017), another French-Canadian trans woman, politician Julie Lemieux,[61] was elected mayor of Très-Saint-Rédempteur, Quebec—the village's first female mayor, and the first transgender person elected to the mayoralty of any municipality in Canada! Trans women were finally breaking through the other glass ceiling that had historically restricted most openly-trans women from climbing the corporate ladder or attaining public office. Radically-inclusive transfeminism—the opposite of trans-exclusionary radical feminism[62] is imperative to ensure that our trans sisters are equally respected and safe. Over the past 50 years, it has been a troubled trajectory in terms of transgender women's fight for social acceptance as legitimate women—especially from cisgender radical feminists. Hopefully, many more of the new generation of cisgender feminists will be transpositive. Promisingly, many more trans men are becoming transfeminist (see chapter 5).

Given that FACT was not a political lobby group *per se,* we weren't embroiled in such contentious debates, the rhetoric getting shriller and the gender-policing more vicious as claws were bared and fangs showed! The war raged over the next few decades as transfeminism slowly took hold, and at the 2010 Egale Canada Human Rights Trust (ECHRT) annual gala in Toronto, I heard New Zealander, Māori activist Georgina Beyer[63] speak out against violence toward trans women and trans-female sex workers. In 2012, ECHRT commissioned the film, *Courage in the Face of Hate*[64] (along with a toolkit) to help activists and allies fight transmisogyny in Canada.

In addition to the unpaid task of running FACT—I continued to edit *Gender Review* up until June 1981 before handing it over to Susan, who remained as editor until 1985. The newsletter was my baby, but, after three years, I felt I had run my course as editor. I was also experiencing a mild burnout, and wasn't sure how much longer I could run FACT. Fortunately, Susan was eager to succeed me as organizational president and had big plans of her own. She wanted to expand FACT into the USA, officially changing its name to the Federation of American and Canadian Transsexuals, still retaining the acronym for continuity. As a result of this bi-national expansion, chapters would soon be created in the American Atlantic and Pacific regions and, particularly, in western New York State.

Relieved, knowing of Susan's immanent takeover, I decided to take a well-deserved break, and tag along with Rita and her girlfriends on their nights out to the Continental Inn or the London Pub and drink and dance away my burnout blues. The trans street girls took over these heterosexual establishments, using them as their combined party place and base of operations. On Friday nights, after sniffing "poppers" (alkyl nitrites) for the thrilling "rush," they would sing their hearts out up on the dancefloor stage to pop hits, like "Ring my Bell" and "Heaven Must Have Sent You," as they kicked up their heels, wearing skirts slit up to their crotch, their private bits neatly tucked away. Often a T-girl would surreptitiously slip out to the back parking lot to take care of business, making a few bucks on the side. One of these memorable nights, I met Ruthie.

Ruthie was an elegant older trans woman, a hairstylist who owned the Chez Shandra salon in the Beaches. Charming in a classy way, she began making overtures to me because of my van Dyke beard, which reminded her of her recently-deceased husband. Flattered, I responded in kind. Flirting shyly, she sipped a slow shot of rye and I chugged down a couple of beers while we made moony eyes at each other. One thing led to another with Ruthie inviting me to dinner the following Friday: after the main course, we had each other for dessert. After that, we saw each other regularly and on April 1, 1980, I moved into her apartment, which was at the back of her salon, along with her black toy poodle, Shandra. Things went pretty well overall except that, other than that first night of passion and one or two thereafter, our eight-and-a-half-year romance was sexless. She had been used to big cis cock and never quite turned on to my micropenis. Too bad because it's not the size of the prick that does the trick: it's the throb of the knob that does the job!

At this time, I became a human companion to a pet of my own for the first time and I've loved cats ever since. Patches, a sweet white tabby with gray markings, was my pride and joy. When Ruthie's client gave us this six-week-old kitten, she told us that Patches was a girl kitty. We soon found out otherwise, but I loved my boy cat just as much. Take heed, cisgender parents of transgender, intersex, or gender non-conforming children (now, gender-independent or gender-creative kids)[65]—and human companions of genitally-ambiguous pets! Patches was my best friend for 13 years until he died of kidney failure in December 1996. I will always cherish his zest for life: how he loved to tomcat around the back alleys; then, come home and meow for his dinner before curling up to sleep on the couch.

Life was rolling along, me working my blue-collar ass off for a pittance in the salt mines. Still, it was better than being on welfare. I wanted to put my Bachelor's degree in psychology to use. So, I applied to the Children's Aid Society of Toronto as a caseworker. Ruthie lent me one of her choice boy outfits: a three-piece, burgundy Brooks Brothers suit. I felt like a million bucks, strutting my stuff, gold watch and chain hanging off my vest button! I got called for an interview and was excited at the prospect of finally working in my field. Alas, I despaired at being told they could not hire me because I didn't have a Master's degree in social work. Why call me for an interview if they already knew that?! Furthermore, a Bachelor's of psychology degree would have been just as good for this entry level position. Once again, I felt that I had been shafted by the system. Following this rejection, I decided to try once more for a postgraduate degree in either social work or counselling psychology. I applied to three graduate schools—Carleton University, the Adler School of Professional Psychology (Ontario), and Ryerson Polytechnic Institute—but was summarily denied yet again due to my poor grade-point average. So much for further schooling for now: it was back to the salt mines for a bit longer.

The following year, Ruthie and I got engaged, just before sex-reassignment surgeon, Dr. William Lindsay would create her neovagina—her dream come true before she turned 60, a birthday present to herself. I planned to meet her at the Wellesley Hospital on the day of her release to take her home in a taxi. But the goddamn Sherbourne bus only came every 20 minutes, so when I finally got to the hospital, dashing up 14 flights of stairs to her room, she had already left in a huff. I was deflated! When I got home, I gave her a birthday gift of a musical jewellery box, but she was still miffed, giving me the silent treatment for a whole day. We finally made up and things returned to normal.

Throughout the 1980s, in addition to numerous queer and transgender folks, I occasionally crossed paths with cisgender men and women at Vicki's soirées, including a coquettish young woman (KJ), who was looking me over. She was pretty, with long, black wavy hair and a sexy smile, not to mention an irascible wit and irresistible laugh. We were out on Vicki's apartment balcony, underneath the Chinese paper lanterns, when I felt the same spark that must have thrilled Elizabeth Taylor and Montgomery Clift as they embraced passionately on the terrace in the 1951 romantic drama, *A Place in the Sun*. Our pheromones were flowing, but we didn't kiss until sometime later. We managed to meet secretly now and then for our romantic trysts: me reading KJ poetry in her bedroom while her parents were away, us necking by the fountain at City Hall's Nathan Phillip Square, giving each other love bites on the shoulder, me furtively fondling her breasts in the cinema while watching *Victor/Victoria*[66] staring Julie Andrews,[67]—who did *not* look anything like a man as she pretended to be a male impersonating a female! When KJ let out a sexy laugh, "The dykes are gonna go crazy over Julie in her tuxedo, her 'bubbies' protruding as she hits the lower register singing 'Jazz Hot'!", I was besotted! But there was a problem: I was already in a relationship. Ever dancing the dialectic, here I was engaged to a woman almost twice my age (57), while having an affair with another one just over half my age (17)—a 40-year difference between them. At least I wasn't ageist.

I had to do something because the guilt was killing me! Impulsively, I picked KJ, leaving a farewell note for Ruthie. KJ and I met at the fairgrounds, gulping cotton candy while riding the Ferris wheel. Suddenly, I got an intense pang of guilt and called Ruthie. She tearfully pleaded for me to come home. So, silly bugger that I was, I gave in to Ruthie, leaving KJ alone at the fair, crying her eyes out at my desertion. Torn between two women, I felt desolate, but I still thought that I was making the right decision. I somehow got the notion that what KJ and I had was merely infatuation, not true love—perhaps my instinct was misguided. Oh, the folly of youth, with its cruel demands to make the best choices around romance and love. If only I had a crystal ball to foresee my several possible futures!

Ruthie hoped we could wed in the Catholic Church inasmuch she craved religious sanction, but upon consulting her parish priest, we were told point-blankly: "No, I'm afraid not. It would be one thing if only one of you was transsexual; but, both of you…," implying that two trans people would compound the sin. So much for marriage! We continued our platonic relationship, playing house for another seven years—an empty engagement. To make up for my non-lovelife, I focussed on my non-paying activist career, preparing to metamorphose yet again….

Chapter 4 Notes

[1] See: Ginsberg, Allen, *Howl and Other Poems* (introduction by William Carlos Williams), San Francisco, CA: 1956; and Whitman, Walt, *Leaves of Grass*, self-published, 1855 (included multiple revisions until his death in 1892).

[2] Two transpositive feminists were Andea Dworkin and Gloria Steinheim. Transphobic feminists included Mary Daly, Janice Raymond, Sheila Jeffreys, and later, Germaine Greer. Those who were non-committal included Simone de Beauvoir, Sheila Rowbotham, Shulamith Firestone, and Kate Millet. See: Intersectional Bibliography.

[3] I'm using the word "fags" in a celebratory way as many gay/bi men do.

[4] For information on Gay Alliance Toward Equality (GATE), see https://en.wikipedia.org/wiki/Gay_Alliance_Toward_Equality.

[5] The Northwest Territories only fund GCSs on a case by case basis; Nunavut Territory is the only jurisdiction in Canada which provides none at all. Some provinces/territories medically insure only certain of the patient-requested genital or gonadal surgeries (e.g., orchiectomy and vaginoplasty for trans women; pan-hysterectomy and metoidioplasty—or phalloplasty—for trans women), and most do not insure non-genital (auxilliary) surgical procedures (e.g., breast augmentation, tracheal shaving and facial feminization for trans women; male chest contouring for trans men).

[6] These were: Dr. Donald Angus, Dr. Roy MacKenzie, Dr. Marvin Bala, and Dr. Dale Birdsell.

[7] Joanna Clark (aka Sister Mary Elizabeth Clark) transitioned to female in the 1970s and was soon after discharged from the US Army, which she successfully sued. She continued the work of the Erickson Educational Foundation through the Janus Information Facility from 1977 to 1980 (or 1981) with Dr. Paul Walker, then through J2CP Services from 1980 (or 1981) to 1991 (or 1992) with Jude Patton, and finally passed this on to Dallas Denny (AEGIS) in 1991 (or 1992). In 1988, Joanna became a nun and took the name, "Sister Mary Elizabeth Clark," but later left the Episcopalian order and resumed her former name, "Joanna." In 1980, she founded the ACLU (American Civil Liberties Union) Transsexual Rights Committee. In 1990, she built AEGiS (AIDS Education Global information System), the world's largest AIDS database. Joanna currently works in environmental advocacy. Read her life story: Clark, Joanna (Sister Mary Elizabeth), and Margot Wilson, *Before My Warranty Runs Out: Human, Transgender and Environmental Rights Advocate*, Victoria, BC: TransGender Publishing, forthcoming.

[8] Jude Patton was the first and only Consumer Advocate on the Board of the Harry Benjamin International Gender Dysphoria Association (now, the World Professional Association for Transgender Health [WPATH]) in 1979. He worked with Joanna Clark again, co-founding J2CP Services, circa 1980 to 1992. A long-time family therapist and certified physician's assistant serving trans people, Jude is also a pet-facilitated therapist. See his autobiographical writings: "My Story," in Vern Bullough's anthology, *The Frontiers of Sex Research*, Buffalo, NY: Prometheus Books, 1979; and Patton, Jude, and Margot Wilson. *Young Kid, Old Goat: Transgender Journey to Understanding the Man Within*, Victoria, BC: TransGender

Publishing, forthcoming. See also his other two books (anthologies co-edited with Margot Wilson): *Life Trips: Navigating LGBT+ Aging, Illness an End of Life Decisions* (forthcoming); and *Unconditional Love: Stories of LGBTQ+ People and Our Animal Companions* (forthcoming) (both with Transgender Publishing).

[9] See: Kane, Ariadne/J. Ari, and Margot Wilson, *Gender Odyssey: Journey of an Intrepid Androgyne*, Victoria, BC: TransGender Publishing, forthcoming.

[10] These trans-female activists are listed below.

Stephanie Castle (née Sydney Heal, 1925-2017) co-founded the Zenith Foundation in Vancouver, BC in 1993 with Christine Burnham, and Patricia Diewold, a clinical psychologist from the provincial Gender Identity Clinic at Vancouver General Hospital. Stephanie edited the *Zenith Newsletter* (later renamed the *Zenith Digest*). See: Castle, Stephanie, *The Zenith Experience: Encounters & Memories in a Transgender Setting*, Vancouver, BC: Perceptions Press, 2005. Read Stephanie's memoir, *Feelings: A Transsexual's Explanation of a Baffling Condition*, Perceptions Press, 1992 (followed by a second edition, with an introduction by Margot Wilson, ed., Victoria, BC: TransGender Publishing, 2018), and her biography: Wilson, Margot, *Girl in the Dream: Stephanie (Sydney) Castle Heal: A Transgender Life*, Victoria, BC: TransGender Publishing, 2018. She was featured in the Canadian film documentary, *Transforming Gender ("Firsthand"* TV series), (Season 2015-2016, Episode 07), CBC-TV, Nov. 26, 2016. http://www.cbc.ca/player/play/2679573123. Stephanie's collection of papers are preserved in the Transgender Archives. http://transgenderarchives.ca/collections/stephanie-castle/index.php. See also https://www.uvic.ca/research/transchair/home/news/current/stephanie-castle---in-memoriam.php

Patricia Fisher was one of the earliest Canadian police officers to reassign as female on the job. As a representative of FACT Quebec (a chapter of the Federation of American and Canadian Transsexuals [FACT]), she supported transsexual women in Montreal in the 1980s.

Denise Hudson formed Transvestites in Toronto (TIT) in 1979 and published its newsletter, *Skirting the Issue* (a single issue). She was the last person to chair FACT Toronto in 1986, and the last to edit its newsletter, *Transition* (not to be confused with the 1970s-1980s American newsletter for transsexuals edited by cisgender sexologist, Garrett Oppenheim, Director of CONFIDE—Personal Counseling Services, in Tappan, NY).

Susan Huxford-Westall (born 1921) passed away in 2009 at 87. For more information, see https://zagria.blogspot.ca/2009/08/susan-huxford-westall-1921-2009-school.html

Linda T. O'Connell produced the poetry anthologies, *Fighting Back: A Symphony in Words* (self-published in 1978); and "The Greatest Hits of Linda T. O'Connell, Not Available from K-Tel" (unpublished, 1982). The latter was donated by me to The ArQuives https://arquives.andornot.com/en/list?q=Linda+T.+O%27Connell&p=1&ps=20. Linda was likely the first ever transsexual to publish a trans poetry anthology. She suffered from severe multiple sclerosis in the 1980s and had been living in a long-term care facility in Toronto for some years.

Dallas Denny founded the American Educational Gender Information Service (AEGIS) (now Gender Education & Advocacy) in 1990, and from circa 1991 to 1998, carried on the work of the Erickson Educational Foundation passed on by Joanna Clark and Jude Patton (J2CP Services). Dallas wrote and edited several books, including *Gender Dysphoria: A Guide to Research* (Shrewsbury, MA: Garland Publishers, 1994); and *Current Concepts in Transgender Identity* (Garland Publishers, 1998); and has recently written trans-related articles with Dr. Jamison Green. See also https://zagria.blogspot.ca/2010/07/dallas-denny-1949-psychologist-writer.html. Read her mini memoir, "Girl with No Name," in Margot Wilson and

Aaron Devor, eds., *Glimmerings: Trans Elders Tell Their Stories*, Victoria, BC: TransGender Publishing, 2019, 33-42.

Angela Lynn Douglas (1943-2007) founded the militant Transsexual Action Organization (TAO) in Los Angeles in 1970, moved it to Miami Beach in 1972 dissolved it in 1978, and edited its newsletter. In 1982, Angela reverted to male and assumed her birth name (Carl Czinki). See https://zagria.blogspot.ca/2007/06/angela-douglas-1943-2007-musician.html and https://zagria.blogspot.ca/2015/07/history-of-tao-bibliography.html. Trans people rarely (3.8-8.0%) revert to their birth-assigned sex, detransitioning often because they cannot make it in a transphobic world, unable to access loving families, friends and partners. Occasionally, non gender-dysphoric and gender-dysphoric people are misdiagnosed as transgender, or are not (fully) prepared to medically transition (social transition might be a viable alternative). Sometimes detransitioners later retransition once a stable transgender identity, positive self-esteem and societal acceptance are forthcoming. No reliable statistics are currently available on detransitioning and retransitioning.

Heather Peerson co-led Cross-Port, a trans peer-support group in Cincinnati, Ohio in the 1980s and edited its newsletter, *Cross-Port InnerView*.

Phoebe Smith edited *The Transsexual Voice* newsletter from 1981-1995. She self-published *Phoebe: My Story* (1979); and *From Sharecropper's Son to Who's Who in American Women* (2014).

Judith (Judy) Cousins (1917-1993) co-founded the Self-Help Association for Transsexuals (SHAFT) in the UK in 1980 and remained its president until 1988. It was succeeded by the Gender Dysphoria Trust International in 1993 (later renamed the Gender Trust. http://gendertrust.org.uk/). See: Hodgkinson, Liz. *Bodyshock: The Truth About Changing Sex*, London, UK: Columbus Books, 1987, 28, 88, 91; and also https://zagria.blogspot.ca/2011/07/judy-cousins-1917-1993-soldier-sculpter.html

Elaine Barrie created the Elaine Barrie Project, a transvestite/transsexual support group in Altona, Australia in the 1980s, and edited its newsletter.

Rosemary, a former member of the Beaumont Society in the UK, co-founded the Seahorse Club of Australia (later renamed the Seahorse Society of New South Wales) in 1971. Trina, the national secretary, was the first editor of its *Feminique Magazine* (1972-1984). Seahorse still runs and is linked to several other Australian groups for crossdressers and trans people.

Gillian Cox formed Transformation, a transsexual support group in Levin, New Zealand in the 1970s, and edited its newsletter.

[11] In 2000, Eugene had given me a newsclipping on the clinic's closure from either the *Calgary Herald* or the *Calgary Sun*, and I was sure I had donated it to The ArQuives, but neither I nor then ArQuives volunteer Nicholas Matte could track it down! A Google search was also futile. The evidence is now elusive, but I know that I had read of the closure.

[12] "CAMH to 'Wind Down' Gender Identity Clinic After Review of Services." *Canadian Press*, December 15, 2015. https://www.cbc.ca/news/canada/toronto/camh-gender-identity-1.3366424.

[13] See: "Position Statement Regarding the Closure of CAMH's Child, Youth and Family Gender Identity Clinic," Toronto, ON: Rainbow Health Ontario. https://www.rainbowhealthontario.ca/.

[14] Kyle Andrew Smith Scanlon (1969-2012) directed Toronto's Lesbian Gay Bi Trans Youth Line in the late 1990s, and headed the Meal Trans Program at The 519 Community Centre in the 2000s. Kyle won the Grassroots Trans Community Activist of the Year Award in 2001, and was the second trans man to be inducted into The ArQuives.

https://arquives.andornot.com/en/list?q=kyle+scanlon&p=1&ps=20.

[15] Christina (Tina) Strang was the Meal Trans Program coordinator at The 519 Community Centre in Toronto in the early 2000s. She now works as a housing worker with Toronto Community Housing. She has worked on several projects (including a safer-sex booklet for trans sex-workers, and a video documentary on my early trans activism), which are noted elsewhere in the book.

[16] See: Gagnon, Audrey, "Boys Will be Girls: Gender Identity Clinic Event Disrupted by Trans Activists," Toronto, ON: *Xtra*, April 12, 2007. Reprinted here http://ai.eecs.umich.edu/people/conway/TS/Clarke/CAMH%20event%20disrupted%20by%20trans%20activists%204-13-07.htm.

[17] See: Zucker, Kenneth J., and Susan J. Bradley, *Gender Identity Disorders and Psychosexual Problems in Children and Adolescents*, New York, NY: Guildford Press, 1995.

[18] *Bill 77, Affirming Sexual Orientation and Gender Identity Act, 2015*, Toronto, ON: Legislative Assembly of Ontario. https://www.ola.org/en/legislative-business/bills/parliament-41/session-1/bill-77.

[19] See: "Canadian Professional Association for Transgender Health Submission to the Standing Committee on Justice Policy Re: Bill 77, Affirming Sexual Orientation and Gender Identity Act, 2015," Victoria, BC: CPATH, June 3, 2015 (Google online PDF).

[20] See: "Ottawa Rejects Plea for Nationwide Conversion Therapy Ban," Stroh, Perlita, Ottawa, ON: CBC News, March 23, 2019. https://www.cbc.ca/news/canada/the-national-conversion-therapy-federal-petition-1.5066899.

[21] See: "List of U.S. Jurisdictions Banning Conversion Therapy," Wikipedia, August 2019. https://en.wikipedia.org/wiki/List_of_U.S._jurisdictions_banning_conversion_therapy.

[22] For the original 1975 version of *The Rocky Horror Picture Show*, see https://en.wikipedia.org/wiki/The_Rocky_Horror_Picture_Show. For its 2016 remake as a musical comedy, starring African American trans woman, Laverne Cox, see https://en.wikipedia.org/wiki/The_Rocky_Horror_Picture_Show:_Let%27s_Do_the_Time_Warp_Again.

[23] I'm building on American trans man David E. Harrison's eloquent words from the 2005 comedy-drama, *Transamerica* (starring Felicity Huffman), about a trans woman soon to surgically transition. David very briefly appeared as himself in the film. His words, "we walk among you," spoken to a mixed group of cis and trans people at a party, specifically referred to himself and other trans people, underscoring the fact that trans people are everywhere—at times noticeably as transgender, but often not. https://www.imdb.com/name/nm2126827/; and https://www.imdb.com/title/tt0407265/?ref_=nm_flmg_act_3.

[24] My allusion here is two-fold. "Walk on the Wild Side" is the title of American rock singer Lou Reed's iconic song of 1972. https://en.wikipedia.org/wiki/Walk_on_the_Wild_Side_%28Lou_Reed_song%29. *Take A Walk On The Wildside*™ is the name of Paddy Aldridge's Toronto-based, transformational

clothing store catering to male crossdressers and trans women since 1987. Watch the 2017 Canadian film documentary of the same name, produced by Lisa Rideout and Sarah Fisher. https://www.imdb.com/title/tt6293648/.

[25] Dianna Boileau (1930-2014) penned her memoir, *Behold, I Am a Woman!* (as told to Felicity Cochrane), (New York, NY: Pyramid Books, 1972). See Katie Daub's *Toronto Star* news feature https://www.thestar.com/news/insight/2016/03/27/the-woman-who-was-trans-before-her-time.html; and also https://zagria.blogspot.ca/2010/09/dianna-boileau-1930-2014-secretary.html

[26] For more information on Michelle duBarry (aka Russell Alldread), see https://zagria.blogspot.ca/2008/10/michelle-dubarry-1931-performer.html.

[27] For more information on Dr. Betty W. Steiner (1920-1994), see https://zagria.blogspot.ca/2010/09/betty-steiner-1920-1994-psychiatrist.html.

[28] Male transvestites are birth-assigned males who dress in female clothing; female transvestites are birth-assigned females who dress in male clothing. Both might crossdress for sensual or sexual reasons, or alternatively, for gender expression as either feminine or masculine (and, in Canada, are protected under human rights legislation). Some crossdressers might also identify as androgynous, bigender, transgender, genderqueer or gender non-binary. A number might later re-identify as transsexual or transgender, and undergo a social and/or medical gender transition. The current term for "transvestite" is "crossdresser," and it is included under the umbrella term, "transgender."

[29] By reverse misogyny here, I mean the minimalization of birth-assigned females by psychiatrists as less-inclined towards certain sexual practices, such as crossdressing for erotic stimulation (historically psychopathologized as "sexual fetishism"), as compared to birth-assigned males.

[30] My review of Dr. Leslie Lothstein's book was published in *Metamorphosis*, April 1984, 3(2): 3-4, and Lou Sullivan's was published in *Metamorphosis*, December 1984, 3(6): 3-5. I subsequently wrote a revised version, published in *The TV-TS Tapestry*, 1984, (44): 47-50, "Comparative Reviews by a Medical Psychologist and a Female-to-Male Transsexual." Incredulously, Johns Hopkins University medical psychologist Dr. Eileen Higham calls Dr. Lothstein's book on female-to-male transsexuals "a welcome addition to the mental health specialist's library despite its errors and logical flaws." Yet, to her credit, she elaborates on "Lothstein's occasional misinterpretations and outright errors," and delineates the limitations of his theoretical orientation, which "relies heavily on psychoanalytic theories, especially the works of Kohut, Laing, Winnicott, Guntrip, and Stoller, and their contributions to understanding pre-oedipal psychopathology." As for me, I found this trans-unfriendly text "to exude a cold clinical approach, which is at once dehumanizing and devoid of compassion, not to mention insensitive and insulting. For example, the author uses female pronouns exclusively—even when referring to post-operative F-M TSs, who are now, by definition, and for all practical purposes, men!…That's the problem—a difference in perspectives. What's the alternative (psycho-biological) point of view?"

[31] For more information on Dr. Kurt Freund (1914-1996), see https://zagria.blogspot.ca/2008/03/kurt-freund-1914-1996-penile.html.

[32] For information on Dr. Ray Blanchard, see https://zagria.blogspot.ca/2009/11/ray-

blanchard-1945-psychologist.html. See also: Blanchard, Ray, and Betty W. Steiner, *Clinical Management of Gender Identity Disorders in Children and Adults*, Washington, DC: American Psychiatric Press, 1990.

[33] Following a 2007 CAMH internal audit a 2009 report was generated, recommending strategies to improve relations with the LGBTTI2SQQAA community—especially gender non-binary and trans people. http://ai.eecs.umich.edu/people/conway/TS/News/US/Zucker/The_War_Within_CAMH.html. The report resulted in Dr. Ray Blanchard's transfer from CAMH's Adult Gender Identity Clinic to the General Psychiatry section, so that trans patients would no longer be harmed by his transphobic practices.

[34] Dr. Ira Pauly interviewed Louis G. Sullivan from 1988 to 1990, which he videotaped in four parts for the Department of Psychiatry & Behavioral Sciences at the University of Nevada School of Medicine in Reno: "Female to Gay Male Transsexualism: I—Gender & Sexual Orientation," 1988; "Female to Gay Male Transsexualism: II—Living with AIDS," 1988; "Female to Gay Male Transsexualism: III," 1989; "Female to Gay Male Transsexualism: Part IV (One Year Later)," 1990. Dr. Eli Coleman and Dr. Walter Bockting also interviewed Lou. See their paper, "'Heterosexual' Prior to Sex Reassignment – 'Homosexual' Afterwards: A Case Study of a Female-to-Male Transsexual," *Journal of Psychology and Human Sexuality*, February 1989, 1(2): 69-82. See also https://zagria.blogspot.ca/2008/07/louis-gradon-sullivan-1951-1991-pioneer.html.

[35] See: Stoller, Robert J., and Laurence E Newman. "The Bisexual Identity of Transsexuals: Two Case Examples," *Archives of Sexual Behavior*, March 1971, 1 (17):17-28.

[36] "Transmisogyny" is a term coined by trans woman Julia Serano in her book, *Whipping Girl: A Transsexual Woman on Sexism and the Scapegoating of Femininity*, New York, NY: Seal Press, 2007. Essentially, transmisogyny is a discriminatory attitude towards trans women, often perpetrated by cisgender women (especially trans-exclusionary radical feminists) and cisgender men – and sometimes even trans men. See https://rationalwiki.org/wiki/Transmisogyny; and also the note below on "transfeminism."

[37] In his book, *Emergence: A Transsexual Autobiography* (New York, NY: Crown Publishers, 1977), Mario Martino (Tony Tornabene's pseudonym) makes some disparaging comments about the mannish physical aspects (e.g., hairy legs) of some of the trans-female patients in Yonkers Professional Hospital, where he worked as a nursing supervisor.

[38] My trans-historian friend Nicholas Matte calls me out on several transmisogynist, sexist and classist remarks I had written in the past before I readily evolved to become a transfeminist, non-sexist and non-classist advocate. See his chapter, "Rupert Raj, Transmen and Sexuality: The Politics of Transnormativities in *Metamorphosis Magazine* during the 1980s," in Patrizia Gentile, Pauline Rankin, and Gary Kinsman, eds., *We Still Demand! Redefining Resistance in Sex and Gender Struggles*, Vancouver, BC: UBC Press, 2017, 117-136. This indictment of my past ideological "transgressions"—gender and sexual policing—along with similar charges of sexism/transmisogyny against Dr. Tony Tornabene (Mario Martino), and noted criticisms of "anti-transsexual" transphobia against American Jewish activist, (Diane) Leslie Feinberg (see note in chapter 5)—is a tough pill to swallow. I can only say that my mainstream, middle-class, sexist and transmisogynist words were sparked by the conservative moral-majority of the times (the 1970s and 1980s). Although I certainly own my early limitations, I'm also

thankful that I was open enough to readily progress to a more enlightened ethic. In fact, in the 1970s into the 1990s, I was one of a mere handful of trans men in North America who cared enough to champion the rights of our trans sisters—such as Canadian trans prisoner, Katherine Johnson—(see chapter 5), among others—even after I went on to create a new service organization focussing on the needs of trans men in 1982. See chapter 5 for a detailed discussion of trans-male (trans)misogyny and its opposite, trans-male (trans)feminism (as well as its lesser-counterpart, transmisandry), and a humanist-feminist ethic of universal equality. It's too bad that I only became fully aware of Nick's published critique of me in late July 2017—a mere two weeks before my printer's deadline for the first edition of this memoir—or I would certainly have addressed his criticisms. Specifically, I would have first owned my earlier devolved remarks, and then underscored my-paradigm shift to an anti-oppressive gender politics.

[39] See: Daly, Mary, *Gyn/Ecology: The Metaethics of Radical Feminism,* Boston, MA, Beacon Press, 1978.

[40] See: Raymond, Janice, *The Transsexual Empire: The Making of the She-Male,* Boston, MA: Beacon Press, 1979.

[41] See: Greer, Germaine, *The Whole Woman,* New York, NY: Doubleday, 1999; and its predecessor, *The Female Eunuch,* London, UK: MacGibbon & Kee, 1970.

[42] See: Jeffreys, Sheila, and Lorene Gottschalk, *Gender Hurts: A Feminist Analysis of the Politics of Transgenderism,* Abingdon, UK: Routledge (Taylor & Francis), 2014.

[43] The term "transfeminism" was independently coined purportedly by trans woman Diana Courvant, in 1992, or trans man, Pat Califia-Rice, in 1997, or trans woman, Jessica Xavier, in 1999. American intersex activist and trans ally, Emi Koyama, defines "transfeminism" (or "trans feminism") as "a movement by and for trans women who view their liberation to be intrinsically linked to the liberation of all women and beyond." It "is also open to other queers, intersex people, trans men, non-trans women, non-trans men and others who are sympathetic toward needs of trans women and consider their alliance with trans women to be essential for their own liberation." Quoted in Emi Koyama's "The Transfeminist Manifesto," in Rory Dicker and Alison Piepmeier, eds., *Catching a Wave: Reclaiming Feminism for the 21st Century,* Boston, MA: Northeastern University Press, 2003, 244-262. http://eminism.org/readings/pdf-rdg/tfmanifesto.pdf. See also https://en.wikipedia.org/wiki/Transfeminism; and: Intersectional Bibliography.

[44] See: Dworkin, Andrea, *Woman Hating: A Radical Look at Sexuality,* New York, NY: E. P. Dutton, 1974.

[45] See Butler, Judith, *Gender Trouble: Feminism and the Subversion of Identity,* Abingdon, UK: Routledge (Taylor & Francis), 1989. See also Butler's *Bodies that Matter: On the Discursive Limits of Sex,* Routledge, 1993; and *Undoing Gender,* Routledge, 2004.

[46] "Femmephobia" is the fear or hatred of feminine (or effeminate) traits in a birth-assigned male (trans women, male crossdressers, drag queens)—or generally, of female aspects in transgender or cisgender women. Female-impersonator entertainers or gay-male queens performing drag are often exempt from such prejudice because their feminine (or effeminate) expression is contained within a safe milieu (either a gay club or a straight dinner theatre). See

also http://www.sjwiki.org/wiki/Femmephobia.

[47] Stone, Allucquére Rosanne (Sandy), "The 'Empire' Strikes Back: A Posttranssexual Manifesto," 1987. First version published in Kristina Straub and Julia Epstein, eds., *Body Guards: The Cultural Politics of Gender Ambiguity*, Abingdon, UK: Routledge (Taylor & Francis), 1991. Second version (rev.) published in "Camera Obscura," Spring, 1994. Electronic version published on ACTLab ftp site, January, 1994. Third version (text-only). http://sandystone.com/empire-strikes-back. Fourth version published April 9, 2014 in pdf and http versions. http://sandystone.com.

[48] Scott-Dixon, Krista, ed., *Trans/forming Feminisms: Trans-feminist Voices Speak Out*, Toronto, ON: Sumach Press (Canadian Scholars' Press), 2006. For contributors' names, see the Table of Contents. https://www.canadianscholars.ca/books/trans-forming-feminisms#tab_toc.

[49] For more information on the other presenters, see http://cfr.info.yorku.ca/transequity-past-present-and-possibilities-conference/.

[50] Miqqi (Michael) Gilbert co-founded Toronto's transgender group, Xpressions, in 1995 and directed Provincetown's Fantasia Fair from 2005 to 2014. S/he was a contributing editor of *The Transgender Tapestry* in the 2000s and has written scholarly articles on gender theory, including, Gilbert, M. A., "Defeating Bigenderism: Changing gender assumptions in the 21st century," *Hypatia: A Journal of Feminist Philosophy*, 2009, 24(3): 93-112. See the article featuring Miqqi Alicia by Gloria Kim, "Why Be Just One Sex?," *Maclean's* magazine, Sept. 12, 2005, 52-53. http://archive.macleans.ca/search?QueryTerm=Why+Be+Just+One+Sex%3F. And watch Miqqi's talk at the 2018 Moving Trans History Forward Transgender Archives conference (Elders Panel), https://www.uvic.ca/mthf (click "Past Conferences" tab). Miqqi's fonds are housed at The ArQuives. https://arquives.andornot.com/en/list?q=miqqi+gilbert&p=1&ps=20.

[51] See: Gilbert, Michael A., "The Feminist Crossdresser," in Scott-Dixon, *Trans/forming Feminisms*, 105-111.

[52] Dr. Virginia (Charles) Prince founded the Society for the Second Self (Tri-Ess) for male crossdressers in 1960, and was the founding editor of the *Transvestia* magazine from 1960 to 1980. See: Docter, Richard F., *From Man to Woman: The Transgender Journey of Virginia Prince*, Northridge, CA: Docter Press, 2004; and Ekins, Richard, and Dave King, "Virginia Prince: Pioneer of Transgendering," *International Journal of Transgenderism*, 2005, 8(4): 5-15, doi: 10.1300/J485v08n04_02. Co-published, Binghamton, NY: Haworth Medical Press, 2005. See also https://zagria.blogspot.ca/2013/03/virginia-prince-1912-2009-part-1-youth.html; https://zagria.blogspot.ca/2013/03/virginia-prince-part-ii-second-marriage.html; and https://zagria.blogspot.ca/2013/03/virginia-prince-part-iii-femmiphilic.html.

[53] Glenda René Jones was the founding editor of the *Journal of Male Feminism* (formerly *Hose and Heel*), published by the International Alliance for Male Feminism, from 1977 to 1980.

[54] Gabriel, Davina Anne, ed., *TransSisters: The Journal of Transsexual Feminism*, Kansas City, KS: Skyclad Publishing, 1994-1995.

[55] Ross, Mirha-Soleil, and Xanthra Mackay, dirs., *Gender Troublemakers*, Toronto, ON: Vtape, 1993. The title of their porn video was a sardonic allusion to Judith Butler's 1989 book, *Gender Trouble: Feminism and the Subversion of Identity*, noted above.

[56] See: Bornstein, Kate, *Gender Outlaw: On Men, Women, and the Rest of Us*, Abingdon, UK: Routledge, 1994; and Bornstein, Kate, and S Bergman, eds., *Gender Outlaws: The Next Generation*, New York, NY: Seal Press, 2010.

[57] See: Courvant, Diana, "Speaking of Privilege," in Gloria Anzaldua and AnaLouise Keating, eds., *This Bridge We Call Home: Radical Visions for Transformation*. Routledge, 2002, 458-462.

[58] Intersex activist and trans ally, Emi Koyama, wrote the "Transfeminist Manifesto" (2001, rev. 2003). See note above on "transfeminism" for full citation.

[59] See: Pichette, Jade, "Challenging Transmisogyny: From the Classroom to Social Work Practice," in Susan Hillock and Nick J. Mulé, eds., *Queering Social Work Education*, Vancouver: UBC Press, 2016, 148-161. Jade is now the program manager at Pride at Work Canada.

[60] In response to a backlash by some French-Canadian feminists, Quebec Women's Federation new trans-female president, Gabrielle Bouchard, says her "job is to represent all experiences, for all women." http://www.cbc.ca/news/canada/montreal/quebec-federation-women-gabrielle-bouchard-1.4441395.

[61] See French-Canadian, Quebec Mayor Julie Lemieux's photograph https://www.ctvnews.ca/politics/small-quebec-municipality-elects-canada-s-first-openly-transgender-mayor-1.3673643.

[62] Sadly, in 2017, some trans women (like Tara Wolf and others in London, UK), have reacted to trans-exclusionary radical feminists (TERFs), with physical violence, and were subsequently convicted of assault. In 2018, an American trans art collective (The Degenderettes) displayed a tee-shirt in the San Francisco Library exhibition (with the words, "I punch TERFs," on it, and splattered with red dye to imitate blood) which had been worn by singer Mya Byrne during a pride parade. The art exhibition also displayed axes and baseball bats, some covered in barbed wire, painted in the colours of the transgender pride flag. After complaints, the library removed the tee-shirt, but not the other items. https://en.wikipedia.org/wiki/Feminist_views_on_transgender_topics#Feminist_exclusion_of_trans_women.

[63] Read Georgina's story (written with Cathy Casey), *Change for the Better: The Story of Georgina Beyer* (Abingdon, UK: Random House, 1999), which was adapted into a 2001 documentary film, *Georgie Girl*, produced by Annie Goldson and Peter Wells. See also https://zagria.blogspot.ca/2013/01/georgina-beyer-1957-actress-sex-worker.html. Georgina successfully underwent a kidney transplant in March 2017 and subsequently retired from an eight-year political career spanning both municipal and federal politics since 1995.

[64] McLaughlin, Matthew, dir.; and Barb Perry and D. Ryan Dyck, prods., *Courage in the Face of Hate*, Toronto, ON: Bulldog productions, 2012. Produced for the Egale Canada Human Rights, http://courageinthefaceofhate.ca/.

[65] "Gender-creative" and "gender-independent" are recent popular adjectives to describe gender non-binary children (expressing a gender beyond male or female, masculine or feminine)—who might or might not grow up to be transgender. See the Montreal peer-support group, Gender Creative Kids Canada. http://gendercreativekids.ca/.

[66] *Victor/Victoria* is a 1982, British-American, musical comedy, directed by Blake Edwards and produced by Tony Adams. It is a remake of the 1933 German film, *Viktor und Viktoria*. In 1995, it was adapted as a Broadway musical. Like its predecessor, *The Rocky Horror Picture Show* (1975), *Victor/Victoria* is a cult classic within the trans and queer communities because both films foreground bigenderism (dual gender expression) or transgenderism, and transvestism (crossdressing). What distinguishes the 1933 and 1982 films from other impersonation movies (like *La Cage aux Folles*) is the double-entendre of a *woman* playing a man impersonating a woman, thereby, making this female impersonator (Julie Andrews starring as both "Victoria Grant" and "Count Victor Grazinski") unique. See https://en.wikipedia.org/wiki/Victor/Victoria.

[67] When I was 13, I sent a letter to Julie Andrews (in care of her fan club) confiding in her that I was really a boy in a girl's body, and that I was in love with her. I signed the letter, "Robin Hood" (my fantasy alter ego at the time). Disappointingly, she never replied, but I did receive her autographed publicity photo.

5. Metamorphosis…More Schooling…A Special Friendship (1982–1988)

It was February 1982 (my 30th birthday) and time for a change. Last December, I'd finally outgrown FACT, wanting to redirect my support to trans men exclusively (although I still remained a volunteer peer counsellor with FACT Toronto until 1986). So, I founded a new counselling and educational service, Metamorphosis, incorporating it the following year as the Metamorphosis Medical Research Foundation (MMRF). The mandate was, firstly, to educate transsexual men on the latest medical developments about phalloplasty around the world and, secondly, to secure funds for medical-technological research, similar to Dr. Tony Tornabene's earlier aborted attempt to design and manufacture a non-surgical prosthetic penis for trans-males. Towards this end, I compiled a confidential research questionnaire to collect generic data about female-to-male transsexuals and their stated wish for phalloplasty or a viable non-surgical alternative. I also contacted American Medical Systems Inc. in Minneapolis and the Mayo Clinic in Rochester, inquiring about penile prosthetic research, but neither responded. Sadly, MMRF was unable to obtain funding because we couldn't meet the criteria for registered charitable status. To partially compensate, however, I did an excellent job of providing comprehensive information on phalloplasty surgeons, techniques, costs, surgical outcomes, and patient testimonials. A third organizational objective was to provide supportive counselling for trans men and their partners in terms of overall gender transitioning. My motto was: Peer-experienced is the best counsellor. I joined the Harry Benjamin International Gender Dysphoria Association (HBIGDA) to network with gender professionals worldwide. I published a regular periodical, *Metamorphosis: The Newsletter Exclusively for F-M Men*, which sported our logo (the Tao symbol superimposed on the trans logo) and put out a confidential contacts directory so that our trans-male members across North America (and the few we had in the UK, Ireland, continental Europe, Australia, and New Zealand, as well as one or two in Latin America, Asia, Africa and the Middle East) could make meaningful connections in person or by correspondence.

I was President and Susan Huxford-Westall generously agreed to be Secretary-Treasurer. We held our Annual General Meetings (AGMs) at The 519 Community Centre in the Gay Village at the corner of Church and Wellesley. One of our AGMs featured a post-meeting city tour on a vintage 1928 Peter Witt streetcar, for which two couples from the USA showed up. In fact, most of our MMRF members and newsletter subscribers were American. By 1986, my original bi-weekly, eight page newsletter had morphed into a 24 page, quarterly *Metamorphosis Magazine*. Our new logo had the figure of a man inside the male symbol, inscribed with our organizational motto: Towards male integrity.

My specialized service for trans men was the only one of its kind in the world at that time—exceeding even Dr. Tony Tornabene's American-based service in terms of my international scope and information-packed periodical until Lou Sullivan founded FTM, which later morphed into FTM International, in San Francisco nearly five years later in December 1986.[1] Lou and I were the hub for trans-male news and features, reprinting each other's pieces and poetry[2] in our respective newsletters and in later periodicals edited by other trans guys. I corresponded with female-to-male transsexuals around the world, although the majority were Canadian and American. As well as trans healthcare professionals and selected trans women, *Metamorphosis* profiled or mentioned various transsexual and intersex men from North America, the UK, Ireland, continental Europe, Australia, and New Zealand,[3] and also pioneering genderqueers like so-called "ex-transsexual" (Diane) Leslie Feinberg.[4] In addition to my trans-male-focussed newsletter, American trans men, such as Johnny Armstrong, Jerry Montgomery, Jude Patton, Dan Riley, and Lou Sullivan, and Englishman, Stephen Whittle, all published newsletters—a lifeline for transsexual men seeking peer-support before electronic bulletin boards emerged in the 1980s and list serves in the 1990s. To facilitate cross-country community building, we advertised our respective newsletters in each other's periodicals, and occasionally reprinted feature articles, book/film reviews, and letters to the editor.

Not surprisingly, I only received submissions for publication from a very few openly gay or bi trans men: namely, Lou Sullivan, initially a male-loving female-to-male crossdresser, who eventually evolved into a transhomosexual activist; Johnny Armstrong, who morphed from a butch dyke to a gay man to a drag king to a "regular" guy; Erik Julian Clarke, and Kwame (the only openly queer, Black trans man I knew back then—all from the USA. I also received private letters from a trans-male queer couple (like Eugene and me), as well as from four other American queer trans men (three White and one Black), who were then in the closet or on the down low. Two of these transqueers (now out), Khalil Jordache and Steven Wells, submitted several poems for inclusion in my 2017/2018 international trans poetry anthology (more on this later). In my newsletter, I also reprinted an American gay trans comic strip by David Kottler,[5] and the story of an out gay trans man in England named Dorian Carl Munday.[6]

Other than Eugene and myself, I didn't know of any other gay/bi trans men in Canada. I had privately disclosed my gay relationship with Eugene to Lou and several other gay/bi trans men. I also casually mentioned it in my 1983 profile, "My Male Metamorphosis: Man in the Making (A political and personal perspective)," which I published in my newsletter and some others around that time (a later, revised version appeared in Dr. Vern Bullough's 1997 book anthology).[7] I didn't explicitly mention my transqueer (or rather, pansexual) sexual identity, however, in my editorial responses to gay or bi trans men who wrote in to *Metamorphosis*, because I chose to not publicly out myself, wanting to go straight since I was now in a middle-class relationship with a professional, non-disclosing, transsexual woman. We were both leading a double life: out as trans to our local friends (trans men and their cis girlfriends/wives), but otherwise discreet in terms of the mainstream, cisgender, heterosexual world. This is why, in 1982, I regrettably categorically stated in the first issue of my newsletter—naïvely influenced by Tony Tornabene—that transsexual men were heterosexual: my aim being to distinguish them from masculine lesbians, who also liked women. This was my gestational period of heteronormativety and the normative gender binary, which dynamically changed over time (more on this later). Soon after receiving Erik Julian Clark's letter identifying as a gay trans man looking for like others, I reframed my narrow view of the sexual orientation of trans men to one which embraced trans homosexuality and trans bisexuality. I, then, opened up *Metamorphosis* to provide a safe forum not only for straight but also for gay and bi trans men seeking peer support. Moreover, in 1985, I wrote to the Harry Benjamin International Gender Dysphoria Association, asking them to address the issue of heterosexism at their next AGM, but received no response. The professional domain of sexology would not be fully open to non-cisheteronormative sexual identities and non-binary gender identities until the new millennium.

I met a lot of trans guys through *Metamorphosis* and some of them became friends. One became more than a friend. Kwame (who lived in Richmond, Virginia) and I became soul brothers, sharing our love for reading and writing, jazz, blues, R&B, and masculinity. He had a girlfriend at the time but was primarily focussed on men. We exchanged copious letters and I wanted to meet up during my trip along the American east coast meeting several other MMRF members. Sadly, he was away then visiting relatives and we wouldn't meet for another 10 years—a wasted decade! Both men of letters though, we continued our meaningful correspondence, rapturing over music, literature, and gay-male sexuality.

Kwame re-sparked my interest in African American authors and activists. I particularly enjoyed James Baldwin's gay-themed novel *Giovanni's Room* (1956), Alice Walker's lesbian love story, *The Color Purple* (1982), Zora Neale Hurston's autobiography, *Dust Tracks on a Road* (1942), and the sexual and racial poetry of queer writers Langston Hughes and Audrey Lorde. I was further enlightened around race and gender relations by Maya Angelou's seven-volume autobiography (starting with *I Know Why the Caged Bird Sings*, 1969, and ending with *Mom & Me,* 2013), and bell hooks' works on feminism, including, *Ain't I A Woman?: Black Women and Feminism* (1981). As well as the sociodynamics of Black queer identity and Black feminism, I learned about African American existentialism and critical theory: W.E.B. Du Bois's essays, *The Souls of Black Folk* (1897/1903), Ralph Ellison's novel, *Invisible Man* (1952), Toni Morrison's *Playing in the Dark: Whiteness and the Literary Imagination* (1992), and Richard Wright's *The Man Who Lived Underground* (1942).

I avidly read these authors works[8] to get a sense of where they came from, and where they were going in their personal, professional, and activist lives. I wanted to compare and contrast my own writings and activist works—with all of its unique challenges, defeats, and victories—with their respective political and artistic visions and achievements. What further intrigued me was the intersectionality of these multidimensional, Black, social change agents, incorporating race, nationality, class, sex, gender, and sexual orientation. I was also interested in their respective religious/spiritual beliefs, existential/humanist leanings, sexual/gender politics, and political ideologies. Such knowledge of other deep thinkers and doers would hopefully help me to break out of my isolated existence as a mixed-race, pansexual, gender-transgressive trans activist caught in a dominantly Judeo-Christian, cisgender, heteronormative society. It's damn lonely being an existential Outsider and a Gender Worker!

On the home front, Ruthie and I hosted house parties for trans guys and their wives/girlfriends (no openly queer trans men were locally around then). We had some good times. Sadly, we also had some bad times: namely, two suicides of MMRF members, David Aaron Liebman (18 years old) from Florida in 1984 and, later, Michael Elliot (in his late 30s) from Boston in 1988. After David took his life, his sister Maura sent me a poignant eulogical letter and several poems dedicated to her brother for publication in *Metamorphosis* and my international trans poetry anthology, respectively.[9] Michael had penned a memoir, *Crossing the Line* and had sent me the manuscript, asking if I could find a potential publisher. Regrettably, I was unsuccessful so it still languishes, unread by others, in my fonds at The ArQuives.[10] Neither of these deaths was due to dissatisfaction with gender transitioning. Multiple factors contributed to their individual senses of despair: clinical depression, chronic suicidality, and autism in David's case and early stages of cancer and impending divorce in Michael's. Additionally, poor body image plagued both men insofar as each desired genital surgery to enhance their male body image: unfortunately, at that time, penile surgical procedures were still experimental with variable outcomes. I never had the good fortune to meet David (although we wrote extensively) but I did meet Michael and his wife when they drove up to Toronto for one of our get-togethers.

In my trans activism, I alternately worked by myself and with Susan

Huxford-Westall (or others) depending on the circumstances. While I primarily served transsexual men and their loved ones, Susan and I also worked together to support trans women specifically, and trans people, generally. As stated earlier, I was an anomaly in this regard given that, at the time (1970s and 1980s), I was one of a tiny number of known trans-male activists—along with Jude Patton, Steve Dain, Jerry Montgomery, and Steve Parent—who were also committed to actively supporting trans women. Where was the solidarity with our trans sisters from the rest of my trans brothers?

The sociopolitical shift towards trans men caring for our trans sisters and eventually embracing a transfeminist ethic would not come for quite some years, gradually evolving over time. Just as gender/sexual identities can develop over time, so can gender/sexual politics. The personal often informs the political, and *vice versa*. Trans-male feminist perspectives are by no means monolithic, as evidenced by the diverse views put forth in recent (late 1990s into the 2000s) transfeminist anthologies by various spokespeople.[11] Sadly, I missed the call for papers for Scott-Dixon's 2006 *Trans/forming Feminisms* anthology (which includes several trans-male contributors). I would certainly have submitted a provocative piece on trans-male transmisogyny that would hopefully have encouraged a move towards trans-male transfeminism. Surprisingly, it took longer for some transsexual men—ironically, often former self-identified lesbian feminists—than others to ultimately embrace trans women as their rightful sisters. Promisingly, progress continues with the help of trans-female, trans-male, genderqueer, and even some cisgender feminists, particularly those of colour.

York University's 2006 Trans/Equity conference included four trans-male presenters: Dr. Aaron Devor, Zack Marshall, Syrus Marcus Ware, and me. My presentation was not specific to transfeminism, *per se*. Rather, it provided a brief overview of some of my past and recent advocacy efforts for trans women (and trans men), including my advocacy work with the Elizabeth Fry and John Howard Societies on behalf of pre-, mid- and post-transitional trans-male and trans-female prisoners and ex-prisoners in southern Ontario in the 1980s and, more recently, in the 2000s. The latter included my deposition to the City of Toronto's Community Advisory Committee on the Status of Women calling for greater inclusion of services for trans women in 2001; my critical input as a member of the Advisory Committee of the Asian Community AIDS Services' Transgender Women's Outreach Project (which primarily included sex workers) from 2003 to 2005; and the design and delivery of a community-development workshop for older transwomen (50+) at Sherbourne Health Centre in 2005; as well as some suggested goals and strategies for the future.

In the final analysis, trans men—as Dr. Nick Matte so poignantly points out in his 2017 chapter on me—must not fall into the traps of classism, (hetero)sexism, or transmisogyny, being ever mindful of negotiating our (newly) acquired male privilege—especially, if we publicly pass as cis or cis hetero men—in skillful ways so as not to perpetrate traditional cisgender male transmisogyny. We can only do this by being radically inclusive transfeminists, committed to respect for, and protection of, our trans sisters.

Not to detract from the vital urgency of anti-transmisogyny, we can go one step further in this discussion of anti-trans sexism and similarly condemn the transmisandry (a dislike of maleness in transgender men) perpetrated by some male crossdressers and transsexual women,[12] not to mention by many cisgender women and men. Although not quite parallel to transmisogyny—being less prevalent and less intense—trans men, notwithstanding, are also victimized by transphobic violence: witness the 1993 brutal rape and murder of 21-year-old, American trans man Brandon Teena. Following the legacy of earlier Black, queer feminists (womanists), Audrey Lorde and Alice Walker, contemporary African American, feminist, integrationist activist bell hooks[13] urges an all-embracing ethic of equity for *every* gender and *every* sex. We would do well to heed her call to action and extend this universal standard to also include *every* gender identity and *every* sexual orientation—as well as Indigeneity, race, ethnicity, nationality, culture, class, age, and (dis)ability.

One of the substantially underserved populations for which Susan and I advocated comprised trans people incarcerated in provincial or federal penitentiaries, as well as paroled ex-convicts. There were two, in particular. One was Jayson de Maeyer, a pre-transitional trans man, whom I visited in the Prison for Women (P4W) in Kingston, Ontario at the request of his cisgender girlfriend (who was also incarcerated there) and who wrote about his life inside a female prison for *Metamorphosis Magazine*.[14] The other was Katherine Johnson,[15] a mid-transitional trans woman, whom I also visited in P4W, before she requested a transfer to Millhaven Institution—an all-male maximum-security prison in Bath, Ontario—in order to be with her cis boyfriend who was incarcerated there. Susan and I did consulting work with the directors of the Elizabeth Fry Societies and the John Howard Societies, in Kingston, Ottawa, Toronto, Hamilton, and Kitchener. This consultation was followed by a professional development training session that we delivered to managers and frontline staff at a Canadian Association of Elizabeth Fry Societies (CAEFS) conference in 1984. Susan and I each drafted a proposal—one for trans women and one for trans men, respectively—recommending specific supports for the rehabilitation and imminent social reintegration of transsexual inmates still inside a penal institution, as well as those recently paroled or released. CAEFS Executive Director advised us she would consider incorporating our respective recommendations into their prisoner support programs. Along with Susan, and later on my own, I advocated for similar provisions for incarcerated trans women (many of whom were racially-profiled sex workers of colour or Indigenous, street-active women). More trans prison advocacy work would soon follow.

Even while operating MMRF, I never stopped serving the larger transgender community (including transsexual women, transgenderists, and male crossdressers) by providing extensive (North American) resources on medical, psychological, counselling, and legal services, as well as international trans support groups. Looking for a more efficient way to achieve this monumental task, I conceived another brainchild: a Gender Dysphoria Liaison Centre—my proposal for a publicly funded, trans-specific, information clearinghouse and community centre. Dr. Maxine Petersen,[16] then a pre-transitional trans woman and psychological associate at the Clarke's Adult Gender Identity Clinic, rejected me out of hand when I asked for a letter in support of my application to the City of Toronto for seed money to fund such a centre. I suppose I could have also asked Dr. Steiner, but I intuited that she was cut from the same cloth as most of the other Clarke clinicians: conservative, complacent, paternalistic, pathologizing. I then appealed to Dr. Michael Barrett, head of the Sex Information and Education Council of Canada. He wrote a letter all right: but, to my dismay, it was non-supportive, recommending *against* my proposal because I lacked professional experience! These powerbrokers invalidated my visionary initiative. Why should I have expected anything else? Dialectical Dancer that I am, I'm constantly straddling idealism and cynicism, ever-striving for the middle road of optimistic realism.

Beaten down once more—would I ever learn my lesson? Evidently not. I approached Raj Anand, Assistant Commissioner of the Ontario Human Rights Commission (OHRC), to ask if the OHRC would enact legislation to protect transsexuals, transgenderists, and transvestites. He pretty much brushed me off, saying that, insofar as the Commission had not received any complaints of discrimination or harassment against trans people, he did not perceive this population as a potential target for societal abuse. I later appealed to Evelyn Gigantes, the NDP MP for Ottawa-Centre, who informed me that a pre-surgical trans man had approached her for assistance to change his legal sex-designation on his identification. I asked her if she would appeal to the OHRC to amend the Ontario Human Rights Code to include gender identity as a protected ground against discrimination. Unfortunately, she vacillated inasmuch as she was on her way out of politics and, therefore, hesitant to take up the fight—bad timing, again! Not to be thwarted, however, I then reached out to Svend Robinson, the NDP MP for Vancouver-Burnaby, BC, who was the first Canadian MP to come out as gay in 1988. At first, he was eager to take up my fight, but his enthusiasm quickly waned because he told me he was going through a period of burnout. Alas, we were both suffering from chronic compassion fatigue! So, in sheer frustration, I gave up. Why do all these politicians (three in succession so far) either burn out or leave politics just when I need them?! Governmental gears grind ever so slowly, so we trans Canadians had to wait another three decades to finally win our political rights as equal citizens—with amendments to the Ontario Human Rights Code (2012), the British Columbia Human Rights Code (2016), and the Canadian Human Rights Act (2015, 2017) (see chapter 11).

So far, 1984 had been a year of disappointments—with the exception of my trans prisoner advocacy work—badly bruising my ego. But, my confidence remained unshaken as I waited for things to look up. Two years later, they did—twofold! My American transgender therapist colleague Dr. Roger Peo[17] nominated me for inclusion in *The International Who's Who in Sexology* (First Edition) (1986), compiled by The Institute for Advanced Study of Human Sexuality in San Francisco. This was my first formal recognition by my professional peers in the then controversial discipline of sexology. I had finally arrived as a contender on the professional scene. Look out world of science, Rupert Raj is here!

My second public acknowledgement was the Man of the Year Award, created especially for me by Sharon Ann Stuart and co-organizers of the annual Spring Fling! for crossdressers and transsexuals. The event was organized by the Gateway Gender Alliance's Chicago chapter in 1986 and I let the cooling breeze of that windy city waft over me as I gratefully accepted my award.

All work and unpaid activism makes Rupert a compromised academic. So, later that year, I gravitated once again towards further education. I enrolled in journalism at Humber College. The dawn of the computer age, one day students were using electric typewriters and the next they were word processing on computers. You should have heard the blue smoke (cursing) when we forgot to save our WordStar files before shutting off the computer! I decided to buy a Compudor 640K computer for MMRF to produce my *Metamorphosis Magazine* and the myriad letters I had to write. After my first year of the journalism program, I switched to the public relations program because I was intrigued by the whole liaising with the public thing, whether corporate or government. I earned my public relations certificate in 1986. I spent $200 photocopying 400 résumés and mailing these to public relations firms and communications departments in the Greater Toronto Area. The few government interviewers I saw preferred a woman or a person of colour (I was the "wrong sex" and also invisible as a White-appearing male). Other positions required either fluent French or possession of a car. Neither was viable for me, being an Anglophone who could not afford a vehicle. Back to the drawing board!

Meanwhile, like James Baldwin and other activist writers, my activism continued as the righteous fires for social justice alternatively raged and smouldered. I, too, was both activist and writer—and also researcher and educator—as they often intersect. At this time, my writing consisted of articles for *Metamorphosis Magazine* and *The TV/TS Tapestry Journal* (later renamed *The Transgender Tapestry*), as well as the compilation of my international trans poetry anthology, *Of Souls and Roles, Of Genes and Gender: A Treasury of Transsexual, Transgenderist, and Transvestite Verse*,[18] which I had begun in 1982. This compilation consisted of nearly 400 poems from 170 people from Canada, the USA, the UK, Ireland, Australia, and New Zealand. I was very excited about this project because it was awesome to be entrusted with the raw emotions (some tragic, some comic) of people from all over the world experiencing gender conflict or confusion (gender dysphoria), and hopefully also, gender resolution (gender euphoria). My American friend, Kim Elizabeth Stuart,[19] wrote the foreword. It was a six-year labour of love—sporadically, adding several more poems over the next three years—and my first full-length work. Shortly afterwards (in 1991), I began my life story, which I soon shelved because, at the time, it was still too triggering to write about all those often traumatic past events. I ultimately resumed this arduous (and oh so bittersweet) task 22 years later in my pre-retirement years.

In addition to my own writing projects, I engaged with others in trans-focussed research initiatives.

The first was inspired by my idea to compile a transgender encyclopedia. A couple of queer encyclopedias existed, but they barely mentioned trans people or events. I embarked on this ambitious endeavour with a trans friend. We began to create biographical entries for trans people worldwide by gleaning morsels of information from books about, and periodicals by, transsexual, transgenderist, and transvestite people, as well as written responses to a mailed research questionnaire. Not too far along though, we abandoned the project, daunted by the sheer magnitude of the task, not having the modern convenience of the Internet. Oh well., Wikipedia came along a couple of decades later, rendering the need for a print encyclopedia irrelevant and saving me years of even more unpaid work!

The second consisted of helping my professor friend, Dr. Aaron Devor, recruit research subjects (including me) for his second book, *FTM: Female-to-Male Transsexuals in Society* (1997). Some years earlier (in 1989), I had positively reviewed his first book about women passing as men: *Gender Blending: Confronting the Limits of Duality*:[20] but, Indiana University Press was not sufficiently impressed to publish my review. I had arranged for a place at my friend's apartment for Aaron to interview several local transsexual men inasmuch as he was travelling to Toronto and other North American cities to collect research data for his book. I wanted to offer my own residence in the interest of scientific research, but my lesbophobic trans-male roommate forbade me to allow a lesbian—as pre-transition Devor appeared to the world until he transitioned as Aaron in 2002 at age 51—to defile our home! My roommate was unaware of Aaron's real (trans-male) gender identity, but he might still have objected because Aaron did not present publicly as male at the time. Not only was transphobia rampant within the lesbian community, lesbophobia was prevalent in the trans community. These border wars between trans men and dykes waged not only in Toronto, Montreal, and Vancouver, but also in New York, Los Angeles, and San Francisco—and beyond into the UK, Ireland, Australia, and New Zealand—each group competing for personal and political identity, self-empowerment, and communal space, firing off almost volatile identity politics or queer theory as ammunition. Even now, in the 2000s, a recent casualty of war was my then transitioning, trans-male friend, who was ousted from the lesbian-only motorcycle club (the Amazons) in Toronto by two trans dykes because he was no longer female, even though he had co-founded the club as a former butch dyke! A tragic example of transmisandry by our (lesbian) trans sisters! Why didn't they have the generosity of spirit to grandparent him and let him stay on as an ally and mascot?

It's bad enough that many cisgender individuals are transphobic, but I cringe in shame when my trans peers exhibit similar reactionary behaviour! I understand the fear, anger, guilt, and shame derived from internalized transphobia, but projected hatred is, nonetheless, unconscionable. Nowadays, more straight trans people are confronting their societally programmed homophobia, lesbophobia, and biphobia, learning how to negotiate private and shared spaces with cisgender queers—and vice versa. One success story is Pride Toronto's Trans* Pride Team—originated by Luka Sidaravicius, Evana Ortigoza, Den Temin, and others—which worked closely with the historically cisgender Pride Toronto Board[21] in 2013 and 2014 to create a sustainable Trans* Pride March, Trans* Community Fair, and Trans* Space as annual events within the LGBTTI2SQQAA community. When Aaron's groundbreaking, transpositive FTM book (in diametric opposition to Dr. Lothstein's transphobic text) finally came out, he formally acknowledged (in print) my small part in bringing together several interview participants. Collaborative research efforts can pay off.

Besides Aaron and Susan, I intellectually engaged with my trans woman friend, Denise Hudson, who carried on FACT Toronto and its newsletter (*Transition*) until they both folded in 1986. Before she left Toronto with her husband for greener pastures in 1991, Denise and I had some intriguing talks about all things transsexual and transvestic, while sampling tasty pastry and a glass of wine to prime the pump at the Queen Mother Café. Susan had recently moved back to Hamilton and in 1987, she launched a new counselling, educational, and research service, GenderServe, and edited its newsletter.

Transsexuals, transgenderists, and transvestites were prolific when it came to publishing periodicals, although some of the early ones lacked a masthead naming the editor(s) and the year—an unfortunate form of unintentional erasure. Back then, print was the primary medium for information dissemination and community connection: very labour-intensive and sometimes costly. Now, it's electronic media; virtually effortless and free!

I attended the last FACT Toronto meeting on September 13, 1986, which seceded from the parent FACT organization that day to become a new group, Transition Toronto—soon after renamed Transition Support.[22] It was one of the longest-running, active trans groups in Canada—formed not too long after the two Montreal groups, *L'Aide aux Transsexuel(le)s du Québec* (ATQ) and *Travestis à Montréal* (TAM), started in 1980, and before the Ottawa-Gatineau group, Gender Mosaic/*Mosaiques de Genres*[23] began in 1988. Notwithstanding, peer-support and advocacy groups for transsexual/transgender French Canadians has played a vital role for the past four decades, and continues to the present. At this auspicious meeting, I met Marg, a trans woman who would play a major role in my life two years down the road. Overall, FACT had had a good eight year run, starting in Calgary in 1978 as a dedicated Canadian association and ending in Toronto in 1986 as a joint Canadian-American federation. The other chapters had already started to wind down after Susan's resignation in February 1986. We gave her a send-off at FACT Toronto's combined retirement celebration and Valentine's Day party at The 519. After the Transition Support co-founders declined my offer to merge their new group with MMRF, I accepted a goodwill position as Transition Support Liaison Coordinator, liaising between our two groups in terms of shared events and promotion of our respective services to potential new members.

MMRF finally found a holistic health promoter, Gosnell Duncan from Brooklyn, NY, who created a prototype prosthetic penis (a peeing packer) as an alternative to phalloplasty for trans men. I and two other MMRF members tested it out, giving our critical input to Gosnell, who made minor modifications and sent us a second prototype. We tested this model, but the limitations—lack of durability and stiffness during penetration, and uric acid eating through the rubber penis following urination—seemed insurmountable given the state of genitourinary technology at the time. We were deflated at the poor outcome because this was one of the primary purposes of the Metamorphosis Medical Research Foundation. Our dream was shattered!

Trans warrior that I was, I picked up the pieces of my disillusionment. There was still the bigger battle of improving quality of life for all trans people, not only trans men. I decided to continue my advocacy efforts for prisoners and ex-prisoners by accepting the invitation of Michael J. Ashford (a gender dysphoric, birth-assigned male incarcerated in a Marysville, Ohio prison), to help facilitate his brainchild, Transsexuals In Prison (TIP), a correspondence network to link up trans inmates across North America. Members would receive the *TIP* newsletter as well as a complimentary subscription to *Metamorphosis Magazine*. Classism[24] was—and sadly, still is—prevalent within the trans community, and I received flak from several trans men and their wives for dabbling with prisoners, My comeback to these elitists was the poignant piece, "First They Came...,"[25] penned by German Lutheran Pastor Martin Niemöller (1892-1984), which mentions the persecution by the dominant group (Nazis) of vulnerable minority groups—socialists, trade unionists, and Jews—who dared to speak out against the immoral majority. The author ends the poem with himself as the final victim: "And there was no one left to speak for me." I later adapted this powerful plea for radical inclusivity, adding into the mix our diverse human family of gay, lesbian, bisexual, transsexual, transvestite, transgender, and intersex people. I can't recall if my focus was then wide enough to include *Hijra* and Two-Spirit people, and those who identified as transensual, pansexual, or asexual.[26] In Canada, PASAN (Prisoners with HIV/AIDS Support Action Network) supports transgender prisoners and parolees, and Black trans-male activist, Syrus Marcus Ware, founder of the Prison Justice Action Committee in the 2000s, lobbies for prison reform for racially-profiled Canadian inmates and those with disabilities.[27]

On November 3, 1986, I appeared with my sister on *The Sally Jessy Raphael Show*[28] along with my trans activist friend, Sister Mary Elizabeth Clark (Joanna Clark) and her father, Dr. Nancy Ledins[29] (an ex-priest who gender reassigned as female), and our cisgender ally Tomye Kelley (director of the Gender Identity Center of Colorado). Wearing my light blue, three-piece suit, I was nervous as hell because this was my first encounter with a big-name talk show host on American television. The producer assured us that the show's tone would be normalizing and affirming: however, although trans-friendly overall, it was still sensationalist, exoticizing "sex changes" while minimizing the real lives and challenges of trans people and their loved ones. Dismayed, Arjuna sent a letter of complaint to the program's producers critiquing their (in her view) mistreatment of serious topics like gender dysphoria and gender reassignment. I, too, did not expect such a questionable treatment insofar as my talk show experiences in Canada up to that point had been respectful and sensitive. I vowed to never again let some talk show diva diminish my reality or that of my loved ones, even for the sake of public education. Consequently, I have only appeared on a few radio and television shows since. I did make the mistake though, in 2004, naïvely trusting the producers to do a fair portrayal of their planned episode for the Canadian CBC-TV newsmagazine, *The Fifth Estate: Becoming Ayden*.[30] Totally unexpectedly, however, the program trashed the featured trans teenager, Ayden Scheim, and the medical director of Sherbourne Health Centre (SHC) where I was working as a mental health counsellor in the LGBT program. The show's assistant producer (a lesbian) promised to portray trans people and SHC in a positive light. Instead, the centre came off looking like a back-street abortion clinic: whereas, CAMH's Adult Gender Identity Clinic was depicted as transpositive, despite being anything but!

The Sally Jessy Raphael Show was filmed on location in New Haven, Connecticut, so I was able to reconnect with Rev. Canon Clinton R. Jones who came to watch the live show. Rev. Jones was a long-time canon of Hartford's Christ Church Cathedral and an affiliate of the Gender Identity Center of New England. He staunchly supported the Twenty (XX) Club, a hub for New England's trans community. He was a rare example of a transpositive, religionist, cisgender ally.

Following my disappointing efforts with American media, I nonetheless persevered in my trans advocacy south of the border. I was elected first alternate to the Board of Directors of the International Foundation for Gender Education (IFGE) in 1987, having already served on the Steering Committee (from 1983 to 1985) of its predecessor, the Tiffany Club of New England. I attended the IFGE conference in Wayland, Massachusetts, where, I finally met a number of my network correspondents:[31] primarily male-to-female transsexual and transgenderist activists, the iconic movers and shakers of early trans organizing in North America. I also crossed paths with two iconic male crossdressers: Carol Beecroft[32] and Dr. Virginia (Charles) Prince,[33] co-founders (in 1960) of the Society for the Second Self (Tri-Ess)—formerly the Foundation for Personality Expression (FPE). Virginia published the *Transvestia* magazine and wrote several books for male transvestites and their wives. She condemned psychiatry's pathologization of men who dressed in female clothing but castigated transsexual women for transitioning to the female sex! She conspiratorially professed to me that, in her opinion, most post-op male-to-female transsexuals ended up badly after sex reassignment surgery; whereas, in general, most females-to-males fared better after surgery. I voiced my disagreement but she was adamant. Naturally, she was lambasted by the T-community for her transsexual-unfriendly views. Prince's prejudice is yet another example of transmisogyny, similar to Dr. Tony Tornabene's condemnation of trans women. Ironically, as a church-going Christian, Tony was admired by Susan Huxford-Westall (a devout Anglican); yet she, too, was guilty of selective transmisandry, saying some untrue and unkind things about me and another trans man—and even sent character-assassinating letters about us to our partners! Evidently, anti-oppression analysis was not prevalent until some decades later. Still, even today, I see a glaring gap between principle and practice, and recoil at the gender and sexual policing within the queer cisgender *and* transgender communities!

I served only a year on the IFGE Board, departing its ranks early on as I felt somewhat erased—perhaps because I was the only trans man at the table and not always assertive enough when confronting the overpowering personalities of some of the more domineering divas. Most of the male transvestites and transsexual women were lovely, but it only takes a few bad apples to spoil the barrel. I fully admit my shortcomings as an often-unassertive advocate: however, I was still fairly new to down and dirty trans politicking, something of a late developer when it came to skilled negotiation and conflict resolution. But, I would learn, in time.

In January 1987, Denise and I travelled to New York City to attend the one year anniversary of the death of our beloved Dr. Benjamin, fondly dubbed the father of transsexuals. Dr. Harry Benjamin was born in Berlin on January 12, 1885 and died on August 24, 1986 at 101 years of age. This compassionate physician had served as an architect of hope for countless trans people across Europe and North America since 1948, including many famous early transsexuals. Sadly, I never got to meet the good doctor but, in 1985, he sent me a copy of his book on transsexualism, signing it, "In praise of your work." He also lent me a photograph of him to reprint when I profiled him in my newsletter. At the celebration, we mingled with many notable sexologists:[34] but, disappointingly, we weren't able to engage with the shy, trans ophthalmologist, Dr. Renée Richards.[35]

Metamorphosis Medical Research Foundation ran for six years, officially winding up May 31, 1988. I was so burned out that I should have checked into a hospital: but, I carried on as usual. The residue of this debilitating compassion fatigue fired me up, some years later, to write a book chapter on trans activism and burnout in order to help activists develop effective preventative and ameliorative strategies (more on this later). Sadly, nobody was willing, or able, to take over from me; thereby, leaving a huge gap. There would be no dedicated group specifically for trans men in Canada until the BC FTM Network[36] was founded in Vancouver nine years later in 1997—soon followed by the formation of my trans-male group in Toronto in 1999. The non-sustainability of trans community resources back then was a crying shame! Just before we folded, the Lesbian and Gay Community Appeal (now Community One Foundation)[37] donated $200 to our cause. At least some cis gay men and women thought us trans guys were cool dudes!

Chapter 5 Notes

[1] "Trans cultural imperialism"—appropriation or erasure of trans Canadians (and also of trans Britons, Australians and New Zealanders, not to mention *Hijra* Bangladeshis, East Indians, Nepalese, and Pakistanis)—by trans Americans is disconcertingly prevalent even now, but especially so in the early days. Is this due to zenophobia, Americentrism, or merely ignorance of the world at large? Typically, the AmericentricWikipedia provides scant coverage of Canadian and other non-American transgender, intersex, and Two-Spirit people, so I have recently provided University of Toronto history professor, Dr. Elspeth Brown, with the names of some 50 Canadian trans, intersex and Two-Spirit activists who are not—but should be—on Wikipedia. Moreover, I have noted several instances where Lou Sullivan was credited with founding the first FTM organization, despite the fact that my Metamorphosis counselling services for female-to-male transsexuals was founded in February 1982—and incorporated as the Metamorphosis Medical Research Foundation in 1983—and ran until the end of May 1988. My *Metamorphosis* Newsletter, cum *Metamorphosis Magazine*, also ran regularly during that time. Lou founded the FTM group and its newsletter in 1987, which later became the *FTM International Newsletter* circa 1994. My point here is not to detract from Lou's remarkable achievements on behalf of transsexual men until his untimely death in 1991—especially his expanded outreach of FTM to international proportions, and his pioneering portrayal of gay trans men in print and audiovisual media. Sadly, though, this cultural erasure of trans Canadians is not limited to trans Americans insofar as even some trans Britons have presumably unintentionally perpetuated the historical mis-fact that Lou's FTM group was the premier organization for trans men in the world, thereby obviating both Tony Tornabene's Labyrinth Foundation Counseling Service established in Yonkers, New York circa 1969, and my Metamorphosis counselling services formed in Toronto in 1982. Conversely, thanks to American trans activists/historians Dr. Jamison Green, Dr. Susan Stryker, and Dr. Brice Smith (and, to some extent, Garin Wiggins, Mac Amos and Rocco Kayiatos), and Canadian trans historians Dr. Nick Matte and Dr. Elspeth Brown (a cis ally), the record has finally been set straight in terms of the true sequence of events of trans-male historical activism in North America! For more on American trans cultural imperialism, see the notes in chapter 9 and chapter 12. And, I hate to admit that even some trans Canadians are culpable when it comes to presumably unintentionally dis-acknowledging their Canadian trans predecessors! See note below on Gender Mosaic.

[2] For example, I am almost certain that Lou Sullivan's poem, "From A Female-To-Male To The Girl Within," premièred in *Metamorphosis*, April 1983, vol. 2(2), reprinted in my international trans poetry anthology, Raj, Rupert, ed., "Of Souls & Roles, Of Sex & Gender: A Treasury of Transsexual, Transgenderist & Transvestic Verse from 1967 to 1991," unpublished, Jan. 1, 2017, rev. July 1, 2018, 154.
https://www.uvic.ca/transgenderarchives/assets/docs/Rupert%20Raj%20anthology.pdf;
https://www.digitaltransgenderarchive.net/files/hm50tr87t.

[3] Mini bios of these transsexual men are included below. Except for the first person named (Canadian Aaron Devor) and the last two (Englishmen Mark Rees and Stephen Whittle), the others are American.

    Dr. Aaron Devor founded the world's largest Transgender Archives at the University of Victoria in BC in 2011, and was appointed World's First Chair in Transgender Studies in 2016. Aaron wrote/co-edited five books, including *Transgender Archives: Foundations for the Future*. Victoria, BC: University of Victoria Libraries—Special Collections, 2014.

http://transgenderarchives.ca/; and (with Ardel Haefel-Thomas), *Transgender: A Reference Handbook*, Santa Barbara, CA: ABC-CLIO, 2019. He was featured in a Canadian film documentary series, *Transforming Gender. (Firsthand*: Season 2015-2016, Episode 07), Ottawa, ON: CBC-TV, Nov. 26, 2016. http://www.cbc.ca/player/play/2679573123.

Johnny Armstrong (aka Johnny Science, etc.) (1955-2007) formed the F2M Fraternity, a group for transsexual men and female-to-male crossdressers, in Tenafly, NJ in the late 1980s, and edited its newsletter, *Rites of Passage*. He produced the 1989 musical porn video, *Linda/Les and Annie: The First Female-to-Male Transsexual Love Story*, with post-transitional trans man, Les Nichols, and cisgender porn star, Annie Sprinkle. http://www.vtape.org/video-catalogue-basic-search? See also https://zagria.blogspot.ca/2011/01/johnny-science-196-2007-musician.html.

Dr. Jason Cromwell, now a retired anthropology professor, wrote *Trans Men & FTMs: Identities, Bodies, Genders and Sexualities*, Chicago, IL: University of Illinois Press, 1999. In the 1980s, he facilitated a trans group at the Ingersoll Gender Center in Seattle, WA (established in 1977), which published the *Emerald City News*.

Steve Dain (1940-2007) was a girls' Physical Education teacher in Emeryville, CA, who was fired for transitioning to male, but then re-hired following his lawsuit for wrongful dismissal. He later counselled trans people in the San Francisco Bay area through his private practice. Steve was featured in director Lee Grant's 1985, HBO-TV, "America Undercover Series, *What Sex Am I?*, USA: Joseph Feury Productions, 2005. See also https://zagria.blogspot.ca/2009/11/steve-dain-1940-2007-gym-teacher-ftm.html.

Jerry Montgomery and his wife, Lynn, incorporated the Montgomery Medical and Psychological Institute for trans people in Decatur, GA in the 1980s, and edited its *Insight* newsletter.

Steve E. Parent co-led the Twenty (XX) Club for trans people in Hartford, CT (associated with the Gender Identity Center of New England) in the 1980s, and operated a private therapy practice (Transcend Counseling Services) in Springfield, MA. Steve passed away in his 40s sometime in the 1990s due to kidney failure.

Dan Riley (partner of trans woman Yvonne Cook-Riley) published *Adam's Word*, the short-lived newsletter of The Adam Society, a 1980s group for female-to-male transsexuals and female crossdressers in Waltham, MA.

Lou Sullivan also published the pioneering pamphlet, *Information for the Female-to-Male Crossdresser and Transsexual*, in 1980 (published by the Janus Information Facility in Galveston, TX). This was followed by a second expanded edition in 1985 (published by Zamot Graphic Productions in San Francisco, CA)—into which he had incorporated some additional resources from my 1983 unpublished document, "Information for the Female-to-Male Transsexual" (provided as a bonus to my Metamorphosis Medical Research Foundation members)—as well as illustrations and new historical data. I had invited Lou to co-edit his second booklet with me—making it a joint American-Canadian work—but he declined, wishing to retain sole ownership of the copyright. Too bad because our pooled resources would have benefitted FTMs in both countries. Later, in 1989, I revised my original 1983 document to an expanded introductory resource booklet, but for some reason, I never published it. In 1991, a third edition of Lou's booklet was published by the Ingersoll Gender Center in Seattle, WA. Some of these versions are preserved in The ArQuives.

Read Mark Rees's autobiography, *Dear Sir or Madam*, London, UK: Bloomsbury Publishing, 1996. See also https://zagria.blogspot.ca/2014/05/mark-rees-1942-part-i-sailor-dental.html; and https://zagria.blogspot.ca/2014/05/mark-rees-1942-part-ii-activist.html.

Dr. Stephen Whittle formed the FTM Network for British trans men in 1989 and edited its newsletter, *Boy's Own*. In 1992, he co-founded Press for Change, an advocacy group to lobby the UK government to reform laws for trans Britons. In 1998, he published a mini manual on gender transitioning for British trans men, *The White Book*, Manchester, UK: Press for Change (for the FTM Network). The August 5, 2002, BBC-Radio (Channel 4) documentary, *Make Me A Man*, followed his life as he underwent phalloplastic surgeries from 2001 to 2003. http://www.bbc.co.uk/radio4/womanshour/2002_32_mon_01.shtml. He was President of the World Professional Association for Transgender Health (WPATH) from 2007 to 2009. His publications include: Whittle, Stephen, *The Ultimate Practice Guide to Transgender and Transsexual Human Rights and Equality Law in the UK*, London, UK: Press for Change, 2016; and Stryker, Susan, and Stephen Whittle, eds., *The Transgender Studies Reader*, Abingdon, UK: Routledge (Taylor & Francis), 2006. Stephen was awarded an Order of the British Empire (OBE) in 2005. Regrettably, he had to cancel his scheduled participation at the 2018 Transgender Archives conference Elders' Panel due to a worsened condition of his multiple sclerosis.

[4] Diane Leslie Feinberg received a lot of criticism by many trans men for her 1980 *Journal of A Transsexual*, published by the World Workers Party in New York, NY. Leslie had undergone male hormone therapy and male chest constructive surgery only to later de-transition to become a feminist genderqueer woman, dropping hir first name, "Diane," and using the gender neutral prononouns "ze" and "hir." Leslie then became a champion of transsexual, as well as genderqueer, intersex and gender non-binary, people, co-founding (with Rikki Wilchins) Camp Trans in 1994 (see note in chapter 9). I initially distributed Feinberg's autobiographical journal of a misdiagnosed non-transsexual (hirself) to self-identified, pre-transitional trans men as a precautionary warning before taking the irreversible step of transitioning to the male sex in case the person was really, instead, a butch dyke. Soon afterwards, however, I discontinued this at the urging of Lou Sullivan, who persuasively argued that the anti-transsexual journal might deter truly transsexual men from transitioning.

[5] See David Kottler's transqueer cartoon, "I'm Me," in Gay Comix #3, published by Kitchen Sink Press in Princeton, WI in December 1982.

[6] Dorian Carl Munday reached out to other potential queer trans-males in his article, "Coming Out as a Gay Transsexual." Published in the *SHAFT (Self-Help Association for Transsexuals)* newsletter, August 1987. Reprinted in *Metamorphosis Magazine*, February 1988, 7(1).

[7] Raj, Rupert, "My Male Metamorphosis: Man in the Making (A personal and political perspective)," in Vern Bullough, Bonnie Bullough, and James Elias, eds., *Gender Blending*, Buffalo, NY: Prometheus Books, 1997, 480-484.

[8] For full citations of these Black writers, see: Intersectional Bibliography.

[9] Maura Liebman's eulogical letter for her deceased trans brother, reads as follows: "David was a beautiful person—too beautiful for the ugliness of the world. Someday, when I've collected myself enough, I'll write his story. I'm grateful to you for your help—thank you for reaching out to David. He admired and respected you and your work. I'm glad there are transsexuals who do make it. I just wish people weren't so judgemental and cruel. If there's something I can do to help, please let me know." Published in *Metamorphosis Magazine*, February 1985, 4(1). Read her three poems: "For David Aaron," "Fight It with Love" and "The End of Denial," in Raj, "Of Souls & Roles, Of Sex & Gender," 183-186. https://www.uvic.ca/transgenderarchives/assets/docs/of-souls-0-rolesj-of-sex-0-gender-revised-july-1j-2018---numbered.pdf; https://www.digitaltransgenderarchive.net/files/hm50tr87t.

[10] See: Elliot, Michael, *Crossing the Line*, unpublished, 1980s, in The Rupert Raj fonds, The ArQuives. https://arquives.andornot.com/en/list?q=Elliot%2C+michael&p=1&ps=20.

[11] These included: Canadian trans men, S. Bear Bergman, Joshua Goldberg, Dr. Dan Irving, Dr. Bobby Noble, Jake Pyne, Kyle Scanlon, and reese simpkins; and Canadian female-embodied, gender non-binary, transfeminist, Louis Esmé Cruz; American trans men, Jacob Anderson-Minshall, Pat Califia-Rice, Dr. Dean Spade, and Max Wolf Valerio; and American female-embodied, gender non-binary, transfeminist, Judith/Jack Halberstam. For a list of transfeminist writings from 1996 to 2015 by the aforementioned (and others), see the Intersectional Bibliography.

[12] In the early 1990s, IFGE's *TV-TS Tapestry Journal*'s editorial staff disputed whether or not to feature a transman on the magazine's front cover instead of its usual cover girl because most readers (male crossdressers, transwomen and cisgender admirers) preferred to see a feminine persona (and the more feminine, the better!). So, the staff were concerned about potential low retail sales. *The Tapestry*'s editorial mandate did (and does) not automatically exclude transmen or female crossdressers—as stated in its masthead: "for all persons interested in crossdressing and transsexualism"—so was this initial reluctance a case of transmisandry, or simply a dislike of masculinity (trans and cis) and a penchant for ultra-femininity? In any event, happily, then editor-in-chief, Vivian D. Allen, did issue a cover photo of transman, Taylor Montgomery, alongside cover girl, Michelle Lynn, in *The TV-TS Tapestry Journal*, 1993, (65). His cover story, "Or Do With It What You Will," was featured on page 30. https://www.digitaltransgenderarchive.net/files/w9505047s.

[13] See: hooks, bell, *Feminism is for Everybody: Passionate Politics*, Boston, MA: South End Press, 2000.

[14] See: de Maeyer, Jason, "The Incarcerated Pre-op Transsexual," *Metamorphosis Magazine*, May-June 1987, 6(3): 6-8.

[15] Katherine Ann Johnson (1949-2014) was doubly-imprisoned: as a woman trapped in a male body, who, in turn, was incarcerated in mostly Canadian male federal penitentiaries. Read her story (with Stephanie Castle), *Prisoner of Gender: A Transsexual and the System*, Vancouver, BC: Perceptions Press, 1997. On page 50, she mentions me (not by name, but by my then title of FACT Director) offering her ongoing support. Kathy wrote a piece, "Life on the Inside," for *Gender Review*, June 1981, (11): 4-5, and a poem (accompanied by a drawing), "Life in Jail," for *Gender Review*, June 1983, (3): 5. As our resident-artist, she drew illustrations for *Metamorphosis*.

[16] For more information on Dr. Maxine Petersen, see https://zagria.blogspot.ca/2011/07/maxine-petersen-195-psychologist.html.

[17] As one of a very few self-identified transvestite psychotherapists at the time, Dr. Roger Peo was selectively out and actively participated in the transvestite community, writing gender-affirming articles ("Roger's Notebook") for *The TV-TS Tapestry*, inspiring me, many years later, to publish my own "TransPositive Therapeutic Model" in 2002. See: Peo, Roger E, "The 'Origins' and 'Cures' for Transgender Behavior," *The TV-TS Tapestry*, 1984, (42). His Poughkeepsie, NY counselling service for transsexual women, male crossdressers and their wives was delightfully dubbed "Androgyny Unlimited," and had the same logo (a Tao symbol superimposed on the trans symbol) as mine for *Metamorphosis*. Great minds think alike!

[18] I later changed the anthology's name to "Of Souls & Roles, Of Sex & Gender: A Treasury of Transsexual, Transgenderist & Transvestic Verse from 1967 to 1991," incorporating the titles of two of its poems: "Of Souls & Roles" and "Sex & Gender" (see Appendix I). The unpublished manuscript was completed January 1, 2017, and slightly revised July 1, 2018. A free pdf is available online from the Transgender Archives. https://www.uvic.ca/transgenderarchives/assets/docs/of-souls-0-rolesj-of-sex-0-gender-revised-july-1j-2018---numbered.pdf; and the Digital Transgender Archive. https://www.digitaltransgenderarchive.net/files/hm50tr87t.

[19] Kim Stuart was one of the first lay people to write a research-based book on transsexual people, *The Uninvited Dilemma: A Question of Gender* (Portland, OR: Metamorphous Press, 1983), which also included a companion volume of the analyzed research data.

[20] Devor, Aaron H., *Gender Blending: Confronting the Limits of Duality*, Bloomington, IN: Indiana University Press, 1989.

[21] Trans women activists, Susan Gapka and Rachel Lauren Clark, have both been Pride Toronto Board members in the recent past, struggling to keep this chronically troubled organization trans-inclusive and trans-responsive in practice, not merely in principle. Rachel Clark is president of Queer Liberals, chair of Amnesty International's LGBTI Action Circle, a TD Bank Group technology strategist and a University of Toronto theology student. She was featured in *Toronto Life*, October 26, 2015. http://torontolife.com/city/life/what-its-like-to-be-transgender-in-toronto.

[22] The early founders of Transition Toronto (renamed Transition Support) included Carolyn Middleton, Connie R., and others. Shadmith Manzo has been facilitating the group from about 1999 to the present. The *Transition Support Newsletter* ran until 1989 and then changed its name to *Trans News*.

[23] According to its website, Gender Mosaic/*Mosaiques de Genres*, Inc. claims to be "Canada's oldest transgender social and support group which started out in 1988…a member of the Tri-Ess Society for the Second Self—a U.S. based organization." In August 2016, I wrote to Gender Mosaic's president and another group member, advising them of their factual misrepresentation—a minimization of their Canadian still-current predecessor groups—but am still awaiting a response. Sadly, trans Americans and Britons are not the only ones guilty of trans cultural appropriation or erasure!

[24] Ironically, I had also been guilty of classist views; not towards trans prisoners, but towards trans women who were strippers, sex workers, ex-prisoners, welfare recipients or psychiatric patients, and also towards female impersonators, as some pre-transitional, transsexual women have performed. I had expressed these views in an 1985 article, "Woman or Queen?," in *Metamorphosis*. See: Matte, Nicholas, "Rupert Raj, Transmen, and Sexuality: The Politics of Transnormativity in *Metamorphosis Magazine* during the 1980s," in Gentile, Kinsman, and Rankin, *We Still Demand!*, 117-136. Soon afterwards, I deeply regretted my incomprehensible, narrow-mindedness because I was, for the most part, Left-leaning and generally non-classist in my worldview, and thereafter espoused more-evolved identity politics, a paradigm shift towards radical acceptance.

[25] Many variations of Pastor Martin Niemöller's poem have been published in English. See https://en.wikipedia.org/wiki/First_they_came_.

[26] I know that I printed my trans/queer adaptation in some trans periodical, but disappointingly, I can't find it anywhere.

[27] See: Ware, Syrus, Joan Ruzsa, and Giselle Dias, "It Cannot be Fixed Because It Isn't Broken: Racism and Disability in the Prison Industrial Complex in Canada," in Liat Ben-Moshe, Chris Chapman, and Allison C. Carey, eds., *Disability Incarcerated: Imprisonment and Disability in the United States and Canada*, New York, NY: Palgrave Macmillan, 2014.

[28] *The Sally Jessy Raphael Show*, USA: Multimedia Entertainment. Aired November 3, 1986 on WTNH-TV in New Haven, CT.

[29] For more information on Dr. Nancy Ledins, see https://zagria.blogspot.ca/2008/11/nancy-ledins-1932-priest-electrologist.html.

[30] Caloz, Marie, and Andrew Culbert, prods., "Becoming Ayden," *Fifth Estate*, Ottawa, ON: CBC-TV. https://www.cbc.ca/fifth/episodes. Aired October 13, 2004. See also: Smith, Evan, "Hana Gartner Don't Know Trans: How I Got Bitten by a TV Documentary," *Xtra*, October 27, 2004. https://www---master-lcaulhwpdi2bg.us.platform.sh/hana-gartner-dont-know-trans-40794.

[31] These male-to-female transsexual/transgenderist activists are listed below:
    Then transgenderist, Merissa Sherrill Lynn (1942-2017), was co-founder of the Tiffany Club in 1978 and IFGE in 1986, and founding editor of *The TV/TS Tapestry*. She initially identified as a male-to-female transgenderist, but later re-identified as a transsexual woman, and surgically transitioned to female.
    Transsexual woman, Yvonne Cook-Riley co-founded IFGE, and co-edited the *The Tapestry*. For more information on Yvonne and the controversy over who coined the term "transgenderism," see https://zagria.blogspot.com/2011/09/tg-word-and-concepts-part-4-myth-that.html#.XTJIhXt7mik, https://zagria.blogspot.ca/2011/09/tg-word-and-concepts-part-4-myth-that.html, https://zagria.blogspot.ca/2011/09/tg-word-and-concepts-part-5-backlash.html, and https://zagria.blogspot.ca/2011/09/tg-word-and-concepts-part-6-conclusion.html (and the three preceding parts).
    Dr. Ariadne Kane is a former (openly crossdressing) gender therapist, who co-founded Fantasia Fair (an annual event for transvestite, transgenderist and transsexual people in Provincetown, MA) in 1973, and established the Outreach Institute for Gender Studies in 1975. She is also a Unitarian Universalist. Read her memoir, Kane, Ariadne (J. Ari), and Margot Wilson, *Gender Odyssey: Journey of an Intrepid Androgyne*, Victoria, BC: TransGender Publishing, forthcoming. See also https://zagria.blogspot.ca/2012/05/ariadne-kane-1936-teacher-activist.html.
    Then transgenderist, Dr. Sheila Kirk, was an endocrinological gynecologist/gynecological surgeon, who wrote medical manuals on hormone therapy for transgender patients. Sheila originally identified as transgenderist, then later, as transsexual, and underwent vaginoplasty. Dr. Kirk co-founded the Transgender Surgical and Medical Center in Pittsburgh. As clinic director (1998-2000), Dr. Kirk was the first transsexual physician/surgeon to offer gender-confirming surgery (GCS) to trans patients. Dr. Marci Bowers was the second transgender surgeon to perform GCS (in Trinidad, Colorado in 2003 and San Mateo, California in 2010), followed by trans GCS surgeon, Dr. Christine McGinn (in New Hope, Pennsylvania in 2007). Dr. Kirk also treated trans people with HIV/AIDS and co-

edited (with Dr. Walter Bockting) *Transgender and HIV: Risks, Prevention, and Care*, Binghamton, NY: Haworth Press, 2001.

Then transgenderist, JoAnn Roberts (1948-2013), was co-founder of the Renaissance Education Association in King of Prussia, Pennsylvania in 1987. She co-founded (with Cindy Martin and Jamie Faye Fenton) the online Transgender Forum in 1996 (which became TG Forum circa 2006). http://www.tgforum.com/. JoAnn wrote *Coping with Crossdressing: Tools & Strategies for Couples in Committed Relationships*, King of Prussia, PA: Creative Design Services, 1991 (rev. 1992, 1993).

[32] Tri-Ess Director Carol Beecroft edited the *Transvestia* magazine from 1980-1986 through Chevalier Publications (Los Angeles, CA), after Virginia Prince's run as editor from 1960 to 1980. There is a photo of Carol and me (sporting a full beard)—taken during the 1987 IFGE Convention—in my report, "Coming Together—Working Together: A Milestone in the Transgender Community," *The TV-TS Tapestry*, 1987, (50) 26-29. The photo also appears in this book, following chapter 8.

[33] See also: Docter, Richard F., *From Man to Woman: The Transgender Journey of Virginia Prince*, Northridge, CA: Doctor Press, 2004; and Ekins, Richard and Dave King, eds., "Virginia Prince: Pioneer of Transgendering," *International Journal of Transgenderism*, 2005, 8-(4): 1-15. Co-published, Binghamton, NY: Haworth Medical Press, 2005. See also https://zagria.blogspot.ca/2013/03/virginia-prince-1912-2009-part-1-youth.html, https://zagria.blogspot.ca/2013/03/virginia-prince-part-ii-second-marriage.html,and https://zagria.blogspot.ca/2013/03/virginia-prince-part-iii-femmiphilic.html.

[34] These notables included my one-time endocrinologist, Dr. Charles Ihlenfeld, as well as other American and European gender experts: Dr. Richard Green, Dr. Leah Schaefer, Dr. Christine Wheeler, Dr. Hans Lefeldt, Dr. Walter Futterweit, Dr. Joel Fort, Dr. Albert Ellis, and Garrett Oppenheim.

[35] Read Dr. Renée Richards' autobiography, *Second Serve: The Renée Richards Story* (with John Ames), New York, NY: Stein and Day, 1983. The book was adapted into a 1986 TV biopic of the same name, directed by Anthony Page. In her book sequel, *No Way Renée: The Second Half of My Notorious Life,* New York, NY: Simon & Schuster, 2007, Renée emphasizes her other identities as an eye doctor and a professional tennis player. A second docudrama, *Renée*, followed in 2011, directed by Eric Drath, in which she played herself.

[36] The BC FTM Network was co-facilitated by various trans men, including: Lukas Walther, Dr. Julian Young, Kevin W., Keenan P., and Joshua Goldberg. The group is still going today.

[37] Community One Foundation awards Rainbow Grants to the LGBTTIQQ2S communities, and each year, presents the Steinert-Ferreiro Award to an outstanding community member. http://communityone.ca/.

6. Gender Worker/Gender Consultants...First Marriage (1988–1990)

Even before I quite gave up MMRF, my brain had already jump-started another project several months before. I wanted to transition from a non-profit foundation to a profitable small business, offering gender consulting/ counselling services to trans people and crossdressers, as well as support to fellow gender resource providers (both lay peers and helping professionals). My inner entrepreneur had inevitably emerged as I was tired of working for free given that I was still only earning minimum wage in my day job. I also wanted to come full circle to support trans women and male crossdressers again, not just trans men and female crossdressers. Why can't I just stick to one thing? I suppose it's because I want to do it all. In September 1987, I established a private consulting firm, Gender Worker (with a new motto: "Working towards gender conflict resolution"). I also founded a 16-page *Gender NetWorker* newsletter, providing a resource for trans peer-counsellors as well as professional therapists, and gender clinicians. I reverted to my original combined Tao-trans symbol for the front-page logo. I announced my new consulting service at the 1988 IFGE convention (and described it in an editorial, "Not Quitting the Game—Just Switching Sides" in *The TV-TS Tapestry*),[1] advising of my dual shift, returning to an all-gender clientele with a fee-for-service payment structure, and introducing a professional networking communication service.

In my new capacity as a paid professional networking with other paid professionals, I published an editorial in *Gender NetWorker* "Healing the Breach: GD Consumers, Professional Providers Working Together."[2] In my editorial, I voiced my plea to gender clinicians and transsexual patients alike to make a commitment to work together within a collaborative professional relationship based on mutual trust. Such a trust relationship could help to repair the damage of decades of transphobic psychopathologizing by mental health and primary care practitioners and clinical social workers.

Earlier that month, I had asked IFGE's Board members if they would publish my international trans poetry anthology: but, even though they told me it had merit, they lacked funds to produce such a large publication. I was crushed! Six years of blood, sweat, and tears down the drain! I added several more poems over the next three years, and from 1992 to 1994, I pitched it to several transgender organizations—Dallas Denny's American Educational Gender Information Service (AEGIS), JoAnn Roberts's Creative Design Services, Marsha Botzer's Ingersoll Gender Center, and *FTM*'s newsletter editor, Kevin Horowitz, as well as three small Canadian presses—but all to no avail. So, I put it on the back burner until, ultimately, it re-emerged 20 years later (more about this later).

Around this time, the Clarke's Adult Gender Identity Clinic conducted a one-year pilot program for Ontario trans men seeking penile surgery (I was still holding off in hopes of future medical-technological improvements). Twelve trans guys were approved for OHIP coverage for phalloplasty. As there were no phalloplasty surgeons in Canada then, Canadian trans men had to cross the border to access one of these surgeons.³ All of the 12 trans men with whom I followed up post-surgically were quite satisfied psychosocially, if not 100% surgically. Some empirical outcome studies focus solely on surgical results (aesthetic appearance, urinary function, sexual performance), while others primarily measure psychosocial outcomes (enhanced body-image and self-esteem, improved quality of life personally, socially, and romantically). Several trans guys understandably had to return for surgical repairs because it would take years for genitoplastic surgeons to achieve better results. Unfortunately, the Clarke AGIC did not extend the pilot program to a permanent one because Dr. Steiner concluded that the surgical results were not good enough despite many trans-male patients' reporting overall satisfaction. This is yet another instance of trans patients being denied consumer choice around treatment options when it comes to emerging medical technology and experimental interventions. Too bad that MMRF's potential prosthetic penis had not worked out as a viable non-surgical solution! Timing and technology simply didn't coincide back then: however, relatively viable prosthetic penises for trans men would ultimately emerge in the USA and Germany in the 1990s, and, later, in the UK.⁴

As for my love life throughout my eight-year non-romance with Ruthie, I occasionally got a sexual itch and would indulge in one-night stands with trans or cis friends, but only when inebriated because if I had been sober, my guilt at cheating would certainly have impeded my pleasure. These brief encounters temporarily sated my lust, but never filled the underlying void that was crying out for a life-long relationship, combining emotional and sexual intimacy.

Then something happened to dispel my romantic blues: an invitation to our trans friend Marg's birthday party in Ottawa. A tax accountant with Revenue Canada, she was turning 40 and wanted to celebrate big time. That September (1988), as we took the train to the national capital, I had no inkling of the turn my life was about to take. Upon arriving, we embraced Marg and settled into the guest room of her townhouse. We had a blast with her other houseguests, especially a mutual trans man friend, Tyler, with whom Marg had just broken up. The original spark between Ruthie and I had long ago extinguished. Nonetheless, she reacted badly when I told her so, vindictively taking back the clothes and furniture she had given me and all the photographs of us together—her way of trying to eradicate our former relationship. Unrequited love is always painful!

But, another spark was soon to kindle between Marg and me. We had only met twice before but I knew that there was something there worth pursuing. I felt hopeful once more: romance was still within my grasp. Marg wanted to see me again during her upcoming business meeting in Toronto, so we met at the downtown Delta Chelsea Inn. Following some excruciating shyness, we professed our fondness for one another and began dating. After many long-distance phone calls, Marg invited me to come and live with her and her roommates for three months until she could get transferred to Toronto. In the interim, I would still hang onto my apartment, paying my roommate my rent portion so that Marg could move in with me on New Year's Eve. I was ecstatic: a new love at 36!

Marg wanted a transfer because her employer (the federal government) would not allow her to use the women's washroom in the building, even though she had filed a grievance with the Public Service Alliance of Canada and a complaint with the Ontario Human Rights Commission, seeking protection as a trans woman-in-transition (this was two decades before *"Toby's Act"* would become law in 2012). To Marg's dismay, her union did not adequately support her. She hired a lawyer and, ultimately, won her case and transferred to a similar post in Toronto. I was proud of Marg, who proved herself to be a successful self-advocate.

She had also proved effective as a community activist, having previously chaired FACT Ottawa for a while (even before we met). Now, as a gender consultant, she became my business partner as Gender Worker morphed into Gender Consultants. Earlier, while I was living in Marg's home in Ottawa, her transgender teenage roommate asked me, "How does one become a 'gender worker'?" I responded, "You just jump in and do what needs to be done, learning the skills as you go along." The required skills included: providing information, resources, peer-counselling, support, and advocacy to transsexuals, transgenderists, transvestites, and their loved ones; offering Trans 101 training to psychological, medical, and legal professionals in their offices and at formal seminars; and educating the public through mainstream and alternative media gender dysphoria and gender transitioning. So far, Marg and I had 12 paying clients—mostly local transsexual women, and male crossdressers and their wives—at $20 per hour. We also sponsored a voice-coaching workshop for 17 trans women in our home. Undaunted by national borders, two American couples (each consisting of a transsexual man and his wife) travelled all the way to Toronto to access our two-and-a-half-hour consultation and comprehensive resource package on reconstructive genital surgery (phalloplasty and metoidioplasty) for trans men. The lengthy consultation involved comparing the pros and cons of each of the two alternative surgical techniques, both still being experimental procedures.[5] We were one of a tiny number of providers (lay or professional) in North America to offer such a comprehensive specialty service for trans people, crossdressers, and their partners. I was gratified to finally be receiving financial remuneration after 15 years of unpaid community service! Money isn't everything but a paycheque sure is validating!

To supplement this meagre sideline, I needed a day job to pay the bills: so, I temped with Kelly Girls (later renamed Kelly Temporary Services as more men were hired) for several weeks. The gendered name of the employment agency was unfortunate, but I took it in stride, enduring razzing by a male acquaintance: "So, you're a Kelly Girl, right?" Stroking my beard for emphasis, my retort was appropriately abrasive: "Yeah right! Do I look like a girl to you?" My reprieve came when I got hired on permanently at CP Hotels' corporate office as a word processor. It was back to the business suit for me. I did not really like the work: but, it brought home steady pay until I could land something better. And there were perks: complimentary stays at CP heritage hotels across Canada from British Columbia to Newfoundland.

From the 1970s into the 2000s, I visited Montreal often (sometimes by myself and sometimes with Marg), hanging out with English and French Canadian trans activists[6] old and new, and with my trans woman friends, Lynne Pellerin (den mother for the T-girls), Janine (with her dog-sledding Huskies), and Jean and her cis wife Stella. I would often accompany my trans gal pals to Cléo's (Café Cléopâtre), an iconic cabaret and sex-club on rue Saint-Laurent, a haven for drag queens, female impersonators, transvestites, and transsexuals since the 1970s. We sipped highballs as we watched an outrageous drag show or shook our booties as we danced to the disco beat. One Christmas, I was invited to a yule log tea by some older trans girls in their 60s, all dolled up in greasepaint, teased hair, mini-skirts, and go-go boots, who still occasionally sold sexual favours for mad money. "Happy trans hookers"?[7]

That spring, Marg and I visited Jakub and his wife, Lilly, and their son in Pittsburgh. They welcomed Marg as my openly transsexual wife, having accepted my gender transition two decades earlier. I had already met Marg's brother, who unreservedly accepted his new sister. But, I had not yet met her mother who still resisted Marg's gender change and her upcoming sex surgery scheduled for the fall.

The long-awaited day finally arrived. Approved by the Royal Ottawa Hospital's gender program, Marg took the train to Montreal to have sex reassignment surgery (now gender-confirming surgery) with Dr. Yvon Ménard. I drove up the next day to be there when she came out of the anaesthetic. Unfortunately, I had to return to Toronto the following day to go to work and to look after our cat. After being discharged, Marg took the train back to Ottawa to stay with her lesbian friend while recovering. Marg was over the moon now that she had finally become a fully-physical female just two weeks before her 41st birthday—what better gift could a girl ask for?

We planned to elope to Ottawa right after her surgery, have a low-key marriage ceremony with a secular celebrant (Marg was turned off by most religionists after her recent excommunication by the Mormon Church), witnessed by my sister and some friends, and, then, stay overnight at a nearby hotel. Our friend, Jean, hitchhiked from Montreal to attend the ceremony. Me in my light-blue dress shirt, bow-tie, and indigo tux; Marg in a white lace wedding dress, gold necklace and matching bracelet. Following the celebrant's official words, we each read our personal vows, exchanged rings, kissed, cut the cake, laughed, and then danced to Latin music with our guests; then, dashed off during a sudden downpour to the nearby Chateau Laurier Hotel for our wedding night. I felt that I had finally arrived: Marg would be my loving partner for life!

We celebrated our honeymoon in Cleveland, Ohio, while we attended the Harry Benjamin International Gender Dysphoria Association (HBIGDA) symposium sponsored by Case Western Reserve University's gender identity program. There I came across several eminent gender clinicians,[8] including the controversial Dr. Leslie Lothstein, and a number of transgender and cisgender psychotherapists,[9] including my friends Dr. Ariadne Kane and Dr. Roger Peo. Susan Huxford-Westall was there too. I had submitted a proposal for a presentation on transgender issues: but, as I had merely a Bachelor's degree in psychology, rather than a Master's degree, one of the symposium organizers, psychiatrist Dr. Aaron Billowitz, turned me down. He invited me to do a poster presentation instead: but I declined his conciliatory offer as too little too late. Besides, I wanted to actively participate in a formal discussion with sexologists, psychologists, and gender clinicians in the field.

Denied entry into this inner sanctum of the virtually all cisgender clinical/academic elite, I was permitted only to listen to their often-sanctimonious pronouncements on what causes transsexualism or transvestism, and their psychopathologizing presumptions that a number of trans people sexually abuse adults or fantasize about molesting children. Professional annihilation was my penalty for being uncredentialled, not to mention being non-cisgender (once again, an Outsider). Real life experience as a trans person with a proven track-record as a paraprofessional gender worker (peer counsellor, researcher, and educator) counted little against these heavy-weight contenders (endocrinologists, surgeons, sexologists, psychiatrists, psychologists, psychotherapists). Moreover, Susan, my trans peer and supposed colleague, disloyally supported their summary dismissal of me! How many ignominious defeats can one man withstand before bitter cynicism burns up all compassion? The world-wearying wounds of so many wars seemed at times too much to bear. Would trans erasure within clinical science and academia ever end?

In fact, some years later, disgruntled trans community members would crash the 1997 HBIGDA symposium in Vancouver, demanding to be invited to the party. Too bad I wasn't there! Conciliatory talks ensued and 10 years later, HBIGDA changed its name to the World Professional Association for Transgender Health (WPATH) as it finally shifted to a gender-affirming collaborative care model, focussing on health, not disease (i.e. a psychiatric disorder), and, for the first time, became trans-inclusive in terms of its leaders. This milestone paradigm shift was essentially due to the advocacy efforts of two trans-identified presidents: Dr. Stephen Whittle of Manchester, UK (2007-2009) and Dr. Jamison Green of San Francisco (2014-2016). Both world-renowned trans activists, the trans community is deeply indebted to these two powerhouse social change agents for favourably altering the course of trans healthcare. Indeed, the old paradigm (from the 1960s through the mid 1990s) in which most transgender behavioural scientists and mental health practitioners had to hide their identity due to discrimination—eventually began to shift in the late 1990s and early 2000s. Finally, trans-identified, mental health professionals and gender clinicians were/are allowed to openly take up their rightful place alongside their cisgender peers and effectively advocate for transpositive healthcare. This paradigm shift in trans-related psychomedicine and trans healthcare gradually extended to law and politics as more transgender, intersex, and Two-Spirit lawyers, judges, politicians, and public officials[10] openly advocated for human rights for themselves and their gender peers.

But to be fair, I wasn't always excluded or erased. In 1990, I was awarded a lifetime membership in the National Gender Dysphoria Organization of America (based in Dearborn, Michigan), by Justina Williams,[11] one of only two openly Black, transsexual women I knew of back then besides Sharon Davies.[12]. Since then, several more trans-female, African American memoirs have recently come out.[13] And, occasionally, I was called upon to appear on a TV talk show, to speak to a community group, or take part in a conference panel—like the one Marg and I were invited to by the Sex Therapy Training Institute affiliated with the University of Guelph. Paddy Aldridge,[14] owner of the Toronto-based store, Take A Walk On The Wildside™ and founder of the Canadian Crossdressers Club, was also a panelist. A cisgender transensualist, Paddy was an ardent admirer of trans people, having dated, married, and divorced several male crossdressers and postsurgical transsexual women. When a student sex therapist at the institute asked about her relationship experiences, Paddy joked that she too was a kind of sex therapist, conducting her own brand of sex therapy by trying to bring to climax both crossdressing men—who were often into bondage-and-discipline sex play—and post-op trans women—who were often more traditional, but at times open to exploration. Then, she added, with sincerity, that she really cared about these people as unique individuals, wanting to give them the gift of emotional and physical intimacy, and validating them—possibly for the first time—as their authentic selves and as sexy sexual beings. I added some complexity to the mix by stating that I knew of several post-transitional trans men who sometimes dressed in female lingerie for kicks, as well as some post-transitional trans women who periodically donned male underwear as an expressive form of kink (transgressive sex-play). Quite an eye-opener for these mostly cisheteronormative students, this anecdotal lesson in sexological science was no less real than empirical fact and not to be found in any curriculum textbook!

We crossed paths with Paddy, several times more. The first time was when she hired Gender Consultants to talk about anything and everything trans to the LGBT youth group that she was facilitating at The 519 Community Centre. I pleaded with these young people to accept gay and bi-trans men into the cisgender gay male community, and lesbian and bi-trans women into the cisdyke community. As stated earlier, the latter was quite transphobic back then, especially many of the cis rad fem lesbians. To augment my advocacy, I brought along a transdyke friend to speak her lived truth to these young cisqueers, who proved to be heartwarmingly receptive. In lieu of cash payment, Paddy promised us a keg of Heineken beer: a fair trade for beer-lovers like us.

The second time we saw Paddy was in Springfield, Massachusetts, where she had temporarily relocated her female image makeover business for male crossdressers with her then partner, Veronica Brown, a trans woman from Hartford, Connecticut, who co-led the Twenty (XX) Club. They soon moved back to Canada and Paddy sponsored Veronica for immigration. Unfortunately, they divorced not long afterwards with Veronica returning home to the USA. Previously, Paddy had invited us to stop over in Springfield *en route* to the Tiffany House in Wayland where we were going to stay with Merissa Sherrill Lynn and other house guests who Marg wanted to meet. So, we spent a few luxurious days in the hotel where Paddy and Veronica were staying. After a delicious meal, we jumped into the hot tub on the hotel roof, toking, joking, and laughing as a warm rain sprinkled down. Time stopped for a brief *satori* moment: me and my loving wife and two friends. Life is good!

The next day we called on my trans therapist friend, Steve Parent, who invited Marg and me to dine with him and his wife, Gloria, at their home. Sadly, not much later, Steve passed away of kidney failure, following lengthy dialysis treatments. In 1990, I sent him a Gender Worker Award plaque thanking him for his trans advocacy over the years, a small token for this gentle man, one of the unsung trans heroes.

Our stay at Tiffany House was memorable. At night, in bed, we listened to the haunting cry of loons in the nearby lagoon, rising in the morning to the smell of fresh coffee and homemade biscuits. During the day, we took long walks in the surrounding countryside and then sat around the piano singing, drinking, and toking with the trans women and crossdressers there; one minute, deep in conversation about discrimination and trans rights and, the next, laughing raucously at naughty limericks. We later drove into Boston to savour some famous home baked beans. Tiffany House in 1989 was truly an intentional trans community. Thank you, Merissa Sherrill Lynn and company!

The third time we saw Paddy was back in Toronto at her wedding reception at the Buddies in Bad Times theatre. She was tying the knot with Roxy, a male crossdresser, with Rev. Dr. Brent Hawkes officiating the ceremony. Sadly, Roxy died some years later from alcoholism, despite having first acquired 10 years of sobriety. In a wedding photo of the four of us, Paddy and Roxy towered over Marg and me, dramatizing the variations of size and shape when it comes to cis and trans folks. But whether big or small, short or tall, we can all have big hearts if we care about each other.

Gender Worker/Gender Consultants had a short run from September 1987 to July 1990. Effective July 1st, we ceased all gender services, primarily due to my massive burnout but also because of a lack of paying clients. As for the newsletter, we only had 20 subscribers and we needed at least 50 to break even. Just as I was closing shop, I had to return a cheque for membership dues to *Metamorphosis* for Jamison Green. I advised him that MMRF had folded two years earlier and that I was giving up trans activism for good! Trans saturated, I was burned to a crisp and needed a good long rest.

Chapter 6 Notes

[1] Published in *The TV-TS Tapestry*, 1988, (52).

[2] Published in *Gender NetWorker*, June 1988, (1).

[3] These American phalloplastic surgeons included: Dr. Michael Brownstein, Dr. Ira Dushoff, Dr. Milton Edgerton, Dr. David Gilbert, Dr. Charles Horton, Dr. Donald Laub, Dr. Toby Meltzer, and Dr. Charles Reynolds. Dr. Brownstein performed both metoidioplasty and phalloplasty for trans men, depending on their preference, and performed one of the first metoidioplasties for Lou Sullivan in 1986.

[4] For information on non-surgical, (typically silicone) prosthetic penises, including soft (non-penetrating) and hard (penetrating) packers, and non-peeing and peeing (stand-to-pee devices) packers, as well as customized enhancement underwear, see: Underwood, Thomas. "A Guide to Packers For Transmen," *FTM Guide*, May 9, 2016. http://ftm-guide.com/guide-to-packers-for-transmen/. Several trans-male-owned companies in North America and Europe sell commercial packers and "pee-ers" online. Alternatively, some trans men use a clitoral or penile pump to enlarge their clitoris or microphallus.

[5] For a comparison of phalloplasty versus metoidioplasty, see https://www.verywellmind.com/what-is-a-metoidioplasty-4153084.

[6] These French-Canadian gender activists are listed below.

Trans woman, Marie-Marcelle Godbout, was the founding president of *L'Aide aux Transsexuel(le)s du Québec* (ATQ). See: Burke, Nora Butler, and Viviane Namaste, (translated and revised by Natalie Duchesne), "'What Is Missing in Our Community, Is Self-Love': An Interview with Marie-Marcelle Godbout, Founder of of *L'Aide aux Transsexuel(le)s du Québec*," in Irving and Raj, *Trans Activism in Canada*, 109-114. See also https://zagria.blogspot.com/2008/11/marie-marcelle-godbout-1944-magician.html.

Trans man, Nick Lalonde, was ATQ's vice-president.

Trans woman, Michelle de Ville, was the self-styled "first-door bitch" for queer/trans clubs in Montreal. See: Namaste, Viviane, "'We Paved the Way for Whatever Tolerance They have in Their Lives': An Interview with Michelle de Ville, 'The First Door Bitch in Montreal'," in Irving and Raj, *Trans Activism in Canada*, 19-25. See also https://zagria.blogspot.ca/2014/05/michelle-de-ville-1958-performer.html.

Beverly Pride was the secretary of *Travestis à Montréal* (TAM), and David Cassidy was TAM's treasurer and newsletter editor. At the time, they both identified as male crossdressers.

Trans woman Patricia Fisher was the FACT Quebec representative. Inge Stephens and Jackie C. were FACT Quebec members.

Trans man, Dale Altrows, was the Canadian liaison for FTM International. From 1996 to 1999, he successfully battled the Quebec government to be legally recognized as male. See: GAIN and Dale Altrows, "Transman Wins Sex Change on Birth Certificate," April 19, 1999. http://www.ifge.org/news/1999/apr/nws99apr19.htm#story4.

Dr. Viviane Namaste, Nora Butler Burke, and James McKye were/are members of Action Santé Travesti(e)s et Transsexuel(le)s du Québec (ASTTeQ) and of CACTUS Montréal.

Hélène (formerly Micheline) Montreuil is a trans-female lawyer and politician. She is also a teacher, writer, radio host, and trade unionist, who has struggled for her legal rights in front of the Canadian Human Rights Tribunal, the Superior Court, and the Court of Appeal in Quebec. In 2007, she was the first openly-transgender person in Canada to be nominated as an electoral candidate by a major political party (the New Democratic Party), but was subsequently dropped. Read "Transgender Girl," Hélène's story of a transvestite becoming a transsexual, http://www.micheline.ca/page62-transgenre-e.htm.

Josée was a trans-female queer/trans nightclub owner, who had a private helicopter.

Joëlle-Circé Laramée is an intersex activist and trans ally, and a fine-arts painter.

[7] I'm making a tongue-in-cheek allusion to Canada's first safer-sex booklet for trans sex workers and trans women: Strang, Christina, *The Happy Transsexual Hooker: A Healthy Resource Guide for Transsexual and Transgendered Sex Workers*, Toronto, ON: The 519 Church Street Community Centre, circa 2000. See the updated version: Page, Morgan M., *Brazen: Trans Women's Safer Sex Guide*, Toronto, ON: The 519 Church Street Community Centre, 2013. http://librarypdf.catie.ca/PDF/ATI-20000s/26424.pdf.

[8] These gender clinicians included Dr. Walter Bockting, Dr. Collier Cole, Dr. Eli Coleman, and Dr. Paul Walker.

[9] These psychotherapists' works are listed below.

Brown, Mildred L., and Chloe Ann Rounsley, *True Selves: Understanding Transsexualism—For Families, Friends, Coworkers, and Helping Professionals*, San Francisco, CA: Jossey-Bass, 1996. Reprint, 2003.

Fraser, Lin, "Psychotherapy in the WPATH Standards of Care for Transsexual, Transgender and Gender Non-Conforming People," *Journal of Sexual Medicine*, September 2013, 10: 283-283.

Miller, Niela, *Counseling in Genderland: A Guide for You and Your Transgendered Client*, Boston, MA: Different Path Press, 1996.

Rachlin, Katherine, "Transgender Individuals' Experiences of Psychotherapy," *International Journal of Transgenderism*, 2002, 6(1). http://web.archive.org/web/20070708184341/http://www.symposion.com/ijt/ijtvo06no01_03.htm.

(My clinical research paper on my transpositive therapeutic model appeared in the same volume as Kit's paper: true validation for me—as a neophyte gender clinician—to rub shoulders, within the confines of this scholarly journal, with my cisgender professional peer!)

Lev, Arlene Istar, *Transgender Emergence: Therapeutic Guidelines for Working with Gender-Variant People and their Families*, Binghamton, NY: Haworth Press, 2004. (I favourably reviewed Arlene's book: Raj, Rupert, "Review: 'Transgender Emergence: Therapeutic Guidelines for Working with Gender-Variant People and their Loved Ones,'" *Journal of GLBT Family Studies*, 2006, 2(3&4), Binghamton, NY: Haworth Press).

[10] Since the early 2000s, an outpouring of self-identifying, transgender and non-binary people (including *Hijras* in India) have successfully run for political or public office in many countries, including Canada: Albertan legislative member, Estefania Cortes-Vargas (2015), Manitoban judge, Kael McKenzie (2015), and Québécois political activists, Gabrielle Bouchard (2017), Julie Lemieux (2017), and Hélène (formerly Micheline) Montreuil (2008). Others have unsuccessfully run for office in the past: British Columbians, Jamie Lee Hamilton (1996, 2008, 2011, 2014) and Morgane Oger (2017, 2018), Manitoban, Shandi Strong (2017), and Ontarians, Enza Anderson (2000, 2002, 2003, 2010), Susan Gapka (2006, 2010, 2013, 2014, 2018), and Nichola Ward (circa early/mid 2000s).

Canada also boasts a number of recent/current openly transgender or Two-Spirit professional legal advocates: Shannon Blatt (currently, Vancouver lawyer, and Trans

Liberation March organizer; formerly, Trans Human Rights Campaign Ottawa liaison), Marie Laure Leclercq (currently, Montréal intellectual property lawyer, and Canadian Bar Association (CBA) Board of Directors member; formerly, CBA Sexual Orientation & Gender Identity Conference co-chair), Judge Kael McKenzie (currently, Manitoba court judge; formerly, Winnipeg lawyer and crown prosecutor in family, commercial and civil law), Hélène (formerly Micheline) Montreuil (currently, Québec business and management lawyer, and Université du Québec à Rimouski Nursing Department ethics lecturer, and Department of Management Sciences law and management lecturer; formerly, a federal politician), N. Nicole Nussbaum (currently, London, ON family law, human rights and trans rights lawyer, CBA Sexual Orientation & Gender Identity Conference co-chair, and Trans* Legal Needs Assessment Ontario project lead; formerly, Canadian Professional Association for Transgender Health President: 2013-2014), and Prof. Samuel Singer (currently, Kamloops, BC LGBTQ rights lawyer, Egale Canada Human Rights Trust Legal Issues Committee member, and Thompson Rivers University assistant professor of law; formerly, Montréal's Trans Legal Clinic founder and supervising lawyer in 2014).

[11] See: Cheers, D. Michael, "Interview with Justina Williams," *Jet Magazine*, November 1, 1979. http://transgriot.blogspot.ca/2007/02/justina-williams-1979-jet-magazine.html.

[12] Sharon Davis's memoir was the first-ever published by an African American trans woman, *A Finer Specimen of Womanhood: A Transsexual Speaks Out*, New York, NY: Vantage Press, 1985. See https://transgriot.blogspot.com/2011/12/sorry-toni-sharon-davis-book-was-first.html.

[13] See: Lady Chablis, and Theodore Bouloukos, *Hiding my Candy: The Autobiography of the Grand Empress of Savannah*, New York, NY: Pocket Books, 1996; Mock, Janet, *Redefining Realness: My Path to Womanhood, Identity, Love & So Much More*, New York, NY: Atria Books (Simon & Schuster), 2014; Newman, Toni, *I Rise - The Transformation of Toni Newman*, Self-published, 2011; and Watson, Tenika, and Jennifer Daelyn, *My Life is No Accident: A Memoir by Tenika Watson, as told to Jennifer Daelyn*, published by Jennifer Daelyn, 2014. See also the biography of Black, American trans woman, Jackie Shane: Maynard, Steven, "Introduction: 'A New Way of Lovin': Queer Toronto Gets Schooled by Jackie Shane," in John Lorinc, Jane Farrow, Stephanie Chambers, Rahim Thawer et al., eds., *Any Other Way: How Toronto Got Queer*, Toronto, ON: Coach House Books, 2017, I1-I10.

[14] Paddy (Patricia) Aldridge founded the Toronto Crossdressers Club in 1991, and edited *Toronto CDC News* (renamed the *Canadian Crossdresser Magazine* in 1992 to reflect the club's new name: the Canadian Crossdressers Club), and the *Drag Queens International* magazine in 1993. Co-producers Lisa Rideout and Sarah Fisher's 2017 Canadian film documentary, *Take A Walk On The Wildsid* (the name of Paddy's "transformational" clothing store) portrays Paddy as a cisgender ally to male crossdressers and trans women since 1987. See https://www.imdb.com/title/tt6293648/.

7. Intense Burnout…Secular Humanism, Ethical Vegetarianism, Career Counselling…A Brief Affair and Divorce (1990–1998)

Yes, I certainly needed a well-deserved rest. It would take me almost a decade to recover from 19 years of burnout and vicarious traumatization; the debilitating effects of working in a marginalized community severely impacted by poverty and violence, societal discrimination and internal strife. Like the wounded warrior and the wounded healer, I, too, would heal in time. To speed my recovery, this burnt-out Gender Worker took a leave of absence from the T-community. I unlisted my phone number so that trans people, their loved ones, and trans care professionals could not find me either to pick my brain for gender resources or pull at my heart-strings for emotional support. Beyond my retreat from the trans scene, specifically, I also needed to withdraw from the larger LGBTTI2SQQAA community. So, I mainstreamed in the cisgender straight world for nine years. Compassion fatigue is the risk that activists commonly face when working and playing within the same community—with nowhere to hide except to go underground, lay low, regroup, renew. It's remarkable that I did not commit myself to the rubber room at the Clarke (now CAMH)! Instead, I simply suffered a mini-breakdown (brownout) while still working and studying: business as usual. The ever-energizing RuBear!

Before I could completely retire from gender work though, I had one last task to perform: to pay tribute to a selected few fellow trans activists. So, I presented 12 Gender Worker Award plaques and 50 Certificates of Merit[1] to outstanding transgender community leaders in Canada, the USA, and the UK.

The first award was presented to Lou Sullivan in January 1990. He wrote me back on February 6, 1990:

> *Dear Rupert,*
> *I'm very honored and truly appreciate your thoughtfulness and the energy you put into this commemoration. I hardly feel worthy of this award, compared to your many years of service to the F-M community, and think YOU should be the one receiving it, not me! Thank you from the bottom of my heart, Rupert….Again, Rupert, I really appreciate the Gender Worker Award. It's hanging on the wall, right in front of me at this very moment….Makes me all the more proud of my newsletter (going on Issue #11), and amazed at your dedication in putting* Metamorphosis *together for all those years. We see them come and go, but you and I are still there, hey, Rupert ?!!*

Earlier, in 1987, I had presented Lou with an Honourary Life Membership in MMRF, which he likewise appreciated. With characteristic humility, he declined my request to nominate him for inclusion in the 1982 edition of *The*

Book of Lists,[2] citing 10 renowned transsexuals—including Mario Martino and Jude Patton. I can't recall if I was included, but likely not if it was exclusively American. As far as I can glean from my files, the aforementioned letter to me from Lou was the final correspondence from him, dated May 4, 1990. In June 1989, I had advised him of an HIV/AIDS research study conducted by psychologist Dr. Christian Crandall at Yale University, who Lou then contacted. He also participated in several other such research studies. Sadly, my good buddy Lou died of MAI (an HIV/AIDS-related infection for which there was no cure at the time) on March 2, 1991, although I didn't find out until quite some time later as I had been out of touch with the trans community. Earlier, I had hoped to be able to visit him in April 1983, and again, in April 1989 during the IFGE convention in San Francisco. Alas, we never did connect because time and money never seemed to coincide (another lifelong regret). Even so, I did call him long distance once (international telephone rates were fairly high at the time) and we had (like Jude Patton and I) a special bond as very close pen pals. A bright light in my life for a time, I still miss you, Lou.

Considering that validation was very important to me, could I do any less than accord my trans peers the acknowledgement they so richly deserved? Three years earlier, in April 1987, I had saluted several fellow trans advocates in an open letter to Phoebe Smith's newsletter, *The Transsexual Voice*, entitled "Burnout: Unsung Heroes and Heroines in the Transgender World,"[3] which called upon trans community members to please honour those few of us mostly unpaid peer-supporters—along with a handful of those with professional credentials—who constantly risk burnout and mental breakdown by devoting our lives to our trans sisters and brothers and by sacrificing our privacy as publicly professional transsexuals (gender workers). A year later, Susan Huxford-Westall wrote a similar piece, "Burn Out and the Gender Worker," in her *GenderServe* newsletter.[4] Prompted by her piece, I wrote an editorial in *GenderNetWorker*, entitled "The Gender-Reassigned Resource Worker: Doubly Damned or Warmly Welcomed?"[5] bemoaning the fact that, whether peer counsellor or professional therapist, we are often caught between a rock and a hard place: unappreciated by transgender clients and gender clinicians alike! Dallas Denny accused me of fouling the nest with my venting, but Kim Stuart commiserated. She perfectly understood my intense frustration and embittered cynicism; the result of two decades of burnout with little formal recognition. Yes, I was an activist; but, still, merely a man. Not a god or a machine! Once Superman, in my prime, my kryptonite had since run out. I urge all trans people to be mindful of this fact. Even the most resilient of activists are vulnerable, so we must nurture—not neglect—our community leaders, those people of action who get things done often by making personal sacrifices for the greater good. If the transgender movement is to flourish, we must stop the in-fighting—as my late friend, Kyle Scanlon, wholeheartedly agreed—and focus on defeating the common enemy: societal transphobia.

This task completed, I was now free to put trans activism aside. I sought refuge as a part-time student, enrolling in a one year course in magazine journalism at Ryerson Polytechnic Institute in 1991. Although it ultimately didn't lead to a profession in journalism, it satisfied my creative journalistic talents for a while.

Trans-spent, but still interested in social justice work, I searched for a completely new cause: mainstream politics. I worked for then city councillor, Jack Layton, on his 1991 mayoralty campaign, ghost-writing a newspaper article on homelessness in Toronto. Regrettably, Jack lost the municipal election to June Rowlands but, in 2003, he became the federal leader of the New Democratic Party (NDP) until his sad passing in 2011. Along with former Prime Minister Pierre Elliott Trudeau, Jack Layton was one of Canada's most loved national leaders. Following this brief stint of political activism, I hungered for more.

In 1992, I applied to The City of Toronto's Committee on Sexual Diversity and Race Relations, only to be beaten out by a Progressive Conservative businessman favoured by Mayor Rowlands. I was so disappointed! Why does corporate clout almost always trump community commitment? What about power to the people? Repeated rejection spells recurrent dejection.

Beaten, but not broken, I rose up again—like the eternal Phoenix rising from the ashes—and looked elsewhere to ply my activist skills. So, after reading a series of secular humanist books on anti-religionism,[6] I joined the Humanist Association of Canada (HAC) (later renamed Humanist Canada). HAC promoted the separation of religion from public policy; fostered the development of reason, compassion, and critical thinking through secular education and community support; and supported the advancement of scientific, academic, medical, and human rights efforts. Founded in 1968, HAC's first president was renowned pro-choice advocate Dr. Henry Morgentaler, who had been fined and imprisoned for performing abortions for Canadian women. He and I had a lot in common: he was an atheist, Polish Jew; and I was an atheist, half-Polish, recovering Catholic, and, more so, we were both secular humanists. Henry reminded me a lot of Dr. Viktor Frankl, Austrian-Jewish, existential psychiatrist, and Holocaust survivor. Philosophical ideals (existential humanism), not religious beliefs (Frankl was theistic)—as well as respect, compassion, and humility—were what linked these two social change agents. I became HAC Secretary in 1993 and helped lobby the Canadian government to legislate much-needed prison reform. I also wrote a feature article for *The Humanist in Canada* magazine entitled "The Feminist Face of Humanism."[7] To my dismay, however, the female editor changed my title to a gendered one: "The *Feminine* Face of Humanism." The perils of advocacy journalism and all too prevalent gendering! Hopefully, my intended message that men can be feminists too came through. Taking the less-travelled road of the non-supernatural demands of us naturalistic, critical freethinkers (a minority) the unflagging courage of our convictions as we continuously challenge the entrenched religious majority. And, as isolating as this quest for truth often is, as the religionists have their communion of saints to intercede in their dark night of the soul, we have—as British philosopher, mathematician, and agnostic, Earl Bertrand Russell,[8] observed—our communion of philosophers (both living and departed) to help dispel our despair and lighten our heavy hearts.

This was the year I turned 40. I craved a family reunion with my four siblings, a time when we could hopefully all come together since we went our separate ways in 1969. They all showed up, along with my sister-in-law, Lilly, and nephew, Sergei, except for Casimir, who had abruptly severed relations with the entire family many years ago in the mid-1970s because of certain sibling conflicts. I was disheartened that he would not let go of his longstanding grudge, hoping for greater family cohesion after this passage of time. Oh well. At least the rest of us came together to celebrate my birthday complete with chocolate cake and assorted gifts.

That fall, Kwame finally came up from Richmond for a visit. Our deep, 10-year friendship had recently evolved into a torrid romance. Marg was unaware of our romantic feelings and I was conflicted. Feeling guilty at breaking my marriage vows to Marg (whom I still loved), I was also enthralled by Kwame. I was caught in the middle (yet again), dancing the dialectic between passion and regret. When I saw him at last, eagerly awaiting me at the Voyageur Colonial bus terminal, beaming shyly in his red sweater and short hair (cropped especially for me), my heart jumped. Weak-kneed, I felt like a randy schoolboy! We walked to the Eaton Centre for a couple of beers where he furtively fondled my thigh under the table: then we rode the streetcar home. After we devoured Marg's delicious dinner, Kwame smoked some "weed" before retiring for the night. After Marg went to work next morning, I wanted to make love to Kwame, but he feared that she might come home early, catching us in the act. Eventually, he got up his nerve and we fucked. It felt damn good and the gay side of me reared up again, ready to play! During his visit, his boyfriend called from Virginia, checking up on him because he suspected that Kwame had more than friendly feelings for me even though Kwame had destroyed all my love letters and denied any lingering feelings for me to his boyfriend. We had a passionate five-day rendezvous; then it was time to part. I was beside myself but I had to let him go. The morning before his departure, following a shared shower, we slow-danced—our bodies pressing hotly together—to Barry Manilow's saxy bittersweet song, "One More Time." Like some coquettish queen doing a striptease, I tore away the towel covering my nakedness: "This is the last time you'll see my sexy body for I don't know how long!" Later that day, when I saw him off at the bus terminal, tears welled up as I ran after his fleeting image in the bus window.

We corresponded for six months afterwards, making plans to leave our partners and form a long-distance relationship. I sent him a loonie (a Canadian $1 coin) in each passionate tear-stained letter to eventually string together into a love necklace as a token of our bond.

Around this time, my earlier inclination towards bisexuality (or rather, pansexuality) poked through again and I bought several bisexual books from Glad Day Bookshop in pursuit of my evolving multisexual identity. At the time, there were no books on pansexuality (still a relatively new term even though some people had been practising it for some time), so I had to settle for bisexuality. Serendipitously, I found chapters in two books by sex researchers intersecting bisexuality and transsexualism![9] I re-read Coleman and Bockting's paper on transhomosexuality. Their piece inspired me to write my own paper on being transqueer and transbi (two terms I independently coined) when American sexologist Dr. Vern Bullough[10] invited me to present at the 1995 First International Congress on Gender, Crossdressing, and Sex Issues, sponsored by California State University at Northridge. Crestfallen, I had to decline due to work obligations and lack of funds. It's damn hard to be an academic when you're struggling financially. A fellow secular humanist, Vern and I chummed with like others, including Dutch sociologist and gay rights activist Dr. Rob Tielman[11], battling homophobic and transphobic religionists through scientific research and education.

Vern asked me if I would compile a biographical anthology of selected number of prominent trans activists. Regrettably, I had to decline this monumental task, still spent after my relentless run of non-stop activism. Too bad, because if anyone was a candidate for the job, it was me, the networker supreme, the resource man! Vern then asked Dr. Ariadne Kane (aka J. Ari Kane-DeMaios) to co-edit the book, which eventually came out some years later: *Crossing Sexual Boundaries: Transgender Journeys, Uncharted Paths* (2005). Other trans people, in particular, trans academics have also taken on the task of tracing the biographical, historical, sociocultural, political, and/or psychosexual dimensions of transgender people, eventually forming the new intersectional discipline of trans studies. A year later (in 1996), Vern requisitioned my mini-autobiography for a chapter in another book he was co-editing on gender blending (more about this later). That much I was able to do.

In terms of my budding multisexual identity, I reached out to the Toronto Bisexual Network to meet others like me but I never became an active member, because of Marg's explicit biphobia. She directed me not to tell people that I was bisexual (the self-descriptor I chose because I was only selectively out as trans). She feared guilt by association: possibly of being found out as a birth-assigned male, thereby compromising her legitimacy as a (gender reassigned) female. Her biphobia was internalized—rather than external—because she later confessed that she had once gone to bed with a woman during our married life. And, she had previously had sexual relations with her ex-wife. Still, her occasional, conflicted bisexual impulses did not deter her from socializing with gay and bi women. In fact, Marg had many lesbian friends and we both joined the Woman's Common lesbian club to increase connections with the dyke community. At the end of the day, I think that she really was bisexual (or pansexual)—as many trans people are—but she felt obligated to conform to the cisheteronormative world in order to be credible as a real woman.

In any event, further expressions of bisexuality or homoeroticism were momentarily quashed as my romantic relationship with Kwame finally ended. The romance fizzled out for two reasons: my guilt at playing around behind Marg's back, and Kwame's doubts about the practicality of our getting together permanently given the international border dividing us. I urged him to leave his boyfriend in Richmond and move to Buffalo so that we could take turns visiting each other—Toronto being fairly close—but he balked at the thought of being alone in a strange city with nobody to support him. So, that was that: insurmountable logistics had dashed our dream! Devastated by our failed plans, we still remained friends long afterwards.

That summer of 1993, I got a rude shock when CP Hotels fired my ass! I had been struggling for four-and-a-half years to advance within the company, applying for positions in the public relations and human resources departments to no avail, despite my public relations certificate, writing features for the corporate newsletter, and completing a credit course towards a human resources management certificate. The human resources director disliked me because I did not fit her ideal corporate image. Perhaps she sensed that I was countercultural. Even though they had succeeded in keeping me down, maintaining my *status quo* as a lowly clerk, I was not permitted to get angry at the management. The perennial Angry Man, I expressed my resentment anyway, confronting them head-on instead of swallowing my pride and controlling my anger impulse. Marg was furious at my dismissal, blaming me and not speaking to me for a whole day before finally relenting. It's lonely at the bottom! Demoralized, I asked a human rights lawyer if I could sue for unwarranted dismissal, but he told me that I did not have a good case because I had shown anger—the inviolate taboo! So, I collected employment insurance for a year, temping occasionally at clerical and factory jobs. A social democrat, I didn't regret my break with corporate Canada given that capitalism doesn't fit for me (nor does communism). To survive, I needed to find another way to fit into the mainstream world.

So, I started my own business, WordWrite, a word-processing service typing and copyediting books and papers. I did this for half a year before finally giving it up out of sheer boredom. I needed a creative challenge to tax my talents, so I opted to do some writing of my own, embarking on a book project on spec entitled, "Gender Crossings: An Historical Anthology of Women Who Have Become Men & Those Who Have Passed as Men."[12] I pursued this project diligently for six months before packing it in, my initial momentum flagging. Was it lingering trans-saturation or a larger feeling of existential malaise?

To get unstuck, I decided to take care of some unfinished business. So, in the winter of 1995, I returned to school part-time to complete the human resources management certificate that I had begun five years earlier. As with my journalism and public relations certificates, this didn't lead to a viable vocation but it did satisfy my hunger for certain knowledge. I loved learning and probably should have pursued an academic career in the footsteps of my father.

Later that year, I resigned from the Humanist Association of Canada prompted by an unfulfilled need for the inclusion of animals in the fight for freedom. As a budding ecofeminist and an ethical vegetarian[13]—which I had become in 1991, following my exposure to eye-opening undercover videos of unspeakable cruelty to enslaved animals in chicken batteries, pig abattoirs, bullpens and slaughterhouses—I found secular humanism overly focussed on humans, excluding animals entirely. Given my holistic nature and my love for Mother Earth and all her sentient beings, I needed to become "trans-speciesist," transcending the so-called evolutionary-based moral hierarchy of human animals over non-human animals. Further enlightened by the concept of "pseudo-speciation,"[14] I also had to become anti-speciesist.

> *Speciesism is morally objectionable, because, like racism, sexism, and heterosexism, it links personhood with an irrelevant criterion. Those who reject speciesism are committed to rejecting racism, sexism, heterosexism and other forms of discrimination as well.*
>
> Gary L. Francione, 2014[15]
> www.AbolitionistApproach.com/

After reading Australian animal rights activist Peter Singer's *Animal Liberation: A New Ethics for Our Treatment of Animals* (1975), I considered getting into ecological advocacy and animal liberation. I contacted various eco-activist and animal rights organizations, such as Action Volunteers for Animals, People for the Ethical Treatment of Animals (PETA), and the Toronto Vegetarian Association. Sadly, I didn't follow through with animal rights advocacy at the time because I feared a recurrence of burnout. Still, I hoped to pursue this worthwhile cause sometime down the road and eventually, did so in my pre-retirement years (see chapter 12).

When I was not studying, working, or writing, I managed to eke out a travel holiday now and then. As we both loved the west coast, Marg and I planned a trip to BC that summer. We spent time in Vancouver and Victoria, and drove through Kelowna and the Okanagan Valley, Marg taking the steep mountain turns like a revved-up race car driver (she had raced stock-cars in her pre-transitional days). We loved the mountains and the ocean so much that we hated having to return back east. Marg had hoped to visit her two teenage boys in Vernon, whom she hadn't seen in 10 years, but her cisgender ex-wife would not hear of it. This is often the case for divorced trans parents, although custody laws and visiting rights for trans parents in Canada (and elsewhere) are gradually becoming fairer.[16]

That fall, I returned to school (part-time) yet, once again—this time to earn my career and work counsellor diploma. I loved the program but it was a killer: two evenings a week and all-day Sunday for three long years—on top of irregular temp assignments! A school widow, Marg spent more time with her cis lesbian and trans women friends, attending Woman's Common and the Canadian Crossdressers Club to fill the hole created by my absence.

Even before graduating, I landed a job as a career counsellor at Goodwill Industries, helping job-seekers with disabilities prepare to look for work. I was only there for three months before being terminated for alleged poor performance. In truth, I was let go because a jealous female co-worker resented me, spitefully setting me up to fail. Machiavellian, she cunningly convinced my boss that I was a liability to the organization. I protested, but my boss sided with my spiteful colleague. The reason for my dismissal was due neither to transphobia nor biphobia because, so far, I hadn't disclosed my dual identity as a bi trans man in the workplace. Was it racism? I doubt it because I don't think they even knew that I was mixed-race, being perceived as White (even though "Raj" is a common South Asian surname). Was it sexism? Yes, I think so given that I sensed a misandrist attitude. These women disliked men whom they found sexually unappealing (not hot) and disrespected those who were non-assertive (wimpy): both easy prey for bullying. Presumably, I was perceived as one of those men, contrary to my positive self-image. I will never know the reason for sure, but bigotry is still bigotry, no matter what the reason.

On the home front, Marg was still trying to get her mother to accept her as a woman. Following four years of estrangement, her mother finally, albeit grudgingly, came around: a remarkable feat for this thoroughly-prejudiced parent. My then mother-in-law hated everyone, including me—berating me for becoming a vegetarian even though she had been one herself previously, and accusing me of being a gold-digger, going after Marg's retirement pension! Naïvely, I did not realize how bad to the bone she was until it was too late. I had suggested that Marg invite her mother to join us on our upcoming Christmas vacation in Mexico. In December 1996, we flew to Puerto Vallarta for what we hoped would be a week of fun in the sun. While on a Caribbean pirate-ship cruise, my mother-in-law—who seemed to be bipolar, borderline, and narcissistic!—threw a temper tantrum over some minor incident. A heated argument ensued between her and me, which the ship's captain tried to mediate. Caught in the middle, poor Marg was distraught, threatening to see her therapist and her lawyer on our return home.

After this upsetting altercation between her mother and me, Marg sank into a depression and began to withdraw emotionally. I managed to get her help at The Adler Counselling Centre run by Dr. Linda Page (a Jewish lesbian psychotherapist and secular humanist). I too engaged a therapist there (Dr. Mel) for support with my personal issues: anxiety, anger, relationship dynamics, frustrated vocational aspirations, and overall life stress. I talked with Mel about sexuality issues as my gay side pushed to the fore, following my brief affair with Kwame. I was hard-pressed to quell fantasies of gay male sex. Although I was still in love with Marg, my homoerotic urges were unsatisfied and I wasn't sure that I could stay in a straight relationship. Polyamory was not an option. Intellectually, I embraced the idea of open marriage, but emotionally I did not feel that it would work for me. Regardless, I knew that Marg wouldn't go for it. I was stuck!

Between jobs, I diligently sought permanent work, arranging networking meetings with managers at various community agencies, and doing volunteer work to augment my job-seeking efforts. I was somewhat demoralized though, but Marg's situation was far worse and her depression deepened. She slowly turned away from me, gravitating towards a trans woman, Sarah, in Rochester, New York, whom she had found in an online chatroom. They became close friends. Sarah drove up to Toronto for biweekly visits, their friendship gradually evolving into a romantic relationship. Feeling conflicted, Marg asked me to go for couples counselling, initially hoping to save our marriage. We had previously had a few couples counselling sessions soon after we were married but, alas, had stopped these prematurely. Because we were the first trans-trans couple our therapists had encountered, they had asked us for some helpful resources. I gave them the only thing I knew of: a book about a 1982 British, trans-male/trans-female couple, who were also parents.[17] Their specific situation, however, did not help our therapists to help us.

Unfortunately, however, Marg had a quick change of heart about staying married to me prior to our scheduled therapy session, but she hid her true feelings from me. Secretly planning to have only one therapy session, her explicit agenda was to persuade me, with the help of her therapists, to let Sarah visit her every week, feeling the need to have her close by much more often. Grudgingly, I conceded. But, feeling more jealous and increasingly threatened, I asked Marg to resume couples counselling. When she declined, I sensed that this was the beginning of the end.

A slim ray of sunshine brightened an otherwise dismal year. My autobiographical piece, "Metamorphosis: Man in the Making (A personal and political perspective),"[18] was published in *Gender Blending* (1997). Seeing my writing in print affirmed my waning self-esteem, providing a counterpoint to my feelings about my troubled marriage.

Another sunny ray piercing the grey clouds was the adoption of Zak and Zoe (double-love brother and sister cats) from the Toronto Humane Society. This feline addition to our family partly filled the huge gap left when Patches departed seven months prior, especially when these two playful youngsters purred perpetually like non-stop motors beside our heads as Marg and I lay in bed!

In the spring of 1997, still in school part-time, I was hired as a career counsellor by the Canadian National Institute for the Blind (CNIB). There, I helped visually-impaired clients develop pre-employment skills and job-search strategies, advised of job leads, negotiated workplace accommodations, coached clients on the job, and liaised between clients and employers. I loved the clients and my bosses, but the organization—like so many corporate and government-funded agencies—did not care enough about its employees to always do the right thing. We were not unionized and following a long-overdue salary review, it came to light that CNIB career counsellors were underpaid by industry standards. Appropriate adjustments had to be made for our rightful back pay. Disenchanted, I stuck it out for another two and a half years before eventually moving on to something better.

Sarah was now a permanent fixture in our household, visiting from Rochester every weekend. Anxious and angry, things were breaking down between Marg and me. Squabbling endlessly, our mutual trust eroded as the relationship grew increasingly strained. Things came to a head in mid-

November. That Saturday morning, before my class, Marg made me breakfast as usual but something wasn't right: she didn't butter the bagels and she was still in her nightie. She looked ashen, a mere spectre. Panic-stricken, I was too scared to probe further when she replied that everything was okay. She told me not to call home from school during my lunch hour because she and Sarah would be out shopping. Even though I had instinctive misgivings, I chose to be in that safe place of denial.

Arriving home that afternoon, I encountered a Dear Rupert letter, advising me that she wanted a divorce and that her lawyer would contact me. Some of the living room furniture was gone. Marg didn't leave me Sarah's phone number, so I couldn't get hold of her. Terrified—and mortified—I felt like a squashed bug: the life had gone out of me. Nausea washing over me, I rushed to the bathroom to throw up. Splashing cold water on my face, nothing seemed real. I felt as if I wasn't there. At first, I didn't know what to do. Then, I called our mutual friend Michelle Duff,[19] who had recently been in touch with Marg. When I asked her as to Marg's whereabouts, she told me that Marg had gone to Rochester with Sarah but that she didn't have her number. Scrambling through the phone bills, I eventually found Sarah's number. Dialing it with trembling fingers, Marg answered the phone in tears: "I don't want to think about the past or the future, only the present." Asking her if she loved Sarah, she replied, "Maybe, I don't know. But from now on, I'll never be left alone again." Earlier, she had intimated that she felt that only Sarah could give her the emotional and financial security she so desperately sought.

Then, I called Arjuna in Victoria and, afterwards, Kwame in Richmond. Kwame was less empathic than I would have hoped: but, my sister was a gem, as always. She really saved me, calling me every week over the next few months, offering much-needed emotional support. I owe my life to Arjuna; I could not have made it without her. Philip and several other friends came over to make me a meal now and then because I was not eating and was losing weight. Once I had a panic attack riding on the subway. My doctor told me that it was due to the acute stress sparked by the sudden loss of my wife and the reality of being single again. I asked Jakub to lend me $500 to help pay the rent as Marg had left only minimal funds in our joint account. Even now, I'm still grateful to him for helping me at the time my world came crashing down. Yet, despite the support of family and friends, I still felt somewhat lost and alone. That old sense of abandonment, triggered by my parents' death all those years ago, suddenly surged over me. I truly felt like a motherless child.

Then, my despair partially dissipated. Mother Earth had sent me a helper. My co-worker Ralph—a bisexual co-worker I had recently befriended—moved in with me on Christmas Eve. Like so many things in life, this was a mixed blessing, I was gaining a temporary human companion to assuage the lonely heartache of losing my wife, but at the cost of having to give up my two feline kids just before New Year's Eve due to Ralph's worsening cat allergy. I couldn't help crying when I had to hand over Zak and Zoe to their new human parent. Fortunately, a kitty-lover, she really took to Z and Z.

At first, Ralph and I did everything together: dining out, browsing in bookstores, visiting the library, listening to jazz and blues, watching film noir, talking about bisexuality. Growing increasingly closer, I asked Ralph to be my boyfriend: but, he vacillated. Initially acquiescent, he soon reneged; wanting, simply, to mutually masturbate. Without hesitation, I declined. I wanted a romantic partner, not a fuck-buddy. Before long, though, his dark side emerged (he had borderline traits). He became ultra-possessive and once, feigning illness, threatened to kill himself if I didn't leave work right away to come home to look after him. Ralph was also jealous of my friends, wanting me to spend all of my time with him. Over Easter, I spent two days with him and one with Eugene, who was now living in Toronto and we had recently reconnected. Ralph went berserk, not wanting to share me with anyone else. Another time, it got so bad that I had to stay at Eugene's place for a while because I was afraid to go home. Ralph's crazy-making tactics—taping threatening messages to the bathroom mirror—scared the hell out of me! One day, our boss sent us home early, without pay, ordering us not to return to work until we had sorted out our personal differences. I had to take drastic measures. I decided to move out and rented an apartment in a high-rise close to the gay village. No pets were allowed, so I had to live all by myself for the first time in years, with no human or animal companion to cheer me up. A sparse existence! But, business as usual, I still had to work and attend classes. Finally, after three long years, I was about to earn my career and work counsellor diploma.

Remarkably, at my invitation, Marg came to my graduation, but left right after the ceremony without staying to chat with me and my fellow graduates. Earlier, we had asked our respective therapists to arrange a closure meeting, still hoping to be friends following the divorce. The day of our scheduled therapy session, fortified by strong drink, I waited in the reception area while Marg laughingly carried on in her therapist's office. Dr. Mel was running late, still in session with another client. Knocking on his office door, he did not respond: so, I asked the receptionist to intervene, but she refused. Rightfully pissed off—I had been waiting over half-an-hour—I took off. Marg raced after me. Outrunning her, she flagged a cab, following me to my apartment building. As I entered the lobby, she begged me to come back to the therapists' office. My blood still boiling, I told her to forget it. So, that was that! I fired Mel's ass at our next individual therapy session, feeling betrayed by this so-called therapeutic healer. Undeterred, I was determined to find another therapist because I sure as hell could use the emotional support. After a diligent search, I fortunately found Dr. Paul Wozniak, with whom I worked therapeutically for almost two decades, from my middle into my senior years. During the course of our professional relationship—one based on mutual trust—we discussed many sensitive issues while I developed several positive coping strategies to help me deal with the challenges of life and love.

The saving grace was that Marg and I eventually had our closure meeting after all—two months later at the Hot House restaurant. My friend Roger accompanied me for moral support. Marg was quite emotional when I gave her a greeting card and told her that I had really loved her and hoped that we could still be friends. Tearfully, she echoed the sentiment. We saw each other only three times after that—the last time was in June 2005 when I visited Marg and Sarah in their London, Ontario home. There were also a few sporadic e-mails over the next few years. So much for a close friendship! In any event, I was soon to embark on a new chapter in my life. But before that, I had a wedding to attend.

My youngest brother Andrzej was getting married in New York City. Thrilling for him. But, sad for me because it was the same month that Marg and I had wed nine years earlier. I didn't let my fragile state deter me though, as it was vital that I be there for my brother on his special day. Sparked by my own recent sexual revolution, I wore my Pride pin to signify my re-emerging queer identity and, indirectly, my recent break with Marg and the straight life. People ending a long-term union often feel fragile if the identity of one partner has been enmeshed with that of the other. Pondering, as a single-again individual, "Who am I now?" I was bent on re-establishing myself as a sexual person in my own right, a bisexual man once more exploring the possibility of relations with another man.

I flew to NYC, where Andrzej greeted me affectionately and drove us to his Bleecker Street loft in Noho. Arjuna, Jakub, my sister-in-law, Lilly, and my nephew, Sergei, were already there. I met Andrzej's fiancée, Olesya, a recent Russian immigrant. A Trinidadian Hindu friend of my brother performed the wedding ceremony. There was plenty of food and wine, music and dancing. I was pleased for my brother and his new wife, but I felt twinges of regret, recalling my own marriage to Marg and our hopes for a lifelong union. Back home again, I was ready to begin a new leg on my journey.

Chapter 7 Notes

[1] The Gender Worker Award plaque recipients included: Canadian trans woman, Susan Huxford West all; 10 Americans trans activists: Louis Sullivan, Stephen Parent, Jude Patton, Sister Mary Elizabeth (Joanna Clark), Dr. Ariadne Kane, Dr. Sheila Kirk, Merissa Sherrill Lynn, Dr. Roger Peo, JoAnn Roberts and Phoebe Smith; and English trans woman, Judy Cousins. I now wish that I had also been able to include more Canadians (Stephanie Castle, Michelle de Ville, Marie-Marcelle Godbout and Linda O'Connell), and more trans men (Americans Johnny Armstrong, Steve Dain and Jerry Montgomery, and Englishman, Dr. Stephen Whittle, as well as Dallas Denny and Georgia Saunders (American trans women), but I had to cap the numbers due to stringent finances. Regrettably, Dr. Aaron Devor didn't ostensibly meet my strict criteria of having to be transsexual, transgender(ist) or transvestite given that he did not disclose his trans status to me until much later. Nonetheless, many others (including some of the above) were duly recognized through my 50 Certificates of Merit.

[2] See: Wallechinsky, David, Irving Wallace, and Amy Wallace, *The Book of Lists*, Los Angeles CA: Self-published, 1982.

[3] Published in *The Transsexual Voice*, April 1987; reprinted in *Metamorphosis Magazine*, June 1988, (1): 2-3.

[4] Published in *GenderServe*, May 1988, 4(1): 4.

[5] Published in *Gender NetWorker*, August 1988, 1(2): 2-3.

[6] See: Lamont, Corliss, *Humanism as a Philosophy*, New York, NY: Philosophical Library, 1949 (https://www.corliss-lamont.org/philos8.htm); Allen, Jr., Norm R., ed., *African-American Humanism: An Anthology*, Buffalo, NY: Prometheus Books, 1991; Ilaiah, Kancha, *Why I Am Not a Hindu: A Sudra Critique of Hindutva Philosophy, Culture and Political Economy*, Kolkata, India: Samya, 1996; Russell, Bertrand, *Why I Am Not a Christian - and Other Essays on Religion and Related Subjects*, Abingdon, UK: Routledge, 1927; Sand, Shlomo, *How I Stopped Being a Jew*, Brooklyn, NY: Verso Books, 2014; Singh, Bhagat, "Why I Am an Atheist," Lahore, India: *The People*, 1930; and Warraq, Ibn, *Why I Am Not a Muslim*, Buffalo NY: Prometheus Books,1995.

[7] Raj-Gauthier, Rupert, "The Feminine Face of Humanism," in *The Humanist in Canada*, Ottawa, ON: Canadian Humanist Publications, Spring 1995, (112): 5-7. Founded in 1968, the Humanist Association of Canada later changed its name to Humanist Canada. https://www.humanistcanada.ca/

[8] See: Russell, Bertrand, *The Autobiography of Bertrand Russell* (vols. 1-3), London, UK: Allen and Unwin, 1967-1969. Earl Russell was also a humanist, a pacifist, a liberal, a socialist, a social critic and a political activist. One of his books criticizing Christianity is noted above.

[9] See: Garber, Marjorie B., "Androgyny and Its Discontents," in Garber, Marjorie B, *Vice Versa: Bisexuality and the Eroticism of Everyday Life*, New York, NY: Simon & Schuster, 1995, 207-236; and "Transsexual Bisexuals," 59-65; and "Change and the Transsexual

Bisexual," 230-238, in Martin S. Weinberg, Collin J. Williams, and Douglas W Pryor, *Dual Attraction: Understanding Bisexuality*, Oxford, UK: Oxford University Press, 1994.

[10] An intersectionalist (American secular humanist, cisgender sexologist and transgender researcher, Dr. Vern Bullough put out a plethora of books published by Prometheus Books in Buffalo, NY, including: *Crossing Sexual Boundaries: Transgender Journeys, Uncharted Paths*, (co-edited with J. Ari Kane-DeMaios), 2005; *Cross Dressing, Sex and Gender* (co-edited with Bonnie Bullough), 1993; *Gender Blending* (co-edited with Bonnie Bullough and James Elias), 1997; and *Frontiers of Sex Research*, 1979.

[11] Another intersectionalist (Dutch secular humanist, queer cisgender sociologist and HIV/AIDS researcher), Dr. Robertus (Rob) Albert Petrus Tielman published books on secular humanism, bisexuality, and queer rights: *Humanistische Sociologie: een Paradox als Paradigma* (Dutch), Amsterdam, NL: Amsterdam University Press, 1987; *Bisexuality and HIV/AIDS: A Global Perspective* (co-edited with Manuel Carballo and Aart C. Hendriks), Buffalo, NY: Prometheus Books, 1991; and *The Third Pink Book: A Global View of Gay and Lesbian Liberation and Oppression* (co-edited with Aart C. Hendriks and Evert van der Vee), Buffalo, NY: Prometheus Books, 1993. Rob was knighted in 1987.

[12] My unfinished manuscript is preserved in The Rupert Raj fonds in The ArQuives. https://arquives.andornot.com/en/permalink/descriptions16420.

[13] See: Walters, Kerry S., and Lisa Portmess, *Ethical Vegetarianism: From Pythagoras to Peter Singer*, Albany, NY: SUNY (State University of New York) Press, 1999.

[14] Deriving from his beliefs and values as a humanist, pacifist, and social democrat, German-American, Dr. Erik Erikson (who was also a developmental and social psychologist), created the concept of "pseudo-speciation": a false hierarchy of presumed superiority of certain types of human beings over others in terms of race, ethnicity, class, or religion. Going one step further, Austrian ethologist, zoologist, and ornithologist, Konrad Lorenz, theorized that humankind is the exception in nature because of the suppression of the "instinctive mechanisms normally preventing the killing of fellow members of the species…and is the cause of war." (Quoted in Erikson, Erik H., and S. Schlein, eds., *A Way of Looking at Things: Selected Papers*, New York: W. W. Norton, 1987, 498).

[15] Gary L. Francione's quote on speciesism is cited here. www.AbolitionistApproach.com/.

[16] Thanks to initiatives like the Trans Family Law Project co-founded by Dr. Rachel Epstein, Dr. Jake Pyne, and Dana Baitz of SHC's Trans Parenting Network. See: Pyne, Jake, *Transforming Family: Trans Parents and their Struggles, Strategies, and Strengths*, Toronto, ON: LGBTQ Parenting Network, Sherbourne Health Centre, 2012. https://rainbowhealth.wpengine.com/wp-content/uploads/woocommerce_uploads/2014/08/Transforming_Family_-_Report.pdf.

[17] See: Johnson, Chris, and Cathy Brown (with Wendy Nelson), *The Gender Trap: The Moving Autobiography of Chris & Cathy, the First Transsexual Parents*, London, UK: Proteus Publishing, 1982.

[18] Bullough, Bonnie, Vern Bullough, and James Elias, eds., *Gender Blending*, Buffalo, NY:

Prometheus Books, 1997, 480-484.

[19] Read Michelle Ann Duff's memoir, *Make Haste, Slowly: The Mike Duff Story* (Coldwater, ON: Mad8Publishing (Canada), 1999), relating her gender transition from a male Grand-Prix motorcycle-racer in the 1960s to a trans woman in the 1980s. Michelle was featured twice on CBC-TV's *The Fifth Estate*: in 1984, just as she was beginning her transition, and in 2004, 20 years post-transition. For the latter program, see: Caloz, Marie, and Andrew Culbert, prods., "Becoming Ayden," *The Fifth Estate*,-Ottawa, ON: CBC-TV, October 13. http://radio-canada.mediaspace.kaltura.com/media/Becoming+Ayden/1_rfctkzs2. See also http://zagria.blogspot.com/2008/04/michelle-ann-duff-1939-motorcycle-racer.html.

8. Trans Re-Activism...Even More Schooling...Ricochet Romance (1998-2001)

In the fall of 1998, I began my three-year, part-time program in counseling psychology at The Adler School of Professional Psychology (Toronto campus), while still working full-time at CNIB. This would be an important stage of my life, learning various psychological theories, therapeutic modalities, and life skills to use in my professional clinical practice with future clients as well as in my personal development. A number of innovative new therapies had come out since I first took Psychology 101 nearly three decades ago.

We got an overview of diverse psychological theories,[1] and learned how to apply various psychotherapeutic modalities.[2] A multimodal therapist, I employed most of these modes of healing but I particularly embraced Adlerian therapy (the will to power), Franklian Logotherapy (the will to meaning), humanist and existential therapies, narrative and metaphor therapies, mindfulness-based cognitive behaviour therapy, and dialectic behavioural therapy (DBT). The latter two are especially effective insofar as they marry eastern psychology (mindfulness practice) and western psychology (cognitive behavior therapy). DBT teaches four essential intrapersonal and interpersonal skills: emotional self-regulation, distress tolerance, core mindfulness, and interpersonal effectiveness. This skillset also includes anger-management and impulse-control strategies, which proved beneficial for those of my clients with borderline personalities and those with drug addictions and eating disorders.

Humanistic, existential, narrative, and metaphor therapies were particularly useful in supporting my trans clients, pre-transitionally, mid-transitionally, and post-transitionally. These therapies can also aid genderqueer, intersex, and Two-Spirit clients—gender transgressors by default when negotiating society's gender-binary.

Existential therapy challenges cisgender and transgender clients, alike, to identify their general existential angst at being born human (the human condition), helping them to formulate strategies to navigate a chaotic, confusing, and often cruel world. It can have added value for transgender and gender non-binary clients by addressing their specific gender angst, as American, trans-identified therapist Dr. Anne Vitale terms this form of distress characteristic of people born with gender dysphoria.[3] With male crossdressers—who often also used to identify as transgenderists or androgynes—she would discuss particular challenges faced during their double life as both man and woman—and often also provide couple counselling for them and their wives. For those crossdressers considering transitioning to women—she would guide them through the decision-making process, and continue to support them afterwards. As a mental health practitioner with lived experience as a trans woman, Dr. Vitale also assists her transgender clients in negotiating societal transphobia—and often internalized transphobia. She teaches her trans-female clients to deal with transmisogyny by brainstorming effective ways to exist more safely in our transphobic world. I'm sad to say that internalized transphobia can affect trans clinicians themselves given that I personally know two trans psychologists who seem to still harbour traits of internalized transphobia since the 1980s.[4]

Narrative therapy encourages clients to rewrite the script in terms of their personal back story, having to have lived some of their early, middle, and/or later life according to their birth-assigned sex rather than their authentic self. The rewritten narrative cannot alter the physical fact of birth or erase the trauma of being born transsexual or intersex (gender dysphoria or sexual dysphoria, respectively). Nevertheless, narrative therapy can be a beneficial psychological retrospective reinvention of oneself. Narrative therapy dovetails nicely with metaphor therapy in the sense of being born again as a spirit warrior or rising anew as the mythical Phoenix. *Rewriting the Script: A Love Letter to Our Families* (2001)[5] is a documentary video featuring me and other queer South Asians in Canada and the diaspora. Disappointingly, I was the only trans person featured because, at the time, very few trans South Asians in Canada had disclosed their crossgender identity to their families. My sister provided a voiceover as a fully supportive sibling. The video is a plea to our families to accept us as our true selves as queer and/or trans people. I employ the metaphor of the Phoenix not only in terms of myself personally, as a gender-reassigned trans man, but also professionally, as a healer in my therapy work with clients.

Feminist therapy[6] is often effective for both cis and trans women, but can sometimes also help cisgender and transgender men towards self-empowerment. In addition to the respective treatment strategies of Dr. Carol Gilligan, Dr. Lenore Walker, and other feminist therapists, Dr. Harriet Lerner's dance therapies are especially useful in teaching clients how to constructively manage their anger, fear, and intimacy. Similarly, trauma therapy often can help to heal cisgender as well as transgender and gender non-binary youth and adults. There are various forms of trauma therapy and numerous trauma therapists, many of whom are feminists and/or humanists of all genders.

Another useful therapeutic modality, especially in addressing anger, sadness, rage, or despair, is humour. Historically and crossculturally, humour has been used in morality and folk tales, such as the two lovable lunatics Kanzan and Jittoku[7] in Zen Buddhist literature and paintings, simple-mindedly living in the moment, exulting in nature, oblivious to the world of people and pettiness. There is also the irascible fool/wise man of ancient Persia (or

Turkey), Mullah Nasrudin,[8] depicted in stories by Afghani Sufi scholar Idries Shah. Alternatively, humour can be an instrument—as light satire, philosophical resignation, or gentle deprecation of oneself, others, or life—or a weapon—as biting sarcasm, caustic cynicism, or abrasive deprecation of oneself, others or life. The former can be especially therapeutic—what I refer to as humorous resignation to life, captured in such sardonic songs[9] as "To Life (L'Chaim)" and "Here's to Life (Streetlight Manifesto)."

Those years of grad school, learning about personal management skills in class (augmented by my work with Dr. Wozniak in therapy), provided me a structured opportunity to practice those life lessons we must all learn. Now, I only needed to keep honing those behavioural strategies to mitigate my chronic anxiety and anger!

In the summer of 1998, I met Mirha-Soleil Ross,[10] a sex worker activist and her then lover Xanthra Phillippa Mackay,[11] two gender transgressive visionaries who created the Meal Trans Program at The 519 Community Centre for low-income trans people. Noted militant activists, they made the porn video, *Gendertroublemakers* (1993),[12] featuring a scene of them making love. They published the underground zine, *gender trash from hell* (1993-1995),[13] which contained political commentary, alongside art and poetry, and critiqued the often contentious relationship between trans and cisqueer communities. In 1999, Xanthra hosted a biweekly radio show, *Psychopathia Transsexualis*, featuring people, culture, and politics related to the trans community. As well as being trans activists, Mirha-Soleil and Xanthra were sex worker advocates and animal liberationists. Mirha-Soleil's videos often dramatically depict the intersections of oppression among females, across species: misogynist violence waged against trans women, the criminalization of solicitation by sex workers, and the enslavement and torture of factory farmed and research laboratory animals.

I celebrated Christmas of 1998 in Montreal with Jean and Stella because, still missing Marg, I did not want to be alone. We had a swell time scarfing down seafood, drinking high-test beer, smoking, toking, watching sci-fi flicks, grooving to classic rock, cracking jokes, and walking their bearded collie in the snow-filled streets, amidst the colourful lights of the Quebec yuletide. Nestled within my chosen family, I felt loved and appreciated.

That winter, while working at my day job and attending evening and weekend classes, I undertook a six-month clinical internship at The Adler School's counselling centre, supporting students around depression and anxiety, low self-esteem, poor body-image, drug misuse, eating disorders, dysfunctional relationship dynamics, sexual exploration, and academic challenges.

Around this time a milestone moment occurred for me when Jude Tate (coordinator of the University of Toronto's LGBT Services for students and faculty) and Dr. Lori Ross (Associate Professor in the Department of Psychiatry at the University of Toronto) invited me to train the university health services' psychiatric staff headed by Dr. Victor Likwornik. I taught them about gender dysphoria, gender transitioning, and how to effectively support pre-, mid-, and post-transition students and faculty. The invitation and follow-up thank you letter from Dr. Likwornik was the first validation I had earned as a psychotherapist-in-training—one of my most cherished tokens—which also made me realize that not all psychiatrists were transphobic. Before framing the letter, I included it in my portfolio. I was well on my way to a viable career as a mental health professional.

That spring, I moved into Hugh Garner Co-Op with Xanthra and her rescued cat Jane as Mirha-Soleil was moving out after their nine-year romance. Xanthra was vegan and I was vegetarian, so it should have been a good fit. But, I hadn't counted on entertaining romantic feelings for her. For three months, I lacked the nerve to tell her directly how I felt, although she already knew of my feelings because, previously, Mirha-Soleil had informed her at my request. Despondent that Xanthra did not reciprocate my feelings, we still managed to remain friends. That summer, I threw her a surprise birthday party with the help of Mirha-Soleil and her boyfriend Mark Karbusicky.[14] Shy, but also social, Xanthra exulted in the large turnout of friends. While I was at work or school, Xanthra volunteered at The 519 and took a part-time math course at the University of Toronto.

We led fairly separate lives but shared vegan Sunday dinners, which Xanthra prepared. For the first seven of our 15-month friendship, all went well. But, at the eighth-month mark, we had a big blow-out because I was eating non-vegan popcorn and wearing a leather jacket and leather boots. I had told her that I was vegetarian, not vegan, when I moved in, so I don't know why she reacted the way she did. There was some yelling and swearing, but we eventually reconciled, coming to a new understanding of how to amicably co-exist with slightly divergent values.

Given my South Asian heritage and my raging hormones, I wanted to connect with other Brown queers. So, I joined Khush,[15] a group for South Asian queer men in Toronto (which later included women). Sadly, Khush was winding down as the members felt no further need for the group given the increasingly ethnoracially diverse queer community in Toronto. There went my chances of meeting a South Asian queer man for potential romance! So, I tried another tactic, successfully running for the Board of Directors of the Alliance for South Asian AIDS Prevention (ASAAP). There, I met fellow gay male directors, Dr. Rakesh Ratti, (a clinical psychologist), Dr. Anthony Mohamed (a medical researcher), and Chakra (an accountant), along with ASAAP members Devan Nambiar and Zevare Tengra (HIV/AIDS activists).

ASAAP marched in Toronto's Gay Pride Parade that June, right behind Queer Muslims,[16] and I proudly held up our banner as a Brown (or rather, beige-skinned) queer. Chakra and I had a casual sexual thing going for a couple of months, but it ultimately fizzled out because I wanted a real romance, not a fly-by-night fuck-fest. It sure is hard to find a meeting of minds, hearts, and bodies, all in one person! A sort of fun fling while it lasted, I never really got my sexual needs met as I still wasn't comfortable letting a cis-male touch my genitals. Ass play would have been okay but Chakra wasn't into that: he only wanted me to suck his cock. Overall, a sexually stone experience for me.

My involvement with the queer South Asian community soon dropped off as all the men I tried to befriend were too damn busy! Eventually, I gave up, but not before curating a panel the following year for Desh Pardesh[17]—Khush's annual South Asian cultural event—at Buddies in Bad Times theatre. The panel, "Poignant Lives, Powerful Voices," consisted of Indigenous trans artist Aiyyana Maracle[18] (a transformed woman who loved women), Mexican-born trans woman, Shadmith Manzo (a refugee to Canada and Transition Support group coordinator), mixed-race (East Indian and German) trans man Kaspar Saxena (a video maker), an African Canadian man (name withheld), and me, as moderator. We also showed Boyd Kodak and Cat Grant's short video, *Shadmith Manzo Performance* (1998).[19] This video had served as a 48-hour fundraiser to pay Shadmith's legal costs to bring her back to Canada, following her deportation, in order to seek refuge status based on transphobic abuse in Mexico. Our panelists earned a standing ovation from the 100+ audience members. Sadly, this was the last Desh Pardesh event due to lack of sustainable funding. We made sure to go out with a bang, our voices powerful, our lives poignant.

Mirha-Soleil had approached me sometime earlier to revive a group for trans men in Toronto because there had been a vacuum in this regard ever since I wound up Metamorphosis 11 years earlier. Was I the only T-boy in Toronto up for running a trans group? No wonder the few of us who do this work burn out so fast! When she had first asked me, I was too busy settling into grad school, but now I was ready. After a nine-year hiatus, Rupert Raj was back in town! That first Friday in June of 1999, my co-facilitator, James Nattal (a young trans man in mid-transition), and I launched the first meeting of the Trans Men/FTM Peer-Support Group at The 519 Community Centre. It was a sell out as 33 trans guys from Toronto and beyond crammed into a tiny room on the top floor (we had to move to a larger room on the second floor). Each week, we had a topic relevant to the lives of trans men and females-to-males (FTMs). These included: gender-identity exploration; disclosure management (telling one's partner, family, friends, classmates, co-workers, community members); identity management (legally changing one's name and/or sex-designation); male hormone therapy; sex-reassignment surgeries; transitioning at school, work, and in the community; negotiating family and relationship dynamics; finding and keeping a transpositive partner; biologically parenting or adopting children; breaking down social isolation and connecting to other trans people; overcoming societal transphobia and/or internalized transphobia; creating ways to engage in trans activism; and simply surviving.

I ran the group for a year, but James left halfway through, preferring to be a member rather than a facilitator. I had to carry on by myself for the remaining six months. Burning out again, I could hardly wait to pass the baton, inviting Kyle Scanlon (in mid-transition himself) to lead the group. After dropping off the Pride t-shirts for the group at the front desk, I couldn't even stay for the last session to bid the group farewell, despite being the one who had brought plastic surgeon Dr. Hugh McLean to talk about chest surgery that evening! Burnout was epidemic as Kyle also gave up leadership of the group after a year, handing it over to James Brown, another young trans guy. James ran the group for two years before handing it over to Greg, yet another young trans man. The group still continues to meet today—alternatively led by my trans friend, Levy—but, usually, only one or two guys show up. Where is the community leadership? The sustainability?

Besides leading the group, I participated in trans-focussed training again, including a plenary at the University of Guelph's sexuality conference and a panel at Central Toronto Youth Services, sharing my lived experience and my community advocacy. I could now also add my clinical experience as a student therapist, speaking about mental health issues, sexual trauma, addictions, and all things trans, including surviving transphobic violence and celebrating one's transgender identity. Yes, I was back in good form: my creative juices were flowing and I was raring to go! I asked Trish Salah, a trans woman I met at The 519, to put on an interactive workshop with me for trans people. Enthused, she suggested a street theatre format. That September, we put on one of the best workshops ever, "Gender Dysphoria, Self-Esteem and Body-Image." Forty-five trans folks came together to learn practical ways to feel better about themselves and their bodies. Some were still waiting to transition and some had already done so. Gratifyingly, for some of the participants, our workshop inspired hope for a better future as trans women and trans men seeking their niche in a sexist, genderist society.

In the fall of 1999, Xanthra Mackay and I premièred *Rupert Remembers* (1999, 2000),[20] a video documentary tracing my trans activism in Toronto from 1979 to 1999, at the third Counting Past 2 trans cultural event,[21] organized by Mirha-Soleil Ross, her partner, Mark Karbusicky, and Xanthra. The video was directed by Xanthra, filmed by Christina Strang, and edited by Jack Jupiter. This important piece of trans history, tracing the early activism of a Canadian trans pioneer (me), was shown again the following spring at Toronto's Inside

Out LGBT Film Festival. Thank you, Xanthra, Christina, and Jack.

Immediately following my film debut, I was hired as a career counsellor at the AIDS Committee of Toronto (ACT), where I served HIV/AIDS clients for the next year and a half. It was the first job where I felt free to be out as both queer and trans, finally emerging from the shadows of my previous double-life. I was chosen to be the trans poster-boy for the upcoming AIDS Candlelight Vigil in June at The 519, where I and others read out the names of trans and queer people who had died of AIDS during the past year. At ACT, I worked in the Ontario Disability Support Program (Employment), doing the same things I had done at CNIB, helping differently-abled clients get ready to look for work. I helped them assess their personal stress levels around their physical disability (HIV/AIDS) and their mental health (depression, anxiety, anger, trauma, addictions, etc.), while striving for a healthy work/life balance once they had found employment. An exceptional few of my clients eventually became ill enough to be referred to The Casey House AIDS Hospice. Still, I did have occasion to support them during their transitional stages of less severe illness, stabilized health, and return to wellness. When discussing their mixed feelings about work, life, dying, and death, I employed Dr. Elisabeth Kübler-Ross's classic grief model (denial, anger, bargaining, depression, acceptance),[22] and also consulted Dr. Walter Bockman and Dr. Sheila Kirk's healing work with HIV transgender patients.[23] Overall, my career counselling work with people with HIV/AIDS—most of whom were queer cis men and trans-female sex workers—was both humbling and inspiring.

That Christmas of 1999, I flew to Victoria to spend the holidays with my sister, Arjuna. We rang in the new millennium together, hoping for a more peaceful one than the last. My New Year's wish for 2000? Some love and joy for a lonely boy. My wish came true. That winter, Eugene and I rekindled our flame after 21 years! So much time had passed since I had left him in Calgary in 1979. My heart had shattered when he had taken up with Cassie. So, I was overjoyed at the prospect of a reunion as I had given him up as a long lost love. In September, we moved into an apartment in the gay village. His cat, Rusty James, in tow, we settled into life together (older, but no wiser).

Several months earlier, I had met Susan Gapka,[24] a trans woman in early transition. We began a collegial relationship as fellow activists (initially, with me as mentor), and over the next few years, we collaborated on substantial trans work: leading support groups for trans people, putting on community workshops, writing research papers on trans health, training healthcare professionals, consulting with lawyers and politicians, and educating the public through the media. We delivered two training workshops at CAMH for mental health clinicians and students, grounded in my TransPositive Therapeutic Model™ (more about this later). We also formed The Thursday Night Group, a support group for trans people who misuse alcohol or drugs.

Disappointingly, it was short-lived due to waning attendance. Susan proved to be a strong asset as a group leader, having beaten alcohol and drugs herself after 10 years on the street, maintaining sobriety through harm-reduction strategies; then, going back to school to earn a political science degree, eventually running for city councilor, and becoming one of Canada's most successful trans activists. A case of the student surpassing the teacher!

In the spring, I began another half-year clinical internship at CAMH's Rainbow Services (addiction treatment program for LGBTTI2SQQAA people), supervised by then program coordinator Farzana Doctor, a South Asian lesbian therapist. I co-led (with social worker Chris Haddon) an addictions recovery group for gay and bi men, and also facilitated an anti-oppression group for queer and trans clients who misused substances to combat sexual orientation and gender identity discrimination, brainstorming healthier alternatives for surviving in a homophobic and transphobic world.

Work, school, community activism: this was my tripart existence. Getting back into the swing as a trans activist, I strove to expand my community connections, applying for a position on the community advisory committee of David Kelley Services (DKS), a gay/lesbian and HIV+ counselling service. Incredibly, I was declined for being the *wrong* sex! DKS wanted (and got) a trans woman, so I had to wait for a future vacancy, eventually reapplying successfully in 2007. Disappointed, I took this initial rejection in stride, however, because I wanted my trans sisters to have a fair playing field given the rampant sexism in society, particularly transmisogyny. This is why, sometime later, I urged Toronto's Sherbourne Health Centre (SHC) to follow the examples of The 519 Community Centre in Toronto and Québec Trans Health Action (*Action Santé Travesti(e)s et Transsexuel(le)s du Québec—AST(e)Q*) in Montreal, to hire more trans women given that, over time, SHC had employed three times as many trans-males as trans-females. It took some time, but eventually, Rainbow Health Ontario (RHO)—a partnership between Sherbourne Health Centre and the Rainbow Health Network—hired a trans woman, on contract, in 2016. My urging then new RHO director, Devon MacFarlane,[25] might have helped, but I know he would have done so regardless. Gender equity is the measure of a progressive organization!

Farzana also invited me to join Rainbow Services' program advisory committee and asked me to review the first draft of a resource manual for mental health and addiction professionals serving trans and queer clients.[26] She exemplified radical acceptance, the radical inclusivity (originally a Buddhist value embracing all sentient beings) practiced by a number of humanists and feminists, especially those who do not exclude trans women. Farzana flung open the doors of addiction services at CAMH to the trans/intersex/Two-Spirit community that had been pathologized for three decades as a psychiatrically-disordered patient population by the transphobic regime of both the adult and youth gender identity clinics: thereby, leaving the community feeling unsafe to access other CAMH programs, such as mental health, addictions, and specialized housing. There should be a post-trauma support group for CAMH gender clinic survivors! Rainbow Services was a milestone in terms of trans-inclusivity: we need more cisgender allies like Farzana. Fortunately, others soon emerged.[27]

Continuing to educate the public, I appeared on a Canada-wide, TV documentary series, *Skin Deep*.[28] Eugene and I discussed our "sexistential" relationship as bi trans men in Episode 8 (2000). Kyle Scanlon was also filmed for this segment, while undergoing top surgery performed by Dr. Yves Ménard at the Montreal Gender-Reassignment Surgery Clinic. The following year, I was again featured in *Skin Deep* (Episode 31, 2001), with Susan Gapka (at the Ontario Provincial Legislature) and several other trans women.

Eugene and I celebrated our one-year anniversary at Zippers, a disco club in the gay village, with my trans friends Levy and Curtis (then a couple) partying along with us. Sadly, my romance with Eugene was winding down due to recurring relationship problems. As the music blared to the house beat, we had our last dance as a couple. Still, we managed to remain roommates for a little while longer.

That fall, I panicked because our school did not arrange our internships, and I had yet to come up with my last one. Scrambling after being declined by several agencies lacking available supervisory personnel, I convinced Gail Flintoff, a social worker at Casey House to supervise my remaining clinical hours. She saved my ass as I counselled four trans clients for the duration of my program.

Come spring, a lightning bolt struck me when my boss asked for my resignation after one and a half years on the job. I was devastated! My dismissal was prompted by a complaint from a domineering (cis straight) female supervisor, claiming that I wasn't cut out for the job after all. Micromanaging me and my co-workers, she had charmed our boss, a meek gay man, who finally gave in to her trumped-up criticisms of my work performance and let me go. I later learned that she used the same intimidation tactics against my gay-male successor! I appealed to the Canadian Union of Public Employees (CUPE), but, remarkably, my union steward proved counterproductive, more pro-management than pro-employee. So, I advocated for myself, negotiating with the executive director to lay me off so that I wouldn't forfeit my employment insurance benefits. I also requested multiple photocopies of my résumé and a send-off to say goodbye to my co-workers. He readily agreed to all of my requests, no thanks to my unsupportive union steward (a gay woman). So much for queer solidarity!

Previously, my boss had not fully supported me when I had tried to reach out to the transgender community, objecting that trans outreach wasn't a part of my job. No wonder it took ACT—historically, an agency staffed by White, middle class, cisgender, gay men—so long to become trans-inclusive! Nonetheless, I kept on urging the powers that be to start caring about trans people because so many of our brothers and sisters were dying on the streets. This being 2001, would trans care at ACT ultimately happen in the new millennium? Fortunately, trans inclusive programs were eventually developed sometime later.[29] I didn't need agency affiliation, however, to help me carry on my gender work. That September, I drove to Peterborough with my York University philosophy professor friend, Miqqi (Michael) Gilbert to co-present at Trent University's TransIdentities Symposium. That's where I probably first met Dr. Karleen Pendleton Jiménez,[30] an associate professor in Trent's School of Education, whose academic and artistic contributions to the gender non-binary include her work on tomboyism and butch lesbianism as often unrecognized distinctive gender/sexual identities. Unexpectedly, however, I came across Dr. Norman Barwin, my physician in Ottawa, who had given me my second shot of life-saving T 30 years previously!

Not having to worry about work, I could now focus exclusively on my studies, finishing up my classes and my major clinical paper on trans therapy (an expanded version of which I would later publish in the *International Journal of Transgenderism*). My final exam was in August: I couldn't wait to graduate. Utterly exhausted after three years of intense coursework and 600 hours of clinical internships, I passed with flying colours. However, the examiners did fail one of my classmates for his presumptuous attitude. In the healing profession, humility—as well as respect, empathy, and compassion—not merely a grasp of psychological theories and therapeutic modalities—is critical. To be an effectual mental health practitioner, one must invoke all three minds: reasonable mind, emotional mind, and wise mind (per dialectical behavioral therapy). We need "the whole shebang": logic *and* emotion, facts *and* feelings—and intuitive wisdom. Moreover, the human touch is paramount to effective client care.

My schooling finally all done, I boarded a plane for Victoria for my anticipated stay at Arjuna's health spa: 10 days of R&R, winding down from my intense three year academic/clinical regimen. Mentally and physically fatigued, my sister was the cure for what ailed me. It took me a good three months to renew, but, as always, resilience prevailed.

As a long overdue reward for my 30 years of trans activism, I earned two back-to-back Lifetime Community Achievement Awards[31] in October and November of 2001. The first was presented at the Sexin' Change: Reclaiming our Genders and Bodies conference at Toronto's Ryerson University—the first ever national trans conference in Canada—organized by trans activists Dr. Dan

Irving and our cis ally, Dr. Nicola Brown. The second was presented at the Trans Planet Awards ceremony sponsored by the Supporting Our Youth program's Trans-Fusion Crew (a support group for trans and gender non-binary youth). Basking in the light of my trans peers and cis allies, public recognition was well worth the wait!

Finally, my long-awaited convocation day arrived! Capped and gowned, I walked up the aisle to proudly accept my degree (Master of Arts in Counseling Psychology), as Eugene and several of my friends, Levy, Susan, Cheryl, and Kay applauded my hard-won achievement. I had finally made the grade as a psychotherapist—a professional therapeutic healer!

Chapter 8 Notes

[1] These psychological theories included: behavioural psychology, social psychology, psychodynamic psychology, Adlerian individual psychology, Freudian psychology, Jungian psychology, Gestalt psychology, and humanistic and existential psychology.

[2] These therapeutic modalities included: Adlerian Therapy, Franklian Logotherapy, client-centred therapy, cognitive behavioral therapy, mindfulness-based cognitive behavior therapy, dialectical behavioral therapy, acceptance and commitment therapy, solution-focussed brief therapy, narrative therapy, metaphor therapy, feminist therapy, and trauma therapy, as well as addictions counselling, couple counselling, family therapy, and group therapy.

[3] See: Vitale, Anne, "The Therapist versus the Client," in Gianna E. Israel and Donald E. Tarver, II, MD, eds., *Transgender Care: Recommended Guidelines, Practical Information & Personal Accounts*, Philadelphia, PA: Temple University Press, 1997, chapter 23.

[4] One psychologist did not openly identify as transgender to their trans clients, doubted the existence of core gender identity, and did not challenge the psychoanalytical theories and aversion therapies of a transphobic cisgender psychologist! The other one was openly transgender but did not sufficiently advocate for their gender-dysphoric clients seeking gender transition services—either on an individual case, or an organizational level—and also supported the research and treatment of a non-transpositive psychiatrist and psychologist (both cisgender)! Intentionally not named here to protect their privacy, I only wish they had used their professional positions of power to be effective allies of their trans peers.

[5] Friday Night Productions, *Rewriting the Script: A Love Letter to Our Families*, Toronto, ON: Vtape, 2001. https://www.youtube.com/watch?v=b2lMb-58MH4.

[6] For books by feminist therapists, Dr. Carol Gilligan, Dr. Lenore Walker, and Dr. Harriet Lerner, see: Intersectional Bibliography.

[7] For more information on Kanzan and Jittok (Japanese Zen Buddhist pilgrims derived from their Chinese Buddhist predecessors, Hanshan and Shide), see https://en.wikipedia.org/wiki/Hanshan_and_Shide.

[8] For more information on the Middle Eastern wise fool, Mullah Nasrudin, see https://en.wikipedia.org/wiki/The_Exploits_of_the_Incomparable_Mulla_Nasrudin.

[9] For lyrics to the song, "To Life (L'Chaim)," written by Sheldon Harnick for the 1964 Broadway musical show, *Fiddler on the Roof*, see https://www.stlyrics.com/lyrics/fiddlerontheroof/tolife.htm; and https://en.wikipedia.org/wiki/To_Life_(song). For lyrics to the 2001 (or 2003) song, "Here's to Life (Streetlight Manifesto)," written by Kalnoky Tomas, copyright by Kandur Bandi Publishing, see https://www.paroles-musique.com/eng/Streetlight_Manifesto-Heres_to_Life-lyrics,p02945153. The latter song references French, absurdist existential philosopher, Albert Camus—one of my favourite inspirational role models.

[10] Mirha-Soleil Ross (born to a Métis mother in Montreal, Quebec) was formerly known as

Jeanne B. before she moved to Toronto. In 2001, she was elected Grand Marshal of Toronto's Pride Parade and, in 2011, she was inducted into Canada's Q Hall of Fame. She has since moved back to Montreal. Mirha-Soleil's fonds are housed at The ArQuives in Toronto. https://arquives.andornot.com/en/list?q=mirha-soleil+ross+Fonds&p=1&ps=20. See: "Interview with Mirha-Soleil Ross," in Viviane Namaste, *Sex Change, Social Change: Reflections on Identity, Institutions, and Imperialism*, Women's Press (Canadian Scholars' Press), 2005, 86-102. See also https://zagria.blogspot.ca/2014/09/mirha-soleil-ross-1969-sex-worker.html.

[11] The cultural artifacts Xanthra Phillippa Mackay (1956-2014) co-created with Mirha-Soleil Ross are part of Mirha's fonds at The ArQuives and the LGBTQ Oral History Digital Collaboratory. See the iconic photo of these two gender troublemakers, happy together. http://digitalcollections.clga.ca/exhibits/show/gendertrash/item/870.

[12] Ross, Mirha-Soleil, and Xanthra Mackay, dirs., *Gendertroublemakers*, Toronto, ON: Vtape, 1993. http://www.vtape.org/video?vi=3636.

[13] Ross, Mirha-Soleil, and Xanthra Phillippa Mackay, eds., *gender trash from hell*, Toronto, ON: genderpress, 1993. https://www.digitaltransgenderarchive.net/files/xg94hp65x; http://digitalcollections.clga.ca/exhibits/show/gendertrash/item/767.

[14] Tragically, Mark Karbusicky took his life in 2007 at 35. Mike Hoolboom's short film, *Mark*, Toronto, ON, 2009. https://vimeo.com/139616710), pays tribute to this gentle animal rights activist, political vegan, punk maestro, and life partner of Mirha-Soleil Ross.

[15] As well as monthly meetings held throughout the late 1980s and 1990s, Khush organized queer South Asian cultural events, including its landmark annual Desh Pardesh festival, which ran until 2001. Khush also put out periodicals, including *Khush Khayal* (the first South Asian gay/lesbian newspaper in Toronto, founded in 1989) and a quarterly zine, *Avec Pyar*.

[16] Salaam: Queer Muslim Community (https://www.salaamcanada.info/) originally started as Salaam: A Social/Support group for Lesbian and Gay Muslims, in Toronto in 1991, founded by Islamic immigration lawyer, El-Farouk Khaki, who has now established the Toronto Unity Mosque. See: Khaki, El-Farouk, "Building the Unity Mosque," in John Lorinc et al., eds., *Any Other Way*, 321-323. *Salaam* (which means "peace") advocates for social justice for the Muslim queer/trans community and is a member of the Global Queer Muslim Network.

[17] Fernandez, Sharon, *Desh Pardesh: A Festival with Attitude*, in John Lorinc et al, *Any Other Way*, 261-264.

[18] Multimedia artist, Aiyyana Maracle (1950-2016), was profiled in words: Cross, Kathleen, ed., *The Trans Biography Project: Stories from the Lives of Eleven Trans People in B.C.*, Vancouver, BC: The Women/Trans Dialogue Planning Committee and Trans Alliance Society, 2001. http://www.transalliancesociety.org/education/documents/01transbiosmall.pdf; and interviewed on Tranzister Radio 29 (CKUT 90.3 FM), October 9, 2014. https://drive.google.com/file/d/0B0KGgCD3_zjTMjVXT2ZvM1J0VnM/edit.

[19] See: Kodak, Boyd, and Cat Grant, prods., *Shadmith Manzo Performance*, Toronto, ON: Vtape, 1998. http://www.vtape.org/video?vi=4417.

[20] Mackay, Xanthra, dir., *Rupert Remembers*, Toronto, ON: Sexy Voice Video Production,

Vtape, 1999, 2000. http://www.vtape.org/video?vi=4390.

[21] Counting Past 2 ran four times from 1997 to 2002. Performers included Aiyyana Maracle, Max Wolf Valerio and other trans people. As a transsexual/transgender film, video, performance and spoken-word festival, it provided a space for trans people to portray themselves without pandering to cisgender audiences or being subsumed by the larger gay/lesbian/bisexual artistic community. See: Salah, Trish, "Notes Toward Thinking Transsexual Institutional Poetics," in Eva C. Karpinski, Jennifer Henderson, Ian Sowton, and Ray Ellenwood, eds., *Trans/Acting Culture, Writing, and Memory: Essays in Honour of Barbara Godard*, Waterloo, ON: Wilfred Laurier University Press, 2013, 167-189.

[22] Read Dr. Elisabeth Kübler-Ross's *On Death and Dying*, 1969; and *AIDS: The Ultimate Challenge*, 1988 (both published by Macmillan Publishers in New York, NY).

[23] See: Bockting, Walter O., PsyD., and Sheila Kirk, MD, eds., *Transgender and HIV: Risks, Prevention, and Care*, Binghamton, NY: Haworth Press, 2001.

[24] Watch out for *Act Three* (working title: *Susan Gapka: A Documentary Film*) (in production), a Canadian film by Lisa Rideout, director/producer, and Sarah Fisher, producer, documenting this trans woman's life story from a pre-transitional, homeless addict to an effective trans activist and politician, who has (unsuccessfully) run for public office multiple times from 2006 through 2018. I successfully nominated Susan in 2004 for The City of Toronto Access, Equity and Human Rights Pride Award, and in 2017, the Canadian Centre for Gender & Sexual Diversity presented her with the Youth Award.

[25] See Devon MacFarlane's two chapters: "Happy Tranny Day" (with Tien Neo Eamas), in Irving and Raj, *Trans Activism in Canada*, 137-147; and "One Step at A Time: Moving Trans Activism Forward in a Large Bureaucracy" (with Lorraine Grieves and Al Zwiers), in Irving and Raj, 195-207.

[26] See the revised version, Barbara, Angela M., Gloria Chaim, and Farzana Doctor, *Asking the Right Questions 2: Talking with Clients about Sexual Orientation and Gender Identity in Mental Health, Counselling and Addiction Settings*. Toronto, ON: Rainbow Services, Centre for Addiction and Mental Health, 2004, 2007. https://cdn.dal.ca/content/dam/dalhousie/pdf/campuslife/studentservices/healthandwellness/LGBTQ/asking_the_right_questions.pdf.

[27] From about 2001 to 2017 (2017 being the year I finished the first edition of this memoir), these Toronto-based cisgender allies (among others) included: Anna Travers, Carole Baker, and Billee Laskin at Sherbourne Health Centre; Bev Lepischak and LeeAndra Miller at Central Toronto Youth Services; Kirsten Schmidt-Chamberlain at Fred Victor Centre; Lorraine Gale and Krin Zook at the Children's Aid Society of Toronto; Dick Moore (and later, Steven Little) at The 519 Community Centre; Ranjith Prasanna Kulatilake at Access Alliance Multicultural Health and Community Services; Bill Worrell and Dr. Louie Chan at East Mississauga Community Health Centre; Lori-Ann Green-Walker and Jothi Ramesh at Women's Health in Women's Hands Community Health Centre; Sue Hranilovic, NP, Dr. Abbas Ghavam-Rassoul, and Celia Schwartz at St. Michael's Hospital; Dr. Chris McIntosh and Dr. Nicola Brown at the CAMH Adult Gender Identity Clinic; Dr. Nick Mulé and Richard Hudler at the Rainbow Health Network and Queer Ontario.

[28] Episode 7 of the TV documentary, *Skin Deep*, Toronto, ON: Inner-City Films (2000), featured several trans women, including trans activist, Christina Strang, who succeeded Mirha-Soleil Ross as the Meal Trans Program coordinator at The 519 Community Centre in Toronto.

[29] The AIDS Committee of Toronto (ACT) ran a trans-male group for a brief time in the mid 2000s, and currently runs several trans-inclusive groups. http://www.actoronto.org/programs-services/groups. The Gay, Bi, Queer Trans Men's Working Group (http://www.queertransmen.org/) offers resources such as *Primed: The Back Pocket Guide for Transmen & Those Who Dig Them*, Toronto, ON: Gay Men's Sexual Health Alliance, 2007, and *Primed^2: A Sex Guide for Trans Men into Men*, 2015). http://www.catie.ca/en/resources/primed-sex-guide-trans-men-men.

[30] Read lesbian tomboy Dr. Karleen Pendleton Jiménez's memoir, *How to Get a Girl Pregnant*, Toronto, ON: Tightrope Books, 2011; and her children's picture book, *Are You a Boy or a Girl?*, Toronto, ON: Green Dragon Press, 2000, rev. 2006. See also: Jiménez, Karleen Pendleton, and Isabel Killoran, eds., *Unleashing the Unpopular: Talking About Sexual Orientation and Gender Diversity in Education*, Association for Childhood Education International, 2007. https://acei.org. And watch her film, Taylor, Barb (creator), and Karleen Pendleton Jiménez (writer), *Tomboy* (English & Spanish), Toronto, ON: Coyle Productions, 2008. https://vimeo.com/10772672.

[31] Disappointingly, I mislaid the only known photograph taken of me (with Eugene) at my first Lifetime Achievement Award ceremony in October! Happily, I salvaged a photo of me at my second award ceremony in November—sounding my rally cry, "Trans Pride! Trans Power!"—which follows this chapter.

Me (R) and my brother, Casimir.
Ottawa, Ontario, 1972

Showing off my hairy torso three years after top surgery.
Vancouver, BC, 1975
(Photo: James Loewen)

__Posing with my coquettish friend, Louise.__
__Vancouver, BC, 1975__
(Photo: James Loewen)

Embracing a rare moment of "existential ease"
and "gender euphoria."
Vancouver, BC, 1975
(Photo: James Loewen)

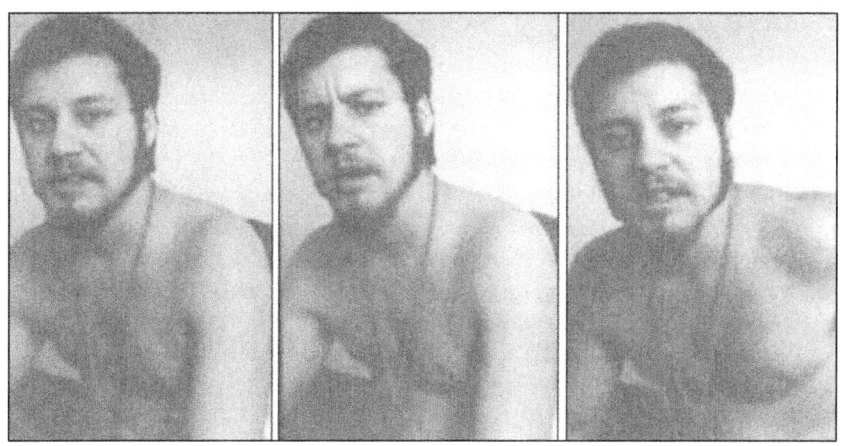

The many moods of Rupert Raj.
Vancouver, BC, 1975
This photo appeared in Gender Review *(June 1978)*
under my former name, Nicholas Ghosh.
(Photo: James Loewen)

Me (R) and my brother, Jakub.
Vancouver, BC, 1976

A hairy "RuBear" wearing spectacles just like my father's.
Calgary, Alberta, 1977

In my androgynous, "hippie" mode, complete with long hair, beard,
earring, ankh pendant, and saffron Indian shirt.
Calgary, Alberta, 1979

Projecting my professional persona as the "corporate man."
Toronto, Ontario, 1982
This photo accompanied my life profile in Metamorphosis *(February 1983).*

Rupert Raj (R) and Susan Huxford-Westall (C)
delivering a training seminar on trans ex-prisoners to the Elizabeth Fry Society.
Kingston, Ontario, 1983

*Partying with trans and cis friends at
Vicki Bellefeuille's Rosedale apartment.
Toronto, Ontario, 1985*

*Ever the dashing "dandy" with open-necked shirt and gold chain.
Toronto, Ontario, 1986*

Rupert Raj and Tri-Ess Director Carol Beecroft at the first annual International Foundation for Gender Education (IFGE) convention. Chicago, Illinois, 1987
(Photo: *The TV-TS Tapestry* 1987, [50]: 27)

Me, wearing my trademark red Doc Martens, with my sister, Arjuna. Victoria, BC, 1999

*Sounding my rally cry, "Trans Pride! Trans Power!,"
at my Lifetime Achievement Award ceremony
(Supporting Our Youth Program, Trans Planet Awards).
Toronto, Ontario, 2001*

Part III:

Therapeutic Healer, Teacher & Writer

* * *

THERAPEUTIC HEALER

Healing the hearts and minds
of the wounded and the weary–
witnessing self-actualization
through sexual transition
as we travel together
on their own gender journey.

* * *

TEACHER

Teaching the cisgender world about
transgender identity is challenging
because of our divergent lived experience–
yet "intentional acceptance" of a trans person
does not require full understanding when
respect and compassion bridge the knowledge gap.

* * *

WRITER

Despair rends my heart
and fire rages in my bowels
as ink flows through my veins.
Writing saves my sanity–
"creative resistors"
zapping right and left brains!

* * *

9. Psychotherapy...Gender Consulting...Second Marriage and Divorce (2001-2011)

Newly-equipped with my Master's degree, I finally secured employment after applying to several postings. It was a five-month contract with the Children's Aid Society of Toronto (CAST), job-sharing with Lorraine Gale, the LGBT Youth Program Director. My duties were to research information towards drafting a policy for timely access to healthcare for gender non-conforming youth in care—including puberty-suppressant agonists or cross-sex hormones—and gender-affirming education for foster/adoptive parents. I joined CAST's transsexual/transgender advisory committee and my preparatory work informed the agency's affirmative practice guidelines regarding queer and gender-variant youth in care.[1] I also delivered a Trans 101 seminar to managers and staff, and, over time, participated in two more inter-agency trainings.

That December of 2001, Susan Gapka and I put on a professional-development workshop for mental health practitioners through The Adler School of Professional Psychology. Twenty-five professional colleagues came out to learn about my TransPositive Therapeutic Model™, based on my journal paper (in-progress). My first trans focussed training as a full fledged psychotherapist. I was in my prime! Exactly three decades had passed since my humble beginnings as a peer counsellor/researcher/educator in 1971. Now, officially welcomed into the fold as a professional peer, I would prove to be a valuable asset as a gender consultant, helping (mental) health practitioners build expertise in trans care.

In February 2002, I celebrated my 50th birthday with Eugene and some trans friends in a low-key gathering. Half a century old, I had already achieved many of my life ambitions and goals: personally (gender transitioning, romantic relationships, pet companionship, travelling, writing), professionally (higher education, private clinical practice, gender consulting, professional training, academic teaching, research, writing, editing), and as an activist (community building, political lobbying, public education, media liaison, writing, editing). Writing is the unifying thread; hence, this memoir. But a few more goals still remained.

First on the list, post-graduation, was making a living. My CAST contract completed, I needed another job to pay my way. I applied to several likely places: CAMH's Cocaine Services, Family Service Association of Toronto's counselling services, David Kelley Services, LGBT and HIV counselling services, and Homeward (a community agency for people with mental health issues in conflict with the law). Landing three interviews but no job offers, I was getting worried! So, I started up RR Consulting, a private psychotherapy practice targeting an LGBTTI2SQQAA clientele. I rented office space in the west end: but, struggling to find paying clients, I ended up undercharging, barely breaking even.

Between my struggling private practice and ongoing search for an organizational employer, I persevered with my research paper, my diligent efforts finally paying off. "Towards a Transpositive Therapeutic Model: Developing Clinical Sensitivity and Cultural Competence in the Effective Support of Transsexual and Transgendered Clients"[2] was published in the *International Journal of Transgenderism* in 2002. My first clinical paper in print—Rupert, the researcher! The reviewers called it a "scholarly work." Acclaim by my academic/clinical peers was indeed gratifying!

In 2003, I produced a second paper, "The Trans Health Project"[3] with co-investigator Susan Gapka and a workgroup of the Ontario Public Health Association (OPHA). Our study researched social determinants of health within the trans community, identified healthcare needs and service gaps, and proposed recommendations, some of which OPHA has already implemented. Susan and I hope our trans peers and cis allies appreciate this labour of love, having given up at least two statutory holidays, countless weekends, and a folk-music festival to meet the deadline! We further hope that our recommendations will improve the quality of life of some trans Ontarians in certain small ways. There's no personal glory in community-based participatory action research: however, our efforts can pay off if the findings and recommendations are applied in practice.

Eventually, I got a job with Homeward as a caseworker, providing therapeutic support to incarcerated males with mental health issues in the nearby Don Jail. I was relieved to eventually leave this position because I abhorred the racist, sexist, genderphobic jail guards. The women were just as bad as the men. I was nervous that they might discover my secret—I had reverted to living a double life for this prison job, while still appearing on TV shows—and harass me. I also feared for my psychological and physical safety, even though I was partially postsurgical. After five months at Homeward, I was finally free to pursue my dream job—the one I had hoped for ever since graduating university in 1975!

Right before my new job was to start, I presented a trans-focussed workshop at the Gay and Lesbian Medical Association (GLMA) conference in Toronto. My presentation was a clinical plea to cisgender queer mental health practitioners to be truly transpositive when counselling trans clients who are either questioning their sexual orientation, or who already identify as gay, lesbian, bisexual, or pansexual *as their identified sexual identity, even before medical gender-reassignment.* Such a client-centred approach unconditionally accepts a pre-transitional trans dyke for who she is and a pre-transitional trans fag for who he is despite their unique body configurations at the time. My choice of presentation was inspired by Dr. Joanne Springer, a trans-identified physician and psychotherapist in NYC, who shared with me her past struggles with GLMA and with certain trans-unfriendly cisqueer healthcare professionals. It was my responsibility to advocate for my queer-identified and queer-questioning trans peers given the then prevalent transphobia and "transqueerphobia" perpetrated by many cisgender healthcare professionals. Most people (initially) resist change, and when it comes to accepting transqueers, cisqueers are no exception! Thankfully, LGBTTI2SQQAA primary care, mental healthcare, sexual healthcare, and social work practice have been steadily changing for the better due to clinical advocacy for better practices in the form of books and published papers by transgender, Two-Spirit, and cisgender health researchers, healthcare practitioners, psychotherapists, and social workers.[4] Psychiatry has made some recent headway in terms of queer-affirming treatment,[5] but still has a way to go to be truly gender-affirming! Between jobs and nearly broke, I also advocated for myself, asking the organizers to waive the $300 USD conference fee as I was not only a presenter but also a recent starving graduate.

Samuel Lurie, an American trans-identified therapist, presented his workshop immediately following mine on our shared panel; the audience (standing room only) loved us. Carrie Davis, a trans-female social worker from Callen-Lorde Community Health Center in NYC, was there with her co-workers. Serendipitously, my family doctor (Dr. Abbas Ghavam-Rassoul) and my new boss-to-be (Anna Travers) were also present: a milestone moment. I could feel the love of my chosen family and I couldn't wait to start my dream job at Sherbourne Health Centre! Given my limited success with my private practice and my yearning to reclaim my weekends after seven years of virtually no personal or social life, I closed up shop after nine months and devoted myself entirely to my new full-time job.

I began work at Sherbourne Health Centre (SHC) in November 2002 as a mental health counsellor, serving queer, transsexual, transgender, genderqueer, intersex, and Two-Spirit adults, gender non-conforming youth, and their loved ones. An interdisciplinary centre,[6] the managers and front-line staff included a number of cisgender queer and transgender/genderqueer people. It was validating to work with a trans physician, trans/genderqueer nurses, a trans client resource worker, trans psychotherapists, trans/genderqueer receptionists, and a trans program coordinator. Two of these were trans people of colour or mixed race: Dr. Sydney Tam,[7] a Eurasian, primary care physician, and Yasmeen Persad,[8] an African Canadian trans program coordinator. I provided individual, couple, and family therapy, and co-facilitated two groups: TransFormations—an arts-based group for trans youth—with LeeAndra Miller, and Gender Journeys—a psychoeducational group for people considering gender transitioning—with Yasmeen Persad. I also co-designed and co-delivered several community educational workshops for various subpopulations: older trans women, older trans men, transforming couples, and transforming families, and a combined workshop for trans people of colour and Two-Spirit people. Additionally, I conducted workshops on specific topics such as: body image issues for trans men, internalized transphobia, trans activists learning and working together, and intergenerational engagement between Black/Brown transgender/genderqueer youth and elders.

From the outset, SHC has been a leader in creating safety when welcoming trans people into historically trans-exclusionary gendered spaces (such as the Michigan Womyn's Musical Festival,[9] the Vancouver Rape Relief Society,[10] and Toronto's Spa Excess gay male bathhouse,[11] to name only a few). Two examples of intentionally trans-inclusive spaces at SHC were created by my LGBT counsellor colleagues: Carole Baker's Outside the Lines expressive-arts group for isolated queer and trans women, and Dr. Peter Hall's trauma recovery group for queer and trans men. It's heartwarming when our cisgender allies proactively create change for the better!

Besides my functions as a psychotherapist and group facilitator, I continued my advocacy role as a community builder by spearheading SHC's annual Trans Pride Day (later renamed Trans, Intersex & Two-Spirit Pride Day) beginning in 2004. This was one of several major trans community events in Toronto, often bringing out 50-100 people (including partners, parents, children, friends, community members, healthcare and social service providers, and even politicians) every year in a celebration of trans culture and gender diversity. One year, we hosted a workshop on Indigenous Two-Spirit people (more about this later). Not surprisingly, a number of Indigenous people also identify as transgender[12] and some Indigenous trans people identify as Two-Spirit, or as "third, fourth, fifth, or sixth gender." Non-transgender, Two-Spirit activists[13] are often transpositive allies. Similarly, there are non-Indigenous trans activists who are allies of Indigenous trans people and Two-Spirit people.[14]

Along with counselling support, group work, program development, and community outreach, I was also involved in advocacy research and joined Sherbourne's Trans and Primary Care Working Group—formed by then LGBT manager, Anna Travers—which included a doctor, a nurse, and two trans community members. The group's mandate was to create hormone therapy protocols for our trans clients, which were published in 2009.[15] The working group was later succeeded by the Trans PULSE project,[16] a government-funded research project, initiated by Anna, Kyle Scanlon and me, to survey the social determinants of health of trans Ontarians and their access to healthcare and social services. Trans PULSE's 433 respondents generated important research data: higher risks for suicidality, self-harm, problematic substance use, (under)employment, poverty, homelessness, and inequitable access to transpositive healthcare and social services.

An undetermined number of our transgender-identifying clients and local community members were also intersex. However, not always feeling included or supported—either at SHC or elsewhere in the community—intersex people often did not openly identify as such. Sometimes, their intersex identity was suppressed because of shame (internalized "intersexphobia"). Fortunately, such shame is now absent in a growing number of people who have publicly disclosed their dual transgender/intersex identity.[17] For deceased trans/intersex people, their invisibility and shame was likely even greater, given the lack of scientific knowledge and attendant public non-acceptance. Wanting to educate others at SHC about this mostly-invisible population, I asked Susan Gapka to co-present a workshop for our managers, staff, and students. Our Intersexuality 101 included the showing of a Canadian TV special on the subject.[18] This would be the first of two knowledge transfers on intersex at SHC spearheaded by me, despite the resistance of several managers and staff, who protested that SHC wasn't (and shouldn't be) experts in the field, even though our centre had already developed, from scratch, trans-specific programming within our overall LGBT program. I wasn't asking for clinical expertise, *per se*, only for greater visibility and inclusivity, as a few other LGBTTI2SQQAA centres were doing in North America and Australia (more about this later).

Undeterred, my limited allies (several co-workers) and I persisted in our efforts to educate and advocate towards greater awareness and inclusivity within our diverse client populations and communities, specifically for intersex and Indigenous folks. As self-admitted, non-expert allies, Susan and I delivered a follow-up workshop in 2004 on Intersex Awareness Day (October 26)[19] in collaboration with CAMH's LGBTI Caucus. Regrettably, we did not have the resources at the time to arrange for an intersex participant but, some years later, I invited intersex-identified activist/academic Dr. Morgan Holmes to present at Sherbourne (more about this later). Several other Canadian intersex activists (who also identified as trans or Two-Spirit) were also starting to speak out, including Alec Butler and Martine Stonehouse.[20] (To learn about my intersex advocacy at SHC, see chapter 11).

Having settled in at Sherbourne Health Centre, I could now resume my other activist efforts outside of the centre. I approached Susan again, and together with Michelle Hogan, Martine Stonehouse, JoAnn Nevermann, Darla S., and Shadmith Manzo, we formed the Trans Health Lobby Group (THLG), which later became a subcommittee of the Rainbow Health Network.[21] We lobbied Greenpeace Canada Executive Director, Peter Tabuns, and several Members of Provincial Parliament (MPPs) (Gerard Kennedy, Tony Rupprecht, George Smitherman, Marilyn Churley, and Cheri DiNovo) to reinstate Ontario Health Insurance Plan (OHIP) coverage for sex-reassignment surgery (SRS) for trans Ontarians. Caught in the political fallout, Michelle and Martine (also A.B. and Andy McDonald) had filed a joint Ontario human rights complaint against the Ontario Ministry of Health, protesting that the 1998 SRS delisting had disrupted their medical gender transitions. In 2007, Michelle, Martine, and A.B. won their joint suit, including funding for surgery and general damages for discrimination. We finally succeeded in getting SRS relisted as an insured provincial government health service in 2008. At that time, there was a huge backlog of trans people awaiting assessment and approval for insured surgeries. Over the next few years, THLG would help win other legal victories for trans Ontarians, including Bill 33 (*Toby's Act*) (more about this later). We also lobbied to have the sex designation removed from the Ontario health card and driver's license, and federally-issued passports (for the latter, we had to wait almost another decade for such gender positive legislation).[22]

Beyond activism and work, I had a home life, interacting with the human and animal members of our household. That year, Eugene's orange calico, Rusty James, passed on in his sleep after 23 years of good living. We eventually adopted three other cats from the Toronto Humane Society: Angie (a two-year-old, black kitty with the softest fur and a playful disposition), Pinky (a four-year-old, skittish tabby with white fur and pinkish ears), and Max (a 15-year-old gray tabby with a bushy tail and a kitten's personality). A senior myself, I deliberately chose the oldest cat there (Max), countering the rampant ageism in our society that discounts the elderly. All three felines delighted in scampering up and down their kitty condo, getting high on the catnip-filled toy mice in their grip, before contentedly curling up to sleep. For now, all was quiet on the home front.

Periodically overwhelmed by the dual challenges of clinical work and community activism, I had to ensure my self-care (Physician, heal thyself!). So, I took a brief holiday every year, visiting family or friends in various provinces or states in order to get away from the local scene, affording me a needed break from office politics and trans politics alike, too close to home. In February 2003, I visited my trans-female friend, Heidi, and her cisgender girlfriend in Orlando, and in April 2004, I visited my Black trans-male friend, Jiles, in Atlanta. Both trans people were former activists who had long since retired from the gender community; so, happily for me, no trans political talk. One of them had even changed their name to hide their trans identity after going stealth. The former had been active in the American northeast in the mid to late 1980s and the latter had been a co-organizer of the annual Southern Comfort trans conference in Atlanta in the early 1990s. Sometimes, I vacationed in Ontario, travelling north to cottage country and lakeside campsites. That summer, in 2004, I attended my first LGBTQ camp.

Organized by the Out & Out club, the annual, weeklong Jamboree camp took place northeast of Toronto on a private lake near Haliburton. Apparently, I was the only trans person there that season and, as the bunkhouses were gender-segregated, I had to sleep and shower with the men. Bunking in the all-male cabin was fine, but having to expose my privates in a common shower room with all those naked gay guys was daunting! I asked a camp counsellor, Flo, if I could shower in his private cabin and he graciously consented. I also urged the Jamboree organizers to implement trans-friendly procedures for future campers to ensure comfort for guys (or gals) like me who hadn't had bottom surgery. Except for my canoe upturning and me nearly drowning—I can't swim!—I had a fabulous time with my chosen queer family. I felt that I really belonged: just one of the bi guys who happened to be trans. Jamboree sharply contrasted with my childhood Red Pine Camp experience as a gender-distressed 13-year-old when I had to fake it (that oh so disingenuous false positive in smiling photos), pretending to be having a good time while wearing that hated feminine bathing suit!

Now that I had more money and more time, I could finally meet some of the trans people I had networked with around the world over the years. My world was starting to open up and soon I would travel to distant destinations like the British Isles. A longtime Anglophile, I would finally see the UK and Ireland after a 30-year wait. As the Sixth International Congress on Sex and Gender Diversity was being hosted by Dr. Stephen Whittle at Manchester Metropolitan University, I seized the chance to combine work with play. My presentation, "Trans Care at Sherbourne Health Centre," was delivered to a receptive audience of international academics, clinicians, and activists. Besides Stephen, two other trans activist friends were also presenting: Nick Matte, then a doctoral candidate in history at the University of Toronto, and Jamison Green, then a doctoral student in law at Manchester Metropolitan University under Stephen's supervision. I have a memorable photo of the four of us: Canadian, American, and British trans activists-cum-professionals smiling in solidarity. This was truly a milestone moment in academia, only recently welcoming transgender studies as a legitimate sub-discipline of women's and gender studies. Trans-identified professionals were finally breaking through the bastions of cisheteronormative society.

In addition to Stephen, who co-founded (with Mark Rees, Myka Scott, and Krystyna Sheffield), the British trans-advocacy organization, Press for Change (PFC), in 1992, I met two other PFC members: Christine Burns[23] and Claire McNab. For their contributions towards securing respect and equality for trans people in the UK, Stephen was awarded an Order of the British Empire (OBE), and Christine, Claire and physicist Angela Clayton (1959-2014) each earned a Member of the British Empire (MBE). PFC's lobby work with the UK government helped bring about the Gender Recognition Act

(2004), the Equality Act (2010), and, recently, the Transgender Action Plan (2011). Kudos to Stephen, Christine, Claire, and other fellow activists across the pond! Alas, I never got to meet Mark Rees[24] to congratulate him for having the balls to file a lengthy (1972 to 1986) human rights suit against the UK government. I also appreciated American Indian (Lakota) anthropologist Dr. Kenneth Dollarhide's gender-affirming presentation: "The Heart/Spirit, Not the Head/Mind: Being Transgendered is a Spiritual Phenomena, Not a Psychological Condition." A cisgender ally, who celebrated transgender and gender non-binary people, Kenneth also wrote articles on Two-Spirit people.[25]

I lived on the memories of my Albion adventures for the next few months, right up to my 53rd birthday. Even that day (February 10, 2005), I was gender working! The constant activist, I was part of a national trans forum in Toronto hosted by Egale Canada helping to strategize ways to lobby the federal government to amend the Canadian Human Rights Act. We wanted the Act to include both "gender identity" and "gender expression" as protected grounds for any Canadian who transcended society's gender-binary norms of male and female. Such an amendment would prohibit transphobic and genderphobic discrimination against transsexual, transgender, intersex, and Two-Spirit people, as well as genderqueers, crossdressers, and other gender non-conformists. Some years later, both Ontario and British Columbia would lobby for similar amendments to their respective provincial human rights codes (more about this later). Spearheaded by Egale Canada president Helen Kennedy, and Laurie Aaron (then chair of the same-sex marriage committee), this history-making forum was attended by then Toronto Mayor Barbara Hall, as well as eminent cisqueer lawyers and noted trans activists from across Canada.[26] Another milestone moment, transgender activists and cisgender allies were working together towards positive change (more about this later).

Following this intense bit of advocacy on top of my usual work, I was ready for another vacation. So, come spring, I got my ass to San Francisco after three decades of anticipation! I was thrilled to finally see, in person, the city I had vicariously cherished for its celebrated queer (and trans) character—my existential home. I had the good fortune to meet Gianna Israel—a trans-identified therapist and co-editor of *Transgender Care: Recommended Guidelines, Practical Information & Personal Accounts,* 1997—before she died of a brain tumour the following year. A caring person, Gianna's passing was a real loss to our community.

I was also looking forward to meeting again several other American trans colleagues. Dr. Jamison Green[27] met me at the airport and over a few beers, we playfully vented about the troublemakers in the trans community: the moochers, whiners, divas, and flakes who push our buttons! Dr. Susan Stryker[28] showed me the final rushes of her film before rushing off to Australia to show it in Sydney. Max Valerio[29] and I hung out, worrying about Gianna and reminiscing how much we missed Lou Sullivan. Jordy Tackitt-Jones[30] and I talked on the phone but weren't able to connect in person this time around. I toured the GLBT Historical Society in San Francisco where the Louis Graydon Sullivan papers are archived, which contained our respective trans newsletters and our mutual correspondence. Brice D. Smith, a trans doctoral history student at the time, was just starting his research for his biography of that courageous, gay trans-male pioneer, *Lou Sullivan: Daring To Be A Man Among Men* (2017).

I was eager to see the renowned Tom Waddell Urban Health Center—the counterpart of our Toronto Sherbourne Health Centre—which opened the same year in 2002. The striking difference though, was that Tom Waddell employed many more trans women (a sad commentary on Sherbourne). I was privileged to meet the medical director, Dr. Barry Zevin, who gave me a tour of their transgender clinic and invited me to sit in on one of their team meetings with several trans healthcare staff,[31] a gracious gesture of welcome! I also met Dr. JoAnne Keatley, director of the Center for Transgender Resources and Neighborhood Space, where she spearheads a program for trans people of colour. And I can't forget Ms. Alexis, the flamboyant hostess of Divas, a transgender nightclub in the Polk district, as well as talented trans musician Coleman, who sang and played at Eros, a gay bar in the Castro district. I was sad to have to leave my new San Franciscan friends. Happily, I accepted an invitation to present at the Gay and Lesbian Medical Association Conference being held there the following year, giving me another glimpse of the city by the bay.

Back home in Toronto again with Eugene, I grew progressively worried about the risk of fire because he smoked in bed after taking medicinal morphine for multiple sclerosis, which caused drowsiness. Finally, in the summer of 2005, I bought a one bedroom condominium up the street: my first property! On the corner of Jarvis and Gerrard, it was home to me and my cats for eight years. Eugene and I stayed friends for awhile until I regrettably had to cut him out of my life when he began stalking me and harassing me on the phone. Somehow he even managed to get past the concierge in my building and repeatedly banged on my door until he finally gave up when I wouldn't answer. So much for our ricochet romance! Sadly, I never had a chance to repair our relationship before he passed away some years later in the fall of 2017.

Over the next 10 years, on top of my regular counselling job and ongoing trans advocacy, I kept busy researching and writing, consulting and training. Presenting at sexological conferences and mental health workshops in Canada, the USA, and the UK, I shared my four trans-focussed clinical models with professionals and students in the evolving field of trans care. And all this without a PhD! I do laud my trans peers though, who worked so hard to earn their post-Master's degrees.

My psychiatrist friend, Dr. Solomon Shapiro,[32] and I co-presented one of these workshops at the 2005 University of Guelph sexuality conference: "TransForming Couples and Families: A TransFormative Therapeutic Model™ for Providers Working with the Loved Ones of Trans-Identified and Gender-Divergent People."[33] My model built on an earlier one we had delivered to the Toronto Transceptance group for parents of trans children: "From Denial to Acceptance to Celebration: An Educational Workshop for Parents of Trans Children," which incorporated a staged continuum of acceptance given that change is an incremental process.

In 2006, The Adler School of Professional Psychology invited me to teach a half credit elective course based on my TransPositive Therapeutic Model™. Battling bronchitis over the two Saturday classes, I taught six eager students effective therapeutic modalities to support trans people and gender non-conforming youth. Students witnessed pre-taped testimonials of transgender or genderqueer teenagers challenged by gender distress, dissociative trauma, psychiatric abuse, parental neglect, truancy, and homelessness, as well as long-time married husbands transitioning to female in their 50s or 60s with the struggling support of their wives and children. The students' exam answers reflected their wide range of understanding as they slowly began their learning curve in trans therapy.

The following year, I presented another one of my therapy models at the 2007 World Professional Association for Transgender Health (WPATH) symposium in Chicago: "Transactivism as Therapy: A Client Self-Empowerment Model Linking Personal and Social Agency."[34] This was yet another milestone moment for me because this time my proposal was accepted—nearly 20 years after my 1989 abstract had been rejected due to my lack of higher educational credentials. I was finally invited (read: allowed) to deliver a clinical presentation as a *bona fide* member of the international professional community. Validation at last! I met some other trans guys also working in trans healthcare.[35]

In 2008, Dr. Shapiro and I reprised our workshop on gender non-conforming youth, featuring our guest panelist, the TransParent Canada founder (who prefers anonymity), at the first Canadian Professional Association for Transgender Health (CPATH) conference in Toronto. As a conference organizer, with then CPATH President Dr. Gail Knudson (who became WPATH president in 2016), Dr. Trevor Corneil, Dr. Joan Quinn, my social worker friend, Jim Oulton, and a steamrollering trans person (who shall be nameless), I found the experience gratifying. But, I would never again take on this formidable task!

Other affiliations with gender-creative youth included Dr. Nicola Brown referencing me as a professional therapeutic resource in a guide for parents put out by Central Toronto Youth Services (Pride & Prejudice Program) in 2007.[36]

As an independent gender specialist apart from my SHC work—even though I had not yet officially resurrected RR Consulting—I was a powerhouse of knowledge on all things trans, presenting at national and international conferences, delivering professional development workshops at hospitals and health centres in southern Ontario, customizing classroom presentations for universities and colleges, and tailoring corporate trainings for companies in which an employee was transitioning.

My trans advocacy work paid off because in December 2007, I was awarded The City of Toronto Access, Equity and Human Rights Pride Award by then Mayor David Miller at Toronto City Hall. Several fellow activists came out in support, including Susan Gapka and Martine Stonehouse of the Trans Health Lobby Group. Central Toronto Youth Services' Pride & Prejudice Program was also honoured for the same award. The only thing that marred the occasion was a blundering remark made by then City Councilor Kyle Rae (a not too trans informed cisgender gay man), asking why we needed the acronym LGBT and why "trans" should be distinguished from "queer." At that moment, I didn't deign to enlighten him with a Trans 101 mini seminar, but now I wish that I had, creating an educational opportunity to explain that gender identity should not be conflated with sexual orientation. Moreover, not all trans people are queer (although many are). These basic distinctions should be self-evident! Some cisgender queer (and many straight) people still have a lot to learn about gender identity, transgenderism, the gender non-binary, transitioning, and transphobia.

Speaking of distinctive comparisons, sometime later, I chose to focus on the links between trans people of colour and Two-Spirit people—and some individuals embrace a dual trans (or genderqueer) person of colour and Two-Spirit identity, like Lukayo Faye Catherine Estrella,[37] Monica Forrester,[38] and jd (see below). Accordingly, I spearheaded two learning opportunities. One was a roundtable discussion, with multidimensional intersex, Two-Spirit, trans man Alec Butler, on identities, sexualities, HIV, trauma, social isolation, and discrimination at the Native Canadian Centre in Toronto. The other was a community workshop, with jd (a Black, Two-Spirit, trans man), and Johl Whitewolf Ringuette (an Anishinaabe, Two-Spirit, trans man), at Sherbourne Health Centre, "*Maawnjidwin*/Coming Together: An Anti-Oppression Workshop for Trans People of Colour and Two-Spirit People." We discovered each population had more differences and more similarities than we had expected. We urged these crosscultural groups to collaboratively brainstorm creative solutions to combat racism and anti-Indigeneity, as well as homophobia, biphobia, and transphobia.[39]

A promising trend is that increasing numbers of politicians and public officials worldwide are now openly identifying as transgender and/or intersex people of colour,[40] as *Hijra*,[41] or as Indigenous transgender and/or Two-Spirit people.[42] This trend of gender diverse politicians publicly disclosing their gender identity is fairly recent. For example, African American politician, Althea Garrison—the first trans person to serve in state legislation in the USA—did not so disclose when she was elected to the Massachusetts House of Representatives in 1992. She was outed sometime later. There is no privacy for trans public officials who prefer to be stealth!

Further forward movement for trans (and queer) people of colour and Indigenous trans (and queer) and Two-Spirit people are two recent initiatives in the form of political and artistic activism, one local and one global.

The first is the Toronto-based Marvellous Grounds:

> *A book and web-based project that seeks to document and create space to vision the ways that QTBIPOC (queer and trans, Black, Indigenous and people of colour) create communities, innovate projects and foster connections within Toronto/Three Fires Territories and beyond. This collection brings together art, writing and research that engages with space-making and is in the service of community-building.*
>
> http://marvellousgrounds.com/

In addition to an online journal and a short video, the diverse Marvellous Grounds collective publishes book anthologies.[43]

The second is Black Lives Matter (BLM), a global network "working for the validity of Black life and to rebuild the Black liberation movement." With chapters in the USA, Canada, the UK, and Australia, all the co-founders (Opal Tometi, Alicia Garza, Patrisse Cullors, and Elle Hearns) are African American women and Elle Hearns is transgender. BLM "goes beyond extrajudicial killings of Black people by police and vigilantes" and, embracing intersectionality, "affirms the lives of Black queer and trans folks, disabled folks, black undocumented folks, folks with (police) records, women, and all Black lives along the gender spectrum." BLM includes direct-action events, social media, songs and films.[44] Genderqueer Torontonian janaya khan is co-founder of Black Lives Matter–Canada (BLM-C) and international ambassador for the Black Lives Matter Network. janaya and Yusra K. Ali (aka Yusra Khogali) co-founded Black Lives Matter–Toronto (BLM–TO) in October 2014 following the police killing of Jermaine Carby in Brampton, Ontario. Since then, they have worked to resist anti-Black racism in the Greater Toronto Area, including a half-hour sit-in, disrupting Toronto's

Pride Parade in June 2016, demanding that Pride Toronto improve its relationship with LGBTQ people of colour, and that Toronto police officers be banned from marching in the parade while in uniform.[45] Yusra, a highly-controversial figure, has been alternatively condemned as a Black supremacist for her anti-White racist rhetoric, and congratulated for her activism against anti-Black racism by The City of Toronto, which awarded her The Pam McConnell Award for Young Women in Leadership in March 2018. Hailed by some as the new civil rights movement, and awarded the Sydney Peace Prize in May 2017 for its non-violent protest of the mistreatment of Australian Aborigines by the police and government, the BLM movement also has its critics: White, Black, and Jewish-American.[46]

Intersecting my roles of therapist, trainer, consultant, and researcher, I published several clinical papers on transgender issues. Also wanting to write a book on trans activism, in June of 2008, I invited fellow trans activist Dr. Dan Irving (Associate Professor in the Sexuality Studies Minor program at Carleton University in Ottawa) to co-edit an anthology on Canadian trans activism, incorporating individual, community, organizational, political, and clinical advocacy. He readily accepted my invitation, excited to help me break new ground. My long history of recurring burnout was the original impetus to write such a book, which I had originally envisioned as a practical manual for trans advocates, warning of the pitfalls of burnout and vicarious traumatization, and offering viable suggestions for prevention or amelioration. Upon deliberating with Dan, however, my initial brainchild morphed into our wider creative vision: a collection of voices from contributors across the country. My original idea for guidelines around burnout and self-care would materialize as a chapter in the book,[47] partly based on a 2008 community workshop I had co-presented with Michelle LeClaire, Terri Mathews, and Yasmeen Persad: "Trans-Generational Trans Activists Working Together."

Dan and I spent six years on the book project, and almost didn't get published because a peer-review committee deemed our book to be a duplication of similar previous work. Fortunately, we managed to convince our prospective publisher (Canadian Scholars' Press) otherwise! We eventually launched our book, *Trans Activism in Canada: A Reader*,[48] in May 2014 to much acclaim. Compiling an anthology is an arduous undertaking and Dan did the lion's share of the editing, taking an unpaid leave to complete the manuscript. For his generous gesture, I'm forever indebted. We were justly proud of our accomplishment: a tangible legacy of the lived experiences of diverse transsexual, transgender, intersex, and Two-Spirit Canadians, personifying their challenges, defeats, and victories in a genderphobic world— alongside examples of effective trans advocacy by transgender and cisgender activists, working together. Although a number of our contributors were Indigenous or people of colour, disappointingly, none of them self-identified as intersex (even the one whom I knew to be trans-intersex). This was another opportunity to put Canada on the map as a viable player in trans advocacy—showing the world that trans activists have existed beyond the USA since the early 1970s (and before), despite most Canadians being "unsung hero(ine)s."[49] Often undocumented and missing from Wikipedia, in 2015, I provided my professor friend, Dr. Elspeth Brown, with a list of 50 noteworthy Canadian trans activists who should be publicly recognized, hoping that she might assign this task to some of her history students. (A good start was made with the Wikipedia entry of iconic activist, Mirha-Soleil Ross, and hopefully others will soon follow.)

Things were going well for a while: then, personal tragedy struck. In early 2008, Max, my cherished older cat, suddenly got ill with lymphatic cancer. Following a grueling battle with diagnostic tests and ineffective medications, he lost his bodily functions to the point where euthanasia was the only option. Max fought to the very end; a life affirmer, like me. Tears welling up, I felt so bad for my beloved buddy: but, I was glad that I had been able to give him four-and-a-half more years of a good life. Max was my second feline family member to die. I love kitties with a passion. Still, it's heart-wrenching to lose them.

Thinking about loss, I had never quite gotten over my romance with Kwame. Ever since our last contact in May 1998, when my unopened letter was returned (no longer at this address), I had tried unsuccessfully to discover his whereabouts. Just about to give up, I finally found his ex-boyfriend's address. I immediately wrote to him, asking him to pass on my letter to Kwame. Upon returning home late one Friday night, I excitedly retrieved a voicemail from Kwame telling me that he really wanted to talk to me but had to wait until Sunday because he was off to a play party to hook up with a sexy dude. I was beside myself with joy! I arranged to visit him the last week of August in Richmond, Virginia, where he and his ex-boyfriend lived, sharing a house with friends. I could stay with my older brother, sister-in-law, and nephew, who had relocated to Richmond the year before. Kwame sent me a picture of a male bodybuilder, saying that his pecs now looked like his. I requested a photo of his bare chest, but he said that he didn't have one. Ashamedly, he later confessed that, fearing surgery, he hadn't had male chest reconstruction. Regardless, I was so excited that I could hardly wait until it was time to leave. During the flight to Virginia, I eagerly anticipated my reunion with Kwame, whom I hadn't seen for 16 years! I hoped that it would be a momentous occasion, fulfilling my fondest dreams. I also looked forward to seeing Jakub, Lilly, and Sergei again after an entire decade.

Jakub met me at the Richmond airport and drove me to their modest mansion in the upscale part of town. The first part of my stay seemed to go smoothly—except for an unexpected, somewhat cool reception by my sister-in-law. I got to see some of the local tourist attractions: the Holocaust museum in the city, a drive to Fredericksburg with my brother to see a heritage plantation, and a commuter-train ride with my nephew, Sergei, to Washington, D.C. to see the spy museum and tour the Capitol Building. Then, totally unexpectedly, my brother got uppity, objecting to Kwame calling me at his home and expressing disapproval of me giving money to Kwame, a so-called underprivileged person, who lived in the housing projects. I was thrown for a loop by this uncharacteristic classist putdown from Jakub, who had assured me, back in the 1970s, that classism was an even worse crime than racism! I didn't realize until that very moment how badly his Americanized, materialistic mentality and snobbery had polluted his previously open mind (while he still was living in Canada). But, my protest was calculatedly moderate because I didn't want to create tension while I was still a guest in his house. Things went from bad to worse as I shockingly witnessed how unfeelingly my hosts treated their pet dog, shutting him away in an upstairs bedroom while they dined downstairs with me and four invited friends, all the while ignoring his pitiful howls. Incredibly, the poor dog was not even allowed to run free in their backyard for fear that he would get dirty rolling in the grass. On top of this hoity-toity pet constraint (read: pest control), I had to endure the inane atrocities of one of my sister-in-law's dinner guests gleefully boasting about taking pot-shots at the squirrels scampering across his yard to the admiring guffaws of all, save me! Once again (counter-instinctively), I choked back my indignation, not wanting to engender conflict, and wishing the remainder of my visit would pass quickly.

 Despite this unexpected domestic discontent, I buoyed myself up by anticipating my reunion with my long lost lover. Although my relatives knew that I would be meeting with Kwame, I neglected to tell them that I planned to stay overnight with my newly re-found paramour. Arriving at the downtown Holiday Inn for our scheduled rendezvous, I kept looking out for Kwame, but there was no sign of him anywhere. Desperately trying to hold back my tears, he suddenly appeared from out of the past (like the classic film noir of the same name)[50]; looking old, yet also, young, both masculine and feminine, a curious, but comely, combination. He hesitated shyly in the hotel lobby, alternately glancing at me and then away, grinning and squirming in mixed discomfort and delight. "Kwame," I gushed, hugging him like a long-lost teddy bear, nearly crushing his bones. We checked into a room so that we could be alone and get reacquainted. Barely undressing, we fell onto the bed, kissing and hugging; then made mad, passionate love. Two guys together, locked in embrace.

 I could only afford a 10-day stay in Richmond so we made the most of it. He showed me the sights: the downtown core, the riverside beach, boats on the canal, museums tracing the history of slavery and the Civil War, and the rich cultural contributions of African Americans. We checked out several jazz and blues joints: I loved the old stuff but Kwame preferred the new sounds of Boyz II Men. He also dug hip-hop. Richmond was largely populated by Black folks, so this was the first city other than Baltimore or Cleveland where I found myself to be a racial minority. A weird and wondrous experience! Richmond being neither overtly homophobic, nor overly queer-friendly, we held hands walking down the street, but guardedly so. Our trepidation, however, was due less to being seen as a same-sex couple than appearing as a Black-White couple. I was perceived as White—not Brown—which would have altered societal perception in terms of race politics. As a beige-skinned, mixed-race person, I was invisible in my Whiteness. And, in this city, neither of us were out as trans. Kwame was selectively out as gay to certain cis gay men. Richmond has several gay bars (we went to two), and two trans support groups and a trans-friendly health clinic. Even so, we had to dance the dialectic as the Other, trying not to lose our own rhythm within the dominant culture, especially those cisheteronormative cultures of the traditional American South and the conservative Canadian North.

Overall, I had a great time except for the occasional red flag: factual inconsistencies, contradictions, and half-truths. Gently confronting him, Kwame denied any falsehood or wrongdoing. Smitten, I filtered out these worrisome annoyances. Why spoil our fun with potential problems? Denial is the deadliest downfall for us poor, self-deluded humans! Alas, there's always a price to pay for romantic idealization. My retribution would come sometime later as I now indulged myself in blissful ignorance. When our brief tryst ended and it was time to go, the agony seemed unbearable. Were we two doomed players in the game of love, acting out our noir roles like Robert Mitchum and Jane Greer? Which one of us was the *femme fatale* (or rather, *l'homme fatal*) in this ill-starred love affair? And, which one of us was the moth inexorably drawn to the all-consuming flame?

As for my brother and sister-in-law, our relationship became strained even further when they confronted me as to why I had stayed out overnight, disapproval dripping from their collective voice. With no desire to get further embroiled in this overblown family drama, I decided to cut my stay short and depart first thing in the morning. To my chagrin, Lilly (the self-appointed mouthpiece of my brother) accosted me early next morning while I was waiting on the front porch for the taxi to take me to the airport. Cajolingly, she guilt-tripped me into waiting a bit longer until Jakub could drive me there himself. Grudgingly, I complied. I uttered a constrained thank you to Lilly, and warmly hugged Sergei goodbye. Emotionally distraught as we drove to the airport, I was mostly at a loss for words as Jakub grilled me regarding the reasons for my (to him, unacceptable) actions. The emotional tone of our farewell was visibly strained as we tentatively hugged before parting. Was this to be an irreconcilable rupture of our 56-year relationship?

Back home in Toronto, I tried to focus on work and everyday life, but it was damn hard! In October, I visited Jean and Stella in Montreal for Thanksgiving, expecting congratulations and good wishes, but was taken aback at their sexual policing of me for my partner choice: a trans-gay male. Despite the fact that they were a lesbian couple, the same standard seemed not to apply to my same-sex relationship with Kwame! Exactly the same thing had happened to me before, when two separate trans (ex)friends had condemned me as abnormal for hooking up with another trans man (Eugene)—my transqueer identity apparently tainting their heteronormative image of trans people. Did they judge all those other queer and pansexual trans folks around the world too? Disheartened by their betrayal, this marked the end of our long friendship: a heavy loss for me. Would there be more losses to come?

Sadly, yes. Jakub (prompted by his control-queen wife, Lilly) wrote me a venomous Dear John letter, cussing me out for apparently exploiting him as a tour guide and mis-using their hospitality as a free bed and breakfast. Very soon after, they permanently cut me off—immediately after my sister had hung up on Lilly, who had called Arjuna to complain about my so-called bad behaviour. Thereupon, I drafted a lengthy rebuttal, complete with my own remonstrances and resentments. At the last minute, however, I chose not to send it, deterred by the inevitability of escalation and never-ending wrangling. I did send a copy to my nephew though: but, feeling caught between his parents and me, Sergei never responded. I'm still sad, even now, that my developing relationship with him ended up as a regrettable casualty of the fallout with his parents. I both liked and respected Sergei, who appeared to be cut from a different cloth than his hard-hearted parents. In the end, I lost a second brother—and my nephew too! Now, only two siblings remained: Arjuna and Andrzej. Other than the consistent connection I have with my sister, Arjuna, this recent family dissolution made it even more vital for me to have a life partner.

Kwame and I continued our romance across the border, writing torrid letters, making love over the phone (sometimes he would be high on coke), and me sending him books on Black literature, CDs on jazz and blues, and DVDs on gay erotica to satisfy the dual sexual and spiritual desires of his constantly-conflicted nature—body and soul waging a war neither would win. We talked about marriage. I wanted to wait until we had been together at least a year to see how the relationship was progressing, but he persuaded me otherwise, and I (silly bugger) gave in. We tied the knot on his birthday, February 12, 2009 (two days after mine). He was 49 going on 19, and I was 57 going on 17: two middle-aged teenagers in love!

We wed at Richmond City Hall, officiated by a pastor and witnessed by Kwame's niece and her boyfriend. Disappointingly, neither my sister nor Kwame's mother or siblings were able to attend. Kwame looked adorable in his silver specs, black braids, and purple sweater. I didn't look too shabby either, in my navy blazer, dark tie, and gray pants. When we requested the use of the identifier "partner" instead of "wife" because Kwame identified as a (trans) man, the homophobic pastor threatened to walk out, but relented when Kwame conceded to the gender-binary label, continuing the cisheteronormative wedding vows. We should have quit the ceremony right then and there: but, we just wanted to get on with it (a grievous mistake!). Ironically, at the same time, on the front steps of the building, a local gay rights group was lobbying for same-sex marriage in Virginia! I spoke to one of the advocates, extending my support while expressing my pride that Canada had already endorsed same-sex marriage in 2005.[51] Gay and lesbian Virginians finally won the right to be married under state law in October 2014.[52] Kwame and I could have wed in Toronto, but not as a same-sex couple because his legal sex-designation was still female, even though he had been taking male hormones and living as a man for many years. The bane of government bureaucracy when it comes to sex and gender, especially for trans and intersex folks!

Financial constraints restricted our international travel but I persuaded Kwame to come to visit me that September, sending him money for the bus fare. Together again in Toronto, we spent most of our time by ourselves; although we visited briefly with friends (Carole, Yasmeen, and King). I took Kwame to several blues bars and an iconic jazz club (The Rex), where we raptured to the riffs amidst beer and brandy toasts. Indulging our love for food, he cooked me scrumptious seafood and vegetarian dishes, including Cajun blackened catfish and sweet potato pie. We watched some of my favourite gay movies, starring Dirk Bogarde and Montgomery Clift. Mixed in with the good times, we had some blow-ups about drugs (I wasn't really into weed and certainly not coke) and sex (I wasn't into kink or rough play). Romantic rationalizer that I was, I discounted these troubling frictions, focussing instead on the sexual frisson and our mutual love. Alas, rationalization all too often messes with our minds and breaks our hearts!

A long-distance relationship is trying, and we only had phone contact, no Skype or Facebook. I invited Kwame to visit me over Christmas, again sending him money for the bus fare. Another red flag waved when he told me soon after that he had used it to buy drugs! For some inexplicable reason (love is illogical), I gave him another chance. Perhaps it was because I was a professional healer and believed in the possibility of positive change, even for people (like many of my clients), who have suffered early emotional or sexual trauma, or struggled with chemical or sexual addictions. Or was it simply my ego that made me think that I could help Kwame change his self-sabotaging ways?

Wanting to be together for our upcoming birthdays in February, he took the Greyhound bus to Toronto. I eagerly anticipated his arrival but my hopes were dashed when he called me, crying, from Buffalo. Canadian border officials were denying him entry because of a recent cocaine conviction. He was desperate and I resentful. Still, what could I do but leave my cats to their own devices for a few days and hop a Megabus to spend some time together in Buffalo? The city was smothered in snow: so, we holed up at a Holiday Inn for four days, conversing, watching TV, listening to music, eating, drinking, and having sex. My OCD shot through the roof when Kwame insisted on smoking and toking in our non-smoking hotel room! I was afraid that if the smoke detector went off I would be charged a fee for violating a city ordinance. I certainly could not afford a criminal record given my line of work! Overall, it was not a very satisfying birthday weekend: yet, parting at the bus station was brutal. Little did I know that this would be our last time together.

Amidst the chaos of my turbulent love life, I still had to carry on—business as usual. I was scheduled to present a workshop ("Internalized Transphobia") at the 2010 CPATH conference in Montreal, suggesting therapeutic interventions to help affected clients resolve their guilt, shame, or embarrassment at being born transgender. I hoped to co-author a clinical paper on this all too prevalent issue with my psychotherapist colleagues, Dr. Roberta Timothy and Mercedes Umana, of Continuing Healing Consultants, combining our clinical models; my TransPositive Therapeutic Model™ and their Anti-Oppression Psychotherapy Model™.[53] What most intrigued me about their intersectional model was the core practice of "creative resistance"—a non-violent, transformative, direct reaction to oppression that is well-suited to those who transgress the gender binary and are punished for daring to counter cisgender heteronormativity. Trans resistance must prevail!

During the conference, Susan Gapka and I attended Trans Pride Day (*Fierté Trans*) at the Université du Québec à Montréal, organized by *L'Aide aux Transsexuel(le)s du Québec (ATQ)*. Several French-Canadian academics and activists attended, including Nora Butler Burke, Dr. Viviane Namaste, and (if memory serves) Micheline (Hélène) Montreuil and Joëlle-Circé Laramée. My colleague, Dr. Françoise Susset, then incoming CPATH President (and a cisgender clinical psychologist working with gender-creative kids and their parents at the Montreal Sexual Minority Health Institute) was there too. That evening, along with other conference delegates and local trans activists, we drank and danced at Cleo's, where I reconnected with some trans gals from the old days, including Marie-Marcelle Godbout and Michelle de Ville.

Back home, in Toronto, once more, I continued my long-distance relationship with Kwame, but I felt torn, battling urges of wanting to stay but needing to go. Grabbing at one last chance to salvage our faltering relationship, I suggested that we holiday for a week in NYC as we both appreciated the city's queer vibe and wanted to check out the Village scene. I reserved my plane ticket with Air Canada and a room at the Hotel Marrakech on Broadway in the Upper West Side. I also arranged to see Andrzej so that my youngest brother could meet my new husband. Susan offered to look after my cats, so I was all set. But that morning, Kwame called, timidly telling me that he couldn't make it after all because he had spent the bus money that I had sent him on cocaine. He added, in ashamed defeat (or resigned indifference?), "I guess this means that we're over, huh?" My world fell out from under me as I crumpled into mush. Mind-shattered, I raged: "Fuck you! We're over all right. Don't ever contact me again!" And slammed down the phone.

Heartbroken, I still had the presence of mind to cancel the hotel reservation but lost the cost of the airfare. My emotional impoverishment far outweighed the financial though. I was a wreck! I called Susan, who, a loyal friend, came right over, commiserating as I chain smoked and downed endless beers, venting angry tears. The bond with Kwame was irrevocably broken: I had to cut my losses and run. I called a lawyer to start divorce proceedings, relieved that I would eventually be free. Thankfully, I could extricate myself from an impossible situation and move on with my life. Still, I felt crushed by grief as I mourned the loss of a long lost lover and potential life partner. Does the hurting ever stop?

A month later, more loss. Pinky came down with a chronic kidney disease and had to be taken to the vet every other day for subdermal saline injections to stabilize her enzyme levels. Fortunately, the clinic was only 10 minutes from my condo and I was blessed by a compassionate vet (Dr. John), who gave me discounted treatments. Still, the ordeal would last for nearly two years.

My grief was temporarily offset when, on October 22, 2010, I was presented with the Steinert & Ferreiro Award by Community One Foundation in Toronto. This award recognizes outstanding leadership within the Canadian LGBTQ community, acknowledging leaders' contributions towards increasing social acceptance of queer and trans people. So far, recipients had included George Hislop, Dr. Beverly Bain, El-Farouk Khaki, Rev. Dr. Brent Hawkes, Dr. Rachel Epstein[54]—and now me. I was the first trans person to win but would not be the last.[55]

Arjuna flew in from Victoria and many friends, colleagues, and community members came out to celebrate my hard-won honour. Two of my nominators were on hand: Anna Travers, Rainbow Health Ontario director, and Susan Gapka, Trans Lobby Group president. Disappointingly, the other two couldn't make it: Dr. Gail Knudson, CPATH president, and Gens

Hellquist, Canadian Rainbow Health Coalition president. It was a fabulous affair with 300 guests, including prominent politicians Barbara Hall, George Smitherman, and Kyle Rae, local businesspeople, community members, and the media. I had spent hours crafting my acceptance speech because this would be the first time that I would talk about me in *all* my dimensions: personal, professional, and activist. Nobody ever wants to know about one's personal life unless it's a prurient interest in one's sexual proclivities or whether a post-transitional person can climax! People are not generally concerned with one's existential or spiritual beliefs and values. That day, I told my captive audience my whole story: the Dialectical Dancing, the Gender Working, the Therapeutic Healing, Teaching and Writing, and the Rainbow Warrioring to come. I alluded not only to my past trans activism but also to my pending ecofeminist activism. My speech was entitled, "The Phoenix Rising: The Transformative Power of Change through Community Action."

Soon afterwards, my divorce papers arrived and a weighty burden was finally lifted. I could now send Kwame my farewell letter expressing all my feelings of love and betrayal, hurt and anger, hope and disappointment, as a way to get emotional closure to this sad affair. Although I was still hurting, I hoped that Kwame would continue to say yes to life like his inspiration, James Baldwin, even if he couldn't quite commit to me. In a cleansing ritual, I shredded all the letters and photographs of our 28-year association, leaving the past behind so that I could now move forward. Immediately after mailing this final missive, I stood tall again, ready to face new challenges and embark on new adventures. Open to the possibility of a new romance, I put out a wish to Mother Earth to send me a sweet lady to love (I was so over men!). A self-determinist, I augmented this wish with a practical strategy of my own.

I applied to participate in the Bisexual Pride/Anti-Stigma Poster Campaign launched by CAMH's Re:searching for LGBTQ Health and Rainbow Health Ontario. I was selected along with three other bisexuals: Danielle, a pregnant mother, Antony, a Black teenager, and Laureen-Blu Waters, a Two-Spirit woman. I was to be the senior trans-male poster-boy, identifying as bi (even though I had recently gone off men after my failed experiments with Eugene and Kwame). The photographer made me look better than ever: posing with a rakish air, one hand tucked into the pocket of my jeans, the other flinging my denim jacket cavalierly over my shoulder, my clean-shaven, boyish face showing a coy, sexy half-smile. I looked considerably younger than my 59 years, improving my chances of catching a new lady-love as my hopefully enticing visage appeared on the worldwide web.

I was back on track: the love-worn, wounded warrior all patched up again, ready for the fight. Rupert, the resilient, rides again!

Chapter 9 Notes

[1] Gale, Lorraine, *Out and Proud Affirmation Guidelines: Practice Guidelines for Equity in Gender and Sexual Diversity*, Children's Aid Society of Toronto, 2011. http://www.torontocas.ca/sites/torontocas/files/CAST_Out_and_Proud_Affirmation_Guidelines_2012.pdf.

[2] Gapka, Susan, Rupert Raj, and the Public Health Alliance for Lesbian, Gay, Bisexual, Transsexual, Transgendered, Two-Spirited, Intersexed, Queer and Questioning Equity (a working group of the Ontario Public Health Association), *Trans Health Project*, Toronto, ON: Ontario Public Health Association, 2003, revised 2004. http://www.opha.on.ca/Advocacy-and-Policy/Position-Paper,-Resolutions-and-Motions.aspx.

[3] Raj, Rupert, "Towards a Transpositive Therapeutic Model: Developing Clinical Sensitivity and Cultural Competence in the Effective Support of Transsexual and Transgendered Clients," *International Journal of Transgenderism,* 2006, 6(2). http://web.archive.org/web/20070429132659/http://www.symposion.com/ijt/ijtvo06no02_04.htm.

[4] For a list of Canadian, American, and other authors© works on trans healthcare, gender transitioning, and related issues, see the specific sections in the Intersectional Bibliography.

[5] See: Peterkin, Allan, MD, and Cathy Risdon, MD., *Caring for Lesbian and Gay People: A Clinical Guide*, University of Toronto Press, 2003. Although Dr. Peterkin (a gay psychiatrist to whom I've referred former trans and queer clients for clinical assessments or treatment), is transpositive, the book itself, has very little to offer about transgender patients.

[6] For information on Sherbourne Health Centre's multidisciplinary program and services, see https://sherbourne.on.ca/. For trans healthcare services, see https://sherbourne.on.ca/primary-family-health-care/lgbt-health/trans-health-care/.

[7] Dr. Sydney Tam won the Gay and Lesbian Medical Association Provider of the Year Award in 2007. Around the same time, Sydney guest-appeared, with her wife and son, on the Oprah Winfrey Show. A few years earlier (before I had bottom surgery in 2012), I was invited to be a guest on the show, but I emphatically declined because the vice-producer wanted to bill me as "a trans-male therapist with a vagina"!

[8] Yasmeen Persad is currently the Education and Training Facilitator at The 519 (formerly, The 519 Community Centre), and is also a peer on the centre's Trans People of Colour Project. http://www.the519.org/programs/trans-identified-person-of-colour.

[9] The Michigan Womyn's Music Festival (MWMF) (1976-2015) has been censured for its virtual exclusion of trans women since 1991 by founding organizer, Lisa Vogel. So, as a "creative resistance" response in 1994, Leslie Feinberg and Rikki Ann Wilchins co-founded Camp Trans across the road, a cultural event welcoming all women (trans and cis), with an annual protest of MWMF's exclusionary policies—joined in 1999, by the Boston and Chicago Lesbian Avengers.

[10] In 1995, Canadian transfeminist, Kimberly Nixon, successfully sued the Vancouver Rape Relief Society for not allowing her to volunteer as a peer-counsellor for women (even though she herself had been abused by men), stating that she was "not a woman." In 2002, she won a BC Human Rights Tribunal award in damages, but in 2003, VRRS won a judicial review in its favour, overturning the earlier decision because the BC Supreme Court stated that VRRS had the right to decide who is or is not "a woman." In 2004, Kimberly appealed, but lost because the BC Court of Appeal stated that because VRRS was an organization benefitting women (a group protected by the BC Human Rights Code), VRRS was not obliged to protect trans people even though they are protected under the Code! Notwithstanding, Kimberly and her lawyer, barbara findlay, successfully campaigned every other women's organization in BC and Canada to become trans-inclusive—losing a battle, but winning the war! The Nixon case is briefly documented in barbara findlay's paper, "Acting Queerly: Ruminations on Being a Queer Lawyer and Activist," in Irving and Raj, *Trans Activism in Canada,* 93-102. In an inevitable backlash, English, transphobic, feminist journalist, Julie Bindel, wrote a scathing article, "Gender Benders, Beware." *The Guardian,* January 31, 2004. https://www.theguardian.com/world/2004/jan/31/gender.weekend7. See also https://zagria.blogspot.ca/2012/04/kimberly-nixon-1957-activist.html.

[11] The late Peter Bochove, former co-owner of the Spa Excess bathhouse for men, initially resisted the inclusion of trans men who either did not have surgically-constructed male genitals (metoidioplasty or phalloplasty, often referred to as "junk" in the vernacular) or did not have a male sex-designation on their birth certificate when Kyle Scanlon and I approached him in 1999. He eventually relented, but public (and private) gay-/bi-male sex-specific spaces for trans men without bottom surgery are still challenging! By contrast, the Toronto Women's Bathhouse (aka the Pussy Palace), founded in 1998, welcomed trans women right from the start. Even so, there were tensions between a number of cisgender and transgender women participants at its first hosted sex party—and some trans women felt marginalized or unsafe.

[12] These Indigenous trans people (many of whom also identify as Two-Spirit) are described below.

Torontonian Mayan Chilean Danielle Araya is coordinator of The 519's Trans Youth Mentorship Program. http://www.the519.org/programs/trans-youth-mentorship-program.

See Alec Butler's autobiographical videos: *Trans Mission: Get Yer Motor Runnin'* (2003), the trilogy, *Misadventures of PussyBoy: First Love* (2002), *Sick* (2003) and *First Period* (date unknown), and *Audrey's Beard* (2002). (Audrey was Alec's birth name). See also *Trans Cabaret: The Video* (2011), featuring trans, intersex and Two-Spirit Torontonians. Alec was the first trans person (who also identifies as intersex and Two-Spirit) to be inducted into The ArQuives in 1998. https://arquives.andornot.com/en/list?q=alec+butler&p=1&ps=20. He was featured in *Toronto Life,* October 26, 2015. http://torontolife.com/city/life/what-its-like-to-be-transgender-in-Toronto.

Louis Esmé Cruz is a Mi'kmaq, Acadian, Irish, Two-Spirit, trans poet, writer, visual artist and activist, and also a member of Toronto's Native Youth Sexual Health Network's Two-Spirit and Indigenous LGBTQQIA Mentors, Elders and Grandparents' Support Circle. See: Cruz, Louis Esmé, and Qwo Li Driskill, "Puo'winue'l Prayers: Readings from North America's First Transtextual Script," in Mark Rifin, Daniel Heath, Daniel H. Justice, and Bethany Schneider, eds., *GLQ: A Journal of Lesbian and Gay Studies,* Durham, NC: Duke University Press, April 1, 2010, 16(1-2): 243-252. https://doi.org/10.1215/10642684-2009-021. And: Cruz, Louis Esmé, "Medicine Bundle of Contradictions: Female-man, Mi'kmaq/Acadian/Irish Diasporas, Invisible disAbilities, masculine-Feminist," in Jessica Yee, ed., *Feminism FOR REAL: Deconstructing the Academic Industrial Complex of Feminism,* Ottawa, ON: Canadian Centre for Policy Alternatives, 2011, 49-60.

Read Jamie Lee Hamilton's piece, "The Golden Age of Prostitution: One Woman's Personal Account of an Outdoor Brothel in Vancouver, 1975-1984," in Irving and Raj, *Trans Activism in Canada*, 27-32. And Barb Daniel's biography, *She's No Lady: The Story of Jamie Lee Hamilton*, Toronto, ON: Cormorant Books, 2005. Jamie Lee was the first transsexual to stand for public office in Canada, running for Vancouver City Council in 1996. Watch her talk at the 2016 Moving Trans History Forward (MTHF) conference (Founders Panel). www.uvic.ca.mthf (click on "Past Conferences"). See also https://zagria.blogspot.ca/2010/10/jamie-lee-hamilton-1955-sex-worker.html.

Read Elizabeth "Raven" James's personal account, "Gender Strike! It's an Offence," in Irving and Raj, *Trans Activism in Canada*, 45-49.

Shaun LaDue is a Canadian, Indigenous trans-male actor, writer and artist descended from the Tlingit, Tagish, Kaska and Mountain Slavey First Nations. In 2015, Shaun won a human rights complaint against the Yukon Territory government to change his sex-designation from female to male (even though he had not undergone genital surgery) on his driver's licence, thereby setting a precedent for other trans people in the territory.

Read Sandy Leo Laframboise's story, *Finding My Place: The High Risk Project Society*, in Irving and Raj, *Trans Activism in Canada*, 51-56. She was portrayed in the 2014 Canadian web series, *The Transgender Project*, on ichannel (co-produced by Kevin O'Keefe), featuring photo essays of Sandy, Rupert Raj and other trans people.

See: Maracle, Aiyyana, "A Journey in Gender," *Torquere, Journal of the Lesbian and Gay Studies Association/Revue de la Société canadienne des études lesbiennes et gaies*, 2000, 2: 36-57. https://torquere.journals.yorku.ca/index.php/torquere/article/view/36587/33238 and also a brief excerpt from her unfinished autobiography, *Chronicle of a Transformed Woman*, n.d. http://www.connect.ecuad.ca/~grunt/art1.html. Watch her films: *Death in the Shadow of the Umbrella*, Vancouver, BC: 2015. https://vimeo.com/137714829; and: *Whispers from the Grandmothers* (First Story TV series), (directed by Renae Morriseau), Vancouver, BC, 2001.

Kiley May is an Indigenous Mohawk and Cayuga shaman, creator, storyteller, writer, poet, journalist, photographer, dancer, fashion designer, performance artist, and also a Two-Spirit, trans, queer and genderqueer human being. Kiley's gender pronouns are "they" and "their," and "she" and "her." Kiley May was Toronto Pride's youth ambassador in June 2017. Watch their short film, *"You Are Not Your Genitals,"* Toronto, ON: 2017. https://www.youtube.com/watch?v=kqp_bKb94cA.

Kole Peplinskie is a queer Algonquin Indian, and Two-Spirit coordinator for the Canadian Centre for Gender & Sexual Diversity;. https://ccgsd-ccdgs.org/kole-peplinskie/.

Johl Whitewolf Ringuette worked as a volunteer coordinator for Toronto's 2-Spirited People of the 1st Nations in 2005, before he became an entrepreneur and established Nishdish Marketeria & Catering.

Tami Marie Starlight (aka Tami Cameron) was formerly Egale Trans Issues Committee co-chair, and currently, is executive director of the Vancouver Transgender Day of Remembrance Society. She organized Vancouver's Trans Celebration and Liberation March in 2011, scheduling the event to take place on July 29, two days before the Pride parade (an extrapolation of the 2010 Trans Pride March, which also wasn't affiliated with Pride) because she believed the Vancouver Pride Society was not trans-inclusive.

Judge Kael McKenzie co-chaired the Canadian Bar Association (CBA)'s Sexual Orientation and Gender Identity Conference from 2012 to 2014, and has served as the Manitoba Bar Association vice-president, the CBA Manitoba Branch chair, and as Winnipeg's Rainbow Resource Centre president. See also http://www.cbc.ca/news/canada/manitoba/transgender-judge-kael-mckenzie-manitoba-appointment-1.3446720.

"Trans grandmother," Kira Vallen, of the Saugeen First Nation identifies as both transgender and "third gender." She believes that people are more accepting of Indigenous trans people in cities than on reservations. https://tvo.org/article/current-affairs/shared-values/why-lgbtq-indigenous-communities- struggle-with-healthcare-for-the-homeless.

[13] These Indigenous, non-transgender, Two-Spirit allies are listed below.

Gloria May Eshkibok is a multi-talented artist and performer from Manitoulin Island, Ontario. https://arquives.andornot.com/en/list?q=gloria+eshkibok&p=1&ps=20.

Ty Nolan is a Native American storyteller, community scholar, and HIV/AIDS activist. He is involved in social justice work in Seattle: affordable housing, disability advocacy, and promoting the needs of Indigenous Elders. See his website http://ty-nolan.blogspot.com/. Read his piece, "The Origin of Corn and Other Stories," in Margot Wilson and Aaron Devor, eds., *Glimmerings: Trans Elders Tell Their Stories*, Victoria, BC: TransGender Publishing, 2019, 94-115.

Read Nicole Nanku Tanguay's piece, "In the Spirit of Beth: Queering Indigenous Space," in John Lorinc, et al., *Any Other Way*, 73-75.

Bisexual Wolf Clan member, Laureen Blu Waters (of the Cree, Métis and Mi'kmaq Nations), is Elder advisor to Canadian Commissioner Brian Eyolfson of the National Inquiry into Missing and Murdered Indigenous Women and Girls. Read Laureen's piece, "Time Capsule" in Jin Harawortin, Ghaida Moussa, and Syrus Marcus Ware, eds., *Marvellous Grounds: Queer of Colour Histories of Toronto*, Toronto, ON: Between the Lines, 2018, chapter 6.

Art Zoccole was formerly Executive Director of Toronto's 2-Spirited People of the 1st Nations. Read his piece, "Agokwe," in John Lorinc, et al., *Any Other Way*, 26-28. See also: Ristock, Janice, Art Zoccole, and Lisa Passante, *Aboriginal Two-Spirit and LGBTQ Migration, Mobility and Health Research Project* (*Final Report*), Winnipeg, MB: University of Manitoba, 2010. http://www.2 spirits.com/MMHReport.p.

[14] Two examples of trans-identified allies of Indigenous Two-Spirit people are noted below.

Transqueer-male Grey Kimber Piitaapan Muldoon is an ally of Indigenous transgender and Two-Spirit people, who has recounted the gender/sexual identity experiences of several of the latter who reside in northern Ontario. See: Muldoon, Grey Kimber Piitaapan (with Dan Irving), "A Sense of Place: Expressions of Trans Activism North of Lake Nipissing," in Irving and Raj, Trans Activism in Canada, 71-84.

Trans man and former University of Washington anthropologist professor, Jason Cromwell, wrote a chapter for this book anthology, Jacobs, Sue Ellen, and Wesley Thomas, eds., Two-*Spirit People: Perspectives on Native American Gender* and *Sexuality*, Chicago, IL: University of Illinois Press, 1997.

[15] The first version (2009) was co-written by primary care practitioner, Dr. Kate Greenaway, and client resource worker, Vlad Wolanyk. For the revised version, see: Bourns, Amy, MD, *Guidelines and Protocols for Comprehensive Primary Health Care for Trans Clients*, Toronto, ON: Sherbourne Health Centre, 2015. https://sherbourne.on.ca/guidelines-protocols-for-trans-care/.

[16] We initially invited trans women, Michelle Boyce and Rebecca Hammond, to join our Trans PULSE Project team, and later, trans men, Dr. Jake Pyne and Nik Redman. Cisgender principal co-investigators, Dr. Greta Bauer (Associate Professor in Epidemiology & Biostatistics at Western University) and Dr. Robb Travers (Assistant Professor in Psychology at Wilfrid Laurier University), were other team-members. For the research project report, see http://transpulseproject.ca/research-type/project-report/.

[17] Descriptions of these intersex activists follow below.
Caroline Cossey (1954) has Klinefelter's syndrome (with an XXXY genotype). Read: *I Am a Woman* (London UK: Sphere, 1982), by "Tula" (Caroline's modelling name), written with a sensationalizing ghost-writer; and *My Story* (London UK: Fabre and Fabre, 1991), wholly penned by Caroline herself, for a truer version. She surgically reassigned as female in 1974. See also https://zagria.blogspot.ca/2008/10/caroline-cossey-1954-model.html.

American gender/intersex activist, Mx. Anunnaki Ray, is a writer, educator and speaker advocating for intersex people and transgender and gender non-conforming children who are being harmed and have no voice:. https://anunnakiray.com/about/.

Del LeGrace Volcano, an American, polymorphous-perverse, queer, gender non-binary, trans man, visual artist and speaker on queer and intersex issues (e.g., "the Critical Sexology Seminars" in London), describes their intersexuality as "self-constructed." See also: Halberstam, Judith, and Del LaGrace Volcano, *The Drag King Book*, London, UK: Serpent's Tale, 1999.

[18] Brough, Brad, dir., "Intersexuality: Redefining Sex," SexTV, Season 2, Episode 24, Toronto, ON: Chum Television. Aired July 22, 2000.

[19] In 2005, Intersex Day of Remembrance (aka Intersex Solidarity Day) (November 8) was subsequently initiated by Joëlle-Circé Laramée, then Canadian spokeswoman for Organisation Intersex International (OII) (http://www.intersexualite.org/), to mark the birthday of Herculin Barbin, a 19th century, French intersex person. OII sought community solidarity by discussing intersex genital mutilation and the violence of the binary sex and gender system. While Intersex Awareness Day on October 26 is celebrated more in English-speaking countries, particularly in North America, Intersex Day of Remembrance is marked mostly in Europe; some countries (e.g., Australia and South Africa) mark both events and the days between as 14 days of intersex.

[20] See: *Transfixed* (2015), a Canadian docudrama featuring Martine Stonehouse and her husband, John Gelmon, directed by Alon Kol and written by Christopher Behnisch. In this film, however, Martine does not speak about her intersexuality. I successfully nominated Martine in 2012 for The City of Toronto Access, Equity and Human Rights Pride Award. https://www.youtube.com/watch?v=QsPQOVGCsuY.

[21] The Rainbow Health Network (Lesbian, Gay, Bi, Trans, Two-Spirited, Queer and Intersex Health) (not to be confused with Rainbow Health Ontario) was formerly called the Coalition for Lesbian and Gay Rights in Ontario (CLGRO). For Queer Ontario (a political advocacy group), see http://queerontario.org/.

[23] Read Christine Burns's books: *Trans Britain: Our Journey from the Shadows*, Unbound, 2018; and *Pressing Matters:* vols. 1 & 2, Self-published, 2013 & 2014. Watch her talk at the 2018 MTHF Transgender Archives Conference (Elders Panel) https://www.uvic.ca/mthf (click "Past Conferences" tab).

[24] See: Rees, Mark (with Katherine O'Donnell), "Taking to the Law," in Burns, *Trans Britain*, 135-160.

[25] See: Dr. Kenneth Dollarhide's other writings: "Native American Spirituality: Understanding Gender As Sacred," *The Transgender Tapestry,* (115) 2008 (http://difecta.blogspot.com/2009/10/gender-as-sacred.html); "Concept of Gender among

Selected Native American Traditions." *The Transgender Tapestry*, (99), Fall, 2002 (http://www.ifge.org/magazines/99_fall02.htm); and "Lakota Winkte," *The Transgender Tapestry*, (94), Summer, 2001 (http://www.ifge.org/catalog/product_info.php?products_id=94). See also this trans person's memorial tribute https://thetmplanet.com/the-ally-i-knew-remembering-dr-kenneth-dollarhide/.

[26] The cisgender lawyers who attended Egale Canada' national forum were barbara findlay, Cynthia Petersen, and Susan Ursel. Trans activists who attended included Trans Health Lobby Group members, Susan Gapka, Martine Stonehouse, Shadmith Manzo, and me, Egale Trans Issues Committee co-chairs, Jessica Denise Freedman and Tami Marie Starlight, and The 519 Community Centre's Meal Trans Program coordinator, Kyle Scanlon, among others. I believe that trans lawyers, Hélène Montreuil and Shannon Blatt, were also in attendance. Shannon won *Capital Xtra's* Political Activist of the Year Award in 2007 for her legal advocacy for trans and queer people in Ottawa and beyond. https://www.dailyxtra.com/community-celebrates-heroes-at-awards-gala-17572. Relocating to Vancouver in 2009, she helped organize the city's annual Trans, Two-Spirit, Genderqueer and Intersex Liberation and Celebration March.

[27] See his memoir, Green, Jamison, *Becoming a Visible Man*, Nashville, TN: Vanderbilt University Press, 2004.

[28] See her book, Stryker, Susan, *Transgender History: The Roots of Today's Revolution*, New York, NY: Seal Press, (1st ed.), 2008, (2nd ed.), 2017. And her film, Silverman, Victor, and Susan Stryker, dirs., *Screaming Queens: The Riot at Compton's Cafeteria*, San Francisco, CA: Frameline, 2005. Film documentary of the first transgender protest against the police.

[29] Read his life story, Valerio, Max Wolf, *The Testosterone Files: My Hormonal and Social Transformation from Female to Male*, New York, NY: Seal Press, 2006.

[30] Jordy Tackitt-Jones is a trans scholar, curator, artist, activist, and writer. He wrote a book about his friend, Alan Selby, San Francisco entrepreneur, activist, and founder of the iconic Mr. S Leather Store on Folsom Street: *The Mayor of Folsom Street: The Auto/Biography of "Daddy Alan" Selby, aka Mr. S.*, Fair Page LLC, 2017.

[31] These included Dr. Linette Martinez (a primary care physician), Mary Monihan (a nurse), and Robyn Stukalin (a social worker).

[32] Child/adolescent psychiatrist, Dr. Solomon Shapiro, founded the former Gender Identity & Sexual Orientation Services (GISOS) at Toronto's Hincks-Dellcrest Centre (a mental health centre for youth) in the early 2000s as an alternative to the Child, Youth and Family Gender Identity Clinic at CAMH (which was discontinued in 2015: see more in chapter 4). In 2016, Hincks-Dellcrest integrated its mental health services with the Hospital for Sick Children under its new name, SickKids Centre for Community Mental Health. A 2019 Google search does not bring up GISOS, so I'm assuming it closed.

[33] Raj, Rupert, "Transforming Couples and Families: A Transformative Therapeutic Model for Providers Working with the Loved Ones of Trans-Identified and Gender-Divergent People," *Journal of GLBT Family Studies*, 2008, 4(1): 133-163. doi. 10.1080/15504280802096765.

[34] Raj, Rupert, "Transactivism as Therapy: A Client Self-Empowerment Model Linking Personal and Social Agency," *Journal of Gay & Lesbian Psychotherapy*, 2007, 11(3-4): 77-98. doi. 10.1300/J236v11n03_05.

[35] These trans-male health professionals are noted below.
  Dr. Nick Gorton is a family physician, who drafted (with Dr. Jamie Buth and Dr. Dean Spade, Esq.) *Medical Therapy and Health Maintenance for Transgender Men: A Guide for Health Care Providers,* 2005. https://www.researchgate.net/publication/239573753_Medical_Therapy_and_Health_Maintenance_for_Transgender_Men_A_Guide_For_Health_Care_Providers.
  Dr. Randall Ehrbar is a clinical psychologist, who was then part of the task force assigned to revise the "gender identity disorder" classifications for the 2013 *DSM-5*.
  Reid Vanderburgh is a former psychotherapist, and author of *Transition and Beyond: Observations on Gender Identity,* Portland, OR: Q Press, 2007.
  André Wilson is a trans man who was then studying health policy: he has since earned his doctorate and now works as a health advocate. See also: Wilson, André A., MS, and Jamison Green, PhD, "Health Insurance Coverage Issues for Transgender People in the United States," University of California, San Francisco, June 17, 2016. https://transcare.ucsf.edu/guidelines/insurance.

[36] See: Miller, LeeAndra, and Lindsay Elin, *Families in TRANSition: A Resource Guide for Families of Transgender Youth* (2nd ed), Toronto, ON: Central Toronto Youth Services, 2016.http://www.ctys.org/wp-content/uploads/2016/03/CTYS-FIT-Families-in-Transition-Guide-2nd-edition.pdf.

[37] Lukayo Faye Estrella is a mixed-race, Filipino/a (Bikol diaspora) and Indigenous (Anishinaabe, Haudenosaunee and Wyandot), genderqueer educator, healer and "wordslinger" (essayist and poet), who travels between Ottawa and Toronto. http://lukayo.com/about/. Read their essay, "Alternative: Moving Towards Liberation & Anti-Oppression," in Douglas Gosse, ed., *Out Proud: Stories of Pride, Courage, and Social Justice*, Egale Canada Human Rights Trust (Ottawa, ON), St. John's, NL: Breakwater Books, 2014.

[38] Monica Forrester is an African Canadian, Two-Spirit, sex worker activist and the founding director of Trans Pride Toronto. She formerly worked with the Trans Sex Worker Outreach Program at The 519, and is currently Program Coordinator of the Aboriginal Sex Workers Education and Outreach Project at Maggie's: The Toronto Sex Workers Action Project. See the Monica Forrester fonds at The ArQuives. https://arquives.andornot.com/en/list?q=MONICA+FORRESTER&p=1&ps=20. She also co-produced (with Viviane Namaste) a film documentary featuring trans sex workers in Montreal; see: Ross, Mirha-Soleil, dir., *Madame Lauraine's Transsexual Touch,* Toronto, ON: Vtape, 2001. http://www.vtape.org/video?vi=4811. See also: Ware Syrus Marcus, "Organizing on the Corner: Trans Women of Colour and Sex Worker Activism in Toronto in the 1980s and 1990s (interview with Monica Forester and Chanelle Gallant)," in Jin Harawortin, Ghaida Moussa, and Syrus Marcus Ware, eds., *Marvellous Grounds: Queer of Colour Histories of Toronto*, Toronto, ON: Between the Lines, 2018, chapter 1.

[39] See: Lagartera, Reece, "ShoutOut Against Homophobia, Biphobia, Transphobia and Heterosexism," Winnipeg, MB: Rainbow Resource Centre, 2009. www.rainbowresourcecentre.org/; https://www.rainbowhealthontario.ca/wp-content/uploads/woocommerce_uploads/2014/ 08/ShoutOut.pdf.

[40] These trans people of colour are noted below.

Estefania Cortes-Vargas is a Colombian-Canadian Member of the Legislature (MLA) in Alberta's New Democratic Party (NDP), who formally came out as gender non-binary in the legislature in December 2015 during debate on the inclusion of transgender rights in the provincial Human Rights Code. Hear them speak on the second reading of the Alberta Human Rights Amendment Act, 2015 (Bill 7). https://www.youtube.com/watch?v=WDq78cjzABI.

In November 2017, Andrea Jenkins became the first Black, openly-transgender woman elected to public office in the USA (Minneapolis City Council, 8th Ward). https://www.washingtonpost.com/news/the-fix/wp/2017/11/08/meet-andrea-jenkins-the-openly-transgender-black-woman-elected-to-public-office-in-the-u-s/?noredirect=on&utm_term=.3d5d7b25393e. Read her book, *The T is Not Silent: New and Selected Poems*, Self-published, 2015. Andrea's election is a long time coming since Justina Williams—(likely) the first out African American, trans-female activist of four decades earlier, soon followed by Sharon Davis (see chapter 6).

In the same month as Andrea Jenkins (see above), Philippe Cunningham became the first (Black) openly-transgender man elected to public office in the USA—and in the same city! (Minneapolis City Council, 4th Ward). https://www.advocate.com/politics/2017/11/08/trans-man-has-also-been-elected-minneapolis-city-council.

Kim Coco Iwamoto, a Japanese-American, Hawaiian trans activist, editorialist and philanthropist, ran in Hawaii's August 11, 2018 primary election as a Democratic candidate for Lieutenant Governor. She supports same-sex marriage, and her passion helping LGBTQ homeless youth inspired her to become a licensed therapeutic foster parent.

Adela Hernández, a former nurse and electrocardiogram technician, is the first trans person elected to political office in Cuba, specifically, the municipal council of Caibarién in Villa Clara Province in 2012. She helped lawmakers pass legislation in 2013 to protect Cuban lesbian/gay employees from workforce discrimination.

Alejandra González Pino was the first elected transsexual councillor in Chile (and in Latin America), elected to Lampa's City Council in 2004 under her former name, Felipé. In 2016, she was nominated for the Municipal Council for the fourth time, but (according to Wikipedia) her "comrades" of the New Majority dared not nominate her as a mayoral candidate of Lampa, otherwise she could potentially have been Chile's first trans mayor. She promotes women's rights, HIV/AIDS prevention, and gender-identity and sexual-orientation diversity.

Zuliana Alejandra Araya Gutiérrez was the first trans politician to be elected in Chile, serving as Councilwoman for Valparaíso from 2012 to 2016. Since 2001, as regional president of Chile's Afrodita union for trans people, and as a member of the international Network for Human Rights (representing 25 Latin American countries), she has fought against the discrimination of transgender sex workers.

Luisa Revilla Urcia became the first openly-transgender person elected to public office in Peru, winning a seat on the local council in La Esperanza in 2014. A trans/queer activist, she hopes to build a home for people living with HIV/AIDS.

Michelle Suárez Bértora is Uruguay's first trans woman lawyer, and in 2014, became the first transgender politician elected to the Uruguayan legislature. As an obese, body-image activist, she believes the "youthful, eternally-beautiful" stereotype is oppressive for all women, and especially challenging for some trans women. In 2017, she resigned her seat in the senate after she was found guilty of forging legal documents while working as an attorney. Read Sofía Formoso's biography, *Michelle Suárez: La Primera Abogada Trans de Uruguay*, Uruguay: Sin Etiquetas, February 9, 2015. Spanish-language edition only. See also https://zagria.blogspot.com/2018/02/michelle-suarez-bertora-1984-lawyer.html.

Tamara Adrián Hernández became the first trans politician elected to office in Venezuela (the National Assembly) in 2015, and as of that year, was only the second transgender member of a national legislature in the Western hemisphere. She intends to promote proper access to public records on identity, same-sex marriage and human rights. See also https://zagria.blogspot.com/2011/04/tamara-adrian-hernandez-1954-lawyer.html.

Aya Kamikawa, a Tokyo municipal official, is the first openly-transgender person elected to office in Japan. She served from 2003 to 2007, and was re-elected for a second term from 2007-2011. Her platform was to improve rights for women, children, older, disabled and LGBT people.

Tomoya Hosoda, a former medical technologist, is the first trans man to be elected to office in Japan (to the City Council of Iruma, Saitama) on March 21, 2017. Tomoya plans to focus on the rights of trans, queer, disabled and elderly people. The March 17, 2017 *Gay Star News* article headlines Tomoya as the "first ever trans man to be elected to public office in the world," but incredibly, fails to mention the previous (December 17, 2015) appointment to public office of Canadian-Métis, trans and Two-Spirit man, Kael McKenzie, the first openly-transgender judge in Canada—yet another form of American erasure of trans Canadians!

Hazreen Shaik Daud, a former NGO worker, is Malaysia's first transgender politician, appointed as political secretary to Tanjung Bungah state assemblyman, Teh Yee Cheu, of the Democratic Action Party in 2013. Her appointment was met by mixed reactions in Muslim-majority Malaysia. As a human rights activist and a member of Penang State's transgender committee, she works hard to alleviate the stigma of her fellow trans Malaysians.

Niluka Ekanayake, a former astrologer, is the first transgender woman to hold the post of governor in a Sri Lankan province: appointed as the 10th Governor of Central Province in 2016, and as the ninth governor of Sabaragamuwa Province in 2018. Following the protest of her appointment, on the basis of gender, by one of Sri Lanka's main Buddhist institutions (the Asgiriya chapter), she promotes the importance of religious tolerance and the rule of law for all.

"Nok" Suanyot, a trans-female activist, was elected to represent Mueang Nan District on the Provincial Administration Organization of Nan Province in Thailand in 2012. Previously, Suanyot had been a beauty queen and a member of the pop group, Venus Flytrap, performing under the name, Nok. Suanyot is Founding Chair of the TransFemale Association of Thailand and advocates for the rights of Thai trans women. See also https://zagria.blogspot.com/2017/08/yollada-nok-suanyot-1983-activist.html.

Geraldine Batista Roman, a practicing Catholic, became the first openly-transgender Congresswoman in the Philippines (Representative of the 1st District of Bataan) in 2016. She officially approves of same-sex marriage, opposes conversion/reparative therapy for LGBT people and aims to introduce a bill for sex-reassignment surgery for trans people.

[41] It's noteworthy that four of India's elected political officials (Shabnam "Mausi" Bano, Kamla Jaan, Kamala Kinnar, Madhu Bai Kinnar) have either been *Hijras* (third gender) or former *Hijras* (who later identify as trans women and often under go vaginoplasty). Regrettably, two were subsequently ousted from public office due to genderphobia. From 1998 to 2003, Shabnam "Mausi" Bano (the first transgender Indian to be elected to public office) was an elected member of the Madhya Pradesh State Legislative Assembly. In 2000, Kamla Jaan of India's Katni district became the world's first "eunuch" (sic) mayor, and in 2009, Kamala Kinnar of the Sagar district won the mayoralty. Sadly, both were pejoratively termed "eunuchs" or "castrated transgenders" by the media, and within two years of being in office, their respective town courts declared their candidacies "null and void" for contesting in the female category, so they had to step down. Things eventually improved when, in 2014, India's supreme court ruled *Hijras* as a legally-recognized "third gender," and shortly after, a TV station recruited India's first-ever transgender news anchor (Padmini Prakashi) to work for

the Tamil Coimbatore-based Lotus News Channel. http://matpal.com/2014/12/padmini-prakash-biographytransgender-news-anchor.html. In 2015, Madhu Bai Kinnar was elected as mayor of the Raigarh Municipal Corporation in Chattisgarh, India. Overall, a positive strike for gender identity. Homosexuality, however, still remains a criminal offence in India, and those caught in sexual acts are imprisoned.

[42] These Indigenous transgender and/or Two-Spirit people include Canadians, Jamie Lee Hamilton and Kael McKenzie, and New Zealander, Georgina Beyer.

[43] See: Jin Haritaworn, Ghaida Moussa, and Syrus Marcus Ware, with Alvis Choi, Amandeep Kaur Panag, and Río Rodríguez, "Marvellous Grounds: QTBIPOC Counter-Archiving against Imperfect Erasures," in John Lorinc et al, *Any Other Way,* 219-223. And the two book anthologies: Jin Haritaworn, Ghaida Moussa, and Syrus Marcus Ware, eds., *Marvellous Grounds: Queer of Colour Histories of Toronto*, Toronto, ON: Between the Lines, 2018; and Jin Haritaworn, Ghaida Moussa, and Syrus Marcus Ware, with Río Rodríguez, eds., *Queering Urban Justice: Queer of Colour Formations in Toronto*, Toronto, ON: University of Toronto Press, 2018. And watch: *Marvellous Grounds (Short Film),* 2018. https://vimeo.com/269198618.

[44] See https://blacklivesmatter.com/.

[45] See: Khan, Janaya, and LeRoi Newbold, "Black Lives Matter Toronto Teach-In," in Haritaworn, Moussa, and Ware, eds., *Queering Urban Justice*, chapter 7. See also https://blacklivesmatter.ca/.

[46] See https://en.wikipedia.org/wiki/Black_Lives_Matter.

[47] See: Raj, Rupert, "Zening the Art of Trans Activism," in Irving and Raj, *Trans Activism in Canada*, 85-91.

[48] For a list of the book's chapters and contributors, see https://www.canadianscholars.ca/books/trans-activism-in-canada#tab_toc.

[49] Hopefully American readers will own, in good faith, the overall cultural imperialism and appropriation inherent in the Americentric mindset—even extending, at times, to xenophobia! This includes the habitual non-acknowledgement—either by assimilation or erasure—of Canadian (and at times even other non-American) trans activists. Promisingly, there is a growing number of exemplary trans Americans, especially Dr. Jamison Green, who are not guilty of such tunnel vision, often serving as effective goodwill ambassadors in terms of North American and international trans relations. As a mixed-race (East Indian and Polish) Canadian, dancing the dialectic between East and West, I am somewhat of a cultural integrationist, an eclectic citizen of the world, embracing selected aspects of diverse cultures, with a view to their sociocultural history, philosophical beliefs, religious values, scientific progress, political ideologies, human rights activism, and cultural arts.

[50] For more information on their trauma-informed Anti-Oppression Psychotherapy Model™, see http://antioppressionpsychotherapy.blogspot.com/.

[51] For same-sex marriage legislation in Canada, see https://www.chrc-ccdp.gc.ca/eng/content/submission-standing-committee-justice-and-human-rights-same-sex-marriages.

[52] For same-sex marriage legislation in Virginia, see https://tv.arlingtonva.us/same-sex-marriage-legal-in-virginia/.

[53] The 1947 film noir, *Out of the Past*, was directed by Jacques Tourneur and produced by RKO Radio Pictures. Robert Mitchum (as "Jeff Bailey") and Jane Greer (as "Kathie Moffat") played the two doomed lovers. Jeff was the *l'homme fatal*, and Kathie was the *femme fatale*. See https://en.wikipedia.org/wiki/Out_of_the_Past.

[54] Dr. Rachel Epstein led the LGBTQ Parenting Network at the Family Service Association of Toronto (David Kelley Services) and Sherbourne Health Centre in 2006. She conducted research and provided education and community programs for cisqueer and trans parents and their families. Read her book, *Who's Your Daddy?: And Other Writings on Queer Parenting*, Toronto, ON: Sumach Press (Canadian Scholars' Press), 2009. It includes information on trans parenting.

[55] Subsequent trans winners (all Canadians of colour) of the Steinert & Ferreiro Award were Syrus Marcus Ware (in 2012), Vivek Shraya (in 2014), Nik Redman (in 2015) and Monica Forrester (in 2018).

See Black trans activist Syrus Ware's paper, "All Power to All People?: Black LGBTTI2Q Activism, Remembrance, and Archiving in Toronto," in Susan Stryker and Paisley Currah, eds., *TSQ (Transgender Studies Quarterly): The Issue of Blackness*, May 1, 2017, 4 (2): 170-180. https://doi.org/10.1215/23289252-3814961.

Vivek Shraya is a South Asian, trans, queer, musician, writer, and visual artist. She currently lives in Alberta, working as Assistant Professor in Creative Writing at the University of Calgary. Read her first children's picture book and other publications. https://vivekshraya.com/books/.

Nik Redman is a Caribbean-Canadian, Black trans man, artist, dj, film festival curator, activist and community worker. He has been involved in trans and queer (sexual) health, prison reform, and people with HIV/AIDS advocacy. Nik is the partner of, and co-parent with, Syrus Marcus Ware.

Monica Forrester (a Black, trans-Two-Spirit, sex worker activist) was one of the Trans* Pride Honoured Individuals for World Pride 2014 in Toronto. She is interviewed here. https://www.youtube.com/watch?v=LT7T1Yt9RH8. Monica's fonds are located in The ArQuives. https://arquives.ca/newsfeed/whats-new-in-the-archives-monica-forrester-shines-a-spotlight-on-trans-history/.

10. RR Consulting Redux…Even More Surgery…The Love of My Life (2011–2013)

On the work front, having been at Sherbourne Health Centre for just over eight years, I was coming to the sad conclusion that this once intentional community was a failed experiment—not for patients/clients, but for many employees. Staff physicians were treated as VIPs (as were Board members and patients/clients), but the adulation stopped there. Loyalty to managers and non-physician staff was apparently not an organizational value and is likely why a number of dispensable employees were let go or felt driven to leave. I had really hoped that SHC would be a workplace that invested value in its people resources, encouraging them to maximize and fostering their growth and advancement. Sadly, this hope was brutally dashed once I realized that organizational validation of, and loyalty to, its employees had eroded over time. Resilient I was, but vulnerable too, like the strong as steel bamboo tree that is still bent by the wind. Dancing the dialectic between resilience and vulnerability, I was eventually overpowered by unexpected organizational dynamics.

Recalling the adage, "a prophet is not without honour save in his own country,"[1] I had recently been feeling undervalued as a staff member—apart from some notable exceptions—especially when it came to pushing beyond my basic job description to take on related activities at work. These included: enhanced client advocacy (testifying as an expert witness in refugee hearings for trans and queer people victimized by violence in their homelands, and in human rights tribunals for trans people harassed in Canada); consulting (proposing trans-inclusive policy changes and legal amendments to corporate directors, government ministers, lawyers, and politicians); training (enhancing professional development for healthcare and social service providers through workshops requested beyond the required conference presentations, transferring knowledge to university/college educators and students); public education (informing the public about trans issues through mass media); media advocacy (recommending best practices for media coverage of trans people to journalists and students); and publishing (writing trans-focussed, clinical research papers for scholarly journals, co-editing a comprehensive anthology on Canadian trans activism).

As a bright light trying to take a leadership role in the centre, some managers were put off by my creative vision; one that transgressed the conservative complacency of the organizational culture. It was that same old dialectical dance: a progressive frontline staff blocked by a reactionary bottom line management. My intuitive sense of being seen as an undesired agitator was borne out as two of my proposals were summarily dismissed as not viable for the organization.

The first was an anti-oppressive/diversity new hire mentorship program incorporating the proven 80/20 Model and my own 7/10 Rule. The former is an applied research model[2] (successfully implemented in Regina, Ottawa, and several other Canadian cities), which allots senior nurses 20% of their time as administrators, mentoring junior nurses and new hires, and the remaining 80% as clinicians, fulfilling typical nursing duties. The 7/10 Rule is an efficacious hiring strategy: provided the candidate has at least seven of the 10 job requirements and seems a good fit, a dedicated committee (I offered myself as a potential member) mentors the new hire over six months until they have attained the required benchmark. I conceived this idea as a proactive response to the reality that many members of marginalized communities (namely, transgender, intersex, and Indigenous people) frequently did not apply for competitive employment, and if they did, were often not hired. If they did manage to land the job, they did not always pass the probation period, and even if they managed that, many eventually resigned or were dismissed due to poor job performance, a bad attitude, or unacceptable behaviour. I hoped that coaching the new hires from the outset would help them gradually grow into the job and, with ongoing support, they would become effective employees of the Sherbourne family. The outcome would be a richer workforce, reflecting our diverse communities.

My second proposal was an employee appreciation program, whereby every employee, from the CEO right down to the housekeeping, maintenance, and security staff would be honoured within their own team once a year—each month featuring one of the 12 teams. I believed that my two proposals were brilliant, innovative strategies—perfectly viable for the cutting-edge organization Sherbourne was reputed to be.

Further disappointments followed. I was not chosen for SHC's Quality Improvement Award, for which a colleague had nominated me for my work providing one-off, trans information sessions for people on our lengthy counselling waitlist. Such timely access to a single session provided knowledge-hungry clients with psychomedical resources on all relevant aspects of gender transitioning, including how to navigate both primary care and mental healthcare and how to access clinical assessments offered by Sherbourne Health Centre and CAMH's Adult Gender Identity Clinics. The other extra-mile service I provided was conducting readiness assessments for cross-sex hormone therapy and gender confirming surgery, not only for SHC trans clients but also those referred to me by St. Michael's Hospital and Toronto East General Hospital.

Due to this under appreciation of my true value and also to supplement my limited salary while still working at SHC, I reinstated my former, part-time private practice. Through this, I provided counselling, consulting, and training around gender identity and gender transitioning, mental health and addictions, and other issues. This time I did it right, contracting a webmistress (Pam Sloan) to design my website, RR Consulting. It took $900 and six months to finally get it off the ground, with the home page proudly declaring: "Rupert Raj is back on track!"

It took time to build up my clientèle and I only worked on weekends but advertising in *Psychology Today* helped. I even received inquiries from south of the border—especially from parents of gender non-conforming youth—and from abroad—including two psychologists from Germany and Poland, respectively, and from trans people from the Middle East immigrating to Canada. I made damn sure not to overwork myself, having previously learned my lesson about the ever-present threat of burnout. I loved being (partly) self-employed because it meant not having to constrain my practice to fit stifling organizational parameters or being forced to work with undermining co-workers or potentially litigious clients. My private clients (and most of my Sherbourne clients), however, have always validated me much more than my agency co-workers. Many of my colleagues outside of the centre think very highly of me: a professional fellowship based on mutual respect and trust. In addition to counselling and therapy, I provided consulting services for healthcare and social service professionals, offering clinical supervision and case conferencing around gender identity and sexual orientation issues, including the challenging question of how to effectively support gender-independent kids or trans teens and their parents. I delivered professional development trainings for physicians, nurse practitioners, nurses, psychologists, psychotherapists, and social workers. My skills-building workshops were grounded in the transpositive/transformative therapeutic models I had evolved over the previous 10 years (and there was still one more to come—more about this later).

I enjoyed being my own boss with no worries of being micro-managed. RR Consulting was back with a vengeance! I couldn't survive financially, however, on my private practice fees alone. So, like it or not, I had to keep working for a health agency during the work week. So, why not apply for work at another organization? In fact, I had contemplated applying to St. Michael's Hospital or CAMH: but, ultimately, I would rather be a big fish in a little pond. At least SHC validated me (some of the time) for my professional expertise as a mental health clinician, my lived experience as a trans man, and my years of community activism. Such validation (albeit limited) would be hard to give up for a few dollars more and a change of venue that might not prove to be that much better in the long term. Besides, I only had eight more years to go before retiring and I wasn't up for such an upheaval.

As an independent gender specialist, I commanded respect on the international scene and in May 2011, then WPATH president Dr. Lin Fraser invited me to serve on WPATH's International Advisory Committee to review proposed revisions for the upcoming (7th) version of the *Standards of Care* for the Health of Transsexual, Transgender, and Gender-Nonconforming People. The new trans affirming *Standards of Care* (SOC)[3] were released to enthusiastic acclaim at the September 2011 WPATH symposium in Atlanta, which I regrettably missed due to a severe bout of bronchitis. The World Health Organization subsequently asked the committee to make recommendations for the upcoming (11th) version of the *International Classification of Diseases (ICD-11)*,[4] in terms of its diagnoses for crossgender identity (the latter was declassified as a psychiatric disorder in 2018).

February 2012: my 60th birthday approaching, I decided to visit New Orleans, a long-time dream. I asked my friend, Philip, to come along and he jumped at the idea. We went for one week, right after *Mardi Gras,* staying in a hotel 20 minutes from the downtown core. In the French Quarter, we dined in Cajun restaurants, drank in gay bars, and boogied the night away in blues clubs. We browsed art galleries and bought local artwork at flea markets. An artist in his own right, Philip was in seventh heaven! We saw nature up close, riding the bayou in a swamp-tour boat, and witnessed vestiges of the destruction wreaked by Hurricane Katrina six years prior. We loved N'awlins: its sax-sensual bluesmen and *avant-garde* artists, its mouth-burning Cajun cooking and thirst quenching beer, the swooping pelicans and grasping 'gators in their primal bayous, its townspeople's gracious generosity, and the constant beat of the city. My trip to the American South was a great way to start the year, but there were some sad times to come.

After a two-year ordeal trying to keep alive my kidney-compromised kitty, Pinky decided that it was her time to go, crawling into a hiding place in my condo. Eventually finding her after a frantic search, I rushed her to the vet that sad day in May only for him to tell me that she needed euthanasia right away to end her suffering. So, heartbroken, I had to let her go. Amidst a gush of rare tears, I said goodbye to my poor sweet kitty with the pink ears: yet another pet to mourn.

As well as my feline daughter, I lost two trans friends: Lynne Pellerin, who died of liver cancer January 10, 2012 at 68, and Kyle Scanlon, who took his life July 3, 2012 at age 40. Lynne had been increasingly ill for some time, having twice undergone radiation and chemotherapy in Montreal. Kyle had been depressed and suicidal for a long time, waiting only for his elderly cat to die before quitting this life in good conscience. Lynne's passing, even though she will be sadly missed by her family and many friends across Canada, was not unexpected, but Kyle's sudden death was a shocking loss to many of us as he had been a mainstay of the Hamilton and Toronto trans communities since the 1990s. His demise was likely exacerbated by burnout as a longtime activist, continuously exposed to vicarious trauma and bearing the burden of having to be a constant beacon of hope to other trans people. The 519 Community Centre held a memorial, and together with his family, founded a trust in Kyle's name to benefit future trans people. I grieved the loss of these two friends who had done so much for so many and will always treasure their memories in my heart. Over the next two years, there would be even more losses.

Yet, the world goes on: the dance of life-and-death never-ending, sorrow and joy juxtaposed. Although I had just lost two friends, Mother Earth answered my plea for someone to love. May brought an unexpected e-mail from KJ, the woman with whom I'd had a brief romantic fling in Toronto 31 years before. Out of the blue! She had been living in Australia since 1985, working in the post office and in social services, getting married and divorced, adopting pet Chihuahuas, gardening, swimming, and travelling in the South Seas. This was our first contact in all that time: a welcome surprise! KJ wanted to visit her elderly mother near Port Elgin, Ontario and her brother in Toronto, not having seen either of them for some years. In a flash, she thought of connecting with me as well. An animal lover too, she commiserated with me over my loss of Pinky and readily accepted my offer, inviting her to stay over at my place during her visit to Toronto. Before her arrival, we Skyped like crazy despite the 14-hour time difference, chatting eight hours at a time, catching up on the last three decades. She played me a selection of love songs from the 1960s and 1970s (the Supremes, Karen Carpenter, Dusty Springfield, Abba, etc.). Relating some rib-cracking joke, she threw her head back in a sexy laugh, just like the old days. That did it: I came undone, lost to her charms! I was falling for her all over again.

KJ's flight was due at Toronto Pearson Airport on June 12. I could hardly wait, counting the hours impatiently like a love-sick schoolboy! When she finally arrived, her full skirt billowing like Marilyn Monroe's, my heart thumped. We embraced, long and lovingly, then headed off to my condo. I made her a pasta dinner, then we retired to the boudoir for a private tryst. Fireworks went off that night, exploding rockets and all! Everything seemed brand new as if we were getting to know each other for the first time. We talked up a storm over the next few weeks, discovering things we had in common, including a concern for the environment and the welfare of factory farmed animals. Committed to animal liberation, we had both been ethical vegetarians for extended periods but were now pescetarians—how we love seafood!—although we still struggle not to eat other animal flesh. I introduced KJ to my friends, colleagues, and members of the queer, trans, intersex, and Two-Spirit communities. I didn't know all that many straight or cisgender people but she was fine with that because she likes someone for their personality and shared values—not for their sexual orientation or gender identity (or their race or religion). Moreover, being pansexual (like me), she has dated cis and trans men and women and befriended all colours of the rainbow.

Pride Week arrived so we attended both the trans and dyke marches, but exhausted by Sunday, forewent the Pride Parade. I had been asked to speak at the trans march with such notables as American trans activist Kate Bornstein and a number of local community leaders: Alec Butler, Susan Gapka, Martine Stonehouse, Monica Forrester, Morgan M. Page, Kenji Tokawa, Nik Redman, and Syrus Marcus Ware.

Following Pride, we drove a rental car north to Lake Huron to visit KJ's mom. Her mother (who did not recognize me from all those years ago) graciously invited me to visit anytime. We stayed for 10 days, wandering through the Bruce County resort town, strolling on the boardwalk by moonlight. Although KJ tried to teach me how to swim, water and I just didn't seem to go together. But my Aussie dolphin was a born water baby and loved to swim in the lake. We had a lovely time, despite the bugs, nestled together on the beach after a refreshing dip, enraptured by the glorious sunset framed by the twin lighthouses. That summer was splendorous, honeymooning with my sexy lady!

Since fall was approaching, it was back to work for me. In September, I flew to Winnipeg for the CPATH conference, where my social worker colleague, Celia Schwartz, and I presented our paper, "A Collaborative Preparedness and Informed Consent Model: Guidelines to Assess Trans Candidates for Readiness for Hormone Therapy and Supportive Counselling throughout the Gender Transitioning Process."[5] The positive feedback from other healthcare professionals was gratifying because Celia and I were committed to our clinical approach in our work with transgender/genderqueer clients. To our indignation, however, we were unprofessionally castigated by one Sherbourne Health Centre and two Rainbow Health Ontario trans employees,[6] the latter two having previously maligned cisgender transcare physicians. Sadly, not all professional trans people are courteous towards other professionals, transgender or cisgender. The oppressed as oppressor! And yet, why can't we trans folks set an example for our often less-evolved cis peers? During the conference, wracked by a bad cold, I somehow got through our presentation, coughing my guts out all the while. While in Manitoba, we met Reece Lagartera, a trans man of colour working at the local Rainbow Resource Centre, and several Indigenous Two-Spirit men and women. I missed KJ so badly that I couldn't wait to return to my baby's comforting embrace!

Now 60 (in 2012), I had been contemplating having my final surgery (genital reconstruction) ever since OHIP had relisted gender confirming surgery four years previously. I had initially hesitated because of my age, the trauma of surgery, the lengthy recovery process, and limited results. Last year, however, comparing the pros and cons, I had reached the decision to go ahead with bottom surgery, choosing metoidioplasty over phalloplasty. To qualify for this procedure, a trans candidate must apply to CAMH's Adult Gender Identity Clinic for approval, which subsequently required OHIP endorsement. It was embarrassing (and mind fucking) for me—a trans man who had been publicly living as male for 41 years—to have to prove that I had been living full-time as a man simply to fulfill CAMH's criteria of the Real Life Experience! I had to produce documentation showing that I had legally changed my name to Nicholas and then to Rupert, and had changed my legal sex-designation to male, as well as a letter from my employer verifying that I had worked there for at least a year in the male gender role. Moreover, I had to attend three sessions with two psychiatrists (Dr. Robert Dickie and Dr. Wayne Baici) and a psychological intern to demonstrate my ability to give informed consent to undergo surgery. Even WPATH's *Standards of Care* were more reasonable, not imposing counter-intuitive logic and burdensome bureaucratic red tape on people who had partly surgically transitioned years ago, grand-parenting these trans people accordingly.

Metoidioplasty is a type of genitoplastic surgery for trans men that is less invasive, less time-consuming, and less expensive than phalloplasty. Given my advanced age and my aversion to being a professional patient for the next few years, necessitating missing a lot of work (and my clients), I chose the metoidio as only two stages are required. The first involves removing the vaginal lining, releasing the clitoris from the underlying ligament, elongating and rerouting the urethra, and creating the scrotum (if the patient opts for all of these procedures). During the second stage, six months later, artificial testes are inserted into the scrotal sac. Within three months after the first stage of surgery—if all goes well—the trans man should be able to stand to pee and to climax with his new microphallus. Nevertheless, about 10-15% of postsurgical trans men lack erotic sensation in their new minipenis and/or cannot achieve penile orgasm. I so hoped not to be among those few! I chose the Gender Reassignment Surgery (GRS) Clinic (*Centre Métropolitain de Chirurgie Plastique*) in Montreal, operated by Dr. Pierre Brassard and Dr. Maude Bélanger, because, even though I had to travel outside of Ontario, it was closer than the other OHIP-approved genitoplastic surgeons.[7] Travel takes time and money.

Prior to my surgery date, KJ enrolled in SHC's eight-week educational and social group offered by the Trans Partner Network[8] for partners of trans or genderqueer folks, facilitated by LeeAndra Miller. The group provided a valuable resource for KJ, alleviating her anxiety somewhat by obtaining peer-support from other partners in the group. This helped her to psychologically prepare for the major ordeal ahead, including supporting me through the surgery and recovery process, and dealing with her own feelings seeing me so compromised.

November 6, 2012 was my scheduled surgery day: exactly four decades after my first surgery when I was 20. I was both nervous and excited. On Hallowe'en, KJ and I took the Megabus to Montreal to stay with our friend (my former counsellor colleague at SHC), Carole Baker, for two weeks. Meeting for the first time, KJ and Carole clicked right away. Carole, along with KJ and my sister, made up our four member family. Next day, we attended the pre-surgical consultation with Dr. Brassard at the GRS Clinic. Waiting an hour and a half in a room overflowing with patients, we had barely 20 minutes to ask the all-important questions about the upcoming surgery. Then, Dr. Brassard examined me to see what he had to work with. We found him pompous and cavalier, but, at the time, he was the only gender confirming surgeon in Canada! Even though I had contracted a bad bout of bronchitis—which both KJ and Carole caught—I still wanted to go ahead because I had waited so long for this final step of my gender transition. The night before the operation, KJ gushed a waterfall of tears because—although she fully supported me as a trans man—she did not like the idea of me being cut up, worrying about the surgical outcome. My heart went out to her: "It'll be okay, Sweetie, don't worry"—but she did. Fortunately, our caring friend, Carole, emotionally supported KJ throughout the ordeal, teaching her some mindfulness meditation to help ease her anxiety. Carole, we are eternally indebted to you!

The following morning, I was wheeled into the operating theatre and hours later, I woke up groggily in the recovery room, panicking because I couldn't move my lower body following the epidural anaesthesia. It's absolutely terrifying feeling numb from the waist down! Returning to my hospital bed, KJ was waiting there, worriedly. Comforting me, she helped me to throw up into the pan—the nausea was sickening(!)—and encouraged me to slowly move my feet, then my legs, to regain sensation. In the crunch, my partner is always there for me and I'm so grateful for her support. The nurses and orderlies were also attentive and I thanked them for their care.

Three days later, I was transferred to the aftercare centre adjoining the hospital with 10 other trans patients from across Canada, including two trans men who were undergoing phalloplasty. The nurses there were equally responsive, and there was an exceptional orderly: however, many were not fluent in English, sometimes making it hard to understand references to specific anatomical parts and medications—scary when it's your body and your health! On Sunday evenings, there was only one nurse, who seemed extremely stressed. The housekeeping and kitchen staff were friendly but the food was atrocious: underdone chicken, rubber-like cannelloni. A nightmare for vegetarian/vegan patients as most meals were meat-based. I complained to the kitchen staff, but their overcooked tofu alternatives were equally inedible. And this unsatisfactory service is paid for by my OHIP premiums! Trans people are often treated poorly when it comes to comprehensive healthcare and related services because we are not viewed as a viable (voting) constituency. Hopefully, trans healthcare in Ontario and the rest of Canada will improve in the near future as we're embarrassingly lagging behind other countries like The Netherlands and the UK. Promisingly, there has been some further progress in trans care since 2012, but it has mostly been limited to the richer provinces and the larger urban centres.

Overall, the bronchitis, epidural, constipation, my cold bedroom, and the inedible meals, all made for a miserable experience. Not to mention the excruciating pain when the doctor and nurse pulled out my drain plug: I shrieked almost like an animal being abused! And, the surgical outcome up to this point was far from satisfactory: the scrotal sac was positioned too low. I didn't yet know about my urinary or sexual functioning as the catheter had to be in for 28 days, and erotic sensation would not be forthcoming for about three months, if ever.

Back home again, sexual sensation thankfully returned within 12 weeks and I could still climax, but my glans was too sensitive: a livewire precluding protracted or multiple orgasms. But, at least my alien entity (the vagina) was finally gone! I could pee fine once the catheter was removed (notwithstanding a post-urination dribble), but alas, I never managed to pee at a public urinal. I had first tried standing to urinate in the stall a few times, but got over-anxious that I might dribble onto my underwear and the last thing I wanted was pissy pants!

Traumatized by the whole experience at the clinic, I chose not to come back for the second stage (testicular implants), so my balls are still virtual. Well, at least I don't need to worry about physical emasculation or testicular cancer. Even though innovative medical technological advances have been made since I decided to hold off in 1978, genital surgical outcomes for trans men are still variable, depending on surgeons' skills, surgical techniques, complications and repairs, postsurgical recovery, and patient expectations. Some trans men are more satisfied than others.[9] If I had known the outcome in advance, would I have still gone ahead with surgery? It's hard to say, having eagerly awaited this for most of my life; but, possibly not, given all the aggravation I had to go through. Well, what's done is done and I now have to live with the less than ideal result. Still, despite the imperfect cosmetic appearance, I feel intact as a male.

But it wasn't over yet: the surgery and recovery were only the first part of this ordeal. The second part was the self-advocacy I undertook: firstly, a constructively critical report to the GRS Clinic and, secondly, a series of five complaints to both Ontario and Quebec medical/psychological personnel and government officials over 12 months. Initially, I emailed a Patient Satisfaction Survey in December 2012 to the GRS Clinic's Head Nurse and the Assistant

Executive Director/Director of Nursing. In my feedback, I critiqued and made recommendations on seven distinct categories relating to the clinic's professional standards, operating practices, patient care, and related issues. These recommendations included: the need for a comprehensive patient-information package in equally literate English and French, adequate bathroom facilities, viable vegetarian/vegan meals, fluently bilingual written and electronic communication, fluently bilingual staff, an improved catheter design, and a postsurgical buddy system. In response, the assistant executive director agreed that I had raised some valid points, which he hoped to address. I offered my consulting services to help out in this regard, but, unfortunately, he did not take up my offer. If he had, and the specific problems had been resolved, these pages would not need to be set forth here, exposing the clinic's unremorseful shame for all the world to see! I, then, followed up on their complacent attitude with a formal complaint, citing six individuals at the Montreal GRS Clinic who were less than professional in their treatment of me (and certain other patients). These included the two surgeons, the head nurse, the assistant executive director/director of nursing, and the two medical secretaries. The clinic's response was essentially a mixture of denial and minimization of my concerns.

Undaunted, that July, I complained to CAMH's Adult Gender Identity Clinic Director, Dr. Chris MacIntosh, and staff psychologist, Dr. Nicola Brown. Dr. Brown sympathized, urging me to file a formal complaint with the Ontario Ministry of Health and Long-Term Care (OMHLTC). When I requested a formal investigation of the Montreal GRS Clinic, the OMHLTC Health Services Branch Manager directed me to the *Collège des Médecins du Québec* (the governing body regulating physicians in Quebec). So, in September, I complained to the *Collège's Office of the Syndic Directeur*. The process was psychologically triggering as I had to record all the events and my negative reactions. The Director finally responded that an inquiry had been conducted into the two surgeons named, and upon reviewing the *Collège's Code of Ethics of Physicians,* she concluded: "There are no grounds to support a disciplinary complaint against the physicians concerned." Notwithstanding, the investigators had neglected to adequately address four of my additional stated complaints: a postponed presurgical consultation, misapplication of the term "female orgasm" for trans men (I have never had a female orgasm in my life!), inadequate postoperative follow-up, and a violation of electronic communication privacy. The *Collège* had totally missed the salient points of my arguments, discounting the evidence cited for each complaint: neither had it referenced my charges against the four other clinic staff, including the assistant executive director/director of nursing, who was responsible for overseeing the quality of patient care.

In December 2013, I filed another complaint with the *Collège's Review Committee Coordinateur*, challenging the initial decision: but, alas, the committee's decision was likewise unfavourable: "There is no cause to lodge a complaint with the disciplinary council against the two surgeons named." My self-advocacy had not succeeded, the old boys' network (including its female members) winning out over the little guy. Even though they had followed due legal process, I found the investigation to be merely a bureaucratic exercise, not one truly committed to patient justice. I was dissatisfied with the outcome, hoping, instead, that it would have brought a show of good faith: an admission of accountability and agreement to make reparation. No such luck! I was equally disappointed that certain other trans patients and their partners, who had vehemently complained to me about their unsatisfactory experiences at the clinic, were not brave enough to formally complain as I had done. When our rights (and dignity) are being threatened, we must summon the courage to claim what is rightfully ours.

A morally responsible citizen, I chose legal means, rather than criminal violence, to convey my displeasure, unlike disgruntled Kelowna, BC trans woman, Jayne Ellen Heideck, who fire-bombed the Montreal GRS Clinic three-and-a-half years later, on May 2, 2016, following her gender confirming surgery there four months earlier.[10] Despite her complaints that the clinic had not provided her with proper care, it is unconscionable to resort to violence, jeopardizing the lives of patients and staff. Fortunately, nobody was injured but there was extensive damage to the property and the clinic was shut down for a few days. The RCMP arrested Jayne and she is now serving time in a federal prison in BC. Hopefully, she will get the psychotherapeutic help she needs towards remorse and rehabilitation. It's noteworthy that only a smaller percentage of trans people commit crimes and that the majority of these are solicitation for prostitution or drug-related offences.

My colleague at the Ontario Human Rights Commission, Jacqui Pegg, suggested that I complain to the Quebec Privacy Commission but, by then, I was so emotionally spent that I gave up on any further self-advocacy, cutting my losses for the sake of my sanity.

Ultimately, I'm not telling trans people whether they should or should not go to the Montreal GRS Clinic. What I'm saying is that, at the time I published my original memoir (2017), it was still discriminatory—a violation of the Canada Health Act—that there was only one clinic in this country for trans people to access genitoplastic surgery. Moreover, the Montreal clinic was the only viable option for most trans people in Canada, given that the American, European and Asian clinics required costly travel and extended postsurgical care. It was also discriminatory that most trans Canadians had to travel outside of their own province or territory—and some even had to travel abroad—for proper medical treatment! Our federal government should have treated its transgender citizens as well as it treats its cisgender ones by providing all trans Canadians with equal access to medically essential, funded healthcare throughout the country—rather than endorsing a monopoly health service (gender confirming surgery) based in a single province! Happily in response to pressure from trans activists and our cisgender allies, two new clinics just recently began performing gender confirming surgeries in central Canada (Toronto) and western Canada (Vancouver).[11]

On a personal note, my gender transition was one of the longest in history, spanning 41 years from age 19 to 60! Born into the wrong body, then surgically corrected to confirm my true gender, I'm now me: genes, genitals, and all. Like the song from *La Cage aux Folles,* "I Am What I Am!"[12] And proud to be me.

Chapter 10 Notes

[1] "Words spoken by Jesus to the people of Nazareth, the town where he grew up. They refused to believe in his teaching because they considered him one of themselves and therefore without authority to preach to them." https://www.dictionary.com/browse/a-prophet-is-not-without-honor-save-in-his-own-country. Of course, I'm not claiming to be a religious prophet, only a bright light with a creative vision.

[2] See: Bournes, D.A., and M. Ferguson-Paré, "Human Becoming and 80/20: An Innovative Professional Development Model for Nurses," *Nursing Science Quarterly*, July 2007, 20(3): 237-53. https://www.ncbi.nlm.nih.gov/pubmed/17595405.

[3] See: World Professional Association for Transgender Health (WPATH), *Standards of Care for the Health of Transsexual, Transgender, and Gender-Nonconforming People* (7th version), 2011. https://www.wpath.org/publications/soc.

4 See: World Health Organization, *International Classification of Diseases and Related Health Problems* (11 edition), 2018. http://www.euro.who.int/en/health-topics/health-determinants/gender/gender-definitions/whoeurope-brief-transgender-health-in-the-context-of-icd-11. This latest version declassified "gender incongruence" (gender variance or transgenderism) as a psychiatric disorder—provided it's not related to a paraphilic disorder—effectively depsychopathologizing trans people in Europe.

[5] On May 1, 2015, I uploaded our unpublished paper on my RR Consulting website (defunct as of December 2016), then subsequently donated it to the Canadian Centre for Gender & Sexual Diversity, which was finally uploaded on January 21, 2019 to its revamped website and new educational resources page. http://ccgsd-ccdgs.org/resources/; http://ccgsd-ccdgs.org/launch-of-rupert-raj-resources/.

[6] Like American trans activist, Buck Angel, most of the "agro" (unconstructive criticism and downright nastiness) I encounter comes from other T-boys! Whatever happened to male bonding and drumming in the woods brotherly love? Of course, sometimes T-girls give me grief as well.

[7] These genitoplastic surgeons included Dr. Marci Bowers, Dr. Curtis Crane, Dr. Sherman Leis, and Dr. Toby Meltzer in the USA; Mr. Nim Christopher in the UK; and Dr. Stanislaus Monstrey in Belgium.

[8] Back in 2009, I had facilitated a home at Sherbourne Health Centre for the Trans Partner Network's (http://www.transpartnernetwork.com/) semi-yearly group cycle by helping LeeAndra Miller and the other three co-founders—all members of the former SOFFA Voices (Significant Others, Friends, Family, Allies) formed in 2001 at The 519 Community Centre—to successfully pitch a solid proposal to the management, and it's now one of the core groups of SHC trans programs.

[9] See Trystan Cotten's two book anthologies, in which he interviewed postsurgical trans-male patients: *Below the Belt: Genital Talk by Men of Trans Experience*, San Francisco, CA: Transgress Press, 2016; and *Hung Jury: Testimonies of Genital Surgery by Transsexual Men*, Transgress Press, 2012.

[10] See the June 3, 2016 *Planetransgender* post, "Jayne Ellen Heideck Wanted for Arson at Montreal Gender Reassignment Surgery Clinic."
https://www.facebook.com/planetrans/posts/1016971051724359.

[11] In Toronto, the Trans Health Expansion Partnership (THEx)—headed by medical director, Dr. Yonah Krakowsky—was launched in 2018 at Women's College Hospital. THEx organizational partners include Sherbourne Health Centre, Rainbow Health Ontario, and the Centre for Addiction and Mental Health. The first full Transition-Related Surgery (TRS)—in this case, vaginoplasty—was performed on a trans woman in June 2019. Non-genital TRSs are also available. My former genderqueer co-worker from Sherbourne Health Centre, Emery Potter, recently joined the TRS team as a nurse practitioner.
http://wearewomensreport2018.womenscollegehospital.ca/portfolio-view/ontarios-first-comprehensive-gender-transition-program/index.html;
https://www.womenscollegehospital.ca/programs-and-services/Transition-Related-Surgeries/.

In Vancouver, the Gender Surgery Clinic at Vancouver General Hospital (VGH) opened the end of September 2019. The surgeons are Dr. Genoway (plastic and reconstructive surgery) and Dr. Kavanagh (reconstructive urology). Bottom surgeries will take place at VGH; top surgeries will continue at UBC Hospital and other Vancouver Coastal Health sites, including Lions Gate Hospital. http://www.phsa.ca/transcarebc/about/news-stories/2019/gender-surgery-clinic;
https://mail.google.com/mail/u/0/?zx=6k1j0ls8xhas#sent?projector=1.

[12] The song is the finale number of the 1983, French Broadway musical, La Cage aux Folles, performed by the character of "Albin Mougeotte," first played by George Hearn. "Folles" is a slang term for effeminate gay men (queens). Composed by Jerry Herman, this cult-classic song was sung by Gloria Gaynor, Shirley Bassey, Amanda Lear, and others. See https://www.stlyrics.com/lyrics/lacageauxfolles/iamwhatiam.htm;
https://en.wikipedia.org/wiki/I_Am_What_I_Am_(Broadway_musical_song); and
https://en.wikipedia.org/wiki/La_Cage_aux_Folles_(musical).

11. Archival Accolades…Trans Anthologies…Intersex and Two-Spirit Inclusivity…Mental Breakdown (2013-2017)

Following my recovery, I resumed work at Sherbourne Health Centre, welcoming an opportunity to clinically supervise another psychotherapy student. Max Carney, a trans man then enrolled in the University of Toronto's Master of Education in Counseling Psychology program, counselled our LGBTTI2SQQAA clients and co-led the Gender Journeys group with Supporting Our Youth program coordinator Kusha Daduil and me. My penchant for mentoring aspiring activists was equalled only by my love for coaching students, especially Max, because he was passionate about his work and deeply invested in transgender, genderqueer, intersex, and Two-Spirit communities.

On May 3, 2013, I earned the first of three archival accolades when I was inducted into The ArQuives in a memorable ceremony in Toronto, featuring the unveiling of my portrait (painted by Maya Suess)—now part of The ArQuives CLGA National Portrait Collection (NPC). My portrait joined those of other eminent Canadian LGBTTI2SQQAA activists and artists in the NPC, including my then boss, Bev Lepischak (a lesbian activist, former social worker, and Sherbourne Health Centre's then LGBT Health program director), Gloria May Eshkibok (a Two-Spirit actor, singer, and community activist), and two local trans activists Alec Butler (a playwright and filmmaker), and the late Kyle Scanlon (a peer researcher, educator, and trainer). My friends, Dr. Nick Matte and Dr. Solomon Shapiro, nominated me for this prestigious honour. KJ, friends, colleagues, and community members were all present to salute my 42 years of trans activism across this continent. Sadly, my sister could not make it but she was there in spirit. I shared this auspicious day with veteran queer activist Richard Hudler, who founded the Homophile Association of London, Ontario (HALO) in 1981, leading the group until it folded in 1995. A fellow Rainbow Health Network member, Richard is also part of Queer Ontario, still lobbying for legal reform all these decades later. Both the Richard Hudler fonds and the Rupert Raj fonds—consisting of our respective materials on queer and trans people, and our fight for rights over the years—are housed in The ArQuives.

In my fonds was the unpublished manuscript of my aforementioned international poetry anthology, *Of Souls and Roles, Of Genes and Gender*, from which I read a few selections at The ArQuives Poetry Salon (along with two other poets/multimedia artists[2]) the following week. As I read aloud several transgender-themed poems written by people around the world in the late 1960s into the early 1990s, I realized that I was not only a trans political activist and a trans clinical activist, but also a trans historical and trans cultural activist too! And, I was a multidisciplinary writer activating trans genres from personal narratives to political activism to psychological health to sociohistorical biography to poetry and free verse. Writing was my life blood, a fire burning inside!

Sometimes, I wished that I had a cloning machine for those times when I had to be in two places at once—which happens a lot when you're not only a community activist but, also, a professional and a person. How to juggle all those balls without stumbling, hoping they don't all go crashing down onto the floor! May 6 was one of those days. I had been scheduled to give a talk on the recent legal victories for trans people in Ontario at the Dare to Stand Out Gender & Sexuality Youth Forum put on by Jer's Vision: Canada's Youth Diversity Initiative[3] at Glendon College in Toronto. Then, almost a year later, just before the event, I was asked to appear as a witness at a Human Rights Tribunal of Ontario (HRTO) preliminary hearing for Sheila Samuels, a trans woman client suing an allegedly transphobic community health centre (CHC) in Toronto's Parkdale Village. I had to honour my prior commitment, which, thankfully, Sheila understood. Besides, I had already submitted a letter to her lawyer, supporting her allegations to be read aloud in court. Sheila valiantly fought her case: however, the outcome was sealed in court, which meant that the CHC could not be named or the decision cited in case law. Shortly afterwards, certain positive changes took place at the CHC in accordance with Sheila's recommendations: additional trans-sensitivity training for its managers and front-line staff, and an organizational policy amendment to ensure a safe space for trans clients. This essentially meant operationalizing equitable access to healthcare by making it trans-inclusive, trans-sensitive, and trans-responsive (the three "T"s of my TransPositive Therapeutic Model™) in everyday practice. Too bad the CHC had not followed Sherbourne Health Centre's example of proactive transpositive healthcare instead of having to be legislated to do the right thing. Complacency rarely escapes ultimate compliance!

Ever busy in my professional life, I managed to eke out a few hours of quality time now and then with my new partner as we solidified our relationship. Feeling crowded in my one bedroom condo, we decided to buy a house: a first for me. Following an extensive search in Greater Toronto, we snapped up a two bedroom bungalow in the east end—a real find given the prohibitive prices: but, there was one drawback—the 90-day closing time. This was a potential problem because KJ's mother, at 90, was rapidly declining in the care centre in which she lived and we wanted to see her before her dementia worsened. She had resisted eating and had taken several bad falls: so, the nurses had to coax her to eat and had to restrain her overnight so she wouldn't fall out of bed. KJ and I were there, visiting every day, right until the end. Despite the pain of seeing her mother so compromised, KJ was steadfast in her vigil and lay beside her dying mom during those last few moments. Per my mother-in-law's wishes, there was no funeral. Instead, we hurried back to Toronto as the movers were due the following week. Sadly, we couldn't bring Angie with us as KJ's cat allergy was worsening and she did not react well to anti-allergy medication. Distressing as it was to part with my beloved kitty, at least we were able to find her a loving home. We settled into domestic life in the inner 'burbs, cocooning in our cozy cottage, far enough away from the chaos of the city centre.

On the work front, I continued to counsel, case conference, and advocate for my clients. Like me, Max was genuinely concerned about intersex, Indigenous, and Two-Spirit people: so, together we advocated on their behalf to Sherbourne Health Centre. As the driving force for more awareness and inclusivity of these marginalized populations within the larger LGBTTI2SQQAA sector, we employed an incremental approach, starting with intersex people first, appealing to SHC managers to expand our LGBT program to formally include intersex people. Australia and New Zealand are miles ahead of Canada in terms of their intersex inclusivity, recently producing two intersex-affirming documentary films,[4] and establishing the Victorian Pride Centre in Australia, Melbourne's first intersex-inclusive, health-based community centre (modelled after San Francisco's LGBTI Community Centre). I spearheaded an Intersex Training Planning Committee in 2013, aimed at providing in-service trainings on intersex issues for our managers, staff, and students. I invited renowned intersex academic-activist Dr. Morgan Holmes[5] (Professor of Sociology at Wilfred Laurier University) to present an introductory workshop on intersex. It was well attended, although one physician was defensive when Dr. Holmes disclosed the intersexphobia she had encountered from several medical practitioners from childhood onwards. I hoped that we could put on future learning opportunities to increase cultural and clinical competency around intersex clients. Such knowledge transfer and capacity-building was not an unreasonable aim given that we were a teaching centre known worldwide for our excellence in LGBT healthcare.

Following on our minor success in this area, Max and I hoped to share our advocacy skills with healthcare practitioners and social service providers in the wider community so that they too might become advocates for potential intersex clients. We submitted an abstract to the conference organizers of Rainbow Health Ontario (RHO) for a skills-based training workshop: but, our submission was declined for no explicit reason!

Earlier, my request to post my research papers on RHO's online research page was denied, simply because I was not affiliated with a university. I found this criterion to be classist because, even though I did not have a PhD or teach at a university, I had already published four trans-focussed clinical research papers (three in scholarly journals), with one more in the works! The overvaluing of academic credentials and university affiliation in trans research, and of clinical credentials in trans programming (such as group facilitation in non-therapy groups), is yet another form of erasure of uncredentialled trans people with otherwise valuable lived experience (including street smarts), creative talents, and life skills. This is why I advocated for Susan Gapka to be my co-investigator on OPHA's Trans Health Project (THP), even though the research committee had initially resisted because she only had a bachelor's degree in political science. Susan's previous proposal to present at the 2010 RHO conference on the successful efforts of the Trans Health Lobby Group (THLG) to relist sex reassignment surgery in Ontario was also declined because RHO conference organizers told her they were looking for (what they deemed) a higher standard of presentation. This was even more elitist, as well as contradictory logic, given that Susan had already proven herself to be an effective published researcher by virtue of our THP paper! Ultimately, Karmic law prevailed and Susan and THG later earned two well-deserved accolades.[6] Moreover, the four trans women (three of whom were people of colour and one a former sex worker) who had unsuccessfully applied for voluntary positions with RHO—or paid jobs at Sherbourne—were subsequently hired at The 519 Community Centre for their real-life knowledge of social determinants of health (racism, sexism, classism, transphobia, poverty, homelessness, etc.) and related practical survival skills. Which organization can rightfully claim to have higher standards?

But, they can't keep a good man down! So, in 2014, Max and I pitched our proposed presentation to the organizers of the sexuality conference at the University of Guelph and the Dare to Stand Out Conference at Ryerson University. Both welcomed our proposal. Our presentation was called "Walking the Razor's Edge: Balancing Client/Community Advocacy and Clinical Practice when Working with Trans, Genderqueer, Intersex and Two-Spirit People." We had a good turnout with engaged participants—a good start toward enhancing clinicians' advocacy skills towards inclusivity of intersex, Indigenous, and Two-Spirit people. These subpopulations often fall through the cracks of basic LGBT services in the same way that bisexual and trans people were previously underserved in queer programs. It's about time the new kids on the block received their fair share of services too!

Towards this goal of building cultural competency and clinical sensitivity in our professional teams, I searched online for a film to show our staff and came across a crosscultural TV program on trans, gender fluid, and intersex people: *A Transgender HBO Biography Special—Middle Sexes* (2009).[7] I wanted to screen this documentary sometime between Intersex Awareness Day

(October 26) and Trans Day of Remembrance (November 20) but was summarily quashed by senior management, who wanted to wait until our second go-round of the Accreditation Canada process was completed on November 20. So, I never got to air the show: a missed opportunity for organizational development and intersex inclusivity. My activist resolve was wearing down as my motivation dissipated. My head was getting awfully sore from banging it against the bastions of intransigent managers!

As a two-tiered organization, our community conscious frontline staff was pitted against a corporate minded senior management. The former largely represented a forward thinking vision that empowered employees (through formation of a union) and clients (through proposals for expanded programming), the latter a reactionary conservatism bent on preserving the *status quo* in order to maintain fiscal solvency. One does not necessarily preclude the other. This split organizational dynamic was one reason so many staff (and many managers) left over the years. Too bad, because this corporate conservatism resulted in substantial brain drain. Sadly, this culture of complacency is a critical flaw of most corporate and government organizations. In fact, it's endemic to our entire society, our whole planet, as self-evident to those few of us (Outsiders) with a modicum of intelligence and wisdom, conscience, and compassion. Complacency is the worst of all human failings: a form of psychic suicide and homicide. We must fight this epidemic infecting humankind! Or, we might as well all give up right now! One way to combat the complacency virus is through activism, locally and globally. Certainly, the social justice movement (like Amnesty International), the environmental movement (like Greenpeace International) and the animal liberation movement (like Animals International) demonstrate the efficacy of such advocacy. A combined movement lobbying for change for both humans and animals is now gaining momentum: a long time coming, but better late than never!

Despite my ongoing frustrations at Sherbourne, two years later I renewed my efforts to advance the agenda of intersex, Indigenous, and Two-Spirit inclusivity—specifically, inclusion in the upcoming 2015 CPATH conference in Halifax. Then CPATH president Devon MacFarlane (a trans man) invited me to join the planning committee in response to feedback I had given the 2012 conference organizers about the need for greater inclusivity of intersex, Indigenous, and Two-Spirit issues and people in future conferences. The 2015 conference organizers did reach out to these populations but, regrettably, only a few turned out. So, CPATH is redoubling its efforts to make meaningful connections with these communities. Poor physical and mental health precluded my attendance at the conference: an ongoing problem, exacerbated by episodic burnout. That was it for intersex inclusivity so far.

As for Indigenous inclusivity within Sherbourne, Max and I organized a community workshop on Two-Spirit people and culture, inviting Dr. Raven Sinclair (*Ótiskewápiwskew*)[8] (Associate Professor in Social Work and Indigenous Studies at the University of Regina) to present. The workshop took place on the same day as our 10th annual Trans Pride Day (expanded that year to explicitly include intersex, Indigenous, and Two-Spirit people), and was a standing room only success. We invited our then CEO, Suzanne Boggild, to open our new and improved Trans, Intersex & Two-Spirit Pride Day. We had three keynote speakers: Nicole Nanku Tanguay (a Two-Spirit, gender-neutral lesbian), Alec Butler[9] (a Two-Spirit, intersex trans man), and me (a mixed-race, pansexual trans man). We felt good about the greater representation of Indigenous, Two-Spirit, and intersex community members, including several who spoke or sang at our event: a solid start. Following my retirement a couple of years later, Max worked towards creating specific programs for Indigenous trans and Two-Spirit people at SHC with the help of two new managers, SHC's Adam Benn and RHO's Devon MacFarlane. Too bad that SHC's human resources management didn't try harder to ensure that Max would be hired on as my successor in the LGBT mental health program, even though I had worked diligently to try to make this happen in ample time. My program manager, Bev Lepischak, had also advocated for Max. The centre let a valuable resource slip through its fingers because of, yet again, a lack of vision and proactive action. Is this the future for the organizational sustainability of its trans, intersex, and Two-Spirit employees? But, a partial consolation is that my counselling successor is Rahim Thawer, a transpositive, South Asian gay man—a professional, personal, and community ally who is moving forward the agenda of gender non-binary people.

On a personal note, my professional advocacy on behalf of gender non-binary people (not only intersex and Two-Spirit people, but also genderqueer adults and gender-creative youth) subtly influenced my own gender identity as I became more androgynous—even somewhat pangender. I captured my still-evolving, combined gender and sexual identity in a poem, "Pansexual Pangender Person."[10]

Around this time, I resumed two of my writing projects. The first was a revision of Celia Schwartz's and my paper, "A Collaborative Preparedness and Informed Consent Model,"[11] which we submitted to the *International Journal of Transgenderism (IJT)* having become tired of waiting for Sherbourne Health Centre to respond about potentially incorporating it into its revised trans care guidelines. Regrettably, *IJT* declined our paper because some reviewers saw it as a duplication of WPATH's 2011 *Standards of Care*, which it wasn't. Rather, it was a customized approach to the Canadian context. Undeterred, on May 1,

2015, we published it on my (former) RR Consulting website, providing free access to trans care professionals and to trans people (most of whom cannot afford to subscribe to online journals or pay for online papers).

My second project was the writing of my life story, which I began and then abandoned a long time ago (in 1988). Turning 62, it was time to give it another go. Up until now (2014), I believe there have been only three other book-length life stories published by trans men in Canada[12] and 14 or so of trans women:[13] so, my story certainly wouldn't saturate the market. And, so far, I had come across only one other autobiography by a Eurasian trans man (Belgium-East Indian American Dhillon Khosla[14]) and only one trans-themed novel by a Eurasian-Canadian trans woman (British-Chinese Canadian Jia Qing Wilson-Yang.[15]) Of course, my intention is not to duplicate Khosla's unique life story and, indeed, my Canadian context sets me apart from his lived reality. My aim, rather, is to reference my own mixed-race cultural heritage within a Canadian context: but, more so, to be racially and culturally inclusive in my sociohistorical (auto)biography of trans people of colour, mixed race trans people, *Hijras*, Indigenous trans people, and Two-Spirit people. I try to do this by citing specific instances of erasure and/or (re)emergence of certain transgender and gender non-binary populations (including African American and Iranian trans people and South Asian *Hijras*) and by highlighting selected Black, Brown, Red, Yellow, and Beige activists and their works.[16]

Ever reclusive, I chose to celebrate my birthday with no one but KJ. The celebration was marred though, because, sadly, on February 9, 2014, my friend, Xanthra (then 57), had a fatal heart attack. She was the third trans activist friend to die within the past two years. I mourned her loss while still grieving my two other recently departed friends, Lynne and Kyle.

Cumulative loss. A sad start to the year. But, I had to go on. So, I wrote. Writing saves my sanity: a creative endeavour that takes me to another world; a welcome diversion from the same shit, different day reality as I try to stave off monotony and madness, complacency and cynicism.

My writing projects continued to roll out, but little did I suspect that the long-buried manuscript of my trans poetry anthology from 1991 would re-emerge again as it did last year at my ArQuives induction. I never expected that *Of Souls and Roles, Of Genes and Gender* might find its way into print after all! Nonetheless, a year later, I got another chance to read from my long-lost labour of love at the Writing Trans Genres Conference held at the University of Winnipeg in Manitoba. The conference (the first of its kind in North America) was organized by Professor of Women's and Gender Studies, Trish Salah.[17] Presenters included international cultural icons.[18] I was privileged to be a part of this inaugural gathering of trans-genre literary genii.

Before inviting me to read from my poetry anthology at the conference,

Trish asked if I still wanted to publish it and I replied with a resounding "Yes!" An award-winning, published poet,[19] Trish offered to help me find a publisher and I invited her to write the foreword. We had hoped to get the book into print by 2018, but daunted by the prospect of yet another interminable publishing schedule, in late 2016, I opted to donate the unpublished manuscript to the Transgender Archives (affiliated with the University of Victoria Library) in Victoria, BC. On top of my clinical/academic papers and trans activist anthology, it was groovy to also be a compiler of poetry, satisfying my Bohemian bent!

Following directly on my trans poetry book project was the May launch of our aforementioned anthology, *Trans Activism in Canada*. I was on a roll! Six years in the making, Dan Irving's and my groundbreaking anthology traces transsexual/transgender/Two-Spirit advocacy in Canada from the 1970s to the present, with a foreword by Dr. Aaron Devor and an afterword by Dr. Viviane Namaste. Trans and queer academic activists, Dr. Susan Stryker, Dr. Dean Spade, Esq., and Dr. Sheila Cavanagh wrote enthusiastic back cover testimonials. There are other books on and by Canadian trans people,[20] but these notable contributions to the overall canon are all single authored works. *Trans Activism in Canada* is unique in that it pulls together multiple perspectives from 54 diverse contributors across the country, both transgender and cisgender.

Contributors include Indigenous transgender people and Two-Spirit people, people of colour and of mixed race, people living in northern Ontario,[21] youth with intellectual disabilities,[22] sex workers, gay/bi men, and cisgender allies (healthcare and legal professionals). Disappointingly, there were no self-disclosing intersex contributors, although I knew of at least one. The book features diverse foci on gender non-conforming children, trans parents, labour unions, high school education, law, healthcare access, nursing, substance misuse and harm reduction work, sexual health (HIV/AIDS), mental health, social work, homelessness and shelter advocacy, public health (participatory action research), and the intersectionality of trans and animal rights. The diversity of papers includes personal narratives of early and present day activists, as well as academic and clinical reports on various aspects of transgender advocacy. In terms of historical activism, Dr. Nick Matte's chapter, "Rupert Raj and the Rise of Transsexual Consumer Activism in the 1980s" (which also briefly references my 1970s work under my former name, Nick Ghosh) is an important record of early trans advocacy in this country before the Internet. My chapter, "Zening the Art of Trans Activism," is a mini-manual for both established and aspiring activists, containing dedicated subsections: gender work; community connection and empowerment;

transphobia and trans activism; focussing; anti-oppression; and burnout, vicarious traumatization, and self-care. Dr. Trish Salah's chapter, "Gender Struggles: Reflections on Trans Liberation, Trade Unionism, and the Limits of Solidarity," is an edifying account of how labour unions can be effective allies for trans people.

We had two launches: one at Brock University in St. Catharines and one at The ArQuives in Toronto, which was crowded to the rafters. Our publisher is pitching the book to North American universities for inclusion in curricula for gender and women's studies, social work, and political science; and approaching libraries and bookstores to put our trans reader on their shelves. Dan and I will never get rich from royalties but, at least, the writing/editing exercise quenched the fire in our belly for now. I later presented signed copies to Canadian Prime Minister Justin Trudeau, Ontario Premier Kathleen Wynne, British Columbia Premier Christy Clark, and federal MP Randall Garrison. So, now, they all have a trans reader to which they can refer when considering future political reforms for trans Canadians. I also gifted copies to former Ontario MPP, Cheri DiNovo, former Ontario Premier, George Smitherman, former Ontario Human Rights Chief Commissioner, Barbara Hall, former federal MP, Bill Siksay, and former BC Human Rights Chief Commissioner, Mary-Woo Sims as a thank you for their previous trans advocacy. Even cisgender politicians (our allies) deserve validation!

This particular time was crazy busy. From April through June, I pulled off 11 gigs over eight weeks in six cities and two provinces. These included: two book launches, a workshop, five conference presentations, and three private practice trainings: a marathon on the non-stop trans circuit! Of these various educational encounters, two are especially noteworthy: the workshop I delivered to the Toronto-based Iranian Queer Organization (IRQO) at The 519 Community Centre and the workshop King and I put on for the Aging LGBT Conference co-sponsored by the Senior Pride Network and The 519.

The first was topical because although gay and lesbian relationships are illegal (punishable by death) in Iran, gender confirming surgeries are permitted given that, in 1983, Islamic leader Ayatollah Khomeini passed a fatwa allowing sex reassignment operations as a cure for diagnosed transsexuals.23 In spite of this recent legalization, however, many pre- and post-transitional, Iranian trans women (and some trans men) still choose to immigrate to Canada, and many come to Sherbourne Health Centre, Access Alliance, The 519, and the IRQO for medical, legal, counselling, and community resources. As a result, my workshop focussed on how to support trans Iranian immigrants.

The second workshop was Trans-Generating!: Black & Brown Trans/Queer Elders & Youth Working Together. The two Black (gender)queer youth told us about their relations (and non-relations) with their parents, grandparents, and other older people. As community elders, King (Black, genderqueer person) and I (Brown/Beige, queer trans man) spoke about the vital need for older and younger LGBTTI2SQQAA people to teach and learn from each other, considering that Canada, at the time, was lagging behind the UK and the USA in terms of intergenerational community involvement in the trans and queer community. Towards this end, my colleague, King—a team member of SHC's Supporting Our Youth program (SOY)—and I had recently co-founded the LGBTI Intergenerational Network with Heather Bain (coordinator of the Senior Pride Network and the Older LGBT Program at The 519), Hannah (a social work student at Ryerson University), and Sarah Singh (a volunteer with Senior People's Resources in North Toronto [SPRINT]). Regrettably, after only four meetings co-chaired by King and me, both of us had already burnt out. As a result, we had each, separately, gone on medical leaves of absence and, upon our return, were seeking others to take over the function of network co-chairs. At the workshop, we again invited interested others to step up to the plate but, sadly, there were no takers. Happily, since then, intergenerational LGBT programming has now been established and, in March 2017, I was invited to participate in The 519 and Senior Pride Network's Tell It Like It Is intergenerational, community speaker series, showcasing LGBTQ elders. Interviewed by an elder trans mentor and a queer youth mentee—the filmed interview explored various themes, including: one's chosen family; aging and disability; aging as a person of colour; transgenderism and aging; and a life of activism. Feisty Trinidadian dyke activist, LeZlie Lee Kam, and I were the first up to be interviewed by local trans artist Nichola (Nicki) Ward, with trans intersex activist, Martine Stonehouse, and veteran queer/AIDS activist, Tim McCaskell, following.

The inevitable aftermath of this whirlwind of activity was that I burnt out so badly that I didn't even make it out to World Pride (held in Toronto) that July! My partner feared for my sanity: so, I vowed to never again get so overwhelmed with training obligations. We must all strive for a healthy work/life balance or end up at the Gerstein Crisis Centre! Somehow avoiding a nervous collapse, I got some R&R by taking off all of July. KJ and I escaped the chaos of the city with short trips to Port Elgin, Barrie, Peterborough, Kingston, Cobourg, and Ottawa. I took another brief holiday in October when my sister came to visit: the first time we had seen each other in four years. This was a chance for Arjuna and KJ to finally meet. I was so pleased that my two favourite women hit it off!

The Toronto Trans Alliance (TTA) invited me to speak at the annual Transgender Day of Remembrance (TDoR) on November 20, 2014. History was made that day at Toronto City Hall as our new mayor, John Tory, and

TTA members proudly raised the first-ever Toronto trans flag. TDoR was recognized as an official day in Toronto, following the example 13 years earlier of Vancouver—the first Canadian city to celebrate TDoR in 2001. A frigid wind was blowing, so we bundled up to mourn the many transgender, genderqueer, intersex, and Two-Spirit people around the world whose lives have been tragically cut short by their own hand (suicidal desperation) or taken by another (brutal murder). Two-Spirit, trans man, Alec Butler, welcomed us, acknowledging that we stood on the occupied lands of our Indigenous ancestors. Several government officials were present,[24] including then Ontario Human Rights Chief Commissioner, Barbara Hall. Metropolitan Community Church of Toronto pastor, Rev. Dr. Brent Hawkes, spoke briefly, followed by several trans activists,[25] including me.

Stark examples of societal transphobia and widespread abuse against trans people necessitated a commemorative event such as TDoR, from the brutal murder of African American trans woman, Rita Hester, on November 28, 1998 right up to the recent human rights violations of a Toronto trans man. Boyd Kodak (aka Jan Joseph Waterman), a post-transitional trans man, was suing the Toronto Police Service and the Ministry of Community Safety and Correctional Services. His lawsuit cited multiple transphobic violations by police officers and prison guards: incarceration in a women's instead of a men's jail—where he should have been assigned in accordance with his legal male status—a humiliating strip search, being paraded in public while forced to wear a female prison gown and female undergarments, and passing around his prosthetic penis (packer), mocking it as if it was a sex toy (dildo) rather than a male extension of his anatomy. Would these men have done this if they had lost their penises to war trauma, accident, or penile cancer? Bullies are always cowards! This psychological abuse severely traumatized Boyd, who was one of countless trans inmates victimized by police and prison brutality over the years in Canada.

I'm hopeful that this mean-spiritedness of some police (and correctional) officers will soon shift given that there has been an LGBTQ Community Liaison Police Officer within the Toronto Police Service for the past few years. Time will tell. Current LGBTQ Community Liaison Police Constable, Danielle Bottineau (a cisgender lesbian), has reached out to trans women (and to me) at the Trans Lobby Group, The 519's Meal Trans Program, and Sherbourne's Mature Trans Sisters group because she is concerned about police violence against trans and queer people in Toronto and is working toward changing police attitudes.[26] Ironically, P.C. Bottineau and other police officers were present at the event, standing apart in a non-intrusive manner. Yes, time will tell. Paradigm shifts happen slowly and only when the dominant societal group is consistently confronted by the Other (racial, ethnic, religious, political, sexual, gendered, and other minorities). Countercultural in beliefs and values, these disenfranchised Others must employ strategies of creative resistance as freedom fighters Mahatma Gandhi, Nelson Mandela, and Martin Luther King, Jr. did in their respective fights for national sovereignty and civil rights—and as the Compton Cafeteria and Stonewall Inn rioters did in their battles for equality around sexual orientation and gender identity. As fellow activist, Dr. Dean Spade, Esq. (Associate Professor of Law at Seattle University and founder of the Sylvia Rivera Law Project in New York City), asserts, trans resistance will inevitably triumph![27]

Boyd called on me to appear as an expert witness at his Human Rights Tribunal of Ontario (HRTO) hearing scheduled for 18 months later. Fortunately, on June 2, 2016, a settlement was reached at the pre-hearing[28] so my presence was not required. However, beforehand, I had given a will-say statement (written testimony) to Boyd's legal counsel, Khizer Anwar, providing helpful background information for the case. Drawing on my earlier personal experience as a trans man who had worn a prosthetic penis for 41 years prior to undergoing genital surgery, as well as my recent professional expertise as a gender specialist counselling countless trans men, I mentioned the paramount significance of Boyd's prosthetic penis for his male body image and his basic right to dignity by being allowed to wear a male prison uniform. I underscored his basic need for comfort by ideally being permitted incarceration in a men's prison in accordance with his male gender identity (but conceded that a male jail, ultimately, would not be safe). Several North American prisons contain a dedicated wing for trans/intersex/Two-Spirit inmates. But most prisons do not: instead, they house trans prisoners in solitary cells with tiny windows where they could spend up to 23 hours a day if they choose not to make use of the common areas with other potentially transphobic inmates. PASAN has advocated for trans and queer prisoners/ex-prisoners in Ontario since 1991: but, change is slow. HRTO ordered the Toronto Police Service to undergo further trans focussed training and to revise their *Guide to Policing for the Trans Communities* in collaboration with the Ontario Human Rights Commission and experts from the trans community.[29]

In December 2014, I asked The 519 Community Centre's program director, Becky McFarlane, to reinstate the group for older (45+) trans men and their allies. The 2013 pilot group, co-led by Jim M., only ran for three months before fizzling out due to lack of funds. Becky suggested that I start with three workshops from February through April, to give her enough time to apply for grant money for an ongoing group if the need was there. I was thrilled because even though Sherbourne Health Centre had finally got a group going for older trans women—10 years after my community education workshop for trans women 45+ in 2004 (and after I and others had advocated for such a group since day one)—there was none for older trans men. I wanted The 519 to fill this gap and, feeling unappreciated at my own workplace, I decided to bestow my talents and energy where I was valued.

I designed a train-the-trainer model, where I would briefly work with several other older trans guys before passing on the baton to ensure sustainability. Our inaugural series for older trans guys and their loved ones/allies comprised three workshops entitled: Social Isolation: Breaking Out and Building Community, Societal & Internalized Transphobia: Strategizing Towards Self-Empowerment, and Getting Older: Effectively Planning for Our Future. My respective co-presenters were Jim M., King, and Kaspar. Sadly, we did not get the turnout we had hoped, likely because older trans men are less prone to come together as a group than either younger trans men or older trans women. Unfortunately, I wasn't able to review the post-workshop evaluations with Becky because immediately following the final workshop (I could barely get through it!), I broke down mentally and could not pursue this further until we met again a year later.

At that time, Becky suggested that we could probably work with several 519 trans and genderqueer folks (Older LGBT Community Services Coordinator Rosalyn Forrester and psychotherapists Robyn Letson and Sly Sarkisova[30]) to assess the needs of older trans men and their significant others with a view towards hiring facilitators to lead a regular support group for this underserved population.[31] In addition to this hoped-for group specifically for trans men, I was also gratified that older trans/intersex/Two-Spirit people, in general, were finally being recognized as worthy of population-based research,[32] client programs and community resources,[33] and public/community education.[34] We trans elders have now won a place of honour within our gender communities![35]

These last four years—anticipating my retirement in early 2017—have been extremely challenging as I hung on by a thread! In addition to being under-appreciated by some managers and co-workers on my two teams at Sherbourne Health Centre, two of my clients tragically committed suicide, making it impossible for me to simply dismiss these human losses with professional detachment insofar as these clients were flesh and blood people, not merely clinical cases or health service users. I did suffer substantial stress, however, from a few exceptional clients from hell, who perpetuated virtual violence—by sending harassing e-mails to SHC or posting character assassinations of SHC staff on the worldwide web. Several of these particularly challenging clients even threatened to sue if their unreasonable demands were not met, and a couple actually did file human rights complaints. These complaints were directed not only against me personally; but also targeted one or more of my co-workers and managers, and the agency itself. Needless to say, even though I (and the other employees involved) were duly exonerated, the impact on me of these few problematic clients was irrevocable, seriously compromising my increasingly vulnerable emotional state. Mental health and addiction work—especially when serving minority groups and trauma survivors—involves both professional and personal risks. My psychological collapse was partly prompted by the cumulative effect of suicides by several clients over the past 13 years, and was further exacerbated by the recent aggressive behaviours of the aforementioned clients.

Consequently, I kept super busy in an effort to fend off both my workplace stress and my increasing disenchantment with SHC—inevitably too busy to prevent ultimate burnout. In fact, I succumbed to the big "B" yet again in early 2015, suffering a severe mental breakdown, complete with major depression, anxiety (including panic attacks), and anger. So, against my initial disinclination, I went on psychotropic medication on the advice of my family doctor and my G.P. psychotherapist, and intensified my therapy sessions to help stabilize my mood. Then, I took a 20-week short term disability leave to alleviate the intense stress of my clinical work, academic pursuits, and community activism, and to effectively address my serious mental and physical health issues. In September, at the urging of Sherbourne Health Centre's Human Resources to either retire early or apply for a Long-Term Disability (LTD) pension, I opted for the latter. I was hoping to eventually resume my part-time private practice if my mental health substantially improved in the near future. My decision to leave SHC 18 months before I had planned was informed by the reality that we were no longer a good fit and who wants to stay where they are not appreciated? Moreover, too burnt out to continue, LTD seemed a viable solution, allowing me the time and resources to hopefully get better before I could officially retire at 65.

Two days after my departure from SHC (September 20, 2015), my collection (The Rupert Raj fonds) was officially launched at The ArQuives by my friend, Dr. Elspeth Brown (The ArQuives Board member and Professor of History at the University of Toronto)—who had painstakingly catalogued my collection over a year and a half and to whom I am eternally grateful! She and her colleagues compiled a Finding Aid[36] to readily access specific items in my fonds. Some of my materials are being digitalized for donation to other LGBT archives such as the Transgender Archives in BC and the Digital Transgender Archive in Massachusetts.[37] When The ArQuives volunteer, Harold Miller, emailed me, advising that I would be issued a charitable tax receipt for my donated papers (fonds), he added a personal thank you note:

> *In my view, this receipt is a small thank you for the enormous amount of work you have done for our communities over the years and for your diligence in preserving the record of your activities. There is no set of personal papers like it elsewhere in Canada and only a couple that are remotely comparable in the US.*

Actually, this is not quite true, insofar as there are a number of Canadian and American collections in the Digital Transgender Archive, the University of Victoria Transgender Archives, and The ArQuives itself. The ArQuives has now processed the fonds of Mirha-Soleil Ross, and will soon be processing those of several more trans activists: Monica Forrester, Susan Gapka, Denise Hudson, Rachel Lewis,[38] Martine Stonehouse, and Regina's OneSong Transgender Support Services.

Needless to say, I was moved by this unexpected validation. It reminded me how vital it is for transgender, genderqueer, intersex, and Two-Spirit people to preserve our history and culture as a testimony to our vulnerability and our resilience—namely, our creative resistance against genderphobic violence, and our pride in who we are as a collective community. This is why the LGBTQ Oral History and Digital Archives Collaboratory[39] is so important. I was privileged to be interviewed for this project on several occasions by Dr. Brown and Dr. Nick Matte, respectively. The Trans Pathfinder,[40] an even more comprehensive virtual finding aid to help researchers and community members locate specific trans related artifacts in the archives, was launched at the same time by its primary creator, Dr. Matte. Sixty people came out to celebrate this milestone in Canadian trans history. There would be a third community event honouring me (and selected others) at another archives—the Transgender Archives in Victoria, BC—next year. I was now being repeatedly acclaimed for my work in the trans world over the past four and a half decades and it felt damn good!

Two months later, SHC threw me a retirement party at the Churchmouse Pub in the nearby gay village, saluting my career as an LGBTTI2SQQAA therapist and trans activist. My former boss, Anna Travers, and my then current boss, Bev Lepischak, highlighted my achievements over the past 13 years at the centre—and before. I was disappointed that my clients were not permitted to participate because I really wanted to say goodbye to them. Even so, I was gratified by the ample turnout of managers, co-workers, and the CEO; but, sad that only three of the 15 trans/genderqueer staff came out to acknowledge my work and wish me well. So much for community support! Overall though, I was glad that I went to my farewell celebration because I was determined to go out with a bang, not a whimper. I very much appreciated those certain occasions when SHC did honour me for services rendered and I would not have missed my time there for the world! Although I have a love-hate relationship with Planet Sherbourne, I believe that it still offers affirming healthcare for both its transgender and cisgender clients. Nevertheless, more trans staff are needed now that at least 10 of us have left. In order to mitigate my mixed feelings about my dream job, I learned to draw upon my humanity and humour, which helped me to let go of my feelings of bitterness and betrayal, and to honour my positive experiences and connections there.

In November, KJ flew back to Australia to look after a close elderly friend and to escape Toronto's harsh winters. She had lived in the South Pacific for nearly 30 years. We shed no tears as we hugged goodbye at the airport, knowing that we would be together again in a year and a half. Of course, we missed each other's physical presence over those 18 long months, but we exchanged virtual caresses and a laugh and a song or two via Skype every day. Our connection was stronger than ever as we held on to each other across the ocean.

For the next six weeks, I holed up in my warm house to avoid the frigid wintry weather outside and, working like a mad artist, I focussed on my two outstanding writing projects. These included incorporating Dr. Trish Salah's revised foreword into *Of Souls & Roles, Of Sex & Gender* (so that Dr. Aaron Devor and University of Victoria archivist Lara Wilson could upload it to the Transgender Archives website), and revising 22 of my 25 original trans resource documents—accessible on my RR Consulting website until I discontinued it in December 2016—and creating three new resource documents on gender transitioning for gender non-binary youth and trans teens, their parents, and helping professionals, which I donated to the Canadian Centre for Gender & Sexual Diversity.[41] I felt gratified to be able to freely share my intellectual property with my peers and the world at large for the good of the gender community. Those two writing tasks wrapped up, I was now free to review the first revisions of my memoir (which I had begun in 2013) made by my literary editor, Lynne Stahl. My initial editor, Loren Bornstein, had to abandon the project after several months due to health-related issues. We were only in the first round of edits and I wanted to get the completed manuscript to the publisher (an American trans press) by the fall so that we could hopefully launch the book in San Francisco in February 2017—what better 65th birthday present?—with follow-up launches in Portland, Seattle, Vancouver, Victoria, Toronto, Ottawa, Montreal, and New York. But, alas, my plans didn't pan out.

At this time, I asked my friend, Elspeth, if she would nominate me for an honourary doctorate degree through the University of Toronto; she told me she would look into it in the fall when the nominating committee convened. She wasn't too hopeful but I figured, what the hell, I already have a number of published works under my belt and several in progress: three books (including one unpublished but soon accessible online, and one in press), three book chapters (including one in press), five clinical research papers (including one unpublished but soon accessible online), three trans newsletters/magazines (accessible through the archives), and numerous articles in North American and British transsexual/transgender periodicals. Not too shabby for a PhD-less writer!

In February, I celebrated my 64th birthday at the Pear Tree restaurant in Cabbagetown with 25 friends, trying (not too successfully) to patch in KJ via Skype. Although grayer, balder, arthritic, and burnt out, I still had enough energy to party hearty, stuffing myself with seafood quesadilla and quaffing a few Coronas to mark my life so far. I had celebrated my 60th in New Orleans. Where would I be for my 65th? San Francisco? Toronto?

In March 2016, I flew to Victoria to present at the Moving Trans History Forward Transgender Archives Conference. I was on the Founders Panel^{42} along with three other trans pioneers: Jamie Lee Hamilton from Vancouver, BC, Yvonne Cook-Riley from Asheville, North Carolina, and Dr. Jason Cromwell from Hoodsport, Washington. One of the original panelists, Aiyyana Maracle, was too ill to attend.^{43} Dr. Aaron Devor was the moderator. We spoke about the history of the North American trans movement since the 1970s, tracing past successes, identifying present issues, and anticipating future challenges. The conference featured two keynote speakers: American trans activists Dr. Jamison Green and Dr. Martine Rothblatt. Jamison, outgoing president of the World Professional Association for Transgender Health, spoke about the triumphs and challenges of transgender people around the world.44 He has done more global trans advocacy than any other activist, exemplifying a refreshing exception to the all-too-prevalent Americentrism of US trans people. Thank you, Jamison! Martine, a lawyer, entrepreneur, and Co-CEO of United Therapeutics, envisions a future of "transhumanism,"45 where gender dimorphism would become obsolete, human bodies optional, and human consciousness would have the potential to become immortal through advancements in artificial intelligence. Three other presenters (out of many) included African American trans activist Andrea Jenkins,46 Swedish trans activist Maria Sundin47 and local Vancouver trans activist, M. Gayle Roberts.48 Overall, I had a fabulous time, reminiscing with old-time activists and meeting up-and-coming young advocates.

I was disheartened though, that I wouldn't be able to make the June WPATH symposium in Amsterdam—because I wasn't allowed to leave the country while collecting my disability pension. I had so looked forward to reconnecting with those two charming Dutch trans men, Thomas Wormgoor[49] and Alex Bakker,[50] and with transpositive and intersex-positive Dutch psychologist, Dr. Peggy Cohen-Kettenis[51]—all of whom I had met at the 2007 WPATH symposium in Chicago. I would have liked to have seen Alex and Dr. Cohen-Kettenis jointly open the 2016 WPATH symposium—transgender and cisgender people collaborating, not competing. Oh happy day! I also would have liked to have seen The Netherlands up close, this progressive land with its humanist ethic, this homeland of gay, humanist sexologist Dr. Rob Tielman, and the birthplace of that bisexual mad artist, Vincent van Gogh. Yay for the Dutch!

Winding down my trans community involvement, I selectively attended a few trans events over the next few months, including several historical milestones. On May 17, I proudly watched Toronto Mayor John Tory raise the Canadian trans flag (designed by Ottawa designer Michelle Lindsay) at Toronto City Hall on International Day Against Homophobia, Transphobia, and Biphobia. On June 1, I cheered as openly gay, Ontario Premier Kathleen Wynne raised the Rainbow Pride flag at Queen's Park the first day of Toronto's Pride Month (I'll be asking Ontario Premier Wynne, BC Premier Clark, and Canadian Prime Minister Justin Trudeau to simultaneously raise the trans flag in 2018). On July 1, I marched in the Trans* Pride Toronto March, proudly carrying the Trans Coalition Project (Toronto) banner with coalition partners Toronto Trans Alliance leader, Stephanie Woolley, Trans Lobby Group leader, Susan Gapka, and others. On August 4, just before I led *Fierté* Simcoe Pride's Trans* Rally/March in Orillia, Ontario along with trans youth leader, Brandon Rhéal Amyot, I urged all trans community members to walk the talk towards true solidarity, transcending racism, classism, sexism, genderism, ableism, and ageism—and to support Trans Black Lives Matter-Toronto.

It is gratifying that trans advocacy is moving ahead (with or without me), and the past nine years (2008-2017) were watershed years for trans Canadians in terms of winning long-awaited, insured health benefits (gender confirming surgery), and human rights. In terms of human rights legislation, no less than three transgender bills became law from 2012 to 2017, as outlined below.

In 2012, Ontario New Democrat MPP Cheri DiNovo's Bill 33 (*Toby's Act*, 2012)[52] amended the Ontario Human Rights Code to include both "gender identity" and "gender expression," thereby protecting not only transsexual and transgender people (including crossdressers), but also genderqueer, intersex, and Two-Spirit people, and all others transgressing the gender binary—apparently, the first law of its kind in North America!

In 2015, British Columbia NDP MPs Bill Siksay and Randall Garrison's private member's federal bill to protect trans people on the grounds of "gender identity" and "gender expression" (Bill C-279) passed third reading in Parliament, but incredulously, the bill included a last-minute amendment by a transphobic senator denying trans people the right to sue if they were challenged while using a gendered bathroom in a federally funded building. So, on May 17, 2016, Liberal Justice Minister Jody Wilson-Raybould (with the support of the Trans Coalition Project) introduced a subsequent federal bill (Bill C-16) declaring it a hate crime to discriminate against transgender Canadians, effectively superseding Bill C-279 with its transphobic bathroom-restriction clause. A year later, on June 15, 2017, Bill C-16 received Royal Assent as a legal amendment to the Canadian Human Rights Act and the Criminal Code.[53]

A year earlier, on July 25, 2016, transgender British Columbians scored a long overdue legal victory as Bill 27 (BC Human Rights Code Amendment Act[54]) was passed to include "gender identity or expression" among the Code's protected grounds.

What a tragic irony that at the same time 15 American states were trying to impose a "bathroom bill" [55] to limit the basic human rights of trans people in the wake of North Carolina's successful lead, and, jumping ahead to 2018, the term "transgender" could be defined out of existence by American President Trump, who rolled back protections of trans people under US federal civil rights law.[56] Sadly, I'm ashamed to admit that we Canadians also have our own trials and tribulations of transphobia in this country. Witness University of Toronto physics professor A. W. Peet's so far unsuccessful demand that self-admitted politically-incorrect, U. of T. psychology professor, Jordan Peterson, refer to the gender non-binary Peet with gender neutral pronouns such as "they" (per Bill C-16 gender identity/gender expression human rights legislation).[57] Also witness, two years later, trans-female, BC NDP political candidate Morgane Oger's legal battle against fellow BC religionist politician, Bill Whatcott (a homophobic, transphobic, anti-abortion, Christian fundamentalist), for allegedly trashing her human rights as a legal woman, with a right to run for political office.[58] Further, in 2018 and 2019, witness the vitriolic actions of another bigotted, right-wing, Christian politician in British Columbia: namely, People's Party of Canada member, Laura-Lynn Tyler Thompson (Anita Bryant reincarnated!), who campaigned against the new, provincial Sexual Orientation and Gender Identity (SOGI) program[59] to make schools safer for LGBTTI2SQQAA students and teachers in BC (and Alberta).[60] Notwithstanding all this raging religious and political controversy, I have faith that our politicolegal system will prevail on the side of right as I take heart that my native land of Canada is still a socially-democratic society.

At this point in my life (2017), winding up a half century of gender advocacy, I wish to share a series of 20 empowering, ongoing paradigm shifts, both within and outside of gender communities, locally and globally (at least in some of the more democratic nations):

1. Anti-racism/Indigenous affirmation: a revolution of trans people of colour, *Hijras*, Indigenous trans people, and Two-Spirit people (re-)emerging from erasure and invisibility to visible presence, and ongoing anti-racist/anti-Indigeneity work.
2. Anti-sexism/(trans)feminism: an evolution from cisgender, *transphobic,* "radical feminism" to transgenderist "male feminism" to cisgender and transgender, *transpositive* transfeminism (including trans women and trans men), and ongoing anti-(trans)misogynist and anti-(trans)misandrist work, although trans-exclusionary radical feminism (TERF) is still an ongoing issue.
3. (Dis)ability empowerment: some limited better understanding of how we need to empower our differently-abled gender community members, but we still need to do much more work in this area, including hiring (dis)abled (differently abled) people from the gender communities for both paid (preferred) and volunteer work.
4. Intergenerational engagement: a recent trend of community collaboration across all ages, bringing together older, middle-aged, and younger LGBTTI2SQQAA people for mutual teaching and learning.
5. Transqueer affirmation: more transqueer (gay, lesbian, bisexual, transensual, and pansexual) trans, intersex, and Two-Spirit people are finally feeling safe enough to come out of the closet to their own gender, sexual, ethnoracial, cultural, religious, and secular communities, and to the world. Transqueerphobia is finally dissipating somewhat. Most genderqueer (gender non-binary) people are also queer, but many do not consider themselves transgender, so they don't identify with the term, transqueer.
6. Genderqueer/gender non-binary affirmation: more genderqueer/gender non-binary (androgynous, pangender, gender neutral) youth and adults are transgressing societal, binary gender norms in various gender progressive countries. Some gender non-binary youth are separating from the overall trans community—sad given that we need cohesion and cooperation, not separation and competition (like the lesbian separatists). We can all work towards integration without assimilation, coming together while still preserving our unique identities.

7. Intersex affirmation: more intersex and dual-identity, trans-intersex people are (re-)emerging from obscurity in Canada and worldwide by means of political, academic/clinical (scientific papers), cultural (film documentaries), and professional sports activism (see #17 below). Intersex people are also gradually becoming more integrated into LGBTTI2SQQAA healthcare and social service programs—in which the "I" is often more than mere tokenism. Now we need intersex education and advocacy in schools and in faith communities.
8. Cross-community alliances: there has been closer cooperation between the historically conflicted gender non-binary (crossdressing/ transsexual/transgender/ genderqueer/intersex/Two-Spirit) and sexual-minority (gay/lesbian/bisexual/pansexual/asexual) communities and, also, a slowly unfolding allyship of transsexual/transgender and intersex people, with a greater appreciation of dual or multiple sexual/gender identities (or multiple) gender and sexual identities.
9. Societal integration and visibility: trans/genderqueer/intersex/Two-Spirit people in many countries are openly entering all spheres of society: science, technology, medicine/healthcare, psychology/ psychotherapy, social work/social services, law/law enforcement, politics, public administration, academia/education, religion, arts/ culture, sports, and the media—now empowered to make positive changes. Some specific areas are reflected below.
10. Canadian trans presence vs. (American) trans erasure: following on the recent appointment of the world's first and only Chair in Transgender Studies (see note 11 below), the recent establishment of the world's largest transgender archives (based at the University of Victoria), and the recent formation of Canada's only trans focussed press, TransGender Publishing (founded by University of Victoria Associate Professor Emerita Margot Wilson), along with recent international media coverage of a number of transgender, genderqueer, and Two-Spirit Canadians—party politicians (Estefania Cortes-Vargas, Julie Lemieux, Héléne Montreuil, and Morgane Oger), public officials (Gabrielle Bouchard and Judge Kael McKenzie), university academic Professor A. W. Peet, and professional athletes (Rachel McKinnon and Kristen Worley, among others)—has finally put Canada on the world map, offsetting our longstanding, trans erasure by the USA and other nations!
11. Depsychopathologization/gender affirming healthcare and social services: the international Stop Trans Pathologization campaign has been fighting to normalize gender variance worldwide since 2009. A greater number of trans, genderqueer, intersex, and Two-Spirit

primary care health professionals, mental health professionals, and social workers, are supporting like others in collaboration with cisgender providers. And, there are now more prescribing psychologists (with pharmacological certification) who are transpositive—and will, hopefully, one day, replace psychiatrists!
12. Gender studies and Indigenous studies: transgender and Two-Spirit academics have either initiated or infused these academic studies at the university/college level and, hopefully, this emerging trend will also continue in the elementary and secondary school curricula with the help of teachers from the gender and Indigenous communities. We still need greater intersex and genderqueer (gender non-binary) education, professors, and teachers. In Canada, sociology professor Dr. Aaron Devor, Director of the Transgender Archives at the University of Victoria, is the world's first and only Chair in Transgender Studies!
13. School safety/student support: increased safety, support, and advocacy guidelines for students have been implemented in schools, from Kindergarten through university. Recent anti-bullying legislation has been enacted to protect students vulnerable to violence—especially LGBTTI2SQQAA students, those of colour, and Indigenous students—in Canada and the USA. Moreover, mandatory gender and sexually diverse educational programs are now being introduced into schools.
14. Gender-affirming religious/spiritual communities: a number of diverse faith communities around the world have become more welcoming of gender non-binary people. Even so, there has been a regrettable backlash against trans people by the Christian Right (and a minority of Roman Catholics) in North America and beyond. Moreover, *Hijras* in Pakistan have recently been oppressed by Christians and Shia and Sunni Muslims in Pakistan—and are unknown in Sri Lanka because the Buddhist sects there condemn them as "sexually abnormal."
15. Genderpositive human rights legislation: several recent gains in terms of trans rights have been made in Canada and beyond. More lawyers, judges, politicians, and public officials worldwide, who identify as transgender, intersex, or Two-Spirit, including people of colour and Indigenous people, are supporting human-rights reforms for like others.
16. Gender diverse arts/culture: a larger percentage of trans and intersex people are entering the various cultural arts. Examples include more

transgender memoirs, novels and poetry, trans stand-up comedians, gender-themed artistic installations, popular trans TV series, trans rock bands, etc.
17. Trans and intersex inclusive sports: finally, trans and intersex athletes are being legitimized in professional sports, thanks to policy reforms in various countries' athletic (including Olympic) protocols. These now need to expand to an international jurisdiction.
18. Genderpositive media: a number of cisgender newspaper reporters/editors, film and TV directors/producers, and media program instructors are finally portraying trans people in a more realistic light. Cisgender employers need to become more gender-inclusive in the dramatic/visual arts, by hiring more trans, genderqueer, intersex, and Two-Spirit actors, directors, and producers. Although we do have a few trans radio programs and web podcasts, we need more gender transcenders in both mainstream and queer media.
19. Humanistic universal alliance: there is increased allyship of cisgender and transgender people (specifically, among families, friends, colleagues, and mainstream and alternative community members). Notwithstanding, we still need a clear commitment from politicians, government officials, lawyers, judges, law enforcement officers, prison officers, human resources directors, school officials, and faith community leaders to be part of all-encompassing, meaningful, anti-violence work, fighting against homophobia, lesbophobia, biphobia, transphobia, intersexphobia, genderphobia, and femmephobia as well as racism, anti-Indigeneity, sexism, classism, ageism, and ableism.
20. Intersectional trans eco-activism: there exists a watershed ecoconscientious movement to work towards overcoming both genderism—transphobia, intersexphobia, femmephobia, etc.—and speciesism—the commodification, abuse, and neglect of non-human animals—by linking the societal oppression of non-cisgender people (particularly, trans women of colour, Indigenous trans women, and trans sex workers) with the anthropocentric violence waged against animals on factory farms, in slaughter houses, research labs, pet mills, zoos, circuses, and in sports. This resolve to one day free all of Mother Earth's sentient beings incorporates an ongoing battle against the limits of both "all-knowing" scientism and religionism. Happily, more transgender/genderqueer youth and adults are becoming deep ecologists: ethical vegetarians, vegans, and harm-reduction pescetarians who respect planetary life.

Of course, we haven't yet reached our preferred standard in all of these areas, and there's still lots more work to do, especially much-needed reform for gender non-binary prisoners/ex-prisoners, sex workers, disabled, un(der)employed, poor, underhoused/homeless people, and immigrants/refugees.

On another note, I'm very happy to be done with litigious clients, intransigent managers, and steamrollering/backstabbing trans co-workers! Official retirement imminent, 2017 is going to be my transitional year to a new life chapter and a new brand of activism.

Chapter 11 Notes

[1] Muslim trans man, Kusha Dadui, came to Canada in 1995 as a refugee and now supports other trans/queer refugees in Toronto. See: Dadui, Kusha, "Queer and Trans Migration and Canadian Border Imperialism," in Jin Haritaworn, Ghaida Moussa, and Syrus Marcus Ware, eds., *Marvellous Grounds: Queer of Colour Histories of Toronto,* Toronto, ON: *Between the Lines*, 2018, chapter 9.

[2] These two multimedia artists included Two-Spirit, trans woman, Kiley May (see her mini bio in the collective note on Indigenous activists in chapter 9), and Jewish, American-Canadian trans man, S. Bear Bergman. He is a trans poet, writer, lecturer, storyteller, workshop presenter, and stand-up comedian, and lives with his trans-male partner, J Wallace Skelton and their son. For a list of his published children's books, see http://www.sbearbergman.com/.

[3] It was later renamed the Canadian Centre for Gender & Sexual Diversity: www.ccgsd-ccdsg.org/. Based in Ottawa, it was founded in 2005 by Jeremy Dias, a young, bilingual, South Asian gay man, who won a lawsuit against the Sault Ste. Marie Catholic School Board for disallowing a Gay-Straight Alliance club in his high school. Jer should get the Governor-General of Canada's Award if there's any justice! The CCGSD trains teachers, students and activists to fight homophobic, biphobic and transphobic bullying and discrimination in schools across Canada, especially in the rural areas.

[4] See: Lahood, Grant, dir., and John Keir, prod., *Intersexion*, Auckland, NZ: Ponsonby Productions, 2012. https://www.imdb.com/title/tt2157302/; and Hart, Phoebe, dir./prod., *Orchids, My Intersex Adventure*, Coorparoo, Queensland, AU: Hartflicker Moving Pictures, 2010. https://www.imdb.com/title/tt1757830/.

[5] Dr. Morgan Holmes's prolific publications include: *Critical Intersex*, Abingdon, UK: Routledge, 2009; *Intersex: A Perilous Difference*, Selinsgrove, PA: Susquehanna University Press, 2007; and "Cal/liope in Love: The 'Prescientific' Desires of an Apolitical 'Hermaphrodite,'" *Journal of Lesbian Studies*, 2007, 11(3-4): 223–232.

[6] The Trans Health Lobby Group changed its name to the Trans Lobby Group (TLG) in 2009 or 2010. (TLG) was officially recognized in 2011, as Pride Toronto's Honoured Dyke Group—even though I, a founding member, was not a dyke(!)—and in 2013, as the INSPIRE Award's Community Organization of the Year. Regarding the 2011 award, I had asked advocacy journalist, Andrea Houston, to feature a news story on the TLG, focussing on why I was the only trans-male in the group (and one of the original co-founders), but she kept putting me off, questioning if this angle was truly newsworthy. Another instance of erasure for me—and a missed opportunity to reach out to other potential trans-male members, pleading for more trans-female/trans-male political collaboration!

[7] Thomas, Antony, dir./prod., *Middle Sexes: Redefining He and She*, USA: Deep Stealth Productions; UK: Granada TV/Films. Aired in Canada, USA & UK in 2005. https://www.imdb.com/title/tt0495729/. Rebroadcast in 2009 as *A Transgender HBO Biography Special – Middle Sexes*.

[8] See: Sinclair, Raven, Michael Hart, and Gord Bruyere, eds., *Wícihitowin: Aboriginal Social*

Work in Canada, Vancouver, BC: Langara College, 2011 (6th of six editions since 2009).

[9] See: Butler, Alec, "Black Friday...With or Without the Question Mark," in John Lorinc, et al., *Any Other Way*, 208-211.

[10] For my poem, "Pansexual Pangender Person" (2012), printed on page 293 of my 2017/2018 trans poetry anthology, see https://www.uvic.ca/transgenderarchives/assets/docs/of-souls-0-rolesj-of-sex-0-gender-revised-july-1j-2018---numbered.pdf.

[11] Raj, Rupert, and Celia Schwartz, "A Collaborative Preparedness and Informed Consent Model: Guidelines to Assess Trans Candidates for Readiness for Hormone Therapy and Supportive Counselling throughout the Gender Transitioning Process," unpublished, Sept. 12, 2012 (rev. May 1, 2015), Ottawa, ON: Canadian Centre for Gender & Sexual Diversity. https://ccgsd-ccdgs.org/resources/.

[12] In chronological order, life stories have been published by these trans men: French Canadian, Yanni Kin (2002) and Patrick Verret (2005); and Engish Canadians, S. Bear Bergman (semi-autobiographical anthology) (2006), and just recently, Lorimer Shenher (2019). For full citations, see the Intersectional Bibliography.

[13] I've already mentioned a number of these life stories: Dianna Boileau, Stephanie (Sydney) Castle Heal, Michelle Ann Duff, Jamie Lee Hamilton and Katherine Ann Johnson. Others include French Canadians: Alain, Madeleine Charest, Frances Olympe Cormier, Guilda Monette, Brigitte Martel and Marie-Claude Paquette; and English Canadians: Alexandra Highcrest, Erica Rutherford and Lisa Salazar. See https://zagria.blogspot.ca/2013/06/canadian-autobiographies.html. Mandy Goodhandy's came out in 2018 and Kristen Worley's in 2019. Two forthcoming memoirs by English Canadians are M. Gayle Roberts and Dawn Angela Wensley. For full citations, see the Intersectional Bibliography.

[14] Khosla, Dhillon, *Both Sides Now: One Man's Journey through Womanhood*, New York, NY: J. P. Tarcher, 2006. Dhillon is an American attorney and lectures on gender transitioning.

[15] Read Jia Qing Wilson-Yang's award-winning novel, *Small Beauty* (Montreal, QC: Metonymy Press, 2016), about a mixed-race, trans woman in a small Ontario town navigating racism and transphobia, and desiring queer community. https://metonymypress.com/story-behind-small-beauty/.

[16] For a list of print and audiovisual works by and about transgender/genderqueer people of colour (including those of mixed race), Iranian trans people, Latin American trans people, South Asian *Hijras*, Indigenous trans people and Two-Spirit people, see specific sections (and subsections) of the Intersectional Bibliography.

[17] My friend, Trish, was the only conference organizer I know who arranged to refund the costs of travel and accommodation for all of the many presenters—on top of an honorarium! Dr. Salah is now Assistant Professor in Gender Studies at Queen's University in Kingston, ON.

[18] For information on all the conference presenters, see

http://www.writingtransgenres.com/conference-schedule/. Several are highlighted below.

Aiyyana Maracle (one of four keynote speakers) was a Canadian, Indigenous sovereign Haudenosaunee woman, multimedia artist, scholar, educator and great-grandmother. Her keynote address was entitled "Ruminations on The Tangled Roots of Today's Garden of Gender Multiplicity." Her many multimedia works are housed at the Transgender Archives. https://www.uvic.ca/transgenderarchives/collections/maracle/index.php. See also: Intersectional Bibliography.

Nathanaël is a gender non-binary, bilingual, French-Canadian author and translator. Their keynote address was entitled "*Mein abendes N.*" See also https://en.wikipedia.org/wiki/Nathana%C3%ABl.

Dr. Rachel Pollock is a prolific, Jewish, American writer across many genres (including novels, essays, science fiction and comic books) and a creative writing program instructor at Goddard College. Her keynote address was called, "Writing to Each Other"—Discovering and Creating A Literature From Within Trans Experience." Some of her works include: "The Transsexual Book of the Dead: Osirus and the Trance Man," in Dean Kotula, ed., *The Phallus Palace: Female to Male Transsexuals,* New York, NY: Alyson Books, 2002, 131-145; "The Varieties of Transsexual Experience," *Transsexual News Telegraph,* 1997, 18, 20; and "Archetypal Transsexuality," 1995. https://web.archive.org/web/20080705185602/http://www.annelawrence.com/twr/archetypal.html. See also https://zagria.blogspot.com/2011/12/rachel-pollack-1945-novelist-poet-tarot.html#.XXWCISipFAE, https://zagria.blogspot.com/2011/12/rachel-pollack-1945-novelist-poet-tarot.html#.XXWCISipFAE.

Dr. Jay Prosser is a British author, and Reader of Humanities at the University of Leeds in West Yorkshire, UK. See: Prosser, Jay, *Second Skins: The Body Narratives of Transsexuality,* New York, NY: Columbia University Press, 1998. His keynote address was called "Digital Trans." For more of his works, see his website http://www.skinterlocutors.org/jay-prosser.html.

Morgan M. Page is a Canadian writer and artist. See her fiction and non-fiction works listed on her website https://www.odofemi.com/writing/.

Tom Léger and Riley MacLeod are American co-authors and publishers. See their anthology, *The Collection: Short Fiction from the Transgender Vanguard,* New York, NY: Topside Press, 2012. See also https://topsidepress.submittable.com/.

Trace Peterson is a poet, editor, and publisher. See: Peterson, Trace, and T. C. Tolbert, eds., *Troubling the Line: Trans and Genderqueer Poetry and Poetics,* New York, NY: Nightboat Books, 2013; and Peterson, Trace, ed., *EOAGH: A Journal of the Arts.* http://eoagh.com.

Max Wolf Valerio is a German-born, Hispanic/American Indian writer and poet. After his autobiography, he published his poetry book, *The Criminal: The Invisibility of Parallel Forces,* Brooklyn, NY: EOAGH Books, 2018. See also https://en.wikipedia.org/wiki/Max_Wolf_Valerio.

[19] Trish Salah has written two poetry collections: *Lyric Sexology, vol. 1,* New York, NY: Roof Books, 2014; and *Wanting in Arabic: Poems,* Toronto, ON: TSAR Publications, 2002, 2013.

[20] These books on trans people by trans Canadians include Dr. Aaron Devor's *FTM: Female-to-Male Transsexuals in Society* (Bloomington, IN: Indiana University Press, 1997); Dr. Viviane Namaste's *Sex Change, Social Change: Reflections on Identity, Institutions, and Imperialism* (Toronto, ON: Women's Press/Canadian Scholars' Press, 2005); and *Invisible Lives: The Erasure of Transsexual and Transgendered People* (Chicago, IL: University of Chicago Press, 2000); and Dr. Bobby Noble's *Sons of the Movement: FtMs Risking*

Incoherence on a Post-Queer Cultural Landscape (Toronto, ON: Women's Press/Canadian Scholars' Press, 2006); and *Masculinities Without Men?: Female Masculinity in Twentieth-Century Fictions* (Vancouver, BC: UBC Press, 2003).

[21] See: Muldoon, Grey Kimber Piitaapan (with Dan Irving), "A Sense of Place: Expressions of Trans Activism North of Lake Nipissing," in Irving and Raj, *Trans Activism in Canada*, 71-84. Grey identifies as a Two-Spirit ally and talks about the Indigenous community near Sudbury, an oasis for gender non-binary people in Ontario North, given the latter's social isolation, conservative Catholic heritage and relative lack of resources.

[22] See: Marshall, Zack, Marcus Burnette, Sonia Lowton, Rainbow, Romeo Dontae Treshawn Smith, Jay Tiamo, Onyinyechukwu Udegbe, and Tess Vo (illustrations by Elisha, Lim), "A Conversation about Art and Activism with Trans and Genderqueer People Labelled with Intellectual Disabilities," in Irving and Raj, *Trans Activism in Canada*, 125-136.

[23] Watch these two recent Iranian trans films, Azarbayjani, Negar, dir., and Fereshteh Taerpoor, prod., *Facing Mirrors* (Persian), Box Entertainment, 2011 (Canada), 2012 (Iran). https://iranianfilmempire.wordpress.com/2016/12/12/transgender-in-iranian-cinema/. Drama about a pre-transitional trans man and his girlfriend in Iran. And Eshaghian, Tanaz, dir./prod., *Transsexual in Iran (Be Like Others)* (Persian), Iran: The Film Collaborative, 2008. https://www.youtube.com/watch?v=qHmi3WAieew. Documentary on trans women in Iran.

[24] Former Health Minister/Energy Minister George Smitherman and several Toronto city councillors also attended. Member of Provincial Parliament, Cheri DiNovo, wasn't able to make it due to illness, but was represented by her assistant, Andrea Houston, a cisqueer advocacy journalist.

[25] Trans activists who spoke included Susan Gapka, Shadmith Manzo, Nichola Ward, Curt Pullan and Boyd Kodak.

[26] See Arshy Mann's news feature on police constable, Danielle Bottineau, "The Gay Cop Trying to Fix the Relationship between Toronto's LGBT Communities and the Police," Toronto, ON: *Xtra*, Aug. 3, 2018. https://www.dailyxtra.com/the-gay-cop-trying-to-fix-the-relationship-between-torontos-lgbt-communities-and-the-police-106729.

[27] See: Spade, Dean, *Normal Life: Administrative Violence, Critical Trans Politics, and the Limits of Law*, Durham, NC: Duke University Press, 2011, (rev. ed.), 2015.

[28] For Boyd Kodak (Jan Joseph Waterman)'s Ontario Human Rights Commission settlement, see http://www.ohrc.on.ca/en/summary-waterman-v-toronto-police.

[29] The guide was revised by the Toronto Police LGBT Community Consultation Committee on December 2016: *A Guide to Police Services in Toronto: Dedicated to our Trans Communities*. https://www.torontopolice.on.ca/publications/files/guide_to_police_services_trans_community.pdf. Interestingly, the Community Consultation Committee members are unnamed(!) but I'm sure that LGBTQ Liaison P.C. Danielle Bottineau headed the committee. However, I had expressed to Boyd (and P.C. Bottineau too,

if memory serves) my interest in being part of the community consultation process prior to the formation of the committee, but regrettably, no one invited me to join. See also the June 16, 2016 *Xtra* news story on Boyd Kodak. http://www.dailyxtra.com/toronto/news-and-ideas/news/ one-man-changing-toronto-police%E2%80%99s-trans-policy-195715.

[30] See: Sly Sarkisova's chapters, "Under A Queer Blue Sky," in John Lorinc, et al., *Any Other Way,* 283-284; and "Resisting the Binary: The Role of the Social Worker in Affirmative Trans Health Care," in Brian J. O'Neill, Tracy A. Swan, and Nick J. Mulé, eds., *LGBTQ People and Social Work: Intersectional Perspectives,* Toronto, ON: Canadian Scholars' Press, 2015, 255-274.

[31] Sadly, The 519 never conducted the proposed needs assessment, and, as of 2019, there's still no group specifically for older trans men. There is only the Mature Men's Book Club—a group for cisqueer and trans men who are 50+.

[32] Empirical research on older Canadian trans people is being conducted by doctoral students Kelsey Rounds (a trans-male nurse), and Kimi Dominic (a genderqueer student)—under the supervision of World Chair in Transgender Studies Dr. Aaron Devor—at the University of Victoria in British Columbia.

[33] Examples of community supports/resources for older trans people in Toronto include gender non-binary facilitator King© Mature Trans Sisters group at Sherbourne Health Centre (https://sherbourne.on.ca/get-involved/community-groups/), and American cisgender therapist Loree Cook-Daniels's Transgender Aging Network, an educational website for trans people in the USA (https://forge-forward.org/aging/).

[34] An innovative vehicle for public and community education is American, gender non-binary photographic artist Jess Dugan and American, cisgender social work professor Vanessa Fabbre's combined print and online project, *To Survive On This Shore: Photographs and Interviews with Transgender and Gender Non-Conforming Older Adults,* Heidelberg, DEU: Kehrer Verlag, 2018. http://www.jessdugan.com/publications; https://www.tosurviveonthisshore.com.

[35] See: Wilson, Margot, and Aaron Devor, eds., *Glimmerings: Trans Elders Tell Their Stories,* Victoria, BC: TransGender Publishing, 2019. For a list of the 15 Canadian and American contributors (many of whom were early activists), see https://transgenderpublishing.ca/glimmerings-recognition-authenticity-and-gender-variance/.

[36] Brown, Elspeth, "Finding Aid for The Rupert Raj fonds," 2015, The ArQuives. https://www.archeion.ca/rupert-raj-Fonds-4

[37] The Digital Transgender Archive (DTA) was spearheaded by Dr. K.J. Rawson, a trans man, and Associate Professor of English at the College of the Holy Cross in Worcester, MA. K.J. is the director of DTA, which is based at, and funded by, the College. https://www.digitaltransgenderarchive.net/about/overview.

[38] Rachel (formerly Sally) Lewis facilitated Xpressions (established 1992), a Toronto-based, social and support group for crossdressers, transsexuals, transgenders, genderqueers and their loved ones, for about 15 years. https://xpressions.org/. Formerly, a male-to-female crossdresser, Rachel transitioned to a woman in 2013.

[39] Collaborators include: Dr. Elspeth Brown (University of Toronto), Dr. K.J. Rawson (College of the Holy Cross), Dr. Elise Chenier (Simon Fraser University), Dr. Sara Davidmann (University of the Arts London), Dr. Aaron Devor (University of Victoria) and Dr. Karen Stanworth (York University). The project manager is Dr. Nick Matte. The ArQuives is one of several archival partners, along with the Archives of Lesbian Oral Testimony, the Transgender Archives and the Digital Transgender Archive.

[40] Matte, Nick, "The Trans Pathfinder," 2016. The ArQuives.

[41] "Hormonal Therapies for Gender Non-Conforming Youth & Trans Teens," "Paediatric Endocrinologists & Paediatric/Adolescent Medicine Physicians for Gender Non-Conforming Youth & Trans Teens," and "Child/Adolescent Psychiatrists & Psychologists for Gender Non-Conforming Youth & Trans Teens" (all compiled by Rupert Raj); submitted in November 2016, and finally uploaded January 21, 2019: "Educational Resources for Transgender, Intersex & Two-Spirit People (including Gender Non-Conforming Youth & Trans Seniors)." http://ccgsd-ccdgs.org/resources/; http://ccgsd-ccdgs.org/launch-of-rupert-raj-resources/. Canadian Centre for Gender & Sexual Diversity staff/volunteers will be responsible for updating my resources given that I'm now finished with clinical research.

[42] Watch my talk ("Rupert Raj's 41-Year Gender Journey & 45-Year Trans Activist Career"). https://www.youtube.com/watch?v=KG4RPJEHrtw&index=5&list=PLjWymvKNnUWKX-Z2tkf_T5UGbrkbvZWzi&t=10s. For talks by the other Founders Panelists and the two keynote speakers at the 2016 Moving Trans History Forward conference, go to https://www.uvic.ca/mthf (click "Past Conferences" tab). The first Founders Panel (renamed the Elders Panel in 2018) in 2014 featured Canadian activist, Stephanie Castl,e and American activists, Dr. J. Ari Kane and Rikki Swin (with Jude Patton moderating). Keynote speakers included Canadian activists (Dr. Viviane Namaste) and American activists (Dallas Denny, Dr. Susan Stryker, and Colonel Jennifer Pritzker). The 2018 conference featured two keynote speakers: African American trans politician, Andrea Jenkins, and Manitoban Two-Spirit artist, Kent Monkman. The Elders Panel included international activists, Christine Burns (UK), Miqqi Alicia Gilbert (Canada), Aidan Key (USA), and Maria Sundin (Sweden).

[43] Aiyyana Maracle, who was then living in Ohsweken, ON, passed away a month later on April 24 at age 65. My dear friend was indeed "a fierce soul with a gentle but powerful voice": see Paul Couillard's *In Memoriam: Aiyyana Maracle*, 2016. http://7a-11d.ca/in-memoriam-aiyyana-maracle/#_ftnref7.

[44] Watch Jamison Green's keynote address at the 2016 MTHF TGA Conference. https://www.uvic.ca/mthf (click "Past Conferences" tab).

[45] Watch Martine Rothblatt's keynote address at the 2016 MTHF TGA Conference. https://www.uvic.ca/mthf (click "Past Conferences" tab). See also https://zagria.blogspot.ca/2009/10/martine-rothblatt-1954-lawyer-broadcast.html. Read Martine's books: *From Transgender to Transhuman: A Manifesto on the Freedom of Form*, Self-published, 2011; and *Virtually Human: The Promise - and the Peril - of Digital Immortality*, New York, NY: St. Martin's Press, 2014. For the record, although I condone the limited use of prosthetics, robotics and android devices, I condemn the kind of "transhumanism" (human mind cloning and "technoimmortality") advocated by Martine (a

biocyberethicist) and by cyberengineers because, firstly, even though I am quite cerebral, I wouldn't want a disembodied human "consciousness" without the all-important vitality of the visceral body, and secondly, why further pollute our planet and the universe by replicating and promulgating the not-too-conscientious consciousness of our doubly-unwise species ("Homo unsapiens unsapiens") instead of simply letting humankind die an evolutionary natural death, finally leaving Planet Earth and the cosmos in peace?!

[46] Andrea Jenkins (with Erica Fields) put on a dramatic performance ("Countering Historical Erasure of Transgender Narratives from Mainstream LGBT History"), and two years later, delivered a keynote address ("The 'T' is NOT Silent in LGBT") at the 2018 MTHF TGA Conference. https://www.uvic.ca/mthf (click "Past Conferences" tab).

[47] Maria Sundin (a sexologist, social worker, past co-chair of Transgender Europe and past Board member of the Swedish Federation for LGBTQ Rights) spoke about Swedish trans politics in the 1960s, and two years later, highlighted her 25 years of advocacy for Swedish trans people at the 2018 MTHF TGA Conference (Elders Panel). https://www.uvic.ca/mthf (click tab: "Past Conferences").

[48] Read M. Gayle Robert's autobiography, *From Shame to Freedom: A Gender Variant Woman's Journey of Discovery*, Victoria, BC: TransGender Publishing, 2019. See also: Wells, Kristopher, M. Gayle Roberts, and Carol Allan, *Supporting Transgender and Transsexual Students in K-12 Schools: A Guide for Educators*, Ottawa, ON: Canadian Teachers' Federation, 2012. http://gendercreativekids.ca/wp-content/uploads/2013/10/Supporting-Transgender-and-Transsexual-Students-web.pdf.

[49] Thomas Wormgoor is a developmental psychologist, trans care psychotherapist, and a healthcare lawyer in Amsterdam. https://nl.linkedin.com/in/thomas-wormgoor-2156744b. Formerly, he was a director and a board member of Transgender Netwerk Nederland, an advocacy organization for Dutch trans people. https://www.transgendernetwerk.nl/.

[50] Read Alex Bakker's life story, *My Untrue Past: The Coming of Age of a Trans Man*, Victoria, BC: TransGender Publishing, 2019. (Originally published in Dutch as *Mijn vales verleden: Het autobiografische verhaal van een man geboren alsmeisje*), Amsterdam, NL: Nieuw Amsterdam Publishers, 2014. www.nieuwamsterdam.nl. See also: *Transgender in Nederland: Een Buitengewone Geschiedenis* (Dutch), Amsterdam, NL: Boom Publishing House, 2018. www.BUA.nl, www.Boomgeschiedenis.nl. And watch his opening talk with Dr. Peggy Cohen-Kettenis at the 2016 World Professional Association for Transgender Health (WPATH) Symposium in Amsterdam. https://av-media.vu.nl/VUMedia/Play/27b2497ee5a449248f9379e6e94d3c901d?catalog=2d190891-4e3f-4936-a4fa-2e9766ae0d0d.

[51] See: Cohen-Kettenis, Peggy T., and Friedemann Pfäfflin, *Transgenderism and Intersexuality in Childhood and Adolescence: Making Choices*, Thousand Oaks, CA: Sage Publishing, 2003.

[52] For Ontario's Bill 33 ("Toby's Act," 2012), see: "Gender Identity and Gender Expression— Something to Celebrate in 2012," *Annual Report (2012-2013)*, Ontario Human Rights Commission. http://www.ohrc.on.ca/en/annual-report-2012-2013-rights-partners-action/gender-identity-and-gender-expression-%E2%80%93-something-celebrate-2012; and "Passage of Toby's Act (Bill 33) an Historic Achievement for Ontario's Trans Community," Ottawa, ON: Egale Canada Human Rights Trust, June 13, 2012. https://egale.ca/passage-of-

tobys-act-bill-33-an-historic-achievement-for-ontarios-trans-community-2/.

[53] For **Canada's** federal gender identity bill ("Bill C-16: An Act to amend the Canadian Human Rights Act and the Criminal Code"), see https://www.parl.ca/DocumentViewer/en/42-1/bill/c-16/royal-assent; and https://egale.ca/billc16/.

[54] For British Columbia's Bill 27 ("BC Human Rights Code Amendment Act, 2016"), see http://www.bclaws.ca/civix/document/id/lc/billsprevious/5th40th:gov27-3; and https://www.lawsonlundell.com/newsroom-news-847.

[55] North Carolina was the only state to pass—and then repeal (in 2017) legislation (House Bill 2) restricting access to multiuser restrooms, locker rooms, and other sex-segregated facilities on the basis of a definition of sex or gender consistent with sex assigned at birth or "biological sex." To track the progress of this transphobic "bathroom bill" in other American states, see: National Conference of State Legislatures. http://www.ncsl.org/research/education/-bathroom-bill-legislative-tracking635951130.aspx.

[56] The Trump administration is considering narrowly defining "gender" as a biological, immutable condition determined by genitalia at birth! https://www.nytimes.com/2018/10/21/us/politics/transgender-trump-administration-sex-definition.html.

[57] Listen to the October 3, 2016, CBC Radio interview as Prof. A. W. Peet (listed on Wikipedia) debates Prof. Jordan Peterson. https://www.cbc.ca/radio/asithappens/as-it-happens-friday-edition-1.3786140/i-m-not-a-bigot-meet-the-u-of-t-prof-who-refuses-to-use-genderless-pronouns-1.3786144. And, watch the October 28, 2016, TVO debate, "Genders, Rights and Freedom of Speech," as U. of T. Transgender Studies Lecturer, Nicholas Matte, butts heads with Prof. Peterson https://www.youtube.com/watch?v=kasiov0ytEc.

[58] Canadian politician, Morgane Oger, is chair of the Trans Alliance Society in Vancouver, BC, and a member of the Vancouver Board of Education's Pride Committee and The City of Vancouver's LGBTQ2+ Advisory Committee. On Nov. 27, 2016, she became the first trans person to be nominated by a major political party in British Columbia (BC New Democratic Party, Vancouver-False Creek), but was unsuccessful in the 2017 election. In 2018, she lost the race for both Vancouver mayor and Vancouver School Board trustee. In December 2018, she filed a provincial human rights complaint against Bill Whatcott for circulating allegedly "transphobic" flyers, and outing her as a (birth-assigned) "male." https://www.straight.com/life/1176021/tribunal-hearing-discrimination-complaint-brought-former-bc-ndp-candidate-and-trans. See also: "Toxic Trans: The Strange Case of Morgane Oger and the BC NDP," July 28, 2018. https://www.newcenter.ca/news/oger-ndp. Morgane recently established a foundation to fight hate crimes. https://www.ogerfoundation.ca/.

[59] For information on the provincial Sexual Orientation and Gender Identity (SOGI) educational program, see https://sogieducation.org/.

[60] British Columbian, anti-SOGI, religionist politician, Laura-Lynn Tyler Thompson, lost the electoral race for a Burnaby schoolboard trustee in 2018, and again, for a federal seat in Parliament (as the People's Party of Canada candidate) at the Burnaby South federal by-

election in 2019. https://vancouversun.com/news/local-news/anti-sogi-activist-to-run-for-maxime-berniers-new-federal-party-in-burnaby-south-byelection. I made damned sure to vote for a non-transphobic, non-homophobic candidate each time!

(L to R) International trans activists: Dr. Nick Matte, Rupert Raj, Dr. Stephen Whittle, and Dr. Jamison Green at the Sixth International Congress on Sex and Gender Diversity. Manchester, UK, 2004

Rupert Raj (L) and American genderqueer activist, Leslie Feinberg, at hir book launch of Drag King Dreams. *Toronto, Ontario, 2006*

Mayor David Miller (R) and City Councillor Kyle Rae (R) presenting Rupert Raj with the 2007 City of Toronto Access and Equity Human Rights Pride Award.
(Photo: Jocelyn Richards, The City of Toronto)

Rupert Raj and fellow Trans Lobby Group (TLG) members, Susan Gapka (L) and Martine Stonehouse (R), at Toronto City Hall, 2007.
(Photo: Jocelyn Richards, The City of Toronto)

Rupert Raj and New Zealander trans activist, Georgina Beyer, following her human rights speech at the Egale Canada gala.
Toronto, Ontario, 2010

Rupert Raj (with sister, Arjuna), proudly holding his Steinert & Ferreiro Award, presented by Community One Foundation for 39 years of outstanding contribution to the LGBT community.
Toronto, Ontario, 2010

*Rupert Raj (L) and Richard Hudler
beaming during their joint induction into The ArQuives
(formerly Canadian Lesbian and Gay Archives).
Toronto, Ontario, 2103*
(Photo: Canadian Lesbian and Gay Archives)

Rupert Raj (R) and Dr. Dan Irving launching their trailblazing book,
Trans Activism in Canada, *at The ArQuives.*
Toronto, Ontario, 2014

My trans activist anthology (co-edited with Dan Irving, PhD), published by Canadian Scholars' Press in 2014.

(L to R): Rupert Raj, Dr. Nick Matte, and Dr. Elspeth Brown launching The Rupert Raj fonds and The Trans Pathfinder at The ArQuives. Toronto, Ontario, 2015
(Photo: Canadian Lesbian and Gay Archives)

In solidarity (L to R): Jude Patton, Dr. Jamison Green, Dr. Nick Matte, Dr. Aaron Devor, John Helle Otto, and Rupert Raj at the Moving Trans History Forward conference. Victoria, BC 2016
(Photo: Transgender Archives, University of Victoria)

Part IV:

Rainbow Warrior

* * *

<u>R<small>AINBOW</small> W<small>ARRIOR</small></u>

Lobbying for trans rights
fighting for animal liberation–
the battle's one and the same.
All Earthly creatures, great and small
reflect their radiance from the rainbow
shining over Terra Firma.

* * *

12. Retirement…Eco-Activism & Animal Liberation (2017-)

Still more transitions! The dance of life never stops until we hang up our dancing shoes, passing through one life stage and then another and another. So now, fast approaching 65, I was transitioning from a lifetime of work and a recent medical disability leave to official retirement. I would soon be making a further transition from trans activism to eco-activism and animal liberation.

To mark my 65th birthday and my retirement, The 519 Community Centre hosted a party for me in honour of my activism and my 38-year relationship with the centre. I am so thankful to Program Director, Becky McFarlane, and Counselling Services Coordinator, Robyn Letson, for giving me this gift. An unforgettable evening of validation galore, 100 or so invited guests came out to help me celebrate my twin milestone, including prominent politicians, community leaders, former clients, colleagues, and friends. Sadly, my partner and my sister could not attend, but they were both there in spirit. We unsuccessfully tried to patch them in via Skype but technology failed us once again. Paddy Aldridge was the Mistress of Ceremonies and my photographer friend, Davina Hader, filmed the event for posterity—eventually to be uploaded to The 519 website and possibly later posted to Facebook. Lucas Silveira of The Cliks sang two songs for us as we revelled, ate, and drank—and as I shone in my glory! Several guests paid tribute to me, acknowledging my activist work, including Metropolitan Community Church of Toronto pastor Rev. Dr. Brent Hawkes, former Ontario Health Minister/Energy Minister George Smitherman, Ontario Member of Provincial Parliament Cheri DiNovo and Toronto City Councillor Kristyn Wong-Tam. Cheri and Kristyn each presented me with an official certificate of achievement for my many years of community service. Kristyn humorously reacted to my comment of being "trans saturated" by asking me to come back to work in the trans/queer community if I ever became "poly un-trans-saturated." Former federal/municipal politician, Olivia Chow, was unable to make it because she was hosting a party herself at the same time, but she sent me a lovely orchid bouquet as a token of her esteem.

The highlight of my special night was the Youth Role Model of the Year Award—in the form of a pink elephant embossed on a medallion and tied to a Rainbow ribbon. The award was jointly presented to me by Canadian Centre for Gender & Sexual Diversity director, Jeremy Dias, and my nominator, Ander Negrazis, whom I had met 11 years earlier when they were a homeless, genderqueer youth moving from Sudbury to Toronto. Ander has a multidimensional identity, with lived experience as "an autistic, neurodivergent, disabled, queer and trans therapist, artist, and organizer."[1] What a tremendous transition from then until now! I thanked them both for this touching tribute: an apt token to mark my "transjectory" from trans youth to trans elder (1971-2017). I mentioned that I was privileged to be there that night, alive and kicking, as many trans people don't even make it to 65, often dying prematurely from minority stress (psychosocial/psychosomatic stress experienced by minority groups). For those elders who do survive, we can teach our youth valuable life lessons about survival, vulnerability, and resilience.[2] So, just before a gratifying standing ovation, I gave my own gift of love to my gathered guests by reading aloud three affirmations—previously penned for my former clients—attesting to the dialectical dynamic of vulnerability and resilience: "The Bamboo Tree," "Power of the Human Spirit" and "Dancing to the Beat of A Different Drummer" (see Appendix II).

Following my party, several of my friends and I walked down Church Street to Glad Day Bookshop, where a launch for Dr. Gary Kinsman's book, *We Still Demand! Redefining Resistance in Sex and Gender Struggles* (2017),[3] was winding down. Gary pointed out a 1977 photo of me in a chapter on me: "Rupert Raj, Transmen, and Sexuality: The Politics of Transnormativity in *Metamorphosis Magazine* during the 1980s."[4] It was written by my friend Nick Matte, who, unfortunately, couldn't make it to my party, but had previously emailed me:

> *Did you know there's a book launch at the same time at Glad Day for another book in which I've published a (more academic) chapter about your early work? I unfortunately can't attend that event either but I wanted to make sure you're aware of it and I'm excited about the fact that you will be being celebrated up and down Church Street that night! Congratulations and I will be celebrating with you in spirit for sure!*

After being passed over many times in the past,[5] such a watershed of present-day validation is certainly appreciated[6]—thank you, Nick, for writing about me in two books in three years.

My party took place a week before my actual birthday on February 10 because that was the day my long term disability pension expired. Finally freed from my 18-month restriction of no travel outside the country, I flew to Mexico—turning 65 on the plane—for two and a half weeks in Lake Chapala (just south of Guadalajara) to escape Toronto's deep freeze. Wishing KJ was with me to share this tropical paradise, I exulted in the Mexican flora and fauna, culture and cuisine, and the community-minded local residents. A few of the Canadian and American tourists and ex-pats were really fine, but many infuriated me as insufferable boors, still obsessed with the trivialities of their former lives back home (and party politics!), instead of focussing on the exciting things of their new homeland. For my part, anthropological adventurer that I am, I exulted in the exploration of new people and places (Lake Chapala, Guadalajara, and Tlaquepaque), clumsily practising the Spanish I had recently begun to learn in Toronto. In Lakeside, I shopped at the weekly fairs, ambled along the pier, or lounged about in the plaza, savouring salsa-spiced quesadillas and sipping lime-ringed margaritas while serenaded by local Mariachi bands. I was hard-pressed to leave this Latin American haven and couldn't wait to return soon with my ladylove.

Back in Toronto in March, I resumed my writer role, working like mad on the last draft of my memoir, pushing myself 24/7 to meet my August 7 deadline, caught between a computer crash and the still lingering aftermath of my 2015 mental breakdown! That month I was also called upon to fulfill my poet role, reading excerpts from my international trans poetry anthology at The ArQuives' Open Box: Poetry In and Out of the Archives hosted by Glad Day Bookshop. Other poets included queer trans women, Trish Salah and Kiley May, among others. Then, later in July, in my role as a social historian, I read aloud my short essay, "Worlds in Collision," published in *Any Other Way: How Toronto Got Queer* (2017),[7] alongside other trans, genderqueer, Two-Spirit, and queer contributors. I was honoured to be included in this cultural milestone: a politicohistorical anthology of Canadian activists and artists, highlighting transformative experiences and events in Toronto from before the 1950s to the present. Soon, I would be reciting once again from my written works—this time at the Glad Day book launch of my memoir only four weeks away on August 23.

* * *

Now, officially retired from my job, and after a long career as a gender worker, it seemed time for a change—another cause. I still had some of the fighting spirit left. Certainly I wasn't the first (nor would I be the last) trans activist to switch focus. Three people, in particular, come to mind: Georgina, Joanna and Joshua.

New Zealander Māori activist Georgina Beyer has "changed for the better"[8] many times: from cabaret performer to sex worker to actress (1980s) to school board official to party politician as the municipal mayor (1995-1999) and federal Parliament member (1999-2007, 2014-2017). American activist Joanna Clark (formerly, Sister Mary Elizabeth) has also evolved through multiple personae over the years: army officer (1970s), trans activist (1970s and 1980s), Episcopalian nun (1980s), AIDS researcher (1990s), and now ecological advocate. Canadian activist, Joshua Goldberg, first worked with people with HIV/AIDS for nine years, then supported trans people for another nine,[9] and now advocates for poor/homeless people. He once told me that he could not pursue all of his many social concerns at once because he would burn out even before he got started. We activists have to be mindful of where we focus our energies because we can't save the whole world!

Their experiences echo my own life situation as a multidimensional man—a Canadian, mixed-race, pangender, pansexual person and a trans activist, psychotherapist, gender consultant, and published researcher—often reduced by the world to the sole entity of trans man. It's noteworthy that most trans people are known exclusively for their transgender identity, with little or no recognition of their other identities, personal and professional achievements, and community activism beyond transgender. My trans identity is both *integral* to my overall identity as an evolving being in the world (a child of Mother Earth) and *incidental* to my combined identities as a transfeminist, ecofeminist, deep ecologist, democratic socialist, existential humanist, and atheist Zenist.

Specifically, this means my intentional identity as an ethical non-meat eater and animal liberationist, who fights for the rights of oppressed animals, and embraces all female sentient beings as equal to males. As a transfeminist and ecofeminist, I further embrace humans and animals who transgress sex or gender, such as offspring bearing male seahorses, sex switching female clownfish, and certain homosexual, transsexual, and intersex people, and animals referenced in Dr. Joan Roughgarden's *Evolution's Rainbow* (2004).

In keeping with this theme of natural compassion, I began re-reading some of my Taoist and Zenist books—including those containing *haiku* (Zen poetry)—and paintings of animals, humans, and nature inscribed with Chinese calligraphy. I hoped someday to try the Zen arts of tea drinking and *bonsai* (growing miniature trees). I also renewed my interest in Native spirituality and Earth medicine, reading shamanic healer Jamie Sams's *Earth Medicine: Ancestors' Ways of Harmony for Many Moons* (1994), and wise woman Paula Gunn Allen's *The Sacred Hoop: Recovering the Feminine in American Indian Traditions* (1986).

What intrigued me about these diverse ways of being was their common value system—an eco ethic that respected all life forms, embracing Mother Earth in an ever expanding circle of compassion. I vowed to renew my commitment to ethical eating. I had ceased all carnivorous consumption in 1991, but in 2000, I had shifted to pescetarianism[10]—eating seafood, vegetables, tofu, and minimal dairy—and, so far, except for a few lapses, have maintained my meatless intentions. My commitment is inspired by my fellow non-meat eaters, in particular, trans-identified, Canadian, animal-rights activists Mirha-Soleil Ross, the late Xanthra Mackay, and Calvin Neufeld and, also, my transqueer vegan/vegetarian friends, Tom Cho, Dan Irving, Jude Patton, Nick Matte, and James Loewen. It's also promising that so many trans, genderqueer, and queer youth are going vegan or vegetarian.

Both Mirha-Soleil and Xanthra were members of the Animal Liberation Front, rescuing doomed dogs and cats from inhumane pet stores or owners, and rodents, rabbits, and other death destined animals from experimental research laboratories. Mirha-Soleil hosted *Animal Voices,* a weekly animal advocacy and vegan lifestyle radio show (1996-2001), and produced the video, *Yapping Out Loud: Contagious Thoughts from an Unrepentant Whore* (2002),[11] drawing parallels between the violence waged against sex workers and animals, and exposing the horrific crimes committed against research laboratory animals in the name of science and against factory farmed animals in the name of agribusiness. Of course, we can also add animal abuse (torture, murder) in the name of religion, such as: fundamentalist Islamic (*halal*) and Orthodox Judaic (*kosher*) ritual animal slaughter.[12] These practices by oppressive patriarchal (and certain other) religions are yet another ethical reason to reject religionism! The only real hope animals have—inextricably caught between science and religion—are the philosophical principles and practices of ecofeminism and deep ecology. Three notable exceptions to such oppressive science and religion, are: the Earth sciences (specifically, the Gaia principle), environmentally-engaged Buddhism, and Native spirituality.

Dan Irving and I included Calvin Neufeld's thought-provoking paper on animal liberation, *Choosing Better than Oppression,* in our 2014 trans activist reader.[13] Calvin's paper links the intersectional oppression of transgender people and animals, wherein both are often voiceless victims of violence, although some trans people, over time, are able to source their own power, enabling them to fight back against their oppressors. He cites Marjorie Spiegel's book, *The Dreaded Comparison: Human and Animal Slavery* (1996) (a must read for everyone on this planet), comparing the dehumanizing brutality of the African and American slave trades with inhumane animal cruelty and exploitation, whereby cages and prisons become transferrable across species. Enslaved livestock and experimental research laboratory animals are powerless unless compassionate human agents help them to attain their freedom. Calvin's passionate compassion palpitates throughout his paper. He also wrote a provocative animal rights booklet for children: *Sanctuary: A Children's Story for All Ages* (2000), and edited a poignant book for adults written by his mother, Franceen Neufeld, *Suffering Eyes: A Chronicle of Awakening* (2000). Book sale profits help to rescue factory farmed animals and place them in lifetime sanctuaries. So far, the Suffering Eyes Project[14] has raised more than $20,000 towards emancipation of enslaved livestock in Ontario. Calvin also co-founded Evolve Our Prison Farms, a proposed model for a dairy farm worked by prison inmates—which would also be an animal sanctuary driven by plant-based agriculture. This project takes the form of a Canada-wide justice movement advocating ethical prison farms to feed prisoners—not promote multinational trade—and to rehabilitate inmates compassionately, without harming them or the farmed animals: an inspired intersection of prisoner and animal justice. To date, 75% of the prisoners surveyed[15] at Joyceville Institution in Kingston, Ontario want just such an ethically evolved prison farm model; one based on health, sustainability, and loving kindness—not exploitation and slaughter. On February 27, 2019, Calvin was invited to televise this groundbreaking project in conversation with world-renowned, Canadian biologist and eco-activist Dr. David Suzuki.[16] An early activist, Calvin earned the Governor-General's Award upon graduating from high school in 1998. Calvin e-mailed me that he had told his son that I was one of his favourite people because of our shared beliefs around animal liberation.

Interestingly, in 1993, I wrote a similar article on spec for *The Humanist in Canada* magazine as an alert to speciesism and a call for trans-species activism, transcending the food chain hierarchy by linking the oppression of humans and animals. American ethologist/psychologist Dr. Gay A. Bradshaw founded trans-species psychology[17] (a subdiscipline of psychology and ethology[18]), researching cognitive and emotional commonalities in humans and animals. I never completed my article: perhaps cynicism got the better of me? I had also penned a poem on the rights of our animal co-tenants on planet Earth, and sent it to Canada's own lesbian, country singer k.d. lang—a vegetarian animal liberationist—hoping that she might adapt it to music: but, to my disappointment, she never responded. Too bad, it might have been a catchy chart topper and a positive blow for animal rights!

Essentially, animal liberation and environmental activism (termed deep ecology when the two are intersected) derive from the intuitive philosophies of ecofeminism,[19] environmentally engaged Buddhism, and the direct sensory experience of Zen Buddhist and Taoist practice. Ecofeminism can alternatively manifest as mystical religion, empirical science, or political activism—or an intersectional approach of all three. This deeper way of engaging with the world of primal nature (and of civilized culture) involves a radically inclusive, anti-oppression approach embracing humans and animals alike—with a particular focus on the female principle *(anima/yin)*. Also included are the plants, trees, rocks, and all of Mother Earth's elements (earth, water, fire, air). Zen Buddhism replaces air with wind, and adds a fifth element of space or void; Taoist elements include: wood, fire, earth, metal, and water. This ever-widening circle of compassion combines certain values of Native Earth Medicine, Taoism, Zen Buddhism, environmentally-engaged Buddhism, Hinduism, Jainism, Greek/Celtic paganism, humanist existentialism, ecofeminism, trans-speciesism, animal rights, ethical vegetarianism/veganism, deep ecology, and social democracy. Its proponents have periodically tried to come together as an intentional community—a galvanizing force ready to fight for our planet's survival and her underdogs.

French feminist Françoise d'Eaubonne coined the term "ecofeminism" in 1974. Other leading ecofeminist voices[20] from then up until now ring out from diverse women around the world, including Earth scientists, Buddhist ecophilosophers, Indigenous spiritual warriors, and African American activists. Black activist, Alice Walker sums it up nicely, "The animals of the world exist for their own reasons. They were not made for humans any more than Black people were made for White, or women created for men."[21]

An aspiring animal liberationist and eco-activist, this year (2017), I recently came upon a website[22] citing Mayan, Cree, Hopi, Sioux, and other prophecies of the rainbow warrior coming to reclaim Mother Earth. Disconcertingly, I found out that these so-called Rainbow Warrior prophecies do not derive from Indigenous legend, but were culturally appropriated by anti-Semitic, early Christian evangelical missionaries. Notwithstanding this post-colonialist cultural appropriation of Indigenous peoples, I'm still drawn to the descriptor, Rainbow Warriors—the colloquial name for Greenpeace activists and their fabled ship, not to mention LGBTTI2SQQAA activists referencing the rainbow flag: an intuitive intersectionality given the nature of oppression. Such interrelatedness is exemplified by activists like Calvin, Mirha-Soleil, Xanthra, and others who combine the fight for the rights of trans people (and/or sex workers) with those of animals.[23] A multi-issue political campaign was the original vision of gay/lesbian activists in the early 1970s—one that would also address (beyond queer rights and men's rights) the needs of women and children, Indigenous people, people of colour, people with disabilities, youth, and seniors, etc.—but, regrettably, this holistic commitment soon devolved to single issue sexual orientation causes, often eroding the needs of the gender community and others. Nevertheless, I laud authentic rainbow warriors' eco ethic and their call to action to save our dying planet. As Mother Earth's caring son, Rupert, the Rainbow Warrior, is ready to join the fight!

This way of being in the world resonates with a number of existential Outsiders—specifically, those empaths with an eco-conscience and a trans-planetary vision. These select few existential empaths[24] are numbered among society's visionaries, teachers, healers, wise fools, spirit warriors, peacemakers, life dancers, and world lovers. Happily, some are also LGBTTI2SQQAA folks. The rest of the world are part of the unthinking mass, extreme examples of what I've sardonically dubbed *"Homo unsapiens unsapiens."* As history has shown, these doubly unwise humans often become so (morally) complacent that they easily succumb to peer pressure or the newest fad, congealing into a mass hypnotic state of group think—akin to Hitlerian fascism or Stalinist communism—or religious cult frenzy—like

Peoples Temple leader Jim Jones's dictated mass suicide and homicide—or even (albeit to a much lesser extent), sexually-driven, pop celebrity worship, such as Elvis or Beatle mania.

Rather than moral complacency, a more enlightened way, I believe, is a paradigm shift to a worldwide system of anti-oppressive, radically inclusive, ecologically conscientious, existential humanist, feminist, pacifist, social-democratic, economically sustainable, communal society. This means a species inclusive, humanly diverse, passionately compassionate, democratic social system that forbids the oppression of either animals or people; condemns violence against transgender, genderqueer, intersex, *Hijra*, Two-Spirit, gay, lesbian, bisexual, pansexual, and asexual people; prohibits male circumcision, female genital mutilation, or surgical "correction" of indeterminate sex organs; and punishes all other abhorrent violations of people, animals (and trees). The foregoing abuses are typically based on either religious or scientific fundamentalism. The former type of fundamentalism implicate hypocritical religionists, the latter, pseudoscientists. Such a progressive society would be one that allows free enterprise with government sponsored social safety nets in place for its less fortunate members, and one that consistently works towards a sustainable economy, based on principles and practices of ethical vegetarianism/veganism and equality for both animals and people. As East Indian, ethical vegetarian activist Mahatma Gandhi asserted, "The greatness of a nation and its moral progress can be judged by the way its animals are treated."[25]

What I mean by an economically sustainable society goes even beyond traditional social democracy to an eco-conscientious one. In other words, a system of "eco-communalism"[26]—comprising a loose collection of semi-autonomous ecological communes like the connecting nodes on a spider web's concentric circles that would include our animal planetary co-tenants. These self-sufficient, agrarian micro-economies would ideally comprise an interdependent network of self-governing intentional communities or eco-collectives similar to Indigenous reserves, East Indian ashrams, Israeli kibbutzim, and Hippie/post-Hippie communes in North America, Europe, Australia, and New Zealand. The back-to-the-land movement has been recently revitalized by grassroots eco-activists around the world. The dawn of a new era? Perhaps. Of course, for this to work human beings must become humbler, wiser, and kinder—not only to our own kind, but also to animal kind. An incredible challenge for our anthropocentric species—but not an impossible one, if we make it our collective promise to planet Earth.[27]

But, back to the animals themselves. Respect and compassion, safety and comfort are their individual and collective right, not only as living organisms sharing our biosphere, but also often as endangered species, and as vulnerable creatures with perceptions and sensations. Let us listen to their voices and look into their eyes so that we might hear and see them, not as an abstract group, but as individuals with their own unique personalities. We commonly assign unique names and attribute individual personality traits to animal cartoon characters and stuffed toy animals, so why not do the same with real live, sensate creatures? Let's just be careful when anthropomorphizing because real life animals don't deserve to be maligned by the all too prevalent imposition of predominantly negative human behavioural traits. Certain animals, however, do share some traits (and some positive ones) with humans.[28] Our responsibility, as the more powerful, reasoning, and supposedly morally enlightened species, is the task of collaborative stewardship of the animal and plant world. It is our sacred duty to preserve and protect our animal earthlings, not a libertine license to wantonly abuse our power, raping and pillaging Mother Earth! New Zealand recently officially recognized animals as sentient beings by amending animal welfare legislation, including a ban on the use of animals for cosmetic testing. A milestone breakthrough for animal rights!

You might think that I am elitist and self-righteous, and you are absolutely right! Yet, I'm one of the most eclectic, diverse, all-inclusive, dialectical elitists on Earth. Like Maya Angelou, "I have no modesty, none...What I hope I have...is humility."[29] My elitism transcends intellectual egotism as I purposefully craft a moral blueprint, following my unique existential life path, striving to practice the principles I espouse. A man of conviction? Absolutely! As an imperfect (flawed) human being, I do not always rise to my higher (ideal) self: yet, I never lose sight of my ideals. We must all take ourselves to task—gently but firmly—when behaving badly as a doubly-unwise human species: acting aggressively not only towards our own kind, but also committing cruel acts against our animal co-earthlings. We need to evolve towards a more advanced species: curious humane beings open to understanding more about, and sharing more with, all creatures: spiders and snakes, seahorses, sharks, seagulls, and swans. Following Gandhi's practice of *ahimsa* (non-violence), we must strive to peacefully co-exist with all living, feeling organisms (and all earthly elements) in a spirit of cooperation.

The inspiration for my eco-consciousness (and eco-conscience) largely derives from British chemist Dr. James Lovelock's Gaia principle,[30] a radical, Earth systems theory formulated in the 1970s and, subsequently, proven and co-developed with American geoscientist/microbiologist, Dr. Lynn Margulis,[31] and from Austrian-American physicist/deep ecologist, Fritjof Capra's living systems theory.[32] The Gaia principle postulates that organisms interact with their inorganic surroundings to form a self-regulating, complex system that contributes to maintaining conditions for life on our planet: ergo, the name "Gaia" after the mythical, Greek, primordial deity believed to personify our planet; hence known as Mother Earth. Lovelock's hypothesis—originally blocked by the academic apartheid of fundamentalist scientists—is intriguing in its intuitive approach to the interconnectedness of life on earth. All the elements within our biosphere are planetary players in the game of life. When I first became an ethical vegetarian in 1991, I read about the revolutionary Earth science of Gaia, but I never had time to pursue this line of inquiry until now.

In my retirement, I can devote myself to the quest for knowledge, delving into science (quantum physics, brain neuroplasticity, evolutionary biology, psychology, sociology, anthropology), religion (Taoism, Buddhism, Zen, Sufism, Kabbalism, Native spirituality/Earth medicine), and philosophy (ethics, logic, metaphysics, epistemology, phenomenology, existentialism, secular humanism, ecofeminism). Ever the truth-seeker, my integrative approach to truth embraces west and east, synthesizing my own brands of humanist-socialist ecofeminism and socially/environmentally engaged Buddhism.

My interest in the latter was inspired by Allan Badiner's *Dharma Gaia: A Harvest of Essays in Buddhism and Ecology* (1990), and Ken Jones's *The New Social Face of Buddhism: A Call to Action* (2003). Welsh Buddhist activist, Jones, compares socially and environmentally engaged Buddhists' mindful market economy to British economist Ernst Schumacher's 1973 green model.[33] He also references the Buddhist metaphor of Indra's net (cosmic interpenetration), which materialized as Gandhi's network of village republics. Jones also cites the Buddhist Soka Gakkai International's Earth Charter: "To eradicate poverty and promote social justice and a culture of peace and ecological sustainability."[34]

An aspiring eco-activist, I'm expanding my knowledge even further by reading the works of American ecophilosopher/Buddhist scholar Joanna Macy[35] and other activists who approach deep ecology intersectionally, incorporating ecofeminism, Earth science (Gaia), environmentally engaged Buddhism, and/or Native spirituality (Earth medicine) across cultures and countries, traversing east and west. I'm joining these auspicious Rainbow Warriors as I walk my own path of Dr. Arrien's Four-Fold Way®. This year (2017), I started attending some ethical eating and eco-conscientious events, such as local vegetarian/vegan food festivals and environmental action activities. Responsible engagement (ecological stewardship) is the essential dynamic for fruitful inter-human and inter-species relations.

Turning 65 (when I first wrote this chapter in February 2017), I'm taking stock of my life: where I've been, where I am now and where I'd like to go from here. As well as some remaining life goals, I have some lingering resentments—as the angry older man—embittered by the past but also many things for which to be grateful—as the mellowing older man—hoping for a brighter future. Sometime ago, I designed a therapeutic tool for my clients: an Emotional Life Ledger, balancing regrets/resentments on the left side of the worksheet, with contrasting "gratitudes/appreciations" on the right. I also use this ledger myself, employing this dual perspective of negative and positive to record my own emotional life milestones: facts and feelings pertaining to family, friends, partners, and pets, as well as vocational, academic, clinical, and community advocacy matters. In this way, each disappointment/dissatisfaction is counterbalanced by a concomitant contentment/satisfaction, thereby providing the pivotal counterpoint for the dialectical dance of life. This visual record of life events (facts) and corresponding emotional reactions (feelings) help me maintain a realistic perspective as I review my life objectively, giving me the courage and commitment, the determination and drive to persevere despite ongoing challenges, and to hopefully fulfill my outstanding goals.

Inspired by Alice Walker's "The Gospel According to Shug,"[36] I drafted my own Guiding Life Directives:

1. Be passionate about life and compassionate toward all life forms.
2. Always operate in good faith, and try to live your life authentically.
3. Exude a generosity of spirit and, whenever possible, forgive, even if you can't forget.
4. Resist oppression creatively, embracing vulnerability *and* resilience and, whenever possible, without violence.
5. Laugh and cry often to dissipate righteous rage and dark despair, benefitting from the healing balm of humour and the cleansing catharsis of tears.
6. Entertain a healthy cynicism, exulting in gently sardonic humour, never letting cruelty crush kindness. But temper cynicism with optimistic realism, reckoning the risks versus the rewards, the losses against the gains.
7. Be grateful for the positives in life (oneself, other people, animals, Mother Earth, adequate food and shelter, relatively good health, enough money to survive, creative diversions), and try not to focus on regrets and resentments.
8. When feeling hopeless in the moment, keep faith that hope will soon return.
9. Harness the transformative power of the collective unconscious, invoking archetypal rituals, symbols and metaphors (like the fiery phoenix and others), using whatever works for you.

10. Effectively balance all three minds: reasonable mind (logic), emotional mind (feelings), and wise mind (intuition).
11. Move strategically from head (thoughts), to heart (feelings) to feet (actions), being mindful of the ethical sequence of intentions to actions to impacts.
12. Realize the full potential of all dimensions of your identity: visionary, teacher, healer, and warrior (per The Four-Fold Way®) as they might apply to you.
13. Be humble, as we share this planet with all other species, ever-mindful in our co-stewardship of Mother Earth and all her sentient beings to exercise our power benevolently, according to our eco-conscience.

Ideally, these moral directives, based on my core beliefs and values, will help me to become a better person and a more evolved sentient being, guiding me through life as I strive to live my truths according to my eco-conscience. And, on a very modest scale, I am hoping to become a Rainbow Warrior, volunteering with Animals International and Greenpeace International. I might even write a book on animal liberation, ethical eating, and eco-activism. The ink in my veins is still flowing. Was I born to write, to work, to teach, to fight, and to heal? Absolutely! My life mission is to offer the world a vision, humble perhaps but, hopefully, inspiring. As stated earlier, my inspiration partly springs from fellow atheist visionary, John Lennon, whose signature song is indelibly engraved on my imagination.

One of my original goals upon retiring was to immigrate to Australia (sponsored by my dual-citizen partner) because KJ and I abhor the harsh Canadian winters. Aussies are progressive around rights for queer, trans, and intersex people. They also boast a vital animal liberationist community and I was looking forward to volunteering with Animals Australia and Greenpeace Australia. Alas, our hopes were dashed as our 2015 application was denied in early 2016. KJ and I were naturally disappointed; but suspected as much because my advanced age, multiple health issues, and disability pensioner status made me a poor candidate, a potential burden on the system. We decided not to appeal because of time, money, and poor chances for success. Instead, we seriously considered moving to Vancouver as we both love BC and the west coast—and it would be close to my sister in Victoria and also to San Francisco. But, we soon abandoned this idea because of the excessive house prices there and the cool, wet winters. California should have gone to Canada in an idealized, more equitable longitudinal split when the continent was divided up as there's no place here that's hot all year round. "Trumpland," of course, was out of the question: so, we finally decided to move to Mexico as

KJ was fluent in Spanish (a real asset) and I would soon pick up the language. July 31 was our targeted moving date to our new frontier land.

It would be a clean break from both Canada and the USA—except for the occasional excursion to Victoria or Vancouver, or Seattle, Portland or San Francisco—and a final farewell to the trans/queer community insofar as I intend to go stealth from now on. I am so relieved to finally be giving up being a trans poster-boy for nearly 50 years! If someone happened to see me on Wikipedia and commented on my trans status, I would respectfully ask them to keep my trans and queer identities discrete, explaining that that was my former life and avocation as a community activist, gender consultant, and mental health practitioner, but that my present life now focusses on the other aspects of my multifaceted identity: cultural explorer (travelling anthropologist) and Rainbow Warrior (ecological activist/animal liberationist)—and, of course, a continuation of my lifelong identity as Dialectical Dancer (existential Outsider). Not wishing to be the typical, post-colonialist capitalist exploiter, my partner and I want to give back to the Latin American community as new immigrants, offering our time and talents as appropriate: volunteering in an animal rescue shelter, working in a community garden, reading to elderly shut-ins, teaching local residents English, or whatever seems right.

My home for nearly 40 years, I will certainly miss Toronto (the most diverse city in the world), but I have now outgrown this too Americanized megapolis. I need a change of pace and scenery—and a break from both party and identity politics! Still, I will miss Canada, my homeland for 65 years. I am hoping my Canadian and American friends and fellow trans community members will be gracious enough to let me go with their blessing as this is my time to travel to the next milestone on my life journey—my next rite of passage. Now, officially off the clock as Gender Worker, I'm morphing into Rainbow Warrior with my fellow eco-warrior, KJ, who, like me, prefers animals to humans. And, we both revere Mother Earth.

If San Francisco was not part of the USA—progressive oasis that it is and still a haven for trans and queer folks—KJ and I would move there in a heartbeat, despite the damp cool winters. Even so, Mexico seems like a viable alternative with opportunities for new adventures, and travels throughout Latin America. In consolation, however, we decided to treat ourselves to a second honeymoon and get married in San Francisco, keeping it a secret from everyone except for my sister as we prefer our privacy. So, in mid-May, after a year and a half apart (while KJ was caring for her elderly friend in Australia), we were reunited once more in San Francisco, so happy to be together again. On May 18, 2017, we were wed in a low-key civil ceremony at San Francisco's city hall with only the Commissioner of Oaths present. Dressed down in jeans, this was merely a formality to confirm our five-year union, but still a semi-public ritual allowing us to reaffirm our vows of love and loyalty. A romantic reunion by the Bay was our much needed respite from all the logistics of managing an 18 month long-distance relationship—and a rebalancing of romance versus realism! We also had a delightful dinner with my charming-as-ever friend, Jamison Green, and his lovely wife, Heidi.

But, work (realism) must come before play (romance) and I first had to take care of business: listing our house for sale, packing our possessions, and putting the first edition of this memoir to bed.

As for the latter, I suffered lots of sleepless nights throughout the course of that book project: firstly, my initial publisher was not being up front with me around estimated timelines. Even though I had informed him at the outset of my need to publish before my scheduled moving date, he still left me hanging for eight months. On top of this, he was dissatisfied with a proposed photograph of me for the book's front cover (over which I lost the trust of a long-time photographer friend). Feeling let down and running out of time, I ultimately cancelled our publishing contract, opting to self-publish through Amazon's CreateSpace. This last minute decision actually allowed me to exceed the original publisher's 70,000 word limit and return to the original 100,000 word count, thereby providing me the opportunity to elaborate further on selected people, important events, and relevant resources, as well as particular points of philosophy, psychology, anthropology, mythology, religion, spirituality, gender, sexuality, feminism, deep ecology, ecofeminism, environmentally engaged Buddhism, Native Earth medicine, and animal liberation. I was also able to add an extensive, cross-referenced bibliography for the edification of my readers (the librarian in me). Essentially, this is what my original creative vision was: an existential intellectual autobiography along the lines of those written by serious existential philosophers Hazel Barnes[37] and Colin Wilson,[38] and zany, Zen Buddhist philosopher Alan Watts[39]—with trans activism and animal liberation thrown into the mix. So far, so good, but then, to my dismay, my laptop crashed just as I was about to send off my manuscript to selected trans activists, asking each one to write a testimonial to help me promote my book. The perils of publishing! Not to mention the stress this put on relations with my partner, frustrated as she also was with the whole process. There's no glamour or money in writing, only blood, sweat, and tears!

Self-determinist that I am though, not relying on gods/goddesses or the Fates to solve my problems, I did some furious fast dancing, exerting brain and brawn to fulfill all my tasks in a timely manner—without going mad—as I could not afford a recurrence of the mental breakdown I had recently suffered. So, I paced myself, breaking things down incrementally. Focussing with my wise mind (aka the third eye)—the intuitive mind overarching our reasonable mind (left brain) and our emotional mind (right brain) (as if perched on top of a triangle), I was able to envision the entire reactive process from concept to completion. I continuously dance the dialectic between my thinking left brain (the psychologist and anthropologist in me) and my feeling right brain (the psychotherapist and activist in me), often hovering in my insightful overarching brain (the philosopher and would-be mystic in me). The unfixed, dynamic writer, editor, and poet in me traverses all three. I wholeheartedly recommend this interactive three-mind model, which forms the essence of Dialectical Behavioral Therapy (DBT).[40] This tripart model of change provides an effective strategy to help one reduce debilitating anxiety or sense of "stuckness" by switching one's perspective from a problem focussed one to a solution focussed one in a dynamic way (usually over time). But the problem solving part (logical thinking) only comes after first taking the time needed to sit mindfully with one's problematic feelings, without moral judgement or critical discernment as in mindfulness meditative practice. The next stage of the DBT process invokes the wise mind: helping to soothe one's troubled emotions by trusting one's gut instinct (intuition) that one can positively change one's attitude or behaviour (or achieve one's desired goal), over time, while still allowing myself to have some lingering self doubts. Buddhists call this skillful practice, but, in their case, a person's wise mind would trust in the Universal Mind or cosmic consciousness. This dialectical dynamic of dancing between the polar opposites—while centring myself in the middle as needed— is what saves me from monotony and madness. Ergo, the Dialectical Dancer.

Dancing the dialectic, spinning at the centre like some dizzying whirling dervish, I embrace the tension of polar opposites (cynical despair and rage versus optimistic, realistic hope and compassion), ever-striving for the Middle Way: the Zen zone of and/or, both/neither. Ambivalence personified. Multidimensional man…pangender pansexual person…Rupert, the growly bear (but cute and cuddly too). Ultimately, my self-determinism and eco-existential vision, my persistence and creative resistance, have enabled me to fulfill many life goals. Over my lifespan, I have been a Dialectical Dancer; Gender Worker; Therapeutic Healer, Teacher and Writer; and, now, a Rainbow Warrior; integrating all aspects of my self per The Four-Fold Way®. Self-made man, sentient being, child of Mother Earth. As a responsible human being among all the other species co-inhabiting Mother Earth (Gaia), I have deliberate intentions, resulting in specific actions, which have variable impacts not only on myself but on all other life forms in our interconnected eco-system.

I'm now closing this word dance with a plea to you, dear reader. Please be kind to all creatures, great and small, and to our planet Earth (aka Turtle Island in Indigenous tradition).

I'm also passing along some parting words of encouragement. When dreading those dark nights of the soul—so lost and alone—take heart, fellow life sojourner. Dig deep down into your core and draw up from that well of loneliness the courage and compassion waiting there to light a flame of faith and hope. And if the flickering flame should fail, "Don't curse the darkness, relight the candle" (to paraphrase the wise old Zen monks). And as the new flame burns brighter and brighter, take heart in the traditional Inuit blessing: "May you always have warmth in your igloo, oil in your lamp, and peace in your heart."

Chapter 12 Notes

[1] Ander Negrazis is quoted here. http://www.holdingittogether.com/about-ander-negrazis/. Trans woman, Martine Stonehouse, is also autistic and believes there is a link between autism and crossgender identity. Trans man, Dr. Jake Pyne, is researching the intersection of autistic and transgender life and the implications for our understanding of "humanness." https://news.uoguelph.ca/2019/09/u-of-g-researcher-wins-top-sshrc-award/.

[2] My abstract, which I had submitted in 2016 for presentation at the October 2017 CPATH (Canadian Professional Association for Transgender Health) conference, was accepted in March 2017, but regrettably, I had to decline as I would be fully retired by then, hopefully living the good life in Mexico. As it turned out, I was able to rework my proposed paper ("Vulnerability & Resilience Across the Lifespan: A Trans Elder's 'Dialectical Dance' from Trans Youth to Trans Activist, Therapist, Trainer & Writer") and present it at the 2018 Moving Trans History Forward Transgender Archives Conference. https://www.uvic.ca/mthf (click "Past Conferences" tab, then "Program" tab, then "Saturday, March 24, 2018 tab," then scroll down to Concurrent Sessions: Session 23").

[3] Gentile, Patrizia, Gary Kinsman, and Pauline L. Rankin, eds., *We Still Demand! Redefining Resistance in Sex and Gender Struggles*, Vancouver, BC: UBC Press, 2017.

[4] See pages 117-136 for Nick's chapter on me. I have deliberately tried to refrain from publicly shaming (by withholding their real names) most of the trans activists critiqued in this memoir for their past transgressions—only calling into account (by name) two transsexual activists (Dr. Tony Tornabene [Mario Martino] and Susan Huxford-Westall), and two non-transsexual transgender activists ([Diane] Leslie Feinberg and Dr. Virginia [Charles] Prince). So, too, Nick Matte had no intention of publicly "calling me out" when he set out to write this chapter, and indeed, tried to be objective and fair overall. Nonetheless, I wish that, as a fellow trans activist, he had let me know, at the outset, that he had unearthed some controversial published writings by, and about, Tony, Virginia, Leslie, and me. Moreover, I wish that Nick had invited me to take part in a primary-source (retrospective) oral trans history recorded interview—to ensure a robust sociopoliticosexual historical research methodology of gender and sexual identity politics that, while focussing on the 1980s, also overviews the 1970s, 1990s and early 2000s—so that I could have, retrospectively, put into perspective my space-and-time limited words and actions (and those of the others noted above) by offering a context and rationale (in my own words) for my now-regrettable, printed words about trans men and trans women, respectively. That way, (while still owning my past culpability), I could still save face by clearly demonstrating that I had evolved in my trans identity politics soon afterwards, and I was now anything but classist, heterosexist, sexist or transmisogynist.

I further wish that Nick had provided me with a draft copy of his chapter to check for factual accuracy insofar as there were several minor errors (mostly dates) pertaining to FACT/*Gender Review* and MMRF/*Metamorphosis*, as well as an incomprehensible reduction of my then almost 46 years of trans activism to a mere 25 in the last sentence. Finally, I also wish that, in this final sentence, when Nick sums me up by stating that I "had been framing and reframing transnormativities, trans communities and trans politics for over twenty-five years," he had referenced my chapter, "Zening the Art of Trans Activism" (Irving and Raj, 85-91), in which I had outlined a series of key components of effective trans advocacy in dedicated subsections. For example, in the subsection, "Anti-Oppression" (Irving and Raj, 88-

89) I wrote about the systemic oppression of trans people, cisgender privilege and power relations, as well as the intersectionality of identities and issues—and recommended a series of anti-oppression principles and practices. Reviewing it now in 2019, I wish I had enriched this subsection by providing specific examples of anti-oppression.

[5] For example, why was I never rated good enough to make the front cover of *Xtra: Toronto's Gay & Liberation News*—although I did make it into the "bowels" of the paper at least half a dozen times—or at least earn an entry in its last print issue (#791, February 19-March 4, 2015). This final issue featured a number of local trans and queer activists—but none of them had been active as long as me—except for longtime queer and AIDS activist, Tim McCaskell, who has twice before been a co-panelist with me—and some of the newbies had only been around for five minutes! Media representation is not always about merit, credibility or longevity—often favouring instead a youthful pose, a pretty face or a sexy story—but rarely an older person (even a community Elder), no matter how substantial their contribution over countless years! Perhaps Canadians (and other non-Americans) should compile an annual list of Trans 100, like the one started in the USA in 2013 to honour living trans activists, including those doing good work behind the scenes without any formal recognition.

And, in terms of American trans erasure, why didn't I rate highly enough to earn the IFGE Trinity Award even though I had served on IFGE's Steering Committee and Board of Directors from 1983 to 1988, and had been a transgender trailblazer not only in Canada, but also in the USA (by virtue of my North American reach and international scope)? And why wasn't I invited to deliver a keynote address at the Seattle Gender Odyssey Conference despite my recent repeated requests to the conference organizer as a mixed-race Trans Elder?

Moreover, why are my trans-related publications and video/TV appearances rarely cited in works by other trans activists, academics, and clinicians? Bitter grapes? You bet! Hopefully, though, by writing this memoir, I can try to let go.

In fact, I did manage to partly let go when I finally met Gender Odyssey conference organizer, Aidan Key, at the 2018 Moving Trans History Forward (MTHF) Transgender Archives conference, where we had a healing dialogue just minutes before his talk as part of the Elders Panel (https://www.uvic.ca/mthf—click "Past Conferences" tab. He bought a copy of my memoir and to show my appreciation for his considerable work with trans youth and their families over the years—and especially, his gratifying relationship repair with me—I invited him to put on an interactive training workshop with me at the next MTHF conference around creating strategies towards resolving tensions/conflicts among trans activists. Disappointingly, however, he had to decline because of multiple prior commitments. The tragic reality, even today, of being a non-mainstream activist: inevitably spread too thin with the risk of burnout ever immanent! See Aidan's co-authored publications: Mayo, Cris, Scott Gust, and Aidan Key, "Transgender Student Advocacy and Support: Evolving Ethics in a Time of Devolving Policy," *Groundworks: A Publication of the Philosophy of Education Society Committee on Professional Affairs*, 2017. https://www.philosophyofeducation.org/publications; and Olson, Kristina R., Aidan C. Key, and Nicholas R. Eaton, "Gender Cognition in Transgender Children," *Psychological Science*, 26 (4): 467–474, 2015.

[6] Of course, I had been briefly mentioned (and/or my works cited) in previous books by fellow transgender activists, Dr. Aaron Devor, Dr. Jamison Green, Dr. Brice D. Smith and Dr. Susan Stryker, and by cisgender researchers, Dr. Darryl Hill and Arlene Istar Lev. I had also been profiled, in the past, in a number of trans periodicals, including (more recently) *Original Plumbing: Trans Male Quarterly Magazine*, (The Hero Issue), Spring 2013, the *FTM International Newsletter* (Winter 2001, 13), and the *Zenith Digest*, 1999, 7 (6): 1, 10, as well

as a couple of cisgender, queer periodicals: *QA: The Queer Archivist*, Canadian Lesbian and Gay Archives (now The ArQuives), 2009, 8-10; and *PinkPlayMags* "Springplay!" Spring 2017, 11-14.

[7] The book's title was inspired by a 1962 ballad sung by African American, R&B singer, "Little Jackie Shane," a femmy gay man-cum-trans woman, who used to come up from the USA to perform at the Sapphire Tavern and other venues in Toronto in the 1960s and early 1970s (see: Maynard, Steven, "Introduction: 'A New Way of Lovin': Queer Toronto Gets Schooled by Jackie Shane," in John Lorinc et al, *Any Other Way*, 11-110).

[8] I'm alluding here to the title of her memoir, *Change for the Better: A Story of Georgina Beyer*, Auckland, NZ: Random House (NZ), 1999.

[9] Joshua Goldberg co-created the Vancouver Coastal Health's Transgender Health Program in 2003 following the closure of Vancouver General Hospital's Gender Dysphoria Clinic, headed by psychiatrist, Dr. Diane Watson, in 2002.

[10] Some ethical vegans/vegetarians critique ethical pescetarians as being hypocritical because they're still eating animal flesh. Perhaps they're right, and I'm hoping, one day, to give up seafood, thereby dispelling my conflictedness. For this form of non-meat diet, see https://en.wikipedia.org/wiki/Pescetarianism.

[11] Ross, Mirha-Soleil, and Mark Karbusicky, dirs., *Yapping Out Loud: Contagious Thoughts from an Unrepentant Whore*, Toronto, ON: Vtape, 2002. http://www.vtape.org/video?vi=5043.

[12] For halal, kosher, and other forms of ritual animal slaughter, see https://en.wikipedia.org/wiki/Ritual_slaughter.

[13] Neufeld, Calvin, "Choosing Better than Oppression," in Irving and Raj, *Trans Activism in Canada*, 103-108.

[14] For the Suffering Eyes farmed-animal sanctuary project, see www.sufferingeyes.com/.

[15] For the Evolve our Prison Farms' Joyceville Institution prisoner survey, see https://evolveourprisonfarms.ca/prisoner/.

[16] Watch trans/animal rights activist, Calvin Neufeld, and Canadian zoologist/eco-activist, Dr. David Suzuki on TV on February 26, 2019. https://www.youtube.com/watch?v=aMycz95kFHw&feature=youtu.be&fbclid=IwAR2h_2KORBmbXeXybsl5cKZp3QftrByJMBUmGNn8bs2jgB8PNUB5gIol1.

[17] See: Bradshaw, Gay A., *Elephant Trauma and Recovery: From Human Violence to Trans-Species Psychology*, Santa Barbara, CA: Pacifica Graduate Institute, 2005. See also https://en.wikipedia.org/wiki/Trans-species_psychology.

[18] Ethology is the scientific and objective study of animal behaviour, usually under natural conditions, which is viewed as an evolutionary adaptive trait. Comparative psychology also studies animal behaviour, specifically in the context of what is known about human

psychology. In contrast, ethology researches animal behaviour in the context of what is known about animal anatomy, physiology, neurobiology, and phylogenetic history. I firmly believe that such core learnings as psychology (the study of human behaviour), comparative psychology and ethology should be introduced to young minds in elementary school before anthropocentrism (a belief that humankind is the central or most important element of existence, above even God or animals) and anthropomorphism (the attribution of human characteristics or behaviour to a god, animal, or object) can warp their worldview of human and non-human animals and the false hierarchy (immoral imperative) that we humans unwisely (counter-intuitively) impose on often instinctively wiser animals!

[19] See: Diamond, Irene, and Gloria Feman Orenstein, eds., *Reweaving the World: The Emergence of Ecofeminism*, San Francisco, CA: Sierra Club Books, 1990; and Warren, Karen, and Nisvan Erkal, eds., *Ecofeminism: Women, Culture, Nature*, Bloomington, IN: Indiana University Press, 1997. See also https://en.wikipedia.org/wiki/Ecofeminism.

[20] These ecofeminists include: Vandana Shiva, Evan Bondi, Val Plumwood (formerly Routley), Greta Gaard, Petra Kelly, Rosemary Radford Ruether, Marie Mies, Sallie McFague, Charlene Spretnak, Starhawk, Buddhist ecophilosopher, Joanna Macy, Earth scientist, Dr. Lynn Margulis, Native spiritualist, Paula Gunn Allen, and (to some extent), African American activists, bell hooks and Alice Walker. Of course, men can also be ecofeminist, even if they don't employ this self-descriptor. Some prime examples include: Dr. Fritjof Capra, Tom Cho, Dr. James Lovelock, Dan Irving, Mark Karbusicky, Nick Matte, James Loewen, Calvin Neufeld, Jude Patton—and me.

[21] See Alice Walker's quote https://www.goodreads.com/quotes/20942-the-animals-of-the-world-exist-for-their-own-reasons.

[22] The original website (www.rainbowwarrior.org.uk/) can no longer be found. See https://en.wikipedia.org/wiki/Legend_of_the_Rainbow_Warriors.

[23] Sex worker activism is often intersected by such issues as poverty, homelessness, HIV/AIDS, drug addiction, and trauma induced by violence perpetrated by police, pimps and johns. A prime example of an intersectional activist is American, trans sex-worker activist Christine Tayleur, who served on the board of Community United Against Violence and was a representative on the San Francisco Task Force on Prostitution. She co-founded Transgender Nation (an offshoot of Queer Nation) in 1992. Many other sex worker activists also identify as transgender, intersex, *Hijra*, Two-Spirit or a woman of colour (namely, Sylvia Rivera, Mirha-Soleil Ross, Monica Forrester, Jamie Lee Hamilton, Elizabeth "Raven" James, Sandy Leo Laframboise, Georgina Beyer, A. Revathi, etc.). And, like Christine, they often focus on issues relating to transphobia, homophobia, misogyny, racism, anti-Indigeneity, violence, etc.

[24] One of the character traits of an empath is an affinity for nature. Although not all existential Outsiders might be empaths, in Aletheia Luna's book (co-authored with Mateo Sol), *Awakened Empath: The Ultimate Guide to Emotional, Psychological and Spiritual Healing* (self-published, 2017), she refers to empaths as "eternal outsiders who are in the world but not quite of the world," and writes of their "existential depression" (https://www.goodreads.com/review/show/2151779475), which definitely describes existential Outsiders.

[25] Mahatma Gandhi is quoted here. https://www.goodreads.com/quotes/search?q=gandhi+animals.

[26] My notion of eco-communalism (predicated on principles of ecology and social democracy) is not at all like Communism, given that the former's core principle is an anti-speciesist one, with equality for animals alongside humans as its primary aim, rather than an economic, anti-classist one solely for the benefit of human beings (specifically, the working class). American trans activist, Leslie Feinberg, was a lifelong member of the Marxist-Leninist Workers World Party (and a number of other trans people are Marxists). French existentialist-humanist philosophers, Albert Camus, Jean-Paul Sartre and Simone de Beauvoir, and American Black civil rights activists, Ralph Ellison and Richard Wright, all initially embraced communism in the 1950s, but eventually became disenchanted by its duplicitous and autocratic methods ("The means do not always justify the end."). See also https://en.wikipedia.org/wiki/Eco-communalism.

[27] Let's honour our living planet not only on Earth Day (April 22), but every day—by making a concerted effort to reduce our ecological footprint. To join the Earth Day Network, go to https://www.earthday.org/.

[28] See https://www.theguardian.com/science/2016/jan/15/anthropomorphism-danger-humans-animals-science.

[29] Quoted in Wagner-Martin, Linda, *Maya Angelou: Adventurous Spirit*, London, UK: Bloomsbury Publishing PLC, 2015. The full quote is: "I have no modesty, none. It's a waste of time. It's a learned affectation stuck on from without. If life slams the modest person against the wall, he or she will drop that modesty quicker than a stripper will drop her G-string. What I hope I have and what I pray for is humility. Humility comes from within."

[30] Read James Lovelock's books: *Gaia: A New Look at Life on Earth*, Oxford, UK: Oxford University Press, 1979; and *The Revenge of Gaia: Why the Earth Is – and How We Can Still Save Humanity*, London, UK: Allen Lane (Penguin Random House), 2006.

[31] See: Margulis, Lynn, *Symbiotic Planet: A New Look at Evolution*, New York, NY: Basic Books, 1998.

[32] See: Capra, Fritjof, *The Web of Life: A New Scientific Understanding of Living Systems*, New York, NY: Anchor Books, 1996.

[33] See: Schumacher, Ernst F., *Small Is Beautiful: Economics as if People Mattered*, New York, NY: Harper, 1989.

[34] See: Buddhist Soka Gakkai International (Buddhism in Action for Peace), "Earth Charter." http://www.sgi.org/resources/ngo-resources/education-for-sustainable-development/sgi-and-the-earth-charter.htm.

[35] See: Macy, Joanna, *World as Lover, World as Self: Courage for Global Justice and Ecological Renewal*, Berkeley, CA: Parallax Press, 1991.

[36] See: Walker, Alice, "The Gospel According to Shug," in Alice Walker's *The Temple of My Familiar*, San Diego, CA: Harcourt Brace Jovanovich, 1989, 287-289. See also

https://alicewalkersgarden.com/2019/04/the-gospel-according-to-shug-to-bless-is-to-help/.

[37] See: Barnes, Hazel E, *The Story I Tell Myself: A Venture in Existentialist Autobiography*. University of Chicago Press, 1997.

[38] See: Wilson, Colin, *Voyage to a Beginning: An Intellectual Autobiography*, London, UK: Cecil & Amelia Woolf, 1969; and *Dreaming to Some Purpose: An Autobiography*, London, UK: Century Publishing, 2004.

[39] See: Watts, Alan, *In My Own Way: An Autobiography*, New York, NY: Pantheon Books (Random House), 1972.

[40] The diagram of the three minds (schematized as two intersecting circles) is on one of the dialectical behavioral therapy (DBT) worksheets-at the back of Marsha Linehan's *Skills Training Manual for Treating Borderline Personality Disorder*, New York, NY: Guilford Press, 1993. For online images of the three minds, see https://www.solutionfocusedparenting.com/a-lesson-in-mindfulness-the-3-states-of-mind/; and http://vimms.info/worksheets/. For DBT skills training, see: https://en.wikibooks.org/wiki/Dialectical_Behavioral_Therapy/Core_Mindfulness_Skills/Wise_Mind/Experiencing_Integration_and_Intuition.

My international trans poetry anthology finally went online in 2017. The 2018 revised version is available on the Transgender Archives and the Digital Transgender Archive websites.

Canadian Centre for Gender & Sexual Diversity Director Jeremy Dias (R), with Ander Negrazis (C) pinning the Youth Role Model of the Year Award medallion on Rupert Raj at his 65th birthday/retirement party at The 519 Community Centre. Toronto, Ontario, 2017

The Canadian Centre for Gender & Sexual Diversity's Youth Role-Model-of-the-Year Award medallion.

Trans Rainbow Warriors: Rupert Raj and Canadian animal liberationist, Calvin Neufeld (R)—co-founder of the Suffering Eyes Project and the Evolve Our Prison Farms project—are committed to end farmed-animal suffering by choosing not to eat meat.

Epilogue (2017-2019)

The following is a chronological recap of selected events since the publication of the first edition of my memoir just over two years ago.

August - December 2017

August was an incredibly stressful time for both KJ and me. I was rushing to finish my memoir in time for my book launch, while in the midst of chaos: packing our things to move to Mexico, dealing with problematic bureaucrats at the Toronto Mexican Consulate, being harassed by a litigious sociopathic next door neighbour, coming down with a cold at the eleventh hour, and bidding farewell to our friends—and my home of 38 years. Caught in the centre of the cyclone!

A week after self-publishing the first edition of my memoir (August 15, 2017), I read excerpts from my book and sold signed copies at the Glad Day Bookshop in Toronto. About 35 people attended my book launch, which then ArQuives staff-member, Jade Pichette, moderated. This was my third book (the second of two within the year): another milestone for Rupert, the writer!

On August 31, having sold our bungalow in Toronto, we moved to Ajijic (a tiny resort town near Lake Chapala in Mexico). Soon after arriving there, I learned that my ex-partner Eugene (a fellow founder of FACT, who had used the pseudonym, Chris Black) had just died. Since publishing the first edition of my memoir, I also found out about the recent passing of two other Canadian trans activists I had known: Katherine Ann Johnson and Stephanie Castle (aka Sydney Heal). Departing American activists since that time have included Merissa Sherrill Lynn and, no doubt, others. Lots of loss of our transgender, genderqueer, intersex, *Hijra*, and Two-Spirit pioneers. At 66, I felt like I was living on borrowed time.

After spending two months (September and October 2017) in Mexico, we realized this was not a good fit for us. It was too chaotic, corrupt, unsafe, and too Americanized. Nevertheless, we did like some of the Mexican people and Canadian and American expatriates we met there. We befriended several. We also appreciated the Spanish language and Latinx cultural artwork and architecture, as well as some of the less raucous Mexican music and less spicy Mexican cuisine. So, on October 31, we moved back to Canada—to a new city (Vancouver, BC)—so glad to be home again! Now, living in the same province—"the best place on Earth" (according to the BC tourist slogan)—as my sister, we are able to visit Arjuna in Victoria much more often (and vice versa). In December, she saw the year out with us in our downtown Vancouver apartment.

January-December 2018

In February, after several weeks of house hunting in the rain or snow, KJ and I bought a townhouse in Vancouver, right by the Skytrain—very handy considering we don't have a car. By that time, I was too burnt out house hunting and setting up our new home to celebrate my 66th birthday with friends. So, KJ and I settled for a quiet lunch for two.

In March, I was able to present again at the Moving Trans History Forward conference at the University of Victoria, presided over by Dr. Aaron Devor, Chair in Transgender Studies, networking with fellow advocates and selling signed copies of my memoir. There, I was privileged to meet Margot Wilson (then retired University of Victoria associate professor emerita and founder of TransGender Publishing), who agreed to publish the second edition of my memoir. Trans elders—especially Canadians, who have been far less visible than our American neighbours—now have an enduring way to share their personal journey and life's work with trans youth and other aspiring gender activists. As referenced at the close of chapter 11, I'm proud to salute both Aaron and Margot for creating these three Canadian milestones: the world's first and only chair in transgender studies and the world's largest transgender archives (Aaron), and the sole transgender publishing company in Canada (Margot). I also fortuitously crossed paths (for the second time) with two fellow international trans historians (Englishwoman Christine Burns and Dutchman Alex Bakker), as well as several longtime American friends (Dallas Denny, Dr. J. Ari Kane, and Jude Patton) and befriended a fellow Vancouverite (M. Gayle Roberts).

On May 18, KJ and I marked the one-year anniversary of our marriage. To celebrate, we went on a combined Alaskan cruise and Yukon railway tour, exploring the American and Canadian northland. (Yukon Territory and Labrador are two of the only remaining relatively unspoiled frontier lands in North America).

In July, I was able to sell copies of the first edition of my memoir at Vancouver's Little Sister's Book & Art Emporium in the gay village. The bookstore was made famous in the 1999 cult film, *Better Than Chocolate,*[1] which relates the story of the banning of the store's lesbian pornographic books by Canada Customs and features a well-loved trans woman character named Judy. Although a much smaller turnout than my Toronto book signing, several of my local trans and cis friends came out to support me.

On August 20, 2018, I marked the 50th anniversary of the loss of my parents in a fatal automobile accident when I was 16 years old. In terms of family, I am now alone; except, thankfully, for my wife, KJ, my two siblings, Arjuna and Andrzej—and a few old and new friends.

In December, KJ and I celebrated our second winter equinox with my sister, who visited with us for a week. Although we don't celebrate Christmas, Chanukah, or Kwanzaa, we did enjoy the natural beauty of several nearby parks (including Stanley Park) and dined out at the all-vegan, South Asian restaurant/bakery/store, Sweet Cherubim, in downtown Vancouver—with dahl soup and chapattis, and spicy samosas to die for!

January - October 2019

In January, I started revising my memoir with Margot Wilson in order to produce this second edition for publication in 2020. I had originally planned to wait until I was 70, but then decided to go ahead and publish it two years earlier so that I could get it out to the world, and hopefully also academia (on the curricula of women's, gender, and sexuality studies) all that much sooner insofar as I wanted this second (expanded and updated) edition to be an educational resource for academics, educators, and students; a research aid for journalists, writers, and filmmakers; and a teaching tool for existing and aspiring gender identity activists and animal liberationists, respectively.

In February, KJ and I celebrated my 67th birthday with a few friends at a nearby Vancouver restaurant. Still a crazy Canuck after all these years!

In May, KJ and I took the Rocky Mountaineer tourist train, travelling through the Rockies from Vancouver to Kamloops, BC, then on to Lake Louise, Jasper, and Banff in Alberta. The majestic mountains and shimmering lakes were breathtaking! It was KJ's first time in Alberta and well worth the trip.

In early September, Arjuna celebrated her 65th pre-birthday with us in Vancouver. Happily, I've managed to preserve my close relationship with Arjuna over the many years since we were children. This is largely because we share many ecohumanist/ecofeminist values and traits (including reason, wisdom, and compassion), and a radical acceptance of, and loving kindness towards, all sentient beings, including people who are different (Outsiders) or disenfranchised (underdogs)—and animals. Unlike most of my American relatives, who often manifest a typical nationalistic narcissism, abrasive arrogance, and obnoxious conceit, my sister expresses an all too rare humility, empathy, and generosity of spirit.

Later, that month, KJ and I took a train trip to Seattle and Portland—two particularly progressive cities in the American northwest—our first time in each. My friend, John Helle Otto,[2] showed us some of the city sights of Seattle, but we never made it to the LGBTQ Center. Unfortunately, we also didn't get to see my fellow trans activists, Aidan Key and Jason Cromwell, who are both always super-busy! Lura Frazey[3] drove us around some of the neighbourhoods in Portland and took us to see the queer/trans Q Center. Regrettably, I forgot that my trans friend, Reid Vanderburgh, lived there or we would surely have called on him. We also paid a visit to Jamison and Heidi Bruin Green in Vancouver, Washington (just outside of Portland), where they had recently relocated from San Francisco. Jamison had just returned from a gender conference in Iceland—another committed activist still on the go at 71!

Although KJ and I met many friendly people in both cities, we were appalled at how uninformed about Canada and Canadians many Americans are—considering that the two countries are geographical and cultural neighbours, if not political ones. Canada—although not utopic, and disconcertingly, becoming more Americanized—ranked #1 in 2018 and 2019 as the country with the best quality of life, and rated sixth out of 10 ethical destinations in the world in which to live, while the USA was critiqued as a "flawed democracy" for the past two years running.[4] No wonder a lot of American queer and trans emigrés are leaving their so-called God's country for greener pastures in Canada. I'm thankful that I have a number of ethically evolved American friends—Democrats, who actually put into practice the principles of democracy.

Now that we're both retired, KJ and I have time and money to travel, so our next trip will be to Spain and Portugal, but we'll be back in time for the Moving Trans History Forward conference in April 2020, where Margot and I will be launching this second edition of my memoir.

The following section continues this two-year recap in the form of a generic summary of certain aspects and actions of my Four-Fold nature since the first edition came out on August 15, 2017.

Dialectical Dancer (philosopher, psychologist, anthropologist)

A lifelong learner, I recently began re-reading a series of spiritual classics[5]: the *I Ching (The Book of Change),* the *Tao Te Ching (The Way)* by Lao Tzu, the *Dhammapada* by the Buddha, the writings on Zen Buddhism by Thich Nhat Hanh, and on Tibetan Buddhism by the Dalai Lama, Chögyam Trungpa, and Pema Chödrön, *The Prophet* by Kahlil Gibran, and the mystical poetry of Mevlâna Jalâluddin Rumi (the Persian Sufi mystic). Although I'm a secular naturalist (not a supernaturalist)—and am still inspired today by Einstein's classical physics[6] and Hawking's quantum physics,[7] and further enlightened by recent advances in parapsychology,[8] with its apparent affinity to quantum physics—both the scientist and the would be mystic (as well as the philosopher and poet) in me can appreciate the ancient, pre-scientific ways of wisdom. These wise ways are helping me to transform my chronic anxiety and anger to (more) compassion and loving kindness by means of a rhythmic dance of alternatively first letting in and then letting go of both positive and negative energy. This energy transfer is done through a mindfulness meditation practice: drawing into myself energy from the world out there and, then, releasing it back into the world again. I'm also appreciative of Chögyam Trungpa's optional method of secular enlightenment for non-religionists like me,[9] as well as the paradoxical works of Indian-British, irreligionist philosopher Jiddu Krishnamurti,[10] who transcended both religion and science. Overall, my inclination is to dance the dialectic amidst science, philosophy, and religion—roughly paralleling the three minds: reasonable mind (left brain), emotional mind (right brain), and wise mind (the intuitive third eye). My tripart mind trips the light fantastic as I re-visit Fritjof Capra's 1975 book[11] comparing western physics and eastern Taoism, and as I newly savour Thomas McFarlane's 2003 compilation of parallel sayings[12] by two of the world's wisest truth seekers: western physicist Albert Einstein and Prince Siddhartha Gautama (the Buddha).

Moreover, as I reread the dissenting works of certain other prominent people[13]—activists, philosophers, religionists, psychoanalysts, and psychologists—who were often ideologically at odds with one another and with their peers, I cherish both their (and my) all too rare human propensity for critical thinking, as well as our (less than universal) democratic rights for freedom of thought, speech, written words, and actions—as long as none of these contravene the basic human rights of others. This capacity to constructively critique our professional peers and fellow activists is also prevalent among sexual and gender rights activists, as well as ecological and animal rights advocates—too many to cite here.

An eclectic music-lover, I started to listen again to the music of acclaimed Canadian songwriter, singer, and musician, Loreena McKennitt, who pleasures our ears with the melodic sounds of Celtic, Mediterranean, world, and new-age music as she serenades us while playing the piano, harp, and accordion.

Gender Worker (trans activist, intersex, and Two-Spirit ally)
My advocacy on behalf of transgender, intersex, and Two-Spirit people over the past two years has been limited to writing (see below), presenting at the biennial Moving Trans History Forward conference, and networking with other activists in North America and Europe—either in person or by email—but not through Facebook as I have neither the time nor the inclination for social media. Notwithstanding, I did participate in a research study (see below), and in August 2019, I took part in a virtual roundtable on trans activism in Canada (past, present, and future) with Toronto *Xtra* senior editor Erica Lenti and Black trans activist, Tatiana Ferguson.[14] These days, I've simply not felt up to doing any other kind of work, such as political lobbying or direct action, and rarely attend any transgender, intersex, or Two-Spirit community events—the cumulative result of half a century of burnout! Even so, I contend that my intentional acts of researching, writing, publishing, presenting, networking (supporting other activists), and voting (against bigoted, religionist politicians) constitute worthwhile forms of advocacy.

Therapeutic Healer, Teacher, & Writer (former psychotherapist, gender consultant, researcher, educator/trainer, writer/editor)

Now retired, of course, I no longer practice psychotherapy. However, I still act, at times, as an informal gender consultant, researcher, and educator in various ways. In June 2018, I participated in the LGBTQ Aging Study, conducted by University of British Columbia kinesiology professor Dr. Laura Hurd Clarke, which surveyed the experiences of older trans and queer people in terms of their health, body functionality, and any discrimination due to age, sexual orientation, or gender identity.[15] And, as aforementioned, I presented at the Transgender Archives conferences in 2016 and 2018, and plan to again in 2020.

And, not surprisingly, I still write. In addition to revising my memoir, I recently finished writing a feature article[16] on the past 50 years of transgenderism in Canada—and its recent depsychopathologization in Europe—for the Canadian Centre for Gender and Sexual Diversity, as well as a chapter for each of three books for TransGender Publishing: *Glimmerings: Trans Elders Tell Their Stories* (edited by Margot Wilson and Aaron Devor), June 2019; *Unconditional Love: Stories of LGBTQ+ People and our Emotional Bonds with Companion Animals*; and *Life Trips: Navigating LGBTQ+ Aging, Illness, and End of Life Decisions* (the latter two, in progress, are edited by Jude Patton and Margot Wilson). My longtime activist friend since 1976, Jude responded to my last chapter submission in 2018 with a plea:

> *I just wish that we all lived in a world where whatever/whoever we are is valid—and to be celebrated. I think this is why you and I continue our work.*

Yes, Jude (now 79) and I (now 67) are two trans elders of a dying breed, still here, after all these years, making our mark on the world.

And, once again, I followed up with my professor friends, Elspeth Brown and Dan Irving, asking them if they were still going to nominate me for an honourary doctorate degree. Elspeth suggested Carleton University (my *alma mater*) as a better bet than the University of Toronto. It would be so validating if I were to win this prestigious honour. Given my prolific output of trans-focussed publications (newsletters/magazines, feature articles, information pamphlets, clinical research papers, book chapters, book anthologies, poetry compilations, and memoirs), numerous professional development training seminars, conference presentations, and community education workshops, as well as much print and broadcast media representation over the past 50 years, I should be a good candidate for such accreditation. Perhaps not quite as prodigious as some, my career was still fairly impressive for a non-academic!

Rainbow Warrior (eco-activism, animal liberation)

My eco-activist and animal liberation efforts are unfolding on a less energetic level than I had hoped for, partly due to age-related fatigue and cumulative stress from the past four transitional years—pre-retirement disability, moving to a new country and then back again (to a new province). Even so, I still subscribe to the Animals Australia, Greenpeace Canada, and other international animal rights mailing lists, and I attended a number of vegan festivals in Toronto and Vancouver over the last two years. And I have willed money to three animal welfare organizations to help carry on their good work on behalf of exploited factory farmed, research laboratory, and recreation/sport animals after our passing. To reduce the environmental burden on our already polluted planet, I have been researching two new cutting-edge, end-of-life alternatives to traditional burials and standard cremations: flameless/water cremation (biocremation) and human composting (green burial).[17]

My envisioned book on ecological activism/animal liberation still remains merely a vision (mapped out in my brain and tentatively sketched as a template on my computer) at this point, so I'll just have to see how this plays out, depending on my limited energy.

In any event, I'm pleased to say that I'm still maintaining my ethical pescetarianism. My diet consists of seafood (and I've occasionally eaten shrimp made from algae), and only "beyond meat" soya burgers, veggie dogs, and fake peperoni. Now, several major North American, fast-food chains are promoting these plant-based alternatives to meat products, including vegan beef, pork, and chicken,[18] and consumers can even order beyond meat products online from a new Vancouver-based, vegan company.[19] This is my ongoing commitment towards harm reduction in terms of eating flesh—one which does not require butchering farmed animals—and hopefully, one day, I'll go one step further and give up seafood too. And now, finally, cruelty-free "cultured," meat is being researched, produced, and sold in the USA, the UK, The Netherlands, Israel, and Australia. Cultured meat involves growing boneless meat in a test tube from the cells of a host animal. I fervently hope this cutting edge, new technology will, eventually, become the dominant form of meat production and consumption in the world, thereby decreasing the enslaving, torturing, and slaughtering of trillions of non-human sentient beings. And eventually, perhaps, this humane methodology will extend to growing cruelty free seafood. Oh, happy day!

Dear reader, my parting wish is that you will have passion for learning, living, and loving and that you will have compassion for all of Mother Earth's creatures, human and animal. Go gently!

Rupert Raj
October 1, 2019
Vancouver, BC

Epilogue Notes

[1] *Better Than Chocolate*, Anne Wheeler, dir., Peggy Thompson and Sharon McGowan, prods., 1999. Filmed in Vancouver, BC. Although the bookstore is not named in the film, it is listed in the credits. See https://en.wikipedia.org/wiki/Better_Than_Chocolate.

[2] See John Helle Otto (standing beside me) in the group photo of six trans men, taken at the March 2016 Moving Trans History Forward Transgender Archives conference in Victoria, BC—the last photo immediately following chapter 11.

[3] Cisgender ally, Lura Frazey, co-authored Lei Ming's life story, *Life Beyond My Body: A Transgender Journey to Manhood in China*, San Francisco, CA: Transgress Press, 2016.

[4] For Canada, see https://www.usnews.com/news/best-countries/quality-of-life-rankings; and https://www.google.com/search?q=10+most+ethical+countires&oq=10+most+ethical+countires&aqs=chrome..69i57j33.12969. For the USA, see https://www.washingtonpost.com/outlook/2019/03/05/why-is-american-democracy-danger/; and https://www.theguardian.com/commentisfree/2018/aug/07/american-democracy-crisis-trump-supreme-court.

[5] For full citations of these spiritual classics, see: Intersectional Bibliography.

[6] See: Einstein, Albert, and Leopold Infeld, *The Evolution of Physics: First Concepts to the Theories of Relativity and Quanta*, (translated from the German by Maurice Solovine), Paris, FR: Flammarion Group (Éditions Gallimard), 1938. Reprint, Amazon, 1983 (Kindle Edition).

[7] See: Hawking, Stephen, *The Theory of Everything: The Origin and Fate of the Universe*, Beverly Hills, CA: New Millennium Press, 1997.

[8] See: Broughton, Robert S., *Parapsychology: The Controversial Science*, New York, NY: Ballantine Books, 1991.

[9] See: Trungpa, Chögyam, "Secular Enlightenment," in Chögyam Trungpa, *The Pocket Chögyam Trungpa*, Boulder, CO: Shambhala Publications, 2017, 26.

[10] See: Krishnamurti, Jiddu, *The Core of the Teachings*, UK: Krishnamurti Foundation Trust Ltd., 1980. https://www.jkrishnamurti.org/about-core-teachings.

[11] Capra, Fritjof, *The Tao of Physics: An Exploration of the Parallels Between Modern Physics and Eastern Mysticism*, Boulder, CO: Shambhala Publications, 1975.

[12] McFarlane, Thomas, ed., *Einstein and Buddha: The Parallel Sayings*, Berkeley, CA: Ulysses Press, 2003.

[13] These dissenting thinkers and writers included: African American activists, James Baldwin and Richard Wright, French philosophers, Albert Camus and Jean-Paul Sartre, Russian religionists, Fyodor Dostoyevsky and Leo Tolstoy, and Austrian psychoanalysts, Sigmund Freud, Alfred Adler, and Viktor Frankl (of the third Viennese school of psychotherapy), and Swiss psychologist, Carl Jung.

[14] *Xtra* staff, "A Millennial and Senior Trans Activist Discuss the Future of Trans Advocacy in Canada: Rupert Raj and Tatiana Ferguson Talk Community Organization, Early and Late-Life Transition," Toronto, ON: *Xtra*, August 26, 2019. Part of a series ("Still Fighting") exploring the past 50 years of LGBTQ2 activism in Canada. https://www.dailyxtra.com/a-millennial-and-senior-trans-activist-discuss-the-future-of-trans-advocacy-in-canada-161344.

[15] For UBC Professor Laura Hurd Clarke's research project on older (65+) LGBTQ Canadians, see https://kin-lhc-research-group.sites.olt.ubc.ca/research-project/. She plans to publish at least three academic journal articles from the data and present the findings at various conferences.

[16] Raj, Rupert, "Depsychopathologizing Gender Diversity and Trans Healthcare in Canada," Ottawa, ON: Canadian Centre for Gender & Sexual Diversity, Sept. 10, 2019 (rev. Dec. 6, 2019), http://ccgsd-ccdgs.org/resources/. Since 2009, the international campaign to Stop Trans Pathologization (STP) has been fighting to normalize gender variance worldwide, decreeing October 21 as the International Day of Action for Trans Depathologization. See https://www.ncbi.nlm.nih.gov/pmc/articles/PMC6466167/; and http://tpathealth.org/tag/stp/. Since 2009, the international campaign to Stop Trans Pathologization (STP) has been fighting to normalize gender variance worldwide, decreeing October 21 as the International Day of Action for Trans Depathologization. See https://www.ncbi.nlm.nih.gov/pmc/articles/PMC6466167/; and http://tpathealth.org/tag/stp/.

[17] For biocremation, see https://en.wikipedia.org/wiki/Alkaline_hydrolysis_(body_disposal). For human composting, see https://globalnews.ca/news/5329686/human-composting-green-burial/.

[18] See which fast-food outlets are selling plant-based (beyond meat) products. https://www.buzzfeednews.com/article/summeranne/morality-didnt-turn-people-vegan-capitalism-might.

[19] To order online beyond meat (soya) vegan products, go to https://vegansupply.ca/collections/plantbase-food.

The first edition of my memoir, self-published in 2017.

Long-time friends came out for my book signing at Little Sister's Book & Art Emporium. (L-R): James Loewen, James Nattal, Rupert Raj, Jerry Van Zuuk and partner, Markku Vuorensivu.
Vancouver, BC, 2018

Rupert Raj with international delegates at the Moving Trans History Forward conference (L to R): Alex Bakker (The Netherlands)), Christine Burns (UK), and K.J. Rawson (USA).
Victoria, BC, 2018

Rupert Raj—with Brij Chopra (R), manager of Sweet Cherubim, an all-vegan Indian restaurant and natural foods store— just about to savour some spicy samosas!
Vancouver, BC, 2019

Appendix I

OF SOULS AND ROLES

Born was the child–
spirit of woman
body of man.

The child grew into role
while he gazed upon his soul.
"How can it be?
This is not me!"

Oh, wits of science
don't play with me!
Tell me now…
can this be?

"Look not upon the mind
for logic has no soul.
There is no peace
in an undesired role.

Look upon the heart–
see what there be.
Do not explain it
for it is thee."

And so, the journey begins…
a bumpy exchange of role
an inner peace–
the uniting of soul.
                    ~C. W. M. (1983)

* * *

SEX AND GENDER

Sex and gender
In the blender
Form is female
Matter is male:

Boy inside
Girl outside
Sexual rift
Gender Conflict!

Genes and gender
Do not render
One of a kind
Or peace of mind:

Female genes
In masculine jeans
The world's tomboy
Is an XX boy!

Sex and gender
Torn asunder
Body and soul
Strive to be whole:

Body image—masculine
Fleshly fact—feminine
To integrate is the goal
Gender identity and sex role!

Genitals and gender
Return first to send
Such loathsome gonads
Repulsive doo-dads!

Cunt and clit
And tacky tits
Trade them all
For cock and balls!

Sex and gender congruity
Through creative surgery
Eve's physical form
Into Adam transforms!
                              ~Rupert Raj (1990)

                    * * *

METAMORPHOSIS

There are several kinds of metamorphosis:
Franz Kafka's hero changing into an insect
Ovid's Greeks turning into trees or stars by hex
The butterfly emerging from its chrysalis
And the transsexual surgically changing sex.

This latter sexual transformation
Is, to me, by far the most dramatic
And causes the greatest news sensation
But it can also be quite traumatic!

For, family and friends might not comprehend
And employers and others might discriminate
And a transsexual might feel quite without a friend
"Cos sometimes love is overshadowed by hate.

Two years, at least, the TS transition
(a period of mixed pain and pleasure -
this so-trying time of rehabilitation)
Is the true test of success or failure.

Yet, it's all worth it in the final analysis
(despite the loneliness and stigmatization)
So, blossom forth from your restrictive chrysalis
And express your true gender identification.
                              ~Rupert Raj (1982)

The three foregoing poems are taken from Raj, Rupert, ed., "Of Souls & Roles, Of Sex & Gender: A Treasury of Transsexual, Transgenderist & Transvestic Verse from 1967 to 1991." Unpublished, Jan. 1, 2017, rev. July 1, 2018: Transgender Archives: https://www.uvic.ca/transgenderarchives/assets/docs/of-souls-0-rolesj-of-sex-0-gender-revised-july-1j-2018---numbered.pdf;
Digital Transgender Archive: https://www.digitaltransgenderarchive.net/files/hm50tr87t

Appendix II

THE BAMBOO TREE

*Bent by the wind, beaten by the rain,
yet the bamboo tree thrives—strong as steel.*

Human beings are both vulnerable and resilient…

*Vulnerability to suffering fosters our humility,
empathy, and compassion for ourselves and others.*

*Resilience helps us endure our pain, loss and grief,
while sustaining our courage, hope and faith.*

*Like the perennial bamboo, it is just this
dialectical tension that allows us to prevail.*
~Rupert Raj (2004, rev. 2017)

* * *

POWER OF THE HUMAN SPIRIT

*I'm forever in awe of the unlimited power of the Human Spirit
to overcome Life's adversities, time and time and time again.*

*May there always be wind in your sails
as you navigate the turbulent seas of Life.*

*And never give up Hope that you will reach
that seemingly far-off safe harbour one day soon.*
~Rupert Raj (2004)

DANCING TO THE BEAT OF A DIFFERENT DRUMMER

*If a man does not keep pace with his companions,
perhaps it is because he hears a different drummer.*

*Let him step to the music he hears,
however measured or far away.*

~Henry David Thoreau (1854)

* * *

*Like that independent thinker, Thoreau,
let us each pursue our personal quest to be true to ourself,
dancing to the beat of a different drummer.*

~Rupert Raj (2004, rev. 2017)

* * *

Intersectional Bibliography

This bibliography is roughly ordered according to each of the four parts of the book (Parts II and III combined), with some intersectional cross-referencing. Nationalities are identified in a few selected sections to make these often marginalized non-Americans (especially, Canadians) more visible, thereby providing a more international perspective. "Canadian," for example, can refer either to the author(s) or the subject(s). Racial ancestry is similarly indicated to offset a Caucasian centrism. "Indigenous," for example, can refer either to the editor(s) or the subject(s). Subpopulations (age-related or family-related, for example,) within the overall gender communities are categorized in certain sections to distinguish these specific age groups or family contexts. The categories follow as:

PART I: DIALECTICAL DANCER
    A. Anthropology/Mythology
    B. Religion/Spirituality
    C. Philosophy
    D. Psychology/Psychotherapy
    E. The Occult/Parapsychology
    F. Physics/Cosmology
    G. Existential (Auto)biography/Fiction
    H. Black & Brown (Auto)biography/Fiction

PART II: GENDER WORKER
PART III: THERAPEUTIC HEALER, TEACHER & WRITER
    A. Transsexual/Transvestite/Transgender
        1. Auto(biography)/Literature/Film/Media
        2. History/Sociology/Sexology
            a. Transsexualism/Transvestism/Transgenderism
            b. Transhomosexuality/Transbisexuality
        3. Trans Studies
        4. Feminism/Transfeminism
            a. Transphobic Feminism
            b. Transpositive Transfeminism
        5. Trans Activism
            a. General
            b. Trans Politicolegal/Human Rights
            c. Trans Liberation & Trade Unionism
            d. Trans Health Care Advocacy
            e. Trans Student Advocacy
            f. Police Services & the Trans Community
            g. (Trans) Prisoner Advocacy
            h. Trans Community Activism
            i. Transqueer Activists
            j. Trans Sex-Worker Activists
            k. Trans Female Sports Activists
            l. Trans Activists of Colour
            m. Indigenous Trans Activists
            n. Animal Rights Trans Activists
        6. Earlier Sexology/Psychomedicine
            a. Psychiatric Classifications of Gender Identity
            b. Gender Dysphoria/Gender Identity Disorder
            c. Transsexualism

            d. Transsexualism & Intersex
            e. Transgenderism
        7. Later Trans Health Care
            a. Psychiatric Classifications of Gender Identity
            b. Trans Care Guidelines
            c. Hormone Therapy for Trans Adults
            d. Hormone Therapy for Gender Non-Binary & Trans Teenagers
            e. Gender-Confirming Surgical Patient Care
            f. Gender Detransition/Retransition
            g. Mental Health Therapy/Addictions Counselling
            h. Sexual Health/HIV/AIDS
            i. Population-Based Public Health Research
            j. Trans Health Care Advocacy
            k. Health Insurance
        8. Gender Transitioning (female-to-male)
        9. Social Work
        10. Education
        11. Religion/Spirituality
        12. Cybernetics (transgenderism to transhumanism)
        13. Special Populations
            a. Trans & Queer Youth
            b. Trans & Queer Parents
            c. Trans & Queer Elders
            d. Transforming Partnerships
            e. Transforming Families
            f. Transgender Community
        14. Web-Based Organizations
B. Gender Non-Binary
        1. Androgynous People
        2. Genderqueer People
        3. Gender-Creative Kids/Teens
        4. Gender/Sexual Diversity
C. Intersex (differences of sex development)
        1. Intersex People
        2. Dual Identity, Trans-Intersex People
D. *Hijra* (South Asian)
        1. *Hijra* People
        2. Dual Identity, Trans-*Hijra* People
E. Two-Spirit (Indigenous)
        1. Two-Spirit People
        2. Dual Identity, Trans-Two-Spirit People
        3. Multiple Identity, Trans-Intersex-Two-Spirit People

F. Combined Populations
        1. Trans, Genderqueer & Queer Activists of Colour
        2. Trans, Intersex, Two-Spirit & Queer Elders
        3. LGBTTI2SQQAA People & Companion Animals
        4. LGBTTI2SQQAA Historical Anthologies
G. LGBTTI2SQQAA/Trans Archives & Digital Collaboratories

PART IV: RAINBOW WARRIOR
A. Ecofeminism/Gaia Earth Science/Environmentally-Engaged Buddhism/Native Spirituality
B. Eco-Activism/Animal Liberation/Trans-Species Psychology

* * *

PART I: DIALECTICAL DANCER
A. ANTHROPOLOGY/MYTHOLOGY
Allen, Paula Gunn. *The Sacred Hoop: Recovering the Feminine in American Indian Traditions.* Boston, MA: Beacon Press, 1986.
Campbell, Joseph. *The Masks of God.* Vol. I, *Primitive Mythology,* 1959, Vol. II, *Oriental Mythology,* 1962, Vol. III, *Occidental Mythology,* 1958, Vol. IV, *Creative Mythology,* 1968. New York, NY: Viking Press.

B. RELIGION/SPIRITUALITY
Arrien, Angeles. *The Four-Fold Way: Walking the Paths of the Warrior, Teacher, Healer and Visionary.* New York, NY: HarperCollins, 1993.
Badiner, Allan Hunt, ed. *Dharma Gaia: A Harvest of Essays in Buddhism and Ecology.* Berkeley, CA: Parallax Press, 1990.
Buber, Martin. *I And Thou.* New York, NY: Scribner's, 1937. Reprint, New York, NY: Continuum International Publishing, 2004.
Buddhist Soka Gakkai International (Buddhism in Action for Peace). "Earth Charter." http://www.sgi.org/resources/ngo-resources/education-for-sustainable-development/sgi-and-the-earth-charter.html.
Byrom, Thomas. *Dhammapada: The Sayings of the Buddha.* Boulder, CO: Shambhala Publications, 1993.
Capra, Fritjof. *The Tao of Physics: An Exploration of the Parallels Between Modern Physics and Eastern Mysticism.* Boulder, CO: Shambhala Publications, 1975.
Chödrön, Pema. *Awakening Loving-Kindness.* Boulder, CO: Shambhala Publications, 2017.
Cleary, Thomas, tr., *I Ching: The Book of Change.* Boulder, CO: Shambhala Publications, 1992.
Dalai Lama, with Howard Cutler. *The Art of Happiness: A Handbook for Living.* New York, NY: Riverhead Books, 1998.
Fromm, Erich. *Zen Buddhism and Psychoanalysis.* New York, NY: Harper, 1960.
Gibran, Kahlil. *The Prophet.* New York, NY: Alfred A. Knopf, 1923. Reprint, 2008.
Helminski, Kabir. *The Pocket Rumi.* Boulder, CO: Shambhala Publications, 2001. Poetry by Persian Sufi mystic, Mevlâna Jalâluddin Rumi.
Ilaiah, Kancha. *Why I Am Not a Hindu: A Sudra Critique of Hindutva Philosophy, Culture and Political Economy.* Kolkata, India: Samya Books, 1996.
James, William. *The Varieties of Religious Experience: A Study in Human Nature.* Harlow, UK: Longmans, Green & Co., 1902.
Jones, Ken. *The New Social Face of Buddhism: A Call to Action.* Somerville, MA: Wisdom Publications, 2003.
Jung, Carl G. *Psychology and Religion: West and East.* New York, NY: Pantheon Books, 1969.
Lao Tzu. *The Way of Life (Tao Te Ching).* Translated from the Chinese by R. B. Blakney. New York, NY: New American Library, 1955.
Maslow, Abraham H. *Religions, Values, and Peak Experiences.* Columbus, OH: Ohio State

University Press, 1964.
McFarlane, Thomas, ed., *Einstein and Buddha: The Parallel Sayings*. Berkeley, CA: Ulysses Press, 2003.
Nhat Hanh, Thich. *The Miracle of Mindfulness: An Introduction to the Practice of Meditation*. Boston, MA: Beacon Press, 1975.
Ross, Nancy Wilson, ed., *The World of Zen: An East-West Anthology*. New York, NY: Vintage Books, 1960.
Russell, Bertrand. *Why I Am Not a Christian* - and Other Essays on Religion and Related Subjects. Abingdon, UK: Routledge, 1927. Reprint, New York, NY: Touchstone Books (Simon & Schuster), 1957. Edited by Paul Edwards.
Sams, Jamie. *Earth Medicine: Ancestors' Ways of Harmony for Many Moons*. San Francisco, CA: HarperCollins, 1994.
Sand, Shlomo. *How I Stopped Being a Jew*. Brooklyn, NY: Verso Books, 2014.
Scholem, Gershom. *Kabbalah*. Philadelphia, PA: Jewish Publication Society, 1974.
Shah, Idries. *The Sufis*. London, UK: ISF Publishing, 1964.
Singh, Bhagat. *Why I Am an Atheist*. Lahore, India: The People, September 27, 1931. Reprint, General Press, 2019 (Kindle edition).
Starhawk. *The Spiral Dance: A Rebirth of the Ancient Religion of the Great Goddess*. New York, NY: Harper & Rowe, 1979.
Untilch, Paul. *The Courage to Be*. New Haven, CT: Yale University Press, 1952.
Trungpa, Chögyam. *The Sacred Path of the Shambhala Warrior*. Boulder, CO: Shambhala Publications, 2007.
Warraq, Ibn. *Why I Am Not a Muslim*. Buffalo, NY: Prometheus Books,1995.
Watts, Alan. *The Way of Zen*. New York, NY: Pantheon Books, 1957.
Wilson, Colin. *Religion and the Rebel*. Bath, UK: Ashgrove Press, 1957.

C. PHILOSOPHY
Allen, Jr., Norm R., ed., *African American Humanism: An Anthology*. Buffalo, NY: Prometheus Books, 1991.
Barnes, Hazel E. *Humanistic Existentialism: The Literature of Possibility*. Lincoln, NE: University of Nebraska Press, 1959.
De Beauvoir, Simone. *The Second Sex*. London, UK: Jonathan Cape, 2009.
Foucault, Michel. *The History of Sexuality: The Will to Knowledge*. Paris, FR: Éditions Gallimard, 1976.
Fromm, Erich, ed., *Socialist Humanism*. London, UK: Allen Lane (Penguin Random House), 1965.
Fromm, Erich. *Marx's Concept of Man*. New York, NY: Frederick Ungar Publishing, 1961.
Krishnamurti, Jiddu. *The Core of the Teachings*. UK: Krishnamurti Foundation Trust Ltd., 1980. https://www.jkrishnamurti.org/about-core-teachings.
Lamont, Corliss. *Humanism as a Philosophy*. New York, NY: Philosophical Library, 1949. Reprinted as *The Philosophy of Humanism* (8th ed.). Washington, DC: Humanist Press, 1997. Edited by Beverley Earles and Beth K. Lamont, with gender neutral references. https://www.corliss-lamont.org/philos8.htm.
Nietzsche, Friedrich. *Thus Spoke Zarathustra*. Translated by Walter Kaufmann. London, UK: Penguin Books, 1978.
Raj-Gauthier, Rupert. "The Feminine Face of Humanism," in *The Humanist in Canada*. Ottawa, ON: Canadian Humanist Publications, Spring 1995, (112): 5-7.
Read, Rupert, and M. A. Lavery, ed., *Philosophy for Life: Applying Philosophy in Politics and Culture*. London, UK: Continuum International Publishing, 2007.
Rowbotham, Sheila, Lynne Segal, and Hilary Wainwright. *Beyond the Fragments: Feminism and the Making of Socialism* (3rd ed.). London, UK: Merlin Press, 2012.

Russell, Bertrand. "Why I'm Not A Communist." In *Portraits from Memory and Other Essays* by Bertrand Russell. London, UK: Allen and Unwin, 1956.
Sartre, Jean-Paul. *Existentialism Is a Humanism.* Translated from the French by Carol Macomber. New Haven, CT: Yale University Press, 2007.
Tielman, Rob. *Humanistische Sociologie: een Paradox als Paradigma (Humanist Sociology: A Paradox and a Paradigm).* Amsterdam, NL: Amsterdam University Press, 1987. Dutch-language edition only.
Tolstoy, Leo. *Tolstoy's Writings on Civil Disobedience and Non-Violence.* New York, NY: Bergman Publishers, 1967. Based on Tolstoy's Russian writings published by Thomas Y. Crowell, New York, 1899.
Wilson, Colin. *The Angry Years: The Rise and Fall of the Angry Young Men.* London, UK: Robson Books, 2007.
Wilson, Colin. *Introduction to the New Existentialism.* London, UK: Hutchinson (Penguin Random House), 1966.
Wilson, Colin. *The Outsider.* New York, NY: J. P. Tarcher, 1956.
Williams, Christine V. *Jiddu Krishnamurti: World Philosopher (1895–1986): His Life and Thoughts.* Delhi, India: Motilal Banarsidass, 2004.
Zahavi, Dan. *Husserl's Phenomenology.* Stanford, CA: Stanford University Press, 2003.

D. PSYCHOLOGY/PSYCHOTHERAPY

Adler, Alfred. *The Individual Psychology of Alfred Adler.* Edited by H. L. Ansbacher, and R. R. Ansbacher. New York, NY: Harper & Row, 1956.
Bucke, Richard Maurice. *Cosmic Consciousness: A Study in the Evolution of the Human Mind.* Northbrook, IL: Innes Publishing, 1905.
Ellis, Albert, Russell Greiger, et al., *Handbook of Rational-Emotive Therapy.* New York, NY: Springer Publishing, 1977.
Erikson, Erik H., Joan M. Erikson, and Helen Kivnick. *Vital Involvement in Old Age.* New York, NY: W. W. Norton, 1986.
Erikson, Erik H. *The Life Cycle Completed.* New York, NY: W. W. Norton, 1985.
Erikson, Erik H. *Identity: Youth and Crisis.* New York, NY: W. W. Norton, 1968.
Frankl, Viktor E. *The Doctor and the Soul: From Psychotherapy to Logotherapy.* Translated from the German by Richard Winston and Clara Winston. New York, NY: Vintage Books, 1986.
Frankl, Viktor E. *Man's Search for Meaning: An Introduction to Logotherapy* (3rd ed.). Translated from the German by Ilse Lasch. New York, NY: Touchstone Books (Simon & Schuster), 1984.
Frankl, Viktor E. *Psychotherapy and Existentialism: Selected Papers on Logotherapy.* New York, NY: Simon & Schuster, 1967.
Fromm, Erich. *Zen Buddhism and Psychoanalysis.* New York, NY: Harper, 1960.
Gilligan, Carol. *In A Different Voice: Psychological Theory and Women's Development.* Cambridge, MA: Harvard University Press, 1982
Hayes, Steven C., Kirk Strosahl, and Kelly G. Wilson. *Acceptance and Commitment Therapy: An Experiential Approach to Behavior Change.* New York, NY: Guilford Press, 1999.
Herbert, James D., and Evan M. Forman. *Acceptance and Mindfulness in Cognitive Behavior Therapy: Understanding and Applying the New Therapies.* Hoboken, NJ: Wiley, 2011.
Jung, Carl, G. *Dreams.* Bollingen Series, vol. 20. Translated from the German by R. F. C. Hull. Princeton, NJ: Princeton University Press, 1974.
Jung, Carl. G. *Psychology and Alchemy.* Collected Works of C. G. Jung, vol. 12. Princeton, NJ: Princeton University Press,1968.
Jung, Carl G. *Psychology and Religion: West and East.* New York, NY: Pantheon Books, 1969.

Jung, Carl Gustav, and Aniela Jaffé, eds. *Memories, Dreams, Reflections* (2nd ed). Translated from the German by Richard Winston and Clara Winston. New York, NY: Vintage Books, 1989.
Kopp, Richard R. *Metaphor Therapy: Using Client Generated Metaphors in Therapy.* Abingdon, UK: Routledge (Taylor & Francis), 1995.
Lerner, Harriet. *The Dance of Fear: Rising Above Anxiety, Fear, and Shame to Be Your Best and Bravest Self.* New York, NY: HarperCollins, 2004.
Lerner, Harriet. *The Dance of Intimacy: A Woman's Guide to Courageous Acts of Change in Key Relationships.* New York, NY: HarperCollins, 1989.
Lerner, Harriet. *The Dance of Anger: A Woman's Guide to Changing the Patterns of Intimate Relationships.* New York, NY: HarperCollins, 1985, 2005.
Linehan, Marsha M. *Cognitive Behavioral Treatment of Borderline Personality Disorder.* New York, NY: Guilford Press, 1993.
Linehan, Marsha M. *Skills Training Manual for Treating Borderline Personality Disorder.* New York, NY: Guilford Press, 1993.
Maslow, Abraham H. *The Farther Reaches of Human Nature.* New York, NY: Esalen (Viking Press), 1971.
Maslow, Abraham H. *Toward a Psychology of Being.* New York, NY: Van Nostrand-Reinhold, 1962.
Miller, Alice. The Untouched Key: Tracing Childhood Trauma in Creativity and Destructiveness. New York, NY: Anchor Books, 1988.
Miller, Alice. *The Drama of the Gifted Child: The Search for the True Self.* (rev. ed.). New York, NY: Basic Books, 1994.
Miller, Alec L., Jill H. Rathus, and Marsha M. Linehan. *Dialectical Behavior Therapy with Suicidal Adolescents.* New York, NY: Guilford Press, 2006.
Miller, S. D., M. A. Hubble, and B. L. Duncan. *Handbook of Solution-Focused Brief Therapy.* San Francisco, CA: Jossey-Bass, 1996.
Perls, Frederick, Paul Goodman, and Ralph F. Hefferline. *Gestalt Therapy: Excitement and Growth in the Human Personality.* New York, NY: Julian Press: 1951. Reprint, London, UK: Souvenir Press, 1994.
Piaget, Jean, and Bärbel Inhelder. *The Psychology of the Child.* Translated from the French by Helen Weaver. New York, NY: Basic Books, 1969.
Rogers, Carl R. *Client-Centered Therapy.* Boston, MA: Houghton Mifflin Harcourt, 1951.
Rosewater, Lynne Bravo, and Lenore E. Walker, eds. *Handbook of Feminist Therapy: Women's Issues in Psychotherapy.* New York, NY: Springer Publishing, 1985.
White, Michael, and David Epston. *Narrative Means to Therapeutic Ends.* New York, NY: W. W. Norton, 1990.

E. THE OCCULT/PARAPSYCHOLOGY

Broughton, Robert S. *Parapsychology: The Controversial Science.* New York, NY: Ballantine Books, 1991.
Wilson, Colin. *Super Consciousness*: *The Quest for the Peak Experience.* London, UK: Watkins Publishing, 2007.
Wilson, Colin. *The Occult: A History.* London, UK: Random House, 1971.

F: PHYSICS/COSMOLOGY

Capra, Fritjof. *The Tao of Physics: An Exploration of the Parallels Between Modern Physics and Eastern Mysticism.* Boulder, CO: Shambhala Publications, 1975.
Einstein, Albert, and Leopold Infeld. *The Evolution of Physics: First Concepts to the Theories of Relativity and Quantum.* Translated from the German by Maurice Solovine. Paris, FR: Flammarion Group (Éditions Gallimard), 1938. Reprint, Amazon, 1983 (Kindle Edition).

Hawking, Stephen. *The Theory of Everything: The Origin and Fate of the Universe*. Beverly Hills, CA: New Millennium Press, 1997.
McFarlane, Thomas, ed., *Einstein and Buddha: The Parallel Sayings*. Berkeley, CA: Ulysses Press, 2003.

G. EXISTENTIAL (AUTO)BIOGRAPHY/FICTION
Barnes, Hazel E. *The Story I Tell Myself: A Venture in Existentialist Autobiography*. Chicago, IL: University of Chicago Press, 1997.
Camus, Albert. *L'Été (The Summer)*. Paris, FR: Éditions Gallimard, collection Blanche, 1954. French-language edition only.
Camus, Albert. *The Outsider*. London, UK: Hamish Hamilton Publishing, 1946. Reprinted as *The Stranger*. New York, NY: Vintage Books, 1988. Translated from the French by Matthew Ward.
Carpenter, Edward. *My Days and Dreams: Being Autobiographical Notes*. London, UK: Allen and Unwin (3rd ed.), 1918.
https://archive.org/stream/mydaysanddreamsb00carpuoft/mydaysanddreamsb00carpuoft_djvu.txt.
Dostoyevsky, Fyodor. *The Idiot*. Translated from the Russian by Constance Garnett and Alan Myers. New York, NY: Vintage Classics, 2002.
Friedländer, Saul. Franz *Kafka: The Poet of Shame and Guilt*. New Haven, CT: Yale University Press, 2012.
Hesse, Hermann. *The Glass Bead Game*. Translated from the German by Richard Winston and Clara Winston. New York, NY: Holt, Rinehart & Winston, 1969.
Kafka, Franz. *The Complete Novels: The Trial; Amerika; The Castle*. Falmouth, UK: Minerva Press, 1992.
Kafka, Franz. *The Metamorphosis* (or *The Transformation*). New York, NY: W. W. Norton, 2014.
Naifeh, Steven, and Gregory White Smith. *Van Gogh: The Life*. London, UK: Random House, 2011.
Sartre, Jean-Paul. *Nausea*. Translated from the French by Robert Baldick. London, UK: Penguin Books, 1965.
Watts, Alan. *In My Own Way: An Autobiography*. New York, NY: Pantheon Books, 1972.
Wilson, Colin. *Dreaming to Some Purpose: An Autobiography*. London, UK: Century Publishing, 2004.
Wilson, Colin. *Voyage to a Beginning: An Intellectual Autobiography*. London UK: Cecil & Amelia Woolf, 1969.

H. BLACK & BROWN (AUTO)BIOGRAPHY/FICTION
Angelou, Maya. *I Know Why the Caged Bird Sings*. New York, NY: Random House, 1969.
Angelou, Maya. *Mom & Me & Mom*. New York, NY: Random House, 2013.
Baldwin, James. *Giovanni's Room*. New York, NY: Dial Press, 1956.
Du Bois, W. E. B. *The Souls of Black Folk: Essays and Sketches*. Chicago, IL: A. C. Mclurg: 1903. Reprint, New York, NY: Vintage Books, 1990.
Ellison, Ralph. *Invisible Man*. New York, NY: Random House, 1947.
Gandhi, Mohandas K. *An Autobiography or The Story of My Experiments with Truth*. Translated from the Gujurati by Mahadev Desai. IN, 1940. Reprints, Chatham, Kent, UK: Dover Publications, 1983; Boston, MA: Beacon Press, 1993.
hooks, bell. *Aint I a Woman?: Black Women and Feminism*. Boston, MA: South End Press, 1981.
Hughes, Langston. *New Negro Poets, USA*. Bloomington, IN: Indiana University Press, 1964.
Hurston, Zora Neale. *Dust Tracks on a Road*. Philadelphia, PA: J. B. Lippncott, 1942. Reprint,

New York, NY: HarperCollins, 1990.
King, Jr., Martin Luther, and Clayborne Carson, ed., *The Autobiography of Martin Luther King, Jr.* New York, NY: Warner Books, 1998.
Leeming, David A. *James Baldwin: A Biography*. New York, NY: Alfred A. Knopf, 1994.
Lorde, Audry. *Sister Outsider: Essays and Speeches.* Berkeley, CA: The Crossing Press. 1984.
Mandela, Nelson. *Long Walk to Freedom: The Autobiography of Nelson Mandela.* Boston, MA: Little, Brown and Co., 1994.
Morrison, Toni. *Playing in the Dark: Whiteness and the Literary Imagination*. Cambridge, MA: Harvard University Press, 1992.
Rampersad, Arnold. *Ralph Ellison: A Biography*. New York, NY: Alfred A. Knopf, 2007.
Wagner-Martin, Linda. *Maya Angelou: Adventurous Spirit.* London, UK: Bloomsbury Publishing, 2015.
Walker, Alice. "The Gospel According to Shug." In Alice Walker's *The Temple of My Familiar*. San Diego, CA: Harcourt Brace Jovanovich, 1989, 287-289.
Walker, Alice. *The Color Purple*. New York, NY: Houghton Mifflin Harcourt, 1982.
Wright, Richard. "The Man Who Lived Underground." In *Eight Men: Short Stories*, by Richard Wright. Cleveland, OH: World Publishing, 1961.
X, Malcolm, and Alex Haley. *The Autobiography of Malcolm X.* New York, NY: Grove Press, 1965.

PART II: GENDER WORKER &
PART III: THERAPEUTIC HEALER, TEACHER & WRITER
A. TRANSSEXUAL/TRANSVESTIC/TRANSGENDER
1. (Auto)biography/Literature/Film/Media
American
Clark, Joanna (Sister Mary Elizabeth), and Margot E. Wilson. *Before My Warranty Runs Out: Human, Transgender and Environmental Rights Advocate.* Victoria, BC: TransGender Publishing, forthcoming.
Cohler, David. *Freemartin.* Boston, MA: Little, Brown, and Co.,1981. Transphobic novel about a misogynist, trans-male sex slayer.
Denny, Dallas. "Girl with No Name." In Margot Wilson and Aaron Devor, eds. *Glimmerings: Trans Elders Tell Their Stories*. Victoria, BC: TransGender Publishing, 2019, 33-42.
Devor, Aaron H., and Nicholas Matte. "ONE Inc. and Reed Erickson: The Uneasy Collaboration of Gay and Trans Activism, 1964-2003." *GLQ: A Journal of Lesbian and Gay Studies*, 2004, 10(2): 179-209.
Devor, Aaron H., and Nicholas Matte. "Building a Better World for Transpeople: Reed Erickson and the Erickson Educational Foundation." *International Journal of Transgenderism*, 2007, 10(1): 47-68.
Docter, Richard F. *From Man to Woman: The Transgender Journey of Virginia Prince*. Northridge, CA: Docter Press, 2004.
Drath, Eric, dir., USA: ESPN Films. Season 1, Episode 3: *Renée*. Aired October 4, 2011. https://www.imdb.com/title/tt3061972/. TV documentary on American transsexual tennis player Renée Richards.
Ekins, Richard, and Dave King, eds. *Virginia Prince: Pioneer of Transgendering.* International Journal of Transgenderism, 2005, 8(4): 5-15, doi: 10.1300/J485v08n04_02. Co-published: Binghamton, NY: Haworth Medical Press, 2005.
Elliot, Michael. "Crossing the Line." Unpublished, 1980s. Rupert Raj fonds, The ArQuives: https://arquives.andornot.com/en/list?q=Elliot%2C+michael&p=1&ps=20.
Feinberg, Leslie. *Trans Liberation: Beyond Pink or Blue.* Boston, MA: Beacon Press, 1998.
Feinberg, Leslie. *Transgender Warriors: Making History from Joan of Arc to Dennis Rodman.* Boston, MA: Beacon Press, 1996.

Green, Jamison. "Doctor Livingstone, You Presume?" In Margot Wilson and Aaron Devor, eds., *Glimmerings: Trans Elders Tell Their Stories*. Victoria, BC: TransGender Publishing, 2019, 43-57.

Green, Jamison. *Becoming a Visible Man*. Nashville, TN: Vanderbilt University Press, 2004.

Grant, Lee, dir., *What Sex Am I?* HBO-TV: "America Undercover Series." Aired March 1985. USA: Joseph Feury Productions, 2005. TV documentary on Steve Dain, Christine Jorgensen and others.

Halberstam, Judith, and Del LaGrace Volcano. *The Drag King Book*. London, UK: Serpent's Tale, 1999.

Jorgensen, Christine. *Christine Jorgensen: A Personal Biography*. New York, NY: Bantam Books, 1967. Reprint, San Francisco, CA: Cleis Press, 2002. Introduction by Susan Stryker.

Kane, Ariadne/J. Ari, and Margot Wilson. *Gender Odyssey: Journey of an Intrepid Androgyne*. Victoria, BC: TransGender Publishing, forthcoming.

Kane-Demaios, J. Ari, and Vern Bullough, eds. *Crossing Sexual Boundaries: Transgender Journeys, Uncharted Paths*. Boston, MA: Prometheus Books, 2005.

Khosla, Dhillon. *Both Sides Now: One Man's Journey through Womanhood*. New York, NY: J. P. Tarcher, 2006. Life story of a mixed-race (Eurasian) trans man.

Leger, Tom, and Riley MacLeod, eds. *The Collection: Short Fiction from the Transgender Vanguard*. New York, NY: Topside Press, 2012.

Martino, Mario, and harriet. *Emergence: A Transsexual Autobiography*. New York, NY: Crown Publishers, 1977. Angelo (Tony) Tornabene was Mario's real name.

Middlebrook, Diane Wood. *Suits Me: The Double Life of Billy Tipton*. Boston, MA: Houghton Mifflin Harcourt, 1998.

Page, Anthony, dir. *Second Serve: The Renée Richards Story* (aka *I Change My Life*). USA: Lorimar Telepictures. Aired May 13, 1986. https://www.imdb.com/title/tt0091913/. TV documentary based on her 1983 autobiography.

Patton, Jude, and Margot Wilson. *Young Kid, Old Goat: Transgender Journey to Understanding the Man Within*. Victoria, BC: TransGender Publishing, forthcoming.

Patton, Jude. "Why Did I Do It, Or What the Surgery Has Meant to Me." In Vern Bullough, ed., *The Frontiers of Sex Research*, Buffalo, NY: Prometheus Books, 1979, 177-187.

Pauly, Ira B. Pauly, Ira, B. (interview wtih Louis G. Sullivan). See below: iii. Earlier Transhomosexuality/Transbisexuality.

Peterson, Trace, ed., *EOAGH: A Journal of the Arts*. http://eoagh.com.

Peterson, Trace, and T. C. Tolbert, eds. *Troubling the Line: Trans and Genderqueer Poetry and Poetics*. New York, NY: Nightboat Books, 2013.

Pollock, Rachel. "The Varieties of Transsexual Experience." *Transsexual News Telegraph*, 1997, 18, 20.

Pollock, Rachel. "Archetypal Transsexuality." 1995.

Prince, Virginia. "The Life and Times of Virginia." In Margot Wilson and Aaron Devor, eds., *Glimmerings: Trans Elders Tell Their Stories*. Victoria, BC: TransGender Publishing, 2019, 134-164.

Rapper, Irving, dir., *The Christine Jorgensen Story*. USA: Edward Small Productions. Aired June 1970. https://www.imdb.com/title/tt0065549/. Film docudrama loosely based on her 1967 autobiography.

Richards, Renée. *No Way Renée: The Second Half of My Notorious Life*. New York, NY: Simon & Schuster, 2007.

Richards, Renée, and John Ames. *Second Serve: The Renée Richards Story*. New York, NY: Stein and Day, 1983.

The Sally Jessy Raphael Show. USA: Multimedia Entertainment. Aired November 3, 1986, on WTNH-TV in New Haven, CT. TV talk-show on transsexuals Rupert Raj (and his sister),

Joanna Clark/Sister Mary Elizabeth (and her father) and Nancy Ledins.

Smith, Phoebe. *From Sharecropper's Son to Who's Who in American Women*. Self-published, 2014.

Smith, Phoebe. *Phoebe: My Story*. Self-published, 1979.

Sprinkle, Annie, Albert Jaccoma, and Johnny Armstrong. *Linda/Les and Annie: The First Female-to-Male Transsexual Love Story*. 1989. Toronto, ON: Vtape. http://www.vtape.org/video?vi=4246. Docu-porn-drama featuring newly-transitioned transsexual man Les (formely Linda) Nichols and porn star Annie Sprinkle.

Star, H. J./Hammonds, Carl. *My Unique Change*. Chicago, IL: Novel Books, 1965.

Star, Hedy Jo. *I Changed My Sex!* Chicago, IL: Allied Books, 1955. Reissued as *I Changed My Sex!: The Autobiography of Stripper Hedy Jo Star, Formerly Carl Hammonds*. Chicago, IL: Allied Books, 1980.

Stryker, Susan, dir. *Christine in the Cutting Room*. USA, 2013. https://letterboxd.com/film/christine-in-the-cutting-room/. Experimental video documentary on Christine Jorgensen.

Sullivan, Louis G. *From Female to Male: The Life of Jack Bee Garland*. New York, NY: Alyson Books, 1990.

Takeda, Michael, ed., *Brave Boy World: A Trans Man Anthology*. Auburn, MA: Pink Narcissus Press, 2017.

Thompson, C. J. S. *The Mysteries of Sex: Women Who Posed as Men and Men Who Impersonated Women*. New York, NY: Causeway Books, 1974.

Valerio, Max Wolf. *The Criminal: The Invisibility of Parallel Forces*. Brooklyn, NY: EOAGH Books, 2018.

African American

Cheers, D. Michael. "Interview with Justina Williams." Chicago, IL.: Jet Magazine, November 1, 1979. http://transgriot.blogspot.ca/2007/02/justina-williams-1979-jet-magazine.html.

Davis, Sharon. A Finer Specimen of Womanhood: A Transsexual Speaks Out. New York, NY: Vantage Press, 1985.

Jenkins, Andrea. "Interview with Philippe Cunningham." The Transgender Oral History Project. Tretter Collection in GLBT Studies. Minneapolis, MN: University of Minnesota. September 25, 2015. A trans-male, African American, Minneapolis city councillor is interviewed by a trans-female councillor.

Jenkins, Andrea. The T is Not Silent: New and Selected Poems. Self-published, 2015.

Lady Chablis, and Theodore Bouloukos. Hiding my Candy: The Autobiography of the Grand Empress of Savannah. New York, NY: Pocket Books, 1996.

Maynard, Steven. "Introduction: 'A New Way of Lovin': Queer Toronto Gets Schooled by Jackie Shane." In John Lorinc, Jane Farrow, Stephanie Chambers, Rahim Thawer, et al., eds. Any Other Way: How Toronto Got Queer. Toronto, ON: Coach House Books, 2017, I1-I10.

Mock, Janet. Redefining Realness: My Path to Womanhood, Identity, Love & So Much More. New York, NY: Atria Books (Simon & Schuster), 2014.

Newman, Toni. I Rise - The Transformation of Toni Newman. Self-published, 2011.

Timane, Rizi Xavier. An Unspoken Compromise: A Spiritual Guide for LGBT People of Faith. Santa Clarita, CA: Hawkfish Publishing, 2013. Semi-autobiographical account by a Nigerian-born trans man who moved to the USA.

Watson, Tenika, and Jennifer Daelyn. My Life is No Accident: A Memoir by Tenika Watson, as told to Jennifer Daelyn. Published by Jennifer Daelyn, 2014.

British

Allen, Robert. But for the Grace: The True Story of a Dual Existence. London, UK: W. H. Allen, 1954.

Ashley, April. First Lady. London, UK: Blake Publishing, 2006.

Collis, Rose. Colonel Barker's Monstrous Regiment: A Tale of Female Husbandry. London, UK: Virago Press, 2002.

Cowell, Roberta. Roberta Cowell's Story. Portsmouth, NH: Heinemann Publishing, 1954. Her documented intersexuality was possibly falsified by her surgeon so she could legally undergo transsexual surgery. https://en.wikipedia.org/wiki/Roberta_Cowell; https://zagria.blogspot.com/2012/07/betty-cowell-1918-2011-motor-racer-pilot.html#.XZ1FtkapFAE.

Devamitra, Upasaka. Confessions of a Transvestite Buddhist: A Quest for Manhood. London, UK: Achilles Publishing, 2014.

Duberman, Martin. "The Female Husband." In About Time: Exploring the Gay Past, edited by Martin Duberman. New York, NY: Meridian Books, 1986, 24-30.

Duncker, Patricia. James Miranda Barry. London, UK: Serpent's Tail, 1999. Dr. Barry's rumoured intersexuality has been controversially debated, both for and against. https://en.wikipedia.org/wiki/James_Barry_(surgeon); https://zagria.blogspot.com/2008/01/james-miranda-stuart-barry-1795-1865.html#.X.

Fallowell, Duncan. April Ashley's Odyssey. London, UK: Jonathan Cape, 1982.

Hall, Radclyffe. The Well of Loneliness. London, UK: Jonathan Cape, 1928.

Hodgkinson, Liz. Michael née Laura: The World's First Female to Male Transsexual. London, UK: Virgin Books, 1989.

Hodgkinson, Liz. Bodyshock: The Truth About Changing Sex. London, UK: Columbus Books, 1987.

Jacques, Juliet. Trans: A Memoir. London. UK: Verso Books, 2015.

Jivaka, Lobzang/Dillon, Michael. Out of the Ordinary: A Life of Gender and Spiritual Transitions. New York, NY: Fordham University Press, 2016. Written in 1962 and published posthumously.

Kennedy, Pagan. The First Man-Made Man: The Story of Two Sex Changes, One Love Affair, and a Twentieth-Century Medical Revolution. London, UK: Bloomsbury Publishing, 2007.

Make Me A Man. UK: BBC-Radio, Channel 4, August 5, 2002. http://www.bbc.co.uk/radio4/womanshour/2002_32_mon_01.shtml. Radio documentary on Dr. Stephen Whittle.

Morris, Jan. Conundrum. San Diego, CA: Harcourt Brace Jovanovich, 1974.

Rees, Mark. Dear Sir or Madam? London, UK: Bloomsbury Publishing, 1996.

Rees, Mark, and Katherine O'Donnell. "Taking to the Law." In Christine Burns, ed., Trans Britain: Our Journey from the Shadows. London, UK: Unbound, 2018, 135-160.

Simmons, Dawn Langley. Dawn: A Charleston Legend. Charleston, SC: Wyrick, 1995.

Simmons, Dawn Langley. Man into Woman: A Transsexual Autobiography. New York, NY: Macfadden-Bartell, 1971. Her self-identified intersexuality has been contested by author Edward Ball. See: https://en.wikipedia.org/wiki/Dawn_Langley_Simmons; and https://zagria.blogspot.com/2009/10/dawn-langley-simmons-1922-2000-part-2.html#.XZ1GbkapFAE.

Wheelright, Julie. Amazons and Military Maids: Women Who Dressed as Men in Pursuit of Life, Liberty and Happiness. London, UK: Pandora Press, 1989.

Canadian (English)

Bergman, S. Bear. Butch is a Noun. Cleveland, OH: Suspect Thoughts Press, 2006.

Butler, Alec. "Black Friday…With or Without the Question Mark." In John Lorinc, Jane

Farrow, Stephanie Chambers, Rahim Thawer, et al., eds., Any Other Way: How Toronto Got Queer. Toronto, ON: Coach House Books, 2017, 208-211. Alec is a trans, intersex, Two-Spirit activist.

Butler, Alec, dir., Trans Cabaret: The Video. 2011. https://www.youtube.com/results?search_query=Butler%2C+Alec%2C+dir.+Trans+Cabaret%3A+The+Video.+2011.

Butler, Alec, dir., Trans Mission: Get Yer Motor Runnin'. 2003.

Butler, Alec, dir., Misadventures of PussyBoy: First Love (2002), Sick (2003), First Period (date unknown).

Butler, Alec, dir., Audrey's Beard. 2002.

Caloz, Marie, and Andrew Culbert, prods. "Becoming Ayden." Fifth Estate. Aired on CBC-TV, October 13, 2004. http://radio-canada.mediaspace.kaltura.com/media/Becoming+Ayden/1_rfctkzs2.

TV documentary on then teenager Ayden Scheim starting his gender transition.

Castle, Stephanie. The Zenith Experience: Encounters & Memories in a Transgsender Setting. Vancouver, BC: Perceptions Press, 2005.

Castle, Stephanie. Feelings: A Transsexual's Explanation of a Baffling Condition. Vancouver, BC: Perceptions Press, 1992. Reprint, 2nd edition (with an Introduction).Wilson, Margot E., ed., Victoria, BC: Transgender Publishing, 2018.

Cho, Tom. Look Who's Morphing.Look Who's Morphing. Syndey, AU: Giramondo Publishing, 2009. Reprint, Vancouver, BC: Arsenal Pulp Press, 2014.

Coffey, Jennifer. "Out Living History: Three Faces of Sherbourne Health Centre." QA: The Queer Activist newsletter, 8-10. Toronto, ON: Canadian Lesbian & Gay Archives (The ArQuives), 2009. Features Rupert Raj and former co-counsellor Carole Baker.

Colgan, Alex. "Lives in Transition." This Magazine, May 1, 2013. https://this.org/2013-05-01/lives-in-transition/. Features Toronto activists Rupert Raj, Susan Gapka, Morgan Page and Shoshana Pollock.

Cross, Kathleen, ed., The Trans Biography Project: Stories from the Lives of Eleven Trans People in B.C. Vancouver, BC: The Women/Trans Dialogue Planning Committee and Trans Alliance Society, 2001.
http://www.transalliancesociety.org/education/documents/01transbiosmall.pdf.

Daniel, Barb. She's No Lady: The Story of Jamie Lee Hamilton. Toronto, ON: Cormorant Books, 2005.

Duff, Michelle Ann. Make Haste, Slowly: The Mike Duff Story. Coldwater, ON: Mad8 Publishing (Canada), 1999.

Dumaresq, Michelle, Karen Duthie, dir., Diana Wilson, prod., and Lesley Ewen. 100% Woman. Vancouver, BC: Artemis Dreams Productions/Producers on Davie Pictures, and the Canadian Television Fund, 2004. Aired on the Documentary Channel (Television Network Canada) and the Life Network in 2004.
https://www.movingimages.ca/store/search.php?keywords=100%25+woman&x=0&y=0. Video documentary on Michelle Dumaresq, a Canadian trans-female, professional downhill mountain bike champion.

Friedman, Melinda, dir./prod. Safety in Numbers: A Trans History. New York, NY: Spotlight Productions. Aired on Telus Optik VOD, August 27, 2018.
https://www.youtube.com/watch?v=dQwS7LqfJys&t=11s.
https://www.facebook.com/storyhive/videos/1125105184307327/. Film documentary on Rupert Raj, Dr. Aaron Devor, Dr. Ariadne Kane, Jude Patton, M. Gayle Roberts and others.

Goodhandy, Mandy/Taylor, Amanda. *Just Call Me Lady: A Work of Completion.* Pennsauken, NJ: BookBaby, 2018.

Hamilton, Jamie Lee. "The Golden Age of Prostitution: One Woman's Personal Account of an

Outdoor Brothel in Vancouver, 1975-1984." In Dan Irving and Rupert Raj, eds., Trans Activism in Canada: A Reader. Toronto, ON: Canadian Scholars' Press, 2014, 27-32.

Highcrest, Alexandra. At Home on the Stroll: My Twenty Years as a Prostitute in Canada. Toronto, ON: A. A. Knopf (Canada), 1997.

Hutton, Megan. "Our Queer Beginnings." PinkPlayMags "Springplay!," Spring 2017, 11-14. Features Rupert Raj, queer activists Richard Hudler and Rev. Dr. Brent Hawkes, and former Canadian Prime Minister Pierre Trudeau.

James, Elizabeth "Raven." "Gender Strike! It's an Offence." In Dan Irving and Rupert Raj, eds., Trans Activism in Canada: A Reader. Toronto, ON: Canadian Scholars' Press, 2014, 45-49.

Johnson, Katherine, and Stephanie Castle. Prisoner of Gender: A Transsexual and the System. Vancouver, BC: Perceptions Press, 1997.

Keith, Corey. "Glimmerings of Balance." In Margot Wilson and Aaron Devor, eds., Glimmerings: Trans Elders Tell Their Stories. Victoria, BC: TransGender Publishing, 2019, 75-88.

Kim, Gloria. "Why Be Just One Sex?" Maclean's Magazine, Sept. 12, 2005, 52-53. http://archive.macleans.ca/search?QueryTerm=Why+Be+Just+One+Sex%3F. Features Miqqi Alicia Gilbert, Rupert Raj and Alec Butler.

Kodak, Boyd, and Cat Grant, dirs./prods. Shadmith Manzo Performance. Toronto, ON: Vtape, 1998. http://www.vtape.org/video?vi=4417. Video fundraiser for Mexican refugee Shadmith Manzo, initially deported from Canada in 1998, then granted Canadian landed immigrant status in 1999.

Kol, Alon, dir., and Behnisch, Christopher, writ. Transfixed. Toronto, ON, 2015. https://www.youtube.com/watch?v=QsPQOVGCsuY. Video docudrama on trans/intersex activist Martine Stonehouse and her husband.

Laframboise, Sandy Leo. "Finding My Place: The High Risk Project Society." In Dan Irving and Rupert Raj, eds., Trans Activism in Canada: A Reader. Toronto, ON: Canadian Scholars' Press, 2014, 51-56.

Lamb, Sybil. I've Got a Time Bomb. New York, NY: Topside Press, 2014. Fantasy novel about a heroine surviving a hate crime.

Lulu. Rupert's Story. Queer Story Archives at: www.Onmyplanet.ca, January 24, 2016. http://onmyplanet.ca/mundo/page/5/. Videotaped interview with Rupert Raj.

Mackay, Xanthra, dir., Rupert Remembers. Toronto, ON: Sexy Voice Video Production. Vtape, 1999, 2000. http://www.vtape.org/video?vi=4390. Video documentary on Canadian trans activist Rupert Raj.

Mackay, Xanthra, host. Psychopathia Transsexualis: Transsexual News, Information and Culture. Toronto, ON: CIUT 89.5 FM-Radio, 1999-2000. http://www.vtape.org/artist?ai=798.

Muldoon, Grey Kimber Piitaapan, and Dan Irving. "A Sense of Place: Expressions of Trans Activism North of Lake Nipissing." In Dan Irving and Rupert Raj, eds., Trans Activism in Canada: A Reader. Toronto, ON: Canadian Scholars' Press, 2014, 71-84.

O'Connell, Linda T. The Greatest Hits of Linda T. O'Connell, Not Available from K-Tel. Unpublished, 1982. Poetry anthology.

O'Connell, Linda T. Fighting Back: A Symphony in Words. Self-published, 1978. Toronto, ON: The ArQuives. https://arquives.andornot.com/en/list?q=O%27Connell%2C+Linda+T.&p=1&ps=2. Poetry anthology.

O'Keefe, Kevin, prod. Toronto, ON: The Transgender Project. ichannel, 2014. https://www.youtube.com/watch?v=GMW6xRieIo4. Cable TV documentary on Rupert Raj, Kinnon McKinnon, Tien Neo Eamos, M. Gayle Roberts and others.

Plett, Casey. A Safe Girl to Love. New York, NY: Topside Press, 2014.

Raj, Rupert. "Glimmerings of My Trans-Male Identity." In Margot Wilson and Aaron Devor, eds. Glimmerings: Trans Elders Tell Their Stories. Victoria, BC: TransGender Publishing, 2019, 165-182.

Raj, Rupert. Dancing the Dialectic: True Tales of a Transgender Trailblazer (1st ed.). Self-published, 2017.

Raj, Rupert, ed., "Of Souls & Roles, Of Sex & Gender: A Treasury of Transsexual, Transgenderist & Transvestic Verse from 1967 to 1991." Unpublished, Jan. 1, 2017, rev. July 1, 2018. Victoria, BC: University of Victoria Library; and Transgender Archives. https://www.uvic.ca/transgenderarchives/assets/docs/of-souls-0-rolesj-of-sex-0-gender-revised-july-1j-2018---numbered.pdf; Digital Transgender Archive. https://www.digitaltransgenderarchive.net/files/hm50tr87t. Poems by people from Canada, UK, Ireland, Australia and New Zealand.

Raj, Rupert. "My Male Metamorphosis: Man in the Making (A personal and political perspective)." In Vern Bullough, Bonnie Bullough, and James Elias, eds., Gender Blending. Buffalo, NY: Prometheus Books, 1997, 480-484.

Raj, Rupert. "Gender Crossings: An Historical Anthology of Women Who Have Medically Become Men & Those Who Have Passed as Men." Unfinished manuscript, 1995. The Rupert Raj fonds, Toronto, ON: The ArQuives. https://arquives.andornot.com/en/list?q=%E2%80%9CGender+Crossings%3A+&p=1&ps=20.

Raj, Rupert, ed., "Of Souls and Roles, Of Genes and Gender: A Treasury of Transsexual, Transgenderist, and Transvestite Verse." Unpublished, 1991. Rupert Raj fonds, Toronto, ON: The Arquives. https://arquives.andornot.com/en/list?q=OF+SOULS+AND+ROLES%2C+OF+GENES+AND+GENDER&p=1&ps=20.

Rideout, Lisa, dir./prod., and Sasha Fisher, prod. Susan Gapka: A Documentary Film (working title). Toronto, ON: Lifted Eyes Media & Clique Pictures. https://www.kickstarter.com/projects/susangapka/susan-gapka-a-documentary-film. In production.

Rinaldi, Luc. "'I Couldn't Lie to My Children Anymore': Morgane Oger on Embracing Her Trans Identity at Age 41." MacLean's Magazine, June 29, 2014. https://www.macleans.ca/news/canada/morgane-oger-embraces-her-trans-identity.

Roberts, M. Gayle. From Shame to Freedom: A Gender Variant Woman's Journey of Discovery. Victoria, BC: TransGender Publishing, forthcoming.

Rudakoff, Judith, ed., Trans(per)forming Nina Arsenault: An Unreasonable Body of Work. Bristol, UK: Intellect Ltd., 2012.

Rutherford, Erica. Nine Lives: The Autobiography of Erica Rutherford. Charlottetown, PEI: Ragweed Press, 1993.

Salah, Trish. "Foreword." In Raj, Rupert, ed., "Of Souls & Roles, Of Sex & Gender: A Treasury of Transsexual, Transgenderist & Transvestic Verse from 1967 to 1991." Unpublished, Jan. 1, 2017, rev. July 1, 2018, 4-6. Victoria, BC: University of Victoria Library; and Transgender Archives. Previously presented, in part, as "Writing What's Not, Yet: Inscribing Emergence." Department of Gender Studies Graduate Colloquium: "Writing Sexualities: Poetics, Politics, Activism." Queen's University, Kingston, ON, April 25, 2014.

Salah, Trish. Lyric Sexology, Vol. 1. New York, NY: Roof Books, 2014.

Salah, Trish. "Notes Toward Thinking Transsexual Institutional Poetics." In Eva C. Karpinski, Jennifer Henderson, Ian Sowton, and Ray Ellenwood, eds., Trans/Acting Culture, Writing, and Memory: Essays in Honour of Barbara Godard. Waterloo, ON: Wilfred Laurier University Press, 2013, 167-189.

Salazar, Lisa. Transparently: Behind the Scenes of a Good Life. Self-published, 2011.

The Sally Jessy Raphael Show. USA: Multimedia Entertainment. Aired November 1986 in New Haven, CT. TV talk show featuring Rupert Raj, his sister, and others.

Sarkisova, Sly. "Under A Queer Blue Sky." In John Lorinc, Jane Farrow, Stephanie Chambers, Rahim Thawer, et al., eds., Any Other Way: How Toronto Got Queer. Toronto, ON: Coach House Books, 2017, 282-284.

Shenher, Lorimer. This One Looks Like a Boy: My Gender Journey to Life as a Man. Vancouver, BC: Greystone Books, 2019.

Shraya, Vivek. She of the Mountains. Vancouver, BC: Arsenal Pulp Press, 2014.

Skin Deep. Toronto, ON: Inner City Films, 2000. TV documentary series. Episode 7: Christina Strang and others; Episode 8: Kyle Scanlon, Rupert Raj and then partner Eugene; Episode 31, 2001: Susan Gapka and Rupert Raj.

Thom, Kai Cheng. Fierce Femmes and Notorious Liars: A Dangerous Trans Girl's Confabulous Memoir. Montreal, PC: Metonymy Press, 2016.

Transforming Gender. "Firsthand" TV series. Season 2015-2016, Episode 07. Ottawa, Canada: CBC-TV, November 26, 2016. http://www.cbc.ca/player/play/2679573123. TV documentary on Dr. Aaron Devor and others.

Wensley, Dawn Angela, and Margot Wilson. Excerpts from Dawn Angela Wensley's diary. Victoria, BC: TransGender Publishing, forthcoming.

Wilson-Yang, Jia Qing. Small Beauty. Montreal, QC: Metonymy Press, 2016. A novel about a mixed-race, trans woman (Mei) navigating racism and transphobia, and desiring queer community.

Worley, Kristen, and Johanna Schneller. Woman Enough: How a Boy Became a Woman and Changed the World of Sport. Toronto, ON: Random House (Canada), 2019.

Youdan, Caroline. "What It's Like to be Transgender in Toronto." Toronto Life, October 26, 2015. http://torontolife.com/city/life/what-its-like-to-be-transgender-in-Toronto. Features Alex Abramovich, Alec Butler and Rachel Lauren Clark.

Canadian (French)

Boileau, Dianna, and Felicity Cochrane. Behold, I Am a Woman.! New York, NY: Pyramid Books, 1972.

Burke, Nora Butler, and Viviane Namaste. Translated from the French and revised by Natalie Duchesne. "'What Is Missing in Our Community Is Self-Love': An Interview with Marie-Marcelle Godbout, Founder of L'Aide aux Transsexuel(le)s du Quebec." In Dan Irving and Rupert Raj, eds., Trans Activism in Canada: A Reader. Toronto, ON: Canadian Scholars' Press, 2014, 109-114.

Charest, Madeleine. Enfin: La Lumière! Self-published, 2009.

Charest, Madeleine. Le dur Combat d'une Femme. Self-published, 2006.

Cormier, Frances Olympe. Frances with an "E": Our Story! Moose Creek, ON: Pilgrim Publications, 1995. Co-published as France avec un "S": Notre Histoire! Moose Creek, ON: Publications du Pèlerin, 1995.

Daubs, Katie. "The woman who was trans before her time." Toronto, ON: The Star. March 27, 2016. https://www.thestar.com/news/insight/2016/03/27/the-woman-who-was-trans-before-her-time.html. Features Dianna Boileau.

Kin, Yanni. Regarde-Moi, Maman!: Témoignage d'un Transsexuel. Outremont, QC: Lanctôt éditeur, 2002.

Martel, Brigitte. Né Homme, Comment Je Suis Devenue Femme. Montréal, QC: Éditions Québecor, 1981.

Monette, Guilda, and Denis. Guilda: Elle est Moi. Montréal, QC: Éditions Québecor, 1979.

Namaste, Viviane. "'We Paved the Way for Whatever Tolerance They have in Their Lives': An Interview with Michelle De Ville, 'The First Door Bitch in Montreal.'" In Dan Irving and Rupert Raj, eds., Trans Activism in Canada: A Reader. Toronto, ON: Canadian

Scholars' Press, 2014, 19-25.
Paquette, Marie-Claude. 17: Autobiographie. Longueuil, QC: Éditions Médialib, 2002.
Ross, Mirha-Soleil, and Mark Karbusicky, dirs. G-SPrOuT! Toronto, ON: Vtape, 2000. Trans/polysexual vegan-docu-porno video on Mirha and boyfriend Mark.
Ross, Mirha-Soleil, and Xanthra Mackay, dirs. Gendertroublemakers. Toronto, ON: Vtape, 1993. http://www.vtape.org/video?vi=3636.
Stephens, Inge, and Alexis Lefrançois. Alain, Transsexuelle: Vis-à-Vies. Saint-Lambert, QC: Héritage House Publishing, 1983.
Verret, Patrick. Changer de Sexe pour Vivre Enfin: Le Long Combat de Manon devenue Patrick. Laval, QC: Vivre enfin, 2005. Subsequently published as Changing Sex to Finally Live: The Long Struggle from Manon to Patrick. Translated by Chris Duncan. Laval, QC: Vivre enfin, 2006.

Chinese
Ming, Lei, and Lura Frazey. Life Beyond My Body: A Transgender Journey to Manhood in China. San Francisco, CA: Transgress Press, 2016.

Danish
Ebershoff, David. The Danish Girl. London, UK: Allen & Unwin, 2000.
Elbe, Lili/Hoyer, Niels. Man into Woman: An Authentic Record of a Change of Sex. Translated by Henry J. Stenning. Published posthumously London, UK: Jarrolds Publishers, 1933. She was possibly intersex, but this has not been confirmed. See: https://en.wikipedia.org/wiki/Lili_Elbe; and https://zagria.blogspot.com/2015/01/lili-ilse-elvenes-surgery-and-womanhood.html#.XZ1RX0apFAE.
Hooper, Tom, dir., Gail Mutrux, and Neil LaBute, prods. USA. The Danish Girl. 2015. https://www.imdb.com/title/tt0810819/fullcredits. Romantic docudrama on Dutch painter Einar Wegener/Lili Elbe and painter wife Gerda Wegener.

Dutch
Bakker, Alex. My Untrue Past: The Coming of Age of a Trans Man. Victoria, BC: TransGender Publishing, 2019. Originally published in Dutch as Mijn vales Verleden: Het Autobiografische Verhaal van een Man Geboren Alsmeisje. Amsterdam, NL: Nieuw Amsterdam Publishers, 2014.

French
"Coccinelle"/Jacqueline Charlotte Dufresnoy. Coccinelle par Coccinelle (Ladybug by Ladybug). Paris, FR: Éditions Filipacchi, 1987.
Léotard, Axel. Mauvais Genre (Wrong Gender). Paris, FR: Éditions Hugo & Cie, 2009. Autobiographical fiction. French-language edition only.

Iranian
Azarbayjani, Negar, dir., and Fereshteh Taerpoor, prod. Facing Mirrors (Persian). Box Entertainment, (Canada), 2011; (Iran), 2012. https://iranianfilmempire.wordpress.com/2016/12/12/transgender-in-iranian-cinema/. Film drama about a pre-transitional trans man and his girlfriend in Iran.
Eshaghian, Tanaz, dir./prod. Transsexual in Iran (Be Like Others) (Persian). Iran: The Film Collaborative, 2008. https://www.imdb.com/title/tt1157609/. Film documentary on Iranian trans women.

New Zealander
Beyer, Georgina, and Cathy Casey. Change for the Better: A Story of Georgina Beyer.

Auckland, NZ: Random House (NZ), 1999.
Goldman, Annie, and Peter Wells, dirs. Georgie Girl. New Zealand: Occasional Productions, 2001. https://www.wmm.com/catalog/film/georgie-girl/. Film documentary on trans activist Georgina Beyer based on her 1999 autobiography.

Uruguayan
Formosa, Sofía. Michelle Suárez: La Primera Abogada Trans de Uruguay (Michelle Suárez: The First Transgender Lawyer in Uruguay). Uruguay: Sin Etiquetas, February 9, 2015. Spanish-language edition only.

2. History/Sociology/Sexology
a. Transsexualism/Transvestism/Transgenderism
American
Allen, Mariette Pathy. *Transcuba*. Self-published, 2014. http://www.mariettepathyallen.com/. Photographic anthology.
Allen, Mariette Pathy. *The Gender Frontier*. Self-published, 2003. Photographic anthology.
Allen, Mariette Pathy. *Transformations: Crossdressers and Those Who Love Them*. New York, NY: E. P. Dutton, 1989. Photographic anthology.
Bolin, Anne. *In Search of Eve: Transsexual Rites of Passage*. Westport, CT: Praeger Publishers (Greenwood Publishing Group), 1987.
Bullough, Vern. *Cross Dressing, Sex, and Gender*. Buffalo, NY: Prometheus Books, 1993.
Bullough, Vern, ed., *The Frontiers of Sex Research*. Buffalo, NY: Prometheus Books, 1979.
Bullough, Vern, Bullough, Bonnie Bullough, and James Elias, eds. *Gender Blending*. Buffalo, NY: Prometheus Books, 1997.
Cotten, Trystan T., ed., *Transgender Migrations: The Bodies, Borders, and Politics of Transition*. Abingdon, UK: Routledge (Taylor & Francis), 2012.
Cromwell, Jason. *Trans Men & FTMs: Identities, Bodies, Genders & Sexualities*. Chicago, IL: University of Illinois Press, 1999.
Denny, Dallas, ed., *Current Concepts in Transgender Identity*. Shrewsbury, MA: Garland Publishers, 1998.
Denny, Dallas, ed., *Gender Dysphoria: A Guide to Research*. Shrewsbury, MA: Garland Publishers, 1994.
Garber, Marjorie B. *Vested Interests: Cross-dressing and Cultural Anxiety*. London, UK: Psychology Press, 1997.
Jennex, Craig, and Nisha Eswaran. *Out North: An Archive of Queer Activism and Kinship in Canada*. Vancouver, BC: Figure 1 Publishers, 2020. Includes a piece on early transsexual groups and photos of Rupert Raj.
Keig, Zander, and Mitch Kellaway, eds. *Manning Up: Transsexual Men Finding Brotherhood, Family and Themselves*. San Francisco, CA: Transgress Press, 2014.
Kotula, Dean, ed., *The Phallus Palace: Female to Male Transsexuals*. New York, NY: Alyson Books, 2002.
Kulick, Don. *Travesti: Sex, Gender, and Culture among Brazilian Transgendered Prostitutes*. Chicago, IL: University of Chicago Press, 1998. Photographic anthology.
Meyerowitz, Joanne. *How Sex Changed: A History of Transsexuality in the United States*. Cambridge, MA: Harvard University Press, 2002.
Pollock, Rachel. "The Transsexual Book of the Dead: Osirus and the Trance Man." In *The Phallus Palace: Female to Male Transsexuals*, In Dean Kotula, ed., New York, NY: Alyson Books, 2002, 131-145.
Prosser, Jay. *Second Skins: The Body Narratives of Transsexuality*. New York, NY: Columbia University Press, 1998.
Stryker, Susan. *Transgender History: The Roots of Today's Revolution*. New York, NY: Seal

Press, (1st ed.) 2008, (2nd ed.) 2017.
Stuart, Kim E. *The Uninvited Dilemma: A Question of Gender.* Portland, OR: Metamorphous Press, 1983.
Valentine, David. *Imagining Transgender: An Ethnography of a Category.* Durham, NC: Duke University Press, 2007.

British
Burns, Christine, ed., Trans Britain: Our Journey from the Shadows. London, UK: Unbound, 2018.
Burns, Christine. Pressing Matters: vols. 1 & 2. Self-published, 2013 & 2014.

Canadian
Devor, Aaron H. FTM: Female-to-Male Transsexuals in Society. Bloomington, IN: Indiana University Press, 1997.
Devor, Aaron H. "More Than Manly Women: How Female-to-Male Transsexuals Reject Lesbian Identities," In Vern Bullough, Bonnie Bullough, and James Elias, eds., Gender Blending, Buffalo, NY: Prometheus Books, 1997, 87-102.
Devor, Aaron H. Gender Blending: Confronting the Limits of Duality. Bloomington, IN: Indiana University Press, 1989. Compares and masculine women and trans men.
Devor, Aaron H. "Gender Blending Females: Women and Sometimes Men." American Behavioral Scientist, 1987, 31(1): 12-40.
Hill, Darryl B. Trans Toronto: An Oral History. New York, NY: William Rodney Press, 2012.
Namaste, Viviane, ed., Sex Change, Social Change: Reflections on Identity, Institutions, and Imperialism. Toronto, ON: Women's Press (Canadian Scholars' Press), 2005, 86-102.
Namaste, Viviane. Invisible Lives: The Erasure of Transsexual and Transgendered People. Chicago, IL: University of Chicago Press, 2000.
Noble, Jean/Bobby. Sons of the Movement: FtMs Risking Incoherence on a Post-Queer Cultural Landscape. Toronto, ON: Women's Press (Canadian Scholars' Press), 2006.
Noble, Jean/Bobby. Masculinities Without Men?: Female Masculinity in Twentieth-Century Fictions. Vancouver, BC: UBC Press, 2003.
Raj, Rupert. "Worlds in Collision." In John Lorinc, Jane Farrow, Stephanie Chambers, Rahim Thawer, et al., eds., Any Other Way: How Toronto Got Queer. Toronto, ON: Coach House Books, 2017, 154-157.
Rose, Fabien. "A History of That Which Was Never Supposed to Be Possible: Rethinking Gender Passing in History." In Patrizia Gentile, Gary Kinsman, and Pauline L. Rankin, eds., We Still Demand! Redefining Resistance in Sex and Gender Struggles. Vancouver, BC: UBC Press, 2017, 165-184. An activist treatise on identity politics.
Shelley, Christopher. *Transpeople*: *Repudiation, Trauma, Healing*. Toronto, ON: University of Toronto Press, 2008.

Dutch
Bakker, Alex. Transgender in Nederland: Een Buitengewone Geschiedenis. Amsterdam, NL: Boom Publishing House, 2018. https://www.bua.nl/; https://www.boomgeschiedenis.n/.
Ben-Zeev, Avi, and Pete Bailey, eds. *Trans Homo...Gasp!: FTM and Cis Men on Sex and Love*. San Francisco, CA: Transgress Press, 2017.
Coleman, Eli, and Walter O. Boctking. "'Heterosexual' Prior to Sex Reassignment - 'Homosexual' Afterwards: A Case Study of a Female-to-Male Transsexual." Journal of Psychology and Human Sexuality, February 1989: 1(2): 69-82.

b. Transhomosexuality/Transbisexuality
Male Transsexualism: Part III. 1989; *Female to Gay Male Transsexualism: Part IV (One Year Later).* 1990. Dept. of Psychiatry & Behavioral Sciences, University of Nevada School of Medicine. Edited by Rev. Megan M. Roher. 1988-1990. Video documentary on American gay trans man Louis G. Sullivan, interviewed by Dr. Ira Pauly.

Stoller, Robert J., and Laurence E. Newman. "The Bisexual Identity of Transsexuals: Two Case Examples." *Archives of Sexual Behavior,* March 1971, 1 (17):17-28.

Sullivan, Louis G. *From Female to Male: The Life of Jack Bee Garland.* New York, NY: Alyson Books 1990.

Towers, Sara. *Transgender Lesbians.* Self-published, 2015.

Weinberg, Martin S., Collin J. Williams, and Douglas W. Pryor, "Transsexual Bisexuals." In Weinberg, Williams, and Pryor, *Dual Attraction: Understanding Bisexuality*. Oxford, UK: Oxford University Press, 1994, 59-65.

Weinberg, Martin S., Collin J. Williams, and Douglas W. Pryor, "Change and the Transsexual Bisexual." In Weinberg, Williams, and Pryor, *Dual Attraction Understanding Bisexuality.* Oxford, UK: Oxford University Press, 1994, 230-238.

3. Trans Studies
Martínez-San Miguel, Yolanda, and Sarah Tobias, eds. *Trans Studies: The Challenge to Hetero/Homo Normativities.* Rutgers University Press, 2016.

Stryker, Susan, ed., *TSQ: Transgender Studies Quarterly.* Durham, NC: Duke University Press. https://www.dukeupress.edu/TSQ-Transgender-Studies-Quarterly.

Stryker, Susan, and Aren Aizura, eds. *The Transgender Studies Reader 2.* Abingdon, UK: Routledge (Taylor & Francis), 2013.

Stryker, Susan, and Stephen Whittle, eds. *The Transgender Studies Reader.* Abingdon, UK: Routledge (Taylor & Francis), 2006.

4. Feminism/Transfeminism
a. Transphobic Feminism
Cisgender-Female Transphobic Feminists
Bindel, Julie. "Gender Benders, Beware." *The Guardian,* January 31, 2004. https://www.theguardian.com/world/2004/jan/31/gender.weekend7.

Daly, Mary. Gyn/Ecology: The Metaethics of Radical Feminism. Boston, MA, Beacon Press, 1978.

Greer, Germaine. *The Whole Woman.* New York, NY: Doubleday, 1999.

Greer, Germaine. *The Female Eunuch.* London, UK: MacGibbon & Kee, 1970.

Jeffreys, Sheila, and Lorene Gottschalk. *Gender Hurts: A Feminist Analysis of the Politics of Transgenderism.* Abingdon, UK: Routledge (Taylor & Francis), 2014.

Raymond, Janice. *The Transsexual Empire: The Making of the She-Male.* Boston, MA: Beacon Press, 1979.

b. Transpositive Transfeminism
Cisgender-Female Trans(positive)Feminists
Anzaldúa, Gloria, and AnaLouise Keating, eds. *This Bridge We Call Home: Radical Visions for Transformation.* Abingdon, UK: Routledge (Taylor & Francis), 2002.

Butler, Judith. *Undoing Gender*. Abingdon, UK: Routledge (Taylor & Francis), 2004.

Butler, Judith. *Bodies that Matter: On the Discursive Limits of Sex.* Abingdon, UK: Routledge (Taylor & Francis), 1993.

Butler, Judith. *Gender Trouble: Feminism and the Subversion of Identity*. Abingdon, UK: Routledge (Taylor & Francis), 1990.

Dworkin, Andrea. *Woman Hating: A Radical Look at Sexuality*. New York, NY: E. P. Dutton,

1974.

Enke, Anne, ed., *Transfeminist Perspectives in and Beyond Transgender and Gender Studies.* Philadelphia, PA: Temple University Press, 2012.

findlay, barbara. "Acting Queerly: Lawyering for Trans People." In Krista Scott-Dixon, ed., *Trans/Forming Feminisms: Trans-feminist Voices Speak Out.* Toronto, ON: Sumach Press (Canadian Scholars' Press), 2006, chapter 13.

hooks, bell. *Feminism is for Everybody: Passionate Politics.* Boston, MA: South End Press, 2000.

Kolmar, Wendy K., and Frances Bartkowski, eds. *Feminist Theory: A Reader* (2nd ed.). Boston, MA: McGraw-Hill Higher Education, 2005.

Scott-Dixon, Krista, ed., *Trans/forming Feminisms: Trans-feminist Voices Speak Out.* Toronto, ON: Sumach Press (Canadian Scholars' Press), 2006.

Steinem, Gloria. "Op-ed: On Working Together Over Time."Advocate.com. October 2, 2013. https://www.advocate.com/commentary/2013/10/02/op-ed-working-together-over-time.

Swain, Gloria. "300 Hours: What I Learned About Black Queer and Trans Liberation at BLMTO Tent City." *Marvellous Grounds: Queer of Colour Spaces in Toronto,* 2016, no. 1: *QTBIPOC Space – Remapping Belonging in Toronto.* marvellousgrounds.com/blog/300-hours.

Yee, Jessica, ed., Feminism FOR REAL: Deconstructing the Academic Industrial Complex of Feminism. Ottawa, ON: Canadian Centre for Policy Alternatives, 2011.

Female-Embodied, Gender Non-Binary Transfeminists

Cruz, Louis Esmé. "Medicine Bundle of Contradictions: Female-man, Mi'kmaq/Acadian/Irish Diasporas, Invisible disAbilities, masculine-Feminist." In Jessica Yee, ed., Feminism FOR REAL: Deconstructing the Academic Industrial Complex of Feminism. Ottawa, ON: Canadian Centre for Policy Alternatives, 2011, 49-60.

Halberstam, Judith/Jack. Gaga Feminism. Boston, MA: Beacon Press, 2012.

Halberstam, Judith. In a Queer Time and Place: Transgender Bodies, Subcultural Lives. New York, NY: New York University Press, 2005.

Halberstam, Judith. "Transgender Butch: Butch/FTM Border Wars and the Masculine Continuum." In Wendy K. Kolmar and Frances Bartkowski, eds., Feminist Theory: A Reader (2nd ed.). Boston, MA: McGraw-Hill Higher Education, 2005, 550-560.

Halberstam, Judith. Female Masculinity. Durham, NC: Duke University Press, 1998.

Trans-Female Transfeminists

Bettcher, Talia Mae. "Understanding Transphobia: Authenticity and Sexual Violence." In Krista Scott-Dixon, ed., Trans/Forming Feminisms: Trans-feminist Voices Speak Out. Toronto, ON: Sumach Press (Canadian Scholars' Press), 2006, chapter 18.

Bornstein, Kate. Gender Outlaw: On Men, Women, and the Rest of Us. Abingdon, UK: Routledge (Taylor & Francis), 1994.

Courvant, Diana. "Speaking of Privilege." In Gloria Anzaldúa and AnaLouise Keating, eds., This Bridge We Call Home: Radical Visions for Transformation. Abingdon, UK: Routledge (Taylor & Francis), 2002, 458-462.

Dubois, Lynnette. "Safe at Home: Redefining the Politics of Rape and Its Aftermath." In Krista Scott-Dixon, ed., Trans/Forming Feminisms: Trans-feminist Voices Speak Out. Toronto, ON: Sumach Press (Canadian Scholars' Press), 2006, chapter 19.

Gabriel, Davina Anne, ed., TransSisters: The Journal of Transsexual Feminism. Kansas City, KS: Skyclad Publishing, 1994-1995.

Hardie, Alaina. "It's a Long Way to the Top: Hierarchies of Legitimacy in Trans Communities." In Krista Scott-Dixon, ed., Trans/Forming Feminisms: Trans-feminist Voices Speak Out. Toronto, ON: Sumach Press (Canadian Scholars' Press), 2006, chapter 11.

McKinnon, Rachel. "The Epistemology of Propaganda." Philosophy and Phenomenological Research, March 7, 2018, 96(2): 483-489. https://doi.org/10.1111/phpr.12429. Analysis of anti-trans women propaganda by cisgender, trans-exclusionary radical feminists (TERFs).

McKinnon, Rachel. "Allies Behaving Badly: Gaslighting as Epistemic Injustice." In James Kidd, José Medina, and Gaile Pohlhaus, Jr., eds., The Routledge Handbook of Epistemic Injustice. Abingdon, UK: Routledge (Taylor & Francis), 2017, chapter 15. Discussion of trans women's experiences with so-called "allies" acting in bad faith.

McKinnon, Rachel. "Stereotype Threat and Attributional Ambiguity for Trans Women." Hypatia: A Journal of Feminist Philosophy, March 31, 2014, 29(4): 857-872. https://doi.org/10.1111/hypa.12097.

Pichette, Jade. "Challenging Transmisogyny: From the Classroom to Social Work Practice." In Susan Hillock and Nick J. Mulé, eds., Queering Social Work Education. Vancouver, BC: UBC Press, 2016, 148-161.

Serano, Julia. Excluded: Making Feminist and Queer Movements More Inclusive. New York, NY: Seal Press, 2013.

Serano, Julia. Whipping Girl: A Transsexual Woman on Sexism and the Scapegoating of Femininity. New York, NY: Seal Press, 2007.

Stone, Allucquére Rosanne (Sandy). The Empire Strikes Back: A Posttranssexual Manifesto. 1987. First version published in Kristina Straub and Julia Epstein, eds. Body Guards: The Cultural Politics of Gender Ambiguity. Abingdon, UK: Routledge (Taylor & Francis), 1991. Second version (rev.) published in "Camera Obscura," Spring, 1994. Electronic version published on ACTLab ftp site, January, 1994. Third version (text-only). https://sandystone.com/empire-strikes-back.html. Fourth version published April 9, 2014 in pdf and http versions. http://sandystone.com.

Transgenderist Transfeminists (male-to-female crossdressers)

Gilbert, Michael A. "The Feminist Crossdresser." In Krista Scott-Dixon, ed., Trans/forming Feminisms: Trans-feminist Voices Speak Out. Toronto, ON: Sumach Press (Canadian Scholars' Press), 2006, 105-111.

Jones, Glenda René, ed., Journal of Male Feminism (formerly, Hose and Heel). International Alliance for Male Feminism, 1977-1980.

Non-Gender, Intersex Transfeminists

Koyama, Emi. "The Transfeminist Manifesto." In Rory Dicker and Alison Piepmeier, eds., Catching a Wave: Reclaiming Feminism for the 21st Century. Boston, MA: Northeastern University Press, 2003, 244-262.

Trans-Male Transfeminists

Anderson-Minshall, Jacob. "The Enemy Within: On Becoming A Straight White Guy." In Shira Tarant, ed., Men Speak Out: Views on Gender, Sex and Power (2nd ed.). Abingdon, UK: Routledge (Taylor & Francis), 2013, 28-33.

Bornstein, Kate, and S. Bear Bergman, eds. Gender Outlaws: The Next Generation. New York, NY: Seal Press, 2010. S. Bear Bergman is a trans-male transfeminist.

Califia-Rice, Pat. "Feminism and Sadomasochism." In Stevi Jackson and Sue Scott, eds., Feminism and Sexuality: A Reader. New York, NY: Columbia University Press, 1996, 230-237.

Goldberg, Joshua, and Caroline White. "Anti-Violence Work in Transition." In Krista Scott-Dixon, ed., Trans/forming Feminisms: Trans-feminist Voices Speak Out. Toronto, ON: Sumach Press (Canadian Scholars' Press), 2006, 217-226. Caroline White is a cisgender female ally.

Irving, Dan: "Elusive Subjects: Notes on the Relationship between Critical Political Economy and Trans Studies." In Anne Enke, ed., Transfeminist Perspectives in and Beyond Transgender and Gender Studies. Philadelphia, PA: Temple University Press, 2012, 153-169.

Irving, Dan. "Book Review: Trans/forming Feminisms: Trans-feminist Voices Speak Out." Toronto, ON: Sumach Press (Canadian Scholars Press), 2006. Journal of International Women's Studies, 2008, 9(3): 363-368.

Noble, Bobby. "Trans. Panic: Some Thoughts toward a Theory of Feminist Fundamentalism." In Anne Enke, ed., Transfeminist Perspectives in and Beyond Transgender and Gender Studies. Philadelphia, PA: Temple University Press, 2012, 45-59.

Noble, Bobby. "Our Bodies Are Not Ourselves: Tranny Guys and the Racialized Class Politics of Embodiment." In Krista Scott-Dixon, ed., Trans/forming Feminisms: Trans-feminist Voices Speak Out. Toronto, ON: Sumach Press (Canadian Scholars' Press), 2006, 95-104.

Pyne, Jake. "Transfeminist Theory and Action: Trans Women and the Contested Terrain of Women's Services." In Brian J. O'Neill, Tracy A. Swan, and Nick J. Mulé, eds., LGBTQ People and Social Work: Intersectional Perspectives. Toronto, ON: Canadian Scholars' Press, 2015, 129-150.

Scanlon, Kyle. "Where's the Beef? Masculinity as Performed by Feminists." In Krista Scott-Dixon, ed., Trans/forming Feminisms: Trans-feminist Voices Speak Out. Toronto, ON: Sumach Press (Canadian Scholars' Press), 2006, 87-94.

simpkins, reese. "Feminist Transmasculinities." In Krista Scott-Dixon, ed., Trans/forming Feminisms: Trans-feminist Voices Speak Out. Toronto, ON: Sumach Press (Canadian Scholars' Press), 2006, 79-86.

Spade, Dean. "What's Wrong with Trans Rights?" In Anne Enke, ed., Transfeminist Perspectives in and Beyond Transgender and Gender Studies. Philadelphia, PA: Temple University Press, 2012, 184-194.

Valerio, Max Wolf. "Now That You're a White Man: Changing Sex in a Postmodern World – Being, Becoming, and Borders." In Gloria Anzaldúa and AnaLouise Keating, eds., This Bridge We Call Home: Radical Visions for Transformation. Abingdon, UK: Routledge (Taylor & Francis), 2002, 239-254.

5. Trans Activism
a. General
American

Currah, Paisley, Richard M. Juang, and Shannon Price Minter. *Transgender Rights*. Minneapolis, MN: University of Minnesota Press, 2006.

Currah, Paisley, and Shannon Price Minter. *Transgender Equality: A Handbook for Activists and Policymakers*. San Francisco, CA: National Center for Lesbian Rights/The Policy Institute of the National Gay and Lesbian Task Force, 2000. http://www.nclrights.org/legal-help-resources/resource/transgender-equality-a-handbook-for-activists-and-policymakers/.

Rudacille, Deborah. *The Riddle of Gender: Science, Activism, and Transgender Rights*. New York, NY: Anchor Books (Random House), 2005.

Spade, Dean. Normal Life: Administrative Violence, Critical Trans Politics, and the Limits of Law. Durham, NC: Duke University Press, 2011, rev. 2015.

British

Burns, Christine, ed., Trans Britain: Our Journey from the Shadows. London, UK: Unbound, 2018.

Burns, Christine. Pressing Matters: vols. 1 & 2. Self-published, 2013 & 2014.
Whittle, Stephen. The Ultimate Practice Guide to Transgender and Transsexual Human Rights and Equality Law in the UK. London, UK: Press for Change, 2016.
Whittle, Stephen, ed., Respect and Equality: Transsexual and Transgender Rights. London, UK: Cavendish Publishing, 2002.

Canadian
Irving, Dan, and Rupert Raj, eds. Trans Activism in Canada: A Reader. Toronto, ON: Canadian Scholars' Press, 2014. Includes transgender, cisgender and Two-Spirit people.

Dutch
Bakker, Alex. Transgender in Nederland: Een Buitengewone Geschiedenis. Amsterdam, NL: Boom Publishing House, 2018. www.BUA.nl; www.Boomgeschiedenis.nl. Dutch-language edition only.

[Note: The following subsections in this section on Trans Activism all have an exclusive Canadian focus except for e. Trans Student Advocacy, and i. Transqueer Activists.]

b. Trans Politicolegal/Human Rights
Markusoff, Jason. "An Alberta MLA on Battling Gender Identity: Member Cortes-Vargas spoke in the legislature about not being defined by words like 'masculinity' and 'femininity'." *MacLean's Magazine,* December 1, 2015. https://www.macleans.ca/news/canada/for-the-record-an-alberta-mla-on-battling-gender-identity.

Noble, Bobby. "Trans-Ing the Canadian Passport: On the Biopolitical Storying of Race, Gender, and Borders." In Patrizia Gentile, Gary Kinsman, and Pauline L. Rankin, eds., *We Still Demand! Redefining Resistance in Sex and Gender Struggles*. Vancouver, BC: UBC Press, 2017, 270-284.

Singer, Samuel. *Trans Rights, Gender Identity, and Gender Expression in Canada.* Ottawa, ON: Canadian Human Rights Commission, 2017.

c. Trans Liberation & Trade Unionism
Salah, Trish. "Gender Struggles: Reflections on Trans Liberation, Trade Unionism, and the Limits of Solidarity." In Dan Irving and Rupert Raj, eds., *Trans Activism in Canada: A Reader.* Toronto, ON: Canadian Scholars' Press, 2014, 149-167.

d. Trans Health Care Advocacy
See below: 7. Later Health Care: Trans Health Care Advocacy.

e. Trans Student Advocacy
Mayo, Cris, Scott Gust, and Aidan Key. *Transgender Student Advocacy and Support: Evolving Ethics in a Time of Devolving Policy.* Groundworks: A Publication of the Philosophy of Education Society Committee on Professional Affairs, 2017. https://www.philosophyofeducation.org/publications.

skelton, j wallace. *Transphobia: Deal with It and Be a Gender Transcender.* Illustrated by Nick Johnson. Toronto, ON: James Lorimer Publishing, 2017. For middle school students.

wallace, j. "Trans in Class: Trans Activism in a Suburban School Board." In Dan Irving and Rupert Raj, eds., *Trans Activism in Canada: A Reader.* Toronto, ON: Canadian Scholars' Press, 2014, 169-177.

Wells, Kristopher, M. Gayle Roberts, and Carol Allan. *Supporting Transgender and*

Transsexual Students in K-12 Schools: A Guide for Educators. Ottawa, ON: Canadian Teachers' Federation. 2012. https://eric.ed.gov/?id=EJ994926.

f. Police & the Trans Community
Toronto Police LGBT Community Consultation Committee. *A Guide to Police Services in Toronto: Dedicated to our Trans Communities.* December, 2016. https://www.torontopolice.on.ca/publications/files/guide_to_police_services_trans_community.pdf.

g. (Trans) Prisoner Advocacy
Johnson, Katherine, and Stephanie Castle. *Prisoner of Gender: A Transsexual and the System.* Vancouver, BC: Perceptions Press, 1997. Trans woman Katherine Johnson was a longterm prison inmate in Ontario and BC.
Ware, Syrus, Joan Ruzsa, and Giselle Dias. "It Cannot be Fixed Because It Isn't Broken: Racism and Disability in the Prison Industrial Complex in Canada." In Liat Ben-Moshe, Chris Chapman, and Allison C. Carey, eds., *Disability Incarcerated: Imprisonment and Disability in the United States and Canada.* New York, NY: Palgrave Macmillan, 2014. Trans man Syrus Ware founded the Prison Justice Action Committee.

h. Trans Community Activism
Burke, Nora Butler, and Viviane Namaste. Translated from the French and revised by Natalie Duchesne. "'What Is Missing in Our Community Is Self-Love': An Interview with Marie-Marcelle Godbout, Founder of L'Aide aux Transsexuel(le)s du Quebec." In Dan Irving and Rupert Raj, eds., *Trans Activism in Canada: A Reader.* Toronto, ON: Canadian Scholars' Press, 2014, 109-114.
MacFarlane, Devon, and Tien Neo Eamas. "Happy Tranny Day." In Dan Irving and Rupert Raj, eds., *Trans Activism in Canada: A Reader.* Toronto, ON: Canadian Scholars' Press, 2014, 137-147.
Matte, Nick. "Rupert Raj and the Rise of Transsexual Consumer Activism in the 1980s." In Dan Irving and Rupert Raj, eds., *Trans Activism in Canada: A Reader.* Toronto, ON: Canadian Scholars' Press, 2014, 33-43.
Namaste, Viviane. "'We Paved the Way for Whatever Tolerance They have in Their Lives': An Interview with Michelle De Ville, 'The First Door Bitch in Montreal.'" In Dan Irving and Rupert Raj, eds., *Trans Activism in Canada: A Reader.* Toronto, ON: Canadian Scholars' Press, 2014, 19-25.
Pyne, Jake, Kyle Scanlon, Dani Araya, Alec Butler, Jazzmine Manalo, Evana Ortigoza, Julissa Penate, Yasmeen Persaud, and Kenji Tokawa. "Trans Access Project: Running the Gauntlet." In Dan Irving and Rupert Raj, eds., *Trans Activism in Canada: A Reader.* Toronto, ON: Canadian Scholars' Press, 2014, 115-123.
Raj, Rupert. "Zening the Art of Trans Activism." In Dan Irving and Rupert Raj, eds., *Trans Activism in Canada: A Reader.* Toronto, ON: Canadian Scholars' Press, 2014, 85-91.

i. Transqueer Activists
Martin, Ellis, and Zach Ozma, eds. *We Both Laughed in Pleasure: The Selected Diaries of Lou Sullivan, 1961-1991.* Brooklyn, NY: Nightboat Books, 2019. Introduction by Susan Stryker. Acknowledges Rupert RajMatte, Nicholas. "Rupert Raj, Transmen, and Sexuality: The Politics of Transnormativity in *Metamorphosis Magazine* during the 1980s." In Patrizia Gentile, Gary Kinsman, and Pauline L. Rankin, eds., *We Still Demand! Redefining Resistance in Sex and Gender Struggles.* Vancouver, BC: UBC Press, 2017, 117-136. Canadian article on North American queer and queer-positive trans men.

Ross, Mirha-Soleil, and Xanthra Mackay, dirs. *Gender Troublemakers*. Toronto, ON: Vtape, 1993. http://www.vtape.org/video?vi=3636. Canadian porn video of trans-female partners making love.

Silverman, Victor, and Susan Stryker, dirs. *Screaming Queens: The Riot at Compton's Cafeteria*. https://itvs.org/films/screaming-queens. San Francisco, CA: Frameline, 2005. American film documentary of first transgender protest against police, including queer and trans people.

Smith, Brice D. *Lou Sullivan: Daring To Be A Man Among Men*. San Francisco, CA: Transgress Press, 2017. American biography of first openly trans-gay man.

j. Trans Sex-Worker Activists

Daniel, Barb. *She's No Lady: The Story of Jamie Lee Hamilton*. Toronto, ON: Cormorant Books, 2005.

Forrester, Monica, co-prod., *Remember the Living: Monica Forrester on Sisters in Spirit and Indigenous Sex Workers*. Toronto, ON: Maggie's: The Toronto Sex Workers Action Project, October 4, 2012. https://www.youtube.com/watch?v=lPGQNvIlLuQ. Hamilton, Jamie Lee. "The Golden Age of Prostitution: One Woman's Personal Account of an Outdoor Brothel in Vancouver, 1975-1984." In Dan Irving and Rupert Raj, eds., *Trans Activism in Canada: A Reader*. Toronto, ON: Canadian Scholars' Press, 2014, 27-32.

Highcrest, Alexandra. *At Home on the Stroll: My Twenty Years as a Prostitute in Canada*. Toronto, ON: A. A. Knopf (Canada), 1997.

James, Elizabeth "Raven." "Gender Strike! It's an Offence." In Dan Irving and Rupert Raj, eds., *Trans Activism in Canada: A Reader*. Toronto, ON: Canadian Scholars' Press, 2014, 45-49.

Laframboise, Sandy Leo. "Finding My Place: The High Risk Project Society." In Dan Irving and Rupert Raj, eds., *Trans Activism in Canada: A Reader*. Toronto, ON: Canadian Scholars' Press, 2014, 51-56.

McLaughlin, Matthew, dir.; and Barb Perry and D. Ryan Dyck, prods., Courage in the Face of Hate, Toronto, ON: Bulldog Productions, 2012. Produced for the Egale Canada Human Rights Trust. http://courageinthefaceofhate.ca/. Video documentary about violent hate crimes against trans and queer people.

Namaste, Viviane. "Interview with Mirha-Soleil Ross." In Viviane Namaste, ed., *Sex Change, Social Change: Reflections on Identity, Institutions, and Imperialism*. Toronto, ON: Women's Press (Canadian Scholars' Press), 2005, 86-102.

Ross, Mirha-Soleil, dir., Viviane Namaste, and Monica Forrester. *Madame Lauraine's Transsexual Touch*. Toronto, ON: Vtape, 2001. http://www.vtape.org/video?vi=4811. Video documentary on Montreal and Toronto trans sex workers Monica Forrester, Lynne Pellerin (uncredited) and others.

Ware, Syrus Marcus. "Organizing on the Corner: Trans Women of Colour and Sex Worker Activism in Toronto in the 1980s and 1990s. (An Interview with Monica Forrester and Chanelle Gallant)." In Jin Haritaworn, Ghaida Moussa, and Syrus Marcus Ware, eds., *Marvellous Grounds: Queer of Colour Histories of Toronto*. Toronto, ON: Between the Lines, 2018, chapter 1.

[**Note:** Jamie Hamilton, Elizabeth James, and Sandy Laframboise have a dual trans-Two-Spirit identity.]

k. Trans-female Sports Activists

Dumaresq, Michelle, Karen Duthie, dir., Diana Wilson, prod., and Lesley Ewen. *100% Woman*. Vancouver, BC: Artemis Dreams Productions/Producers on Davie Pictures, and the Canadian Television Fund, 2004.

https://www.movingimages.ca/store/search.php?keywords=100%25+woman&x=0&y=0. Aired on the Documentary Channel (Television Network Canada) and the Life Network in 2004. Video documentary on Michelle Dumaresq, a Canadian trans-female, professional downhill mountain bike champion.

Friedlaender, Christina, and Rachel McKinnon. "The Fundamental Attribution Error, Microaggressions, Harassment, and Gaslighting of Transgender Athletes: A Bi-Directional Analysis of the Role of Stereotypes in Transmisogynist Harassment in Single-Gender Sports." In Lauren Freeman and Jeanine Weekes Schroer, eds., *Microaggressions and Philosophy*. Abingdon, UK: Routledge (Taylor & Francis), forthcoming.

McKinnon, Rachel. "Gaslighting as Epistemic Violence: 'Allies,' Mobbing, and Complex Post-Traumatic Stress Disorder, Including a Case Study of Harassment of Transgender Women in Sport." In Lauren Freeman and Jeanine Weekes Schroer, eds., *Overcoming Epistemic Injustice*. Abingdon, UK: Routledge (Taylor & Francis), forthcoming.

McKinnon, Rachel, and Aryn Conrad. "Including Trans Women in Sport: Analyzing Principles and Policies of Fairness in Competition." In Bianca Takaoka and Kate Manne, eds., *Philosophical Topics: Gendered Oppression and Its Intersections*. Fayetteville, AR: University of Arkansas Press, forthcoming.

Worley, Kristen, and Johanna Schneller. *Woman Enough: How a Boy Became a Woman and Changed the World of Sport.* Toronto, ON: Random House (Canada), 2019.

l. Trans Activists of Colour

Dadui, Kusha. "Queer and Trans Migration and Canadian Border Imperialism." In Jin Haritaworn, Ghaida Moussa, and Syrus Marcus Ware, eds., *Marvellous Grounds: Queer of Colour Histories of Toronto*. Toronto, ON: Between the Lines, 2018, chapter 9.

Diverlus, Rodney, Sandy Hudson, and Syrus Marcus Ware, eds. *Until We Are Free: Reflections on Black Lives Matter in Canada*. Regina, SK: University of Regina Press, 2019. Syrus Ware is an anti-racist, Black trans-male activist.

Lagartera, Reece. "ShoutOut Against Homophobia, Biphobia, Transphobia and Heterosexism." Winnipeg, MB: Rainbow Resource Centre, 2009. https://www.rainbowhealthontario.ca/resources/shoutout-against-homophobia-biphobia-transphobia-and-heterosexism/; www.rainbowresourcecentre.org/.

Ware, Syrus Marcus. "Organizing on the Corner: Trans Women of Colour and Sex Worker Activism in Toronto in the 1980s and 1990s. (An Interview with Monica Forrester and Chanelle Gallant)." In Jin Haritaworn, Ghaida Moussa, and Syrus Marcus Ware, eds., *Marvellous Grounds: Queer of Colour Histories of Toronto*. Toronto, ON: Between the Lines, 2018, chapter 1.

[See also: A. Transsexual/Transvestite/Transgender: 1. Auto(biography)/Literature/Film/Media: *African American*; and F. Combined Populations: 1. Trans, Genderqueer & Queer Activists of Colour.]

m. Indigenous Trans Activists

2-Spirited People of the 1st Nations. *Our Relatives Said: A Wise Practices Guide. Voices of Aboriginal Trans-People.* Toronto, ON, 2008. https://www.rainbowhealthontario.ca/resources/our-relatives-said-a-wise-practices-guide-voices-of-aboriginal-trans-people/. Features Indigenous trans people, some of whom also identify as Two-Spirit.

Couillard, Paul. *In Memoriam: Aiyyana Maracle.* 2016. http://7a-11d.ca/in-memoriam-aiyyana-maracle/#_ftnref7.

Maracle, Aiyyana. *Death in the Shadow of the Umbrella.* Vancouver, BC, 2015.

https://vimeo.com/137714829.
Maracle, Aiyyana. Interview with Aiyyana Maracle, Tranzister Radio 29, CKUT 90.3 FM, October 9, 2014.
https://drive.google.com/file/d/0B0KGgCD3_zjTMjVXT2ZvM1J0VnM/edit.
Maracle, Aiyyana. "A Journey in Gender." *Torquere, Journal of the Lesbian and Gay Studies Association/Revue de la Société canadienne des études lesbiennes et gaies*, 2000, 2: 36-57. https://torquere.journals.yorku.ca/index.php/torquere/article/view/36587/33238.
Morriseau, Renae, dir./prod. *Whispers from the Grandmothers*. "First Story" TV series. Vancouver, BC, 2001. Based on an excerpt of Canadian performing artist Aiyyana Maracle's unpublished memoir, *Chronicle of A Transformed Woman*. http://www.connect.ecuad.ca/~grunt/art1.html.
Toms, Colleen. "Six Nations Woman Shares her Transgender Experience." *Brant News*, January 19, 2015.
Ware, Syrus Marcus. "The Sacred Uprising: Indigenous Creative Activisms (An Interview with Rebeka Tabobondung)." In Jin Haritaworn, Ghaida Moussa, and Syrus Marcus Ware, eds., with Río Rodríguez. *Queering Urban Justice: Queer of Colour Formations in Toronto*. Toronto, ON: University of Toronto Press, 2018, chapter 11.

n. Animal Rights Trans Activists
For animal-rights trans activists Calvin Neufeld and Mirha-Soleil Ross, see: Part IV: B. Eco-Activism/Animal Liberation/Trans-Species Psychology: Transgender.

6. Earlier Sexology/Psychomedicine
a. Psychiatric Classifications of Gender Identity
American Psychiatric Association, Washington, DC: *The Diagnostic and Statistical Manual of Mental Disorders (DSM)*. A brief history of *DSM 1* to *DSM 5*. https://www.psychologistpanel.com/diagnostic-statistical-manual-mental-disorders/.
World Health Organization, Geneva, CH: *International Classification of Diseases (ICD)*. A brief history of *ICD 1* to *ICD 11*. https://www.britannica.com/topic/International-Classification-of-Diseases.

b. Gender Dysphoria/Gender Identity Disorder
Steiner, Betty W. *Gender Dysphoria: Development, Research, Management*. New York, NY: Plenum Press, 1985.
Zucker, Kenneth J., and Susan J. Bradley. *Gender Identity Disorders and Psychosexual Problems in Children and Adolescents*. New York, NY: Guildford Press, 1995.

c. Transsexualism
Benjamin, Harry. *The Transsexual Phenomenon*. New York, NY: Julian Press, 1966. Reprint, Düsseldorf, DEU: Symposium Publishing, 1999.
Green, Richard, and John Money, eds. *Transsexualism and Sex Reassignment*. Baltimore, MD: Johns Hopkins University Press, 1969.
Lothstein, Leslie Martin. *Female-to-Male Transsexualism: Historical, Clinical, and Theoretical Issues*. Abingdon, UK: Routledge (Taylor & Francis), 1983.

d. Transsexualism & Intersex
Dillon, Michael. *Self: A Study in Endocrinology and Ethics*. Amsterdam, NL: Elsevier Science, 1946.
Farina, Roberto. *Transexualismo: do Homem a Mulaher Normal Atraves dos Estados de Intersexualidade e das Parafilias*. *(Transsexualism: From Man to Normal Woman*

Through the States of Intersexuality and Paraphilia). São Paulo, BR: Novalunar-Graf, 1982. Portuguese-language edition only.

e. Transgenderism (transsexualism/transvestism)
Peo, Roger E. "The 'Origins' and 'Cures' for Transgender Behavior." *The TV-TS Tapestry*, 1984, (42).

7. Later Trans Health Care
a. Psychiatric Classifications of Gender Identity
American Psychiatric Association, Washington (APA), DC: *The Diagnostic and Statistical Manual of Mental Disorders (DSM).* 2013.
https://www.psychiatry.org/psychiatrists/practice/dsm. This current fifth version, *DSM-5*, still includes classifications of *"Gender Dysphoria"* for both children/adolescents and adults.
World Health Organization (WHO), Geneva, CH: *International Classification of Diseases (ICD)-11-CA and CCI Classifications.* 2018. https://icd.who.int/browse11/l-m/en. This current 11th version, *ICD-11*, de-psychiatrizes Gender Incongruence (06.) (Conditions Related to Sexual Health [17]), excluding Paraphilic Disorders (6D30-6D3Z).

b. Trans Care Guidelines
Bockting, Walter O., and Joshua M. Goldberg, eds. *Guidelines for Transgender Care (Special Issue).* Binghamton, NY: Haworth Medical Press, 2007. Co-published in the *International Journal of Transgenderism*, 2006, 9(3-4).
https://www.tandfonline.com/action/doSearch?AllField=Bockting%2C+Walter+O.%2C+and+Joshua+M.+Goldberg%2C+eds.+%22Guidelines+for+Transgender+Care%22&pageSize=10&subjectTitle=&startPage=1.
Canadian Professional Association for Transgender Health (CPATH).
http://cpath.ca/en/resources/.
Israel, Gianna E., and Donald E. Tarver, II, MD, eds. *Transgender Care: Recommended Guidelines, Practical Information & Personal Accounts.* Philadelphia, PA: Temple University Press, 1997.
World Professional Association for Transgender Health (WPATH). *Standards of Care for the Health of Transsexual, Transgender, and Gender-Nonconforming People* (7th version), 2011. https://www.wpath.org/publications/soc.

c. Hormone Therapy for Trans Adults
Bourns, Amy, MD. *Guidelines and Protocols for Comprehensive Primary Health Care for Trans Clients.* Toronto, ON: Rainbow Health Ontario (Sherbourne Health Centre), 2015.
    https://sherbourne.on.ca/guidelines-protocols-for-trans-care/. First edition (2009) co-written by Kate Greenaway, MD and Vlad Wolanyk.
Dahl, Marshall, Jamie L. Feldman, Joshua Goldberg, Afshin Jaberi, Walter Bockting, and Gail Knudson. *Endocrine Therapy for Transgender Adults in British Columbia: Suggested Guidelines.* Vancouver, BC: Vancouver Coastal Health, 2006, rev. 2015.
    https://www.researchgate.net/publication/250401252_Endocrine_Therapy_for_Transgender_Adults_in_British_Columbia_Suggested_Guidelines.
Feldman, Jamie, and Joshua Goldberg. "Transgender Primary Medical Care: Suggested Guidelines for Clinicians in British Columbia." 2006.
    https://www.researchgate.net/publication/253294860_Transgender_Primary_Medical_Care_Suggested_Guidelines_for_Clinicians_in_British_Columbia.
Gorton, Nick, MD, Jamie Buth, MD, and Dean Spade, Esq. *Medical Therapy and Health Maintenance for Transgender Men: A Guide for Health Care Providers.* USA, 2005.
    https://www.researchgate.net/publication/239573753_Medical_Therapy_and_Health_Ma

intenance_for_Transgender_Men_A_Guide_For_Health_Care_Providers.

Raj, Rupert, and Celia Schwartz. "A Collaborative Preparedness and Informed Consent Model: Guidelines to Assess Trans Candidates for Readiness for Hormone Therapy and Supportive Counselling throughout the Gender Transitioning Process." Unpublished, Sept. 12, 2012, rev. May 1, 2015. Ottawa, ON: Canadian Centre for Gender & Sexual Diversity. https://ccgsd-ccdgs.org/resources/.

d. Hormone Therapy for Gender Non-Binary & Trans Teenagers

Cohen-Kettenis, Peggy T., and Friedemann Pfäfflin. *Transgenderism and Intersexuality in Childhood and Adolescence: Making Choices.* Thousand Oaks, CA: SAGE Publishing, 2003.

de Vries, Annelou L. C., MD, PhD, Peggy T. Cohen-Kettenis, PhD, and Henriette Delemarre-van de Waal, MD, PhD. "Clinical Management of Gender Dysphoria in Adolescents." *International Journal of Transgenderism*, 2006, 9(3-4): 83-94. https://www.tandfonline.com/doi/abs/10.1300/J485v09n03_04.

Holman, Catherine White, and Joshua M. Goldberg. "Ethical, Legal, and Psychosocial Issues in Care of Transgender Adolescents." *International Journal of Transgenderism*, 2006, 9(3-4): 95-110. https://www.tandfonline.com/action/showCitFormats?doi=10.1300%2FJ485v09n03_05.

e. Gender-Confirming Surgical Patient Care

Bowman, Cameron, and Joshua Goldberg. "Care of the Patient Undergoing Sex Reassignment Surgery." *International Journal of Transgenderism*, 2006, 9(3-4): 135-165. https://www.tandfonline.com/doi/abs/10.1300/J485v09n03_07.

f. Gender Detransition/Retransition

Graham, Julie. "Detransition, Retransition: What Providers Need to Know." San Francisco Department of Public Health, n.d. https://fenwayhealth.org › Detransitioning-and-Retransitioning-graham-1.

g. Mental Health Therapy/Addictions Counselling

Barbara, Angela M., Gloria Chaim, and Farzana Doctor. *Asking the Right Questions 2: Talking with Clients about Sexual Orientation and Gender Identity in Mental Health, Counselling and Addiction Settings.* Toronto, ON: Centre for Addiction and Mental Health (Rainbow Services), 2004, rev. 2007. https://cdn.dal.ca/content/dam/dalhousie/pdf/campuslife/studentservices/healthandwellness/LGBTQ/asking_the_right_questions.pdf.

Bockting, Walter, Gail Knudson, and Joshua Goldberg. "Counseling and Mental Health Care for Transgender Adults and Loved Ones." *International Journal of Transgenderism*, 2006, 9(3-4): 35-82. https://www.tandfonline.com/doi/abs/10.1300/J485v09n03_03.

Fraser, Lin. "Psychotherapy in the WPATH Standards of Care for Transsexual, Transgender and Gender Non-Conforming People." *Journal of Sexual Medicine,* September 2013, 10: 283-283.

Gozlan, Oren. *Transsexuality and the Art of Transitioning: A Lacanian Approach.* Abingdon, UK: Routledge (Taylor & Francis), 2014.

Lev, Arlene Istar. *Transgender Emergence: Therapeutic Guidelines for Working with Gender-Variant People and their Families.* Philadelphia, PA: Haworth Press, 2004.

Miller, Niela. *Counseling in Genderland: A Guide for You and Your Transgendered Client.* Boston, MA: Different Path Press, 1996.

Rachlin, Katherine. "Transgender Individuals' Experiences of Psychotherapy." *International Journal of Transgenderism,* 2002, 6(1).

http://web.archive.org/web/20070708184341/http://www.symposion.com/ijt/ijtvo06no01_03.htm.

Raj, Rupert. "Transforming Couples and Families: A Transformative Therapeutic Model for Providers Working with the Loved Ones of Trans-Identified and Gender-Divergent People." *Journal of GLBT Family Studies*, 2008, 4(1): 133-163. doi: 10.1080/15504280802096765.

Raj, Rupert. "Transactivism as Therapy: A Client Self-Empowerment Model Linking Personal and Social Agency." *Journal of Gay & Lesbian Psychotherapy*, 2007, 11(3-4): 77-98. doi: 10.1300/J236v11n03_05.

Raj, Rupert. "Towards a Transpositive Therapeutic Model: Developing Clinical Sensitivity and Cultural Competence in the Effective Support of Transsexual and Transgendered Clients." *International Journal of Transgenderism,* 2002, 6(2). http://web.archive.org/web/20070429132659/http://www.symposion.com/ijt/ijtvo06no02_04.htm.

Raj, Rupert, and Celia Schwartz (2012, rev. 2015). See above: c. Gender-Affirming Hormone Therapy for Trans Adults.

Richards, Christina. *Trans and Sexuality: An Existentially-Informed Enquiry with Implications for Counselling Psychology.* Abingdon, UK: Routledge (Taylor & Francis), 2017.

Roberts, JoAnn. *Coping with Crossdressing: Tools & Strategies for Couples in Committed Relationships*. King of Prussia, PA: Creative Design Services, 1991, rev. 1992, rev. 1993.

Vanderburgh, Reid. *Transition and Beyond: Observations on Gender Identity.* Portland, OR: Q Press, 2007.

Vitale, Anne. "The Therapist versus the Client." In Israel, Gianna El, and Donald E. Tarver, II, *Transgender Care: Recommended Guidelines, Practical Information & Personal Accounts.* Philadelphia, PA: Temple University Press, 1997, chapter 23.

Wong, Wallace. "Using A Family and Multi-Systems Treatment Approach: Working with Gender-Variant Children." In Dan Irving and Rupert Raj, eds., *Trans Activism in Canada: A Reader.* Toronto, ON: Canadian Scholars' Press, 2014, 235-246.

h. Sexual Health/HIV/AIDS

Bauer, Greta, Nik Redman, and Kaitlin Bradley. *Gay, Bisexual and MSM Guys: No Assumptions!* Toronto, ON: Trans PULSE Project, 2012. https://www.ncbi.nlm.nih.gov/pmc/articles/PMC4059421/.

Bockting, Walter O., PsyD, and Sheila Kirk, MD, eds. *Transgender and HIV: Risks, Prevention, and Care.* Philadelphia, PA: Haworth Press, 2001.

Gay, Bi, Queer Trans Men's Working Group. *Primed[2]: A Sex Guide for Trans Men into Men.* Toronto, ON: Gay Men's Sexual Health Alliance, 2015. http://www.catie.ca/en/resources/primed-sex-guide-trans-men-men.

Meal Trans Programs. *The Toronto Trans and Two-Spirit Primer: An Introduction to Lower-Income, Sex-Working and Street-Involved Transgendered, Transsexual & Two-Spirit Service Users in Toronto.* Toronto, ON: The 519 Community Centre, circa 2004.

Page, Morgan M. *Brazen: Trans Women's Safer Sex Guide.* Toronto, ON: The 519 Church Street Community Centre, 2013. http://librarypdf.catie.ca/PDF/ATI-20000s/26424.pdf.

Scheim, Ayden I., Syrus Marcus Ware, Nik Redman, Zack Marshall, and Broden Giambrone. "Sexual Health on Our Own Terms: The Gay, Bi, Queer Trans Men's Working Group." In Dan Irving and Rupert Raj, eds., *Trans Activism in Canada: A Reader.* Toronto, ON: Canadian Scholars' Press, 2014, 247-258.

Strang, Christina. *The Happy Transsexual Hooker: A Healthy Resource Guide for Transsexual and Transgendered Sex Workers.* Toronto, ON: The 519 Church Street Community Centre, circa 2000.

i. Population-Based Public Health Research
Chow, Kathy, Jean Clipsham, Cheryl Dobinson, Susan Gapka, Elaine Hampson, Judith A. MacDonnell, and Rupert Raj. "Public Health Professionals, Community Researchers, and Community-Based Participatory Action Research: Process and Discovery." In Dan Irving and Rupert Raj, eds., *Trans Activism in Canada: A Reader.* Toronto, ON: Canadian Scholars' Press, 2014, 259-268.
Gapka, Susan, Rupert Raj, and the Public Health Alliance for Lesbian, Gay, Bisexual, Transsexual, Transgendered, Two-Spirited, Intersexed, Queer and Questioning Equity (a working group of the Ontario Public Health Association). *Trans Health Project (Report).* Toronto, ON: Ontario Public Health Association, 2003, revised 2004. http://www.opha.on.ca/Advocacy-and-Policy/Position-Paper,-Resolutions-and-Motions.aspx.
Taylor, Catherine. *Nowhere Near Enough: A Needs Assessment of Health and Safety Services for Transgender and Two Spirit People in Manitoba and Northwestern Ontario (Final Report).* Winnipeg, MB: Nine Circles Community Health Centre, 2006. www.turtleisland.org/healing/transgender.doc.

j. Trans Health Care Advocacy
MacDonnell, Judith A., and Robin Fern. Advocacy for Gender Diversity in the Contemporary Canadian Nursing Context: A Focus on Ontario. In Dan Irving and Rupert Raj, eds., *Trans Activism in Canada: A Reader.* Toronto, ON: Canadian Scholars' Press, 2014, 269-285.
MacFarlane, Devon, Lorraine Grieves, and Al Zwiers. "One Step at A Time: Moving Trans Activism Forward in a Large Bureaucracy." In Dan Irving and Rupert Raj, eds., *Trans Activism in Canada: A Reader.* Toronto, ON: Canadian Scholars' Press, 2014, 195-207. About Vancouver Coastal Health's LGBT2SQ initiative, PRISM.
Raj, Rupert. "Depsychopathologizing Gender Diversity and Improving Trans Healthcare in Canada." Ottawa, ON: Canadian Centre for Gender & Sexual Diversity, Sept. 10, 2019 (rev. Dec. 6, 2019). http://ccgsd-ccdgs.org/resources/.
Rowe, Will. "Auditioning for Care: Transsexual Men in Ontario Accessing Health Care." In Dan Irving and Rupert Raj, eds., *Trans Activism in Canada: A Reader.* Toronto, ON: Canadian Scholars' Press, 2014, 209-224.

k. Health Insurance (Canada & USA)
Canadian Professional Association for Transgender Health (CPATH). "Publicly-funded transition-related medical care in Canada." http://cpath.ca/en/resources/ufcw-cpath-state-of-publicly-funded-transition-related-medical-care-in-canada/.
Wilson, André A., MS, and Jamison Green, PhD. "Health Insurance Coverage Issues for Transgender People in the United States." University of California, San Francisco, June 17, 2016. https://transcare.ucsf.edu/guidelines/insurance.

8. Gender Transitioning (male-to-female)
Cameron, Loren. *Body Alchemy: Transsexual Portraits.* San Francisco, CA: Cleis Press, 1996. Photographs of trans men's top and bottom surgeries.
Cotten, Trystan T., ed., *Below the Belt: Genital Talk by Men of Trans Experience.* San Francisco, CA: Transgress Press, 2016.
Cotten, Trystan T., ed., *Hung Jury: Testimonies of Genital Surgery by Transsexual Men.* San Francisco, CA: Transgress Press, 2012.
Raj, Rupert-Gauthier. "Information on Female-to-Male Transsexualism: An Introductory Resource Booklet (revised)." Unpublished, 1989, updated from my original 1983 version. https://arquives.andornot.com/en/list?q=INFORMATION+ON+FEMALE-TO-

MALE+TRANSSEXUALISM&p=1&ps=20.
"The Total Guide to Penile Implants for Transsexual Men." *TransHealth,* May 2, 2013. http://www.trans-health.com/2013/penile-implants-guide.
Underwood, Thomas. "A Guide to Packers For Transmen." San Francisco, CA: *FTM Guide,* May 9, 2016. http://ftm-guide.com/guide-to-packers-for-transmen.
Whittle, Stephen, ed., *The White Book.* Manchester, UK: Press for Change, 1998. Gender-transition manual for females-to-males. Written for the FTM Network (UK).

9. Social Work
Hillock, Susan and Nick J. Mulé, eds. *Queering Social Work Education.* Vancouver, BC: UBC Press, 2016.
Mahood-Greer, Treanor. "A Very Brief Discussion of Social Work and Gender." In Dan Irving and Rupert Raj, eds., *Trans Activism in Canada: A Reader.* Toronto, ON: Canadian Scholars' Press, 2014, 179-193.
Pichette, Jade. "Challenging Transmisogyny: From the Classroom to Social Work Practice." In Susan Hillock and Nick J. Mulé, eds., *Queering Social Work Education.* Vancouver, BC: UBC Press, 2016, 148-161.
Pyne, Jake. "Queer and Trans Collisions in the Classroom: A Call to Throw Open Theoretical Doors in Social Work Education." In Susan Hillock and Nick J. Mulé, eds., *Queering Social Work Education.* Vancouver, BC: UBC Press, 2016, 54-72.
Pyne, Jake. "Transfeminist Theory and Action: Trans Women and the Contested Terrain of Women's Services." In Brian J. O'Neill, Tracy A. Swan, and Nick J. Mulé, eds., LGBTQ People and Social Work: Intersectional Perspectives. Toronto, ON: Canadian Scholars' Press, 2015, 129-150.
Sarkisova, Sly X. "Resisting the Binary: The Role of the Social Worker in Affirmative Trans Health Care." In Brian J. O'Neill, Tracy A. Swan, and Nick J. Mulé, eds., LGBTQ People and Social Work: Intersectional Perspectives. Toronto, ON: Canadian Scholars' Press, 2015, 255-274.
Sinclair, Raven, Michael Hart, and Gord Bruyere, eds. *Wícihitowin: Aboriginal Social Work in Canada.* Vancouver, BC: Langara College, 2011. Sixth of six editions since 2009.

10. Education
Devor, Aaron H., and Haefel-Thomas, Ardel. Transgender: A Reference Handbook. Santa Barbara, CA: ABC-CLIO, 2019.
Jiménez, Karleen Pendleton, and Isabel Killoran, eds. Unleashing the Unpopular: Talking About Sexual Orientation and Gender Diversity in Education. Association for Childhood Education International, 2007. https://acei.org.

11. Religion/Spirituality
Buddhism
DeMaioNewton, Emily. Interview with Caitriona Reed. The Buddhist Review Tricycle, July 26, 2019. https://tricycle.org/trikedaily/caitriona-reed/.
Devamitra, Upasaka. Confessions of a Transvestite Buddhist: A Quest for Manhood. London, UK: Achilles Publishing, 2014.
Jivaka, Lobzang/Dillon, Michael. Out of the Ordinary: A Life of Gender and Spiritual Transitions. New York, NY: Fordham University Press, 2016. Written in 1962 and published posthumously.
Reed, Catriona. "Coming Out Whole." Inquiring Mind, Spring 1998, 14(2). https://www.inquiringmind.com/article/1402_15_reed_coming-out-whole/.

Christianity
Timane, Rizi Xavier. An Unspoken Compromise: A Spiritual Guide for LGBT People of Faith. Santa Clarita, CA: Hawkfish Publishing, 2013.

Indigenous Spirituality
Dollarhide, Kenneth. "Native American Spirituality: Understanding Gender As Sacred." The Transgender Tapestry, 2008, no. 115. http://difecta.blogspot.com/2009/10/gender-as-sacred.html.

Dollarhide, Kenneth. "The Heart/Spirit, Not the Head/Mind: Being Transgendered is a Spiritual Phenomena and Not a Psychological Condition." Presented at the Sixth International Congress on Sex and Gender Diversity at Manchester Metropolitan University, Manchester, UK. September, 2004.

Islam
Khaki, El-Farouk. "Building the Unity Mosque." In John Lorinc, Jane Farrow, Stephanie Chambers, Rahim Thawer, et al., eds., Any Other Way: How Toronto Got Queer. Toronto, ON: Coach House Books, 2017, 321-323.

Judaism
Pollock, Rachel. "Transgender Jews." Lilith, Spring 2002.
Pollock, Rachel. "Aphrodite: Transsexual Goddess of Passion." Journal of Archetypal Psychology, Spring 1995.
Pollock, Rachel. "Abandonment to the Body's Desire." Rites of Passage, 1992. Reprint, Dzmura, Noach ed., Balancing on the Mechitza: Transgender in the Jewish Community. Berkeley, CA: North Atlantic Books, 2010.

12. Cybernetics (from transgenderism to transhumanism)
Rothblatt, Martine. *Virtually Human: The Promise - and the Peril - of Digital Immortality.* New York, NY: St. Martin's Press, 2014.

Rothblatt, Martine. *From Transgender to Transhuman: A Manifesto on the Freedom of Form.* Self-published, 2011. Newly-titled, expanded second edition of *The Apartheid of Sex: A Manifesto on the Freedom of Gender.* New York, NY: Crown Publishers, 1994.

13. Special Populations
a. Trans & Queer Youth
Brill, Stephanie A., and Lisa Kenney. *The Transgender Teen: A Handbook for Parents and Professionals Supporting Transgender and Non-Binary Teens.* San Francisco, CA: Cleis Press, 2016.

Brill, Stephanie A., and Rachel Pepper. *The Transgender Child: A Handbook for Families and Professionals.* San Francisco, CA: Cleis Press, 2008.

Cohen-Kettenis, Peggy T., and Friedemann Pfäfflin. *Transgenderism and Intersexuality in Childhood and Adolescence: Making Choices.* Thousand Oaks, CA: SAGE Publishing, 2003.

Gale, Lorraine. *Out and Proud Affirmation Guidelines: Practice Guidelines for Equity in Gender and Sexual Diversity.* Toronto, ON: Children's Aid Society of Toronto, 2011. http://www.torontocas.ca/sites/torontocas/files/CAST_Out_and_Proud_Affirmation_Guidelines_2012.pdf.

Marshall, Zack, Marcus Burnette, Sonia Lowton, Rainbow, Romeo Dontae Treshawn Smith, Jay Tiamo, Onyinyechukwu Udegbe, and Tess Vo. Illustrated by Elisha Lim. "A Conversation about Art and Activism with Trans and Genderqueer People Labelled with Intellectual Disabilities." In Dan Irving and Rupert Raj, eds., *Trans Activism in Canada*:

A Reader. Toronto, ON: Canadian Scholars' Press, 2014, 125-136.
Olson, Kristina R., Aidan C. Key, and Nicholas R. *Eaton.* "Gender Cognition in Transgender Children." *Psychological Science*, 2015, 26(4): 467–474.

b. Trans & Queer Parents

Epstein, Rachel. *Who's Your Daddy?: And Other Writings on Queer Parenting.* Toronto, ON: Sumach Press (Canadian Scholars' Press), 2009. Includes information on trans parenting.
Hagger-Holt, Sarah, and Rachel Hagger-Holt. *Pride and Joy: A Guide for Lesbian, Gay, Bisexual and Trans Parents.* London, UK: Pinter and Martin Publishers, 2017.
Mallon, Gary P. *Lesbian, Gay, Bisexual and Trans Foster and Adoptive Parents: Recruiting, Assessing, and Supporting Untapped Family Resources for Children and Youth* (2nd ed.). Washington, DC: Child Welfare League of America, 2015.
O'Connor, Wendy, MD. *Transgender Parents: The Ultimate Guide for Teens with Transitioning Parents.* Self-published, 2014.
Pyne, Jake. *Transforming Family: Trans Parents and their Struggles, Strategies, and Strengths.* Toronto, ON: LGBTQ Parenting Network, Sherbourne Health Centre, 2012. https://lgbtqpn.ca/trans-parenting/#report.

c. Trans & Queer Elders

Clark, Joanna (Sister Mary Elizabeth), and Margot E. Wilson. *Before My Warranty Runs Out: Human, Transgender and Environmental Rights Advocate.* Victoria, BC: TransGender Publishing, forthcoming.
Denny, Dallas. "Girl with No Name." In Margot Wilson and Aaron Devor, eds. *Glimmerings: Trans Elders Tell Their Stories.* Victoria, BC: TransGender Publishing, 2019, 33-42.
Dugan, Jess T., and Vanessa Fabbre. *To Survive on This Shore: Photographs and Interviews with Transgender and Gender Non-Conforming Older Adults.* Heidelberg, DEU: Kehrer Verlag, 2018. http://www.jessdugan.com/publications/; https://www.tosurviveonthisshore.com/.
Green, Jamison. "Doctor Livingstone, You Presume?" In Margot Wilson and Aaron Devor, eds., *Glimmerings: Trans Elders Tell Their Stories.* Victoria, BC: TransGender Publishing, 2019, 43-57.
Harley, Debra A., and Pamela B. Teaster, eds. *Handbook of LGBT Elders: An Interdisciplinary Approach to Principles, Practices, and Policies.* New York, NY: Springer Publishing, 2016.
Kane, Ariadne/J. Ari, and Margot Wilson. *Gender Odyssey: Journey of an Intrepid Androgyne.* Victoria, BC: TransGender Publishing, forthcoming.
Keith, Corey. "Glimmerings of Balance." In Margot Wilson and Aaron Devor, eds., *Glimmerings: Trans Elders Tell Their Stories.* Victoria, BC: TransGender Publishing, 2019, 75-88.
Nolan, Ty. "The Origin of Corn and Other Stories." In Margot Wilson and Aaron Devor, eds., *Glimmerings: Trans Elders Tell Their Stories.* Victoria, BC: TransGender Publishing, 2019, 94-115.
Orel, Nancy A., PhD, and Christine A. Fruhauf, PhD, eds. *The Lives of LGBT Older Adults: Understanding Challenges and Resilience.* Washington, DC: American Psychology Association, 2015.
Patton, Jude, and Margot Wilson. *Young Kid, Old Goat: Transgender Journey to Understanding the Man Within.* Victoria, BC: TransGender Publishing, forthcoming.
Prince, Virginia. "The Life and Times of Virginia." In Margot Wilson and Aaron Devor, eds., *Glimmerings: Trans Elders Tell Their Stories.* Victoria, BC: TransGender Publishing, 2019, 134-164.
Raj, Rupert. "Trans, Intersex, Two-Spirit & Queer Elders." In Jude Patton and Margot Wilson,

eds., *Life Trips: Navigating LGBTQ+ Aging, Illness, and End of Life Decisions*. Victoria, BC: TransGender Publishing, forthcoming.

Raj, Rupert. "Glimmerings of My Trans-Male Identity." In Margot Wilson and Aaron Devor, eds., *Glimmerings: Trans Elders Tell Their Stories*. Victoria, BC: TransGender Publishing, 2019, 165-182.

Roberts, M. Gayle. *From Shame to Freedom: A Gender Variant Woman's Journey of Discovery*. Victoria, BC: TransGender Publishing, forthcoming.

Wensley, Dawn Angela, and Margot Wilson. Excerpts from Dawn Angela Wensley's diary. Victoria, BC: TransGender Publishing, forthcoming.

Wilson, Margot E. *Girl in the Dream: Stephanie (Sydney) Castle Heal, A Transgender Life*. Victoria, BC: TransGender Publishing, 2018.

Wilson, Margot, and Aaron Devor, eds. *Glimmerings: Trans Elders Tell Their Stories*. Victoria, BC: TransGender Publishing, 2019.

Witten, Tarynn M., PhD, and Evan A. Eyler, MD, eds. *Gay, Lesbian, Bisexual, and Transgender Aging: Challenges in Research, Practice, and Policy*. Baltimore, MD: Johns Hopkins University Press, 2012.

d. Transforming Partnerships

Ben-Zeev, Avi, and Pete Bailey, eds. *Trans Homo...Gasp!: FTM and Cis Men on Sex and Love*. San Francisco, CA: Transgress Press, 2017.

Green, Jo. *The Trans Partner Handbook: A Guide for When Your Partner Transitions*. London, UK: Jessica Kingsley Publishers, 2017.

McClellan, Joseph. *Trans*Am: Cis Men and Trans Women in Love*. Berkeley, CA: Three L Media (Stone Bridge Press), 2017.

Pfeffer, Carla A. *Queering Families: The Postmodern Partnerships of Cisgender Women and Transgender Men (Sexuality, Identity, and Society)*. Oxford, UK: Oxford University Press, 2017.

Towers, Sara. *Transgender Lesbians*. Self-published, 2015.

e. Transforming Families

Boenke, Mary, ed., *Trans Forming Families: Real Stories About Transgendered Loved Ones* (2nd ed.). New Castle, DE: Oak Knoll Press, 2003.

Boyce, Michelle, and Jessica Boyce. "When Dad Becomes Mom: The Story of One Mother's Love for Her Children, Parent Alienation, and "Happily Ever After." In Dan Irving and Rupert Raj, eds., *Trans Activism in Canada: A Reader*. Toronto, ON: Canadian Scholars' Press, 2014, 59-84.

Brown, Mildred L., and Chloe Ann Rounsley. *True Selves: Understanding Transsexualism – For Families, Friends, Coworkers, and Helping Professionals*. San Francisco, CA: Jossey-Bass, 1996, (rev.) 2003.

Lev, Arlene Istar. *Transgender Emergence: Therapeutic Guidelines for Working with Gender-Variant People and their Families*. Philadelphia, PA: Haworth Press, 2004.

Miller, Lee Andra, and Lindsay Elin. *Families in TRANSition: A Resource Guide for Families of Transgender Youth* (2nd ed.). Toronto, ON: Central Toronto Youth Services, 2016. https://ctys.org/information/resources/ctys-publications/.

Pepper, Rachel, ed., *Transitions of the Heart: Stories of Love, Struggle and Acceptance by Mothers of Transgender and Gender Variant Children*. San Francisco, CA: Cleis Press, 2012.

f. Transgender Community

Erickson-Schroth, Laura, ed., *Trans Bodies, Trans Selves: A Resource for the Transgender Community*. Oxford, UK: Oxford University Press, 2014.

14. Web-Based Organizations
Canadian Professional Association for Transgender Health. www.cpath.ca/.
Centre for Gender Advocacy. http://genderadvocacy.org/.
European Professional Association for Transgender Health. https://epath.eu/.
International Transgender Day of Remembrance. https://tdor.tgeu.org/.
Rainbow Health Ontario. www.rainbowhealthontario.ca/.
Trans Alliance Society. http://transalliancesociety.org/.
Trans Equality Rights in Canada. https://www.transequalitycanada.com/.
Trans Lobby Group. https://www.prod.facebook.com/TransLobbyGroup/.
TransParent Canada. https://www.transparentcanada.ca/?file=welcome.
Toronto Trans Alliance. https://torontotransalliance.com/.
Toronto Trans Coalition Project. http://www.transcoalitionproject.com/.
Trans PULSE Project. www.transpulseproject.ca/.
Transgender Health Information Program (Vancouver Coastal Health). http://www.vch.ca/search#k=transgender%20health%20information%20program.
US Professional Association for Transgender Health. https://www.wpath.org/uspath/.
World Professional Association for Transgender Health. www.wpath.org/.

B. GENDER NON-BINARY
1. Androgynous People
American
Garber, Marjorie B. "Androgyny and Its Discontents," In Marjorie B. Garber, *Vice Versa: Bisexuality and the Eroticism of Everyday Life*. New York, NY: Simon & Schuster, 1995, 207-236.

Kane, Ariadne/J. Ari, and Margot Wilson. *Gender Odyssey: Journey of an Intrepid Androgyne*. Victoria, BC: TransGender Publishing, forthcoming.

Singer, June. *Androgyny: Toward a New Theory of Sexuality*. New York, NY: Anchor Books, 1976. Republished as *Androgyny: The Opposites Within*. Jung on the Hudson Book Series. Lake Worth, FL: Nicolas Hays, 2000.

British
Carpenter, Edward. *The Intermediate Sex: A Study of Some Transitional Types of Men and Women*. London: Swann Sonnenschein, 1908. Reprint, London, UK: Allen and Unwin, 1918. http://www.gutenberg.org/ebooks/53763.

Canadian
Devor, Aaron H. *Gender Blending: Confronting the Limits of Duality*. Bloomington, IN: Indiana University Press, 1989.

Devor, Aaron H. "Gender Blending Females: Women and Sometimes Men." *American Behavioral Scientist*, 1987, 31(1): 12-40.

2. Genderqueer People
American
Bornstein, Kate, ed., *My New Gender Workbook: A Step-by-Step Guide to Achieving World Peace Through Gender Anarchy and Sex Positivity*. Abingdon, UK: Routledge (Taylor & Francis), 2013.

Bornstein, Kate. *My Gender Workbook: How to Become a Real Man, a Real Woman, the Real You, or Something Else Entirely*. Abingdon, UK: Routledge (Taylor & Francis), 1997.

Bornstein, Kate. *Gender Outlaw: On Men, Women, and the Rest of Us*. Abingdon, UK:

Routledge (Taylor & Francis), 1994.
Bornstein, Kate, and S. Bear Bergman, eds. *Gender Outlaws: The Next Generation*. New York, NY: Seal Press, 2010.
Feinberg, Leslie. *Trans Liberation: Beyond Pink or Blue,* Boston, MA: Beacon Press: 1998.
Feinberg, Leslie. *Transgender Warriors: Making History from Joan of Arc to Dennis Rodman*. Boston, MA: Beacon Press, 1996.
Feinberg, Leslie. *Stone Butch Blues*. Ann Arbor, MI: Firebrand Books, 1993. Semi-autobiographical novel.
Naz, Dave. *Genderqueer: And Other Gender Identities*. Los Angeles, CA: Rare Bird Books, 2014. Photo anthology.
Nestle, Joan, Clare Howell, and Riki Anne Wilchins, eds. *GenderQueer: Voices from Beyond the Sexual Binary*. New York, NY: Alyson Books, 2002.
Rajunov, Michah, and A. Scott Duane, eds. *Nonbinary: Memoirs of Gender and Identity*. New York, NY: Columbia University Press, 2019.

Canadian
Jiménez, Karleen Pendleton. How to Get a Girl Pregnant: A Memoir. Toronto, ON: Tightrope Books, 2011. Life story of a Latina lesbian tomboy.

Web-Based Organizations
Beyond Hanky Code. https://beyondhankycode.wordpress.com/.
Genderqueer.me. https://genderqueer.me/.
Genderqueer Australia. http://www.genderqueer.org.au/.
Genderqueer Identities. https://genderqueerid.com/.
Neutrois. http://neutrois.com/.

3. Gender-Creative Kids/Teens
Canadian
Jiménez, Karleen Pendleton. *Tomboys and Other Gender Heroes: Confessions from the Classroom*. New York, NY: Peter Lang Publishing, 2016.
Jiménez, Karleen Pendleton. *Are You a Boy or a Girl?*, Toronto, ON: Green Dragon Press, 2000. Children's graphic book about the author's gender-creative kid.
Taylor, Barb, creator, and Karleen Pendleton Jiménez, writer. *Tomboy* (English and Spanish). Toronto, ON: Coyle Productions, 2008. https://vimeo.com/10772672. Short animated fim partly based on Karleen's book.

Web-Based Organizations
CHEO (Children's Hospital of Eastern Ontario) Gender Diversity Clinic.
  https://www.cheo.on.ca/en/clinics-services-programs/gender-diversity-clinic.aspx.
Gender Creative Kids/Enfants Transgenres Canada. http://gendercreativekids.ca/.
SickKids (Hospital for Sick Children) Transgender Youth Clinic.
  http://www.sickkids.ca/AdolescentMedicine/Programs/Transgender-Youth-Clinic/transgender-youth-clinic.html.

4. Gender/Sexual Diversity
American
Bullough, Vern ed., *The Frontiers of Sex Research*. Buffalo, NY: Prometheus Books,1979.
Bullough, Vern, Bullough, Bonnie Bullough, and James Elias, eds. *Gender Blending*. Buffalo, NY: Prometheus Books, 1997.
Fausto-Sterling, Anne. *Sexing the Body: Gender Politics and the Construction of Sexuality*. New York, NY: Basic Books, 2000.

Herdt, Gilbert H. *Third Sex, Third Gender: Beyond Sexual Dimorphism in Culture and History.* Brooklyn, NY: Zone Books, 1994.
Nanda, Serena. *Gender Diversity: Crosscultural Variations* (2nd ed.). Long Grove, IL: Waveland Press, 2014.
Roughgarden, Joan. *Evolution's Rainbow: Diversity, Gender and Sexuality in Nature and People.* Berkeley, CA: University of California Press, 2004.

Web-Based Organizations
Canadian Centre for Gender & Sexual Diversity. www.ccgsd-ccdsg.org/resources/.
Egale Canada Human Rights Trust. https://egale.ca/.
Gender Variance Who's Who. www.zagria.blogspot.com/.
Rainbow Health Network. https://rainbowhealthnetwork.wordpress.com/.
Rainbow Health Ontario. www.rainbowhealthontario.ca/.
Sexual Orientation & Gender Identity Educational Program. https://www.sogieducation.org/.

C. INTERSEX (DIFFERENCES OF SEX DEVELOPMENT)
1. Intersex People
American
Chase, Cheryl/Bo Laurent, ed., *Hermaphrodites with Attitude.* 1994-2005. Intersex Society of North America. http://www.isna.org/library/hwa.
Now-defunct electronic newsletter for and about intersex people.
Devore, Tiger/Howard. Interviews: "We Who Feel Differently." February 7, 2011. http://wewhofeeldifferently.info/.
Diamond, Milton, and Hazel G. Beh. "Changes in the management of children with intersex conditions." *Nature Clinical Practice Endocrinology & Metabolism.* January 2008, 4(1): 4-5.
Dreger, Alice Domurat. *Hermaphrodites and the Medical Invention of Sex.* Cambridge, MA: Harvard University Press, 1998.
Fausto-Sterling, Anne. *Sexing the Body: Gender Politics and the Construction of Sexuality.* New York, NY: Basic Books, 2000.
Gale, Porter, and Laleh Soomekh, dirs. *XXXY.* Stanford, CA: Stanford University Department of Art & Art History, March 2000. http://www.impossiblehermaphrodites.com/xxxy.html. Video documentary featuring intersex individuals, Kristi and Howard.
Herdt, Gilbert H. *Third Sex, Third Gender: Beyond Sexual Dimorphism in Culture and History.* Brooklyn, NY: Zone Books, 1994.
Koyama, Emi. Introduction to Intersex Activism (2nd ed.). Portland, OR: Intersex Initiative Portland, 2003. http://www.intersexinitiative.org/publications/index.html.
Koyama, Emi. Teaching Intersex Issues (2nd ed.). Portland, OR: Intersex Initiative Portland, 2003. http://www.intersexinitiative.org/publications/index/html.
Thomas, Antony, dir./prod. *Middle Sexes: Redefining He and She.* USA: Deep Stealth Productions; UK: Granada TV/Films. Aired in Canada, USA & UK in 2005. https://www.imdb.com/title/tt0495729/. Rebroadcast in 2009 as *A Transgender HBO Biography Special – Middle Sexes*. TV documentary on intersex, transgender and gender non-binary people.
Viloria, Hida. *Born Both: An Intersex Life.* New York, NY: Hachette Books, 2017.
Wilbur, Gigi Raven. "Walking in the Shadows: Third Gender and Spirituality." In Krista Scott-Dixon, ed., *Trans/Forming Feminisms: Trans-feminist Voices Speak Out.* Toronto, ON: Sumach Press (Canadian Scholars' Press), 2006, 65-71.

Australian
Hart, Phoebe, dir./prod. Orchids, My Intersex Adventure. Coorparoo, Queensland, AU: Hartflicker Moving Pictures, 2010. https://www.imdb.com/title/tt1757830/. Autobiographical film documentary of an Australian intersex activist, and others.

British
"Man, Once Girl, Weds Friend: He was Formerly Woman Athlete." Portsmouth Evening News, August 1936. In Christine Burns, ed., Trans Britain: Our Journey from the Shadows. London, UK: Unbound, 2018, 15. Photostat of news article on Mark Weston, who was quite possibly intersex.

Mason, Gordon, dir., A Girl Called Georgina. UK: ITV, 1995. http://www.bfi.org.uk/films-tv-people/4ce2b7e73bd35. TV documentary on Georgina Somerset, the UK's first public intersex person.

Somerset, Georgina. A Girl Called Georgina: An Illustrated Autobiography, with Study Update. Leicester, UK: The Book Guild, 1992.

"Woman's Physical Transformation: Starting Life Afresh as a Man." Dundee Evening Telegraph, Sept. 11, 1933. In Christine Burns, ed., Trans Britain: Our Journey from the Shadows. London, UK: Unbound, 2018, 14. Photostat of news article on Mark Woods, who was very likely intersex.

Canadian
Holmes, Morgan, ed., Critical Intersex. Abingdon, UK: Routledge (Taylor & Francis), 2009.

Holmes, Morgan. Intersex: A Perilous Difference. Selinsgrove, PA: Susquehanna University Press, 2007.

Holmes, Morgan. "Cal/liope in Love: The 'Prescientific' Desires of an Apolitical 'Hermaphrodite'." Journal of Lesbian Studies, 2007, 11(3-4): 223–232.

"Intersexuality: Redefining Sex." SexTV, Season 2, Episode 24. Brough, Brad, dir., Toronto, ON: Chum Television. Aired July 22, 2000.

Danish
Ebershoff, David (2000).

Elbe, Lili/Hoyer, Niels. Man into Woman: An Authentic Record of a Change of Sex. Translated by Henry J. Stenning. Published posthumously London, UK: Jarrolds Publishers, 1933. She was possibly intersex, but this has not been confirmed. https://en.wikipedia.org/wiki/Lili_Elbe; https://zagria.blogspot.com/2015/01/lili-ilse-elvenes-surgery-and-womanhood.html#.XZ1RX0apFAE.

Hooper, Tom, dir., Gail Mutrux, and Neil LaBute, prods. (2015).

[**Note:** For the first and third entry listed above, see: A. Transsexual/Transvestite/Transgender: 1. (Auto)biography/Literature/Film/Media: Danish.]

Dutch
Cohen-Kettenis, Peggy T., and Friedemann Pfäfflin. Transgenderism and Intersexuality in Childhood and Adolescence: Making Choices. Thousand Oaks, CA: SAGE Publishing, 2003.

French
Barbin, Herculine. Herculine Barbin: Being the Recently Discovered Memoirs of a Nineteenth-Century French Hermaphrodite. Introduction by Michel Foucault. Translated from the French by Richard McDougall. New York, NY: Pantheon Books, 1980.

New Zealander
Lahood, Grant, dir., and John Keir, prod. Intersexion. Auckland, NZ: Ponsonby Productions, 2012. https://www.imdb.com/title/tt2157302/. Video documentary on Mani Bruce Mitchell, New Zealand's first public intersex person, and others.

Polish
Klobukowska, Ewa. https://zagria.blogspot.ca/2009/08/ewa-kobukowska-1946-athlete.html. [Ewa's surname is mis-spelled in url.]

Portuguese
Farina, Roberto. Transexualismo: do Homem a Mulaher Normal Atraves dos Estados de Intersexualidade e das Parafilias. (Transsexualism: From Man to Normal Woman Through the States of Intersexuality and Paraphilia). São Paulo, BR: Novalunar-Graf, 1982. Portuguese-language edition only.

Web-Based Organizations
AIS-DSD Support Group (USA/Canada/SA). http://aisdsd.org/.
Androgen Insensitivity Syndrome Support Group Australia. http://aissga.org.au/.
Androgen Insensitivity Syndrome Support Group UK. http://www.aissg.org/.
Interact: Advocates for Intersex Youth. https://interactadvocates.org/.
Intersex Awareness New Zealand. http://www.ianz.org.nz/.
Intersex Initiative Portland. http://ipdx.org/.
Intersex Society of North America (closed/archived. http://www.isna.org/.
Organisation Intersex International. http://www.intersexualite.org/.

2. Dual Identity, Trans-Intersex People
African American
Cheers, D. Michael. "Interview with Justina Williams." Chicago: *Jet Magazine,* November 1, 1979. http://transgriot.blogspot.ca/2007/02/justina-williams-1979-jet-magazine.html.

Australian
Stirling, Peter. *So Different: An Extraordinary Autobiography.* Melbourne, AU: Simon & Schuster (Australia), 1989.

Austrian
Mayer, Kurt, dir., *Erik(a).* (German). Vienna, AU: Kurt Mayer Films. 2005. https://www.imdb.com/title/tt0443741/. Video documentary on Austrian skier Erik Schinegger's gender transition as based on his 1989 autobiography.
Schinegger, Erik, and Marco Schenz. *Mein Sieg über mich. Der Mann, der Weltmeisterin wurde. (My Victory Over Myself: The Man Who Became a Female World Champion).* München, DEU: Herbig, 1988; *L'Homme Qui Fut Championne du Monde.* Paris, FR: Éditions Michel Lafon, 1989. No English-language editions.

British
Cossey, Caroline/"Tula." My Story. London, UK: Faber and Faber, 1991.
Cossey, Caroline/"Tula." I Am a Woman. London, UK: Sphere, 1982.
Cowell, Roberta (1954). A post-transitional, transsexual woman whose documented intersexuality was possibly falsified by her surgeon so she could legally undergo transsexual surgery. See: https://en.wikipedia.org/wiki/Roberta_Cowell; and https://zagria.blogspot.com/2012/07/betty-cowell-1918-2011-motor-racer-pilot.html#.XZ1FtkapFAE.

Duncker, Patricia (1999). Dr. James Miranda Barry's rumoured intersexuality has been controversially debated. https://en.wikipedia.org/wiki/James_Barry_(surgeon) ; https://zagria.blogspot.com/2008/01/james-miranda-stuart-barry-1795-1865.html #.X.

Simmons, Dawn Langley (1971, 1995). A post-transitional, transsexual woman whose self-identified intersexuality has been contested by author Edward Ball. https://en.wikipedia.org/wiki/Dawn_Langley_Simmons; https://zagria.blogspot.com/2009/10/dawn-langley-simmons-1922-2000-part-2.html#.XZ1GbkapFAE.

[**Note:** For Robera Cowell, Dr. James Miranda Barry and Dawn Langley Simmons, see: A. Transsexual/Transvestite/Transgender: 1. (Auto)biography/Literature/Film/Media: British.]

Canadian

Kol, Alon, dir., and Behnisch, Christopher, writ. Transfixed. Toronto, ON, 2015. https://www.youtube.com/watch?v=QsPQOVGCsuY. Video docudrama on trans/intersex activist Martine Stonehouse and her husband.

Ugandan

Kaggwa, Julius. From Juliet to Julius: In Search of my True Gender Identity. Kampala, Uganda: Fountain Publishers, 1998. Memoir of an African, trans-intersex man, who advocates for intersex and gender non-binary people.

D. *HIJRA* (*SOUTH ASIAN*)

[Most *Hijras* are third-gender (ritually castrated natal males), but a few now identify as female and surgically transition to trans women. Post-transitionally, the latter often retain their *Hijra* community status as sister activists. All of the following are Tamil Indians.]

1. *Hijra* **People**

Bharadwaj, Yogesh, dir., *Shabnam Mausi.* (Tamil). India, 2005.
    https://www.imdb.com/title/tt0459133/. Film documentary on *Hijra* activist Shabnam Mausi.

Nanda, Serena. "*Hijra* and *Sadhin*: Neither Man nor Woman in India and Bangladesh." In Serena Nanda, *Gender Diversity: Crosscultural Variations* (2nd ed.), Long Grove, IL: Waveland Press, 2014, chapter 2.

Nanda, Serena. *Neither Man nor Woman: The Hijras of India.* Belmont, CA: Wadsworth Publishing, 1989.

Sivan, Santosh, dir., *"Navarasa." ("Nine Emotions").* (Hindi). India: 2005.
    https://www.bollywoodhungama.com/movie/navarasa-nine-emotions/critic-review/. Tamil social drama featuring fictional third-gender *Hijra* uncle.

2. **Dual Identity, Trans-***Hijra* **People**

Kathir, V. V., dir., *"Thenavattu" ("Lethargy").* (Tamil). India, 2008. Film documentary on *Hijra*-trans woman A. Revathi.

Kumar, Shiva, dir., *"Paal"("Unisexual").* (Tamil). India, 2008. Film documentary on *Hijra*-trans woman Karpaka.

Lingadevaru, B. S., dir.,*"Naanu Avanalla...Avalu" ("I Am Not A He...I Am A She").* (Tamil). India, 2015. Film documentary based on *Hijra*-trans woman Living Smile Vidya's autobiography.

Living Smile Vidya. *I Am Vidya: A Transgender's Journey.* New Delhi, IN: Rupa Publications, 2014.

Revathi, A., and M. Nandini. *A Life in Trans Activism.* Self-published, 2016.

Revathi, A. *The Truth About Me: A Hijra Life Story.* New Delhi, IN: Penguin Books, 2010.
Vignesh, dir., *"Achchupizhai."* (Tamil). India, 2008. Film documentary on *Hijra*-trans woman Achchupizhai.

E. TWO-SPIRIT (INDIGENOUS)
1. Two-Spirit People
American
Dollarhide, Kenneth. "Native American Spirituality: Understanding Gender As Sacred." *The Transgender Tapestry,* 2008, (115). http://difecta.blogspot.com/2009/10/gender-as-sacred.html.
Dollarhide, Kenneth. "Concept of Gender among Selected Native American Traditions." *The Transgender Tapestry*, Fall 2002, (99). http://www.ifge.org/magazines/99_fall02.htm.
Dollarhide, Kenneth. "Lakota Winkte." *The Transgender Tapestry*, Summer 2001, (94). http://www.ifge.org/catalog/product_info.php?products_id=94.
Driskill, Q.-L., D. H. Justice, D. Miranda, and L. Tatonetti, eds., *Sovereign Erotics: A Collection of Two-Spirit Literature.* Tucson, AZ: University of Arizona Press, 2011.
Jacobs, Sue-Ellen, Sabine Lang, and Wesley Thomas, eds., *Two-Spirit People: Native American Gender Identity, Sexuality, and Spirituality.* Chicago, IL: University of Illinois Press, 1997.
Nibley, Lydia, dir., *Two Spirits.* USA: Say Yes Quickly Productions, June 21, 2009. https://www.imdb.com/title/tt1296906/. Film documentary of the hate-murder of 16-year-old, Navajo Fred Martinez, a Two-Spirit effeminate male or *"nádleeh"* ("half woman, half man") in Cortez, Colorado.
Nolan, Ty. "The Origin of Corn and Other Stories." In Margot Wilson and Aaron Devor, eds., *Glimmerings: Trans Elders Tell Their Stories*. Victoria, BC: TransGender Publishing, 2019, 94-115.
Roscoe, Will. *Changing Ones: Third and Fourth Genders in Native North America.* New York, NY: St. Martin's Press, 1998.
Roscoe, Will. *The Zuni Man-Woman.* Albuquerque, NM: University of New Mexico Press, 1991.
Williams, Walter L. *The Spirit and the Flesh: Sexual Diversity in American Indian Culture.* Boston, MA: Beacon Press, 1992.

Canadian
2-Spirited People of the 1st Nations fonds. Toronto, ON: The ArQuives. https://arquives.andornot.com/en/list?q=2-spirit+of+the+1st+nations&p=1&ps=20.
Cruz, Louis Esmé. "Medicine Bundle of Contradictions: Female-man, Mi'kmaq/Acadian/Irish Diasporas, Invisible disAbilities, masculine-Feminist." In Jessica Yee, ed., Feminism FOR REAL: Deconstructing the Academic Industrial Complex of Feminism. Ottawa, ON: Canadian Centre for Policy Alternatives, 2011, 49-60.
Cruz, Louis Esmé, and Qwo-Li Driskill. "Puo'winue'l Prayers: Readings from North America's First Transtextual Script." GLQ: A Journal of Lesbian and Gay Studies, April 1, 2010, 16(1-2): 243-252. https://doi.org/10.1215/10642684-2009-021. Qwo-Li Driscoll is American.
Forrester, Monica, co-prod., Remember the Living: Monica Forrester on Sisters in Spirit and Indigenous Sex Workers. Toronto, ON: Maggie's: The Toronto Sex Workers Action Project, October 4, 2012. https://www.youtube.com/watch?v=lPGQNvIlLuQ.
Ristock, Janice, Art Zoccole, and Lisa Passante. Aboriginal Two-Spirit and LGBTQ Migration, Mobility and Health Research Project (Final Report). Winnipeg, MB: University of Manitoba, 2010. http://www.2 spirits.com/MMHReport.pdf.
Robinson Margaret. "Two-Spirit And Bisexual People: Different Umbrella, Same Rain."

Journal of Bisexuality, 2017, 17(1): 7-29.

Sinclair, Raven, Michael Hart, and Gord Bruyere, eds., Wícihitowin: Aboriginal Social Work in Canada. Vancouver, BC: Langara College, 2011. Sixth of six editions since 2009.

Tanguay, Nicole Nanku. "In the Spirit of Beth: Queering Indigenous Space." In John Lorinc, Jane Farrow, Stephanie Chambers, Rahim Thawer, et al., eds., Any Other Way: How Toronto Got Queer. Toronto, ON: Coach House Books, 2017, 73-75.

Taylor, Catherine. Nowhere Near Enough: A Needs Assessment of Health and Safety Services for Transgender and Two Spirit People in Manitoba and Northwestern Ontario (Final Report). Winnipeg, MB: Nine Circles Community Health Centre, 2006. www.turtleisland.org/healing/transgender.doc.

Tietz, Lüder. "Two-Spirited People in Canada: Between Triple Discrimination and Empowerment." Paper presented at the 93rd annual meeting of the American Anthropological Association, Atlanta, GA, 1994.

Waters, Laureen Blu. "Time Capsules." In Jin Haritaworn, Ghaida Moussa, and Syrus Marcus Ware, eds., Marvellous Grounds: Queer of Colour Histories of Toronto. Toronto, ON: Between the Lines, 2018, chapter 6.

Zoccole, Art. "Agokwe." In John Lorinc, Jane Farrow, Stephanie Chambers, Rahim Thawer, et al., eds., Any Other Way: How Toronto Got Queer. Toronto, ON: Coach House Books, 2017, 26-28.

Web-Based Organizations
2-Spirited People of the 1st Nations (Toronto, Canada). http://www.2spirits.com/.

2. Dual Identity, Trans-Two-Spirit People
American

Valerio, Max Wolf. *The Testosterone Files: My Hormonal and Social Transformation from Female to Male.* New York, NY: Seal Press, 2006.

Valerio, Max Wolf. "Now That You're a White Man: Changing Sex in a Postmodern World – Being, Becoming, and Borders." In Gloria Anzaldúa and AnaLouise Keating, eds., *This Bridge We Call Home: Radical Visions for Transformation.* Abingdon, UK: Routledge (Taylor & Francis), 2002, 239-254.

Canadian

Benaway, Gwen, ed., *Maiden, Mother, and Crone: Fantastical Trans Femmes*. Winnipeg, MB: Bedside Press, 2019.

Daniel, Barb. *She's No Lady: The Story of Jamie Lee Hamilton.* Toronto, ON: Cormorant Books, 2005.

Estrella, Lukayo Faye C. "Alternative: Moving Towards Liberation & Anti-Oppression." In Douglas Gosse, ed., *Out Proud: Stories of Pride, Courage, and Social Justice.* Egale Canada Human Rights Trust. St. John's, NL: Breakwater Books, 2014, n.p.n.

Hamilton, Jamie Lee. "The Golden Age of Prostitution: One Woman's Personal Account of an Outdoor Brothel in Vancouver, 1975-1984." In Dan Irving and Rupert Raj, eds., *Trans Activism in Canada: A Reader.* Toronto, ON: Canadian Scholars' Press, 2014, 27-32.

James, Elizabeth "Raven." "Gender Strike! It's an Offence." In Dan Irving and Rupert Raj, eds., *Trans Activism in Canada: A Reader.* Toronto, ON: Canadian Scholars' Press, 2014, 45-49.

Laframboise, Sandy Leo. "Finding My Place: The High Risk Project Society." In Dan Irving and Rupert Raj, eds., *Trans Activism in Canada: A Reader.* Toronto, ON: Canadian Scholars' Press, 2014, 51-56.

May, Kiley. *You Are Not Your Genitals."* Toronto, ON, 2017. https://www.youtube.com/watch?v=kqp_bKb94cA. Performance video on Kiley's gender identity.

Muldoon, Grey Kimber Piitaapan, and Dan Irving. "A Sense of Place: Expressions of Trans Activism North of Lake Nipissing." In Dan Irving and Rupert Raj, eds., *Trans Activism in Canada: A Reader.* Toronto, ON: Canadian Scholars' Press, 2014, 71-84. Includes one Indigenous transgender-Two-Spirit (Nakota) person (Christian Thompson).

Pope, Jessica, and Jennifer Norwell. *TransNorth.* Ottawa, Canada: CBC-Radio. www.cbc.ca/sudbury/features/transnorth. Radio program on transgender & Two-Spirit people in northern Ontario, some of whom have a dual identity. Also features trans man Treanor Mahood-Greer.

3. Multiple Identity, Trans-Intersex-Two-Spirit People
Canadian

Butler, Alec. "Black Friday…With or Without the Question Mark." In John Lorinc, Jane Farrow, Stephanie Chambers, Rahim Thawer, et al., eds., *Any Other Way: How Toronto Got Queer.* Toronto, ON: Coach House Books, 2017, 208-211.

[**Note:** For Alec's three autobiographical videos, see above: Transsexual/Transvestite/ Transgender: 1. (Auto)biography/Literature/Film/Media: *Canadian*.]

F. Combined Populations
1. Trans, Genderqueer & Queer Activists of Colour

Estrella, Lukayo Faye C. "Alternative: Moving Towards Liberation & Anti-Oppression." In Douglas Gosse, ed., *Out Proud: Stories of Pride, Courage, and Social Justice.* Egale Canada Human Rights Trust (Ottawa, ON). St. John's, NL: Breakwater Books, 2014.

Friday Night Productions. *Rewriting the Script: A Love Letter to Our Families.* Toronto, ON: Vtape, 2001. https://www.youtube.com/watch?v=b2lMb-58MH4. Video documentary on Rupert Raj (and his sister) and other trans/queer Canadian South Asians.

Haritaworn, Jin, Ghaida Moussa, and Syrus Marcus Ware, eds., *Marvellous Grounds: Queer of Colour Histories of Toronto.* Toronto, ON: Between the Lines, 2018.

Haritaworn, Jin, Ghaida Moussa, and Syrus Marcus Ware, eds., with Río Rodríguez. *Queering Urban Justice: Queer of Colour Formations in Toronto.* Toronto, ON: University of Toronto Press, 2018.

Haritaworn, Jin, Ghaida Moussa, Syrus Marcus Ware, with Alvis Choi, Amandeep Kaur Panag, and Río Rodríguez. "Marvellous Grounds: QTBIPOC Counter-Archiving against Imperfect Erasures." In John Lorinc, Jane Farrow, Stephanie Chambers, Rahim Thawer, et al., eds., *Any Other Way: How Toronto Got Queer.* Toronto, ON: Coach House Books, 2017, 219-223.

Khan, Janaya, and LeRoi Newbold. "Black Lives Matter Toronto Teach-In." In Jin Haritaworn, Ghaida Moussa, and Syrus Marcus Ware, eds., with Río Rodríguez. *Queering Urban Justice: Queer of Colour Formations in Toronto.* Toronto, ON: University of Toronto Press, 2018, chapter 7.

Marvellous Grounds, and Min Sook Lee. *Marvellous Grounds Short Film.* Toronto, ON, 2018. https://vimeo.com/269198618. Multimedia film on queer/trans community organizing in Toronto in the 1980s and street corner activism by trans sex workers.

Ware, Syrus Marcus. "All Power to All People?: Black LGBTTI2QQ Activism, Remembrance, and Archiving in Toronto." In Susan Stryker and Paisley Currah, eds., *TSQ (Transgender Studies Quarterly): The Issue of Blackness.* May 1, 2017, 4(2): 170-180. https://doi.org/10.1215/23289252-3814961.

2. Trans, Intersex, Two-Spirit & Queer Elders
Dugan, Jess T., and Vanessa Fabbre. *To Survive on This Shore: Photographs and Interviews with Transgender and Gender Non-Conforming Older Adults.* Heidelberg, DEU: Kehrer Verlag, 2018. http://www.jessdugan.com/publications/; https://www.tosurviveonthisshore.com/.
Patton, Jude, and Margot Wilson, eds., *Life Trips: Navigating LGBTQ+ Aging, Illness, and End of Life Decisions.* Victoria, BC: TransGender Publishing, forthcoming.
Raj, Rupert. "Trans, Intersex, Two-Spirit & Queer Elders." In Jude Patton and Margot Wilson, eds., *Life Trips: Navigating LGBTQ+ Aging, Illness, and End of Life Decisions.* Victoria, BC: TransGender Publishing, forthcoming.

3. LGBTTI2SQQAA People & Companion Animals
Patton, Jude, and Margot Wilson, eds., *Unconditional Love: Stories of LGBTQ+ People and our Emotional Bonds with Companion Animals.* Victoria, BC: TransGender Publishing, forthcoming.
Raj, Rupert. "Feline Friends, Canine Companions." In Jude Patton and Margot Wilson, eds., *Unconditional Love: Stories of LGBTQ+ People and our Emotional Bonds with Companion Animals.* Victoria, BC: TransGender Publishing, forthcoming.

4. LGBTTI2SQQAA Historical Anthologies
Gentile, Patrizia, Gary Kinsman, and Pauline L. Rankin, eds., *We Still Demand! Redefining Resistance in Sex and Gender Struggles.* Vancouver, BC: UBC Press, 2017.
Lorinc, John, Jane Farrow, Stephanie Chambers, Rahim Thawer, Tatum Taylor, Tim McCaskill, Rebecka Sheffield, Maureen FitzGerald, and Ed Jackson, eds., *Any Other Way: How Toronto Got Queer.* Toronto, ON: Coach House Books, 2017.

G. LGBTTI2SQQAA/TRANS ARCHIVES & DIGITAL COLLABORATORIES
1. The ArQuives: Canada's LGBTQ2+ Archives (formerly, Canadian Lesbian and Gay Archives, Toronto, ON): https: arquives.ca/.
Brown, Elspeth. "Finding Aid for The Rupert Raj fonds." 2015. https://arquives.andornot.com/en/list?q=rupert+raj+-+finding+aid&p=1&ps=20.
National Portrait Collection: Rupert Raj, Alec Butler, Gloria Eshkibok, Kyle Scanlon, etc. https://digitalexhibitions.arquives.ca/exhibits/show/npc/npc_qtos.
Matte, Nick. "Trans Pathfinder." hyperlink forthcoming.
Rupert Raj fonds. https://arquives.andornot.com/en/permalink/descriptions16420a.

2. Digital Transgender Archive (College of the Holy Cross, Worcester, MA):
http://www.digitaltransgenderarchive.org/.

3. Transgender Archives, (University of Victoria, Victoria, BC):
http://transgenderarchives.ca/.
Moving Trans History Forward Transgender Archives conferences, 2014, 2016, 2018. https://www.uvic.ca/mthf2020/. (Click on "Past Conferences" tab for Programs, Keynote Speakers, Founders Panel or Elders Panel & Youth Panel.)
Rupert Raj on 2016 Founders (Elders) Panel. https://www.youtube.com/watch?v=KG4RPJEHrtw&index=5&list=PLjWymvKNnUWKX-Z2tkf_T5UGbrkbvZWzi&t=10s.

4. LGBTQ Oral History Digital Collaboratory:
http://lgbtqdigitalcollaboratory.org/.
Brown, Elspeth. "Trans Oral Histories: The Transgender History Project of the Upper

Midwest." December 30, 2017. http://lgbtqdigitalcollaboratory.org/2017/12/tran-oral-histories-the-transgender-history-project-of-the-upper-midwest.
Brown, Elspeth, et al., "TransPartners Project." 2018. http://lgbtqdigitalcollaboratory.org/projects-2/.
Matte, Nick, and Elspeth Brown. "Rupert Raj Oral History about Trans Health Care Activism." 2016. http://digitalcollections.clga.ca/items/show/626.

PART IV: RAINBOW WARRIOR
A. ECOFEMINISM/GAIA EARTH SCIENCE/ENVIRONMENTALLY-ENGAGED BUDDHISM/NATIVE SPIRITUALITY

Allen, Paula Gunn. *The Sacred Hoop: Recovering the Feminine in American Indian Traditions.* Boston, MA: Beacon Press, 1986.
Badiner, Allan Hunt, ed., *Dharma Gaia: A Harvest of Essays in Buddhism and Ecology.* Berkeley, CA: Parallax Press, 1990.
Buddhist Soka Gakkai International (Buddhism in Action for Peace). "Earth Charter." http://www.sgi.org/resources/ngo-resources/education-for-sustainable-development/sgi-and-the-earth-charter.htm.
Capra, Fritjof. *The Web of Life: A New Scientific Understanding of Living Systems.* New York, NY: Anchor Books, 1996.
Dalai Lama. "A Buddhist Concept of Nature." Address given at New Delhi, India, February 4, 1992. https://www.dalailama.com/messages/environment/buddhist-concept-of-nature.
Diamond, Irene, and Gloria Feman Orenstein, eds., *Reweaving the World: The Emergence of Ecofeminism.* San Francisco, CA: Sierra Club Books, 1990.
Jones, Ken. *The New Social Face of Buddhism: A Call to Action.* Somerville, MA: Wisdom Publications, 2003.
Kaza, Stephanie, and Kenneth Kraft, eds., *Dharma Rain: Sources of Buddhist Environmentalism.* Boulder, CO: Shambala Publications, 2000.
Lovelock, James. *The Revenge of Gaia: Why the Earth Is – and How We Can Still Save Humanity.* London, UK: Allen Lane (Penguin Random House), 2006.
Lovelock, James. *Gaia: A New Look at Life on Earth.* Oxford, UK: Oxford University Press, 1979.
Macy, Joanna. *World as Lover, World as Self: Courage for Global Justice and Ecological Renewal.* Berkeley, CA: Parallax Press, 1991.
Margulis, Lynn. *Symbiotic Planet: A New Look at Evolution.* New York, NY: Basic Books, 1998.
Read, Rupert, and P. Hutchinson. Cambridge, UK: *Cambridge Green Party Local Manifesto.* 2015. https://cambridge.greenparty.org.uk/assets/files/localparties/cambridge/2015%20policies/GPEW_Cambridge_Manifesto_Small.pdf.
Sams, Jamie. *Earth Medicine: Ancestor's Ways of Harmony for Many Moons.* New York, NY: HarperCollins, 1994.
Schumacher, Ernst F. *Small Is Beautiful: Economics as if People Mattered.* New York, NY: Harper, 1989.
Shiva, Vandana. *Making Peace With The Earth.* London, UK: Pluto Press, 2013.
Spretnak, Charlene, and Fritjof Capra. *Green Politics: The Global Promise.* New York, NY: E. P. Dutton, 1984.
Starhawk. *The Spiral Dance: A Rebirth of the Ancient Religion of the Great Goddess.* New York, NY: Harper & Rowe, 1979.
Warren, Karen, and Nisvan Erkal, eds., *Ecofeminism: Women, Culture, Nature.* Bloomington, IN: Indiana University Press, 1997.

Web-Based Organizations
Buddhist Soka Gakkai International (Buddhism in Action for Peace): http://www.sgi.org/.
Dharma Gaia: https://www.dharmagaia.org/.
Earth Medicine Institute: http://earthmedicineinstitute.com/.
Environment and Ecology: Gaia: http://environment-ecology.com/gaia/.
Greenpeace International: http://www.greenpeace.org/international/.
Women and Life on Earth: http://www.wloe.org/.

B. ECO-ACTIVISM/ANIMAL LIBERATION/TRANS-SPECIES PSYCHOLOGY
Cisgender
Bradshaw, Gay A. *Elephant Trauma and Recovery: From Human Violence to Trans-Species Psychology.* Santa Barbara, CA: Pacifica Graduate Institute, 2005.
Singer, Peter. *Animal Liberation: A New Ethics for Our Treatment of Animals.* New York, NY: HarperCollins, 1975.
Spiegel, Marjorie. *The Dreaded Comparison: Human and Animal Slavery.* London, UK: Mirror Books, 1996.
Walters, Kerry S., and Lisa Portmess. *Ethical Vegetarianism: From Pythagoras to Peter Singer.* Albany, NY: SUNY (State University of New York) Press, 1999.

Transgender
Neufeld, Calvin. "Choosing Better than Oppression." In Dan Irving and Rupert Raj, eds., *Trans Activism in Canada: A Reader.* Toronto, ON: Canadian Scholars' Press, 2014, 103-108.
Neufeld, Calvin. *Sanctuary: A Children's Story for All Ages.* Suffering Eyes Project, Perth, ON: Purposeful Publishing House, 2000. www.sufferingeyes.com/.
Neufeld, Franceen. *Suffering Eyes: A Chronicle of Awakening.* Suffering Eyes Project, Perth, ON: Purposeful Publishing House, 2000. www.sufferingeyes.com/.
Ross, Mirha-Soleil, and Mark Karbusicky, dirs. *Yapping Out Loud: Contagious Thoughts from an Unrepentant Whore.* Toronto, ON: Vtape, 2002. http://www.vtape.org/video?vi=5043.
Ross, Mirha-Soleil, and Mark Karbusicky, dirs. *G-SPrOuT!,* Toronto, ON: Vtape, 2000. http://www.vtape.org/video?vi=4462.
Ross, Mirha-Soleil, host. *Animal Voices.* Broadcast 1996-2001. Toronto, ON: CIUT 89.5 FM-Radio (web broadcast: www.ciut.fm).

Web-Based Organizations
Animal Liberation Front: http://www.animalliberationfront.com/.
Animal Rights: The Abolitionist Approach: www.AbolitionistApproach.com/.
Animals International: https://www.animalsinternational.org/.
Evolve Our Prison Farms: https://evolveourprisonfarms.ca/.
Gaia Foundation: https://www.gaiafoundation.org/.
People for the Ethical Treatment of Animals: http://www.peta.org/.
Suffering Eyes Project: www.sufferingeyes.com/.
Toronto Vegetarian Association: http://veg.ca/.

About the Author

Rupert Raj is a Eurasian-Canadian, pansexual, trans man, who transitioned from female to male in Ottawa (Canada's capital) in 1971 as a gender-distressed, transsexual teenager of 19. He has been a trailblazing trans activist in Canada and the USA ever since.

Rupert co-founded a number of transsexual/transgender peer-support groups and gender consulting service organizations: Foundation for the Advancement of Canadian Transsexuals (FACT) (1978-1986), Metamorphosis Counselling Services (1982-1983), Metamorphosis Medical Research Foundation (MMRF) (1983-1988), Gender Worker/Gender Consultants (1988-1990), the Trans Men/FTM Peer-Support Group (1999-), the Thursday Night Group (2000), and TransFormations (2003-2004). He also co-led the Gender Journeys group from 2006 to 2013.

As a Toronto-based gender consultant and psychotherapist from 2001 to 2015, Mr. Raj counselled transsexual, transgender, genderqueer, intersex, and Two-Spirit adults and gender non-conforming youth and their loved ones. Through his private practice (RR Consulting), he provided gender consultation services and transpositive training workshops to healthcare and social service professionals, educators and students, employers and human resources directors, researchers and policymakers, lawyers, and politicians.

A published author, Rupert has (co-)written five trans focussed clinical research papers for scholarly journals and six trans themed chapters for book anthologies, and has (co-)edited three books: *Trans Activism in Canada: A Reader* (with Dan Irving, PhD), Canadian Scholars' Press, 2014; *Of Souls & Roles, Of Sex & Gender: A Treasury of Transsexual, Transgenderist & Transvestic Verse from 1967 to 1991*, unpublished, 2017, revised 2018; and *Dancing the Dialectic: True Tales of A Transgender Trailblazer* (first edition), self published, 2017.

In recognition of his many years of service to the trans/intersex/Two-Spirit community, Mr. Raj was inducted into The ArQuives (formerly, the Canadian Lesbian and Gay Archives) in 2013, where The Rupert Raj fonds are housed. A recipient of multiple honours, including mention in the Institute for Advanced Study of Human Sexuality's *The International Who's Who in Sexology* (first edition) (1986) and The City of Toronto Access & Equity Human Rights Pride Award (2007), he especially cherishes his Youth Role Model of the Year Award (2017) presented by the Canadian Centre for Gender & Sexual Diversity at his 65th birthday/retirement celebration: a fitting tribute to a 46-year transjectory from trans youth to trans elder.

The perennial activist, since 2017 Rupert has been morphing from Gender Worker (trans activist, intersex and Two-Spirit ally) to Rainbow Warrior (eco-activist/animal liberationist), working to free Mother Earth's enslaved farmed and research-laboratory animals, and to expand the circle of compassion to include human and animal sentient beings.

In 2017, he moved to Vancouver, BC to be near the mountains and the ocean. Enjoying his retirement, Mr. Raj travels occasionally, reads avidly, and writes when inspired.

Printed in Great Britain
by Amazon